THE TEXAS RANGERS AND
THE MEXICAN REVOLUTION

THE TEXAS

AND THE MEXICAN

Sergent J.G. Perkins, A.J. Robertson
F.dd. Hollebeke
J.D. McClelland.
S.R. Ikard.
Frank Bla
Texas Ra

The Bloodiest Decade, 1910–1920

RANGERS

REVOLUTION

E. Hunt. W. R. Holland. Santos Duran. B. F. Pennington. T. E. Perkins. Captain Will Davis.

Charles H. Harris III and Louis R. Sadler

University of New Mexico Press | Albuquerque

For Betty

© 2004 by the University of New Mexico Press
All rights reserved. Published 2004

10 09 08 07 06 05 04   1 2 3 4 5 6 7 8 9 10

Library of Congress Cataloging-in-Publication Data
Harris, Charles H. (Charles Houston)
The Texas Rangers and the Mexican Revolution : the
bloodiest decade, 1910–1920 / Charles H. Harris III
and Louis R. Sadler.— 1st ed.
p.   cm.
Includes bibliographical references and index.
ISBN 0-8263-3483-0 (cloth : alk. paper)
1. Texas Rangers—History—20th century.
2. Texas Rangers—Biography.
3. Mexico—History—Revolution, 1910-1920.
4. Texas—Relations—Mexico.
5. Mexico—Relations—Texas.
I. Sadler, Louis R. II. Title.
F391.H28 2004
972.08'16—dc22

2004009059

Printed and bound in the USA by Thomson-Shore, Inc
Typeset in Janson 11 / 14 pt
Display type set in Myriad Tilt, Birch, Giddyup Thangs
Design and composition: Robyn Mundy

T HE law places the Ranger Force of the State under direct command of the Governor, and they operate altogether under his direction, in such manner and in such detachments and in such localities as the Governor may direct.—Governor Oscar B. Colquitt

CONTENTS

Prelude

Part One

The Colquitt Years, 1911–1915

Governor Oscar Branch Colquitt

Part Two

Governor James Edward Ferguson

The Ferguson
Years, 1915–1917

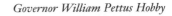

Part Three

Governor William Pettus Hobby

The Hobby
Years, 1917–1921

ILLUSTRATIONS

Maps

Figures

ACKNOWLEDGMENTS

More than a quarter century ago, the authors decided to write a history of the Texas Rangers and the Mexican Revolution. As is the case with many book projects, intervening events delayed the research and writing. However, we kept coming back again and again to the topic. The result is what we hope is a useful monograph.

Because of the time involved in conducting our research, we are significantly indebted to a number of individuals and institutions.

We would like to thank the Weatherhead Foundation, New York City, for their generous financial support of our research. In addition, the Arts and Sciences Research Center at New Mexico State University supported our initial investigations and assisted us in obtaining external funding.

Our research began at the Nettie Lee Benson Latin American Collection at the University of Texas at Austin. The Benson Collection is well known as the finest archive on Mexico in the United States, and we had the great good fortune to both know and consult with the late Dr. Benson during our investigations of the Mexican Revolution. Dr. Benson's staff, including Laura Gutiérrez Witt, Jane Garner, Wanda Turnley and Carman Sacomani, were of considerable assistance over an extended length of time.

Adjacent to the Benson Collection at UT is the Center for American History (CAH), formerly named the Barker Texas History Center. The staff of the CAH were most helpful in our research. Most recently Steven Williams, Kathryn Kenefick and Amy Bowman at the CAH assisted us in obtaining photographs. In addition, the Harry Ransom Humanities Center at UT provided us with a unique photograph.

At the Texas State Preservation Board, photo archivist Lindsey Block was of assistance in obtaining photographs.

At the Lorenzo de Zavala Texas State Library, former Director David Gracey, former Archivist Michael Dabrishus and Mrs. Eddie Williams (now retired) were enormously helpful. Mrs. Williams copied literally thousands of documents for us. Most recently, Photo Archivist John Anderson combed the TSL Archives for photographs for this monograph.

We wish to thank the staff of the Texas National Guard at their headquarters at Camp Mabry in Austin for giving us access to the Texas Ranger papers that they hold.

In Waco, at the Texas Ranger Hall of Fame and Museum, Assistant Director and Archivist Christina Stopka and Librarian Judy Shofner went way out of their way to copy archival documents and photographs for us.

The staff of the Centro de Estudios de Historia de México, Departamento Cultural de Condumex in Mexico City, assisted us in our research in their collections.

Over an extended period of time, a number of archivists at the National Archives—including Timothy Nenninger, Sue Falb, Rick Cox, John Taylor, George Chalou, Rebecca Livingston, Trudy Peterson, and Mitchell Yokelson—were extremely helpful.

The staffs of four Federal Records Centers—Fort Worth (the late George Youngkin), Denver, Laguna Nigel, California, and East Point, Georgia—provided advice as did the staff of the Washington National Records Center. George Youngkin in particular not only advised us on collections that we should consult but also expedited our work.

At Brownsville and Laredo, the staffs of the Office of the District Court Clerk, in Cameron County and Webb County respectively, allowed us to consult their records as did the staff of the Texas Court of Criminal Appeals in Austin.

At the Angelo State University Library, Suzanne Campbell and Alexander S. Cano enabled us to use the West Texas Collection. The Huntington Library allowed us to use a unique photograph. Both the Kansas State Historical Society and the Museum of South Texas History provided rare photographs. We also wish to acknowledge the University of Oklahoma Press, which permitted us to scan photographs no longer available in the public domain from a volume published by the press.

The late State Senator Frank Lombardino of San Antonio intervened in our behalf in securing access to documents as did our friend Paul Harris of Austin.

At New Mexico State University, the chair of the Department of History Ken Hammond was more than helpful to two emeritus historians. History Department Secretaries Patsy Montoya and Nancy Shockley constantly responded to cries for help from the technologically illiterate. Our colleagues in the History Department are undoubtedly ecstatic that they will no longer have to hear more than they ever wanted to learn about the Texas Rangers and the Mexican Revolution.

The authors could not have met their deadlines without the technical help of our colleague and former student Mark Milliorn. Mark is technologically brilliant and always willing to help the computer challenged.

At the Branson and Zuhl Libraries at NMSU, Dean Elizabeth Titus, Associate Dean Cheryl Wilson, Archivists Steve Hussman and Bill Boehm (and before he retired, Austin Hoover), Rose Marie García in Special Collections, Norice Lee and the Inter-Library Loan staff responded to innumerable requests for assistance. Our friend Tim Lawton, the chair of the Department of Geology at NMSU, provided technical advice and located a bright young graduate student, Giovanni Romero, who created our maps. At University Communications Darren Phillips scanned photos for us.

Our friend Ann Atterberry of Plano, Texas, combed the files of the *Dallas Morning News* on our behalf. Art Robertson of Las Cruces, whose dad was a Ranger, allowed us to use a photograph of his father's company. Four old friends, Theo Crevenna at the Latin American and Iberian Institute of the University of New Mexico, Frank Rafalko, political scientist José García, and novelist Ricardo Aguilar, were of considerable assistance to us.

We are indebted to our colleagues Bill Beezley and Alwyn Barr for their excellent suggestions. Fellow historians Michael Meyer, John Hart, Colin MacLachlan, Jeff Pilcher, Daniel Newcomer, John Chalkley, and Jack Wilson each assisted us in a variety of ways. Lawrence Taylor, a friend at El Colegio de la Frontera Norte in Tijuana, located a hard-to-find monograph.

At the University of New Mexico Press, David Holtby for the second time was our editor. We could not have asked for a better one. Managing Editor Evelyn Schlatter, Designer Robyn Mundy, and Editorial Assistant Maya Allen-Gallegos were more than patient with us during the lengthy editorial process. We are indebted to them all.

Finally this book is dedicated to our wives: Betty Harris and Betty Sadler. Both played a significant role in the production. Betty Harris word-processed the manuscript and Betty Sadler helped proof what in typescript was a 900-page monograph. We would like to thank them for their help on the manuscript but mainly for putting up with us all these years.

Charles H. Harris III, Louis R. Sadler
Department of History
New Mexico State University
Las Cruces, New Mexico
June 9, 2004

INTRODUCTION

"One riot—one Ranger." This phrase encapsulates the image of the Texas Rangers—all it takes is a single Ranger to stare down a howling mob. The image is captured in the statue by sculptress Waldine Tauch—a heroic, eight-foot-tall figure wearing two six shooters and standing on a three-foot-tall granite base inscribed "One riot—one Ranger."[1] The phrase continues very much in vogue. For instance, a recent article in the British news magazine *The Economist* entitled "The Future Is Texas" observes that "Texas's minimalistic attitude toward government is embodied in one of the Texas Rangers' favourite mottoes: 'one riot, one ranger.'"[2]

The Texas Rangers are arguably the most celebrated lawmen in the world, their fame ranking with that of the Federal Bureau of Investigation, Scotland Yard, and the Royal Canadian Mounted Police. This is remarkable because the Rangers are a state agency,[3] whereas the others are national organizations; the Federal Bureau of Investigation in 1997 had 10,074 special agents and 13,611 support staff, the Royal Canadian Mounted Police numbered 20,866 in 2001, while in 2003 there were only 118 Texas Rangers. State agencies created in imitation of the Texas Rangers, such as the Arizona Rangers or the New Mexico Mounted Police, existed briefly and in relative obscurity.

Good publicity contributed significantly to the Rangers' reputation. "One riot—one Ranger," with its implication of almost superhuman prowess, is a little gem attributed to Captain Bill McDonald, who happened to be the greatest publicity hound in the history of the Rangers. He had a positive gift for pithy sayings that were immediately seized upon by reporters and that contributed to the glamorous image of the organization. In reality, when a single Ranger arrived to confront rioters it was simply because no more men were available, not because the presence of a single Ranger automatically had an intimidating effect.

Offsetting McDonald's bombast was the Rangers' pathetic performance in the so-called El Paso Salt War of 1877, an inglorious event that is as much a part of Ranger history as "one riot, one Ranger." Ironically, the Salt War began with a real "one riot, one Ranger" episode. When Hispanics in San Elizario, downriver from El Paso, were informed they must now pay to obtain salt from deposits that had traditionally been free, they rioted against Charles Howard, the new owner of the deposits. Since the nearest Ranger company was 500 miles away, the governor dispatched Major John B. Jones, commander of the Rangers, who at the time were organized as the Frontier Battalion, to El Paso to restore order. Jones went to San Elizario and indeed singlehandedly quieted the mob. He returned to El Paso where on November 12, 1877, he mustered in a twenty-man detachment of Company C, Frontier Battalion and then returned to his headquarters in Austin. The El Paso detachment escorted Howard to San Elizario, where they set up camp. The mob reassembled, and a gun battle lasting several days ensued. It ended when the Rangers, who had suffered one man killed and one captured, surrendered and turned Howard over to the mob, who promptly shot him and two of his associates dead. There was considerable enthusiasm for shooting the Rangers as well, but in the end they were just disarmed and shooed back to El Paso. In discussing the Salt War, the distinguished historian Walter Prescott Webb states that Lieutenant John B. Tays, commander of the El Paso detachment, "was not a Texas Ranger," that is, he did not measure up to the finest traditions of the service.[4] (Tays had the dubious distinction of being the only Ranger commander to surrender his force.) This rationalization has been repeated down through the years, notably in the memoirs of William Warren Sterling, *Trails and Trials of a Texas Ranger*—so-and-so was not a "real Ranger" or was a "counterfeit Ranger" because he disgraced the organization.[5] Like it or not, Lieutenant Tays and the others were as "real" as anyone else who ever held a Ranger commission. Furthermore, in defense of the hapless El Paso Rangers it has been pointed out that they were raw recruits after all.[6] True enough, but they had received all the training any Ranger got—none. When a man became a Ranger, or for that matter any other kind of peace officer, he engaged in on-the-job training. It was just naturally assumed that he could handle himself; if not, he did not last long.

Exemplifying the Ranger tradition was Sergeant John Armstrong, who traveled alone to Florida in 1877 after the notorious Texas gunslinger and fugitive John Wesley Hardin. The Ranger located Hardin and four of his desperados on a train. Armstrong killed one, disarmed the other three, knocked Hardin unconscious, and took him back to Texas to stand trial for murder.[7] Among modern Rangers the best known is undoubtedly Frank Hamer, whose most spectacular feat was leading the team of lawmen who tracked down, ambushed, and killed Bonnie and Clyde in 1934. However, Hamer was not a "real Ranger" when he did so. He had been a Ranger and a Ranger captain but resigned in 1933. He was working for the Texas prison system at the time of the ambush.[8] More recently, it was Ranger Drew Carter who in 1999 located and arrested Angel Maturino Reséndez, the serial "railroad killer," rather than—despite its best efforts—the FBI. It is the exploits of men such as these, as well as fictional figures such as the Lone Ranger, that have made the Texas Rangers famous, being celebrated in print, on the radio, on the screen, on television, and even in song. In addition, a town and a professional baseball team have been named for them.

Not only are the Texas Rangers renowned, they are also controversial. The very phrase "Texas Rangers" tends to trigger an emotional response. For most Texans, that is, those of Anglo extraction, the Rangers stand as a symbol of state pride second only to the Alamo itself. Their history is commemorated in the Texas Ranger Hall of Fame in Waco. They are viewed as the handful of courageous men who were instrumental in making Texas a decent place in which to live. This they accomplished by combating, and defeating, Indians, outlaws, and Mexicans. And herein lies the other side of the coin—for Hispanics in Texas the image the Rangers have historically projected is that of the most notorious instrument of repression employed by a racist, Anglo-dominated society. Hispanics, who hated and feared the Rangers, called them *rinches*, and about once a generation or so there would occur in South Texas a *rinchada*—a housecleaning by the Rangers with Hispanics as the target: In the 1850's the Rangers helped crush an insurrection by Juan Cortina in Brownsville; in the 1870's, Captain L. H. McNelly drastically reduced the criminal element in the same area; in the 1890's, Rangers helped smash Catarino Garza's projected invasion of Mexico. And, as we shall see, in 1915 the Rangers conducted a rinchada to end all rinchadas. This was the so-called "Bandit War," a controversial episode in Texas history that until recently has received little attention. All along the Rio Grande the population was predominantly Hispanic, which inevitably meant that most of the criminals were Hispanic, which inevitably injected a racial component into law enforcement—predominantly Anglo peace officers versus predominantly Hispanic outlaws. What tends to get overlooked, however, is that the vast majority of law-abiding citizens in this area were also Hispanics.

The diametrically opposed images of the Texas Rangers can perhaps be illustrated by referring to the "San Benito ambush." On the night of July 31, 1910, a party of lawmen consisting of Rangers Quirl Carnes and J. P. N. "Pat" Craighead and deputy sheriffs Benny Lawrence and Earl West deployed to stake out the anticipated route of a murder suspect. Jacinto Treviño had killed an engineer in San Benito, some twenty miles north of Brownsville, and had fled across the Rio Grande to Mexico. The authorities were informed that Treviño and several friends would cross back into Texas that night, and the officers split up to watch the approaches they might take in coming up from the river. Carnes and Lawrence covered one trail, Craighead and West another. But the ambushers were themselves ambushed—Carnes and Lawrence were killed, and, when they ran to help, Craighead and West were shot and wounded. They managed to kill one of the attackers, but Treviño and his other companions escaped back across the river. The only consolation the Rangers derived from the debacle was that the dead ambusher was the man whose information had led the peace officers into the fatal trap.[9]

Most Texans—primarily the Anglos—were outraged at this further evidence of Hispanic criminality and treachery, whereas Hispanics sympathized with Jacinto Treviño. A *corrido*, or ballad, was even composed about him.[10] In 1971, when the Chicano movement was gaining momentum, a Chicano college in Mercedes, thirty miles northwest of Brownsville, was named for Jacinto Treviño. "Students at the college said they know of Trevino only as a Mexican-American folk hero who had killed a Ranger."[11] Killing a Ranger would indeed make Treviño a folk hero, for Rangers were very hard to kill.

The situation in South Texas in the first two decades of the twentieth century can perhaps best be explained by using present-day Israel as an analogy, with the Anglos as the Israelis and the Hispanics as the Palestinians. The former viewed the latter as conquered people, a fifth column not to be trusted and to be crushed at the least sign of trouble. But one person's terrorist, or in the Texas case "bandit," is another person's freedom fighter. An Israeli history of the State of Israel would differ significantly from a Palestinian history of the same events.

Likewise, conflicting perspectives are reflected in the literature on the Rangers. The most illustrious historian writing from the Anglo point of view was Walter Prescott Webb, whose *Texas Rangers: A Century of Frontier Defense* was published in 1935 and remains the standard work on the subject. The second edition appeared in 1965, with a Foreword by President Lyndon B. Johnson, no less. Webb, whose hometown was, fittingly enough, Ranger, Texas, wrote an account which immeasurably enhanced the heroic image of the organization, for essentially it told the story the way the Rangers would have liked it told.[12] In fairness to Webb, toward the end of his career he did acknowledge that the Rangers had committed excesses.[13] But there was the impression that Webb had said it all. In his introduction to one of Webb's later works, historian Joe B. Frantz declared that:

> *The Texas Rangers* appeared in 1935. Hailed as the definitive history of a frontier law-enforcement agency, it had the faults as well as the virtues of definitiveness. It was overpacked, almost ponderous in its detail; but it hardly left anything for anyone else to say.[14]

The most recent work on the Rangers, Robert M. Utley, *Lone Star Justice: The First Century of the Texas Rangers*, which appeared in 2002,[15] undertakes to present a more balanced view. This first volume of a projected two-volume treatment of the Rangers ends in 1910. Time will tell whether Utley's work will displace Webb.

In recent decades there developed a reaction to Webb, primarily as a result of the Chicano movement. Attempting to redress the balance, Chicano historians have focused on the Rangers as a type of Texas Gestapo. The works emanating from this school of thought stress racism, brutality, and oppression. Rodolfo Acuña, *Occupied America: The Chicano's Struggle Toward Liberation,*[16] and Julian Samora, Joe Bernal, and Albert Peña, *Gunpowder Justice: A Reassessment of the Texas Rangers,*[17] come to mind. Yet in their efforts to debunk the Rangers in general and Webb in particular, Chicano writers have been unwilling or unable to do the kind of massive research that Webb engaged in. Chicanos also tend to view the whole subject with tunnel vision, reducing everything to race: Anglo versus Hispanic. Admittedly, much of it was. No one could accuse Texans of having been overly fond of Mexicans. It could even be postulated that in terms of ethnic relations, Texas history is a case of the Mexicans winning at the Alamo and Goliad and losing at San Jacinto and paying for it ever since. This of course illustrates the historical truism that a good way to avoid oppression, discrimination, and racism is by not losing the war. But viewing everything strictly within a racial context is a bit simplistic, ignoring the socioeconomic and political differences existing within the Hispanic population. Chicanos' accounts of the Rangers tend to be as stereotyped as anything one can find among Anglo writers, which is surprising among those who themselves are so sensitive to stereotyping. Chicano writers are also prone to portray Chicanos in the same overly heroic light that they decry in Webb's treatment of the Rangers.

A word about nomenclature seems in order. During the decade under study, people were referred to as either "negroes" (blacks, Afro-Americans, African-Americans, colored people, people of color), "Americans" (whites, Anglos), or "Mexicans" (Mexicans, Mexicanos, Mexican-Americans, Latin Americans, Chicanos, Hispanics, Hispanos, Latinos/as, Tejanos). Since the politically correct terminology keeps changing, we have settled on "Anglos," "Hispanics" (for the Texas-born), "Mexicans" (for those from Mexico), and "blacks."

Historians have neglected the decade 1910–1920 despite its significance.[18] Since these were by far the most important years in the history of the Texas State Ranger Force, they richly deserve a book of their own, not just a chapter or two in some general history of the Rangers. Because so little has been written about the Rangers in this decade, we have tried to provide a context by discussing the organization and routine operations of the Ranger Force in some detail. When people think of "the Texas Rangers" they have in mind the Regular Rangers— paid by the State of Texas and organized into companies. But the Regulars were only the tip of an extensive law enforcement pyramid. There were, in addition, Special Rangers, who had the same authority as Regulars but were neither paid by the state nor always assigned to a company. And during World War I there was created yet another category of Special Rangers—the Loyalty Rangers, charged with combating disloyalty and subversion. There was frequent movement between the three types of Rangers and between the Rangers and other kinds of peace officers such as sheriffs, deputies, constables, railroad detectives, and brand inspectors for cattlemen's associations. Furthermore, many Rangers resigned to enter federal service, primarily as Customs or Immigration inspectors. Thus it is important to determine whether a man was in fact a Texas Ranger when a specific incident occurred.

But just who were "the Texas Rangers"? The term is an abstraction. To some Hispanic in South Texas any Anglo lawman with a horse, a badge, and a gun was a rinche. But not unless one knows precisely who the Rangers were can they be accurately held accountable for their actions. Previous writers have made little effort to identify them. The present authors have built on the Texas Rangers Service Records in the Archives Division of the Texas State Library to compile dossiers on 1,785 individuals who at one time or another held Ranger commissions between 1910 and 1921. Their tenure ranged from that of Captain John H. Rogers, who served continuously for twenty-eight years, to that of J. William Stewart, who was enlisted and honorably discharged on the same day. One thing the dossiers reveal is the striking number of Rangers who were related to other Rangers; oftentimes one is dealing with law enforcement clans. This phenomenon is especially the case for Wilson County, southeast of San Antonio, which produced a disproportionate number of Rangers, mainly from the Carnes, Shely, Hamer, Brady, Craighead, Webb, Wright, and West families. Over the decades Wilson County produced forty-four Rangers, nearly half of them from the tiny community of Fairview, twelve miles west of Floresville, the county seat. Today Fairview is a ghost town.[19]

By way of illustrating the law enforcement and familial connections that emerge, one need only refer to the participants in the San Benito ambush. Ranger Quirl Bailey Carnes, who was killed, had enlisted in Company A in 1907. He was the brother of Ranger Herff Carnes. After being a farmer, Herff Carnes spent eight years in the Rangers, resigning in 1911 as a sergeant to become a mounted Customs inspector in El Paso. He served for twenty-one years before being killed by Mexican smugglers in 1932. Their brother, Alfred Burton Carnes, was Wilson County sheriff from 1918 to 1938. (Their nephew Tom Carnes was a member of the Border Patrol for many years; nephew Bob Carnes was in the FBI; nephew Don Carnes was Wilson County sheriff from 1953 to 1960; nephew Don Gilliland served in the Rangers in the 1920's.) The wounded Ranger, Pat Craighead, was the brother of Ranger Charles A. Craighead, who was in Company D from 1908 to 1911, when he resigned. Charles Craighead then became a policeman in Marfa and later a mounted Customs inspector. Pat and Charles Craighead were sons of a former sheriff of Wilson County, John S. Craighead. Pat Craighead had been a deputy sheriff before enlisting in the Rangers in 1910. He served until April, 1915. In 1916 he was appointed sheriff of Jim Hogg County, serving in that position until his death in 1921. The wounded deputy sheriff, Earl West, became a Special Ranger in 1918. His father, Milton Crockett West, was a Special Ranger in 1918–1919. His brother, Paul More West, was a Ranger in Company D in 1915. His other brother, Milton H. West, served in Company C in 1911–1912 and held a Special Ranger commission in 1927–1928. Milton H. West, incidentally, became an attorney and later a congressman, succeeding John Nance Garner, who went on to be Franklin D. Roosevelt's vice president.[20]

Besides the documentation establishing who the Rangers were, there is abundant material describing what they did. The basic source is the Adjutant General's Correspondence, which includes the Ranger records, in the Archives Division of the Texas State Library in Austin. In addition, there is a quantity of adjutant general's papers in Austin at Camp Mabry, the headquarters of the Texas National Guard. Another major source is the 1919 legislative investigation of the Rangers, comprising 1,605 typed pages of sworn testimony. The papers of Governors Thomas M. Campbell, Oscar B. Colquitt, James E. Ferguson, and William P. Hobby contain a great deal of material bearing on the Rangers. The fourth indispensable repository is the Walter Prescott Webb Collection at the University of Texas at Austin. The Webb transcripts include a number of items no longer found in the Adjutant General's Correspondence. Supplementing these four main sources is the mass of archival material revealing what other agencies had to say about the Rangers—the Federal Bureau of Investigation's files on the Mexican Revolution; the records of the Department of Justice and the Department of State; the Army's records—that is, the Adjutant General, the Department of Texas, the Southern Department, and the Military Intelligence Division; the Secret Service archive; and hundreds of federal and state court cases. Certain Mexican sources, such as the archives of President Venustiano Carranza and General Pablo González, shed light on some of the Rangers' activities.

The present authors intend to present a full-scale treatment of the Texas Rangers during the decade of the Mexican Revolution. We will examine the Rangers not just as a law enforcement agency but also within a political context, for the Rangers did not operate in a vacuum. They were, in a real sense, the governor's personal police and reported to him through the adjutant general, who supervised both the Rangers and the Texas National Guard.[21] Moreover, the issuance of Ranger commissions became a common method of conferring political favors. The Rangers played a unique role. They were a state constabulary, but they were also charged with helping to defend the American border. And, because ever since 1876, when General Porfirio Díaz used Brownsville as a base of operations, Mexican exiles had used Texas as a sanctuary from which to attempt the overthrow of the Mexican government, the Rangers also became involved in monitoring exile activity and suppressing filibustering expeditions. Thus their activities had an important bearing on the relations between the United States and Mexico.

As T. R. Fehrenbach has observed, "One problem that faces every Texan historian facing a Texas readership is that all nations have their national myths, and Texas became enough of a nation within a nation to formulate its own. Many of Texas's legends, historically unproven and even historically insupportable, are fondly held and fiercely defended. This is not unique to Texas. The American nation has its own mythology."[22] In undertaking this study, our purpose is neither to justify nor to condemn but rather to paint as accurately as possible a portrait of the Rangers, warts and all.

TEXAS

OKLAHOMA

NEW MEXICO

•Amarillo

ARKANSAS

Lubbock•

•Post

Ft. Worth• •Dallas

•Longview

El Paso

•Midland

Ranger•
•Desdemona

Pecos •

Waco •

LOUSIANA

Fort Stockton•

•Marfa

Austin •

•Rocksprings

Houston•

Del Rio•

San Antonio

•Eagle Pass

Corpus Christi

Gulf of Mexico

MEXICO

•Laredo

100 ml

0   100 Km

•Brownsville

UPPER BORDER

NEW MEXICO

Midland •

El Paso
Ciudad
Juarez • Ysleta

• Fabens

• Fort Hancock

• Sierra Blanca

Van Horn •

• Lobo

• Valentine

• Porvenir

• Alpine

• Marathon

• Sanderson

• Shafter

Ojinaga • • Presidio

15   30   60 ml
0   20   40   80 Km

MEXICO

MIDDLE BORDER

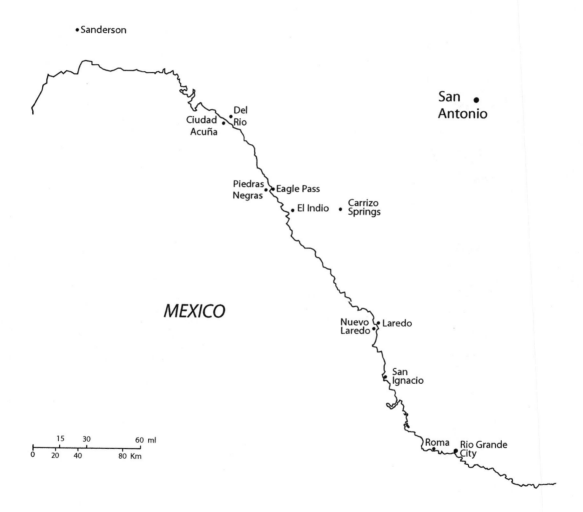

• Sanderson

Del
Rio
Ciudad
Acuña

San
Antonio

Piedras
Negras •Eagle Pass

• El Indio

Carrizo
Springs

MEXICO

Nuevo • Laredo
Laredo

San
Ignacio

Roma   Rio Grande
City

15   30   60 ml
0   20   40   80 Km

LOWER BORDER

San Diego •   • Alice

• Laredo

Kingsville •

Hebbronville •

• Falfurrias

MEXICO

Norias •

Raymondville •

Lyford
Sebastian •

Rio Grande
City •

Edinburg •

Mission   •   McAllen   Harlingen •
Pharr •   • Donna   San Benito
Progreso •   • Mercedes

Matamoros •   • Brownsville

Corpus Christi •

Gulf

of

Mexico

15   30   60 ml

0   20   40   80 Km

Prelude

CHAPTER 1

THE TEXAS STATE RANGER FORCE

THE Texas Rangers have been remarkably resilient. They have existed, with a few interruptions, for 180 years in one form or another. They first appeared while Texas still belonged to Mexico; in 1823, Stephen F. Austin hired ten men to serve as rangers to protect the Anglo settlements from Indian raids. A more formal organization came into being on November 24, 1835, while Texas was struggling for its independence. The revolutionary government authorized the creation of a corps of Texas Rangers commanded by a major and consisting of three companies of fifty-six men each, to protect the frontier.[1] During the Mexican War, 1846–1848, units of volunteer irregular cavalry called Texas Rangers fought with distinction under Generals Taylor and Scott, although they gained a reputation for brutality.[2] From the Rangers' point of view, the war was a splendid opportunity to kill Mexicans and get paid for it. They remembered the Alamo and Goliad with a vengeance.

In the postwar period, "The Texans demanded that the United States should muster the Rangers into federal service, pay them with federal money, and let them run all the Mexicans into the Rio Grande and all the Indians into Red River."[3] The federal government declined to do so. To protect its border with Mexico, Texas in the 1850's periodically mustered in companies "of minute men or Texas Rangers." One of these units, under Captain J. H. Callahan, crossed the Rio Grande and on October 4, 1855, captured the border town of Piedras Negras. As Mexican reinforcements closed in, Callahan burned the town to cover his retreat back into Texas.[4] In 1858–1859, Rangers played a prominent role in combating Indian depredations on the western frontier and in suppressing Juan Cortina's rebellion in Brownsville. Cortina, who came from a wealthy ranching family, made himself a folk hero when on July 13, 1859, he rescued a former servant who was being roughly arrested by the city marshal. Cortina shot the lawman in the shoulder and galloped out of town with his servant hanging on behind him, thus creating a kind of Robin Hood image. Cortina took over Brownsville on September 28. Not until the following spring were the army and the Rangers able to suppress the rebellion.[5]

The Civil War produced the apparent demise of the Rangers in their traditional role of combating Indians and Mexicans. A unit named Terry's Texas Rangers did fight in the Confederate Army. But for the nine years following the end of the Civil War, the Texas Rangers were nonexistent. During Reconstruction, the Republican regime in Austin organized a state police force in 1870, a body that was despised by ex-Confederates but popular among ex-Unionists and blacks. The state police force was abolished in 1873 as soon as the Democrats gained control of the state legislature.

In 1874, since a national guard had not yet been organized, the legislature created two paramilitary forces. One was the Frontier Battalion of Texas Rangers, commanded by Major John B. Jones. Jones reported to the adjutant general and the governor. The Battalion's authorized strength was six companies—A to F—of seventy-five men each, a total of 450 men. A captain commanded each company, assisted by a first lieutenant, a second lieutenant, and a sergeant. The Battalion's primary mission was to fight Indians on the western frontier.[6] The other unit was a Special Force under Captain L. H. McNelly, a Civil War veteran who had been a state police captain. Its mission was to suppress banditry along the lower Rio Grande border. McNelly carried out his mission in spectacular if ruthless fashion. Not only did he eliminate rustlers and bandits, but he even crossed the Rio Grande with thirty men, shot up two ranches said to be dens of rustlers, and managed to recover 500 head of King Ranch cattle.[7]

There is, however, some disagreement as to whether McNelly and his men were in fact Texas Rangers. Walter Prescott Webb stoutly maintained that they were.[8] But Robert Draper argues that:

> Leander McNelly was never a Texas Ranger. Muster rolls, vouchers, and state correspondences indicate that from 1874 until 1876, McNelly was the captain of the Washington County Volunteer Militia, and from 1876 until his departure in January 1877, captain of a brigade worded in state legislation as "special state troops." His troops were structurally and budgetarily set apart from the six companies making up the separately legislated Frontier Battalion of Texas Rangers. McNelly did not report to the head of the Rangers, Major John B. Jones, but rather to Adjutant General William Steele. Occasionally reporters and McNelly referred to his men as Rangers, presumably as a descriptive term — and indeed, McNelly's brigade performed just as bravely as Major Jones's Rangers did. But to say that McNelly was a Texas Ranger

simply because he killed Mexican bandits on behalf of the state would be like saying that Oliver North was a CIA agent simply because he went on a few spying missions.

Yet historians, including the Rangers' eminent biographer-booster Walter Prescott Webb, have woven Leander McNelly into Ranger history with little regard for the facts.[9]

The author of the most recent work on the Rangers, Robert M. Utley, seems to hedge his bets on this question: "Despite its unusual origin, McNelly's Company A, Volunteer Militia of Washington County, compared in most essentials to the companies of the Frontier Battalion. The men regarded themselves as Rangers, and so did the public—'McNelly's Rangers.'"[10] So, since the men thought they were Rangers and the public did as well, Utley follows Webb's lead in so characterizing them.

Besides beating down Indian resistance in the West, the Frontier Battalion's most famous exploit was the killing in 1878 of the notorious outlaw Sam Bass when he tried to rob the bank in Round Rock, an operation that Major Jones personally directed.[11] But by the decade of the 1880's, the Frontier Battalion no longer had a frontier to protect. And with the rise to power of the dictator General Porfirio Díaz, the Mexican side of the border was gradually brought under control. The Texas Rangers now became a state police force whose function was to support local lawmen. The Frontier Battalion had become an anachronism. Nevertheless, the organization remained in being until 1901. Ironically, what Indians, outlaws, and Mexicans had failed to do, the legal profession accomplished. A sharp defense attorney noticed that the statute creating the Frontier Battalion stated that each *officer* had the authority of a peace officer. Thus, technically, only the major commanding the Battalion and the captain and lieutenants of each company could lawfully make arrests. The issue went to the Texas attorney general, who in 1900 ruled that indeed the Battalion's non-commissioned officers and privates had no authority to arrest. The ruling was devastating. The attorney general did hand down a second opinion that allowed the Battalion to reorganize temporarily until the legislature could take appropriate action. The makeshift reorganization reduced the Battalion to a pitiful four companies of six men each, half of them officers, who were the only personnel empowered to make arrests. This shell of a battalion existed from June 1, 1900, to July 8, 1901, when it was replaced by the new Ranger organization.[12]

On July 8, 1901, a law empowering the governor to create a new Ranger Force went into effect. The Texas State Ranger Force's mission was to protect the frontier against marauders and thieves, and to suppress lawlessness and crime. The Force had an authorized strength of eighty-nine men and consisted of four mounted companies, each company having a captain, a sergeant, and twenty privates. In addition there was a quartermaster captain for the entire force who functioned as quartermaster, commissary, and paymaster. The Ranger Force was in effect the governor's personal police, and that would be the single most important fact in the entire history of that organization.

The captains were appointed by the governor and served at his pleasure. Unless the governor removed them, they served for a two-year tour of duty. Captains were paid $100 a month, sergeants $50, and privates $40. The Rangers, usually unmarried, volunteered for a two-year tour. Each officer, non-commissioned officer, and private furnished his own horse, horse equipment, clothing, etc. But if his horse were killed in action, the state would pay for the animal at fair market value. The state furnished:

each member of said force with one improved carbine and pistol at cost, the price of which shall be deducted from the first money due such officer or man, and shall furnish said force with rations of subsistence, camp equipage and ammunition for the officers and men, and also forage for horses.

The Rangers ate well—in theory. Daily rations for each man were:

twelve ounces of bacon or twenty of beef
twenty ounces of flour or corn meal
two and two-fifths ounces of beans or peas
one and three-fifths ounces of rice
three and one-fifth ounces of coffee
three and one-fifth ounces of sugar
one-sixth gill of vinegar or pickles
one-sixth ounce candles
one-third ounce of soap
two-thirds ounce of salt
one twenty-fourth ounce of pepper
four and four-fifths ounces of potatoes
sixteen twenty-fifths of an ounce of baking powder.

One can just imagine a Ranger captain doling out sixteen twenty-fifths of an ounce of baking powder daily to each of his men. In the field, the cuisine was likely to be beans, roasted goat meat, and coffee.

Daily forage for each horse was:

twelve pounds of corn or oats
fourteen pounds of hay
plus two ounces of salt per week.

When the above rations could not be provided, a man received a subsistence allowance not to exceed $1.50 a day. When Rangers traveled by railroad, the state would pay their expenses.

Regarding the all-important matter of who had the power to make arrests, the 1901 Act explicitly stated that:

> The officers, non-commissioned officers and privates of this force shall be clothed with all the powers of peace officers, and shall aid the regular civil authorities in the execution of the laws. They shall have authority to make arrests, and to execute process in criminal cases, and in such cases they shall be governed by law regulating and defining the powers and duties of sheriffs when in discharge of similar duties; except that they shall have the powers, and shall be authorized to make arrests and to execute all process in criminal cases in any county in the State.[13]

Such was the new Ranger Force—on paper. In many respects it retained the paramilitary structure of the Frontier Battalion, although its authorized strength was of course much smaller. Initially this Ranger organization actually numbered only about a fourth of its authorized strength. In theory, the Rangers investigated felonies; in practice, they investigated everything from murder to shoplifting.

Contrary to popular perception, Western Union and the railroads were as essential to the Ranger Force as were guns and horses. The adjutant general controlled the movements of his Rangers by telegraph. This system worked well everywhere except in the Big Bend, where telegraphic facilities were practically nonexistent. Another important aspect of Ranger operations has been mentioned only in passing—their dependence on the railroads, which provided free transportation to peace officers.[14] The popular view is that of Rangers riding horseback, thundering along in pursuit of outlaws. While this was true in earlier times, by 1910 the Rangers did much of their traveling by railroad, which obviously enabled them to cover long distances more quickly than on horseback. They either took their horses with them or acquired horses—or automobiles—as needed once they reached their destination. The adjutant general's department spent a not inconsiderable amount of its time dealing with the railroads, of which there were fifteen in Texas. Each January the adjutant general requested passes for Rangers for that year, but he requested them only from those lines that each Ranger company was likely to use.[15] When emergencies occurred, he had to request additional passes on a crash basis. The adjutant general ensured that the right passes went where and when they were needed, and throughout the year he supervised requests for passes for enlistees and the cancellation of passes for men no longer in the Ranger service.

Although the 1901 Act provided that the state would pay the Rangers' rail expenses, the railroads were pleased to provide free transportation. An appreciative State of Texas reciprocated by issuing Special Ranger commissions to the railroads' detectives, thus giving them jurisdiction throughout the state. Furthermore, the Rangers were available to protect the railroads' property in the event of labor disputes. This mutually beneficial arrangement reflected a principle that applied not just to the Rangers but to any other law-enforcement organization: Those who pay the most taxes get the most protection.

Whatever money the State of Texas saved from free rail transportation certainly did not go to increase the Rangers' budget. Texas might love its brave Ranger boys but it sure hated to spend money on them. The Ranger Force operated on a shoestring—the appropriation for the biennium 1908–1909 was all of $25,000 a year.[16] Low salaries were a perennial problem in trying to attract good men into the Rangers. The $100 a month that a captain made was the same salary as any mounted Customs inspector received. A private's $40 a month was not much more than the average wage for a cowboy, the difference being that cowboys got shot at a whole lot less often.[17] There was, of course, no provision for pensions or other benefits for Rangers. The law provided for compensation in cases of death or injury in line of duty, but if a Ranger got sick he was on his own. As far back as 1876, when Capt. L. H. McNelly was terminally ill with tuberculosis, the adjutant general discharged him because his medical bills were eating up his company's appropriation.[18] The state hadn't gotten much more charitable in the years since. When Sergeant W. J. McCauley, who'd been a Ranger for eleven years, died of natural causes in 1910, the state refused to pay his medical expenses. The state was somewhat more compassionate toward those Rangers who were shot in the line of duty. It paid the funeral expenses for Quirl Carnes, killed in the San Benito ambush. But the $827 medical bill of his partner Pat Craighead, wounded in the same incident, was still outstanding in 1914, and not until 1914 did Craighead get an artificial leg.[19] The state did, however, pay the medical expenses of Ranger Richard C. Hawkins, wounded in 1912. The real compensation for low salaries and the dangers inherent in the job was being able to include "Texas Ranger" on one's résumé. Serving in the Rangers automatically conferred a certain status, as indeed it does even today.

The Rangers were not big on paperwork, but some amount of it is indispensable in any bureaucracy. Every month each Ranger captain certified and submitted a Ration Return for his company.[20] He had received the commodities on credit from a local merchant, who would eventually be paid by a warrant drawn on the state treasury. One imagines that the Ration Return was among the least enjoyable chores a captain performed, for the quartermaster was quick to pounce on any inaccuracies. Besides the Ration Return, each captain filled out a "Pay Roll" form monthly.[21] But the most important form he submitted to the adjutant general, with a copy to the quartermaster, was the Monthly Return for his company.[22] It was through this document that headquarters in Austin could keep track of what was happening in the field. Filled out at the end of the month, the Monthly Return had a section for reporting absences when not on duty and explaining the nature of such absences. There was a section dealing with the "increase and decrease of public property"—here were listed the tents, cots, stoves, and other equipment of the company and its condition, as well as ammunition received from the quartermaster and its disposition. The Monthly Return included a listing of individuals who joined the company, either by enlistment or transfer, those who were discharged, who deserted, who died or were killed, and the reason therefore. The most important section dealt with a listing of arrests made during the month, the name of the prisoner, the charge against him, by whom he was arrested, and the disposition of the prisoner. There was also a narrative report of scouts conducted and arrests made during the month, and the number of miles traveled in the line of duty. In addition, there was a discharge certificate, which a captain filled out in duplicate whenever a Ranger resigned or was discharged. One copy went to the Ranger and the other to the adjutant general's office to be filed with the Ranger's enlistment papers.

Rangers either furnished their own weapons or at their request the assistant quartermaster general, Colonel R. H. Beckham, would order the weapon for them and deduct its cost from their salary. The quartermaster furnished the ammunition. The favorite rifle was the Model 1895 box magazine Winchester carbine firing 30–40 Krag-Jorgensen cartridges. This lever-action weapon was prized because it was rugged and dependable. As for pistols, the Rangers, like many other lawmen, favored the Colt .45 single action revolver with a $5^1/_2$" barrel, which was ideal for "bending" over the head of a recalcitrant offender. This preference for Colt firearms was of long standing, going back to the 1830's when the Texas Rangers adopted the Colt revolver, which they had helped design.[23] But there was certainly room for individuality. Captain Frank Johnson had, as backup to his six-shooter, a Colt .32 automatic, while Captain John Brooks favored a Luger. In 1910, an unidentified member of Company C requested that the quartermaster ask the Colt company the price of a 16-gauge automatic shotgun "with the shortest barrel you make. He wants it for night work and close range."[24] Two years later, Ranger Paul McAlister was using a Colt .45 automatic. And by 1913, the assistant quartermaster general was "recommending strongly to all Texas Rangers that they arm themselves with the new Government Model Colt's Automatic Caliber 45."[25] As with firearms, so with clothing. There was no regulation uniform. The men wore whatever they felt comfortable in, although if somebody had reported for duty in a frock and sunbonnet it probably would have upset his captain.

Rangers used what has been called a "scout belt." A six-inch-wide strip of supple leather was doubled, so the slot could serve as a money belt and hold a small screwdriver to tighten the screws on weapons. Around the outside of the belt were two rows of loops for pistol cartridges and one for rifle shells. The men also had two kinds of pistol holsters—one for use with the scout belt, having a thong to hook over the hammer to keep from losing the pistol when riding through rough country, and the other holster without the thong for town and evening wear.[26]

Although Rangers enlisted for a two-year tour of duty, they could resign or be discharged at any time. They were granted leave at the captain's discretion. This system constituted a grave weakness, for it produced a continual turnover of personnel. Coupled with low pay, the system made it difficult for a captain to build up an effective company. Captains selected their men, but they had difficulty attracting experienced men. The latter served, often for short periods of time, until they could find something better. And when recruits gained experience they too looked for better paying jobs. Thus the pattern for Rangers was that of sporadic periods of service. Few of them served continuously for as much as a decade, and Captain John H. Rogers's twenty-eight-year career was a striking anomaly.

What would make or break the new Ranger Force was its captains. In this respect the organization got off to a splendid start, for its captains were men of exceptional ability. They were experienced, three of them having come up through the ranks of the Frontier Battalion. More importantly, each was a natural leader of men. Taken together, they set a standard of excellence that the Ranger Force would never again achieve. Interestingly, three of the four captains were born out of state: William J. McDonald in Mississippi, John R. Hughes in Illinois, and John A. Brooks in Kentucky. Only John H. Rogers was a native Texan.[27]

John Harris Rogers was born in Guadalupe County on October 7, 1863. He grew up in poverty, with little education. Rogers did what some other poor but ambitious young men did—he enlisted in the Rangers, on September 5, 1882. He resigned from Company B the next year but a few months later reenlisted, this time in Company F under Captain Joe Shely, one of the six celebrated Shely brothers who were Rangers. In 1887, Rogers was badly wounded in a bloody shootout in East Texas with a family of outlaws named Conner. Two years later he was promoted to sergeant of Company F. Rogers saw action on the Rio Grande, participating in crushing Catarino Garza's rebellion in 1891, and on January 1, 1893, he was promoted to captain of Company F. In 1898, he became captain of Company E, and the next year he was again badly wounded. This time he was in Laredo helping to enforce the quarantine laws and was shot in the right shoulder by a man who objected to those regulations. Rogers never fully recovered from this wound, for a section of bone had to be removed from his arm. Thereafter he used a custom-built Winchester carbine whose stock was offset.

Rogers's most famous exploit was the capture—together with mounted Customs Inspector Bill Merriman—of a fugitive who was the subject of the largest manhunt in Texas since the days of Sam Bass. Gregorio Cortez had killed Sheriff Brack Morris (who had been a Ranger in Company F, Frontier Battalion) of Karnes County and Sheriff Robert M. Glover and Deputy Sheriff Henry Schnabel of Gonzalez County. Cortez struck out for the Mexican border, and the hunt for him spanned ten days and eight counties, involving hundreds of heavily armed peace officers and citizens. Cortez nearly made it. But only a few miles from the Rio Grande a Hispanic shepherd disclosed his whereabouts to Captain Rogers and Customs Inspector Merriman, who on June 22, 1901, arrested Cortez as he slept at a goatherd's camp.[28] On July 8, 1901, Rogers was appointed to command Company C in the new Ranger Force.

Rogers certainly did not fit the stereotype of the hard-bitten Ranger captain, for his demeanor was more that of a preacher. And in fact, Rogers was a deeply religious man, a staunch Presbyterian who was a church elder, who never cursed, and who was soft-spoken and modest. He exercised command through his moral authority. A number of criminals found to their sorrow that they had mistaken Rogers's low-key approach to law enforcement for weakness.[29] Like so many other Rangers, Captain Rogers had relatives who were also in law enforcement. His brother Charles served in Company F from 1888 to 1892; his brother-in-law, William M. Burwell, was Rogers's sergeant in Company C and later became sheriff of Potter County; his other brother-in-law, Charles B. Burwell, was sheriff of La Salle County; Charles B. Burwell, Jr., served in Ranger Companies A and I from 1917 to 1919, was a Special Ranger in the 1920's while a brand inspector for the Texas and Southwestern Cattle Raisers Association, and in the 1950's managed the Laureles division of the enormous King Ranch.[30]

Captain Rogers was a man of principle, which he demonstrated by resigning his command on January 31, 1911, because Governor Oscar B. Colquitt opposed Prohibition. Rogers's twenty-eight years of continuous service was a record in the Rangers. Immediately upon his resignation he was appointed deputy U.S. marshal in El Paso, and on April 1, 1913, was appointed U.S. marshal for the Western District of Texas. Unlike his three fellow captains, Rogers returned to the Rangers: On May 15, 1927, he was commissioned as Captain of Company C, a position he held at the time of his death in Scott and White Hospital in Temple, on November 11, 1930. Rogers was comfortably off, having saved his money and made shrewd investments in real estate near El Paso.

Captain William Jesse McDonald was the antithesis of Rogers when it came to personality—McDonald was a showman through and through. He was born in Kemper County, Mississippi, on September 28, 1852. He moved to a farm near Henderson, Texas, in 1866. McDonald had more education than most other Rangers, for he graduated from Soule's Commercial College in New Orleans in 1872. Afterward he was a grocer in Mineola in the 1870's, and in the 1880's a deputy sheriff in Wood and Hardeman Counties, and then a deputy U.S. marshal for the Northern District of Texas. In 1891, he was appointed as captain of Company B, Frontier Battalion. When the Ranger Force was established, he continued as captain of Company B until his retirement in 1907.[31] Without question he was a brave and capable officer, and he had a career year in 1906.

The army decided to station the black troops of the 25th Infantry Regiment in Brownsville, to the intense displeasure of the citizenry. Although the Anglo and Hispanic residents might dislike each other, both groups were agreed on one thing—they despised the black soldiers. Overwhelmingly Hispanic Brownsville considered what the army had done to be a deliberate insult, and the citizens went out of their way to impress on the black troops that they were not welcome. Less than a month after their arrival, the blacks allegedly struck back. It was said that on the night of August 13, some twenty soldiers sallied forth from Fort Brown and shot up the town. They killed a bartender and wounded the lieutenant of police, José Domínguez, whose arm had to be amputated. After a ten-minute rampage, the troops rushed back to the fort and put away their weapons.

The raid naturally caused an uproar in Brownsville. On August 21, Captain McDonald and two of his men arrived to reinforce the two Rangers already on the scene. "The Rangers and the citizens' committee had gathered valuable information which was imparted to McDonald, who spent most of the night in making further investigations and in giving the third degree to a colored ex-soldier who ran a saloon and had knowledge of the raid."[32] The next morning he marched up to the gate of Fort Brown carrying an automatic shotgun and backed up by his sergeant, William J. McCauley, who happened to be his nephew. Boldly facing down the file of armed black troops who barred his way, the Ranger captain entered the fort. It was this act that impelled the commanding officer, Major C. W. Penrose, subsequently to declare that "Bill McDonald would charge hell with a bucket of water." This saying, together with McDonald's "one riot, one Ranger" chestnut, would form the core of the growing McDonald legend. What tended to get overlooked in all this was that ultimately McDonald was unable to serve the arrest warrants he had secured for twelve soldiers and one ex-soldier. He did, however, inform the judge who demanded that he return the warrants that the judge and the local lawmen backing the jurist up "looked like fifteen cents in Mexican money," another eminently quotable one-liner.[33]

The 25th Infantry was transferred out of Brownsville and Captain McDonald went on with his career. The McDonald legend took another jump in November. The captain was ordered to Rio Grande City to investigate the murder of District Judge Stanley Welch. The judge was in town to supervise a bitterly contested election, but on November 6, on the eve of the election, he was shot to death while he slept. On the night of November 7, McDonald, three of his men, and a former Ranger who was now a Customs inspector were traveling toward that town in a rented open hack. They were unaware that coming down the road toward them was another hack with six Hispanics from Rio Grande City who'd gotten liquored up and had decided to ambush the two Rangers they'd heard were on the way. The two vehicles met at the Casitas ranch, and the Mexicans opened fire. In the confused firefight that followed they were decidedly the losers; when the smoke cleared four were dead, and the other two were prisoners. McDonald's party emerged without casualties. Afterward, when McDonald was asked about how many he'd shot in the fight, he modestly allowed as how he hadn't missed any of them. This was true, but it was hardly the truth—McDonald had used one of the newfangled semi-automatic Winchesters, and it had jammed after the first shot.[34]

McDonald resigned from the Rangers in 1907. His exploits were chronicled in a 1909 biography by Albert Bigelow Paine, which further enhanced the captain's reputation.[35] In 1907, Governor Tom Campbell appointed him as the state revenue agent. When Campbell's term ended in 1911, McDonald toyed with the idea of becoming a private detective, and he reportedly turned down an offer to become police chief of Houston. He did, however, become sergeant-at-arms of the Texas legislature. McDonald's career was furthered significantly by his friendship with Colonel Edward M. House, a major political power in Texas. As House's protege, McDonald moved in all the right circles, and when Woodrow Wilson became the Democratic presidential candidate in 1912, House got McDonald hired as Wilson's bodyguard. The former Ranger captain was as quotable as ever. Wilson's entourage were enchanted with "Silent Bill," who wore two six-shooters, and they gushed about his marksmanship to Wilson, telling him that shooting from the hip "he could hit the eye of a mosquito at 500 yards range." Asked if this were really true, McDonald calmly inquired "Which eye?"[36] When Wilson was elected he appointed McDonald as the U.S. marshal for the Northern District of Texas. McDonald died at Wichita Falls on January 15, 1918. He was buried at Quanah with one of his memorable sayings carved on his tombstone: "No man in the wrong can stand up against a fellow that's in the right and keeps on a-comin'."[37]

The third captain was John Abijah Brooks. Born in Bourbon County, Kentucky, on November 20, 1862, he arrived in Laredo in 1882. After a stint working in the nearby coal mines, he became a cowboy. In 1883 he enlisted in the Rangers, in Company F, serving together with the future captain John H. Rogers. In 1885, Brooks was promoted to sergeant. In 1887, he and Rogers were among the Rangers who participated in the gun battle with the Conner family. Like Rogers, Brooks was wounded; he was hit in both hands, losing the two middle fingers of his left hand. Brooks was promoted to captain in 1889, and Rogers became his sergeant. Two years later they helped to quash Catarino Garza's attempt to invade Mexico. This campaign was covered by the famous correspondent Richard Harding Davis in his book *The West From a Car Window*. When the Ranger Force was organized in 1901, Brooks commanded Company A, covering Southwest

Texas. He served with distinction until his retirement on November 17, 1906, after a twenty-three-year career.

Brooks had purchased land south of Falfurrias, and he intended to become a rancher. However, he was elected to the state legislature, where he sponsored a bill to create a new county from the northern part of Starr County. The county was indeed created, in 1911, and was organized in 1912. The county was appropriately named for Captain Brooks, who served as its county judge until his death in 1944.[38]

The last of the captains was John Reynolds Hughes, who was born on February 11, 1855, in Cambridge, Illinois. After an adventurous youth as a cowboy and Indian trader, he finally settled down as a small rancher. But this kind of life was tame, so on August 10, 1887, he joined the Rangers, enlisting in Company D. While a young man in the Indian Territory, his right arm had been crippled in a fight. He had to fire his six-gun with his left hand and his rifle from his left shoulder, being able to raise his right arm just enough to support the weapon. Despite this handicap he proved he could fire well enough to get the job done. He became sergeant of Company D in 1893 and its captain several months later, on July 4, 1893. Hughes's entire career was in Company D (which on February 1, 1911, was redesignated as Company A), whose captain he remained when the new Ranger Force was created in 1901. Most of Hughes's career was spent in West Texas, frequently in the area of El Paso.

When President William Howard Taft and General Porfirio Díaz met in El Paso and Ciudad Juárez in October, 1909, Hughes was a member of the Committee of Public Safety charged with protecting the chief executives during this unprecedented event. One of Hughes's men, Private C. R. Moore, performed one of the most important but least-known feats in the history of the Ranger Force. Moore prevented a major tragedy by arresting a Mexican anarchist armed with a "pencil pistol" before he could approach the heads of state. This foiled a plot by a group of Mexican anarchists to assassinate President Díaz.[39]

Hughes was, next to McDonald, the most publicized of the four captains, mainly because reporters in El Paso were eager to write about the Rangers. And they liked Hughes's pleasing personality and modest demeanor. He was an avid reader and was notably frugal. Hughes wisely invested his meager Ranger pay, plus substantial honoraria from mineowners at Shafter for protecting their property. When he resigned from the Rangers on January 31, 1915, after a career spanning twenty-seven years, he settled down to become an alfalfa farmer at Ysleta, twelve miles southeast of El Paso. He later became chairman of the board and the largest stockholder in a bank in Austin. Hughes was a lifelong bachelor; in failing health, he committed suicide in Austin on June 3, 1947.[40]

The resignations of Captains Brooks and McDonald were regrettable, especially because their replacements were men of lesser stature. There were three applicants for McDonald's job: the (ex-Ranger) sheriff of Wilson County, W. L. Wright, and two Ranger sergeants, W. J. McCauley and Tom M. Ross.[41] The one appointed to command Company B was Ross, who did not fit the stereotype of a Ranger captain: He was the great-grandson of Colonel José Antonio Navarro, a signer of the Texas Declaration of Independence. Ross's other distinction was that he was the only captain with a cork leg, which he always removed before going to bed. Several years earlier his six-shooter had accidently discharged, shattering his leg just below the knee and resulting in amputation.[42] His brother, J. Alexander Ross, served in Company D from 1907 to 1909. Tom M. Ross was born in San Antonio in August, 1871. He enlisted in the Rangers in 1898, serving four years and nine months under Captain Rogers both in Company E of the Frontier Battalion and in Company C of the Ranger Force. In 1902 he transferred to Hughes's Company D, and the next year he was promoted to sergeant. On February 1, 1907, he was again promoted, to captain of Company B. In 1909 the company was stationed in Ysleta. The other replacement captain, Francis Noel "Frank" Johnson, who took over Brooks' Company A on January 28, 1907, was pretty much a nonentity; his claim to fame was that for eight years he'd been sheriff of Mitchell County, whose seat is Colorado City, forty miles east of Midland.[43] The caliber of Ranger captain didn't seem crucial at the time because increasingly the Rangers were only performing routine law enforcement duties.

That traditional troublespot, the Mexican border, was a troublespot no longer. Evidencing this development, the army was in the process of dismantling the chain of forts built in the nineteenth century to protect the border. Between San Diego and El Paso, only Fort Huachuca in Arizona remained, and it had but a small garrison. In Texas, only Fort Bliss at El Paso, Fort Clark near Bracketville, and Fort McIntosh at Laredo remained in service. Forts Hancock, Quitman, Duncan, Ringgold, and Brown had all been deactivated.[44]

This lowering of the U.S. military guard reflected the decades of stability in Mexico resulting from General Porfirio Díaz's seizure of power in 1876. Díaz had seemingly performed the miracle of transforming Mexico from a turbulent and unstable country into a model for developing nations. For one thing, he had made great strides in pacifying the countryside and reducing banditry. This was accomplished largely by Díaz's mounted constabulary, the *Rurales*, who administered summary justice by the application of the *ley fuga*, or law of flight—the practice of shooting prisoners while they were allegedly attempting to escape.[45] Díaz certainly didn't invent the shooting of prisoners, but his Rurales institutionalized the practice. Coupled with pacification, Díaz provided political stability, ruling the country as a dictator and having himself repeatedly elected president, to preserve the facade of constitutional government. He also embarked on an ambitious program of modernization. Among other things he brought Mexico into the railroad age, building three trunk lines linking Mexico City with the United States border at Nogales, El Paso, and Laredo. Díaz's policy of economic development was fueled largely by foreign capital. He welcomed foreign, and especially American, investment. With foreigners being treated as a privileged element, their governments had few complaints about Díaz. Although the dictator would be eighty years old in 1910, he seemed to be as firmly in control as ever. Yet all this was about to change.

CHAPTER TWO

ON THE DEFENSIVE

1910 was not a good year for the Texas Rangers. The decline in leadership that had characterized the preceding decade accelerated, and by the end of the year there was a real crisis. Still, the badly understrength organization gamely soldiered on. In January the Ranger Force was deployed as follows:

Harlingen
    Company A: Capt. Frank Johnson, 1 sergeant, 5 privates   7

Ysleta
    Company B: Capt. Tom M. Ross, 1 sergeant, 4 privates   6

Austin
    Company C: Capt. John H. Rogers, 1 sergeant, 4 privates   6

Amarillo
    Company D: Capt. John R. Hughes, 1 sergeant, 4 privates   6
                                                                    ___
                                                                    25

These twenty-five men had to cover a lot of territory, for Texas is a big place, as expressed in the nineteenth-century saying: "The sun has riz, the sun has set, and here we is in Texas yet." Or, as the adjutant general informed a woman in Oklahoma who wanted the Rangers to locate her husband for her, "The State of Texas is very large and the Ranger Force is very small."[1]

The year 1910 actually began on a positive note—a grand jury in Trinity County took no action against two Company C Rangers who had killed a man by mistake in September, 1909. Rangers Goff White and Hall Avriett had been searching for a notorious criminal near Grovetown. Their story was that one night they encountered a man who fit the description and was armed with a shotgun. They identified themselves and ordered him three times to drop the shotgun. Instead, he aimed it at the Rangers, who immediately shot him dead. Only later did they discover that the deceased, one W. E. Collins, was not the fugitive. The Rangers were released on bond to await the action of the grand jury. When that body convened in January, 1910, White and Avriett were present, accompanied by their captain, John H. Rogers. The grand jury decided there was nothing to warrant an indictment.[2]

Out in West Texas, Captain Ross and Company B were keeping busy. In January, trouble broke out in Colorado City. Local officials sent out an urgent request for Rangers, to prevent the lynching of a man being held for murder. Ross responded with his entire company, and evidently the presence of Rangers caused the leaders of the lynch mob suddenly to remember that they had pressing business elsewhere.[3]

Unfortunately, this success was completely overshadowed by the regrettable Redus affair. Roscoe Redus was sergeant of Captain Ross's company. He decided to have a few drinks with the boys but worked up a real head of steam. He got roaring drunk and rode his horse through a saloon, assaulting the proprietor and shooting up the place. Captain Ross was of course furious and immediately discharged Redus on January 12. As an El Paso newspaper put it, "Redus's downfall followed an attempt on the ranger's part to make a livery stable and a morgue out of the Alamo Saloon recently."[4]

Ross tried to finesse the affair, notifying the adjutant general that he had fired Redus but not giving the reason for doing so.[5] But with the newspaper story the affair was beyond Ross's control. It became a disaster when the *El Paso Morning Times* published a blistering editorial entitled "Let the Rangers Go." The editorial focused on the Redus incident as yet another reason for abolishing the Rangers. It reminded the reader that Ross's company had previously been stationed in Amarillo "and was mixed up in the rows which occurred there and which resulted in its transfer to Ysleta." Acknowledging the great service the Rangers had performed in pioneer days, the editorial called the organization "a relic of the reconstruction days and an insult to the citizens of the state." Not only were the Rangers no longer needed, but the law gave the governor excessive authority to use the Rangers "in arbitrarily superceding the local authorities for his own purposes." That law should be repealed.[6]

This editorial represented the kind of publicity that money cannot buy. When it was brought to Adjutant General J. O. Newton's attention, he was not pleased. Newton sent Ross a curt note enclosing a newspaper clipping and demanding an explanation. He stated that if the account were true, it might cost Ross his position. A contrite Ross ruefully admitted that the article, though exaggerated, was indeed based on fact. Ross went on to say that although Redus was a good man and quite popular, he had no choice but to fire him after such a rampage. As for Ross himself, he said he would hate for the blame to fall on him but he would abide by his superiors' decision.[7] Applying the stern principle that a commander is responsible for everything his men do or fail to do, the adjutant general, after consulting with Governor Tom Campbell, fired Ross on February 12, effective February 28; Ross tendered his letter of resignation on February 19, leaving Sergeant F. C. Wynn as acting company commander.[8] Ross was a capable officer, but the last thing the Rangers needed was the kind of image projected by the Redus fiasco. Despite a petition endorsing Ross's character and conduct signed by thirty-three of the leading citizens of Ysleta, the adjutant general was unmoved.[9]

News of Ross's firing produced several applicants for his job. One was A. W. Brown, an ex-Ranger who was now a brand inspector. He was strongly endorsed by the sheriff of Potter County, W. D. Twichell, who praised Brown's record as a Ranger in and around Amarillo. In addition, John J. Sanders, a former city marshal and currently a sheriff, renewed his application for a Ranger captaincy.[10] After due deliberation, however, the governor on March 1 appointed Marvin E. Bailey, currently sergeant of Company C, thus resuming the tradition of promoting from within the Rangers to fill captaincies.[11] Bailey, born in Riddlesville, Karnes County, in September, 1879, illustrates the pattern of men serving nonconsecutive enlistments. He had been a hotel employee when he joined Company C in 1905. In August, 1906, he resigned to become deputy clerk of Karnes County. But in June, 1908, he reenlisted, this time as sergeant of Company C. He was now captain of Company B, at Ysleta. Bailey would prove to be a dependable but undistinguished captain at a time when outstanding leadership was needed to raise the prestige of the Rangers.

Among his first acts, Bailey demoted Sergeant F. C. Wynn to private and replaced him with J. W. Reese. While it was important for any captain to have the sergeant of his choice, this move further destabilized Company B, which had now had two captains and three sergeants in less than three months. A change of station, however, presented an opportunity to weld the unit together, and to please some residents of Ysleta. The Ysleta correspondent of the *El Paso Morning Times* wrote, "It is reported about town that the rangers stationed here will move their headquarters to Marfa on the first of next month. Oh, joy!"[12] Company B was indeed reassigned from Ysleta to Marfa, in the Big Bend region of Texas. The adjutant general mentioned that from Marfa, Bailey would be able "to look more thoroughly into the mining interests of Presidio County."[13] Marfa was a much more strategic location than Ysleta, for besides Presidio County, Bailey and his men covered much of West Texas from Socorro and Clint downriver from El Paso, to Del Rio, and north to Colorado City. Their scouts were often conducted at the request of and in conjunction with local officers.[14]

The first real test of Bailey's leadership came in late May, when a strike broke out on the Southern Pacific. The railroad's officials immediately began sending urgent requests for Rangers to protect the corporation's property at the small and isolated towns of Del Rio, Langtry, Sanderson, and Valentine. And at the same time Sheriff Chastain of Presidio County wanted two or three Rangers stationed at the mines at Shafter, where a great deal of stealing was going on. With pleas for Rangers increasing, Bailey had to report that

> Some of the men I have now is [sic] of the town kind and while they seem willing and anxious to work they have never had any experience in the kind of work we will have to do here and I believe it would be a good idea for me to pack a mule and take them on a short scout to let them get on to the way it is done.[15]

Since Bailey, like any other captain, had the authority to pick his men, this was a most unusual state of affairs. Not only were some of Company B's five men lacking in outdoor skills, but Bailey desperately needed more manpower. Yet his request to enlist an additional Ranger was denied by the adjutant general, who explained that the Ranger appropriation was nearly all spent and not until after the end of the fiscal year on August 31 would it be possible to add a man.[16]

Bailey would have to do the best he could with what he had. He decided that he just couldn't spare anyone for the mines at Shafter, at least not until the Southern Pacific strike ended. In dealing with that conflict, he "instructed all the men to be very careful in what steps they took and interfere only when the law was violated & under no circumstances talk or take sides with anyone."[17]

Fortunately, the strike produced little violence, the only incident of note occurring in Alpine, where a crowd of strikers intimidated several replacement workers. The latter took the first train out of town, to Marfa. But they returned the next day accompanied by two Rangers, who were soon replaced by a deputy sheriff. In this connection, Bailey reported that the Southern Pacific was paying the deputies protecting its property $4 a day and he proposed asking the company to pay the Rangers' expenses as well. Regarding the strike, Bailey wrote that "it is very disagreeable work but I am handling it as best I can & know how." Captain Bailey was continually deploying and redeploying his few Rangers between Marfa, Sanderson, Langtry, and Del Rio. He himself was also on the move, finally stopping off at a hotel in Del Rio "to get a night's rest as I have not been in bed for the past 3 nights."[18] At the request of the railroad's superintendent he had one man riding the passenger trains between Sanderson and Del Rio. A point of particular concern was the Pecos High Bridge, a vital Southern Pacific installation quite vulnerable to sabotage. Built in 1892, it was the most spectacular railroad bridge in the country. On it the Southern Pacific's main line crossed the Pecos

River canyon some five miles from the Mexican border on a steel structure 1,515 feet long and 321 feet high.[19] Bailey had to detail two of his men to guard the bridge for a time.

The Rangers' presence in the town of Sanderson became controversial—a petition was circulated calling for their removal, and a delegation left for Austin to complain to the governor. According to Bailey, this was all an overreaction to a trivial incident. He pointed out that none of the leading citizens had signed the petition, though he admitted that Sheriff Bean, the county attorney, and the county clerk all sympathized with the strikers. The precipitating incident occurred when one of the Rangers escorted off railroad property a firebrand Methodist preacher and strike sympathizer. The Reverend F. C. Cox, who signed himself "Representing Maintenance of Way Employees," not only delivered impassioned speeches to the strikers but also had fliers printed headed "To All Railroad Employees," in which he bitterly denounced the Rangers as strikebreakers. Among the rhetorical questions he asked was

> . . . Say, bud, did you ever hear of the State Rangers being called out to force the railroad to give the laborers a fair show . . . ? No, you never did, and you never will, as the laws are made to be executed only when the railroad howls. . . . Can't you see that it is the railroad that is benefitted by having these Rangers called out?[20]

Bailey gleefully reported that the Reverend Cox had since left town, without paying the editor of the *Sanderson Times* for the fliers printed at his request. Although he expected no trouble at Sanderson, Bailey decided it would be prudent to leave, at least temporarily. The strikers confined themselves to making speeches, which did have some effect—the Southern Pacific kept shipping in groups of Hispanic track workers, but the strikers kept talking them into quitting. Some 150 had accumulated, and Bailey speculated that if the strike committee could no longer feed them they might cause trouble serious enough to warrant the Rangers' attention. Luckily, nothing like this happened, and by late June the strike was over.

Captain Bailey had performed creditably. He could now resume his ordinary duties, such as pursuing rustlers. In fact, things were so calm that he requested a few days' leave to return home and bring his mother to Marfa, as well as to stop in Austin and confer with General Newton.[21]

Still, Bailey had his problems. As he ruefully informed the adjutant general, "This seems to be an ill fated company." Bailey had just found it necessary to fire the sergeant he himself had selected, J. W. Reese. The sergeant had proved to be undependable; not only Bailey but the rest of the men had lost confidence in him. "I tried to treat him right and do the best I could by him, giving him almost an honorable discharge," wrote the disillusioned captain, who complained that Reese "has turned out to be the most artful liar I have ever had the misfortune to have dealings with." Bailey alerted the adjutant general to Reese's probable fulmination against Bailey but expressed confidence in being able to refute any such allegations. The disgruntled Reese indeed sent General Newton a letter full of vitriolic charges against Bailey.[22] The adjutant general evidently ignored them.

The night before his departure from Marfa, however, Reese had managed to create further trouble for Captain Bailey. The presence of Rangers at elections was not unusual; local officials not infrequently asked their assistance in keeping the peace. What did rile local officials was the presence of uninvited Rangers. On his last night as a Ranger, former sergeant Reese had convinced the sheriff of Brewster County, J. A. Walton, that Bailey and his Company B intended to descend on the hamlet of Terlingua and dictate the outcome of an impending election. Not unnaturally, the sheriff got his hackles up and sent Bailey a terse telegram that it was neither necessary nor proper for Rangers to go to Terlingua, and if Bailey so intended, for him to see Walton and the county judge first. Bailey conferred with them and explained that only he and one of his men would go to Terlingua strictly to keep the peace and in no way to interfere with or try to influence the election. Bailey's action restored good relations with the sheriff and county judge, laying to rest a spate of ugly rumors.[23]

Terlingua was not the only town in West Texas where Rangers patrolled at election time. Even as Bailey was in Terlingua, the adjutant general ordered that two of Bailey's men proceed at once to the town of Fort Hancock to preserve order during an election. Relieving to some extent the demands on his scant manpower, in July Bailey enlisted a replacement for the fired Reese, in the person of Alfred R. Baker, who'd been a Ranger from 1906 to 1909.[24]

While Captain Bailey's Company B operated in West Texas arresting rustlers and a few bootleggers, Company A in Amarillo was arresting bootleggers and a few rustlers. At one level, this was a waste of talent, for the company's commander, Captain John R. Hughes, was the senior Ranger captain and a most able officer. But Prohibition had become the burning political issue of the day in Texas, and Hughes was assigned to enforce the local option liquor law in dry Potter County, spending much of his time arresting bootleggers, pimps, and gamblers.[25] He carried out his duties with his usual diligence, but many of these arrests were for misdemeanor offenses. What contributed to Hughes's frustration was the attitude of the locals. As the adjutant general commented in a letter congratulating him on his misdemeanor convictions, it was "strange that a jury will convict for running a disorderly house but not for selling whiskey."[26] Hughes and his men spent part of their time in district courts, either as witnesses in criminal cases or providing security while the courts were in session. And like Bailey, Hughes and his Rangers were called upon to keep order at election time, on occasion at places as distant as Fort Hancock and Ysleta, Hughes's old stomping grounds.

But sometimes there were more interesting law enforcement challenges. In March, the one-man detachment Hughes maintained at turbulent Colorado City, Ranger C. R. Moore, received a letter with photograph and description of a fugitive wanted by Sheriff Deodoro Guerra of Starr County for rape.[27] And several months later, Rangers C. A. Craighead and Harry Moore arrested a man at Dalhart for carrying a pistol and, God forbid, impersonating a Ranger. But if one had to sum up the activities of Company A in one word, that word would be—routine.

That was certainly not the case regarding Company C, based in Austin and commanded by another veteran officer, Captain John H. Rogers. In March, at the request of the Mitchell County sheriff, Rogers sent Ranger Roy H. Adams under cover to Colorado City to investigate cases of suspected arson and bootlegging. Adams stayed for eighteen days, determining that the fire had been accidental and that there was no bootlegging; there was a lot of drinking going on, but it was legal under local option. Adams concealed his identity so well that the suspects took a liking to him, inviting him back to play on their baseball team.[28]

The following month there was big trouble in Hempstead, forty miles northwest of Houston. This was a rough town that had earned the nickname of "Six-shooter Junction" because in 1905, in the midst of passions generated by the issue of Prohibition and a local option election, a gunfight had erupted. When the smoke cleared, four men lay dead: Congressman John M. Pinckney, his brother, a local attorney, and a farmer; the attorney's son and the congressman's secretary were wounded. The governor had sent in the Rangers.[29] Now, on the night of April 28, 1910, there had occurred another sensational shooting, resulting from a bitter divorce proceeding. This time the passenger depot was the battleground: Two men were killed outright, Sheriff Perry was seriously wounded, and several traveling salesmen were slightly wounded. As it happened, the chief deputy sheriff, ex-Ranger Goff White, was sick in bed. With the local lawmen incapacitated, Captain Rogers did not wait for a request for Rangers but on his own initiative despatched Sergeant Joseph J. Anders and Private Ed Avriett to take charge of the situation. This they did, but feelings were running so high that at the examining trial of the two accused shooters everyone entering the courtroom was searched for firearms. But by May 2, Hempstead was quiet enough for Anders and Avriett to return to Austin.[30]

Captain Rogers again sent Private Adams, who evidently had a flair for such work, on an undercover mission. On orders not just from the adjutant general but from the governor himself, Adams and his colleague R. M. "Duke" Hudson were dispatched to Galveston, which had a well-deserved reputation as a wide-open city. The Rangers were to report for undercover work to the foreman of a grand jury investigating gambling. The foreman instructed them to win the confidence of the leading gamblers, gain access to the big games, and report. The foreman planned to have the games raided, hopefully arresting between seventy-five and one-hundred gamblers. But because of the grand jury's activities, the gamblers prudently suspended their activities. The Rangers returned to Austin but were soon back in Galveston, for gambling had resumed after the grand jury adjourned, though on a smaller scale. The foreman decided to send the Rangers back to Austin once more but had them remain on call. Ranger Hudson again traveled back to Galveston to resume his covert assignment. He learned that a large gambling establishment operated over the Turf Saloon. The enterprising Hudson got himself a job in a leading dry goods store, became an enthusiastic gambler, and was soon able to collect evidence. Captain Rogers then sent another clandestine operative to join Hudson: Private Levi Davis, of Company A. On June 30, the two Rangers raided the gambling den, but it took them awhile to force an entrance, giving those inside time to stampede out a back exit, the result being that the Rangers were able to arrest only six individuals. These they turned over to the chief of police. The Rangers could take satisfaction in the district attorney's assurance that there was ample evidence for convicting the group of felony gambling, and that he looked forward to sending them to the penitentiary.[31]

Governor Campbell continued to take a personal interest in the Rangers' activities. In June, after conferring with the governor, the adjutant general ordered Captain Rogers to send Ranger Ed Avriett to the Kimball County town of Junction, in the Hill Country, to combat some pesky goat rustlers. An organized gang was operating with impunity, and they had stolen lots of goats. Avriett went under cover to gather evidence, but his identity was discovered and he had to be withdrawn. Nevertheless, Captain Rogers planned to assign three Rangers to work openly in Kimball County on the case for several months, perhaps even until after the November election, "after which it is believed the county authorities will be able to handle the situation, as that county will elect a law and order sheriff in November."[32]

Ranger Avriett subsequently carried out what proved to be a dangerous assignment. In July he was sent to Navasota to relieve the city marshal, who had requested a replacement so he could take a short vacation. The city marshal, incidentally, was a twenty-six-year-old former Ranger named Francis Augustus "Frank" Hamer, who would eventually become a legend in Ranger lore.[33] Avriett went through the local criminal element like a dose of salts, arresting a number of petty offenders. Then, on the night of July 17, while he was patrolling the alley behind the post office and bank, someone tried to murder him. The shots missed, and Avriett returned fire, wounding the perpetrator. The latter fled, with Avriett in hot pursuit, but in the darkness Avriett fell down a step and the would-be assassin escaped. It was later speculated that the shooter and an accomplice, who were never apprehended, had been lurking in the alley intending to rob the bank or the post office, or both, and Avriett had come across them while making his rounds.

The next day Avriett received a telephone call from the police at Bryan that a very valuable horse and buggy had been stolen the previous night and were thought to be heading for Navasota. Upon investigation Avriett learned that such a rig had indeed been seen passing through Navasota shortly before Avriett had received the phone message. The Ranger quickly secured an automobile and driver, and, accompanied by a Navasota policeman, gave chase. They caught up with the stolen buggy some twenty miles south of town. The officers forced the buggy to a halt and tried to arrest its two occupants. One whipped out a pistol, whereupon Avriett shot and killed him. The dead man's companion was over-powered, handcuffed, and taken to Navasota. It turned out that the horse thieves were Greek brothers.

This shooting quickly became a cause celebre. It seemed as though the Rangers could not buy a break, for when the incident was reported in the press, it was depicted as yet another example of Ranger brutality. According to the newspaper, two harmless Greek laborers, "unfamiliar with the ways of the Rangers and the English language," were peacefully walking along a road, when a "posse of rangers" in search of those who'd tried to rob the bank in Navasota the previous night came upon the pair. When the command to halt was disregarded because of the Greeks' linguistic ignorance, one of the posse opened fire, killing one Greek and seriously wounding the other. "Then the mistake was discovered and the wounded man was hurried to a hospital and the rangers continued the pursuit."[34] This account immediately produced a savage editorial entitled "The Ranger Curse," which not only recounted the sensational news story but denounced the "constant killings" by the Rangers and devoutly hoped the legislature would abolish that organization. Several politicians were quick to jump on the bandwagon and echo that sentiment.[35] When the real facts became public, the newspaper of course failed to print a retraction. Thus the Rangers had taken a lot of undeserved criticism. The facts were as Ranger Avriett had reported them, and whether the Greeks understood English or not, having stolen a horse and buggy and being stopped by armed officers, it had been a grave error in judgment for the deceased Greek to have pulled a pistol. As for Avriett, after nearly being killed twice, he presumably was happy to see City Marshal Frank Hamer when the latter returned from vacation on July 22. Avriett and the Navasota policeman were tried on November 29, 1910, for the horse thief's killing. The jury deliberated for three minutes before returning a verdict of "not guilty," the officers having acted in self-defense.[36]

Only a week later, Avriett was in the East Texas town of Palestine, where a very nasty situation had developed. Rumors had spread in Palestine, seat of Anderson County, and in the adjoining counties, that blacks were arming themselves to kill Anglos. In reaction, Anglos had armed themselves and a mob of over 100 men had gone on a rampage, slaughtering eighteen blacks. The governor ordered that "all available Rangers" be dispatched to the scene. Those immediately available were Company C Rangers Ed and Hall Avriett and Sergeant J. L. Anders. They took the first train to Palestine, secured horses, and raced to the scene of the worst atrocities, the nearby town of Slocum. The situation was so serious that Adjutant General Newton, Ranger Captain Rogers, Colonel Beckham, and two other officers of the Texas National Guard arrived in Palestine on the morning of the 31st. On telegraphic orders from the governor, Troop C, 1st Texas Cavalry, and Company D, 3rd Texas Infantry were ordered to Palestine that same day. But by the time they arrived by train early the next morning, the crisis was over.[37] The rapid and effective action of the Texas Rangers had dispersed the mob and saved a number of blacks from being killed.

Anxious for reliable news of what was happening, the adjutant general and his party proceeded by automobile toward Slocum but on the way encountered Rangers Ed and Hall Avriett, a deputy sheriff, and a deputy constable. The lawmen were taking four ringleaders of the mob to jail in Palestine. Sergeant Anders had remained behind in Slocum searching for others. Slocum was now quiet, the officers "having ordered everyone to disarm themselves and go home, which they promptly did." The prisoners were jailed, along with, for their own protection, a number of blacks whom the Rangers had also brought along to testify as state's witnesses against the rioters. The Palestine jail was heavily guarded to prevent either the liberation of the prisoners or the lynching of the black witnesses. Sergeant Anders failed to find the fugitives he sought, but they were later arrested by the sheriff, who'd been working with the Rangers. Captain Rogers and several Rangers remained on the scene, arresting a total of eleven men for murder. They also arrested a man for horsewhipping his wife. The Rangers played the leading role in quelling the outrages in East Texas, which gave their image a welcome boost.[38]

A new crisis soon erupted, this one involving Captain Frank Johnson's Company A. In many respects Johnson had the most demanding assignment, for South Texas had always occupied much of the Rangers' attention. From his headquarters in Harlingen, Captain Johnson covered a vast area—along the river from Rio Grande City to Brownsville, and north to Alice, where he had a man stationed to scout Duval and Nueces Counties.

A good part of Johnson's problem was that a lot of men carried guns. Citizens tended to give up their weaponry only when they were confident that the law could protect them. This had never been the case along the lower Rio Grande border, with its tradition of political corruption and endemic violence. The attitude seemed to be that one should go around armed because you never knew when you'd run across somebody who needed killing. In fact, this mentality pervaded the state. As an exasperated newspaper editorial entitled "The Gun Man" put it:

Whenever a man is killed in the State, the killer usually gets on the witness stand and swears that the victim "made a movement toward his hip pocket as if to draw a gun," thus injecting self-defense into the case. Then the jury is at liberty to acquit the shooter if there is a reasonable doubt as to whether or not the victim made a movement toward his hip pocket as if to draw a gun.

Under such circumstances it is truly wonderful that there is ever a conviction for a killing in this State. Any motion of the right hand, when interpreted by a skillful lawyer, becomes a motion toward the hip pocket.[39]

Nothing got the locals' juices flowing faster than a good murder or an election, and Company A repeatedly had to deal with both. In March, when a murder in Falfurrias threatened to produce a serious ethnic clash, Johnson and his Company A arrived to impose order. The trouble grew out of a baseball game, played at Falfurrias between the local team and one from Alice. Heated words led to an affray in which a Hispanic stabbed and wounded an Anglo. Several days later, the stabber, one Baltazar García, who'd been arrested and released on bond, was waiting at the depot to take the train back to Alice, when he was shot and killed by Dave Dolan, a cousin of the man stabbed. Great excitement prevailed, and Dolan narrowly escaped being lynched by a mob of furious Hispanics. He was rushed to Corpus Christi for safekeeping. Falfurrias boiled with hostility and a race riot was imminent. Anglos and Hispanics alike armed themselves, and the situation was so serious that officials of the San Antonio and Aransas Pass Railroad were prepared to send a special train to evacuate Anglo women and children to San Antonio. However, Captain Johnson and four of his Rangers arrived and took charge of the situation. They began by closing all the saloons. They then dispersed any crowds that began to form. Gradually, calm returned to Falfurrias.

Yet there remained the possibility of future trouble when Dolan was brought back for his arraignment. Fortunately, nothing happened. Dolan was released on a $10,000 bond to await the action of the grand jury, scheduled to convene at Rio Grande City in April.[40] The judge who would go from Corpus Christi to preside at the trial, W. B. Hopkins, wrote to the adjutant general that partisans of both victim and killer would descend on Rio Grande City in considerable numbers, and he suggested that Johnson's Ranger company should be stationed there throughout the trial.[41] Judge Hopkins perhaps had in mind the fate of District Judge Stanley Welch, who had been shot to death in Rio Grande City in 1906. From March on, Johnson stationed Rangers Quirl Carnes and Pat Craighead, who operated as partners, in Rio Grande City. Johnson himself, with Sergeant W. J. McCauley and Ranger Gus T. Jones, went to Brownsville in April at the request of Sheriff Celedonio Garza of Cameron County to keep order on election day. Voting occurred without incident, after which Johnson went to Fort Worth to testify in a case, while McCauley and Jones scouted in Cameron and Hidalgo Counties.[42]

Private Gus T. "Buster" Jones soon thereafter had a narrow escape. He was on duty in Harlingen, where drunks had been causing trouble every Saturday night by shooting up the town after the saloons closed. On the night of May 28, there was shooting about 2 a.m. in the *barrio*, the Hispanic part of town. The constable asked Jones to help him find the culprit. They, together with the city marshal and a special officer, set out to investigate; the marshal and constable went one way, Jones and Special Officer Everett Anglin another. The Ranger and officer sighted two Hispanics causing a disturbance. Walking up behind them, Jones grabbed both men and told them they were under arrest for disorderly conduct. One of them, Esteban Cervantes, jerked loose and drew a pistol. Jones was a fraction of a second faster—he fired from the hip and shot Cervantes in the heart. Cervantes's cocked pistol fell to the ground. The other Hispanic was arrested and held as a material witness. Both he and Anglin testified as eyewitnesses to the shooting. At the examining trial the justice of the peace wanted to release Jones, it being a clear case of self-defense and the deceased having been what was then called a "bad Mexican"—in this instance a hard case who was wanted for murder in Mexico. Nevertheless, Captain Johnson insisted that Jones be placed under a $500 bond, for Johnson wanted the "grand jury to act on the case so there will be no hereafter about it." Twenty of the most prominent men in Harlingen signed Jones's bond.[43]

But it was the situation in San Benito that increasingly demanded Johnson's attention. The citizens were most upset by a series of robberies there during the last few months, robberies which neither the Rangers nor the sheriff seemed able to solve.[44] Sheriff Celedonio Garza of Cameron County even attended a mass meeting to try to formulate some plan of action. And as Captain Johnson informed the adjutant general:

> Owing to many requests for Rangers I've sent Carnes & Craighead to scout; think it'd be well to have them at San Benito for a while. The Toughs seems [sic] to have taken charge of the place and I get reports almost daily of some theft down where [sic] the citizens have petitioned me to protect them against it and I think I will let the boys do a little cleaning up there.[45]

A day later Johnson telegraphed that:

> Have investigated situation in San Benito and find it grave; think can handle it by placing men there; people very muchly wrought up over murder of Engineer by Mexicans; will keep you advised.[46]

Captain Johnson was referring to the murder of James Darwin. On May 27, the twenty-six-year-old engineer for the San Benito Land and Water Company was murdered in cold blood. The unsuspecting Darwin was walking to work at the Company's canal head gates on the Rio Grande about seven miles from San Benito when he was shot at close range, the .45 caliber slug passing completely through his head. The murderer escaped. After some confusion, Darwin's killer was identified as one Jacinto Treviño, the natural son of Captain Natividad Treviño, a retired Mexican army officer. The motive for the crime was revenge. The previous day Jacinto Treviño had made inappropriate suggestions to Darwin's wife of four months, and the engineer had beaten him to a pulp. The San Benito Company offered a $500 reward for the capture of the murderer who, as was usual in these cases, had immediately fled across the river to Mexico, where the authorities showed no disposition to arrest him.[47]

The prime mover in posting the reward was Sam Robertson, the San Benito Company's chief engineer. Because of his prominent role in trying to bring Jacinto Treviño to justice, Robertson himself soon became a target. Whether motivated by loyalty to Robertson or by the $500 reward, a longtime trusted employee informed Robertson that Treviño intended to kill him. The employee, as it happened, was Pablo Treviño, a cousin of the fugitive. He said that Jacinto Treviño and some others planned to slip back across the river on the night of July 31 and ambush Robertson as he drove to work the next morning. He even specified the exact spot where they planned to pile logs on the road to stop Robertson's car. Not unnaturally, Robertson took Treviño's story seriously and informed the local authorities.

The authorities leaped at what might be their only chance to deal with Jacinto Treviño on Texas soil. A posse consisting of Texas Rangers Quirl Carnes and Pat Craighead, deputy sheriffs Benny Lawrence and Earl West, and six employees of the San Benito Company was quickly organized. On the night of July 31, they left San Benito between nine and ten o'clock in two autos. When they neared the Rio Grande, they left the autos at a house and split up into four groups, in order to cover all the approaches Jacinto Treviño might use in coming up from the river to the San Benito road. Carnes, Lawrence, and John Zoll, a levee rider for the San Benito Company, made up one of the parties. Carnes and Lawrence were wearing dark coats over white shirts—not the best choice of attire for a night operation. The trio took up station with Carnes on the extreme left, Lawrence a few feet from him, and Zoll on the right. They crouched down, and after a long wait, Zoll informed his companions that he heard men approaching through a clearing. It was a very dark night, and only the dim outlines of figures were visible. According to Zoll, one of the officers hailed the approaching men in Spanish, a language Zoll didn't understand. Someone answered in Spanish and a fusillade erupted. Lawrence and Carnes were cut down as they rose from a crouch. Lawrence died instantly from seven buckshot in the right side of his head; Carnes was mortally wounded by rifle bullets, one entering behind the right ear and exiting through the right eye, and the other in his right arm. As the officers were being cut down, Zoll emptied his weapon at the attackers and ran for his life.

Zoll encountered Craighead and West hurrying toward the scene of the shooting. Craighead instructed Zoll to return to the house and phone for help, while they went on to assist Carnes and Lawrence. They reached the scene of the ambush and, hearing Carnes groan, West walked up to him, put his rifle down, and started to examine him when he heard the click of a rifle being cocked. He dropped and drew his pistol. A rifle opened up from the brush; Craighead and West returned fire but West was hit, the bullet going into his right arm, through his shoulder, and out his back. The firing stopped. West was badly wounded and Craighead decided to go for help. He got to the road and soon heard an auto approaching. A relieved Craighead then fired into the air—the prearranged signal—so the car's occupants could locate him. They did. They opened fire on the hapless Ranger with everything they had. Craighead fell with a rifle bullet through his left thigh and some buckshot in his right leg. Quickly realizing their mistake, the relief party apologized profusely to Craighead and began tending his wounds. He and West were driven back to San Benito for medical attention, as was Carnes, who died at nine the next morning. By daybreak a posse from San Benito hurried to the scene, and they found the body of Pablo Treviño, whose information had led the officers into the ambush. He had evidently taken a bullet in the chest in the initial shooting and had crawled or been dragged into the brush. He had fallen on his right side facing the officers, his rifle tightly clutched in both hands. The rifle had jammed as the dying man had tried to shove in another cartridge. The party also found the tracks of several men headed straight for the Rio Grande.

As news of the ambush spread through San Benito, the town quickly became an armed camp. Not only were angry citizens milling around carrying firearms, but Ranger Captain Frank Johnson and Sergeant McCauley arrived from Harlingen before daybreak; they were later joined by Captain Bailey and two Rangers from Marfa. Some thirty-five members of the Brownsville Rifles, the local militia company, arrived by train during the morning, as did Cameron County Sheriff Celedonio Garza and two deputies, and Brownsville City Marshal José "Joe" Crixell. The next day, August 2, Sheriff William L. Wright of Wilson County (who had been a deputy under Sheriff John Craighead, had been a Ranger, and would become a Ranger captain) arrived from Floresville with seven deputies. The deceased Ranger Quirl Carnes, his badly wounded colleague Pat Craighead, and the wounded deputy Earl West were all from Wilson County. Among Sheriff Wright's seven deputies were one West, two Craigheads, and one Carnes, all of them in an ugly mood. Besides the militia and the peace officers, armed citizen volunteers poured into San Benito from the neighboring towns.

In the event, all this firepower was unused. The militia, Sheriff Wright's posse, and dozens of volunteers deployed to scour the bank of the Rio Grande, with no real hope of catching the murderers, but they had to do *something*. The Rangers, on the other hand, took specific action. On August 1, they went out to the nearby Las Rusias ranch and arrested seven of Jacinto Treviño's relatives living there. The prisoners were taken to the pumping plant and held overnight while being interrogated. They were released early the next morning. As the Brownsville *Daily Herald* put it, there was apparently "no reason for their arrest beyond the fact that they are cousins of Jacinto Treviño . . . who appears to be the black sheep of a very respectable flock."[48] Not only did the Rangers fail to get their man but they got some unmerited bad publicity. On August 3, sensational newspaper stories reported that a youth named Cecilio Arteaga had been caught by the Rangers near the San Benito pumping plant and had been beaten and burned in an effort to make him divulge information about the ambush. Arteaga's employer wrote to the Brownsville *Daily Herald* that Arteaga had actually been scalded by steam in a construction accident, but by then the damage had been done.[49]

In the midst of all the frantic activity and anti-Mexican feeling in San Benito, it was Joe Crixell, the Brownsville city marshal, who actually accomplished something worthwhile. He crossed the river the day after the ambush to conduct a quiet investigation of his own. In the small settlement of Tahuachalito he interviewed some of the participants at a *baile*, or open air dance. They told him that the night of the ambush Jacinto Treviño had been seen heading for the river accompanied by Benjamín Estrada and a man named Loya. At the request of the Cameron County authorities, the Mexican government subsequently issued warrants for the arrest of Jacinto Treviño and Benjamín Estrada. The latter, it turned out, was already wanted for the murder in San Diego, Texas, of a prominent cattleman, John Cleary, whom he had shot down as Cleary ate supper in a restaurant. But despite the cooperation of the Mexican government, and the substantial rewards offered for Treviño and Estrada, they were never caught, disappearing into the maelstrom of the Mexican Revolution. There was a flurry of excitement in June, 1912, caused by a report that Rurales had captured Treviño. Brownsville City Marshal Joe Crixell went to Matamoros and learned that the report was without foundation. And in May, 1914, Treviño was said to be one of the revolutionists encamped across the Rio Grande from San Benito.[50]

Some aspects of the San Benito ambush have never been cleared up. For example, Sam Robertson stoutly denied that his employee Pablo Treviño had lured the officers into the fatal trap.[51] Captain Johnson, however, was of the opinion that the ambush was a carefully arranged plot to assassinate Carnes and Craighead because of their active work in suppressing crime in San Benito and their vigorous efforts to capture Jacinto Treviño. Carnes and Craighead had indeed made a dozen arrests since their arrival in San Benito on May 3, including three men charged with attempting to wreck a passenger train.[52] Yet it was the assistant adjutant general who made the most accurate assessment of the matter: "Ranger

Carnes seems to have lost his life unnecessarily, owing to the fact that the affair was badly planned, and known to too many persons."[53]

Bungled or not, the unsuccessful and tragic attempt to neutralize the fugitive Treviño had the citizens of San Benito hopping mad. Sam Robertson again took the lead in organizing vigilantes to hunt down the ambushers. To command these vigilantes he needed someone both tough and knowledgeable. Robertson found him in the person of Tom Ross, the former Ranger captain. After his dismissal from the service, Ross had returned to San Antonio and had opened a real estate office. But selling real estate was a pretty tame occupation, and Ross readily accepted Robertson's offer, leaving for San Benito on August 30.[54] It would appear, though, that Ross didn't accomplish much once he got there.

The San Benito ambush not only sent a shock wave through the Ranger Force but, more importantly, it set the tone for the ensuing decade. Company A grimly set about trying to apprehend the ambushers. Efforts to extradite anybody from Mexico entailed endless delays and mountains of red tape, but it was suspected that some of the guilty parties had slipped back into Texas, and those the Rangers intended to have. A sergeant and two privates, one of them Pat Craighead's brother, worked out of San Benito, while another sergeant and two privates assisted Captain Johnson's investigation from Harlingen.

That town remained a trouble spot, with Johnson reporting that "there is usually a shooting every night." On September 5, a local bartender, William E. Whitley, who had served in Ranger Company A in 1909–1910, shot and killed Francisco "Pancho" Balli in A. W. Weller's saloon. Whitley was about to leave the saloon when Balli and José María Sánchez entered. As soon as Balli saw Whitley he exclaimed, "Here comes the cousin of Henry [sic] Lawrence," cursed, and drew a .45 Colt pistol. The pistol got hung up in his clothing, and when he fired, he hit his companion Sánchez in the leg. Simultaneously, Whitley whipped out his own pistol—a Luger—and put six rounds into Balli, who fell, dropped his pistol, tried to rise and retrieve his weapon, and pitched over dead. Whitley was a cousin of Deputy Sheriff Benny Lawrence, who had died in the San Benito ambush, and it was Lawrence's Luger that he used on Balli. Whitley's version of the shooting was corroborated by Constable Carl T. Ryan (ex-Ranger and future Cameron County sheriff) who had been getting into Weller's buggy outside and who heard everything, and by Weller himself, who was already sitting in the buggy. Ryan rushed into the saloon, and Whitley surrendered peacefully. Another witness, P. S. Waterwall, who had been about thirty feet away when the gunfight occurred, likewise testified on Whitley's behalf. Balli's companion, the wounded Sánchez, was frightened and told a stupid story of not having seen or heard anything. Although no one knew of any previous trouble between Balli and Whitley, the conventional wisdom in Harlingen was that the killing grew in some way out of the San Benito ambush, speculation given plausibility by Balli's exclamation on seeing Whitley.

The latter pleaded self-defense at his arraignment and was released on $5,000 bond, which was signed by eleven of Harlingen's most prominent citizens.[55]

But even as the Rangers focused on San Benito, they were also needed elsewhere, this time in West Texas, at Post City, the seat of Garza County. The village had been founded in 1907 by the cereal magnate Charles W. Post, who had purchased 200,000 acres of ranch land. He wanted to develop a model town, where alcohol and brothels were prohibited.[56] But the picture-postcard-pretty little town contained some very mean people. On August 12, the county attorney, M. L. Harkey, telegraphed Governor Campbell from Big Spring that the situation in Garza was out of control: Vigilantes were running amok, mob rule prevailed, people were being waylaid and brutally beaten and driven from their homes by death threats, and local peace officers lacked the courage to act. He implored the governor to send Rangers at once. Captain Hughes got the assignment.[57] He and two of his men had just returned to Amarillo from Marlin, where they had helped protect a wife murderer, B. B. Myatt, who had just been given the death penalty by a jury. There had been no mob violence, but the officers had experienced difficulty controlling "the immense crowd of county people who assembled to see Myatt and listen to the proceedings."[58] Now Hughes was ordered to take the first train to Big Spring and report to the Garza County attorney. Hughes took two of his Rangers with him and was even authorized to enlist another man if necessary.

What Hughes found was disturbing. County Attorney Harkey was hiding out in Big Spring, a badly shaken man. Hughes and his Rangers escorted Harkey the sixty miles north back to his office in Post City, and on the way listened to the attorney's tale of terror. Harkey had been vigorously prosecuting lawbreakers, and some of the locals who objected to this had taken direct action. On the night of August 10, as Harkey was returning to town from bird hunting, he'd been jumped by men wearing white hoods and shirts. They dragged the hapless attorney from the car and tied and blindfolded him. The leader of these "whitecappers" informed Harkey that they were going to whip him within an inch of his life, and if he stayed in Post they would kill him. Two men held Harkey, another pressed a pistol to his forehead, while the rest took turns whipping him until his back and legs were covered in blood. They then knocked him unconscious with a six-shooter. The following day the terrified attorney slipped out of town, fled to Big Spring, and wired the governor for help.

Captain Hughes and his men conducted an investigation that resulted in the arrest of six prominent citizens. There was no further trouble, because Hughes announced that he was prepared to stay in Post until he was satisfied there would be no more whitecapping. Sadly, Hughes stayed close to Harkey until the latter could wind up his affairs, resign his office, and leave Garza County forever.[59]

While they were in the area, Hughes's Rangers also cleaned up the little town of Coahoma, twenty-five miles east of Big Spring. A vicious feud had been raging there, and four people had been shot. The law-abiding citizens of Coahoma even signed a warm letter of appreciation for what the Rangers had done. Hughes and his men then returned to Amarillo to more humdrum duty—keeping the peace during a local option liquor election.[60]

Out in the Trans-Pecos region, Captain Bailey and Company B were still based in Marfa, with two-man detachments at Shafter and Comstock, the mining centers. And Bailey was still having personnel problems. This time he had to discharge Ranger C. T. Smith because he was disagreeable, stubborn, contrary, and overbearing; none of the others liked to work with him. Bailey was hoping to enlist a man or two as soon as the new fiscal year began on September 1.[61]

The adjutant general was also hoping this could happen. He proposed on August 31, 1910, that the Ranger appropriation for the 1910–1911 fiscal year be doubled—to $50,000 a year. In justifying this mind-boggling increase, he stated that at present the Ranger Force consisted of four captains, four sergeants, and eighteen privates, but it should be increased to at least fifty officers and men. Requests for the Rangers' services were so numerous that they could be granted only in the most serious or urgent cases. There was enough work to keep 100 or more Rangers busy. During the previous two years the organization had made 1,017 arrests, 458 of them for felonies, the remainder for misdemeanors. The Rangers had traveled a total of 277,871 miles and had recovered thousands of dollars of stolen property.[62]

Not only was the increased appropriation not approved, but the Ranger Force was further reduced: On September 30, 1910, Captain Johnson's Company A was mustered out, perhaps because Johnson wasn't sufficiently deferential to the powerful South Texas political boss Judge James B. "Jim" Wells, Jr. In a confidential telegram, the adjutant general ordered Captain Bailey to transfer his Company B to South Texas; Captain Hughes would now cover North and West Texas. Bailey was authorized to enlist three or four additional men but was enjoined to take his time and select good recruits. In a subsequent communication the adjutant general ordered Bailey to arrive in San Benito by September 30. Captain Johnson would transfer to Bailey all his state property; Bailey would have transferred his own property to Hughes before leaving Marfa. Bailey's horses would be shipped gratis by rail. As the adjutant general pointed out, this arrangement would save considerable transportation expense. When Johnson's company was mustered out, its members would receive honorable discharges. If Bailey wished, he could enlist some of these individuals.[63]

One of these was Daniel Hinojosa, among the handful of Hispanic Rangers. Born in March, 1876, at Bluntzer, Nueces County, he'd been a Cameron County deputy sheriff at Harlingen when he enlisted in Company A on September 6, 1910. Captain Johnson had stationed him in San Benito, "doing secret work in murder cases there."[64] On October 22, 1910, he enlisted in Captain Bailey's Company B.

Hinojosa was discharged on February 1, 1911, because of a reduction in force. He became a special policeman in San Benito, then in 1912–1913 a deputy sheriff there. In 1914 he was a Cameron County constable, and in 1915 again a deputy sheriff at San Benito.

From his new headquarters in San Benito, Captain Bailey soon had an incident to report. On October 1, 1910, he notified the adjutant general that Ranger Charles Craighead had just killed a Hispanic. According to Bailey, Rangers Craighead and Cox, together with Deputy Sheriff Earl West, who had recovered from the serious wound to his arm in the San Benito ambush, went to the house of their Hispanic laundress, Paula Treviño. Craighead stepped inside and was speaking with the woman about his clothes. One Valentín Noyola, whom Craighead and Carnes had arrested back on July 25 for being drunk and disorderly, was sleeping on a bed with his hat over his face. Hearing Craighead, Noyola leaped up and lunged at the Ranger with a knife, slashing the front of his shirt. Craighead sprang back and fired five times, hitting Noyola in the inner thigh, in both shoulders, in the left chest, and in the abdomen. Noyola died on the spot. Bailey said the deceased "has reputation of having been a very bad Mex." Although Noyola had relatives in San Benito, Bailey expected no further trouble, but if it occurred he had eight Rangers available to handle it.[65]

Craighead was arrested by none other than Tom Ross, the former Ranger captain, who was now a deputy sheriff in Cameron County. Craighead was bound over to the grand jury on a $5,000 bond. Commenting on the affair to Captain Bailey, the adjutant general wrote, "It would appear from your letter that Craighead was justified in killing a Mexican, as it was done in self-defense. However, the affair is to be regretted, as it will delay the departure of Sergeant Carnes and Craighead, who are much needed at this time by Captain Hughes."[66]

In order to settle the Noyola affair definitively, Craighead asked to be indicted. At the examining trial in Brownsville, with Captain Bailey in the audience, Craighead was defended by a legal and political heavyweight—Jim Wells, the longtime political boss of Cameron County. The forthcoming trial caused considerable interest; Sheriff Garza was ordered to summon a special venire of 200 men from whom to select the jury. When the trial was held on November 4, Captain Hughes and two of his men were in attendance, for Craighead was a member of Hughes's Company. The trial proved anticlimactic—the district attorney asked the judge to instruct the jury to return a verdict of "not guilty."[67] Charles Craighead was acquitted, but there was more to the Noyola killing than just self-defense. The Brownsville *Daily Herald* indicated that the affair was apparently an aftermath of the San Benito ambush.[68] It seems not improbable that if Craighead believed that Noyola had been implicated in the ambush that wounded his brother and killed his friend, he would go gunning for Noyola. Captain Bailey later reported that a brother of the slain Noyola had threatened

Craighead's life several times; threats were as far as it went. But the Noyola killing further poisoned ethnic relations.

The Craighead trial was not the only source of excitement in Brownsville. Forthcoming elections would be hotly contested, and as so often happened across the state,[69] the Rangers were called in to help preserve order. At the request of District Judge W. B. Hopkins, Captain Bailey stationed three men in Brownsville. But as with so much that occurred in South Texas, things were not always what they seemed. A prominent and well-connected Hispanic attorney and former state legislator from Brownsville, J. T. Canales, wrote a letter to the governor, with a copy to Canales's friend General J. O. Newton, the adjutant general. Canales's letter, although lengthy, is worth quoting, for it provides a marvelous, if partisan, description of the political climate in Cameron County:

Dear Governor:

I presume that you know that we are making an effort in this county to throw off the bossism and dictation of Judge Wells. The time has come when many strong democrats in this community feel that it is their duty to clear our County from the shame that all the officers should be under the control of one man, and also from the palpable corruption that is evidenced from the fact that in Democratic primaries you will see 800 and 900 votes cast for the same candidates from Governor to Constable; this is due to corrupt machine politics, and we deem it our duty as loyal citizens of Texas to take our stand for clean politics and clean government.

In this movement I figure as Candidate for County Judge, and Mr. Lon C. Hill as candidate for Sheriff. I think that our democracy is unquestioned, but when it comes to co-operating in a movement to put in power men whom we know to be corrupt, we feel that it is our duty to make a halt.

Judge Wells is making the strongest efforts to retain the power that he has enjoyed for thirty years and there is talk throughout the County that they will win by fair means or unfair. One of the usual tricks heretofore used, is to intimidate voters by placing armed men at the polls. I will state to you, Governor, and will verify [the?] statement by the testimony of honorable men from this City, that there will be absolutely no disturbance at the polls if Judge Wells and his party will give us a fair and square deal. The rumor has gone throughout the County that the Rangers are here for the purpose of intimidating our voters on the day of election. It is a well known fact that the Mexicans are afraid of the Rangers, and especially so now, because of the Rangers having killed three or four Mexicans in the last two months. The charge is that the Rangers are State officers, and as the State is Democratic, that they are here to see that the Blue Ticket, called the local Democratic

Ticket, shall win. Now the agents of the Blue Club are making these assertions throughout the County in order to intimidate our voters from going to the polls, and I apprehend that a request will be made soon, by the County Judge or other officers of the County, to have the Rangers sent here to protect them. This will be done purely for the purpose of intimidation and nothing else. They have all the officers of the County with them, the sheriff has appointed deputy sheriffs of their own, the District Court is now in session and the District Judge, I know, will appoint thirty or forty of their men to act as peace officers on that day, and so on, and this shows that when they ask for the Rangers, it is not for any purpose other than to carry out the threats which they are now making.

Captain Johnson was one of the most fair minded men that ever came into this country, and they did everything possible to have him removed, and succeeded. He was the only one that understood the law which says that the Rangers shall not meddle in politics, and complied with it to the letter. Now, I do not know this new Captain nor any of his men, but I do hope you or General Newton will instruct the Rangers not to serve as instruments in the hands of Mr. Wells for any unlawful purpose.

I will further acquaint you with this fact; that Tom Ross, a former Captain of the Rangers, is now a deputy sheriff in this County, and he has a great deal of influence with the Rangers. Captain Ross is heart, soul and mind with the Blue Ticket and doing all he can against us, (which he has a perfect right to do). But he is at the same time prejudicing the Rangers against our movement, and he has a great deal of influence on account of his former position as a State Ranger.

I believe it is my duty to acquaint you with these facts because I know you will not co-operate directly or indirectly in any unlawful action. I guarantee to you that there will be absolutely no disturbance at the polls nor necessity for any interference, and I will also call your attention to the fact that all of the officers appointed will be appointed by the Blues; we have absolutely none on our side and if anybody needs protection and needs fair treatment it is our side, and not them. The only way that Mr. Wells and his crowd can beat us is if they succeed in intimidating our voters and keeping them away from the polls, as we have fully 75% of the Mexican voters with us and about the same percent of the American voters. And again I appeal to you, Governor, to give us protection in this, that we have a square election, and that our voters shall not be intimidated, but be allowed to vote according to their honest convictions.

Very truly your friend,

J. T. Canales[70]

It should be mentioned, though, that Canales, the former state representative from the Brownsville district who had been elected by the very Wells machine he was now denouncing, had been the Democratic nominee for county school superintendent in the forthcoming election, but in August he had deserted the party to accept the nomination for county judge on the Independent "Red" (Republican and dissident Democrats) ticket. Given the unforgiving nature of Cameron County politics, Canales had reason to be worried.[71]

The Rangers saw the situation in Brownsville somewhat differently than did Canales. Captain Hughes, who had come for the Craighead trial, informed the adjutant general that "the election is very warm here and it looks like there is sure to be trouble here." Lots of special police were on duty, and it was said that some of them were irresponsible individuals. One of these special policemen was, like Tom Ross, another ex-Ranger captain in reduced circumstances: "Capt. Johnson is here and wearing a pistol and stands on the Main Street and it is rumored that he is a Policeman at a salary of about $35.00 per month—he is very friendly to the Rangers and I don't think that he will be in the way at all."[72] According to Hughes, the citizens of Brownsville were quite uneasy and wanted all the Rangers they could get. Hughes planned to leave two of his men, Carnes and Craighead, in Brownsville to reinforce Bailey's three men until after the election.[73] Moreover, the district attorney and Judge Hopkins, both good Democrats, urged the adjutant general himself to come and oversee the election. They stressed that there were rumors that the local militia unit, the Brownsville Rifles, might be called out. Their objection was that the Rifles's commander, Captain George Head, was a Republican customs officer who, in their opinion, should be removed from command because he was a strong partisan. In his telegram to the adjutant general, Judge Hopkins mentioned the crux of the political controversy—county and city officials were on opposite sides. Adjutant General Newton telegraphed Captain Hughes that he was quite agreeable to going to Brownsville if necessary, and he declared that the "Governor directs that rangers remain perfectly neutral and take no part in election except to assist local officers in preserving order." The thrifty Newton instructed Hughes to show the telegram to the district attorney and Judge Hopkins, as this would save the expense of sending each of them a telegram.[74]

The Rangers found themselves continually caught up in electoral disputes of this kind—what one faction considered intimidation the other faction viewed as merely keeping the peace. Despite whatever orders and good intentions were involved, it was humanly impossible to remain absolutely neutral. Captain Bailey, for example, while assuring the adjutant general of his impartiality, nevertheless inclined in favor of the Blue (Democratic) machine.[75] The November election in Brownsville was so potentially explosive that Adjutant General Newton, Ranger Captains Rogers, Bailey, and Hughes, and all the members of Hughes's and Bailey's companies converged on Brownsville. Rangers were deployed throughout Cameron County to those voting precincts where trouble seemed the most likely. Despite the vicious political atmosphere, some drunkenness and rowdiness, and many threats, the election went off without a major disturbance. Captain Rogers, for one, was convinced that only the presence of the Rangers had prevented bloodshed. And after the election, General Newton ordered Captain Bailey to be on hand to prevent trouble when the Blue Club held their victory parade.[76]

During November, calls for Ranger assistance intensified. The sheriff of Pecos County, Dudley S. Barker (another ex-Ranger who had served under Captain McDonald), sent the adjutant general a petition asking for a Ranger to be stationed permanently at the village of Sheffield to keep order. The sheriff of Atascosa County requested that Rangers be present for the district court session, and Captain Rogers sent two men to Pleasanton to assist the sheriff in keeping the peace. Rogers himself went to Rock Springs, in Edwards County, to investigate a particularly ugly incident.

One Antonio Rodríguez had raped and shot to death in front of her children the wife of a rancher in Edwards County because she "spoke roughly" to him. The murderer was apprehended the next day, and he readily admitted his guilt. He was jailed in Rock Springs. Evidently operating on the principle that justice delayed is justice denied, on the night of November 3 a mob of approximately fifty citizens stormed the jail and seized Rodríguez. The mob was reportedly composed of Anglos and Hispanics, both groups outraged by Rodríguez's brutal crime. They marched the doomed prisoner through town to a nearby hill. There he was tied to a mesquite tree and every man in the mob went forward and laid mesquite branches around Rodríguez. When the funeral pyre was deemed sufficiently large someone splashed the contents of a five-gallon can of kerosene on the prisoner and the brush. A match was lit, and the crowd watched silently while Rodríguez turned into a charred corpse. The crowd then walked in righteous solidarity back to town.

In the aftermath of the lynching a rumor spread that Mexicans were marching on Rock Springs to avenge Rodríguez's gruesome death. On November 16 the governor and the adjutant general ordered Captain Rogers to Rock Springs to assist the sheriff in protecting the town from Mexicans. Rogers and two of his men "found all quiet at Rock Springs, and, after quietly investigating the mobbing of Rodriguez, as directed by the Governor—we returned to Austin, after having been relieved by the Sheriff, and also being assured that the citizens were no longer uneasy. Reached Austin on the 19th."[77] Rogers's report clearly indicates where the priorities lay.

The Rodríguez lynching not only exacerbated ethnic tensions in Texas, but it also reverberated in Mexico. The Mexican ambassador filed a formal protest with the State Department and demanded a thorough investigation and the punishment of those involved. The secretary of state in turn requested the governor of Texas to make such an investigation and furnish the State Department with the results. In addition, the Mexican consul and vice-consul at Eagle Pass, Texas, were to conduct their own investigation. The secretary of state wired Governor Campbell: "The Department also requests that in view of the feeling against Mexicans in that neighborhood every precaution be taken to protect Mexican Citizens." The governor replied that the Mexican consular officials at Eagle Pass would be protected and that the lynching would be thoroughly investigated.[78] In Mexico, violent anti-American demonstrations occurred in Mexico City, Guadalajara, and other urban centers.

These outbursts of popular rage could be discounted by the regime of General Porfirio Díaz as isolated incidents, but they added to the discontent that would erupt as the Mexican Revolution. To all appearances, Díaz, although eighty years old, was still firmly in control of Mexico. The old dictator had been "reelected" in June for his seventh consecutive term as president, an event that he had celebrated in September with lavish ceremonies in Mexico City. But the upstart opposition candidate for the presidency, Francisco Madero, had refused to accept defeat. Díaz had had Madero arrested on a trumped-up charge prior to the election, effectively nullifying his campaign. Madero had been confined to the city of San Luis Potosí awaiting trial, but on October 5, 1910, he escaped and made his way to San Antonio, Texas, where he organized the Mexican Revolution. Madero, a wealthy landowning liberal aristocrat, was a most unlikely revolutionist. He decided to rebel only as a last resort, the alternative being to return meekly to his estates in Coahuila and cease opposing the regime. Madero focused on establishing through honest elections a democratic government as a prerequisite to solving the country's problems, concentration of land ownership being one of the most pressing. From San Antonio, Madero issued his Plan de San Luis Potosí, calling for a nationwide uprising against Díaz to begin on November 20, 1910. This revolutionary manifesto was backdated to October 5, the last day Madero had physically been in the city of San Luis Potosí. It could not very well be titled the Plan de San Antonio, for this would mean Madero had violated the neutrality laws of the United States, a charge he was trying to avoid. The roughly six-week period between his arrival in San Antonio and the date for the outbreak of the Revolution on November 20 was insufficient time to organize and equip a network of revolutionary cells throughout Mexico, and when the Revolution began, it began with a sputter not a roar.

Nevertheless it produced a sharp increase in requests for Rangers. The first came on November 20 itself, when John A. Valls, the district attorney of Webb County, telegraphed the governor from Laredo that General Lauro Villar, the commander of the military zone from Ciudad Porfirio Díaz (today Piedras Negras) to Matamoros, advised that revolutionists were gathering in Zapata County, Texas, to attack the town of Guerrero across the Rio Grande. Valls stated that Rangers were needed. Valls was not the only nervous official in Laredo; the captain commanding the local militia company offered to mobilize his troops. The authorities in Austin thanked him politely but informed him that the governor had no intention of calling out the militia unless it was absolutely necessary.[79]

Responding to Valls's call for Rangers, the governor and adjutant general on November 21 dispatched Captain Rogers, recently returned from Rock Springs, to Laredo to enforce the neutrality laws. Rogers and five of his men arrived there on the 22nd and reported to District Attorney Valls as instructed. Rogers and Valls immediately crossed the river to Nuevo Laredo to confer with General Villar. In their lengthy discussion Rogers assured the general of his cooperation in enforcing neutrality. Upon returning to Laredo, Rogers further conferred with the Mexican consul and the deputy U.S. marshal, offering them his assistance. Having established cordial relations all around, Rogers that same day was informed that some 200 revolutionists were encamped on the United States side of the river some thirty-five miles above Laredo. A more reliable report later reduced the number of rebels to seventy-five. Rogers notified the U.S. marshal and the commanding officer at Fort McIntosh, each of whom wired his superiors for instructions. The next day a company of troops, a deputy U.S. marshal, and Rogers and his five Rangers proceeded by special train to the coal mines at Minero, twenty-six miles upriver from Laredo. The troops refused to go any farther because night was falling, so Rogers's Rangers, the deputy marshal, and a Customs inspector they'd picked up on the way secured horses and continued upriver. When they neared the reported rebel camp, they dismounted, waited for daylight, and proceeded on foot into the thick brush lining the Rio Grande. They found the camp, but it was deserted. Fresh tracks, a few cartridge boxes, and a campfire still smoldering were evidence that the insurgents had evacuated the place only a few hours earlier. Rogers was convinced that sympathizers in Laredo had warned them that American officials were on the way.[80] The lawmen searched some nearby houses and interrogated their Hispanic residents, certain that they had harbored rebels, but unable to prove it. In any case it appeared that the rebel band had numbered only some fifteen men.

Undaunted by their failure, Rogers and his party continued upriver to Palafox, some forty-five miles above Laredo. Rogers and the two federal officers crossed the river to the town of Hidalgo, where they conferred with the garrison commander and a captain of Rurales, Díaz's feared mounted constabulary. After exchanging information, the Americans returned to Texas. For the next several days, Rogers and the others focused on the mines, the Ranger captain commenting that "this place, Minero, is a hot-bed at which this bunch of revolutionists had sprung." The peace officers failed to secure any evidence and decided to return to Laredo. They did, however, enlist a Mexican informant at Minero, and they were told that Madero himself had been in the area the previous week.[81]

In reality, Madero had slipped away from his headquarters in San Antonio and had driven to the Rio Grande, crossing on the night of November 19 to lead in person an attack the next day against Ciudad Porfirio Díaz, thus touching off the Revolution on a highly symbolic note. But instead of the easy victory he anticipated, Madero suffered the humiliation of having to call off the attack because the arms and ammunition he'd paid for were nonexistent, as was the army his supporters had confidently assured him would be ready and waiting. Madero glumly returned to San Antonio to await developments. Given the lack of revolutionary activity, both the Mexican consul in Laredo and District Attorney Valls concluded that the crisis had passed, and they informed Rogers that Rangers were no longer needed. The adjutant general concurred. Rogers and his men returned to Austin.[82]

The adjutant general accepted the conventional wisdom regarding the Mexican Revolution. On November 28 he wrote to Rogers, "From the latest news gleaned from the press, the revolutionists seem to have about spent their force, and there is every evidence that President Diaz will remain in complete control."[83] Yet it was, improbably enough, the *New York Times* that grasped the implications of the Mexican Revolution for the Rangers. That same day, November 28, the newspaper published an editorial entitled "The Texas Rangers." The piece began:

> The historic Rangers of Texas have been busily and worthily employed the last week or so. Texas has lately shown signs of getting tired of Rangers. Of old, the Rangers guarded the frontier, and the Texas of today feels that it has no frontier. Indians have passed into history, or gone into business, and cattle thieves are scarce and no longer picturesque. But Mexico has a northern frontier, and granting the modern Texan idea of the obliteration of that state's frontier, the Rangers have nevertheless been up and active, day and night, on work of the old frontier type.

After sketching the history of the Rangers, the editorial continued:

> Perhaps Texas, because of its recent scare, will conquer its disposition to abolish the Rangers. . . . Let the Texas Rangers be preserved for the good of all of us. While they exist Texas will not permit the Mexicans to whip us. The Texas Legislature is to vote for or against the abolition of the Rangers in January. It is likely that the force will be reorganized and its historic name preserved.[84]

As the *New York Times* perceived, the Rangers would be *needed*. The incipient Mexican Revolution was not dead, it was just catching its breath, and as it gained momentum and spilled over into Texas, the Rangers would play an increasingly important role. But this was in the future; in the fall of 1910 the Revolution didn't seem to amount to much.

Yet there were signs of life. Captain Hughes reported from Marfa in late November that there was a lot of revolutionary talk in that town. Moreover, he had just learned from the sheriff that one of his deputies at Ruidosa, on the Rio Grande north of Presidio, had crossed the river and encountered a band of *insurrectos* 117 strong. They assured the deputy that they would not raid into Texas; their quarrel was with President Díaz. Because the deputy's report had caused some excitement along the Texas side of the river, Captain Hughes transferred the two men he had in Amarillo to Ysleta and planned to "keep them there until after the Revolutionary excitement is over."[85] The Big Bend region of Texas remained an area of concern, for the residents of Brewster and Presidio Counties were becoming increasingly nervous about the possibility of Mexican incursions. Captain Hughes continued to monitor the situation and reported that the county judge in Alpine wanted a company of soldiers to patrol the Rio Grande and protect the citizenry. Hughes was not opposed to the idea. Then in mid-December rumors were flying that rebels were preparing to attack the town of Ojinaga, across the river from Presidio, Texas. This produced a stampede of refugees fleeing Ojinaga for the safety of the United States—a scene that would be repeated many times along the border during the next decade. On the afternoon of December 15, Captain Hughes and Sheriff Milt Chastain were atop the tallest house in Presidio observing through field glasses a column of Mexican troops leaving Ojinaga to fight rebels dug in ten miles up the Rio Grande.[86] As the clash near Ojinaga indicated, it was in the state of Chihuahua that the Revolution was beginning to make headway. It was in the mountainous western part of that state that guerrilla chieftains such as Pascual Orozco and Francisco "Pancho" Villa were defeating small contingents of Díaz's army. With each insurgent victory more and more *Chihuahuenses* flocked to join the revolutionary ranks.

While the ongoing Mexican Revolution was of concern to the adjutant general, a more immediate concern was the festering political situation in Cameron County. The recent elections had not changed the balance of power—Democrats (Blues) controlled the county offices while Independents (Reds) controlled the Brownsville municipal government. The two factions hated each other's guts, and the Texas Rangers were caught in the middle.

The latest round of animosity involved Alfred R. Baker, who had been discharged from Captain Bailey's Company B in November. Private Baker had committed some unspecified but serious offense, for the adjutant general wrote to Bailey that "I am satisfied that you acted exactly right in discharging Ranger Baker, as conduct of this kind is inexcusable."[87] Baker had quickly found employment as a deputy constable in Cameron County.

On the night of December 27, 1910, Baker and his fellow deputy Harry

Wallis, also an ex-Ranger, were involved in a shooting scrape in the White Elephant Saloon in Brownsville. The affray resulted from the ongoing feud between the sheriff's department and the Brownsville police. Earlier that evening a policeman had disarmed a deputy sheriff, Guillermo Sosa, for carrying a gun in Brownsville. The policeman, William Crafts, had acted on the standing order of José Crixell, the city marshal. Deputy Sosa told his story to Baker and Wallis, who decided Officer Crafts had exceeded his authority, and they went to look for him. They encountered Crafts and another policeman, Ignacio Treviño, and demanded the return of Sosa's gun. Crafts insisted he was just following orders, and the group went to the White Elephant so Crafts could use the telephone and ask for further instructions from Marshal Crixell. Both Crafts and Wallis spoke with the marshal, Sosa's gun was returned, and the matter was apparently settled amicably.

But as Wallis and Baker were walking out of the White Elephant, whose proprietor was Alderman Vicente Crixell, the city marshal's brother, firing broke out. It proved to be an exercise in wretched marksmanship: More than a dozen shots were exchanged at close range and nobody got killed. Baker fired five times; Wallis got off four rounds before his pistol, a .32 automatic, jammed. They claimed that Policeman Treviño shot at least twice, as did, interestingly enough, Vicente Crixell, the saloon proprietor, who had a commission as a special policeman. Baker was shot twice from behind, once in the left shoulder and once in the left leg, and he took a third bullet from in front, in the left part of his belly. Still he was able to walk around the corner to Putegnat's Pharmacy for help, from where he was taken to Work's Sanitarium. Policeman Ignacio Treviño received a flesh wound in the abdomen and also left under his own power to seek medical attention.

The stories given by Baker and Wallis on the one hand and Vicente Crixell and the policemen on the other were diametrically opposed, but it would appear that Crixell opened fire as the deputy constables were leaving his saloon, and they whipped around and sprayed the place as the patrons and Crixell fled out the back door. On December 27, each group of participants swore out complaints charging the others with assault with intent to murder. Everybody got arrested and promptly posted bond.[88]

Brownsville was in a high state of excitement over this latest vestige of the Wild West, and the Independent city administration was deeply worried. The mayor, Benjamin Kowalski, and George J. Head, captain of the local militia company, quickly fired off a letter to the adjutant general. After briefly sketching the events leading up to the shooting, they got to the crux of their anxiety: There were in Brownsville four or five Rangers, and in addition at least half a dozen ex-Rangers, including the fearsome A. Y. Baker, who'd come to see why his little brother had been shot up.

Anderson Yancy Baker was a man not to be messed with. He had served in Captain Brooks's Company A, attaining the rank of sergeant. On May 16, 1902, he and several other Rangers were beating through the thick brush on El Sauz Ranch, a component of the enormous King Ranch, in search of rustlers. Baker came upon one Ramón Cerda branding a stolen calf. The Ranger and the rustler fired at virtually the same time; Cerda shot Baker's horse in the head, but Baker shot Cerda in the head. This killing produced a prolonged confrontation between the Cerda family, whose small ranch adjoined El Sauz, and the Rangers. The Cerdas and their political allies, the Red Club, whipped up public sentiment against the "official murder" of Cerda, while the owners of the King Ranch and John B. Armstrong, the ex-Ranger who had captured John Wesley Hardin and who had become a prominent rancher, supported Baker. The latter had no difficulty in posting a $10,000 bond. Public sentiment regarding the Rangers was sharply divided, largely along ethnic lines.

On the night of September 9, Baker and fellow Rangers Emmett Roebuck and Jesse Miller were riding back from Brownsville to their camp about a mile out of town on a ranch belonging to Judge James B. Wells. The trio were bushwhacked by several men using shotguns and Winchesters. Roebuck was killed and Baker was slightly wounded. Captain Brooks and Brownsville city marshal Lawrence Bates, who was a cousin of Baker's, rushed to the scene and began an investigation. Six men, including Alfredo Cerda, were soon arrested for Roebuck's murder and jailed in Brownsville. A lynch mob quickly formed, and the Rangers found themselves in the ironic position of dispersing the crowd in order to protect the men who had killed their comrade.

The deceased Ramón Cerda's brother, Alfredo, who was generally believed to have led the ambush of the Rangers and who had been released on bond, went around Brownsville making threats against Baker, and the Cerdas reportedly put out a contract on him, offering $1,000 to anyone who would kill the Ranger; in 1902, and in Brownsville, $1,000 was real money. Alfredo Cerda was evidently naive enough to think that Baker would simply sit around waiting to be dispatched. Imagine his surprise when Baker killed him.

This occurred on October 3 in the dry goods store of Gerónimo Fernández & Bro. on the corner of Elizabeth and 13th Streets. Alfredo Cerda was sitting by the entrance trying on a pair of gloves and chatting with the proprietor when Baker shot him with a Winchester from the sidewalk in front of the entrance. The bullet entered the right side of Cerda's chest and exited the left side. Cerda, who was not shot in the back as one account alleges, lingered for about an hour before dying. Immediately after the shooting Baker walked up the street to Fort Brown, where he remained through the night. Baker was charged with murder and released on bond. He and Captain Brooks took the stage to Alice, while the rest of Brooks's company remained in Brownsville. Several days after the Cerda killing, an important witness for Baker, one Herculano Berbier, was killed by parties unknown.[89] In 1903, in separate trials in Brownsville in February and September, Baker pleaded self-defense and was acquitted in the deaths of Ramón and Alfredo Cerda. His attorney was Judge James B. Wells.

The Baker case is a prime example of the diametrically opposed views of the Rangers. In writing about the killing of Ramón Cerda, the authors of *Gunpowder Justice* omit any mention of Cerda's branding a rustled calf or his trying to shoot Baker, presumably because Cerda doesn't fit the innocent Mexican image. They merely state that Rangers "came across a Mexican branding a calf. Sergeant Baker shot the Mexican, who proved to be Ramon De La Cerda." These authors do, however, dwell on the details of Alfredo Cerda's killing. Conversely, Webb and Sterling dwell on the details of Baker's killing of Ramón Cerda and the ambush of Baker and his companions but have little to say about Baker's killing of Alfredo Cerda, presumably because it doesn't fit the noble Ranger image. Webb merely states that Alfredo Cerda "was killed on Elizabeth Street by A. Y. Baker against whom he had been making threats." Sterling tries to insinuate that this occurred in some kind of gunfight: "Alfredo Cerda was shot and killed by A. Y. Baker. They met on Elizabeth Street, the main thoroughfare of Brownsville, near the corner of Nineteenth." The contradiction extends to the aftermath as well. According to Sterling, Ranger Winfred Bates, who was Baker's cousin, witnessed the shooting of Alfredo Cerda; Bates, Baker, and Captain Brooks deliberately withdrew to Fort Brown in order to avoid having to shoot a few hotheads in the crowd that had gathered. According to Américo Paredes, Baker ran to a nearby saloon where the other Rangers awaited him, and they ran out the back door and sought refuge at Fort Brown, "to escape a mob of indignant citizens" (which sounds awfully like a Hispanic lynch mob).[90]

After resigning from the Rangers, Baker married and remained in the area. He was now the treasurer of neighboring Hidalgo County, living in Chapin. A lot of Hispanics still hated Baker, referring to him by his translated name—*El Panadero*—but nobody wanted to take him on. Not that they didn't have numerous opportunities, for Baker took no precautions. He habitually sat on the curb chatting with somebody while crowds passed behind his back on the sidewalk. In December, 1910, officials in Brownsville must have breathed a sigh of relief when Baker left town without shooting any policemen.

The Bakers and their relatives, by the way, could have staffed a Ranger company all by themselves. Besides A. Y., his brother Alfred R., who had been fired from Company B in November, 1910, was reenlisted in that company in September, 1911, serving until October, 1912. Their brother, Frank P., served in Companies D and A in 1915–1916 and was a Special Ranger from 1917 to 1919. Their other brother, Joseph E., was in Companies D and G in 1915–1918. Then there were their cousins, the Bates: Lawrence H. (a Ranger from 1899 to 1902 and a Special Ranger in 1917) and Winfred F. (Company A 1902–1904, becoming sergeant, in Company D in 1905, and in Companies C and B in 1915). We will encounter A. Y. Baker again, for in 1912 he was elected sheriff of Hidalgo County.

Mayor Kowalski continued in his letter to the adjutant general:

> Excitement is very high and most of the citizens, as well as the police force, are sure that should any further trouble arise, both the active and ex-rangers would certainly side with Baker and Wallace [sic], and thereby possibly cause a great deal of unnecessary blood-shed.

The mayor urgently requested that the adjutant general ask the governor to withdraw the active-duty Rangers from Brownsville until things quieted down, "as they can be of no earthly use in quieting the situation, but on the other hand, under the circumstances of their relationship to both Baker and Wallace [sic], tend to excite and agitate, by their presence, if for no other reason." Kowalski hoped that the adjutant general would come to Brownsville and see the situation for himself, but in any case withdraw the Rangers at once.[91]

The adjutant general indeed discussed the matter with Governor Campbell and solicited the opinions of District Judge Hopkins and District Attorney Kleiber regarding Mayor Kowalski's letter.[92] In reply, Judge Hopkins commented on the animosity between the county and city authorities. Several Brownsville policemen had been arrested and charged with carrying arms while they were at political meetings in ranches out in Cameron County. The judge understood that all of these men had been tried and discharged. In retaliation, the Brownsville city marshal instructed the police to disarm and arrest all deputy sheriffs who did not reside in Brownsville and who came to town armed. This was what had caused the latest shooting scrape. Judge Hopkins recommended against withdrawing the Rangers, stating that Captain Bailey wouldn't allow his men "to take sides unjustly." Hopkins further commented that ex-Rangers were not under the adjutant general's jurisdiction, and that they had every right to be in Brownsville. The judge reiterated that the Rangers should remain in Brownsville and that "they would only cause trouble to those wanting to make trouble. . . ."[93]

Even before receiving Judge Hopkins's opinion, the adjutant general wrote to Mayor Kowalski that he had shown Kowalski's letter to the governor and had asked for Hopkins's and Kleiber's views. Captain Bailey had been instructed to "caution his men to take no part with either faction in this trouble, except to see that order is maintained and the law enforced." The adjutant general hoped "the matter is now a closed incident."[94] The Rangers stayed.

That same day the adjutant general instructed Captain Bailey to:

Please impress on every member of your company the necessity of not taking sides with either faction in this matter, their duty being to assist in the enforcement of the law without respect to persons or factions.[95]

This was all well and good, but Bailey had his own views on the situation in Brownsville and they were unequivocally supportive of Sheriff Carl T. Ryan, who had served under Captain McDonald and had been a Cameron County constable. It is quite conceivable that Ryan's being an ex-Ranger may have influenced Bailey as he informed the adjutant general that:

The main trouble is on account of the rottenness of the city government, in fact that is where the whole trouble lies. They are fighting Ryan, the sheriff. Ryan is in for [sic] the right, has done all in his power to preserve order, has used good judgement, kept his head & patience & has so far with our help managed to prevent further trouble. A. Y. Baker is here but has been quiet saying & doing nothing in the way of causing trouble. It is all coming from the mayor and City Marshall [sic]. Capt. Rogers can give you some idea as to the kind of men we have to deal with along that line. . . . As I stated before, Ryan is on the right side & has done all he could to keep down further trouble while we have caught several of their "frame ups" and in fact he has to some extent let them run over him.[96]

Acknowledging the adjutant general's order to remain neutral, Bailey nevertheless wrote that "we have taken no sides, are friendly with both factions, but it is all one sided as to right & wrong & law & order. We may be able to hold off trouble while rangers are here, but should we leave I believe it will be pulled off." He had three Rangers with him in Brownsville; two men were at Alice and three at San Benito. For the adjutant general's edification, Bailey enclosed a list of Brownsville policemen: ten policemen and ten supernumeraries; all but two were Hispanic.[97] As we shall see, the situation in Brownsville would get considerably worse before it got better.

The same could be said for the situation of the Ranger Force. The year 1910, which had already been marred by events such as the Redus affair, the San Benito ambush, and the disbanding of Company A, was closing on an ominous note. The Democrat Oscar B. Colquitt was running for governor, and Colquitt was no friend of the Texas Rangers.[98]

Governor Campbell's policy of utilizing the Rangers to enforce the gambling and local option liquor laws whether local officials requested the Rangers' assistance or not was producing a wave of resentment. There was a growing perception that the governor was running roughshod over the rights of local officers and of the citizens. In the 1910 gubernatorial campaign, Colquitt played on this resentment most effectively in his bid to succeed Campbell. In July, for instance, when Colquitt delivered a two-hour speech in the school auditorium in Big Sandy, he blasted the Rangers. Colquitt

> severely denounced the secret police force of the governor, known as the rangers, and referring to the outrage at Amarillo, he said that after that incident, had he been governor, he would have fired the rangers into the middle of the gulf of Mexico.[99]

And a few days later, in a speech at Rogers, Colquitt

> Stated that when he is elected governor, that he won't send the state rangers to usurp the power of the sheriff and trample under foot the rights of people of Bell county under the constitution.[100]

Colquitt's rhetoric struck a responsive chord not only among many citizens but also among state legislators, a growing number of whom echoed the views of a legislator who declared, "The force is not now needed and is not only an incubus but an entirely unnecessary expense."[101] As the campaign wore on, Colquitt hammered away at Campbell's use of the Rangers, and there was speculation that as governor, Colquitt would not abolish the Rangers but he would downsize them in such a drastic fashion that they would be brought to heel.[102]

Although his policy was being sharply criticized, Governor Campbell steadfastly continued to use the Rangers as he thought best. In September, during the traditional fiesta in San Antonio celebrating Mexican independence, there was widespread illegal gambling in that city, and local officials chose to ignore it. They also condoned prostitution on a permanent basis.[103]

Governor Campbell might be unable to suppress prostitution, but he could sure do something about the gambling. He ordered it stopped immediately and sent in the Rangers, announcing that if necessary he would call out the militia.[104] The gambling ceased, but Mayor Bryan Callahan, who had dominated San Antonio politics for nearly twenty years, was furious, and he retaliated in a particularly petty way. On December 11, Captain Bailey was at the police station in San Antonio on business when Police Captain Frank Newman asked him if he was carrying a pistol. Bailey replied that of course he was, whereupon the dumbfounded Ranger was informed that he was under arrest. He was hustled off to the county court, where he was charged with unlawfully carrying a pistol. Fortunately an assistant district attorney heard of the arrest and immediately began habeas corpus proceedings in district court, whose judge ruled that a Ranger was a peace officer and had a right to be armed. Captain Bailey was released. The arrest had resulted from Mayor Callahan's claim that the Rangers had no right to carry a pistol in San Antonio.[105]

The Rangers found themselves in an awkward situation. They had been carrying out Governor Campbell's orders and enforcing the law, but in so doing they had become increasingly unpopular. And when Oscar Branch Colquitt was indeed elected governor in the fall of 1910, the Rangers knew they were in for a rough ride.

Part One

The Colquitt Years, 1911–1915

CHAPTER THREE

REVOLUTION IN MEXICO

COLQUITT as governor began by living up to his fiery rhetoric concerning the Rangers. His attitude was expressed in a letter he wrote on January 11, 1911, to Mrs. W. E. Collins, the widow of the man the Rangers had killed near Grovetown, allegedly in self-defense, in September, 1909: "I think the killing of your husband by the Rangers was a grevious [sic] outrage."[1] Little wonder that H. A. Carnes, sergeant of Company D, would write that "We are in a good deal of suspence [sic] as to what the new Gov. will do with us."[2]

The Rangers could only hunker down, keep doing their job, and hope for the best. They could take some comfort in the fact that although Company A had been mustered out on September 30, 1910, the Ranger Force had undergone only a slight numerical decline: from twenty-five in January, 1910, to twenty-one at the end of December. In January, 1911, the status of the organization was:

San Benito
Company B: Captain M. E. Bailey, 1 sergeant, 7 privates   9

Austin
Company C: Captain J. H. Rogers, 1 sergeant, 2 privates   4

Ysleta
Company D: Captain J. R. Hughes, 1 sergeant, 5 privates   7
_____
     20

As is evident, manpower had been shifted toward the Mexican border.

For the moment at least, Captain Bailey's Company B was in the limelight, and not necessarily for the right reasons: On January 8, Private Roy Adams was discharged for disorderly conduct while in Brownsville.[3] The animosities in Brownsville continued to simmer, and Bailey still had several men stationed there. He reported that ex-Ranger A. R. Baker had substantially recovered from his wounds at the hands of the police and was out and about again. On a more sinister note, Bailey advised the adjutant general that one evening a Mexican had told two Rangers in Brownsville that a fight was going on in the same saloon where Baker had been shot. On their way to investigate, the Rangers encountered two additional Rangers and a couple of sheriff's deputies, and they all proceeded to the saloon. This was fortunate, for when they entered they found no brawl in progress but rather nineteen Brownsville policemen waiting. Words were exchanged, but no bullets. To Bailey, the whole thing smelled like a trap.[4]

At the other end of the border, Captain Hughes, after repeated requests from the sheriffs of Presidio and Jeff Davis Counties, had decided to station some of his men at Valentine, a hardscrabble little cowtown on the windswept plains of West Texas forty miles south of Van Horn: "On account of the revolutionary movement along the Rio Grande, I think the move is a proper one at this time as horse thieves of both nationalities will take advantage of the unrest to commit depredations."[5] Like the other captains, Hughes operated on a very tight budget. He sold a worn-out Company D hack for $5.00, sending the adjutant general a check for that amount. The latter authorized Hughes to purchase a replacement vehicle, but cautioned: "I leave details as to kind, price, etc., to you, for you not only know what is needed for your work, but will save every cent possible for the State."[6]

The state was about to save some money all right, for Governor Colquitt wielded his bureaucratic ax with a vengeance. He and the legislature decided not to abolish the Rangers, but during January the word went out announcing a major reorganization of the constabulary. As of February 1, 1911, Companies C and D were abolished, and Captain Bailey of Company B was relieved of command. Bailey was ordered to inform his men that there was no guarantee that his successor would retain them.[7]

Adding to the personnel turmoil, the veteran Captain J. H. Rogers of Company C resigned on January 31 because of Colquitt's opposition to Prohibition, and he immediately secured a position as a deputy U.S. marshal in El Paso.[8] The other veteran leader, Captain John R. Hughes, commanded a resurrected Company A, which was merely his old but now abolished Company D.

Further weakening the tradition of filling captaincies by promoting from within the ranks of the Rangers, Governor Colquitt appointed as Bailey's successor in Company B an outsider, John J. Sanders, who had several times applied to become a Ranger captain. Sanders was born in June, 1854, in Cold Springs, Polk County. From 1888 to 1898 he had served as city marshal of Lockhart, remaining there from 1898 to 1909 as sheriff of Caldwell County. He was now captain of Company B, and in a rather odd development, his predecessor, M. E. Bailey, was now Sanders's sergeant, but only for a short time. Bailey resigned in May.[9]

The icing on the cake was that Colquitt's adjutant general was not just from out of state, he was from out of the country—Brigadier General Henry Hutchings had been born in Somersetshire, England, in 1865. The following year his parents brought him to the United States. He had been in the newspaper and publishing business in Austin since 1890. In 1885 he joined the Texas National Guard, rising from private to brigadier general. Hutchings had served on the personal staffs of Governors Ross and Hogg. Though his experience in state government was limited—the only office that he had ever held was that of chief clerk in the Department of State—this was more than offset by his having been the secretary and treasurer of the Travis County Colquitt Club during the 1910 campaign. Hutchings maintained an armory and arsenal in the basement of the capitol directly under the adjutant general's department. When some of his subordinates expressed apprehension because Hutchings had just added two carloads of ammunition to what was already in the arsenal, he assured them that none of the ammunition was combustible and there was no danger of an explosion.[10]

Governor Colquitt had turned the Texas Rangers every which way but loose, and when the dust settled, instead of its authorized strength of eighty-nine men, the demoralized Ranger Force consisted of [11]

Ysleta
Company A: Captain John R. Hughes, 1 sergeant, 5 privates   7

San Benito
Company B: Captain John J. Sanders, 1 sergeant, 4 privates   6
_____
13

In terms of manpower, the Rangers had hit rock bottom. Colquitt had certainly kept his campaign promise, reducing the organization to little more than a corporal's guard.

But it soon began to look as if the governor might have acted a bit hastily. The Mexican Revolution continued to gain momentum, especially in the state of Chihuahua. During January, Rangers from Captain Hughes's company were called on to assist federal officers in scouting the Rio Grande near El Paso and in enforcing the neutrality laws.[12] One of Hughes's privates, incidentally, was Pat Craighead, recovered from his serious wounds incurred in the San Benito ambush and back on duty, wooden leg and all. He was serving together with his brother, Charles A. Craighead.

It was in early February, 1911, that the Mexican Revolution began to cause real concern. By February 2, Pascual Orozco, Madero's principal insurgent commander in Chihuahua, was advancing on Ciudad Juárez, across the Rio Grande from El Paso. While Díaz's garrison in Ciudad Juárez prepared to fight, El Paso was in a major uproar. Besides the danger of bullets landing in El Paso if a battle did occur, the city officials were concerned about the Hispanic residents. They numbered more than ten thousand and were staunchly pro-Madero, as, for that matter, were many of their Anglo fellow citizens. Sheriff Peyton Edwards prepared to call out the local militia to assist the few regular troops trying to control the crowds, especially at the two international bridges. In addition, a guard was placed on the militia's armory, located in the basement of the county courthouse, as a precaution against the weapons being stolen and delivered to the rebels. For a week El Paso lived in a state of high tension, until the arrival of government reinforcements in Ciudad Juárez forced Orozco to withdraw his irregulars from the border.[13] Nevertheless, this had been a wake-up call for the Texas authorities—the Mexican Revolution was not going to go away anytime soon.

There wasn't much the Ranger Force could do to influence events, since the organization was barely visible to the naked eye. Captain Hughes's men continued to scout along the Rio Grande, usually as members of patrols consisting of a Ranger or two and mounted Customs inspectors, or "river guards" as they were commonly known, plus a few cavalrymen.[14] As a change of pace, Privates C. R. Moore, Craighead, and Webster made an unsuccessful scout in March with an El Paso policeman, looking for an old muzzle-loading cannon that had been stolen from an El Paso park. It was smuggled out of the city in a farm wagon, taken some thirty-five miles downriver, and delivered to the rebels, who were desperately short of artillery.[15]

At the same time, Captain Sanders's Company B was being withdrawn from the border. On March 11, Sanders established a camp at Harlingen, then on March 26, on orders from Adjutant General Hutchings, moved his company headquarters 175 miles north to Kenedy, only fifty miles southeast of San Antonio. If Hutchings's motive had been to remove the Rangers from the Brownsville area in order to preclude further friction with that city's police, he certainly accomplished his objective. It might be mentioned that in this case, as when Bailey had commanded Company B, what was meant by a "Ranger camp" was a rented house in town.[16]

As the Revolution intensified, the federal government intensified its response. In early February four troops of cavalry were rushed from Fort Meade, South Dakota, to Fort Bliss for patrol duty in the El Paso area. And the United States finally decided that indeed Madero had been using American territory to organize a revolution aimed at overthrowing a friendly government, that of General Porfirio Díaz. Accordingly, a federal warrant charging Madero with violating the neutrality laws of the United States was issued on February 13.[17] Madero, however, managed to make his way from San Antonio to the El Paso area undetected, and he slipped across the Rio Grande into Chihuahua on February 14 to take personal command of his rebel forces.

Governor Colquitt, meanwhile, had embarked on a policy that at first glance appeared to suppress revolutionary activity but in reality was an exercise in smoke and mirrors. On February 11, after conferring with Díaz's emissary, Joaquín Casasús, and Henry Clay Pierce of the Standard Oil Company, he issued a proclamation enjoining Texans to observe strict neutrality with regard to the armed struggle raging in Mexico.[18] The proclamation merely restated the federal statutes on neutrality, whose enforcement was a federal—not a state—responsibility. Furthermore, as Colquitt informed President Taft on February 23, he had ordered Captain Hughes "to keep a sharp lookout for . . . Madero. . . . I have also ordered Captain Hughes to take Madero in custody for violation of the neutrality laws if he can locate him in Texas." Colquitt went so far as to urge Taft to request Díaz's permission for Texas Rangers to cross into Mexico to arrest certain insurrecto chieftains who were fugitives from justice in Texas.[19] At this point Taft surely must have begun to suspect that Colquitt was a loose cannon. As for the Rangers, it was just as well that they were unaware of their governor's madcap plans for them. Had the Mexican government in a fit of whimsy agreed to permit Texas Rangers to arrest its deadly enemies, insurgent chieftains, it would probably have taken more than the dozen Rangers then in existence to get the job done.

Of course one just had to take a man's word that he was a Texas Ranger, at least with regard to Captain Hughes's Company A. As Hughes informed the adjutant general's office:

> Referring to your letter of the 10th, inst. I beg to say that no certificate of authority had been furnished to C. A. Craighead, nor to any of my men, for the reason that several of these certificates have been lost. They do not seem to be necessary, and for that reason the one sent from your office to Ranger M. H. Wright has not been delivered to him. As none of my men have ever been required to show their certificates of authority I thought it better that they should not carry one, run the risk of losing it, and have it fall into the hands of some one who would falsely personate a ranger.[20]

Since most Rangers didn't wear badges, it wouldn't have been difficult to "personate" a member of Hughes's company.

Hughes and his men were keeping busy. On the governor's orders one Ranger was dispatched to Van Horn and another to Kent to keep order during elections in newly created Culberson County. Evidently the presence of a Ranger prevented a disturbance in Kent. But the real excitement continued to center on El Paso and the Mexican Revolution. Hughes reported that his Rangers had good relations with the U.S. cavalry and had made a number of scouts with the troopers, who were actively patrolling the Rio Grande in that area. To the frustration of the army, parties of Mexicans, totaling several hundred, had crossed into Mexico downriver from El Paso to join the Revolution, but as the Mexicans were unarmed the soldiers were powerless to stop them.

Hughes himself traveled frequently to El Paso to monitor the situation. On April 19, he wrote from Ysleta that people expected rebels to attack Ciudad Juárez the next day. Hughes sent three men to El Paso to assist the sheriff, and he himself planned to go there early the next morning: "We will have all our war paint on."[21] Anticlimactically, no attack developed, and Hughes and his men returned to Ysleta. But by April 24, he and several of his Rangers were back in El Paso. Hughes was rotating his men between his camp in Ysleta and El Paso, something that was easy to do because there were three trains a day each way. Mainly, Hughes, like everyone else in El Paso, was watching across the river where Madero and his rebels were now encamped.[22]

Captain Sanders's Company B was still based in Kenedy, from where they covered all of South Texas. On occasion some of Sanders's men were sent to Brownsville to help the sheriff keep order during district court sessions. Sanders and Sergeant Bailey went to Austin in April to confer with Hutchings and Colquitt about enlisting another man in Company B, which seemed like a good idea given the way things were developing. Yet the adjutant general saw no need for another Ranger private.[23]

The major development in May was a full-scale rebel assault on Ciudad Juárez. Madero had been negotiating with the Díaz regime, but the negotiations had become deadlocked. For this reason, and because he feared international complications with the United States if the rebels attacked Ciudad Juárez, on May 7 Madero ordered his forces to withdraw from around the border city. Some of Madero's commanders, notably Pascual Orozco and Pancho Villa, were having none of it; they provoked a firefight with the federal garrison on May 8, a clash which quickly escalated into an all-out insurgent attack. Captain Hughes and his men were interested observers. As he informed the adjutant general, "Wish you and all the force could be here to enjoy the fun."[24] Hughes's attitude mirrored that of the citizens of El Paso, who acted as though the savage battle raging in Ciudad Juárez were an entertainment the Mexicans had thoughtfully put on for El Paso's enjoyment. The citizenry crowded as close to the action as they could get, many of them standing on railroad cars in the freight yard in order to get a better view. But bullets are no respecters of international boundaries and, as Madero had feared, complications with the United States did occur. Rebel bullets landed all over El Paso; six people were killed, and another fifteen were wounded.[25]

After three days of ferocious house-to-house fighting, Ciudad Juárez fell to the rebels on May 10. Madero had to personally escort the defeated federal commander, General Juan Navarro, across the river to El Paso to save him from being shot by Orozco and Villa. The capture of Ciudad Juárez marked the breathtakingly unexpected turning point in Madero's rebellion. The popular image of

President Díaz as the invincible iron-fisted dictator who had controlled Mexico since 1876 shattered, virtually overnight. Madero's seizure of the largest Mexican border city convinced the public that Díaz was a paper tiger. Only two weeks later, by May 25, the tired old dictator had resigned and was on his way to exile in Paris, where he would die in 1915. Madero was now the man of the hour, and he began planning a campaign to be elected president in an honest election.

Following the overthrow of Díaz, conditions in Mexico remained unsettled. Governor Colquitt was especially concerned about the situation in El Paso, and he again engaged in micromanaging the Rangers. On May 15, 1911, he wrote to Captain Hughes that:

> In view of conditions prevailing at Juarez I wish you would take as many of your men as convenient and remain in El Paso until matters quiet down. I want you especially to remain in El Paso as my special representative and keep me advised by wire of the situation if there is danger of a conflict.
>
> I will look into the law and see what right the Governor of the State has to require of the combatants that they do not shoot into the City of El Paso. Please proceed to El Paso upon receipt of this letter and remain there until further advised.[26]

As a reminder that revolutionary unrest existed the length of the Rio Grande border, Sheriff C. T. Ryan wired the adjutant general from Brownsville that because of rebel activity there he thought it necessary to have a detail of men guard the weapons and ammunition of the local national guard company at night. Ryan's deputies were otherwise engaged, so the adjutant general ordered the captain of the Brownsville militia company to mount guard. The latter reported that this had been done from May 24 to June 6 because on three different nights members of the *magonista* revolutionary faction had tried to raid the armory.[27] The *magonistas* were followers of the Mexican anarchist exile Ricardo Flores Magón, who prudently stayed in his Los Angeles headquarters while urging his supporters to join the armed struggle in Mexico.

Adjutant General Hutchings faced a frustrating situation: trying to cope with growing unrest but lacking enough Rangers to do the job adequately. The best he could do was to improve the readiness of the Force. Accordingly he wrote to Captain Hughes that

> At your earliest convenience I desire that you submit a list of such things as are necessary to increase the efficiency of your command. I am of the opinion that the two ranger companies should be completely and adequately equipped out of the present appropriation, which will expire on August 31.[28]

Hughes wrote back that what he most needed was a hack with double harness, two double-bed mattresses, and one tent. In addition, although he wasn't short of ammunition, "it has always been customary to lay in a supply of ammunition before the appropriation expires."[29] Regarding the appropriation, the Rangers continued to have their share of enemies in the Texas legislature. There was vitriolic debate in the appropriations committee, which introduced a bill slashing the appropriation from $25,000 to $15,000, and it was only after acrimonious discussion that the legislators restored the original amount.[30]

Captain Hughes spent much of his time in El Paso assisting the sheriff and monitoring the activities of Mexican revolutionaries. On May 10, the day Ciudad Juárez fell, Hughes had his entire company in El Paso trying to keep onlookers out of the danger zone. On May 22 Sergeant H. A. Carnes and Private C. R. Moore helped Sheriff Edwards restore order among some Mexican revolutionary officers who'd congregated on the El Paso side of the Rio Grande. The altercation resulted from the desire of some of these officers to shoot Col. Giuseppe Garibaldi.[31] The grandson and namesake of the Italian liberator, Garibaldi was serving as a mercenary in Madero's forces, and some rebels, Pancho Villa among them, bitterly resented his presence.

Into the summer of 1911, the Mexican Revolution seemed to be abating. Yet Captain Hughes's Company A was stretched to the limit. In June, for example, Hughes sent three men by train to Big Spring in response to an urgent telegram from the sheriff; one man was assisting the sheriff of El Paso County; one man was stationed at Valentine; and only one private was with Hughes at Ysleta. Hughes speculated that the U.S. cavalry would be withdrawn from the border. He would be sorry to see them go, for they had "taken lots of the work off the hands of the Rangers and local officers." Presciently, though, he added: "I am afraid they are being moved away too soon."[32]

In July, District Judge S. J. Isaacks wired from Pecos asking Governor Colquitt to send two or three Rangers to report to the sheriff at Pecos to assist in maintaining order at the trial of a teenaged Mexican, Leon Cárdenas Martínez, who had confessed to killing a visiting schoolteacher, Emma Brown, at the hamlet of Saragosa when she resisted his amorous advances. The crime had generated enormous outrage, and lynching was imminent. Captain Hughes was ordered to take one man and proceed immediately to Pecos. Hughes took no chances—he was accompanied to Pecos by Privates Moore, Craighead, and Webster. The presence of four Rangers dampened the enthusiasm for lynching, but Cárdenas Martínez was tried in Pecos a week after the murder and was sentenced to death. After the trial two of the Rangers assisted the sheriff in transporting the convicted murderer to jail in Midland for safekeeping. Because of the murderer's age—sixteen—a prolonged legal battle and public opinion campaign was waged to spare his life, but he was hanged at Pecos on May 11, 1914.[33]

Sadly, lynchings were a fact of life in Texas as in some other parts of the country. People favored direct action to avenge the crime, and they were not too concerned about the rights of the accused. Lynchings occurred most often when a member of a minority group was accused of committing murder or rape. In March, 1910, for example, in Dallas a mob of 5,000 men—including both whites and blacks—lynched a black who'd raped a three-year-old girl. The mob stormed the courthouse and hanged the rapist out of a window.[34] But lynchings occurred most frequently in small towns.

On June 20, 1911, there occurred a despicable act in Thorndale, forty miles northeast of Austin. Antonio Gámez, who was either sixteen or fourteen years old, was whittling on a shingle when an Anglo man cursed him as he passed by. The youth reacted by stabbing the man, who collapsed and died. The constable arrested Gámez and left him in the custody of a citizen while he went to get a car in order to transport the prisoner to the county seat. During the officer's absence, a group of half a dozen men went to the house. Four of them beat Gámez, dragged him by a chain around his neck to a light pole and hanged the youth. Because of Gámez's age, this lynching caused widespread revulsion, especially among Hispanics, who held a mass meeting in San Antonio to protest and to appeal to the authorities for justice. An assistant attorney general and Ranger D. W. Cox were sent to Thorndale to investigate, and Cox was able to report to Governor Colquitt that four men were under arrest there facing murder charges.[35]

Colquitt soon had occasion to dispatch Rangers on a similar mission to Farmersville, a hamlet some forty miles northeast of Dallas. The reason for this lynching on August 11, 1911, was truly mind boggling—it occurred because the night telephone operator accused a black man, one Commodore Jones, of insulting her over the telephone—for the third time. The local constable arrested Jones and tried to spirit him out of town to nearby McKinney. Unfortunately he missed the train and had to return Jones to jail. The sheriff came from McKinney for the prisoner but left empty handed, thoroughly intimidated by a mob that had swelled to some 300. They broke into the jail, seized the luckless Jones, and hanged him from a telephone pole in the town square. Governor Colquitt was outraged; he dispatched three Rangers to restore order and threatened to send troops if necessary.[36]

Captain Sanders's Company B, in the meantime, had been engaged in more routine kinds of work. From Kenedy they covered South Texas, scouting all the way to Brownsville. Sanders's men investigated the odd murder, but most of their time was spent chasing rustlers.[37] Ranchers were usually glad to have Rangers around, not only for protection but also because some ranchers were ex-Rangers themselves, such as John Armstrong, of John Wesley Hardin fame. And then of course ranchers paid a lot of taxes, and thus merited a lot of protection. Besides enforcing the law, what was on Captain Sanders's mind was a raise. He had his old friend A. J. Bell, of the law firm of Bell and Lipscomb in San Antonio, sound out the adjutant general on this matter:

> Captain Sanders thinks, as I do, that the Ranger Department is not paid enough for its services, and I told him that I would do what I could to raise the pay of the privates in the services.[38]

The adjutant general concurred, recommending that privates' pay be raised to $60 a month and sergeants' to $75.[39] The legislature didn't see it that way, and no raises were forthcoming. Everybody could have used a raise, because low pay perpetuated the personnel turnover that was a major weakness of the Ranger Force. For instance, in July, Captain Hughes informed the adjutant general that Private W. H. "Harry" Moore of Company A had resigned to become a mounted Customs inspector in the El Paso district. Hughes stated that "I regretted losing the services of Private Moore, as he has made a splendid officer. I have written to another man offering him the vacancy."[40] Hughes suffered a further disappointment when his sergeant, Herff A. Carnes, resigned effective August 8, also to become a mounted Customs inspector.[41] The Ranger Force just could not compete with the federal government, with a mounted Customs inspector making as much as a Ranger captain—$100 a month.

Occasionally a Ranger captain received a signal honor from the State of Texas. In 1911, a new county was created in South Texas: Brooks County, named for the retired Ranger captain John A. Brooks. The new county had been carved out of Starr County, and on September 2, elections were scheduled in Falfurrias and the other precincts in Brooks County. A concerned citizen, Mrs. E. R. Jenson, wrote to the governor requesting Rangers. Mrs. Jenson was a pioneer, having lived on a ranch in Starr County for the last thirty years, and she described the political lineup in the new Brooks County:

> First there are two factions Democrats and Republicans. The Democratic party being the white man's party is composed of white men, while the Republican party headed by Ed C. Lasater and a bunch of Mexicans for a selfish motive contrary to the interest, and peace, to the new formed Co of Brooks. Therefore in order to prevent trouble and for the benefit of a fair election and peace to the Democratic party of the new-formed Co, I honestly request of you that you order a few rangers to Falfurrias and Agua Nueva that their presence may avoid any trouble between the two partys [sic].[42]

Mrs. Jenson was the wife of E. R. Jenson, a Dane who had worked as a "private ranger" (for which read "hired gun") for Captain Richard King, who built the King Ranch into an empire. As one of King's cowboy/rangers, Jenson rode as a volunteer with Captain L. H. McNelly in the 1870's. Around the turn of the century, Jenson established his own ranch—Rancho de Casa Verde—in Starr County. Like many others in the region, he always went around armed. The leader of the wicked Republicans, Ed. C. Lasater, was also a rancher, but on a considerably larger scale. Lasater was one of the cattle kings of Texas, his property covering some 500,000 acres.[43] In her effort to ensure fair play for the Democratic party, Mrs. Jenson wrote not only to Governor Colquitt but also to Mrs. Colquitt: "I take the liberty of addressing the Governor in behalf of the people in the new Co, as you may be absent, and as you said he would help us if he could. . . ."[44] Governor Colquitt instructed Adjutant General Hutchings to get in touch with Mrs. Jenson and determine where she thought Rangers would be needed on election day. The adjutant general's office did so, assuring Mrs. Jenson that they "shall try to comply with your request." A Ranger sergeant and two privates from Company B were ordered to be in Falfurrias by September 1.[45] The election was held the next day. E. R. Jenson was elected a county commissioner, and ex-Ranger Captain Brooks was elected county judge, holding that office until his death in 1944, when he was succeeded by his son, John Morgan Brooks.[46]

As the summer of 1911 wore on, the depleted Ranger Force performed routine law enforcement duties. There were times, though, when Rangers scouted along the Rio Grande for magonistas who reportedly had crossed into Texas. Magonistas were active in El Paso, where they maintained a junta. According to Captain Hughes, they hadn't been able to accomplish much "as they lack the essentials—money and leaders." Two of their principal leaders in Chihuahua had recently been wounded and captured by the Mexican army and were on their way to prison in Mexico City.[47] The magonistas as a revolutionary faction were militarily ineffectual. They had already passed their peak—the seizure of northern Baja California in the spring of 1911; even though that peninsula was a backwater, the Mexican government had regained control of the territory by July, chasing the surviving magonistas into California. Yet their continued activities along the Rio Grande were symptomatic of the unsettled conditions in Mexico.

That being the case, Governor Colquitt came up with an idea that was simply brilliant. Since the now pitifully small Ranger Force was obviously incapable of defending the Texas border, why not persuade the federal government to subsidize the Rangers so they could do the job properly? To that end, Colquitt wrote to President Taft on September 14 requesting a meeting. They conferred on September 26 at Hutchinson, Kansas, during Taft's western trip.[48] Their discussion was a triumph for Colquitt, who jubilantly informed a friend on September 30 that "I have just returned to Austin after a week's absence from the state, conferring with the President with reference to defending the Texas border against Mexican incursions and robber bands."[49] What Colquitt had accomplished was nothing less than persuading Taft to have the federal government defray the cost of expanding the Rangers.[50] For the only time in the history of the United States, the federal government agreed to subsidize a state police force to defend the American border.

Having thus adroitly extricated himself from an extremely awkward political situation, Colquitt on October 1, 1911, ordered that the Ranger Force be immediately increased to three companies, each consisting of a captain, a sergeant, and twelve privates, for a total of forty-two Rangers.[51] During October, federal funds were used to add six privates to Company A, five to Company B, reactivate Company C (one captain, one sergeant, eight privates), and pick up the salary of another captain, who was a one-man Company D. In November, federal dollars brought Company C up to fifteen. The structure of the Ranger Force was now:

Ysleta
Company A: Captain John Hughes, 1 sergeant, 12 privates   14

Kenedy
Company B: Captain John J. Sanders, 1 sergeant, 10 privates   12

Austin
Company C: Captain J. Monroe Fox, 1 sergeant, 13 privates   15

Austin
Company D: Captain William Smith   1

              ——
              42

The two new captains, J. Monroe Fox and William Smith, were both outsiders. James Monroe Fox had been born in Houston in November, 1867. For years he'd been a deputy sheriff and jailer in Travis County (Austin). In 1910 he'd been elected constable, precinct 3, in Travis County. He'd resigned to become Captain of Company C, Ranger Force, on October 5, 1911. Fox's career could best be described as undistinguished. The other new captain, William Smith, was a truly exotic specimen. For openers, he'd been born in Adelaide, Australia. Smith, more commonly known as "Australian Billy," was a gifted athlete. He played left tackle on the first football team in El Paso and was a formidable boxer. The Australian had had a varied career. He'd been a deputy U.S. marshal in New Mexico, had served in the 1st Volunteer Cavalry—Teddy Roosevelt's Rough Riders—during the Spanish American War, and had ended up in El Paso, where in 1899 he became a policeman. By 1902, he was working as a railroad detective for the El Paso and Rock Island Railroad. There followed an eight-year stint as chief city detective in El Paso, then a period of employment with the El Paso Health Department. In May, 1911, he was a private detective in El Paso, working for none other than Francisco I. Madero. He rejoined the local police force as a detective, the position he held when on September 1, 1911, he received a commission as captain of Company C. This was a one-man company, and Smith was used as an undercover detective, investigating violations of the liquor laws in Galveston. On October 5, he was transferred to become captain of a one-man Company D and continued doing the same kind of work.[52]

As part of the reorganization, the State standardized the rifles used by the Rangers, thus simplifying the ammunition resupply. Each of the men enlisted after October 1, 1911, would be issued an 1895 model Winchester, chambered for .30-caliber U.S. Government model 1906 ammunition. The captains would be responsible for requisitioning these weapons, as well as for exchanging for the new rifles all those currently being used by men enlisted before October 1, 1911. Rangers still had to pay for their own rifles, pistols, saddles, and horses.[53]

There was no question as to who ran this expanded Ranger Force. In reporting a request for Rangers by the sheriff of Waller County, Adjutant General Hutchings wrote to Governor Colquitt that "I explained that you personally so far as able directed the Rangers."[54] But now Colquitt directed the Rangers to focus on protecting the border. This was odd in view of his activist policy during the Madero rebellion. At that time he had issued his neutrality proclamation with great fanfare and had ordered the Rangers to arrest Mexican revolutionists. He had even asked for permission to send the Rangers into Mexico after fugitive rebels. As of October, the neutrality proclamation was still in effect, and there was still considerable Mexican exile activity, especially in San Antonio. Plotting against Madero had intensified during the summer.[55] It took a quantum leap in October with the arrival in San Antonio of General Bernardo Reyes, a distinguished member of the old Díaz establishment who had once been viewed as Díaz's probable successor. He had been in Europe during Díaz's overthrow but had returned to Mexico to announce his candidacy for the presidency, in opposition to Madero. Reyes subsequently withdrew from the campaign, alleging that Madero had the forthcoming election rigged. In October, 1911, Madero was indeed elected as the constitutional president of Mexico—in the cleanest election yet held in that country. Reyes, taking a page from Madero's book, made his way to San Antonio to organize a revolution against the new president. It was an open secret that Reyes was planning a rebellion, yet Colquitt did absolutely nothing to enforce his own neutrality proclamation. Why?

The answer lay in Texas politics.[56] With Prohibition being the burning issue of the day, Colquitt relied heavily on the Hispanic vote in San Antonio and along the border to defeat his Prohibitionist opposition. And as it happened, two of the men most responsible for delivering that crucial vote for him were among General Reyes's leading co-conspirators. The governor doggedly looked the other way while they conspired.

The more important of the pair was Francisco A. Chapa, a druggist and man-ufacturing chemist in San Antonio. Born into a prominent Matamoros family, he had become a naturalized citizen of the United States, had earned a degree in phar-macology from Tulane University, and had worked for a time in Monterrey. In 1894 he had become a druggist in San Antonio, building a thriving retail business. His store, on the corner of Houston and Laredo Streets, became a landmark, largely because of a golden lion on a field of green painted on the side of the build-ing.[57] Chapa subsequently established his own laboratory at 816–818 West Commerce Street. The druggist was what in those days was called a "live wire." Besides his pharmaceutical interests, he played an active role in civic affairs. In 1906 he was elected to the San Antonio board of education, later becoming its treasurer. He served on several carnival committees, and in March, 1911, was elected to the board of directors of the International Club, one of San Antonio's most prestigious organizations. Nor was this all; he and Miguel Quiroga published *El Imparcial de Texas*, the state's most influential Spanish-language newspaper.[58] Chapa was also the state's most influential Hispanic politician.[59] As he informed Colquitt in a congratulatory telegram, "The Mexican vote all over Texas voted with the antis to a man not only for principle but because their friend governor Colquitt was supporting the cause."[60] A grateful Colquitt rewarded Chapa by commissioning him as a lieutenant colonel in the Texas National Guard on the governor's personal staff.[61] This was a conspicuous honor, for the twelve lieutenant colonels on the staff were Colquitt's closest political advisors; Chapa was the lone Hispanic among them. The druggist and the governor maintained cordial rela-tions. Chapa advised Colquitt regarding the neutrality proclamation, handled the arrangements for a tour of Mexico that Colquitt was planning, and published flat-tering articles about the governor in *El Imparcial*.[62]

The other Hispanic politician intimately involved in the Reyes conspiracy was Amador Sánchez, the political boss of Webb County. Descended from one of the founding families of Laredo, Sánchez effectively used his family's local prominence to build a political career as a Democrat. He was elected mayor of Laredo in 1900, resigning in March, 1910, to become the sheriff of Webb County. Like Chapa, Sánchez was active in state politics and was an outspoken Colquitt supporter, con-ducting campaign rallies in Spanish on Colquitt's behalf.[63]

In October, 1911, Chapa traveled to New Orleans to meet his old friend General Reyes and escort him to San Antonio. Reyes set up his headquarters in the mansion of Chapa's friend and business partner, Miguel Quiroga. The exiled Mexican general's plans were grandiose—an invasion of Mexico, the main thrust being through Laredo, with simultaneous attacks from El Paso and Brownsville. The conservative Reyes worked out an alliance with the radical magonistas, a clas-sic marriage of convenience between factions which had in common only their hatred of Madero.

Quiroga's mansion was the center of constant activity, as Reyes's supporters streamed in and out to assist the general in his plotting. Among the most frequent callers was Francisco A. Chapa.[64] Any perceptive newspaper reader in San Antonio was aware that Reyes was organizing a revolution. Reyes himself maintained a high profile, being entertained at a civic club luncheon, visiting the points of interest, and attending the fair. The U.S. Army accorded him the honor of reviewing the cavalry at Fort Sam Houston. The highlight of Reyes's public activities was a meeting Chapa arranged with Governor Colquitt in the capitol.

The meeting took place on October 16, when Colquitt received Chapa, Reyes, Miguel Quiroga, and David Reyes Retana. The newspaper accounts of the interview described it as being brief and formal, with other state officials besides the governor being present. A federal Bureau of Investigation informant, however, gave a more tantalizing account of the meeting. He was William Chamberlain, a close friend of Reyes who was privy to the general's plans. According to Chamberlain, Reyes said that Chapa had arranged the meeting hoping to persuade Colquitt not to use the Texas Rangers along the border against Reyes and his associates.[65]

Coincidently or not, the Rangers were deployed in a peculiar manner. As Adjutant General Hutchings stated in mid-October, "the policy of this Department at the present time is to locate them along the Rio Grande border."[66] They were stationed as follows:

Company A: Ysleta, Fort Hancock, and Valentine

Company B: Kenedy and Del Rio

Company C: Sam Fordyce and Harlingen

What is remarkable is that no Ranger detachment was stationed in Laredo, the Paris of Webb County. If Colquitt were serious about enforcing neutrality, it was at Laredo that Rangers were needed, for it was the center of *reyista* activity on the border. And the reyista activity was of a particularly blatant nature: Sheriff Amador Sánchez was running this branch of the conspiracy, and plotters gathered in the Webb County jail, where Sánchez was storing the arms and ammunition they were stockpiling.

Colquitt announced on November 2 that his neutrality proclamation was still in effect and that the Rangers would enforce the neutrality laws to the letter. And he ordered a small detachment of Rangers to Laredo. And that was all. These Rangers were either unaware of or oblivious to Sheriff Sánchez's activities. Not until the federal authorities forced Colquitt's hand did he reluctantly order the Rangers into action.

On November 13, a federal grand jury convened in Laredo to investigate reyista intrigues; on November 16, the jury began returning bills of indictment against Reyes, Chapa, Sheriff Sánchez, and the sheriff's brother, among others. That same day Colquitt conferred at some length with Captain Hughes about the Reyes conspiracy. The press reported that:

> While the details of the conference were not, of course, made public, Governor Colquitt said if these conditions exist he will at once inquire into the situation and the part that is being played in Texas. His proclamation of neutrality, issued when the late revolution was at its height, enjoining Texans from interfering in Mexican troubles and demanding the neutrality laws be enforced by State police along the border, will be considered with attorneys with the view of deciding whether it is sufficient to keep citizens from mixing in the affairs of any juntas that may be working here. . . .[67]

Yes indeed it was, as the Texas attorney general's office informed the adjutant general on November 19.[68] Hopefully Colquitt managed to keep a straight face as he went through the charade of suddenly discovering that Reyes had been plotting and of having to seek legal advice as to whether his own neutrality proclamation applied to Texans.

Now that the Reyes conspiracy was unraveling, Colquitt desperately tried to get the credit for smashing it. First of all he wrote to President Taft on November 17, assuring the chief executive that the augmented force of Rangers was deployed along the Rio Grande, which they were keeping "very well policed." He also mentioned that the adjutant general was maintaining meticulous records of the expense incurred in patrolling the Rio Grande, so there would be no problems with the bill he would present to the government for reimbursement. Colquitt also informed Taft that he was "in receipt of numerous letters advising me of the disquietude in Mexico, and of suspicious movements going on tending to show a prospective revolution in the near future. Conferences, I am advised, are being held, provisions and arms purchased and transported to Mexico for future use." The governor inquired whether Taft had any helpful suggestions to make.[69] That same day Colquitt conferred in Austin with his captains and decided to order virtually the entire Ranger Force to the border. The next day, November 18, he sent Adjutant General Henry Hutchings to Laredo to direct operations. Colquitt immediately telegraphed Taft informing the president of this action and stating that serious trouble was expected at Nuevo Laredo. He reminded Taft that in May, twenty-one Texans had been killed and wounded when the rebels stormed Ciudad Juárez. Should a similar attack develop against Nuevo Laredo, the governor asked for Taft's cooperation to prevent shooting across the river into Laredo, Texas. Taft replied that he had forwarded Colquitt's telegram to the secretary of war with instructions to cooperate fully with the Texas governor. That personage received assurances of cooperation from the commanding general of the Department of

Texas should the governor request it. However, troops would not be rushed to the border unless and until there was a real emergency.[70] Colquitt complained to Hutchings that "The secretary of war does not seem to understand the requests made of me to assist in enforcing the neutrality laws in view of his instructions to General Duncan [the Department of Texas commander]."[71] In his newly found zeal to enforce the neutrality laws, Colquitt even wired Taft, on November 21, asking permission for the Rangers to enforce the immigration laws in order to expedite the deportation of Mexican plotters. Colquitt ordered them cleared out of Laredo within forty-eight hours. Permission for the Rangers to enforce the immigration laws was not forthcoming from Washington. Colquitt finally got the picture. On November 22, he wired Taft stating "I concede that the enforcement of the neutrality laws is [a] Federal question and will act accordingly unless otherwise requested by you."[72]

As mentioned, Colquitt on November 18 had dispatched Adjutant General Henry Hutchings to Laredo to direct the operations of the Rangers there. Yet, curiously enough, on November 13, the very day the federal grand jury convened in Laredo, Captain Sanders had ordered the Ranger detachment in that city to leave for Eagle Pass. The District Attorney, John A. Valls, who was a Republican, and a Hispanic, and a sworn enemy of Sheriff Sánchez, protested vigorously, and the order was countermanded.[73] Still, the incident is suggestive.

Hutchings sent the governor a detailed report of his actions at Laredo. When the adjutant general arrived on November 19, he was met at the train by Major Charles B. Hagadorn, commander at Fort McIntosh. Declining the major's offer of hospitality so as not to be under any obligation to him, Hutchings took a room at the Ross Hotel, which had been the reyistas' headquarters. He proceeded to confer with District Attorney Valls, Captain Sanders, who had just arrived, and the captain commanding the local militia company; he then met again with Major Hagadorn. From these talks Hutchings concluded that "the U.S. marshal was apathetic, the deputies sympathetic until Washington woke them up, and the county and city officials in the main are favorable to Reyes."[74] The "apathetic" deputy U.S. marshal in Laredo was A. J. Barthelow, who had been a state policeman in the early 1870's, a Brownsville policeman, a Texas Ranger under Captain McNelly, a Customs inspector, and Laredo city marshal.[75]

Hutchings and the Rangers assisted the federal authorities in searching suspect houses. Their first raid yielded only knapsacks, leggings, and provisions; the weapons had been removed the previous night. The next search was more rewarding, for the officers seized forty rifles, one thousand cartridges, and sixty dynamite bombs. The occupant of the house, Captain Juan Mérigo, a graduate of the Mexican national military academy and a cavalry officer, was arrested on the spot by Captain Sanders. When taken before the U.S. commissioner, Mérigo made a full confession—he was a representative of General Reyes and the seized munitions were for Reyes's impending revolution. In what appears to be a bit of grandstanding on Hutchings's part, he and a Ranger escorted Mérigo to the guardhouse at Fort McIntosh. Although the Rangers were represented by Captain Sanders, his sergeant, and eight privates from Company B, they continued to play only a supporting role, participating in joint searches with Customs inspectors and the army. The Rangers seized fifty-six horses belonging to Sheriff Sánchez's brother and earmarked for Reyes's invasion. In addition, fifty rifles and five thousand cartridges were confiscated, as well as a quantity of printed Reyes proclamations.[76] And on November 28, the army seized from the luggage of Dr. Samuel Espinoza de los Monteros, Reyes's chief of staff, a list of reyistas. Significantly, General Pascual Orozco was one of the names on the list.[77]

Hutchings telegraphed a supplementary report on November 20. He announced that the "Reyistas here stunned but plotting." The situation in Laredo was under control. As for Sánchez, "Sheriff permitted meetings and storage of arms in jail. Many suggest his suspension from office."[78]

The Reyes conspiracy had been smashed at Laredo, but there was also concern by the officials in Brownsville. On November 20, the sheriff ordered the local militia company to guard the armory.[79] That same day Colquitt ordered Hutchings to send Captain Fox and his Company C to Brownsville, and he told Hutchings to impress on them that their duty was to enforce the laws and "not to become partisans of Mexican factions either on this or the other side of the river."[80] Fox arrived on November 22 with twelve men, almost his entire company, checked his men into the Hoyt Hotel, and reported to the deputy U.S. marshal.[81] Fox's Company C, incidentally, included a Hispanic, Miguel Oyervides, born in 1874 in Lockhart. He had been a clerk before enlisting on October 16, 1911. Oyervides served until January 20, 1912. As it turned out, Fox's Rangers were not needed, and they left on the 26th; the militia company had been relieved of duty on the 23rd. At the governor's request a troop of regular cavalry was sent to Brownsville since things were under control there. Colquitt instructed Hutchings to go to El Paso and report on conditions in that city.[82]

Captain Hughes had been busy. On November 23 he had gone to El Paso with his sergeant and six privates to work on revolutionary cases, remaining there until December 2. Hughes worked closely with federal officers and agents of the Mexican government in identifying the members of the reyista junta in El Paso. On November 26 it was learned that Dr. Rafael Molina, the reyista paymaster, had gone to San Antonio for funds and would return on November 30. The junta, meanwhile, was purchasing dynamite and had rented a room in which to make bombs. The Rangers managed to rent an adjoining room from which they maintained surveillance, hoping the bomb makers next door knew their business and wouldn't accidently blow everybody up.[83] Hughes's investigation culminated on November 30; he and his men, together with Deputy U.S. Marshal John

H. Rogers, who until recently had been a Ranger captain, Special Agent L. E. Ross of the federal Bureau of Investigation, and a special agent of the Mexican government swooped down on the reyista junta, arresting fourteen men for violation of the U.S. neutrality laws. As Hughes later reported: "These men had been under surveillance for some time, and the move against them so timed that none whom we wanted were [sic] allowed to escape."[84] Hughes returned frequently to El Paso to work on revolutionary cases. Company A Rangers J. L. Anders, W. M. Barbee, and Aubrey Shipley would soon arrest three more men for neutrality violations, two of the prisoners being from Valentine, caught with weapons and incriminating documents.[85]

Enforcement of the neutrality laws was anything but a cut-and-dried affair. The statutes provided an effective way to settle old scores. In places like Brownsville, unscrupulous officials were reported to have deliberately manufactured evidence against their enemies in order to secure their indictment.[86] Another aspect of neutrality law enforcement was that on occasion someone arrested as a member of a revolutionary group turned out to be an undercover agent of the Mexican government. But in a larger sense, the Mexican Revolution itself provided a vast umbrella for the settling of political and personal accounts, in Texas as well as in Mexico. As one astute observer commented about Laredo:

> There is another side to all the interest the local Mexicans take in affairs in our sister Republic, and if this is looked into, it will generally be found that the local political factions are always on different sides of matters political in Mexico, and this has a great deal to do with present conditions in Webb County. It is not so much the desire to enforce the laws, as it is trying to get even with some fellow on this side, who is antagonistic or unfriendly.[87]

The Reyes conspiracy had been crushed but, except for Captain Hughes's work in El Paso, the Rangers had played only a supporting role in crushing it. Colquitt's last-minute burst of activity generated a lot of favorable publicity in Texas and boosted his image as a no-nonsense governor, but federal authorities were less impressed by Colquitt's posturing. Not only was his request to have the Rangers enforce the immigration laws denied, but the State Department viewed him with amused condescension:

> The governor of Texas, upon receiving the President's assurance of cooperation, seems to have proceeded to do most of the cooperating himself. He appears to be a little mixed as to the respective functions of the Federal and State authorities, as he refers in his telegram to the State Adjutant General to *my* proclamation, and directs the seizure of arms and ammunition, and the arrest of persons violating the neutrality laws of the United States.[88]

The aftermath of the Reyes affair was truly bizarre. General Reyes was arrested in San Antonio on November 18 and released on a $5,000 bond posted by Chapa. The latter could certainly afford to act as Reyes's bondsman. According to one report, Reyes had given Chapa $165,000 to purchase arms, ammunition, and equipment. When the Reyes conspiracy was crushed, most of this money was unspent, and Chapa allegedly just kept it, later claiming that he'd sent it by messenger to Reyes in Mexico. According to the Bureau of Investigation's informant, "from that day on Chapa has been in the most excellent financial condition."[89] Reyes jumped bond and fled to Mexico on December 13, leaving his fellow conspirators to fend for themselves.[90] In practice this meant getting themselves good lawyers, for their trial began in Brownsville federal court on January 1, 1912. The governor ordered that a detachment of Rangers accompany Chapa to Brownsville "to assist him while his trial was going on."[91] The individual appointed as court interpreter was Tom Ross, the former Ranger captain. The lead attorney for all but Chapa of the twenty-three defendants present was Marshall Hicks, a prominent San Antonio lawyer and former mayor of that city who was the Democratic national committeeman from Texas. Hicks had also been Reyes's attorney in San Antonio. Chapa's lawyer was even more distinguished—Jacob F. "Jake" Wolters of Houston, a fellow lieutenant colonel on Governor Colquitt's staff and the man who had managed Colquitt's successful campaign to defeat Prohibition. Not only did Chapa stoutly maintain his innocence, but Colquitt was also his defender, writing to a friend that "I think myself that Chapa is the victim of a conspiracy. . . ."[92]

The trial was an important test of the federal government's ability to enforce the neutrality laws. The defendants were charged with multiple counts of conspiracy to set on foot a military expedition against a friendly nation.[93] The government presented an overwhelming case: enough seized arms, ammunition, and equipment to fill a boxcar; sixty-nine witnesses, some of them conspirators turning state's evidence; letters and telegrams exchanged between reyistas; proof that Reyes's revolutionary manifestos had been secretly printed on the presses of *El Imparcial*. An embarrassing feature of the testimony was Colquitt's private secretary admitting that in fact the governor had met privately with Reyes and his friends. Perhaps to preclude further awkward revelations, a quick plea bargain ensued. Amador Sánchez and twelve others pleaded guilty; charges were dropped against nine lesser defendants. That left only Chapa. Although he steadfastly maintained his innocence, he was found guilty by the jury. Chapa's punishment was a $1,500 fine, which he paid on the spot.

What is fascinating about the trial is the conduct of Federal Judge Waller T. Burns of Houston. The man was a defendant's dream. He was the picture of solicitude for the defendants, from looking after their welfare in jail, to sending a defendant out to look for another defendant who had fled, to construing the statutes to mean that violating the neutrality laws was only a misdemeanor and not a felony, to lending a defendant the money to pay his fine and inviting him to Houston as his guest, to apologizing for having to sentence the defendants, to sentencing Sánchez and some other defendants who could not pay their fines to serve their time in the Webb County jail, where Sheriff Sánchez put his convicted brother on the payroll as a jailer to supervise the others; those who lived in Laredo were allowed to go home at night. As a bemused journalist covering the trial wrote, it was "the most unusual occurrence ever chronicled in a court of justice in this section of the country. . . ."[94]

With Judge Burns's invaluable assistance, the plotters had received a mere slap on the wrist. But that accommodating jurist had overstepped himself—it turned out that the offenses against the neutrality laws were in fact felonies. Chapa and Sánchez were convicted federal felons. Chapa had the grace to resign immediately from Colquitt's staff. Sánchez, however, adamantly refused to step down as sheriff of Webb County. But as convicted felons, Chapa and Sánchez were now political liabilities for the governor. Not to worry. The Democratic establishment in Texas, including the governor, both senators, Congressman John Nance Garner, the prosecuting attorney, and of course Judge Burns, launched an intense lobbying campaign to secure executive clemency for the pair. Sánchez's application for a pardon was disingenuous: He had been unaware that he was breaking the law by helping his lifelong friend General Reyes, because "this custom of purchasing arms, horses, and munitions of war along the Rio Grande for revolutionaries in Mexico has prevailed ever since I was a boy, and no one has ever been prosecuted for it until the beginning of what was known as the Reyes Revolution." Through the use of some outrageous political shenanigans, the Texas Democratic establishment succeeded not just in persuading Republican President Taft to grant pardons for Chapa and Sánchez, but they even got the mandatory two-year probationary period waived.[95] Chapa immediately resumed his position on Colquitt's staff, and he would be appointed to the staffs of Governors Ferguson and Hobby, remaining the most influential Hispanic in Texas until his death on February 18, 1924.[96] Sánchez remained as sheriff until 1914. Both continued their revolutionary plotting. It was good to have friends in high places.

CHAPTER FOUR

ENFORCING NEUTRALITY

T HE Texas Rangers' role in dismantling the Reyes conspiracy had several
consequences. For one thing, Governor Colquitt felt their services had not
been adequately appreciated. He was miffed, for example, that in the
outrageous Brownsville trial Judge Burns in his charge to the jury had
praised various federal officials but said not one word about the Rangers. In the
governor's view the Rangers had been slighted and their services ignored. He
therefore wrote a letter to Hutchings expressing his appreciation for what the
Rangers had done.[1] This was a far cry from the view he had of the Rangers when
he took office. Hutchings shared the governor's appreciative sentiments with the
Ranger captains but perhaps got a little carried away. As he informed Captain
Hughes, "I have informed his Excellency that to merit his commendation is our
highest aim."[2]

More importantly, ranking federal officials were also unimpressed by the
Rangers' performance. When President Taft asked Secretary of War Henry L.
Stimson for his recommendation on continuing the federal subsidy for the
Rangers, Stimson condescendingly replied:

The arrest of General Reyes and the energetic measures employed by the
Federal, and possibly State, authorities along the border seem to have
allayed the revolutionary sentiment along the Rio Grande, and stopped
efforts to aid and abet revolutionary movements from the American side of
the river.

Conditions along the border appear to be in a normal state, and from
a federal point of view, no reason seems to exist for continuing the increased
force of Rangers along the border.[3]

Colquitt and Hutchings were keenly aware that federal aid for the Rangers was about to end. Though they hardly shared Secretary Stimson's view that "conditions along the border appear to be in a normal state," there was nothing they could do to convince Washington that the Mexican Revolution was just taking another breather. They began to prepare for the imminent reduction in the Ranger Force.

Hutchings reported, on January 10, 1912, that the appropriation for the Ranger Force for the fiscal year ending August 31, 1912, was $20,000. As of December 31, 1911, the balance on hand was $11,470.83; December and January expenses would probably be about $4,000 a month. As of February 1, 1912, the federal government's share of the increased expense would total about $8,000, or about $2,000 for each of the four months since the subsidy began in October, 1911.[4] Hard times were ahead.

At the beginning of 1912, the Rangers were stationed from one end of the border to the other:

Company A: maintained detachments at Ysleta, Valentine, Terlingua, and Austin

Company B: at Comstock, Del Rio, Eagle Pass, and Laredo

Company C: at Rio Grande City, Sam Fordyce, Harlingen, and Brownsville

Company D: (Captain William Smith)—wherever needed

As usual, Governor Colquitt personally directed how the Rangers were employed. On January 8, he ordered that the detachment in Brownsville be reinforced from three men to five, and that to compensate, Captain Fox could abandon one of the towns he was covering. Abandonment was certainly on the mind of Captain Sanders, who wrote a day later that an epidemic of smallpox was raging in Ciudad Porfirio Díaz (Piedras Negras) and its sister city, Eagle Pass. Sanders wanted to move his men out of Eagle Pass immediately. He must have been nonplused when Hutchings informed him that the conditions he reported at Eagle Pass would indicate an even greater need for the presence of a Ranger detachment. The governor ordered the Rangers to stay.[5]

Two days later, though, Colquitt ordered a major redeployment. He notified Hutchings that:

> In view of recent correspondence with the President I think it advisable to begin to muster out a part of the force and prepare for an early reduction of same to the basis at which the membership stood prior to the mustering in of new men.
>
> I beg to suggest also that you abandon the Del Rio and Laredo stations, and that you concentrate at the Ysleta and Brownsville stations the main part

of the ranger force. I think it advisable to keep two or three of your best men here in Austin for emergency use.[6]

On January 22, Taft notified Colquitt that the federal subsidy was ending and asked for a statement of the government's bill so he could send it to Congress. Federal aid formally ended as of January 31, 1912.[7] In February,

Hughes's Company A totaled	7
Sanders's Company B totaled	7
Fox's Company C totaled	7
	21

Captain William Smith, who composed Company D, was kept on as the "Ranger Detective."[8] Despite the reduction in force, the Rangers were somewhat better off than they had been prior to October, 1911, when they had reached a low of thirteen men.

Colquitt was still mad at the government. Reacting to a report by Captain Hughes of renewed revolutionary unrest in the vicinity of El Paso, the governor on February 2 spelled out for Hutchings his new policy:

> At the request of the President the Ranger Force has been reduced to its present basis for the purpose of giving attention to police duties under the Statutes of the State. In view of the charge of the Federal Judge at Brownsville, and the treatment of the Federal officers, and the ignoring of the services of the State, and especially of the Rangers, and the further contention of the Federal authorities that the enforcement of the neutrality laws is for the Federal Government, I wish you would instruct the captains of the Ranger companies that hereafter they will take no part in these matters for the reason that my neutrality proclamation has been cancelled and withdrawn, and the matter of enforcing the Neutrality Laws will be left exclusively to the Federal authorities.[9]

Not only was Colquitt withdrawing the Rangers' cooperation with federal officials, but he soon got his chance to stick it to the arrogant feds.

His opportunity came because of a new crisis at Ciudad Juárez, where there occurred an uprising on behalf of Emilio Vázquez Gómez, who was organizing a revolution to overthrow President Madero. The crisis at Ciudad Juárez began on January 31, when the garrison mutinied, ostensibly because their number was to be reduced by one third. They proclaimed their allegiance to Vázquez Gómez, arrested their commander and the chief of police, released the prisoners from the jail, proceeded to loot stores and saloons, and began firing their weapons indiscriminately. The mutineers effectively isolated the city—they destroyed the telegraph office, blew up bridges on the two rail lines into the city, and barred traffic with El Paso. Captain Hughes reported that General Pascual Orozco was coming to Ciudad Juárez to restore order, but that Orozco's loyalty to Madero was questionable.[10]

With chaos reigning in Juárez, Colquitt promptly telegraphed President Taft urging action. Taft replied that he had "issued orders with a view to meeting the difficulties at Juarez and have invited the attention of the Secretary of War to the necessity for action." Colquitt asked to be kept informed.[11] Colquitt's overriding concern was that there be no repetition of firing into El Paso, as had occurred during Madero's capture of Juárez in May. He ordered Captain Hughes so to notify the commander of the Juárez garrison; Hughes dispatched Ranger Charles R. Moore to deliver the message. Hughes reported that he had prepared an identical communication for the commander of Madero's federal forces, "but was not delivered on account of there being no Federals in the vicinity of Juarez."[12] In any case the situation soon became much calmer, mainly because General Orozco arrived on February 3 and addressed the mutineers. His prestige was so great that the mutineers in effect surrendered. Orozco arrested their leaders.

On February 7, Secretary of State Philander C. Knox informed Colquitt that the Mexican government had requested permission for 500 or 600 of its troops to travel on the Southern Pacific Railroad from Eagle Pass to El Paso. The United States government planned to agree, stipulating that the Mexican soldiers be unarmed, their weapons shipped as baggage, and that they be escorted by a small detachment of American troops. Before notifying the Mexican government formally, Knox requested from Colquitt the "customary formality" that "this course of action will be entirely agreeable to the State of Texas."[13] Evidently Colquitt gave his approval. But on February 9, Hutchings brought to Colquitt's attention newspaper accounts of the Mexican government's request to move troops across Texas, a request the State Department had approved. Both the Treasury and War Departments had been advised that a regiment of Mexican soldiers would travel on February 10 from Eagle Pass to El Paso in order to reach Ciudad Juárez, the center of unrest. Hutchings pointed out that he had no right to assume that Colquitt had not been consulted in the matter, but it appeared to him that the law prohibited such a movement without the governor's permission. He attached a copy of the relevant statute.[14] This reinforced Colquitt's abrupt change of heart. The governor informed Hutchings that he had also received a protest against the move from the *El Paso Times* "and have transmitted the protest to the Secretary of State, Washington, D.C., withdrawing my assent to their passage through Texas until further notice."[15] He could almost hear the squeals of dismay from the effete Washington types. It was a sound to be savored.

Implementing Colquitt's policy of noncooperation, Hutchings immediately telegraphed Captains Hughes and Sanders that "no armed military force shall be permitted to enter this State without the permission of the Governor, unless such force is a part of the U.S. Army. The Governor has withdrawn his permission and if Mexican soldiers with arms cross into Texas you will advise the Department for immediate action." The key words in all this were "with arms." Hutchings added that it was possible the Mexicans might travel unarmed with their weapons securely boxed; in such a case the federal government might have the authority to transport the foreign troops. In that event, he ordered the Ranger captains to ensure that the Mexicans remained unarmed while in Texas territory. Sanders and his men were to escort the Mexicans to El Paso, at which point Hughes and Sanders would ensure that the Mexicans remained unarmed and their weapons secured until they crossed into Mexico.[16] Either Hutchings and Colquitt were not communicating or Hutchings was engaged in some posturing of his own. As for the State Department, it informed Colquitt that it had agreed to the transportation of the Mexican troops on the understanding that they were to be used only for restoring order in Juárez, not for general hostilities. Unless the Mexican government so stipulated, State would withdraw its permission. The Mexican government decided to cancel its request.[17]

Having gotten Washington's attention, Colquitt dispatched Hutchings to El Paso to report on conditions there. Hutchings stopped off in Del Rio and again impressed on Captain Sanders the governor's prohibition against armed Mexicans traveling through Texas. They were to be arrested. When Hutchings arrived in El Paso he intended to ask Mayor Kelly to request that the army move artillery in to protect the city, for he understood there were only four troops of cavalry at Fort Bliss. Hutchings suggested that the governor make his own request for artillery, since such a reinforcement would have a reassuring effect on the citizenry. And he stressed that Colquitt's hard-line border policy was making the governor more popular than ever. The adjutant general suggested that Colquitt order the Dallas national guard artillery battery to El Paso on "maneuvers," which would "keep the federal government guessing from the President down, & the people of the state would understand their purpose if needed."[18]

The federal government was probably not just guessing but was positively apprehensive about what Colquitt might decide to do. In a letter to Taft, the governor stated:

In the light of events, I think it unfortunate, both for Mexico as well as for us, that our treaty stipulations do not provide for the occupation of Juarez by American troops for the purpose of restoring law and order. I believe that if the Mexican Government would consent to the friendly occupation of Juarez with a regiment of Federal troops, for the purpose of preserving order, it would go a very long way towards settling all of the troubles, so far as our side of the question is concerned. I suggested this course to you in a former letter last summer, while the Madero Revolution was in progress, but at the time you did not think it advisable to take up the suggestion with the Mexican Government. I am renewing my suggestion at this time, and believe that course would be a wise policy.[19]

At Fort Bliss, in the absence of the commander, Colonel E. Z. Steever, Hutchings reiterated to the adjutant, Captain W. F. Clark, Colquitt's determination to prevent any more shooting into El Paso. Clark said the Mexicans had already been so informed, and commented that it was a good bluff on Colquitt's part. Hutchings indignantly replied that the governor was not bluffing. Clark inquired as to just how Colquitt proposed to prevent incoming fire, whereupon Hutchings asserted that the governor would take "drastic action." Clark in turn asserted that Texas couldn't take such action, and that the governor would be arrested if he tried.[20] An indignant Colquitt fired off a letter to Hutchings in which he quoted the latter's report about the threat of arrest and informed Hutchings that he was sending a copy to Taft asking if in fact he, Colquitt, would be arrested if he tried to protect the lives and property of Texans. In the letter Colquitt quoted from the Texas constitution, which made the governor the commander in chief of the state's military forces, except when they were called to duty by the federal government. Colquitt ended by stating that in the event of trouble he would first call on Taft to prevent or suppress anarchy, but if the President did not act "I shall not hesitate to do so," and he told Hutchings to tell Captain Clark "that I shall not fear arrest from him either." The governor wrote a covering letter to Taft, a rather conciliatory missive stating that "I desire to co-operate in every way possible with the Federal Government in preserving and enforcing neutrality laws, and I have instructed the members of the Ranger Force, and all of those under my direction, to take no part or parcel in the politics of Mexico." He asked Taft to get the attorney general's opinion as to whether he would be subject to arrest. Fortunately for all concerned, the matter was settled amicably. In effect, the army apologized for Captain Clark's remarks, and Clark said he'd been misunderstood.[21]

Whatever apprehension Taft may have had about the prickly Texas governor had probably increased because on February 15 Hutchings ordered the mobilization of the El Paso national guard company. This was a precaution to restore order in El Paso. An inexperienced army lieutenant and some of his men were riding the street car, not knowing that the line looped through Juárez before returning to El Paso. When they were spotted in Juárez, a riot ensued, fanned by the parents of León Martínez, the teenager who had been sentenced to death for murdering Emma Brown in Saragosa in July, 1911. The disturbance had spread to Hispanics in El Paso, where, Hutchings reported, some 12,000 of them lived. He evidently viewed them as a potential Fifth Column. Hutchings subsequently reported considerable unrest in "the Mexican quarter," that is, south El Paso, along the river.[22] A detail of Rangers was stationed along the river as a precaution.

The situation in Juárez remained fluid—the city now had three competing mayors. At Hutchings's suggestion, Colquitt dispatched two more Rangers to El Paso. In the event of trouble, Hutchings intended to station Captain Hughes and his men at the international bridges. And if Americans attending the Juárez race-track should be attacked, Hutchings was going to send the local national guard company and the Rangers into Juárez to rescue them: "We will go and let the diplomats fix it."[23] It was precisely this kind of thinking that worried the commander at Fort Bliss and President Taft in Washington.

Colquitt told Hutchings to order Captain Sanders to leave one man in Del Rio and bring the rest of his Rangers to El Paso, explaining that this would be cheaper than sending militia. And in El Paso, rumors flew that *vazquistas* could attack Juárez at any time. In fact, correspondents for the Hearst newspapers and for *Colliers Weekly* had arrived to cover the expected battle. The sheriff, Peyton Edwards, asked Hutchings for the loan of 500 rifles and ammunition for use in case of emergency. Hutchings informed him that the state had no spare rifles to lend.[24] Edwards continued making his own preparations. The sheriff began enrolling citizens in a posse, an action that produced unexpected criticism: The Mexican consul in El Paso objected strenuously to the inclusion of Mexicans, Germans, and other foreigners, and blacks, on the grounds that the inhabitants of Juárez viewed this as a menace. Colquitt admonished the sheriff to proceed with caution and hoped he would "eliminate any undesirables as members of your posse."[25]

In his communications with the commander of the Department of Texas, General J. W. Duncan, Colquitt expressed his desire to cooperate "fully and consistently" with the military authorities. What was fueling the new cordiality was the vindication of Colquitt's hard-line policy on defense of the border. The jubilant governor telegraphed President Taft on February 25:

> My heartiest congratulations on action taken by you to protect the lives and property of citizens of Texas. Your demand for a neutral zone and notice that American troops will cross the border if firing by Mexican combatants into Texas is permitted meets my most cordial approval and is what I hoped would be done. I am sure Texas will applaud your action.[26]

In the event, there was no battle for Juárez. After desultory skirmishing, the city surrendered to the vazquista rebels on February 27.

But there was a troubling undertone; according to Captain Hughes, there was bitter feeling between Anglos and Hispanics in El Paso, and the militia guarding the El Paso power plant had been fired on at night—from the Texas side of the

Rio Grande.[27] Moreover, at the town of Canutillo, north of El Paso, there was considerable "anti-American talk and threats of trouble from the Mexicans in case of American intervention." The sheriff had recently made six trips to Canutillo, each time taking Rangers with him. Two Rangers had been stationed there, but they were withdrawn because the surrender of Juárez removed the threat of intervention, and Canutillo had quieted down.[28] The Mexican Revolution was continuing to generate ethnic animosity.

In Ciudad Juárez the rebel vazquista chieftains who had triumphantly occupied the city were soon overshadowed. On March 3, 1912, General Pascual Orozco, the man who had been Madero's principal field commander in the struggle against Díaz, formally announced his adherence to the rebel cause. This was a turning point, not just because of Orozco's military abilities and his wide popularity in the state of Chihuahua, but also because he quickly displaced Emilio Vázquez Gómez as leader of the rebel movement. What had been a vazquista rebellion was now an *orozquista* revolution.[29] Because of the color of their standard, Orozco's rebels were referred to as "red flaggers." Orozco and his supporters were well financed and they naively assumed they could import all the arms, ammunition, and supplies they needed through El Paso. This despite the United States' recent crushing of General Reyes's movement and American diplomatic recognition of Madero as the constitutional president of Mexico. The orozquistas were thus disconcerted when on March 14 President Taft imposed an embargo on munitions shipments to Mexico, an embargo later modified to permit shipments to the Madero regime. Although Orozco didn't yet realize it, he was already losing the most critical battle of his entire campaign—the battle of El Paso. The orozquistas were reduced to smuggling munitions across to Ciudad Juárez, but their efforts were insufficient to keep Orozco's army supplied.

Thus, with Colquitt's enthusiastic support, the Rangers found themselves back in the business of helping to enforce the neutrality laws and the arms embargo. Captain Hughes was his usual active self. For example, he arrested three men working for the Mexican consul in El Paso who were in Ysleta recruiting men to fight for the Madero government against Orozco. The Bureau of Investigation agent whom Hughes consulted decided that a case could not be made against the trio; two were released but one remained in custody for carrying a pistol. But Hughes could not win for losing, as the saying goes. The Mexican consul general in San Antonio complained that the Rangers were said to favor Orozco's rebels. Colquitt reiterated his order that the Rangers be politically impartial. An aggrieved Captain Hughes indignantly rejected the consul general's accusation of pro-Orozco partiality, declaring that for the past month his men had been working "in perfect harmony" with the Madero secret service in El Paso, whose chief would be willing to make a written statement to that effect. A Ranger had just assisted in arresting two Americans for violating the neutrality laws and in seizing 14,000 cartridges destined for Orozco's forces. During March, Hughes's men had helped make fifteen arrests for neutrality violations and had seized 18,761 rounds of rifle ammunition.[30]

Captain Sanders at Del Rio was also incensed by the Mexican consul general's accusation. Sanders minced no words, saying that the "Rangers of Company 'B' are not and never will be in sympathy with a band of outlaws." Sanders emphasized that his men had already been properly instructed to steer clear of Mexican affairs. And he stated that the "Rangers are aware of the fact, that the Federal Government People are very jealous of the work we have been doing on the Border."[31]

There was certainly no lack of work. At Brownsville, Captain Fox was busily preparing for whatever might result from a rumored rebel attack on Matamoros expected within days. But when army headquarters at San Antonio sent an officer to report on the situation, he discounted Fox's anxiety. The officer conferred with a number of officials in Brownsville, then crossed the river to Matamoros, where he interviewed the military commander, an immigration official, and the United States consul. He concluded, perceptively enough, that there was "certainly nothing alarming in the situation here aside from local political feuds in Brownsville which appear to be much more likely to result in serious consequences to the town than an attack on Matamoros could possibly be."[32] In a follow-up report he stated: "Feeling is very high here. Race prejudice is so strong that everything is colored with it." Further, "political and personal feuds are responsible for conditions in Brownsville. As a result many men here are daily taking their lives in their hands when they go about their ordinary business."[33] Brownsville was one tough town, and the presence of Rangers was having little effect.

Adding to the prevailing tension were incidents such as the arrest by Mexicans on March 3 of one José García, a Brownsville resident. It was said that García was a United States citizen.[34] Captain Fox reported that "Mexican officers came over the bridge last night and arrested two Mexicans, Jose Garcia, Arturo Margain. Wire me what steps to take." That was enough to send Colquitt into high gear—a United States citizen had been illegally arrested by Mexicans on Texas soil. The governor immediately wired President Taft and ordered Captain Fox to "prevent such arrests when practicable," whatever that meant.[35] It turned out, however, that the Mexican authorities were completely within their rights. García had been involved with ex-reyistas in a plot to seize Matamoros, which had accounted for some of the rumors buzzing around Brownsville. The Matamoros detachment of Rurales, eighty strong, had cleverly pretended to join the conspiracy, had lured García and his companion out of Brownsville, and had arrested them on the Mexican side of the international bridge.[36] Oh, well.

Unrest extended along the border all the way to El Paso. For example, around Sanderson, on the edge of the Big Bend, a state of lawlessness existed, with rustling, smuggling, and robbery being daily occurrences, the authorities receiving a steady stream of complaints. Armed bands prowled the rugged and sparsely populated region, and it was difficult to know whether they were connected with the Mexican Revolution or were just garden-variety outlaws. Isolated ranches were particularly vulnerable to marauders, and in these conditions it was hardly surprising that virtually every man went around armed. Given the shortage of Rangers, the sheriff had asked the governor for permission to organize a home guard, presumably consisting of Anglos. In Presidio County, in the Big Bend, ranches located near the Rio Grande were repeatedly raided by rustlers, mainly revolutionists from Mexico. These enterprising thieves were stealing cattle in Texas, butchering them across the Rio Grande, and selling the beef to the unsuspecting army detachment stationed at Presidio. The ranchers and the sheriff pleaded with Colquitt to send Rangers. Although he had more calls than he could possibly handle, the hard-pressed Captain Hughes sent his sergeant and a private to Presidio County. That left Hughes shorthanded, because for the past month he had let Sheriff Edwards use three of his Rangers to help him keep order in El Paso.[37]

And in El Paso, order was touch and go. Illustrating the explosiveness of the situation, Hughes reported on March 6:

> Feeling between the Americans and the Mexicans is still bitter here, and a race riot was narrowly averted last night. A Juarez Mexican, said to be a judge on the other side, kissed a white woman, whom he did not know, on the street last night. The timely arrival of the patrol wagon saved him from a mob which quickly gathered around him.[38]

Animosity also surfaced in nearby Canutillo, but the arrival of a cavalry detachment quieted things down.[39]

As usual, much of Captain Hughes's work involved enforcing the neutrality laws. Soldiers as well as civilians sometimes found the money to be made by smuggling ammunition to Ciudad Juárez too tempting to resist. This was the case with a member of the El Paso militia company, who was sentenced to a year's imprisonment. And members of the regular army were not immune. Hughes informed Hutchings that two regulars had just been arrested for smuggling. Hutchings was avid to learn the details, "as it may be of use should slighting remarks be made with reference to the National Guard." Hughes himself participated in raids with federal Bureau of Investigation agents resulting in the arrest of brothers Sabino and Abelino Guaderrama for conspiracy to smuggle 52,000 rounds of ammunition. During April alone Hughes and his men were involved in seizing 390 rifles and 83,760 rifle cartridges. Despite the focus on interdicting smuggling, Hughes had to spend some of his time testifying in federal court against the reyistas he had arrested on December 2, 1911. The presiding judge, incidentally, was our old friend Waller T. Burns, but this time in his new incarnation as a hard-nosed enforcer of the neutrality laws—twenty-three convictions in his court in three days, and not a single acquittal.[40]

In addition to neutrality work, Hughes had to contend with the constant requests for Rangers. He had to dispatch two men to Dickens County in the Panhandle to work on rustling cases and a man to Galveston to testify in liquor cases then join two other Rangers in Sweetwater to help the sheriff keep the peace during the trial of criminal cases. Then two privates were ordered to Big Spring and Coahoma, where feuding had again broken out, with one man killed.[41] Stress seems to have been a pretty constant feature of a Ranger's job.

Downriver at Del Rio, Captain Sanders's Company B was getting its share of excitement. On April 11, word reached Del Rio that a large body of revolutionists had crossed the Rio Grande and were only eight or nine miles from town. Two of Sanders's men, together with a Customs inspector and a couple of other federal officials, were immediately dispatched by special train to investigate the rumor. They learned that earlier that day a dozen men had been sighted running toward the Rio Grande. Upon investigation, the lawmen discovered 213 cartridges, fifteen sticks of dynamite, eight homemade dynamite bombs and slings for hurling them, and some nitroglycerine hidden under a bridge nine miles west of Del Rio. Captain Sanders firmly believed that the munitions were for either blowing up the bridge or, more likely, for a raid on the banks and stores in Del Rio. He was convinced that the miscreants were now under cover in Del Rio and that they were in cahoots with a band of outlaws operating across the Rio Grande.[42]

Farther south, in Brownsville, that running sore on the body politic, factional rivalries had again heated up at election time. The Independents, or Reds, composed of 80 percent dissident Democrats and the rest Republicans, were the political machine who controlled the city. They had repeatedly requested, even demanded, that the Rangers be withdrawn. The Blues, who were straight Democrats, were the Jim Wells machine that controlled Cameron County. They stoutly advocated the need for Rangers to maintain order in Brownsville. With passions rising as the election approached, Colquitt sent Hutchings himself as an observer. Hutchings had an interesting visit. On his first night in Brownsville he was rudely awakened by two gunshots at 4:30 a.m. He leaped from his bed only to learn that they were the hotel signal for a fire alarm. Later that morning the adjutant general duly made the rounds, conferring with political boss Judge James B. Wells, the candidates for local office, the sheriff, and so on. Hutchings tried to impress on everyone that as long as the law was observed the Rangers would merely observe, but in case of disturbance they would act as readily against one faction as the other. Hutchings proceeded to station two Rangers 100 feet from each polling place. Hutchings's account of the voting is revealing:

The two sides had Mexicans corralled in different blocks, with a fence rider, herding them and they were marched up to the polls and remained in line all day. A gentlemen's agreement was made that a Red should vote and then a Blue, and then an American [an Anglo]. This kept up all day, except that the Americans played out frequently, but the supply of Mexicans was inexhaustible.

This was because neither faction scrupled at bringing over voters from Matamoros whenever needed.

Hutchings was there as an impartial observer, but he was quite willing to give a little nudge in favor of the Blues. Voting proceeded uneventfully except at the ballot box for the 4th Ward. The Blues expected to carry it by a majority of 100 to 150. But the Independent city council appointed an election judge who deliberately slowed the process down so much that only a small percentage actually got to vote. "It started out very slowly and Judge Wells and Seabury asked me to stay at that Ward and try to expedite the voting." Hutchings did his best "to secure a large vote, of course without regard as to how they should vote. . . ." After the polls closed, Hutchings reported that "I am sorry that a full vote was not cast in the 4th Ward, Judge Wells seemed to want it so badly, but I certainly did all that I could." The Independents carried the day in a close election. Particularly significant was the reelection of Joe Crixell as city marshal.[43] His tenure as chief of the Brownsville police would be controversial and relatively brief. But for now the city was quiet; Captain Fox's men remained, while the reinforcements brought in from Captain Sanders's company returned to their stations.

Speaking of elections, there was a memorable one in San Diego, county seat of Duval County, in May, 1912. Here, too, politics were taken very seriously. In what the locals would describe as "some right smart gunplay," three men were killed in an election fight. The sheriff at Alice immediately wired for Rangers, and Governor Colquitt ordered that Captain Fox and four Rangers proceed to Alice and report to the sheriff. By the time Fox arrived, the local authorities had the situation under control, and the Rangers returned to Brownsville. Even so, bitter factional feeling remained, for the sheriff and county officers were allegedly partisans of one faction. This made District Judge W. B. Hopkins of Corpus Christi extremely apprehensive, for he was scheduled to hold court in San Diego in June. He planned to make the session as brief as possible, and he urged the adjutant general to have Captain Fox and three or four of his men present. Without the presence of Rangers, violence was a distinct possibility, and Hopkins wanted to get back to Corpus Christi in one piece. The judge got his Rangers—Captain Fox and four of his men.[44] The disputed 1912 election was not just an example of hardball South Texas politics. It was memorable because it marked the rise to power of Archie Parr, who would rule Duval County ruthlessly for decades to come as "the Duke of Duval." He would bequeath his political power to his son, George, and the Parr dynasty would last until 1975.

While the three Ranger companies concentrated on enforcing the neutrality laws and keeping order at elections and court sessions, Captain Smith, the one-man Company D, had been quietly going about his business of assisting local officers in his capacity as detective. As we have seen, he was used to investigate liquor law violations in Galveston. In addition, he participated in raids on brothels in Taylor looking for gamblers and investigated a murder at Georgetown. Hutchings even wanted to enlist him into the Texas National Guard so that in uniform he could be approached by those in San Antonio selling liquor illegally to enlisted men.[45] In many respects, Captain Smith had the best job in the Rangers.

In the spring of 1912, once again it was the El Paso area that caused concern, to the point that in May, Hutchings was dispatched there to make a first-hand report, and Captain Sanders and five of his Company B Rangers arrived to assist Captain Hughes. Although Orozco still controlled most of Chihuahua, contingents of Madero's federal forces totaling some 500 men were converging on Ciudad Juárez. Sheriff Edwards believed that an attack was imminent, with inevitable firing into El Paso. Ominously, there were rumors that if Orozco were defeated by federal troops south of the city of Chihuahua, his partisans intended to provoke United States intervention, presumably by firing into El Paso. Colquitt, of course, intended to urge Taft to warn the combatants not to shoot into Texas. Captain Hughes, however, spoke with a representative of the Madero federal forces who assured him that their intention was to besiege Juárez but not to attack the city. Rather, they hoped to challenge the orozquista garrison to come out and fight like men. The latter declined, and the immediate crisis passed. Nevertheless, Sanders and his men were kept at El Paso, and by June, Sanders was dividing his time between El Paso and Del Rio.[46]

On May 21, a couple of Hughes's men demonstrated remarkable courage. Privates Charles R. Moore and Charles H. Webster were scouting with Troop A, 4th Cavalry, on "Pirate Island" near Fabens. The "Island" was a large tract of land on the south side of the Rio Grande but on the American side of the international boundary, the result of an 1854 shift in the river's channel. When the river flooded, water ran through the dry channel as well as the present channel, thus creating the "Island." The area was traditionally the haunt of outlaws, and it was on the Island that in 1893 Captain Frank Jones of the Rangers had been killed in a shootout with Mexicans. The American patrol spotted an orozquista contingent of some 300 marching parallel to them. The cavalrymen halted some 500 yards from the boundary, while the two Rangers advanced to a spot about 100 yards from the boundary, at which time a shot was fired. The Rangers drew their carbines, galloped into some brush, and dismounted. The cavalrymen fell back another 100 yards. The orozquistas had taken up positions on the roofs of two adobe houses and had formed a line on either side of the buildings. Suddenly about thirty-five mounted rebels with rifles in hand formed a skirmish line and charged.

As the Mexicans bore down on them with blood-curdling yells, the two Rangers started toward them on foot. Moore held up his left hand as a signal for them to halt. He informed the flabbergasted rebels in Spanish that they were about to cross into Texas. Moore then told the rebel commander to send one man forward to parley. The upshot was that the Rangers told them to do their fighting on the Mexican side of the boundary because they would arrest any man who came to the Texas side. The rebels retreated, regrouped, and continued their march parallel to the boundary. Moore reported that the "attitude of the rebels was sullen and menacing," which was, to say the least, an understatement. The Rangers continued to scout with the cavalry. The lieutenant in charge of the patrol was fulsome in his praise of Moore and Webster, saying "I have never known two more fearless men," and he wrote a letter of commendation for Captain Hughes to forward to the governor.[47]

These two Rangers had rather unusual backgrounds. Charles R. Moore was born in 1875 in Indianola, and like many other Rangers, had a brother who also served in the organization—F. R. Moore would be a Special Ranger in 1918–1919. But unlike other Rangers, Charles R. Moore had worked for years as a railroad conductor in Mexico. He moved to El Paso in 1900 and became a deputy sheriff. In 1909 he enlisted in Captain Hughes's Company D. What was striking about Moore was that he was one of the best-read men in Texas. He spent much of his off-duty time reading widely, especially in history.[48] His partner, Ranger Charles H. Webster, was also atypical. He had lived in El Paso for years working first as a stagehand and then as the operator of a vaudeville road show. He later became a peace officer, and on January 13, 1911, a Texas Ranger. There was no question but that, like Moore, Webster was brave. And he performed his duties of enforcing the neutrality laws quite effectively, working closely with the Bureau of Investigation and Madero's intelligence service.[49] Yet there was another side to Webster.

For one thing, Webster was not averse to doing favors for El Paso politicians. To neutralize one of their opponents, Victor Valverde, the political boss of Canutillo, Webster arranged to have Valverde arrested by the army on election day to prevent him from voting his followers. The El Paso federal Bureau of Investigation agent, L. E. Ross, indignantly declared that "This whole transaction was nothing but a frameup by local ring politicians to abuse the confidence of government officers for the purpose of illegally furthering their political ends and it is not the intention to permit this kind of dirty work under any circumstances."[50] Ross's indignation was more apparent than real, however, for he and Webster were business partners.

With all the money to be made from illicit activities such as smuggling, it is hardly surprising that some officers—as they do today—found temptation irresistible. Not all the munitions being seized ended up where they should have. The forty-three-year-old Webster approached a prominent arms dealer, Julius Krakauer, with whom he was friendly, with a proposition in the spring of 1912. Krakauer and his two brothers were the largest munitions dealers not only in El Paso but in the entire Southwest. They owned the firm of Krakauer, Zork, and Moye. Krakauer testified that on April 17, 1912, Webster implored him to buy some ammunition from him, no questions asked. The Ranger assured Krakauer that its origin was legitimate and explained that he needed the money for his daughter, who was in the theater. Although skeptical, Krakauer bought from Webster 2,780 30–30 and 920 7mm cartridges, for $102.35. Webster did not deliver the merchandise personally, for he was out of town when the transaction was concluded. Instead, he sent his associate, L. E. Ross. Krakauer tried to pay by check but Ross demanded cash. So Krakauer obliged him but insisted on getting a receipt, which Ross reluctantly signed. The receipt, dated April 18, listed the ammunition sold and the amount paid.

Webster subsequently offered to sell Krakauer "more of the stuff" that he and Ross had, provided Krakauer didn't ask too many questions. Krakauer declined. Webster then offered to sell at a sacrifice price 30,000 cartridges that belonged to him and Ross. When Krakauer again declined, Webster announced that he'd sell to "the other fellows," presumably referring to the other large El Paso arms dealer, the Shelton Payne Company. This was Krakauer's last encounter with Webster, but he was able to produce the receipt for $102.35 with Ross's signature on one side and Webster's on the other where the order for the cartridges was written.[51] Evidently no action was taken against Webster, and he remained a Ranger until July, 1913, when he resigned.

His associate L. E. Ross was less fortunate. Besides his business ventures with Webster, Agent Ross sold to Shelton Payne ten rifles that he claimed he had found abandoned for $100. His endeavors in private enterprise eventually came to the attention of his superiors, and on October 7, 1912, he was summarily fired from the federal Bureau of Investigation.[52] The very next day he went to work as a secret agent for the Mexican consul. Ross subsequently became an operative for the Western Detective Agency in El Paso. Evidently this line of work didn't pay enough, for on January 14, 1913, Ross and one V. L. Schneider, wearing masks, held up a poker game in a local hotel room, relieving the eleven players of $1,300 in cash and $3,000 in diamonds. The holdup artists were arrested, however, as they left the hotel.[53] Their trial ended in a hung jury.

In the summer of 1912, it seemed that whereas Brownsville would be a constant problem for the Rangers because of local politics, El Paso would be a constant problem because of threats from Juárez. As Madero's field commander, General Victoriano Huerta, inflicted a series of crippling defeats on Orozco, the latter kept falling back toward the city of Chihuahua. The closer he got to Ciudad

Juárez the greater the degree of apprehension there, and consequently in El Paso. On June 17, Sheriff Edwards notified Hutchings that the rebels had reinforced the Juárez garrison with troops and artillery, and that the Madero government was thought to have secretly organized a force in El Paso to storm across the international bridges when the *maderista* forces launched their assault on Juárez. Moreover, the Rangers at Ysleta reported that wounded rebels were being conveyed across the river for treatment there. Once again the sheriff asked Hutchings for instructions on what to do if there was firing into El Paso. Governor Colquitt put Hutchings on standby to go to El Paso. This time the governor ordered the entire Texas National Guard, including the Dallas battery, alerted for instant movement to El Paso, by special trains if necessary. If Mexicans fired on El Paso and the garrison at Fort Bliss did not stop it, the Texas National Guard, the Rangers, and the citizens would. Moreover, Hutchings was ordered to prevent any maderista contingent lurking in El Paso from attacking Juárez. Uncharacteristically, Colquitt also cautioned Hutchings: ". . . don't allow us [to] be drawn in trouble unnecessarily by those interested in bringing about trouble at El Paso." The governor sent the usual telegram to President Taft, who replied with the usual reassurances. Hutchings arrived in El Paso on June 20, having been cautioned by Colquitt to do nothing that would incur expense without first getting the governor's approval. Once again the apparent crisis proved to be a false alarm, and by June 23, Hutchings was preparing to return to Austin.[54]

In all these alarms it was Captain Hughes and Company A who continued to bear the brunt of the workload. By this time Hughes had developed a network of informants. Among them was Sam Dreben, perhaps the most famous soldier of fortune on the border. He had been serving as an expert machine gunner with the orozquistas but had left their employ when they began to lose. He would later sell his services to the Madero government. The Ranger captain also maintained useful relations with George Clements, the Associated Press correspondent covering the orozquistas, and with E. S. O'Reilly, Associated Press correspondent with the Madero federal army. Hughes also received information from Canuto Leyva, the maderista recruiting officer in El Paso; from H. C. Kramp, manager of the Thiel Detective Agency, which was working for Madero; from Mormon bishop O. P. Brown (the Mormon colonies in Chihuahua had been ruthlessly plundered by Orozco's generals); and from E. L. Charpentier, a French mercenary recently returned from a mission to destroy orozquista communications.[55] In a noteworthy development, Private C. H. Webster of Company A on June 9 arrested Gonzalo Enrile, financial agent for the orozquistas, on a charge of embezzlement. Enrile was turned over to United States authorities, who held him for extradition by the Mexican government.[56]

Captain Hughes continued to make good use of his informants. H. C. Kramp, of the Thiel Detective Agency, told the Ranger captain that federal troops advancing from Agua Prieta, Sonora, via Casas Grandes, Chihuahua, planned to attack Ciudad Juárez on July 5 in conjunction with maderistas already secreted in and around the city. This would be in addition to the main federal advance up the rail line toward the city of Chihuahua. Kramp had gotten his information from Powell Roberts, of the Madero intelligence service. Roberts told Hughes directly that about 600 rebels had just left Juárez to meet this threat. Hughes did not simply rely on informants; he arranged for a spy to go to Juárez and report to him on the number and disposition of the rebels' artillery. As Hughes put it, "I am keeping in close touch with the situation, and I think I have good sources of information."[57]

Hughes had been skeptical that Madero's forces could launch an attack on Juárez as early as July 5, and he was proved right. The orozquistas defeated the federals' advance guard near Casas Grandes, and it would be some time before the federals could regroup and resume their advance. There would be no uprising by Madero supporters on July 5. But there was increased anti-American feeling among the rebels in Juárez. And it was rumored that if they were forced to evacuate the city and retreat to Casas Grandes, they would mutiny and fire into El Paso. The rumor was taken seriously; among other precautions, extra guards were placed on the El Paso electric plant. Captain Hughes quietly escorted the commander of the Texas National Guard's Dallas artillery battery who came to El Paso to locate gun positions in case the four-gun battery was needed. With Orozco's military fortunes still declining—he suffered a major defeat at Bachimba, south of the city of Chihuahua, on July 3–4—El Paso was filling up with refugees and orozquista deserters.[58] This of course heightened concern among the city authorities.

As matters moved to a climax in Juárez—Orozco himself arrived on July 11— the rumors and predictions of firing into El Paso proved groundless, to the general relief. Hughes reported that the evacuation of some of the orozquistas to Casas Grandes was under way in a reasonably orderly fashion. Hughes and two privates, however, were ordered to Brownsville in mid-July to work on several cases there.[59] That left Captain Sanders as the ranking Ranger in El Paso. But reinforcements arrived in the person of Captain William Smith, who immediately used his experience as an ex-chief of detectives in El Paso to begin gathering information on the situation in Juárez.[60]

Most of what the Rangers did in El Paso was to help enforce the neutrality laws. During July, for example, they made a number of arrests for neutrality violations, including, on July 20, the head of the orozquista intelligence service in El Paso, Victor Ochoa. They also arrested the brothers Abelino and Sabino Guaderrama once again for smuggling ammunition. During the month the Rangers participated in seizing 20,000 rounds of ammunition and fifty canteens.[61] As might be expected, the ammunition smuggling business was not characterized by high ethical standards. In June, Captain Sanders, Private A. R. Baker, and federal Bureau of Investigation agents had raided a house on El Paso Street and:

Recovered three large coffee boxes laden with cartridge boxes; upon examination discovered that the cartridge boxes were carefully packed with ordinary red brick. Said boxes were prepared to be shipped to Mexico as ammunition.[62]

Although at the time El Paso was the center of ammunition smuggling, contraband activity was taking place elsewhere on the Rio Grande. On July 26, Ranger Richard C. "Red" Hawkins of Company B was scouting near Del Rio with a deputy U.S. marshal and two mounted Customs inspectors when they encountered eight or ten Mexican smugglers. The two sides were equally surprised, and a confused firefight erupted in which twenty to thirty shots were exchanged. No one was hit, and the smugglers made good their escape in heavy underbrush. But the officers seized 4,000 rounds of ammunition, fifteen rifles, and fifteen canteens. This single seizure was almost equal to what Company A confiscated in El Paso during the entire month of August—5,000 rounds.[63]

What the latter number reflected was that the Orozco rebellion was collapsing, so there was little incentive to smuggle ammunition into Juárez. By the third week in July, Juárez was the only important city still under rebel control.[64] Crumbling orozquista resistance to a federal column confidently advancing up the rail line from the city of Chihuahua meant even more refugees pouring into El Paso. Most, of course, were Mexicans, but several thousand were American Mormons from the colonies in Chihuahua devastated by the rebels.

The impending fall of Juárez worsened the problem facing the Rangers— orozquistas were dispersing into small bands in order to wage guerrilla warfare, or simply to rape and pillage. The prospect of these irregulars raiding into Texas caused great concern. Minor skirmishes occurred, and, as usual, Sheriff Edwards sent out a call for more Rangers. Captain Sanders and three privates arrived from Del Rio but had to return there a few days later because of an orozquista threat in that area. Captain Smith also left El Paso, being ordered to Brownwood to investigate an outbreak of arson. That left Captain Hughes, recently returned from Brownsville. The Ranger captain and his men joined Sheriff Edwards and his posse to deal with rebels who'd reportedly crossed near Sierra Blanca. The lawmen sped to Sierra Blanca by special train, mounted up, and scouted along the river. The only rebels they spotted were on the Mexican side of the Rio Grande. Back in Austin, Governor Colquitt was again threatening to mobilize the national guard. He informed the War Department that he had four troops of cavalry that could be rushed to the El Paso area by special train.[65]

Fortunately, Madero's army finally marched into Ciudad Juárez on August 16. For the first time since the beginning of the year, the citizens of El Paso could contemplate life without Juárez constituting a threat. The Orozco rebellion was substantially over, although rebel bands remained at large in northern Chihuahua.

For the next month Orozco led guerrilla raids against federal garrisons. In September he managed to capture the isolated town of Ojinaga, in the Big Bend across from Presidio, Texas. By way of illustrating the isolation of this area, Presidio was seventy miles from the nearest railroad, at Marfa, and communications between the two towns were by an automobile stage line. Orozco captured Ojinaga with ridiculous ease because the maderista garrison offered only token resistance before stampeding across the Rio Grande to Texas, where they were interned. Two weeks later Madero's army recaptured Ojinaga, and it was the turn of the orozquistas to flee in disarray into Texas. Colquitt had instructed the Rangers to arrest Orozco if he entered Texas, to hold him for extradition to Mexico, but with the assistance of sympathizers in the Big Bend the rebel leader managed to elude the authorities. By December, he was back in Chihuahua trying to rejuvenate his failed revolutionary movement.[66]

With no rebel threat to El Paso and a resumption of cooperation with Washington in enforcing the neutrality laws, Colquitt was in a benign mood. When the Madero government again requested permission to transport troops across Texas soil, Colquitt readily agreed. The governor of course stipulated that the troops travel unarmed and be escorted by the U.S. Army. Just to be sure, he ordered that Rangers also perform escort duty. The Mexican government contemplated two troop movements, one involving 1,200 men through El Paso to Douglas, Arizona. This operation proceeded smoothly, with a couple of Rangers riding each troop train from El Paso to the New Mexico line. Second, the Mexican government wanted to send a brigade of troops through Eagle Pass by rail to Del Rio and Marathon, where they would detrain and march the seventy miles through the Big Bend to Boquillas on the Rio Grande. Colquitt agreed but subsequently, at Hutchings's suggestion, withdrew his consent because he did not want Mexican troops marching through Texas, even if they were escorted by American soldiers and by Rangers. The acting secretary of state remonstrated, but to no avail. Washington had no choice but to revoke its permission as well.[67]

Colquitt was not the State Department's favorite governor. Especially since on October 22, Colquitt asked President Taft to inquire of the Mexican government "as to whether they would object to the crossing of Texas Rangers and Texas militia into Mexico, if necessary, to apprehend and arrest bandits and revolutionary bands who periodically cross the Rio Grande River for the purpose of theft and pillage of Texas citizens." The State Department blandly informed Colquitt that they had asked the Mexicans about this, "but with unsatisfactory results."[68] Colquitt just didn't get the picture.

There simply weren't enough Rangers to answer all the requests for assistance they were getting in Texas, let alone carry out Colquitt's idea of hot pursuit into Mexico. Recognizing this, Colquitt authorized an increase in the Ranger Force. Captain Hughes was ordered to enlist five more men. Hughes took his time, for he was "trying to select men who will make good Rangers."[69] The Rangers desperately needed a few more good men. The organization was still trying to adjust to the loss of the federal subsidy. Congress had passed the General Deficiency Appropriation Act on August 26, 1912, under which the federal government provided $9,639.41 to reimburse Texas for the increased Ranger force between October 1, 1911, and January 31, 1912.[70] The money was most welcome, for as of September 13, 1912, the Ranger Force had once again dwindled to:

Company A: Captain Hughes, 1 sergeant, 4 privates	6
Company B: Captain Sanders, 1 sergeant, 4 privates	6
Company C: Captain Fox	1
	13

In terms of manpower the Rangers were back to where they had been in February, 1911. As some kind of commentary on Captain Fox's leadership, the adjutant general observed that Company C "has practically mustered itself out by resignation. . . ."[71]

But there was some reason for optimism. The appropriation for the fiscal year beginning on September 1, 1912, was $20,000. And according to the adjutant general, it cost approximately $1,000 a year to maintain a Ranger, captains included.[72] Therefore, it should be possible to build the Ranger Force back up to at least twenty men.

In October, Adjutant General Hutchings was literally swamped by appeals for Rangers. From San Angelo came a request for Rangers to investigate rustling; Captain Fox, who was the sole Ranger left in Brownsville, got the assignment of being the Ranger detective, and off to San Angelo he went.[73] Sheriff Ryan in Brownsville appealed for Rangers to be stationed there at election time on November 5. A rumor of renewed orozquista activity aimed at Ciudad Juárez meant that Rangers were needed in El Paso.[74] From Cold Springs, in East Texas, came an appeal for three or four Rangers to prevent mob violence at the forthcoming trial of some blacks accused of murder.[75] From Duval County in South Texas, both Archie Parr and the county judge requested four Rangers to keep order preceding and during the November election.[76] All this was in addition to the Rangers' performing their regular duties of scouting, testifying in court, etc.

A harassed Hutchings sent the governor a situation report on October 29. He had ordered Captain Sanders and his four men to Brownsville; Sanders was even more shorthanded than usual, for Private A. R. Baker had resigned on the 23rd. The adjutant general noted that Sanders and company were in Brownsville and Edinburgh on court cases involving Brownsville matters. Hutchings hoped that after the election he could send Sanders back to his base in Del Rio. Captain

Hughes and Company A were scattered all the way from El Paso to Del Rio. Captain Fox had just returned to Austin from his San Angelo assignment, but Hutchings planned to send him to Seminole in the Panhandle, where the local authorities had called for Ranger help to investigate some bank robberies.[77] Even with a Ranger Force that by this time had been increased to fifteen men, it was manifestly impossible to meet all the requests pouring in. Colquitt gave top priority to having peaceful elections. He wrote to Hutchings that:

> I think it would be a misfortune to have an election riot, and if two rangers can prevent it I wish you would send them to Duval County. The other requests for Rangers you will have to write and tell them that you will send them as soon as you can spare them.[78]

Furthermore, in response to an appeal for Rangers from the chairman of the Democratic committee of Brooks County, Colquitt decided to send two of Captain Hughes's men to Falfurrias. And he instructed Hutchings to "grant all other requests for rangers to prevent election riots. I presume we will have to abandon the border question until the election is over." Hughes and all of his available men were ordered to San Antonio as a reserve in case of election trouble. In any event, Captain Fox was at Falfurrias for the election, which was peaceful.[79]

Whatever relief Colquitt and Hutchings may have felt at getting through the November 5 election without major incident proved short-lived. A major flap erupted on the night of November 9 in that traditional trouble spot, Brownsville. The root of the problem was what it had always been: vicious political quarrels between the Independents (Reds), who controlled the city, and the Democratic machine (Blues), who controlled Cameron County. This animosity extended to the law enforcement agencies—the police forming part of the Independent political machine and the sheriff's department forming part of the Blue machine. As we have seen, on occasion this had led to shootings between deputies and police. The Rangers had always been perceived as supporting the Blues, evidenced by the fact that Jim Wells, the Cameron County political boss and leader of the Blues, frequently served as the Rangers' attorney. Furthermore, the sheriff, Carl T. Ryan, was himself an ex-Ranger, having served under Captain McDonald. What added to the prevailing tension was the ethnic factor—the sheriff's men were predominantly Anglo, as were the Rangers, whereas the police were overwhelmingly Hispanic.

The tension level rose appreciably on August 9, 1912. That night about 9:45, City Marshal José Crixell finished his rounds, dismounted, and hitched his horse in front of his brother Teófilo's saloon. A short distance away sitting in a chair in the gutter in front of the Club Saloon was Paul McAlister, an ex-Ranger who was now a Cameron County deputy sheriff. McAlister called out to Crixell, who began walking over toward him. When he was five or six feet away, McAlister whipped out a .45 Colt automatic and emptied it into Crixell, who died in the gutter a few minutes later. Ranger Captain Monroe Fox happened to be sitting in a chair across the street talking with friends. He rushed across the street and disarmed and arrested McAlister, who offered no resistance. Fox hustled McAlister off to the county jail. At the risk of doing Captain Fox an injustice, the account of the shooting as reported in the local newspaper is just too pat. It may indeed have been sheer coincidence that Fox was on the scene when McAlister, who had served under Fox, killed Crixell. But at the examining trial it turned out that another Ranger, Private James B. Mercer—one of Fox's men—also happened to be present, and he accompanied Fox and McAlister to the county jail. What lends credence to this skeptical interpretation of Fox's actions is that his testimony was seemingly aimed at discrediting that of the only eyewitness, a traveling salesman from Chicago who had just stepped out of the Club Saloon.

Not surprisingly, Crixell's death produced a major uproar in Brownsville. The city council appointed another ex-Ranger, Ralph J. Tucker, to succeed Crixell. McAlister was denied bail, and Captain Fox took him to jail in Corpus Christi. Despite the efforts of his attorneys to secure bail for him, McAlister remained in jail until his trial on a change of venue at Halletsville. A number of people from Brownsville attended the trial. To prevent confrontations between McAlister's friends and his enemies, they stayed at different hotels, drank in different saloons, and sat on separate sides of the courtroom. On the stand McAlister proved to be an appealing witness. He pleaded self-defense—it sure looked to him like Crixell was reaching for a pistol. Strengthening McAlister's defense was a witness who suddenly remembered having heard Crixell make threats against McAlister's life. Moreover, the prosecution's case was fatally weakened by its inability to produce the single eyewitness to the shooting—the traveling salesman from Chicago. McAlister was acquitted on November 11, 1913.[80]

In October, 1912, Captain Fox, who may have been a bit nervous at being the only Ranger still stationed in Brownsville, wrote to Hutchings suggesting that he either be reassigned or that a company of Rangers be sent to Brownsville, for things were heating up as the election approached.[81] Hutchings was well aware that because Sheriff Ryan had been a Ranger, the Independents would automatically consider any Rangers sent to Brownsville as being Blue partisans, whether they were or not. But he and the governor decided that the way to handle the situation was to reassign Fox, since one man couldn't do much to influence events, and to send Captain Sanders and his four men to monitor the election.[82] The election on November 5 went off without major mayhem, and a sigh of relief was breathed in Austin.

But on November 10, Captain Sanders wired that:

Was called to arrest an outlaw at 2 o'clock this morning. Made the arrest and on my return to jail with prisoner, self, men, and Sheriff's Department were fired upon by several Mexicans, Policemen who were laying in ambush. Jenkins shot in arm. One Mexican Policeman badly shot and others wounded. No doubt that it was a frame up just like happened in San Benito in June [sic] 1910.[83]

That same day, Sanders provided further details in a letter to Hutchings. It seems that the previous night at about 1:30 a.m., Deputy Sheriff P. D. Haley came to the Rangers' quarters and asked their help in arresting one Ignacio Treviño, a local fugitive wanted for rape and first-degree murder. Captain Sanders readily obliged; together with Rangers Joe Jenkins and Richard C. "Red" Hawkins he accompanied the deputy to Treviño's hideout. Arriving at about 2 a.m., the officers pounded on the door and announced that Treviño had better surrender. The fugitive did not respond, whereupon Sanders kicked in the door, charged into the bedroom where Treviño was hiding, and with the help of Ranger Hawkins, dragged him from the bed and into the street, where they handcuffed him. The party started for the county jail in a hack, but when they'd gone some 200 yards they were suddenly fired upon by four mounted policemen. The first shot hit Ranger Jenkins, inflicting a nasty wound in his upper left arm. The Rangers and deputies returned fire, killing one policeman. Sanders was absolutely certain that the police had intended to murder him and his men. He stated that Treviño was "an ex-policeman and has been shielded by the department at the time since the charge of Rape has been preferred against [him]." Further, Sanders reassured the adjutant general that he had the situation under control and did not need help, barring further hostilities by the police. The Ranger captain had been informed that the supposed instigator of the ambush was the night chief of police, who reportedly had fled to Matamoros.[84] A concerned Hutchings sent two Company A Rangers to Brownsville anyway.

The wounded policeman died on November 13, and Sanders notified Hutchings that Brownsville officials planned to arrest him and his men for murder. Now Hutchings was really worried. He ordered Sanders to give him details of the city officials' intentions so that the Texas attorney general could issue a writ of habeas corpus or other legal protection for the Rangers involved. No help needed, replied Sanders, explaining that Judge Jim Wells and Judge J. R. Jones were at his service day and night. Hutchings instructed Sanders to stay in Brownsville. The adjutant general also asked for Private Jenkins's medical bills so they could be paid promptly, and he alluded to the unsettled accounts resulting from Pat Craighead's medical treatment after the San Benito ambush. The inference was that the state considered the doctors' fees excessive and had refused to pay.[85]

The Brownsville mayor and city council appointed a committee to investigate the death of the policeman, Toribio Rodríguez. Not surprisingly, their version differed significantly from that of Captain Sanders. The committee began its report by complaining that neither Sanders nor Sheriff Ryan would talk with them. According to the committee, between 1 and 2 a.m. on November 10, two gunshots were heard in the extreme eastern part of Brownsville. Three special mounted policemen, one of them the deceased, were on duty in place of regular policemen who were on sick leave. The mounted trio decided to investigate. They spotted a hack coming toward them without lights, in violation of city ordinances. When they called on the driver to stop, the occupants of the hack opened fire on them. At the time the policemen had no idea who the occupants were. The deceased was shot off his horse and, wounded in the right arm, went directly home, leaving his horse, his hat, and his unfired pistol at the scene. His two companions were later arrested by a lieutenant of police. Meanwhile, the deceased had walked the six blocks to his home. Shortly thereafter, a doctor dispatched by the lieutenant of police arrived and found Rodríguez wounded in the right forearm and not a sign of blood anywhere except on his right sleeve. To ease Rodríguez's pain, the doctor gave him an injection in the back "at almost the exact spot where a bullet hole was found later, and he found no wound in deceased's body and no blood on and no hole in his shirt; this shirt was worn by deceased all that night." The doctor later reiterated that when he examined Rodríguez, the latter had only the wound in his arm.

After the doctor left, Rodríguez went to sleep. A short time later, three deputy sheriffs arrived, woke him up, and demanded that he make a statement. They were finally persuaded to leave, but about half an hour later there appeared at the home "from eight to ten rangers and deputy sheriffs," some of whom entered. They hustled the wounded Rodríguez out the door in his sock feet and started on foot up the alley. All the officers were around Rodríguez, and when they'd walked some thirty to forty yards, one of the officers shot Rodríguez in the back. The seriously wounded prisoner was taken to the county jail, and later to the sanitarium. Between 4 and 5 a.m. a doctor was summoned, examined Rodríguez, and found that he had been shot just under the right shoulder blade, the bullet going through his right lung and exiting the body. The deceased, who had been bleeding profusely for some time, died of this wound.

Rodríguez, however, made a deathbed statement at 2:55 p.m. on November 12. He recounted the unprovoked attack by the occupants of the hack, and described how a bullet knocked him off his horse. "The only wound I then received being one in my arm." He went home, was attended by the doctor, and went to sleep. "Then the Rangers and Manuel Saldaña and Andrés Uresti [deputies] came. They got me out of the house and then one of them shot me in the back. I think it was Uresti. The Captain of the Rangers said that if I did not have enough with that to die, they would give me more." After that he was taken to jail in a hack.

"When Dr. Stell examined me I only had the wound in the arm. I understand and believe that I am going to die." Rodríguez signed the statement with his mark.

The committee concluded that those in the hack when the initial shooting scrape occurred were Captain Sanders, two of his men, and deputy sheriffs P. D. Haley and Andrés Uresti, and that they were taking a prisoner to jail. The deceased was wearing a coat at the time, and the coat only had holes on the right sleeve. The coat, which was taken from the deceased's home to city hall as evidence, had no hole in the back. "The officers who took the deceased from his house were Captain Sanders of the Rangers, several of his men, Deputy Sheriff P. D. Haley, Andrés Uresti, Manuel Saldaña, and several others to us unknown." The committee recommended not only that the city council adopt the report, but that the mayor send certified copies to the governor and adjutant general, asking them to have an immediate investigation of the affair conducted by a "competent and unprejudiced person." The committee also recommended sending a copy to the foreman of the Cameron County grand jury.[86] The mayor indeed sent the report to Colquitt, who ordered Hutchings to investigate and report as soon as possible. The governor suggested that the Rangers involved make their statements under oath. Hutchings immediately sent the relevant documents to Sanders and ordered him and his Rangers to make detailed statements under oath.[87]

On November 30, Sanders and R. C. Hawkins gave their sworn and notarized statements. The captain stated that on November 8 and 9, he and his sergeant, Marcus Hines, were away from Brownsville on business, leaving Rangers Hawkins, Jenkins, and Willis in the Rangers' quarters at Fort Brown. When Sanders returned, Hawkins told him of a proposal the city police lieutenant had made, a proposal that to Sanders smelled of a trap. He at once sent for the police lieutenant, who said that Ignacio Treviño, an ex-policeman and fugitive from justice, was in town. The lieutenant proposed that Sanders and his men arrest Treviño after the lieutenant and several of his men had located him in a saloon on the outskirts of Brownsville. The lieutenant later informed Sanders that he had been unable to locate Treviño but would continue searching for him. To Sanders the whole thing was a plot to lure him and his men to an out-of-the-way saloon, where police would be waiting to shoot them down, as had happened to deputy sheriff A. R. Baker some months earlier.

Sanders then recounted how he had been awakened about 1:30 a.m. in his quarters by deputies Pat Haley and Andrés Uresti, asking his help in arresting Treviño. After the arrest, as the party of officers and their prisoner turned a dark corner in their hack, they were confronted by four mounted men. Hawkins asked in Spanish who they were and what they wanted. Uresti did likewise. Without replying, the riders drew their guns and began firing. The officers immediately returned fire; some twenty shots were exchanged in the melee. Sanders said he fired twice, as did Jenkins and Hawkins. "One of the men shot was seen to fall off his horse as though he was dead." The horses pulling the hack bolted, but after about fifty yards the driver managed to stop them. Sanders stayed with the prisoner while Jenkins, Hawkins, Haley, and Uresti went back to search for their antagonists. It was very dark, and all they found was the horse from which the wounded policeman had fallen. Jenkins then announced that he had been shot in the arm. Sanders immediately ordered that they proceed to jail so Treviño could be locked up and Jenkins's arm treated.

About 4 a.m., Sanders, Hawkins, Sheriff Ryan, and a number of his deputies began searching for the ambushers, and they learned that policeman Rodríguez had been wounded and was at home. They descended on the house. As they entered, Sanders remembered hearing someone remark that Rodríguez was very badly wounded. "I arrested him and started to jail with him on foot holding him by the right arm." After they'd gone half a block, Sanders heard a shot. He thought he was being ambushed again. He asked where the shot had come from but no one seemed to know. It was very dark but the shot was not near enough for Sanders to see the flash or locate it, although it seemed to have come from his left rear. According to Sanders:

> I had Rodriguez by the arm at the time the shot was fired, he gave no evidence whatever of having been struck, and I am satisfied that the flesh wound in Rodriguez's right arm, and also the other through his body, from which he died, were both received by him at the time he made the attack on our hack. . . . it was then and there that he received both shots, and that he was not struck by the shot that was fired while we were taking him to jail, from his house.

Rodríguez showed no sign of having been shot, but after walking about four blocks he became very weak, so Sanders had him put in a hack and taken to jail. That was Sanders's story and he was sticking to it.

Sanders stated that he had had the matter thoroughly investigated by the grand jury and was confident that it would exonerate both the Rangers and the sheriff's department. Anything to the contrary was "wholly false, and worked up simply for local political capital, and in order to counteract, and draw public attention from, the attack made upon us, in the hack, . . ."[88] Nor was Sanders's confidence in the grand jury misplaced. That body reported that:

> This grand jury has spent almost half of its time investigating the shooting between the police force, Rangers, and deputy sheriffs in which Toribio Rodriguez received his death wound, and after examining twenty-seven witnesses we have failed to find sufficient evidence to return an indictment in this case. It is the opinion of this Grand Jury that Captain Sanders with his

Ranger Force and the Deputy Sheaff [sic] were unquestionably fired upon by parties unknown to them and that they were justified in defending themselves and their prisoner.[89]

So there. Not only did the grand jury exonerate Sanders and company but, at least from the Independents' perspective, added insult to injury by criticizing the police department. It found that there were forty-four men in Brownsville with commissions as policemen: Chief (or City Marshal) Ralph J. Tucker; two lieutenants, Joaquín Treviño and O. M. Puig; eight regular patrolmen; fifteen supernumeraries; and eighteen special officers, all of whom were permitted to carry a pistol at all times. The grand jury declared that:

> We believe that the Mayor and the City Council have overstepped their authority in commissioning so many men to carry arms and we believe the way to break up so much gun toting and stop so many homicides in this county is to first disarm those men who have commissions just for the purpose to get to carry a gun, and we suggest that the County Attorney investigate this matter thoroughly. . . .[90]

It was no wonder that the sheriff's department was constantly on edge—whereas the police could muster forty-four armed men, the sheriff had only ten deputies. The grand jury felt this was a sufficient number, but:

> we suggest to the sheriff that he re-organize his force of deputies and secure the best men available because we have found in our investigation that there have been a number of times that a deputy sheriff has known the whereabouts of criminals and who had a warrant for their arrest, and have [sic] failed, through lack of courage, to arrest them.[91]

As, for example, in the case of the fugitive Ignacio Treviño, where the deputies had to ask the Rangers for help in making the arrest.

This affair has been discussed at some length because it sheds light on how things worked in Brownsville. The evidence suggests that indeed the special policemen ambushed the Rangers and deputies. This was another in the tit-for-tat shootings between the sheriff's men and the police, who apparently were more interested in fighting each other than in chasing criminals. Second, it is clear that the Rangers did sympathize with the sheriff's department over the police. Third, when the deputies located the wounded Rodríguez, they and the Rangers returned and somebody executed Rodríguez. Fourth, Rodríguez thought that the man who shot him in the back was a Hispanic deputy, not an Anglo Ranger; but the deputy bungled, and Rodríguez lived long enough to make a dying statement. Fifth,

Captain Sanders's story of Rodríguez's death was preposterous, in the face of the doctor's testimony and the policeman's coat, which magically repaired itself to conceal the bullet hole in the back. Lastly, the grand jury bought Sanders's story. What comes to mind is that this was a Cameron County grand jury, and Jim Wells ran Cameron County. Captain Sanders dodged a bullet on this one, both literally and figuratively.

Sanders and his men remained in Brownsville and, not surprisingly, tension remained high. The Ranger captain received an anonymous "warning" through the mail to the effect that one José Marroquín, urged on by Vicente Crixell (brother of the late city marshal José Crixell and a special police officer, as were his brothers Luis and E. C. Crixell), planned to lead a group of desperate characters to massacre Sanders and his Rangers some night. The message said that Sanders and Sheriff Ryan were in danger even on the streets, and that Sanders had better act at once before the plan ripened. The writer said the police force knew of the plot and that Marroquín had been a policeman, adding "I am amongst them know it to be true. . . ." The writer signed himself "A true friend." Sanders informed the adjutant general and said that only he, Sheriff Ryan, Judge Wells, Judge Jones, and his Rangers had been told of the warning.[92] Then on December 24, City Marshal Ralph J. Tucker wired the adjutant general that the previous night there had been "serious trouble" between Captain Sanders and one of Tucker's policemen. Tucker asked Hutchings to come to Brownsville and investigate the matter personally, "as it may be dangerous trouble in the future."[93] Instead Hutchings recommended to the governor that Company B should be split into two detachments, at Sinton and Del Rio, adding that:

> The several trials at Brownsville have been concluded, the troubles that exist there are purely between two rival political factions, and the presence of the Rangers is not required for the safety of the average non-participating citizens in these factions. I do not believe substantially half of the Ranger Force should be situated in Brownsville merely to prevent possible clashes between sworn preservers of the peace in the Sheriff's and City Marshal's offices.[94]

Colquitt approved of Hutchings's suggestion. As 1912 ended, Brownsville remained what it had always been—a tough town for the Rangers.

THE REVOLUTION INTENSIFIES

A FTER his recent difficulties there, Captain Sanders was not at all reluctant to leave Brownsville. In late January, 1913, he and his men were transferred to Del Rio.[1] But, Rangers or no Rangers, the feud between the Brownsville police department and the Cameron County sheriff's office continued unabated. In March there was an altercation when a Hispanic policeman tried to arrest a Hispanic deputy sheriff; they got into a fight. But the feud again reached serious proportions in September. In the early hours of the 19th, there occurred a shooting scrape in Flossie Wescott's whorehouse down by the Frisco freight depot. Winchester in hand, Police Lieutenant Octaviano M. Puig, accompanied by policeman Henry Havre, entered the establishment, ostensibly responding to a complaint about shots being fired. Sitting in the parlor were Sheriff Carl T. Ryan and six of his deputies. Puig informed them that they were all under arrest and commanded them to appear at city hall at 9 a.m. By way of reply, they opened fire, hitting Puig nine times. Remarkably, Puig lived for several hours, long enough to make a deathbed statement. Policeman Havre was wounded in the arm, Sheriff Ryan and Deputy José Longoria in the hand. Predictably, the police and the sheriff's office promptly filed charges against each other and everybody was released on bond. The city council appointed John Natus, a former Ranger and Brownsville policeman, to succeed Puig.[2] In a much less spectacular encounter, in October, policeman Carlos García shot deputy sheriff Encarnación Cuéllar in the hip when they quarreled and blasted away at each other in a local restaurant.[3]

As for the Texas Rangers, 1913 found them still badly under strength: eighteen men in all, with Captain Hughes and Company A at Ysleta, Captain Sanders and Company B at Del Rio, and Captain Fox, who constituted Company C, serving from Austin as Ranger detective. Captain William Smith, who had been discharged in August, was once again an El Paso city detective, later becoming the house detective for the Paso del Norte hotel.[4] And, as usual, there were many more requests for assistance than the Rangers could answer.

Attention focused on the border from El Paso to Fabens. Adjutant General Hutchings was worried about orozquista bands operating in the vicinity of Juárez attacking that city, as well as the possibility of small-scale raids into Texas. Governor Colquitt was also concerned. On January 30, he informed Taft that 1,000 orozquistas under General José Inés Salazar were menacing Juárez, that a battle was imminent, and that Taft should take the necessary steps to prevent firing into El Paso.[5] Colquitt telegraphed Captain Hughes to "keep me advised of the situation and shoot straight if necessary."[6] No battle materialized, but two weeks later Colquitt wrote to Taft:

> The continued disorders and the obligation of the United States to the world under the Monroe doctrine makes it now a duty for our government to intervene in Mexico, not for conquest or territorial gain but to restore order and protect life and property and I respectfully urge this course without delay.[7]

Hutchings recommended, and Colquitt concurred, ordering Sanders and his company from Del Rio to Ysleta to reinforce Hughes, whose men had already had a skirmish with rebels: Sergeant Charles Moore and Private Charles Webster wounded two orozquistas and captured one, plus three horses and some equipment.[8] As Sergeant Moore informed the adjutant general:

> Sir, I have the honor to send you today under another cover, a rebel flag that Pvt. Webster and I captured on Pirate Island on January 29. A deputy sheriff and I shot from his saddle the rebel who had this flag, and as we were only seventy five yards from him when we fired I think we did him some serious damage. There were so many rebels in the thick brush that we could not stop to investigate but I don't think our rebel would be in shape to again use the Mauser carbine we got off his saddle.[9]

Captain Sanders's men arrived in Ysleta, but not Sanders. He was having serious health problems and had gone home to Lockhart for treatment.[10] His recurring bouts of illness would substantially reduce his effectiveness as a company commander.[11] It fell to Hughes to take up the slack. He duly scouted the border downriver as far as ten miles below Fabens, across from the Mexican village of Guadalupe, which was being garrisoned by some 200 federals dispatched from Juárez. And that city was no longer threatened by orozquistas; by early February Hughes felt confident in sending Sanders's men back to Del Rio.[12] He would also deploy his own company far and wide to answer the requests for assistance that had been accumulating:

at Ysleta: Captain Hughes and Private Cline
at El Paso: Sergeant Moore and Private Webster
at Marfa: Private Knight
at Valentine: Private Vaughn
at Hebbronville: Private Craighead
at Dickens: Private Roberson
at Fort Stockton: Private Russell[13]

Having barely settled back into the routine of assisting local law enforcement officers, Hughes and Sanders would have their priorities rearranged by developments in Mexico.

Things seemed to be improving for the Mexican president, Francisco I. Madero. He had withstood General Bernardo Reyes's attempt to overthrow him, and Reyes was now safely imprisoned in Mexico City. Likewise, Madero had overcome the much more serious insurrection by General Pascual Orozco. Even though bands of orozquistas remained at large in Chihuahua, they posed no real threat, nor did the disorganized and financially strapped magonistas. Furthermore, in October, 1912, Madero had triumphed over yet another challenger, General Félix Díaz, nephew of the exiled dictator. Félix Díaz and his followers, the *felicistas*, rose in rebellion at the strategic port city of Veracruz. Díaz issued the obligatory manifesto, calling on the nation for support. Nothing happened. Evidently Félix Díaz could never grasp the fact that prior to November, 1910, being Porfirio Díaz's nephew was an enormous asset; once the Mexican Revolution began, it was an enormous handicap. Because of the public's indifference, Díaz's rebellion collapsed, and by the end of October he had surrendered to the Madero government and was packed off to prison in Mexico City. Only General Emiliano Zapata continued to pose a major problem for Madero. Zapata was leading what amounted to his own Mexican revolution, whose cornerstone was a demand for immediate land reform. But Zapata's rebellion suffered from a crippling weakness—it was centered in the interior of the country, in the state of Morelos adjoining the Federal District and Mexico City. Thus Zapata lacked access to the American border and its crucial supply of munitions; it was no accident that the other major revolutionists—Madero, Villa, Orozco, Carranza, Obregón, and Calles—all came from northern border states. Still, Zapata doggedly fought every regime from his initial rising in March, 1911, to his assassination in April, 1919.

By February, 1913, Madero seemed to be consolidating his rule, although Zapata remained in arms. But in Mexico City itself trouble was brewing for the well-meaning president. Because Generals Félix Díaz and Bernardo Reyes were in separate prisons, Madero believed they were now harmless. Reyistas and felicistas were permitted frequent contact with their leaders. And their leaders, who had plenty of time for reflection, came to the conclusion that their rebellions had failed because they began out in the provinces, giving Madero time to react. Therefore, a well-planned coup in Mexico City should be able to remove Madero before his supporters could rally to his defense. Accordingly, such a coup was organized with the help of several disaffected generals. The plotters struck on February 9, 1913. Reyes and Díaz were liberated, and a column of less than 1,000 men marched through downtown Mexico City to seize the presidential palace and Madero. Their plans miscarried because forces loyal to Madero retained control of the palace. When the rebels advanced on the building, General Reyes was at the head of the column. He had the distinction of being the first person killed when the attack was repulsed. Under the leadership of Félix Díaz, the demoralized rebels barricaded themselves in the *ciudadela*, an arsenal in the downtown area. Madero designated General Victoriano Huerta, the man who had crushed the Orozco rebellion, to command the loyalist units being massed to finish off the rebels.

Instead of finishing them off, however, Huerta cut a deal with Félix Díaz, becoming in effect a co-conspirator in the plot to overthrow Madero. From February 9 to 18, the so-called *decena trágica*, or tragic ten days, rebels and loyalists went through the charade of fighting each other while devastating the heart of Mexico City. Finally, on February 18, Huerta arrested Madero and the vice president, arranged—with the connivance of the American ambassador—a division of the spoils with Félix Díaz, and proclaimed himself provisional president. There remained only the tidying up. On the night of February 22, Madero and the vice president were murdered, and the next day the Huerta regime announced that regrettably the two had been killed when some of their partisans had tried to rescue them—a variant on the ley fuga.

General Huerta was the new strongman of Mexico. In one of the permutations that characterized the Revolution, Huerta was soon joined by General Pascual Orozco, the man he had defeated in 1912; Orozco became Huerta's ally and military subordinate. Huerta's first priority was to consolidate his own position. He quickly shunted Félix Díaz aside and instituted a crash program to enlarge the army significantly.[14] But opposition to Huerta soon materialized. Many Mexicans regarded Madero as a martyr and Huerta as a usurper. Capitalizing on this wave of popular revulsion, the governor of Coahuila, Venustiano Carranza, became the self-proclaimed leader of a rebellion to topple Huerta. He issued his revolutionary manifesto, the *Plan de Guadalupe*, christened his rebels the Constitutionalist Army, and proclaimed himself its First Chief. Carranza quickly began to attract support. One of those rallying to the Constitutionalist cause was General Francisco Villa, who had recently been living in obscurity as an exile in El Paso. Starting with a literal handful of followers, Villa built his command, the

Division of the North, into the most formidable of the Constitutionalist formations. Heretofore the Mexican Revolution in the north had been centered primarily in the state of Chihuahua, but the Constitutionalists encompassed the entire northern tier of states. The Mexican Revolution was entering its bloodiest phase, and it would spill over into Texas to an unprecedented degree. In May, 1913, Carranza established relations with Governor Colquitt for all international matters affecting Texas and Coahuila. Carranza explained that he couldn't deal with Washington because the Mexican foreign minister was a *huertista*.[15] The Wilson administration refused to recognize Huerta as the legitimate president of Mexico, and this policy was of inestimable benefit to Carranza and his fellow rebels.

The immediate concern was the Mexican border towns—whether the Madero officials would recognize Huerta's seizure of power or join the Constitutionalist opposition. Governor Colquitt was especially concerned about rumors involving Nuevo Laredo, and the adjutant general instructed Captain Sanders to dispatch a couple of his men to Laredo to investigate the situation. Sanders sent Sergeant Marcus Hines and Private Joe Jenkins, who returned on February 12 and reported no revolutionary activity around Laredo.[16] On February 15, a group of conservative Mexicans sympathetic to the Huerta regime crossed from Laredo and captured Nuevo Laredo without a shot being fired, as the result of what one observer described as "merely a total change of sentiment" by the population. The conspirators had considerable help while in Laredo. Several of them had slept in the Webb County courthouse, and prominent among the plotters was Sheriff Amador Sánchez.[17] Even as his application for a presidential pardon for his role in the 1911 Reyes conspiracy was being considered by President Taft, Sheriff Sánchez had been up to his eyeballs in intrigue. When the new pro-Huerta city administration was installed in Nuevo Laredo, Sánchez's eldest son was among the notables on the balcony of the city hall.[18]

Two days after the coup in Laredo, Huerta sympathizers took over Matamoros without a fight—the city simply surrendered to them. Although the new regime initially prohibited any contact with Brownsville, by February 18 some 3,000 people had fled across the river to the safety of the Texas city.[19] Since there were currently no United States troops in Brownsville, Colquitt demanded that the army act immediately to protect the city, because if the federal government didn't protect the border the State of Texas most certainly would. When informed that the Huerta commander in Matamoros, Major Esteban Ramos, had threatened Americans in that city, Colquitt, with his usual hyperbole, declared that the life of the Mexican commander would be forfeit if a single Texan were harmed. Colquitt then ordered units of the Texas National Guard to proceed immediately to Brownsville. Although there was some apprehension in Washington that he might order them to attack Matamoros, it would appear that the governor's actions were designed to get the federal government's attention, which they unquestionably did.

The army rushed troops to Brownsville, and as they arrived, Colquitt sent the national guard home.[20]

By February 25, officials in Ciudad Juárez loyal to the late president Madero were fleeing to El Paso, fearing arrest by the pro-Huerta military authorities who had taken control of the city.[21] But this situation was vastly different from that in Brownsville. The mere presence of Fort Bliss served to reassure El Pasoans that the federal government was protecting them.

Events along the border were contradicting Governor Colquitt's optimistic assessment on February 15 that "I apprehend that much of the disorders will now pass away on account of the termination of events in the City of Mexico."[22] While border towns were going over to the Huerta regime, Constitutionalist activity was intensifying in the countryside. Small bands were appearing, arms smuggling across the Rio Grande increased, and some Hispanics were beginning to slip across the river to join the fight. When the Huerta consul in San Antonio brought these matters to Colquitt's attention, the governor replied that the state was powerless to enforce the neutrality laws. Texas was quite willing to cooperate with the federal government, but the latter had not yet indicated that it wanted such cooperation.[23]

The Rangers were simply stretched too thinly to answer all the calls for assistance that were pouring in. On February 18, Captain Sanders at Del Rio deployed his company along the river in conjunction with mounted Customs inspectors and some twenty-five cavalrymen, in response to reports—unfounded, as it turned out—that rebels on the Texas side of the Rio Grande planned to cross to attack Las Vacas (today Ciudad Acuña); nevertheless, the population fled to Del Rio for protection. Calls for help also came from Alpine and Marathon in the Big Bend, where several ranches were reportedly raided. Sanders didn't respond, pointing out that this was Hughes's territory. But on the adjutant general's orders Sergeant Hines and Private Jenkins from Company B were sent to Laredo, to patrol the border from Minerva to Palafox.[24]

Meanwhile, Captain Hughes was responding to appeals from Alpine and Marfa. As it developed, the Mexicans who had robbed the Hancock ranch near Alpine were not raiders from Mexico but had been working in the area for some time.[25] Besides keeping an eye out for Mexican marauders, Hughes was instructed to keep an eye on the army, to "report location of U.S. troops, what they are doing and what seems their intentions."[26] As Hutchings himself already knew, it wasn't too difficult to learn the army's order of battle along the border, for it was published in the *Army and Navy Journal*.[27] As for learning the army's intentions, that was another matter. Hughes pointed out quite reasonably that "General Steever at San Antonio is [the] only one that knows about troop movements."[28] Nevertheless, Hughes did his best, going to Fort Bliss to elicit information from uncommunicative officers, assigning Private Webster to monitor troop movements, and reporting whatever information he could.[29]

The level of tension along the border remained high, as illustrated by a few examples. On March 11, Captain Sanders reported that "the killing of an American at Langtry a few days ago by a Mexican and the killing of a Mexican by an American Lady at Carta Valley last night is causing quite a lot of excitement through out the [border] country."[30] A resident of Palafox wrote that "The town across the river—Hidalgo—has been looted and is now threatened again. The Mexicans show a great deal of unrest, and there is no law prevailing on the other side of the river."[31] Captain Sanders wrote that although reports of Mexican bandits raiding ranches around Laredo were untrue, Rangers Hines and Jenkins having thoroughly scouted along the river, "Being very few Officers in that country the few Americans there are always in constant fear of Mexicans making a raid on their ranches."[32] And speaking of raids, some Constitutionalists attacked Nuevo Laredo on March 17, retreating after a battle lasting over an hour and resulting in twenty dead on both sides.[33] And at Laredo, Sheriff Amador Sánchez was now a zealous enforcer of the neutrality laws, doing everything he could to prevent munitions from being smuggled across the river to the Constitutionalists. They returned the compliment by burning several buildings on a ranch Sánchez owned outside Nuevo Laredo.[34]

In the midst of these alarms and excursions there was a bit of comic relief. Some officious fool in the management of the Saint Louis Southwestern Railway (the Cotton Belt) decreed that its annual passes could be used only "when in uniform and when called into the service of the State." The assistant adjutant general commented dryly that "This is the first time that this road has so favored the Rangers." He instructed Captain Hughes to "Tell the boys that what ever they happen to have on will be in uniform."[35]

Then there was the matter of the Mongolian rangers. Adjutant General Hutchings began receiving inquiries from several army officers about the organization, training, and tactics of the Texas Rangers, the writers explaining that the government of the Chinese republic was considering creating a similar force to combat bandits in Inner Mongolia. They wondered if any of the Rangers might be interested in organizing and staffing such a constabulary. Initially Hutchings was cool to the whole idea.[36] Surprisingly, one of these inquiries was from the major who was the Secretary of the War College Division of the army; he stated that his office had been unable to obtain any information about the Texas Rangers, and he wondered if Hutchings could recommend any experienced men for the Mongolian project and any books or reports on the Rangers and, if so, where they could be obtained.[37] The army's intelligence capabilities left something to be desired.

The whole affair came into sharper focus when Captain James H. Reeves, who had been the military attaché in China for the past five years, wrote to Hutchings saying that his successor requested information about the Texas Rangers. Reeves explained that the situation along the Chinese-Mongolian border was not unlike that along the U.S.-Mexican border, and that the Chinese government's advisor on Mongolian affairs, a Mr. Larson, was the driving force behind the Mongolian ranger project. Larson wanted "accurate information about the organization of the Texas Rangers and their methods of policing the border, keeping down horse and cattle thieves, etc." He also wanted "to know how much it would cost to get a good man for organization work and a number of subordinates as District Commanders." Lastly, Larson wanted "men to go into Mongolia to work, not high salaried individuals who want to live in Peking."[38] By now Hutchings was more enthusiastic about the idea. He provided Reeves with copies of General Orders No. 5, October 2, 1911, under which the Rangers were organized, and of various forms used, such as the Monthly Returns. As to how the Rangers currently patrolled the border with a limited force, they did it by changing the home stations of the command and patrolling in either direction; if the force were larger a constant patrol would be maintained. Thefts of horses and cattle were minimized as much as possible by Rangers familiarizing themselves with brands, which by law had to be filed with county clerks. At times Rangers were sent to work undercover in assisting local authorities. Hutchings now believed it was practicable to organize an efficient force in Mongolia "from officers in the Texas National Guard and from selected Rangers who would go to Mongolia to work for the good of the service." Hutchings said he couldn't estimate costs since he didn't know what the Chinese contemplated paying for transportation, or the cost of living, the terms of service, etc. However, "the greater the inducement, the better the men." His conclusion was that "I think good men can be secured, but I would not like to interest anybody in the project without something more definite, as it might lead to unpleasant notoriety and cause some worthy men to be classed as soldiers of fortune."[39] The Mongolian rangers never came into being, but the very idea of such an organization was eloquent testimony to the fame of the Texas Rangers.

The Rangers continued to focus on the Mexican border, where Constitutionalist activity was increasing. In March, the rebel commander Toribio Ortega was menacing the town of Ojinaga, whose officials and garrison had sworn allegiance to the Huerta government. Most of the population fled across the river to Presidio on learning of Ortega's approach. Besides the Constitutionalist irregulars operating near the border, there was considerable rustling and smuggling going on in the Big Bend.[40] Captain Hughes reported the sighting of small bands along the river. He also passed along the rumors circulating in El Paso, perhaps the wildest being that "six of the northern states will secede. Governor Carranza is to be the Provisional President and he will be financed by the Standard Oil Co., and after they gain their independence they will ask to be annexed to the United States."[41]

Although rebel forces attacked Mier, opposite Roma, Texas, and a sizeable contingent—some 1,000—of rebels was reportedly near Matamoros, it was the Big Bend that required constant attention.[42] The pattern here was one of brief, sharp clashes between small parties of officers and Mexicans. A Ranger or mounted Customs inspector working in this mountainous and desolately beautiful region was keenly aware that if he got into trouble help was a long way away, and one of the highest compliments that a man could receive was that he "was a good man to ride the river with," for riding along the Rio Grande was often hazardous. To illustrate, back in February mounted Customs inspectors Jack Howard and Joe Sitter (a former Ranger) and J. A. Harvick, a brand inspector for the cattlemen's association (and future Special Ranger), were scouting along the Rio Grande near the settlement of Pilares. There they found Francisco "Chico" Cano, one of a band of Mexicans who had been smuggling horses and mules; in September, 1912, Sitter had seized 140 head of stock they had smuggled. The officers arrested Cano, spent the night at the little store in Pilares run by Sabino Hernández, and left the next morning—February 10—to take their prisoner to Marfa to appear before the U.S. commissioner. They had gone about a mile and a half and were riding single file through a deep canyon, Howard in the lead, then two pack animals, then the prisoner, then Harvick, with Sitter bringing up the rear. A high bluff was on their left, while on their right was a higher mountain whose side was strewn with large boulders. Hidden behind the boulders were five or six Mexicans, members of the gang of smugglers, two of them brothers of the prisoner.

When Howard reached a point directly below them, the ambushers opened fire, at a range of about fifty yards. Howard was hit in the chest and his horse was killed; Harvick and Sitter were shot off their horses. Harvick was shot through the left thigh, while Sitter took a grazing bullet that entered above his left temple and exited behind the ear. Despite their wounds, the officers drew their weapons. Howard retrieved his rifle from his dead horse but was too badly injured to use it. Sitter and Harvick were able to return fire, although they couldn't spot their attackers among the boulders. For half an hour the Mexicans did their best to kill the officers. The ambushers finally left, as did Cano, who had bolted to freedom when the shooting started. After waiting to be sure the ambushers had really gone, Sitter and Harvick painfully climbed the bluff on the left side of the canyon. From the top of the bluff they waved, hoping that someone in Pilares would see them. Sitter passed out. Fortunately, the storekeeper Sabino Hernández had indeed seen the wounded men, and he hurried to the scene. He and other Hispanics from Pilares got a wagon and took the lawmen to his store. Hernández then sent a messenger to the nearest army detachment, at Candelaria, thirty-five miles downriver from Pilares. The sergeant commanding the detachment telephoned his commander in Marfa, who notified the local authorities, who alerted the authorities in Valentine, the closest town having a physician. A posse of Rangers and citizens, accompanied by the doctor, rode to Pilares, arriving on the afternoon of February 11. Howard died of his wound on the night of the 12th, but the other two were carried to Marfa, where they were put on the train to El Paso. There they were taken to Hotel Dieu hospital. Both Harvick and Sitter recovered and were released from the hospital on March 3.

The official report of the incident concluded:

> Conditions along the border in the "Big Bend" section where this occurred have gradually grown from bad to worse during the past two years, this occasioned mostly by the chaotic conditions existing in Mexico brought about by the revolution now in progress there, and in my opinion the Customs force in that section should be strengthened and arranged so that they may work in squads of not less than four. Under present conditions two men scouting in the rough country which extends along the river for nearly four hundred miles in this Customs district can be expected to accomplish but little and while at work their lives are constantly in danger and attacks like this may be expected at any time.[43]

This observation of course also applied to the Rangers. In this connection, Ranger Jefferson Eagle Vaughan was considerably luckier than Howard, Sitter, and Harvick. In April, he and another officer, Buck Pool, captured a cattle thief near the Rio Grande. They set out for Marfa but were ambushed by Mexicans trying to free the prisoner. During the firefight the prisoner attempted to escape and the officers shot him while routing their attackers. While it might be suspected that this was an instance of the ley fuga, the officers just disposing of their prisoner and inventing the story of the ambush, it would appear that this was not the case. When Ranger Vaughan reached Shafter, he notified Sheriff Milt B. Chastain in Marfa. The sheriff and Ranger Ira Cline immediately set out to join Vaughan. When Captain Hughes was notified of these developments, he dispatched Sergeant Moore and Private Scott Russell to Marfa as backup.[44] A week later Ranger Cline and Customs inspector O. C. Dowe made a scout resulting in the seizure of forty stolen horses and mules, and the arrest of the rustlers—four Mexicans and one Anglo.[45]

Numerous citizens of Marfa signed a petition on April 14 asking that four Rangers be stationed at the Shafter mines. Governor Colquitt sent the petition to Hutchings with the notation: "Advise if you do not think it best to move Captain Sanders and his station from Del Rio to Marfa." Surprisingly, Hutchings, who usually acquiesced to Colquitt's every wish, replied that Marfa was well within Captain Hughes's territory and advised against stationing what amounted to 25 percent of the Ranger Force at Shafter. "Roughly speaking, Hughes must control from El Paso to Del Rio and Sanders from Del Rio to Brownsville. Territory considered, this must seem somewhat absurd, but it is, so far as I know, the best that can be done." Hutchings added that "It is all a matter of judgement and effort to cover so large a territory and answer so many requests with so few men." He ended by observing that "If men are stationed at Shafter a call will immediately come from Terlingua," a hamlet even closer to the Rio Grande.[46]

Not only was Captain Hughes having to cover an impossibly large territory, but he was having personnel problems. Company A experienced unusually high turnover. First, Hughes lost his very capable sergeant, Charles R. Moore, the man who had faced down the orozquista mounted charge in 1912. Moore liked being a Ranger, but he hoped to find a similar job at better pay: "I am anxious to get a job where I can scout along the [boundary] line, and not have to stay cooped up in an office."[47] In March, 1913, Moore resigned to accept the position of deputy U.S. marshal at El Paso under ex-Ranger captain John H. Rogers, who was now U.S. marshal for the Western District of Texas. Beginning on April 5, 1913, Moore performed his new duties with his usual efficiency, but on April 7, 1914, he died in El Paso as the result of an operation.[48] Moore's colleague, Ranger Charles H. Webster, had been thinking of resigning, but he aspired to do so as a sergeant, and he was anxious to be Moore's replacement. When he was not selected, he resigned in July, 1913. As of 1915, he was an El Paso County automobile inspector. The man Captain Hughes appointed as his new sergeant was H. L. "Hod" Roberson.

Into the summer of 1913, Hughes continued to have personnel problems, this time involving Ranger Scott Russell. Born in Stephenville in 1888, Russell had been a farmer before enlisting in Company A on October 1, 1912. He'd been stationed for several months in Fort Stockton, helping Sheriff Dudley Barker investigate a murder case, but was transferred to Hughes's camp in Ysleta in March, 1913.[49] By late April Russell found himself on duty at the smelter in El Paso where a threatening situation had developed. The smelter, one of the city's principal industries, had been hit with a strike by the overwhelmingly Hispanic work force of some 3,000. Sheriff Peyton Edwards was quite worried and requested Captain Hughes to send as many of his Rangers as possible. The sheriff could only deploy three deputies, a totally inadequate number. At first, the sheriff detailed Ranger Charles Webster to take charge of the numerous smelter guards, hoping that an experienced lawman like Webster would be able to control them, but Webster quickly became disgusted with management's intransigent attitude and informed Edwards that he would no longer perform this function. The law allowed the guards to carry weapons on the smelter premises, but Sheriff Edwards refused to deputize them, for then they could wander around El Paso armed when not on duty. He repeated his appeal for Rangers.[50]

The situation at the smelter became more ominous when management filed suit to evict the strikers who occupied ninety-eight company-owned adobe houses. On the morning of April 22, some fifteen strikers were trying to prevent strikebreakers from entering the plant by stoning them. Some of the strikers rushed a guard and tried to wrestle his rifle away. Ranger Russell ran over to the scene, shot the striker grappling for the guard's weapon in the leg, and dispersed the group, who were later arrested. A pitched battle between guards and strikers had been narrowly averted. But tensions remained high; the next day a quarrel between strike sympathizers and opponents resulted in one man being shot and killed.[51]

Ranger Russell remained on duty in turbulent Smeltertown, notorious for its frequent brawls and general rowdiness.[52] On June 23, Captain Hughes assigned Russell to accompany Deputy Sheriff W. H. Garlick to serve a warrant for the arrest of one Manuel Guaderrama for rustling. This was a sensible precaution, for the Guaderrama clan was well known to law enforcement. In the winter of 1909, for instance, Abelino Guaderrama was arrested for breaking into a boxcar. He was freed on bond. Later the body of a witness in the case was fished out of the Rio Grande—he'd been beaten over the head and a wagon wheel had been tied to his neck. No clue to the murderer was ever found. Since then, Abelino and his brother Sabino had been arrested for conspiring to smuggle arms, for smuggling arms, and for stealing bars of silver bullion from the smelter. Sabino and two others had recently been arrested for rustling.[53]

The two lawmen hoped to find Manuel Guaderrama in Smeltertown at the establishment he and his brother Juan owned. It consisted of a saloon with an adjoining grocery store on the corner, a storeroom, and living quarters in the back. To avoid arousing suspicion, the officers sauntered into the store and asked to buy ten cents worth of tobacco from Juan, who was behind the counter. The only other person in the room was Juan's mother, Marina Guaderrama. Russell and Garlick kept a sharp eye on Juan and on the door to the adjoining saloon. It never occurred to them that Juan's sweet gray-haired mother might be a threat. She sidled up behind Ranger Russell and smashed him in the back of the head with an axe handle. As the stunned Ranger began to fall, Juan whipped out a Luger from under the counter and opened fire, killing both Russell and Garlick. To make sure they were dead, he raced around the counter, pulled down the window shades, and hacked at the fallen officers' heads with a hatchet. Presumably it was only then he discovered that while he was blasting away at the peace officers he had accidently shot his mother in the stomach. She lingered in agony for an hour before dying. Someone—probably Juan's wife—ran in and removed the officers' sixguns and Russell's gunbelt. Garlick's gunbelt was unbuckled but evidently there was not time to take it also. At the same time Juan Guaderrama called the police station to report a fight in his saloon and inform the police that Russell and Garlick were drunk, and had drawn their guns, and had struck his mother. Guaderrama implored the police to come. The police, however, referred him to the sheriff, saying it was out of their jurisdiction. A few minutes later news of the shooting reached El Paso.[54]

Captain Hughes rushed to El Paso and assisted Stanley Good, the chief deputy sheriff, in the investigation. Hughes had no doubt about the circumstances leading up to the killing: "We have plenty of evidence that the killing was planned several days ahead, and that they were prepared for the first opportunity."[55] Conventional wisdom was that the killings were in revenge for the dead officers' role in arresting several Guaderramas for rustling. Governor Colquitt was duly informed of Russell's murder, and besides expressing his regret he directed that the body be prepared for burial and shipped to Stephenville, Russell's hometown, at state expense. Hutchings instructed Hughes to have a Company A Ranger accompany the body—that is, if the budget permitted it.[56] Deputy Garlick's body was sent to Valentine for burial.

In the immediate aftermath of the killings the authorities rounded up many of the Guaderrama clan—everybody they thought could conceivably be involved—thirteen people in all. As the El Paso *Morning Times* reported, "The men under arrest are considered dangerous characters. They are sullen and refuse to make any statement regarding the shooting."[57] The prisoners were held in the county jail, which was surrounded by extra guards to prevent either a rescue or a lynching. Seven of the prisoners were released when a grand jury declined to indict them; the other six—Juan, Jesús, David, and Adolfo Guaderrama, Juan's wife, and Leddio Domínguez—were indicted for murder. The Guaderramas sold their saloon, possibly to raise money for attorney's fees, as they had hired expensive legal talent—Tom Lea, a future mayor of El Paso.[58] The Guaderramas really needed to keep a law firm on retainer. Not only were six members of the family facing capital murder charges, as well as a couple more facing rustling charges, but Manuel was arrested on a charge of seduction and another of wife abandonment, while Sabino and Abelino were arrested in Juárez in connection with an ammunition deal. Sabino was jailed in Juárez, then incarcerated in the penitentiary in Chihuahua for three weeks. After his release he filed a $50,000 lawsuit against the El Paso representative of the Mexican foreign office and a former mayor of Juárez for the treatment he, "a peaceable, honest, and law-abiding citizen," had received.[59]

By the time the eagerly anticipated Guaderrama murder trial began on January 13, 1914, only five members of the family were still under indictment—charges against Leddio Domínguez had been dismissed. Their lawyer, Tom Lea, pulled out all the stops: Mrs. Juan Guaderrama had been pregnant at the time of the killings; she now dandled her baby on her knee, while Juan gazed adoringly at his child. A key witness was a twelve-year-old Hispanic boy who was thoroughly confused by the time opposing counsel had finished grilling him on the stand. Deputy U.S. Marshal and ex-Ranger Charles R. Moore was also a witness. He stoutly denied having hit one of the Guaderramas on the head with his six-shooter the day after the killings but admitted having slapped one in the face in a fit of temper because "the Guaderramas had murdered his friends." Moore also testified that when he and other officers searched the crime scene they found a hatchet with blood and hair on it hidden in a box of corks. The prosecution not only showed the jurors gruesome photos of Russell's bloody head, but also a piece of bone from his skull. The principal defendant, Juan Guaderrama, who one witness said had admitted killing Garlick, gave a highly improbable account of how he killed Garlick in self-defense after the officers had shot his mother, but he left unexplained how Russell met his death. The prosecution suffered a major blow when one of its key witnesses changed his testimony on the stand. He was quickly arrested for perjury. After forty-two hours of deliberation and 116 ballots, the all-Anglo jury informed the judge that it was hopelessly deadlocked. The jurors reportedly agreed that Mrs. Juan and Adolfo Guaderrama were not guilty but disagreed nine to three on the guilt of Jesús and David, and on the sentence that Juan Guaderrama should receive. In view of the hung jury, a second trial was expected.[60]

In preparation for a second trial, friends of the slain Ranger raised money for private counsel to assist the district attorney in prosecuting the Guaderramas. Taking the lead in the movement to secure justice for the late Scott Russell were former Rangers Charles H. Webster and C. R. Moore, who solicited contributions from the smelter management and the cattlemen's association as well as from individuals. One of the latter was Captain John R. Hughes, who pledged $100; another was Sheriff Peyton Edwards, whose deputy W. H. Garlick had been murdered along with Russell.[61] Moreover, Adjutant General Hutchings asked Governor Colquitt if the governor "would be authorized to employ additional counsel out of the appropriation for the executive office for enforcement of law."[62] Captain Hughes also approached the governor. After Colquitt had reviewed the facts in the case, he decided to employ the law firm of state Senator Claude B. Hudspeth of El Paso to help prosecute the Guaderramas. Colquitt agreed to pay the firm $250.[63] Legal maneuvering delayed the second Guaderrama trial until June, 1915. Again the opposing attorneys did everything they could to gain the jury's sympathy. When Mrs. Juan Guaderrama appeared in court holding her baby, the prosecution countered by having Mrs. Garlick hold her own baby. To the disappointment of those seeking justice for the murdered lawmen, the prosecution achieved only a partial victory—Juan Guaderrama was convicted of second-degree murder and was sentenced to five years in prison. While awaiting transfer Guaderrama tried to escape from the county jail, but the authorities found the five hacksaw blades and two fourteen-inch monkey wrenches he had had smuggled into his cell.[64]

Russell's murder had further strained Captain Hughes's resources at a time when conditions in the Big Bend continued to deteriorate and Mexican revolutionary activity increased. In April, Rangers Knight and Vaughan scouted from Marfa down to Shafter, where rustling seemed endemic. They made a swing through Polvo, Presidio, and back to Shafter. In addition, calls for help against rustlers came from Candelaria.[65] In May, Hughes himself took two men and set up shop in Valentine to combat cattle thieves,[66] intending to spend several months there. But a buildup of Constitutionalist forces near El Paso changed his plans. Leaving several men to operate out of Valentine and Marfa, Hughes rushed back to Ysleta, arriving on May 26.

He found that small bands calling themselves revolutionists were active downriver from Ysleta. They gathered at the town of Guadalupe, announcing their intention of attacking Ciudad Juárez in early July. Although Hughes thought this unlikely, he had to patrol the Rio Grande, sometimes in company with mounted Customs inspectors.[67]

The military momentum was swinging in the Constitutionalists' favor at several points along the border. This was a most distressing development for Huerta's partisans in Texas, prominent among whom was F. A. Chapa. Undaunted by his conviction in the Reyes affair, Chapa continued his involvement in Mexican revolutionary intrigues for the remainder of the decade while remaining the leading Hispanic politician in the state and a lieutenant colonel on the staffs of Governors Colquitt, Ferguson, and Hobby. Like his colleague Amador Sánchez, Chapa was now a zealous advocate of strict enforcement of the neutrality laws. He did everything he could to frustrate the Constitutionalists, becoming an informant for the federal Bureau of Investigation in San Antonio.[68] He also instigated the pardon by Governor Colquitt of Gregorio Cortez, who had been imprisoned since 1901 for killing two sheriffs, and who was a Hispanic folk hero. Chapa introduced Cortez to the local Bureau of Investigation office, for whom Cortez readily agreed to become an informant against the Constitutionalists, who were continually trying to recruit him.[69]

To Chapa's intense disappointment, the Constitutionalists steadily became stronger. A major turning point occurred on June 4 when General Lucio Blanco stormed Matamoros and captured the city after a stiff fight.[70] Although the inhabitants of Juárez and El Paso were not yet unduly excited, it became apparent that several Constitutionalist formations were slowly moving within striking distance. Hughes reported in late June that General Francisco Villa was said to be at Guzmán, about seventy miles southwest of Juárez, with 1,000 men, General Toribio Ortega near Villa Ahumada, some eighty miles south of Juárez on the Mexican Central railroad, Porfirio Talamantes with 600 men southeast of Juárez, and a column of 200 under Juan N. Medina coming overland from Agua Prieta, Sonora. Yet the Huerta garrison of 2,000 soldiers was making few preparations for defense.

Not so the El Pasoans: The mayor, army officers, and city detectives reconnoitered in automobiles along the river to plan defensive positions in case of an attack on Juárez. Hughes was contacting all his sources, including Abraham Molina, who had been Madero's intelligence chief in El Paso, and Mormon Bishop

O. P. Brown, who maintained close ties with the Mormon colonies in Chihuahua, in an effort to keep the adjutant general abreast of developments. What really frustrated the Ranger captain was his unfinished work in Valentine, which he couldn't resume until it became clear whether or not there would be a battle in Juárez.[71] On July 2, he wrote that "The rebels have not arrived yet and I am getting very impatient" to get to Valentine.[72] All he could do was to watch the situation and comment on the latest rumors, though on occasion he could forward to Austin something more substantial, such as reports on Mexican conditions provided by H. C. Kramp, manager of the Thiel Detective Agency.[73]

Since Hughes was having to watch developments around El Paso, he could not respond to emergencies in the Big Bend. Captain Sanders began detailing several of his men to handle these calls. In June, Sanders went to San Antonio to visit hospitalized Sheriff Jack Allen of Terrell County, who asked Sanders to assist his deputies at Sanderson "in holding down the Mexicans at that place during his absence." Sanders assigned Private Robert Speed to that duty. Privates Speed and Hawkins had just arrested Jesús Reyes who had murdered John McKay, a prominent rancher, a few days earlier at Sheffield by bashing his head in with a rock. The Rangers were in an automobile, south of Marathon, and they bore down on Reyes, who was desperately fleeing on horseback. When they were about ten yards from him he leaped off his horse and drew his rifle. The officers opened fire. They killed his horse and thought they had killed him: He was hit under the shoulder and through the left leg. Reyes was one tough hombre, though; he was unconscious for some time, but when he regained consciousness he asked for a drink and a cigarette. He was taken to jail at Sanderson.[74] However, he developed blood poisoning in his wounded leg. It was amputated but he died a few hours later.[75]

On July 18, the adjutant general instructed Sanders to be ready to leave Del Rio if Hughes needed his help. On July 20, Hughes did—a strike had broken out among the Hispanic miners at Shafter, and Hughes simply did not have men available to respond. Sanders and Company B took the first train for Marfa.[76] From there Sanders reported the situation at Shafter under control: Five of his men, one of Hughes's men, a deputy U.S. marshal, and twenty-five soldiers were at Shafter to prevent the strike from erupting into violence. The Rangers arrested nine strikers for "fomenting peace disturbances and making incendiary threats" and turned them over to the sheriff. By July 28, most miners had returned to work, and the strike was nearly over. At the request of the sheriff, Captain Sanders left his five men at Shafter for a few more days, but he soon had Company B back at their station in Del Rio. Sheriff Chastain wrote to Colquitt praising the Rangers' role in keeping the peace during the strike and requesting that, because Shafter was remote and near the Rio Grande, two Rangers be stationed there indefinitely. Sanders decided to leave Private Speed there for some months.[77]

Captain Hughes, in the meantime, scouted along the Rio Grande as far down-river as Fort Hancock.[78] He informed Hutchings that not only had the Constitutionalists not raided into Texas, but they were quite friendly to Americans. And "El Pasoans still expect Pancho Villa to attack Juarez, and while I don't know if he'll attack, still I'm afraid to go off and quit watching."[79] The captain had become friendly with a man who made trips to Villa's encampment about once a week, and he relied on this individual for some of his information. Finally, on August 5, Hughes decided that the chances of Villa attacking Juárez were remote, and he left for Valentine. The night of his arrival he informed the adjutant general that "I sent Cline away in the night to try and catch a prisoner who escaped from an officer on the train." What Hughes neglected to mention was that the prisoner was a seventeen-year-old burglar being returned under arrest to El Paso by one of Hughes's own men, Private O. W. "Doc" Goodwin, so nicknamed because he had been the pharmacist at the El Paso smelter hospital before becoming a Ranger. In Van Horn Goodwin had stepped off the train to buy a newspaper, and his prisoner had vanished.[80] Hughes spent as much time as possible in Valentine, sending his men on scouts down to the Rio Grande to combat the rustlers who were driving ranchers in that region to despair.[81]

During much of August, 1913, Hughes reported to the acting adjutant general, Colonel E. R. York, because Adjutant General Hutchings was busy with Texas National Guard affairs. The Texas National Guard was a not inconsiderable organization, consisting of:

3 regiments of infantry

1 squadron of cavalry

1 company of coast artillery

1 battery of field artillery

1 field hospital.

"All," as Hutchings stated, "reasonably well armed and equipped, considering the legislature's limited appropriation."[82] Some units required more attention than others. One was Company L, 2nd Texas Infantry, the Brownsville militia company. Its commanding officer indignantly reported in July that some of his men had arranged to sell all the unit's rifles to the Mexicans, and the plan had been frustrated in the nick of time, the very night they had intended to make delivery.[83] Hutchings was currently focusing his efforts in a lobbying campaign to be appointed as brigade commander of volunteer forces in the event of war with Mexico. To that end, he wrote the entire Texas congressional delegation requesting their support.[84] Since war with Mexico never occurred, Hutchings's ambition remained unfulfilled.

Hutchings reacted petulantly to President Wilson's refusal to invade Mexico, thereby robbing the adjutant general of the chance for military glory. He described himself as being "sweating to go" and declared that:

> As for myself, I am going to join the International Peace Society, and advocate disarmament. Fighting is barbarous. Not only that but it is WRONG—I remember having been "licked" for fighting when I was a small boy. And then the wicked, wicked soldiers might hurt someone if they are permitted to play with rifles and things like that. Oh! I am disgusted! We should employ all the soldiers in digging irrigation ditches and convert our battle ships into floating laundries. Then I want to be the judge in a baby show. . . .[85]

The Ranger captains might have been quite amused by their superior's childish tantrum.

With Hughes better able to cover the Big Bend, Captain Sanders could concentrate on his own territory—the border from Del Rio to Brownsville. There was increased smuggling of munitions to the Constitutionalists, who by September had seized Las Vacas, across from Del Rio, producing a flood of refugees. Sanders reported that both Del Rio and Eagle Pass were crowded with strange Mexicans, over 3,000 in Del Rio alone. The majority were Huerta partisans. A group of Huerta filibusters organized in Del Rio in fact tried to cross the Rio Grande and recapture Las Vacas but were stopped by the army; they were expected to try again.[86] They did, and this time they succeeded.

Nevertheless, the Constitutionalists continued to strengthen their position on the border. They were operating in the vicinity of Nuevo Laredo, which of course made the Huerta authorities in that city quite nervous. The situation in October as described by the commander of the Texas National Guard company in Laredo, was that:

> The Military Authorities in New Laredo have ordered that no one can cross to or from that town without a passport duly signed and countersigned and which has your picture pasted on it; further, you have to be O.K.'d by Mr. [Amador] Sanchez the Sheriff of this county, and if you don't vote for him there is nothing doing in the O.K. line. As a whole I think that the Sheriff is entirely too friendly with the people across the way: he knows of every secret movement that is intended by the Mexican soldiers, and about half of his time is spent over there while other American officers cannot cross at all. He is being closely watched but is a sly hombre and will hardly be tripped up again: while everything that is being said against him is based upon suppositions (suppositions that are based upon his actions) I would not advise

anyone to give him a task that would require secrecy in so far as the Mexican Government is concerned.[87]

In a further commentary, he observed that "The elections are supposed to be held next Sunday [in Nuevo Laredo] and they will probably be a monumental farce, as are most of the elections held in Mexico and in Texas on the border. . . ."[88]

Sheriff Amador Sánchez might be crooked as a snake, but he was still doggedly enforcing the neutrality laws against the Constitutionalists, who torched four frame buildings Sánchez owned near Nuevo Laredo.[89] Sánchez's actions illustrate the complexities of the local political alignments the Rangers had to deal with. Colquitt's policies further complicated their job. The governor reiterated that enforcement of the neutrality laws was a federal—not a state—matter. Thus, Captain Sanders, for one, was uncertain as to just how to proceed. The adjutant general's office assured him that:

> You have full authority to arrest all persons who are violating the law and they should be turned over to the federal authorities. If the Mexicans are organizing on the Texas side for an attack on some other faction it is your duty to advise the federal authorities and to assist in making arrests.[90]

This was all well and good, but enforcement of the law might involve shooting, and Sanders was out of ammunition. He therefore urgently requested the quarterly ammunition allotment for his company, stating that "I have no ammunition on hand and am in great need of ammunition and may be more so at any time now."[91]

By November, the center of action on the border had swung back to El Paso. General Pancho Villa's forces were increasing, and Villa was threatening to wrest control of Chihuahua state from the huertistas. One of his prime objectives was Ciudad Juárez, the largest port of entry on the border. Villa's ascendancy made Sheriff Peyton Edwards most apprehensive, for Captain Hughes reported that: "Sheriff at El Paso has been begging so hard for Rangers to help him that I thought I would stay a few days and help him out."[92] As it developed, Captain Hughes missed out on the real excitement, for he was in San Antonio on another assignment when Pancho Villa captured Juárez. For three days Villa had been launching unsuccessful frontal attacks against the city of Chihuahua, the state capital. When he finally broke off the engagement, the Huerta garrison rejoiced, thinking they had inflicted a crushing defeat on the Constitutionalist commander. But in what proved to be his most spectacular feat of arms, the resourceful Villa captured a freight train going from Juárez to Chihuahua, loaded 2,000 of his troops aboard it, notified the Huerta garrison in Juárez that the train was having to return because of *villista* activity, and by this ruse got his men into the Juárez railroad station at 2:30 a.m. on November 15. They poured from the train, taking the garrison completely by surprise, and by 5 a.m. the city was theirs. Not only had Villa surprised the huertistas, he'd also surprised the Americans. Juárez fell so quickly that Governor Colquitt had no opportunity to issue his usual warnings against bullets landing in El Paso. A few did, but fortunately no one was hurt. Villa's exploit made him an international celebrity overnight.[93] Ten days later at Tierra Blanca, south of Juárez, Villa smashed a huertista column advancing to recapture Juárez.[94] He was well on the way to controlling the entire state of Chihuahua.

Even so, Colquitt informed Hutchings that "I again take the liberty of suggesting that inasmuch as most of our troubles seem to be at points south of Laredo, that Laredo would be a more suitable place for the headquarters of Capt. Sanders's company."[95] Hutchings got the message. He wired Sanders that "The governor directs the removal of your command to Laredo from Del Rio."[96] Hutchings directed that Sanders send two men on temporary duty to Dimmit County, leave Private Anders at Sanderson and Private Speed at Shafter and take up station at Laredo with the rest of his command.[97]

Sanders arrived in Laredo on December 1, and despite some difficulty succeeded in renting a house on the outskirts to be used as the Rangers' camp. He had met all the local peace officers, "who are as nice and accommodating as can be, and as far as I can learn everything is quiet." Sanders also requested permission to purchase a new cookstove, as the old one had burned out and was left in Del Rio. The purchase was approved.[98] A week later Sanders again reported that Laredo was quiet and that "the Sheriff and Mayor have both been very nice to us and have offered to assist us in any way possible."[99] Though things might be lovely in Laredo, conditions at Palafox, some thirty miles northwest, required attention. There were complaints that Mexican refugees were stealing everything they could, and that neither the small army detachment, Immigration officers, nor county officers were doing anything about it.[100] In response to requests for help, Sanders established a two-man Ranger camp at Palafox.[101] Having done so, Sanders went home to Lockhart to recuperate over Christmas, because he had been ill for some time.[102] Referring to Hutchings's reports on the situation at Palafox, Governor Colquitt stated that:

> You refer to the lack of effective enforcement of the Neutrality and Immigration Laws. You understand that our efforts to assist the Federal Government in the enforcement of these statutes have been unsatisfactory, and, in fact, seemingly resented.[103]

Not only was Governor Colquitt irritated with the federal government, he was also unhappy with some of the Hispanics in Texas. Back on September 14,

Captain Sanders had received an urgent assignment from Colquitt himself. The Ranger captain was ordered to proceed immediately to Carrizo Springs with all available men. Sanders and the four Rangers then in camp at Del Rio took the train to Uvalde but missed their connection to Carrizo Springs. Sanders had to hire an automobile for the remainder of the trip; one man had to be left behind in Uvalde because there was no room for him in the car. He caught up with them the next day. Sanders's mission was to help guard fourteen prisoners being held in the Carrizo Springs jail awaiting the action of the grand jury.[104] These prisoners were gunrunners but of an ideologically motivated variety, and their case would have important repercussions.

On the night of September 10, several Dimmit County officers had intercepted near Carrizo Springs a party of ammunition smugglers moving toward the Rio Grande with a cargo of weaponry. The smugglers captured Deputy Sheriff Candelario Ortiz and Deputy Sheriff (and former sheriff) Eugene Buck. For the next two days the smugglers dodged the soldiers and lawmen pursuing them, and during this time they murdered Deputy Ortiz. They were finally run to earth as they neared their goal, the Alamito ford across the Rio Grande. Deputy Buck was rescued, two of the fugitives were killed and fourteen were captured, although Sheriff W. T. Gardner was in favor of shooting them all and being done with it.[105] The leader of the smugglers turned out to be an Anglo, Charles Cline, a member of the radical Industrial Workers of the World. The rest were Hispanics belonging to the Mexican Liberal Party, the magonistas.[106] The grand jury indicted the whole bunch for the murder of Deputy Ortiz.[107] Captain Sanders and his men helped the sheriff transport the prisoners to Pearsall, where they were tried on a change of venue.

The fourteen smugglers were tried individually, receiving sentences ranging from life imprisonment to six years in the penitentiary.[108] By the time the third smuggler had been convicted there were repercussions. A group of 128 Hispanics at San Marcos sent a threatening telegram on November 15, 1913, to Governor Colquitt. Not only did they protest against the sentences being handed down, but they stated that:

> We will not stand by such barbarous state of things and will appeal to the whole Mexican nation if your state want [sic] to murder men loyal to the human race and the liberty of oppressed people. We have notice [sic] that the other men are going to be convicted and sentenced to be hanged and we tell you Mr. Colquitt if such a thing happens Texas will answer before the whole Mexican community of crimes without precedent in legal history.
>
> Committee
> 908 Durango St.
> San Antonio[109]

The telegram made Colquitt mad. He fired off a letter acknowledging receipt of the telegram, pointing out that the smugglers had killed a lawman and wounded others while resisting arrest, that they'd gotten a fair trial under the laws of the state, and that "if any violence should come to American citizens as a result of your threat each of you will be held personally responsible under the law."[110] Colquitt wasn't mollified by receiving a letter from "Various True Mexicans" at San Marcos who denounced those who had sent the telegram: "these people, under the leadership of Juan Ulloa, of evil antecedents in this town, are not Mexicans, since in the meetings of the wicked so-called Liberal Mexican Party they renounce and curse the Mexican flag." They, the "peaceful and honorable San Marcans," indignantly protested against these magonistas.[111] Several days later, Sheriff Gardner of Dimmit County wrote to Colquitt from Carrizo Springs reporting that Mexicans belonging to the I.W.W. were said to be holding weekly meetings in Crystal City. The sheriff requested that at least two Rangers be stationed at Crystal City to cope with "any night-plots which these drifting Mexicans are indulging in."[112] Colquitt ordered that two of Captain Sanders's Rangers be dispatched to Crystal City.[113] All this on top of letters warning that Hispanics throughout Texas were buying Winchesters and ammunition, and that Hispanics in San Antonio were arming,[114] caused Governor Colquitt to shift his attention from protecting the border against Mexicans to combating internal subversion by Hispanics. These reports urgently needed investigating, and the man for the job was the senior Ranger captain, John R. Hughes.

Captain Hughes had already performed unaccustomed duty—the adjutant general had sent him under cover to Galveston to investigate liquor violations. Hughes duly registered at the Fremont Hotel under the alias "J. Reynolds," but he informed Hutchings that he had little hope of accomplishing anything, especially since the Galveston police, who were familiar with conditions, had made little progress. He was anxious to return to Ysleta and Valentine. Hutchings agreed and had Hughes leave Galveston.[115]

Now Hughes approached his assignment of investigating Hispanic unrest with his usual thoroughness. He reported to Colquitt that he had gone to San Antonio, had secured a list of arms dealers, had personally checked some of them, and had Sheriff John Tobin check the rest. There had been no unusual sales of guns to Hispanics, and Tobin would be notified if there were.[116] Hughes also jailed the man who had sent the threatening telegram—J. A. Hernández of San Antonio. Hernández testified before the grand jury that he had gone to San Marcos, had sponsored a dance there, and had persuaded those attending to sign the telegram. Hernández said he belonged to the I.W.W. and to the Mexican Liberal Party.[117] Captain Hughes also followed up leads in San Marcos and elsewhere in the vicinity and was able to gather information on the other signers of the telegram.[118] The upshot of Hughes's extensive investigation was that there existed no sinister conspiracy, and that the threatening telegram had merely been an ineffectual gesture by the I.W.W. and the magonistas. Nevertheless, the publicity surrounding the affair served to strengthen some people's belief that Hispanics' loyalty was questionable at best. This view was expressed by United States Senator Morris Sheppard, who stated that "most of the people living along the river are Mexican Americans who are American in name but Mexican in sympathy."[119]

Figure 1. Texas Governor Oscar Branch Colquitt (1911–1915) initially wanted to abolish the Rangers. However, he soon changed his mind and, in the spring of 1911, was perfectly willing to send all thirteen of his Rangers into Mexico, on a suicide mission, to arrest Francisco Madero, who had at least 400 guerrillas with him at the time. His use both of the Rangers and the Texas National Guard was more like that of president of the Republic of Texas, rather than governor of the State of Texas. *Photo courtesy of Texas State Library.*

Figure 2. Texas Governor James Edward Ferguson (1915–1917) has the distinction of being impeached in 1917 and was unquestionably the most crooked governor in twentieth century Texas history. Ferguson fought off two invasions of his state by Mexican troops in mufti, which in 1915 brought south Texas to the brink of a race war. In particular, he ordered the Rangers to kill the raiders and their sympathizers. Rangers, local lawmen, and vigilante groups killed an estimated 300 without benefit of trial. *Photo courtesy of Center for American History, the University of Texas at Austin, CN#00743.*

Figure 3. Texas Governor William Pettus Hobby (1917–1921) had been lieutenant governor since 1914 and assumed office in 1917, following the impeachment of Governor James Ferguson. Hobby was elected to a full term in his own right in 1918. A prudent and savvy politician, Hobby supervised the Rangers from a distance utilizing his Adjutant General. However, he was not averse to using the Rangers for political purposes. *Photo courtesy of Center for American History, the University of Texas at Austin, CN#00745.*

Figure 4. Brigadier General Henry Hutchings was the Adjutant General of Texas from 1911 until 1917. Hutchings was not even a "real Texan," having been born in England. Obsequious to a fault, he was a mediocre adjutant general. *Photo courtesy of Texas State Library.*

Figure 5. Brigadier General James A. Harley replaced Henry Hutchings as Adjutant General in late September 1917. A state senator at the time of his appointment, Harley was a much more cautious and effective AG than his predecessor. Harley was not adjutant general at the time this photograph was taken. He is on the second row, third from left, wearing glasses. In the front row, third from left, is Brigadier General John A. Hulen, the most prominent Texas National Guard (and Army general in World War I) commander of this era. *Photo courtesy of Texas State Library.*

Figure 6. Adjutant General W. D. Cope, who served from October 1919 until January 1921, standing with his Ranger captains and sergeants for a group photo in the fall of 1919. Front row, left to right, Captain Tom R. Hickman, Captain Jerry Gray, Captain Joe Brooks, Adjutant General Cope, Captain Joseph Lee Anders, Captain William Ryan. Back row, left to right, unidentified, Captain William L. Wright, unidentified, Captain Roy W. Aldrich, and Captain Charlie Blackwell. *Photo courtesy of Texas Ranger Hall of Fame and Museum.*

Figure 7. Resplendent in his uniform as a Lieutenant Colonel in the Texas National Guard, Francisco A. Chapa served three successive governors as a member of their personal military staff. The most powerful Hispanic politician in Texas, Chapa was convicted in 1912 of neutrality violation for assisting his friend General Bernardo Reyes's abortive attempt to overthrow the Francisco Madero government in Mexico. Chapa in a matter of months received an unconditional presidential pardon from President William Howard Taft. The wealthy owner of a chain of drug stores in San Antonio and the publisher of EL IMPARCIAL DE TEXAS, the most important Spanish language newspaper in the state, Chapa throughout the decade remained immersed in Mexican revolutionary intrigue. *Photo courtesy of Texas State Library.*

Figure 8. Claude Benton Hudspeth of El Paso was a two-term member in the House of Representatives before serving twelve years in the Texas State Senate. It was while he was in the State Senate that Hudspeth became a stout defender of the Rangers. Hudspeth played a not insignificant role in arranging the deployment of Rangers in west Texas, often to his ranch in Brewster County. During the 1919 Ranger investigation, he appeared before the committee to denounce those who would attack the Rangers. Hudspeth subsequently was a U.S. Congressman before retiring because of ill health. *Photo courtesy of Texas Preservation Board.*

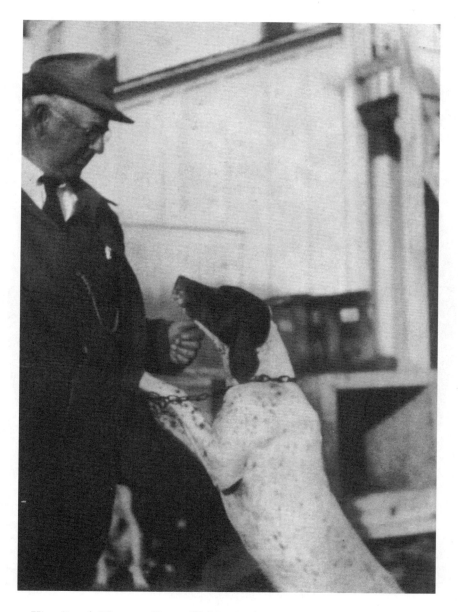

Figure 9. King Ranch Manager Caesar Kleberg is shown petting one of his favorite bird dogs. Kleberg was a politically and financially powerful figure not only in the lower Rio Grande Valley, but throughout Texas. Thanks to Kleberg, an entire Texas Ranger company practically camped on one of the divisions of the King Ranch during the "bandit war" in 1915. The defenders of the Norias subheadquarters during the August 1915 raid remained bitter at Kleberg for years because he refused to come to their assistance. Photo from *Trails and Trials of a Texas Ranger* by William Warren Sterling. Copyright ©1959 by William Warren Sterling. Assigned 1968 to the University of Oklahoma Press. *Reprinted by permission of the publisher.*

Figure 10. State Representative José Tomás Canales of Brownsville in 1919 launched a legislative investigation of the Texas Rangers. Canales fought the Rangers, and the Rangers won. *Photo courtesy of Texas Preservation Board.*

Figure 11. Major General Frederick Funston was a genuine war hero and Congressional Medal of Honor winner in the Philippines for capturing Filipino insurgent leader Emilio Aguinaldo. During the 1915–1916 "bandit war" Funston as commander of the U.S Army's Southern Department was responsible for defending the Texas border. Funston was so angry about the insurgent tactics, including the mutilation of one of his enlisted men, that he requested permission from the Secretary of War to issue "no quarter" orders to his units. *Photo courtesy of Kansas State Historical Society.*

Figure 12. Captain William J. (Bill) McDonald was unquestionably the most famous Texas Ranger Captain of the pre-1910 era. Some of his more notorious exploits—such as the 1906 Fort Brown incident—would create problems for Texas governors with the U.S. Army a decade later. McDonald served as President Woodrow Wilson's bodyguard during the 1912 presidential election campaign and was appointed in 1913 as U.S. Marshal for the Northern District of Texas. This photograph is undated but was probably taken late in his career as a Texas Ranger. *Photo courtesy of Texas State Library.*

Figure 13. Company A Texas Rangers was commanded by Captain Frank Johnson. In 1910, Johnson, who was both big and tall in the tradition of Ranger captains of this era, poses with his company. When being photographed, Rangers, for whatever reason, deliberately poked their gun barrels into the dirt and some put the barrel on the toe of their boot (one presumes the weapons were unloaded). Left to right, unidentified, unidentified, Bill McCauley, Captain Johnson, Crosby Marsden, Oscar Rountree, and Gus T. "Buster" Jones. The date on the photograph is incorrect. Jones did not become a Ranger until 1908 and it is believed that this photograph is dated 1910. *Photo courtesy of Texas Ranger Hall of Fame and Museum.*

Figure 14. While Hispanic Texas Rangers were uncommon, Hispanic Ranger Captains were rare. One was Tom Ross who commanded Company B and was a Ranger for twelve years. Ross was fired in 1911 because his sergeant, Roscoe Redus, got drunk and rode his horse through a saloon. Ross tried to cover up the incident without success. His subsequent career was as a federal court translator and as a special employee and then special agent for the federal Bureau of Investigation. He was fired by the Bureau for excessive drinking. He is shown here in the center flanked on the left by Ranger Jim Dunaway and on the right by Ranger Milam Wright. From *Trails and Trials of a Texas Ranger* by William Warren Sterling. Copyright ©1959 by William Warren Sterling. Assigned 1968 to the University of Oklahoma Press. *Reprinted by permission of the publisher.*

Figure 15. Texas Ranger Captain John R. Hughes was the last of the great captains to retire. Governor James Ferguson fired him in January 1915. Hughes, a popular and highly effective Ranger captain, was dismissed because Ferguson had numerous political hacks who needed a job. This photograph was taken in 1911 in the Adjutant General's office in the state capitol. The clean-shaven Hughes would affect a beard in retirement. *Photo courtesy of Texas State Library.*

Figure 16. Captain J. Monroe Fox, commanding Company C of the Rangers in 1911, is shown standing in front of six members of his company. They are from left to right, R. L. Morris, R. L. Burdett, Sue M. "Mack" Jester, Jim Mercer, R. G. Askew, and M. C. Cathey. Fox resigned in 1918 in protest over the firing of members of his company who carried out the infamous Porvenir massacre. *Photo courtesy of Texas Ranger Hall of Fame and Museum.*

Figure 17. Captain John J. Sanders was tall, pot-bellied, accident prone, and a less than outstanding Ranger captain. He is shown here on the north bank of the Rio Grande in an undated photograph but probably post-1915. Sanders, through no fault of his own, was in the middle of the Clemente Vergara case and the recovery of his body from Mexico. As a result of the 1919 Ranger investigation, Sanders was fired. *Photo courtesy of Texas State Library.*

Figure 18. Captain Henry Lee Ransom, shown seated at the left on the front row, was a cold-blooded killer who had no compunction about shooting anyone who might have been involved in a crime. Ordered by Governor Ferguson to kill raiders and their sympathizers during the "bandit war," Ransom carried out his orders with enthusiasm. Front row left to right, Ransom, M. G. "Blaze" Delling, former Ranger and U.S. Immigration Inspector; R. M. "Duke" Hudson, former Ranger and Sheriff, Anderson County. Second row, Jim Dunaway, Ranger; A. Y. Baker, former Ranger and Sheriff, Hidalgo County. Third row, unidentified; Jules Baker, Ranger; unidentified; Levi Davis, Ranger; and Lee Anders, Ranger. *Photo courtesy of Texas Ranger Hall of Fame and Museum.*

Figure 19. Captain William M. Ryan, a wartime Ranger, was enlisted in November 1917 and served primarily in the Laredo area. *Photo courtesy of Texas Ranger Hall of Fame and Museum.*

Figure 20. Ranger Captain W. L. Barler was a product of the World War I build-up of the Ranger Force. This photograph, showing Barler posing informally, is a rarity among photographs of Ranger captains of this era. Barler's appointment stemmed in part from the patronage of State Senator Claude Hudspeth who liked him. Barler spoke fluent Spanish, had been a rancher, and had spent time in Mexico. *Photo courtesy of Texas Ranger Hall of Fame and Museum.*

Figure 21. Texas Ranger Captain Roy Wilkinson Aldrich was both peculiar and colorful. A former Oklahoma lawman, Aldrich became a Ranger private in 1915, a sergeant in July 1917, and a captain six months later. Aldrich remained a Ranger captain (later as Ranger Quartermaster with the rank of Captain) until 1947 with one two-year interruption—the longest tenure of any Ranger in history. The photograph shows him with fancy horse and saddle regalia. *Photo courtesy of Texas Ranger Hall of Fame and Museum.*

Figure 22. Texas Ranger Captain Will L. Wright was the only Ranger captain of his era who can truly be called great. Wright, a veteran sheriff, was appointed late in the decade but repeatedly proved his worth, particularly against smugglers hauling liquor into Texas from Mexico. *Photo courtesy of Texas State Library.*

Figure 23. Texas Ranger Captain William Martin Hanson (shown here in the back row, second from right, in a white linen suit and a bow tie) was easily the most powerful Ranger during World War I. This photograph shows a group of Army draft dodgers who had resisted an attempt to arrest them, killing one Ranger and wounding another. Hanson took charge of the situation and arrested them without further casualties. *Photo courtesy of Texas Ranger Hall of Fame and Museum.*

Figure 24. William W. Sterling was not only a Texas Ranger captain, but he also became Adjutant General. During the period covered by this monograph, Sterling served as a U.S. Army scout in the lower Rio Grande Valley during the "bandit war." Sterling, who is best known for his autobiography, *Trails and Trials of a Texas Ranger*, in which he rendered judgment on decades of Ranger history, neglected to mention a couple of notches on his .45. This photo shows him in the center with four Knox County, Texas, law enforcement officers. Sterling loved to pose for photographs. *Photo courtesy of Texas Ranger Hall of Fame and Museum.*

Figure 25. Captain Jerry Gray and the fourteen members of Company A pose for this photograph at Marfa in 1918. Gray is second from left (with a holstered pistol on his saddle). Left to right, Rangers Arthur Miles, Gray, Charles Hagler, Bug Barnett, Jack Murdock, Sam Neill, A. G. Beard, Mark Langford, Frank Hillbolt, Dee Cox, Harold King, N. N. Fuller, Frank Crittenden, A. H. Woelber, and Bill Shurman. *Photo courtesy of Texas Ranger Hall of Fame and Museum.*

CHAPTER SIX

INTERNATIONAL COMPLICATIONS

THE new year saw redoubled Constitutionalist military activity, due in no small measure to President Wilson's lifting the arms embargo on February 3, 1914. A strong force under General Pablo González attacked Nuevo Laredo in early January but was repulsed with heavy losses; during the battle only one unfortunate inhabitant of Laredo was killed by a stray bullet.[1] González was the least effective of the Constitutionalist commanders. At the other end of the scale was General Pancho Villa. Following his surprise capture of Ciudad Juárez and subsequent victory at Tierra Blanca in November 1913, Villa occupied the city of Chihuahua in December. The dispirited Huerta garrison, accompanied by a host of civilians fearing Villa's wrath, made a disastrous 125-mile trek northeastward to the border town of Ojinaga. The fugitives represented the whole spectrum of Chihuahua society—from General Luis Terrazas, patriarch of the family that had controlled the state before the Revolution, riding comfortably in his coach, to the ragged wives of common soldiers, many of them with children, trudging barefoot across the desert in the dead of winter. As the survivors straggled into the border town, the huertistas, including General Pascual Orozco, dug in for a last stand, knowing they were completely cut off from reinforcements. Initially Villa delegated the attack on Ojinaga to his subordinates, for he was busy planning his advance southward down the Mexican Central railroad against Torreón, his next major objective on the way to the ultimate prize—Mexico City. The huertistas at Ojinaga, however, put up desperate resistance, and finally Villa himself had to take charge of the battle. It was over quickly, and the town fell on January 10. As had happened before, the defeated garrison, refugees, and townspeople fled across the Rio Grande to Presidio, where the huertista soldiers were disarmed and interned. The army had to march its Mexican prisoners—3,300 Huerta soldiers, 1,067 women, and 312 children—seventy miles north to Marfa, where they could be put aboard trains for transport to a prisoner of war stockade at Fort Bliss.[2] General Pascual Orozco was not among the prisoners. As he had done after his defeat at Ojinaga in 1912, Orozco managed to disappear into the Big Bend, where sympathizers hid him for six weeks. He then made his way to Mexico City, where he arrived in late February.[3]

The Rangers had played only a peripheral role in these events. They had, for example, investigated reports that huertistas from Ojinaga were moving upriver in the direction of Ciudad Juárez. After conducting careful scouts, they were able to assure General Hugh L. Scott, the Fort Bliss commander, that there were no Huerta troops along the Rio Grande between Ojinaga and Juárez. Ranger Robert Speed had participated in the army's internment of huertistas at Presidio, but the Rangers' continued presence at that town was sorely missed.[4] Dr. W. E. Ashton wrote to Colquitt in March describing conditions in Presidio as unsupportable— for Anglos at least. The good doctor complained that there was no law and order and that every night there was shooting by drunken Mexicans. He stressed that the population consisted of ten or eleven Anglos and 1,500 or 2,000 Hispanics and Mexicans. Even though most of them were law abiding, the doctor pleaded for a Ranger because "They are more independent and not controlled by local political conditions."[5]

Colquitt instructed Hutchings to have Hughes's Rangers deal with the situation in Presidio. Not until several weeks later could a man be spared for this assignment. Ranger C. P. Bishop reported that conditions at Presidio were indeed bad, owing to the presence of between 1,000 and 1,500 Mexican refugees, many of whom were armed. Since the army had only a twenty-six-man detachment at Presidio, most of the Anglo population had left as a precaution against trouble. The twelve remaining Anglos would leave if they could but had to remain for business reasons. They wanted more protection. Colquitt immediately contacted the military authorities, who indicated that additional troops would be stationed in Presidio.[6]

In the Big Bend, the pattern of sharp small-scale actions continued. One such incident occurred in early January, when a storekeeper near Candelaria reported that two Mexican rebels had tried to rob his store; he had killed one and captured the other. Deputy Sheriff Kilpatrick, mounted Customs inspector Joe Sitter, who had recovered from his head wound, and several soldiers started for the scene. As they rode along the river below Candelaria, they suddenly came under intense rifle fire from the Mexican side. The Americans scrambled for cover, and Deputy Kilpatrick began returning fire. Fortunately no one in the party was hit although the Mexicans fired hundreds of rounds. Constitutionalists across the Rio Grande later claimed to have mistaken them for a gang of bandits they had just chased into Texas.[7] Inspector Joe Sitter was involved in another incident in March. A posse consisting of himself, Customs inspector J. A. Bannister, and Sheriff Milt Chastain tried to arrest at Pilares one Lino Baeza, who was under indictment for murder. Baeza allegedly pulled a gun and the officers shot him dead. This was viewed as good riddance, for Baeza was a "bad Mexican," and he had been indicted as one of the ambushers who had killed Customs inspector Jack Howard and wounded Sitter. It later developed, though, that Baeza had nothing to do with killing Howard.[8] The people of Valentine certainly weren't upset by Baeza's demise, for

> There is a strong feeling here that the country between the G.H. & S.A. [railroad] and the river should have greater police protection. Mexican desperados frequently cross the river and commit depredations and it is almost impossible for the present small force, though composed of fearless and competent officers, to cope with them.[9]

Two weeks later, reports reached Valentine of Mexican raiders attacking three ranches in the Big Bend and making off with nearly 100 horses. The raids were well planned, timed to take place when the mounted Customs inspectors were appearing as witnesses in a court case.[10] Yet the pattern in the Big Bend and West Texas during the spring of 1914 was one of continual rustling, rather than raids by Mexican marauders.

The Ranger Force, which in early April consisted of eighteen men, was deployed all over the place:[11]

Company A	Captain Hughes	Ysleta
	Webb	Ysleta
	Goodwin	El Paso
	Roberson	Dickens
	Cardwell	Uvalde
	Craighead	Hebbronville
	Cline	Raymondville
	Vaughan	Raymondville
	Bishop	Raymondville
Company B	Captain Sanders	Laredo
	Taylor	Laredo
	Speed	Laredo
	Grimes	Palafox
	Felps	Palafox
	Willis	Carrizo Springs
	Anders	Blocker & Ford Ranch
	Patton	Blocker & Ford Ranch
Company C	Captain Fox	Austin

As is evident, Captain Hughes now had responsibility for both West Texas and the lower Rio Grande Valley, while Captain Sanders covered the middle border. And it was in the middle border that there occurred a killing that exploded into an international incident.

A resident of Webb County, Clemente Vergara, owned a ranch on the river near Palafox, across from the Mexican town of Hidalgo. Vergara also pastured some of his horses on an island in the Rio Grande in front of his ranch, an island that was part of Texas. Several of his horses had been stolen from the island. And on the morning of February 13, four Huerta soldiers and Captain Apolonio Rodríguez crossed to the island and seized eleven more of Vergara's horses, taking them into Mexico. Later, one of the party went to the riverbank opposite Vergara's house and called to the rancher, asking him to cross to the Mexican bank because the captain wanted to arrange payment for the animals. A Texas Ranger who was patrolling that sector of the riverfront advised Vergara not to go. Nevertheless, the rancher and a nephew of his crossed over in a skiff. As the boat touched the Mexican bank, two men leaped from the heavy brush into the skiff, struck Vergara on the head with a pistol several times, and dragged him off. The nephew managed to hide in the brush and subsequently made his way back to the American side. Vergara was taken to jail in Hidalgo by his huertista captors. At 2:00 a.m. on February 15, he was marched a short distance from the town, was beaten, then shot to death, and his body was left hanging from a tree.[12] The body was subsequently buried secretly. It was another in the thousands of small tragedies that occurred in Mexico during the Revolution.

Constitutionalist sympathizers immediately portrayed Vergara as a martyred model citizen, although there were allegations that he had been dealing in stolen Mexican livestock and had a dubious reputation among his fellow ranchers. But what raised the Vergara killing to a different level was the initial report that he had been kidnapped from the island—from Texas soil—and that Texas Rangers had been on the scene when this happened.[13] The very idea that a gang of Mexicans could kidnap a citizen of Texas from Texas soil, take him to Mexico, and brutally murder him produced an explosion of outrage from Governor Colquitt. The immediate target of his wrath was Captain Sanders. Hutchings telegraphed Sanders on February 26 that:

His Excellency the Governor advises me that he has called on you for a detailed telegraphic report with reference to the Vergara case and directs me to censure you for failure to have reported the day Vergara was assaulted and to explain why the Rangers present did not afford assistance when Vergara was assaulted on the Island.[14]

That same day Hutchings fired off another stinging rebuke:

> His excellency the Governor has just been in my office and is considerably wrought up that he is receiving telegrams from about everybody but you. He says I cannot take up this matter with you too strong. He wants all the facts from you by telegraph at once.[15]

The hapless Ranger captain immediately wired the governor an account of the incident as related above. And he added, "I am informed that he had a pass to cross the river signed by Sheriff Sanchez and [Juan] Garza Galan."[16] This was most awkward for the governor because, as we have seen, the unsavory Sheriff Amador Sánchez was a close political ally of Colquitt's. Since beating the rap on the 1911 Reyes conspiracy, Sánchez had not only remained as sheriff but had served as president of the Webb County school board, and he had campaigned vigorously in 1912 for Colquitt's reelection. Sánchez had also been a delegate to the 1912 Democratic national convention, which he attended with his lawyer Marshall Hicks, the national committeeman from Texas. There they had enthusiastically supported Woodrow Wilson's candidacy. And after returning to Laredo, Sánchez had handily won the Democratic primary—the only one that counted—for sheriff although his name didn't even appear on the ballot.[17] He would remain as sheriff through November 1914, surviving an assassination attempt as well as indictments for conspiracy to murder, for having more deputies than the law allowed, and for adultery.[18]

It developed that Vergara had asked Sheriff Sánchez to use his considerable influence with the local Huerta authorities so Vergara could cross the river and retrieve his stolen horses. Sánchez obliged, crossing the Rio Grande and conferring at length with the huertista commander. The sheriff returned to the Texas side and, at Vergara's request, wrote him a recommendation.[19] The evidence indicates that Sánchez set Vergara up. As the sheriff's role emerged, Colquitt ran for political cover by disassociating himself from Sánchez. He wrote that: "I am not responsible for Mr. Sanchez or what he does. The people of Webb County elected him sheriff. . . . You should not hold me responsible for any act of his, taken upon his own motion."[20]

As for Captain Sanders, he followed up his report to Colquitt with a letter of explanation to Hutchings. Sanders said he had not reported sooner because he had had to wait for the American consul, Alonso Garrett, to complete his investigation so that Sanders could obtain the information he had reported to the governor. Absent that, Sanders had only known what he had been reading in the newspaper.[21] Sanders pointed out that contrary to the newspaper accounts, no Ranger was present when Vergara crossed the river; Private Henry Felps was at Palafox and did advise Vergara against going, but he wasn't present when Vergara went.

Moreover, Sanders explained quite reasonably, "as Vergara crossed the river of his own accord and was captured on the Mexican side of the river I did not think it was a case of Kidnap; consequently did not report the matter."[22]

Once again Colquitt had fired from the hip, and he had shot himself in the foot; the assumptions on which he had based his outrage were collapsing at the very time he had publicly been making pronouncements about increasing the Ranger Force and if necessary calling out the national guard to protect the border, and demanding that Vergara's killers be brought to justice.[23] In fact, Colquitt's public pronouncements were so bellicose that former Rangers C. R. Moore and his partner C. H. Webster wrote to the adjutant general offering to reenlist if, as Colquitt had been intimating, he might send the Rangers into Mexico. Moore just wanted enough notice to give him time to resign as deputy U.S. marshal.[24] Having gotten himself out on a limb, all Colquitt could do now was try to salvage something from the debacle of the international incident that wasn't an international incident after all.

Hutchings helped in every way he could. He ordered Captain E. M. Matson, commander of the national guard company in Laredo, to conduct a thorough investigation and prepare a detailed map of the island, to prove that it was indeed Texas territory. Matson did so, being assisted by Ranger Felps.[25] At the same time, Colquitt asked the Texas attorney general for an opinion on the case. The latter replied that the only crime the huertista soldiers were guilty of in Texas was horse theft, and for that Colquitt could seek their extradition.[26] When Colquitt asked the State Department for permission to have Rangers cross the Rio Grande, it was of course immediately denied. And when he asked to which Mexican authority an extradition request should be sent, Secretary of State Bryan replied that it should go to "the chief executive authority" of Mexico. Since the United States recognized neither Huerta nor Carranza, this vague instruction in effect meant that Washington was washing its hands of the matter and Colquitt was on his own. The frustrated governor finally decided to request extradition from both the huertista and *carrancista* governors of the State of Coahuila, with little hope of success despite assurances from the huertista military governor of Coahuila, General Joaquín Maas, that he'd ordered the arrest of the horse thieves wanted in Texas.[27]

The Huerta authorities continued to deny any role in Vergara's disappearance. Moreover, they claimed he was a Mexican, not an American citizen, which was untrue. General Alberto Guajardo, commander at Piedras Negras, declared that he had ordered Captain Apolonio Rodríguez at Hidalgo to release Vergara. Rodríguez denied ever having received such an order. Guajardo then asserted that Vergara had started under guard from Hidalgo to Piedras Negras but on the way had escaped and joined a band of Constitutionalist guerrillas.[28] This was an innovative variant on the ley fuga—not that the prisoner had been shot while attempting to escape but that he had in fact escaped and thus the authorities had no idea where he was.

Where Vergara was was in the cemetery at Hidalgo, buried in a shallow grave, and the recovery of his body caused an uproar in and of itself. Captain Sanders telegraphed to Colquitt from Laredo that "I proceeded to Hidalgo, Mexico, obtained the body of Vergara and now have it here."[29] Everyone naturally assumed that Rangers had crossed into Mexico, and another international incident was in the making. Colquitt coyly refused to say whether Sanders had entered Mexico on his orders, but the clear implication was that no international border would deter the governor when the rights of Texans were at stake. Evidently Colquitt was trying to squeeze some favorable publicity out of the incident, because he knew full well that Sanders had not crossed the river. In both a telephone report to the governor and in his written report, the Ranger captain made that point quite clear. He, Rangers Hines and Felps, Consul Garrett, and several others had gone to Palafox on March 7. Vergara's body was brought across the river on a stretcher about 3:30 a.m. on March 8. Sanders did not know who had exhumed the body, which was identified by Vergara's son and was taken to a mortician in Laredo.[30] Colquitt ordered the body held at Laredo until Adjutant General Hutchings could arrive and personally supervise the examination of the corpse by two physicians.[31] Not only was Hutchings investigating the Vergara affair, but Captain Hughes was called in to assist him.[32] As to who had recovered the body and brought it back to Texas, it was Vergara's brother-in-law, acting for Vergara's widow, who had hired a party of Mexicans to perform that task.[33] The Dallas *News* commented rather cynically:

> The governor claims that he is receiving many telegrams of congratulation over the recovery of the body. *News* says that he probably did not even know that a move to recover the body was in progress. The Ranger captain must be a hero if the Gov. is to have any glory, and Sanders contends that he had nothing to do with the recovery of the body. The *News* says that it is not clear who brought the body, though one is led to infer that it was brought by Mexicans living in Mexico. Report is that it cost the relatives of Vergara $400 to get it—and thus the whole thing becomes a commercial transaction with little glory involved.[34]

When Hutchings reported to the governor on his investigation of the Vergara affair, he explained Sanders's telegram, the "I proceeded to Hidalgo, Mexico, obtained the body of Vergara and now have it here" wire, as being Consul Garrett's fault. It seems that Garrett wired the State Department that he had returned from Hidalgo because he had planned to go to Hidalgo to investigate and the State Department knew the town's location. Garrett feared the Department wouldn't know where Palafox was located. At Sanders's request, Garrett wrote out Sanders's telegram for him and in doing so inadvertently stated "Hidalgo" instead of "Palafox"; Sanders didn't notice the inaccuracy. Hutchings reported that both Garrett and Sanders agreed on this version of events.[35] Army Chief of Staff General Leonard Wood, badly worried that if Rangers had crossed the river a diplomatic incident would result, ordered an extensive investigation. The army concluded that no Rangers had crossed into Mexico.[36]

It appeared that the governor's remaining hope of "glory" now revolved around recovering Vergara's eleven stolen horses. Here again Hutchings was eager to do his master's bidding. He wrote to his assistant from Laredo on March 13 that "I am extremely anxious to recover these Vergaras horses for the credit of the governor & will consequently be delayed a few days yet."[37] Colquitt sent a formal request for delivery of the horses not only to the huertista commander at Nuevo Laredo but also to President and General Victoriano Huerta himself.[38] Huerta ordered that the horses be returned.[39] Colquitt spent what was apparently an inordinate amount of time and energy trying to get the wretched horses back. He fired off communications to various other Mexican officials, kept giving Hutchings detailed instructions on the matter, and finally told the adjutant general to receive the horses individually if the Mexicans wouldn't return them all at once.[40] Hutchings did receive one horse, which he turned over to Vergara's heirs. The adjutant general then detailed Captain Sanders to go to Eagle Pass, where the Mexican consul delivered two more horses and promised that four more would be forthcoming. Vergara's heirs rejected the two animals as not being theirs. Colquitt finally suggested that if the Mexicans for whatever reason did not deliver the rest of the stolen animals, they compensate Vergara's heirs monetarily.[41] There is no indication that the Mexicans either paid for or delivered any more of the horses.

Speaking of delivery, Colquitt offered a $200 reward for the delivery of each of Vergara's five killers to the Texas Rangers or to any jail in Texas.[42] Captain Hughes received information from one of his contacts, H. N. Gray of the Carranza intelligence service, that two of the killers were said to be on a ranch about ten miles from Del Rio. Hughes quickly left Austin to check out this lead, but it proved unproductive. On this same trip, Hughes twice tried to see the Mexican consul at Eagle Pass about the Vergara horses, but both times the consul was unavailable.[43] Meanwhile, the reward offer was causing heartburn in Washington. Officials in both the War and State Departments expressed serious concern; they didn't question Colquitt's right to offer a reward, but they worried that somebody might kidnap the fugitives and take them to Texas, thus causing an international incident. Colquitt stated that "I am not worried over Washington's troubles" and declined further comment about the reward.[44]

As it happened, Washington had good reason to be concerned. Colonel T. W. Griffith, commanding the 19th Infantry at Eagle Pass, reported to Southern

Department headquarters on March 25 that while Adjutant General Hutchings was negotiating with Mexican officials for the return of the horses:

> General Hutchings further admitted to me that while his open mission was to secure the horses above referred to, he was endeavoring under orders from the Governor of Texas, to employ the necessary number of men on this side [of] the Rio Grande to cross and kidnap the following named Mexicans [five men are named] who are the men he holds responsible for the capture and murder of Vergara. General Hutchings left here for Austin at 1:55 PM yesterday saying that he would return here in a few days when he expects to conclude all arrangements for carrying out his kidnaping scheme.[45]

Griffith's report perhaps explains why Colquitt had telegraphed Hutchings at Eagle Pass on the 21st: "All you are trying to do and some things you are not trying to do reported to Associated Press from Eagle Pass. Look out for leaks or our plans will be spoiled."[46]

Brigadier General Tasker H. Bliss, commanding the Southern Department, was not amused by the antics of Colquitt and Hutchings. He issued confidential orders to Colonel Griffith to "resort to whatever measure that may be necessary" to prevent the execution of the illegal scheme. Just so there would be no misunderstanding, Griffith was ordered to "break up this illegal expedition regardless of the character of the persons who may form such an expedition—that is to say whether they be officials of the State of Texas of whatever rank [i.e., Hutchings and the Rangers] or persons employed by the State or whether they be any other persons whatsoever."[47] The army also deployed detachments of the 14th Cavalry to apprehend the members of the proposed expedition should they try to cross the river.

Those who have written about the Vergara case[48] have been unaware of this most startling aspect of the affair—the governor of Texas instructing his adjutant general to arrange multiple kidnapings in a foreign country. Presumably because the army spoiled the fun, Colquitt's plan failed. And the main reason it failed was because Hutchings couldn't keep his mouth shut. But it is much more probable that Hutchings had wit enough to realize that Colquitt's scheme was fraught with peril and deliberately leaked it to the army hoping the military would shut the operation down, as in fact happened. (This scheme brings to mind the kidnaping in Mexico and delivery to the United States of several men allegedly implicated in the kidnaping, torture, and murder of DEA agent Enrique Camarena by a drug kingpin in Guadalajara in 1985.)

Colquitt may have been unpopular with the army, but he was much more unpopular with the Brownsville *Daily Herald*. The newspaper missed no opportunity to ridicule the governor as a jingoistic buffoon interested only in self-aggrandizement.[49] As part of this press campaign, fueled by Colquitt's criticism of President Wilson's Mexican policy, the newspaper acidly commented on Colquitt's desire to expand the Ranger Force for border duty. It jeered at Colquitt's statement: "Give me 100 Texas rangers and I can do more toward keeping law and order in Texas than 10,000 United States troops." The newspaper commented sarcastically: "Doubtless, Governor, but why 100? If the Governor of Texas knows anything about border conditions, he knows that ten Texas rangers can give the border all the protection it needs. The Governor's bluff is a pretty one—and incidentally an utterly ruinous one." The *Daily Herald* petitioned "the Governor to send his hundred rangers to Texarkana or Texline, or some place where they are as badly needed as they are here." The crux of the *Daily Herald*'s fury toward Colquitt was that such a "blatant speech" devastated the price of real estate in the Lower Rio Grande Valley by creating the impression that the border was being laid waste by Mexican marauders. Such an impression scared off homeseekers and investors. The newspaper repeatedly assured its readers that Colquitt was a solitary scaremonger and that substantial peace reigned in the area.[50]

This wasn't quite the case. In the midst of the Brownsville *Daily Herald*'s crusade against Colquitt, Captain Hughes arrived in town. He announced that the citizens of Sebastian and Lyford, villages in northern Cameron County, had appealed to Colquitt for protection following a series of killings, and Hughes was sent to determine whether a Ranger detachment should be stationed in Lyford. He later said that, because the people of Lyford had failed to make acceptable arrangements to house the Rangers, no detachment would be coming, and he returned to Austin.[51] Hughes's version was disputed by the mayor of Lyford, who wrote to the *Daily Herald* that:

> the council at Lyford had arranged for a good house with a large lot for pasture and plenty of good water, besides agreeing to furnish horses and to always have automobiles ready for rangers' service. Hughes was present at the council meeting and knows the facts.[52]

The *Daily Herald* speculated that whereas the appeal for Rangers at Lyford and Sebastian might have been sincere, nevertheless it contributed to the perception of an insecure border region and thus hurt the Valley and retarded its development. In fact, the newspaper suggested, the appeal might have been made just to cripple the Democratic party. "This part of the border has never been as free from depredations as it has been since this war [the struggle against Huerta] began."[53]

There was some justification for the *Daily Herald*'s optimism. Not only had there been no depredations from Mexico, but Brownsville itself was beginning to shed its Wild West past and enter the twentieth century. For instance, the title of "city marshal" was replaced by that of "police chief." Although there were still occasional abuses by the police, and sporadic incidents between the police and the sheriff's departments, their feud was no longer as ferocious and deadly as it had been. In part this reflected a move to increase the number of Anglos in the police department, thus reducing ethnic animosity, and in part it reflected a growing political maturity, with businessmen running for local office on compromise platforms, and the power of bosses such as Jim Wells beginning to wane.[54] The municipal election on April 7 was blessedly peaceful, and Captain Hughes was the only Ranger present.

He was called away the next day:

> Captain Hughes left Brownsville this afternoon for Mission to investigate the occurrence of yesterday when a band of men crossed the Rio Grande and for several hours terrorized the residents of the little town of Madero, on the Rio Grande and 3 miles from Mission.[55]

The *Daily Herald*'s account went on to say that the marauders reportedly consisted of between twenty and forty Constitutionalists, who returned to Mexico after shooting up the town. Although luckily no one had been wounded at Madero, the people in Mission urgently appealed to Austin and Washington for protection. The report of course caused considerable excitement. The excitement quickly subsided when Hughes returned to Brownsville and announced that the events at Madero were greatly exaggerated. The Ranger captain had encountered considerable reticence on the part of the locals, for "Mexicans at this end of the border are reluctant to give information to American officials." Some thirty to thirty-five Constitutionalists had indeed crossed the Rio Grande to Madero, but their intentions had been peaceful; they were not in uniform, they left their rifles behind, and those with pistols left them on the American riverbank. They then proceeded to carry out their mission—to have a few beers at the Madero saloon. There had been no shooting, and the invaders, decorously drunk, had returned to Mexico.[56] The army also investigated the affair and reached the same conclusion, adding that the press reports had been concocted in San Antonio, and that the "people of Mission object to newspaper reports as likely to create [a] false impression of conditions near their town."[57] The flurry of excitement about Madero paled into insignificance, though, by what happened two weeks later.

The Constitutionalist cause rapidly gained momentum. Increasingly, Constitutionalist forces enjoyed both higher morale and superior firepower as they engaged the armies of the crumbling Huerta regime. Adding to the pressure on Huerta, the United States maintained powerful naval squadrons off the coasts of Mexico, ostensibly to evacuate foreigners if necessary. One such squadron was off the strategic gulf port of Tampico, through which Mexican oil was exported.

By early April, Constitutionalists were at the outskirts of Tampico, and the Huerta garrison was understandably nervous. In this charged atmosphere there occurred an incident that would have momentous consequences. On April 9, a whaleboat from the USS *Dolphin* inadvertently docked in a restricted military zone. The whaleboat was seized by huertista soldiers and its crew detained. The American sailors and their boat were soon released with apologies, and that seemed to be that—a minor misunderstanding. But Rear Admiral Henry T. Mayo, commanding the United States squadron, chose to interpret the incident as a deliberate insult to the sovereignty of the United States, for the whaleboat had been flying the American flag. The Tampico affair now became an international incident indeed, with diplomatic communications flying between Washington and Mexico City. The Wilson administration demanded that Huerta formally apologize, punish those responsible, and fire a twenty-one-gun salute to the American flag. The Mexican strongman refused to accede to all the American demands, whereupon the United States bombarded and seized Veracruz, Mexico's largest seaport, on April 21. The American attack produced a wave of patriotic fervor in Mexico, which Huerta unsuccessfully tried to turn to his own advantage. Constitutionalist commanders rejected his plea that they join him in driving out the invaders. And with the U.S. Army occupying Veracruz, Huerta's lifeline to Europe was cut. His days in power were numbered.[58]

With relations between the United States and Mexico in crisis, many of the Anglo inhabitants along the border were terrified that war with Mexico might erupt, producing Mexican raids into Texas coupled with some kind of uprising among the state's Hispanics, whom many considered a Fifth Column. Governor Colquitt announced that he wouldn't hesitate to mobilize the Texas National Guard, which was to be recruited to wartime strength. Moreover, Colquitt urged President Wilson to have the army seize the Mexican border towns.[59]

Colquitt's most ambitious policy for border protection was a plan for a home guard, to be directed by Texas Rangers. After conferring with Hutchings, Captain Hughes, and an assistant attorney general, the governor announced that the Ranger Force would be increased and empowered to organize home guard companies of from twenty to forty men in each border town. One Ranger stationed in every town would command the company and arrange for its armament. Captain Hughes would command the Brownsville district, Captain Sanders the Laredo district, and Captain Fox would presumably be in charge at El Paso. Hutchings requested 500 Springfield rifles from the federal government.[60] This ambitious plan ultimately failed because the federal government wanted no part of it and the state simply couldn't afford it. Still, some communities organized home guards on their own, among them Sanderson, Del Rio, and San Benito, as did, incidentally, several border towns in Arizona.[61] Austin was deluged with appeals for Ranger protection; as Colquitt commented to Hutchings regarding one such petition: "I am getting similar requests from about every community now between El Paso and Brownsville, and it will be impossible for us to furnish Rangers in all instances as requested."[62] There was a similar deluge of requests from those wanting to organize—and command—volunteer units, whether for war with Mexico or for local protection. One of these requests, incongruously, was from the Reverend Ben B. Hunt, of Columbus.[63] There were also many applications for enlisting in the Rangers, applications that had to be rejected for lack of funding.

In the midst of all this excitement, Colquitt took the controversial step of rushing sixteen companies of the Texas National Guard to the Brownsville area. As he later explained:

> I am aware that there are some people who would criticize me regardless of what I might do. If I had failed to send State troops to the border, and Mexican bandits had blown up the pumping stations belonging to the immense irrigation plants in the Brownsville country, or robbed and burned the town of Brownsville, these same people would have blamed me for not sending State troops for the protection of these people.[64]

Colquitt having forced the government's hand, the army moved more than 1,000 soldiers into the area, and as they arrived, the Texas troops were withdrawn.[65]

In the event, war with Mexico did not occur, but the level of tension along the border remained quite high, with the vastly outnumbered Anglo inhabitants remaining apprehensive as to the intentions of their Hispanic neighbors.[66] (The situation was not dissimilar to that of Jewish settlers in the West Bank today.) For example, in May the Valley Protective League was organized to combat widespread thieving from farmers in Hidalgo and Cameron Counties. (There were no black or Hispanic farmers in all of Cameron County). Likewise, cattlemen in the Valley organized a protective association of their own to suppress a rising tide of livestock being rustled into Mexico. Texas ranchers had reportedly lost some 8,000 head of cattle this way during the past year.[67] Captain Hughes commented in early June that just in the last few weeks "nearly 100 horses and numerous head of cattle" had been stolen and driven into Mexico. Hughes expressed the hope that the Rangers and the army patrols along the border would be able to curtail the thieving.[68] The thieves evidently feared the Rangers more than the army, for the governor announced that he would thoroughly investigate "a report reaching him indirectly from the Madero ranch on the Rio Grande that there is a standing reward among Mexicans of five hundred cattle for the head of every Texas Ranger."[69] This proved to be only a rumor, but it provided Captain Sanders with the opportunity to offer a reward of his own—$500 each for the Mexicans who had offered the above reward, delivered on Texas soil.[70]

Although many border residents clamored for the Rangers to come and save them, the organization continued to have its detractors, and periodically Colquitt had to deal with complaints about the Rangers. One was from Mrs. Virginia Yeager, a sturdy widowed ranch woman in McMullen County. She wrote to Colquitt that Oscar Thompson, sheriff of Jim Hogg County, was using the Rangers to further his private interests: "This month he brought a posse of Rangers and other armed men to intimidate me over the possession of some land which I had bought and he had leased." She had refused to let him use the land without payment, which he refused to make. She added that "I am perfectly sure that tho [sic] Thompson is a sheriff he has no right to bring deputies nor State Rangers into a civil case without a court order and there was none." In her opinion Sheriff Thompson was able to act in this arbitrary manner because of her ranch's isolation, and she appealed to Colquitt for help. This was a serious charge, and the governor ordered an investigation.[71] Captain Fox drew the assignment of going to Hebbronville, the county seat of Jim Hogg County, and determining the facts. The man on the spot was not Sheriff Thompson but Ranger Pat Craighead, who had been assigned to assist the sheriff at Hebbronville for more than a year. Craighead had done a good job, according to Sheriff Thompson with whom he had become close friends. Not only did the ranchers in the region, whether Anglo or Hispanic, have confidence in Craighead, but he could discharge many of his duties by using Thompson's automobile, no small consideration for a man who had lost a leg in the 1910 San Benito ambush. But Craighead's Ranger career was now in jeopardy, for he had accompanied Thompson to Mrs. Yeager's place. Fortunately for Craighead, the whole thing turned out to be a misunderstanding on Mrs. Yeager's part. Craighead stated that the only reason he had gone was because Sheriff Thompson had asked him to. Mrs. Yeager had announced that her son would run Thompson off if he came, and the boy had a six-shooter and a Winchester; Thompson wanted no trouble, and he had Craighead go along specifically to prevent any. Craighead was the only Ranger in Thompson's "posse"— the rest were unarmed surveyors the sheriff had hired to check the property line. Besides Craighead's statement, Captain Fox attached to his report a letter from Mrs. Yeager explaining that since she knew Craighead was a Ranger she just assumed the others accompanying Sheriff Thompson were also. Adjutant General Hutchings declared the matter closed.[72] Craighead, incidentally, would succeed Thompson as sheriff in 1916.

The governor received a more serious complaint from a resident of the Big Bend, J. J. Kilpatrick, of the Kilpatrick Milling and Ginning Company at Candelaria. Kilpatrick explained that:

We live on the very banks of the Rio Grande where we have extensive business interests. Beyond us on the Mexican side is a wild, mountainous country infested with thieves, robbers, and murderers. . . . In fact, Candelaria and the Pilares border is the most dangerous along the great river. Owing to the killing of a Mexican prisoner below here nearly a year ago by rangers and the recent killing of a Mexican outlaw by the river guards and others, the Mexican people up and down the river have become greatly stirred up against what few Americans live in this vicinity. Hence any unreasonable and illegal acts now committed against Mexicans in the interior will but add to the bad relations already existing between the two races.[73]

Kilpatrick then proceeded to denounce Ranger Jefferson Eagle Vaughan for having mistreated Mexicans at the town of Valentine about the 13th of April. Vaughan had clubbed a man over the head with his six-shooter until blood was drawn, just because the Mexican had urged his friends not to assist the Anglos in recovering some stolen horses. Not only had Vaughan clubbed the man, but he had thrown him in jail. Then Vaughan had induced Kilpatrick's son, J. J., to file a complaint against the prisoner for having stolen his sixgun. Nor was this all. Vaughan had seized a pair of binoculars and a rifle from the saddle of a second Mexican, who was not even a U.S. citizen. Kilpatrick stated that this individual was the only Mexican who had helped locate the killers of Customs inspector Jack Howard, who'd been Kilpatrick's son-in-law. Ranger Vaughan had also arbitrarily jailed this second Mexican, who was deprived of food and drink for the next twenty-four hours; he had had to perjure himself before the justice of the peace by testifying against the first Mexican in order to gain his freedom. Kilpatrick's son had been able to keep the outraged Hispanic population of Valentine from tearing down the jail and liberating their abused companions. Kilpatrick suggested that the affair was "a shame & would be fine reading for some of your newspaper enemies to holler over the state." Kilpatrick ended by declaring that "We make no complaint against the ranger idea. . . . Our complaint is against the cruel and illegal acts of an individual member for the most part of a useful and excellent body of men." He requested that the governor have Captain Hughes investigate the matter.

The governor did so, and his reply to Kilpatrick was contemptuous. Captain Hughes had informed Colquitt that Kilpatrick was a sleaze—he had been indicted for receiving cattle stolen in Mexico as well as for smuggling guns and ammunition into Mexico. Colquitt informed Kilpatrick that "I think the Rangers have been doing very effective and efficient service on the border, notwithstanding your effort to ridicule them."[74] The governor's view of Kilpatrick's complaint was reinforced as Ranger Vaughan's side of the incident became known. Vaughan stated that "The Mexican Lino Barragan was walking the streets of Valentine with a belt of cartridges buckled on him and a rifle on his saddle." He attracted Vaughan's attention. When the Ranger asked who he was, he learned that Barragán "was one of Kilpatrick's Mexicans and he did not belong on this side but lived in Mexico. I was also told that he was suspicioned of being implicated in the theft of some horses from Mr. Burford who has a ranch near Valentine." Vaughan said he took Barragán's rifle off the saddle as well as a bag partly filled with cartridges and was asking him about the horses when "an other [sic] big Mexican came up to us with a knife in his hand and using vile language towards me and the Gringoes generally. He told Lino not to tell the Gringo Cabrone [sic] any thing about the lost horses, and said the Mexicans ought to steal all the horses the Gringoes Cabrones [sic] had. About this time he walked up close to me in a threatening manner with the knife in his hand still abusing me. I hit him with my pistol and got him on the neck." Vaughan jailed the man, whose name was Guillermo Moreno. The Ranger then asked Jim Kilpatrick what connection he had with the Mexican; Kilpatrick said Moreno had stolen a pistol from him, and he swore out a complaint before the justice of the peace. Kilpatrick also claimed—and received—the binoculars.[75] Mounted Customs inspector Joe Sitter also made a statement corroborating Vaughan's version. Sitter witnessed the altercation between Vaughan and Moreno. According to Sitter, Vaughan hit the Mexican once with his pistol when the latter came at him with a knife. Further, Sitter said Moreno was given water within an hour after being jailed, and that he was fed that evening and the next morning before his release. And, "In regard to the character of Guillermo Moreno will say that about six years ago I arrested him for smuggling a horse, and since that time he has been before the courts several times for violation of the laws. He is considered a dangerous Mexican."[76] Additional support for Vaughan came from L. D. Louthen, a rancher and cattle buyer in Valentine, who was also an eyewitness to the events. He not only corroborated Vaughan's version but said he and the other "law abiding citizenship of this part of the country highly commend Vaughan for what he did. . . ."[77] Captain Hughes in his report stated that everyone he had spoken with in Valentine thought Vaughan's actions were justified.[78] Hutchings forwarded Hughes's report to Colquitt, and that was the end of the matter.

Vaughan's "bending" a gunbarrel on a recalcitrant offender was brutal, but it was nothing unique to the Rangers; pistol whipping was a standard law enforcement technique, used by officers in the absence of a nightstick. When "bending" a gunbarrel over the head of an offender was done properly, as with a Colt .45 single-action pistol with a $5^{1}/_{2}$" barrel, the man dropped like he'd been pole-axed. "Bending" was certainly a more humane way of subduing an offender than was shooting him, although there were lawmen who favored the latter technique. But there was an art to "bending," and if not done right the situation could get messy. For example, Luis Parra, a deputy sheriff from San Elizario, was charged with aggravated assault by Casimiro Reyes, who testified that while Parra was arresting him he struck Reyes eleven times on the head with his six-shooter. "Parra admitted striking the prisoner but said the taps were light ones else Reyes would have been unable to count after the first one." This seemed an eminently reasonable explanation to the jury, who acquitted Parra after only a few minutes' deliberation.[79] Then there was Agustín Salinas, night marshal of Laredo, who was subduing a prisoner by "bending" a pistol over his head. The weapon accidentally discharged and blew the prisoner's brains out.[80]

The most tiresome of the people complaining about the Rangers was also one of the most exotic specimens of the human flotsam that the Mexican Revolution deposited on the Texas border—Dr. C. F. Z. Caracristi. He wired Colquitt accusing American cattlemen of dealing in stolen Mexican livestock, and as a result "I was kidnaped from the Hotel Hamilton, Laredo, by armed cattlemen, taken to Nye Station in [an] automobile, put on a train for San Antonio and threatened with death if I returned."[81] He implied that the Rangers were involved in his expulsion and requested that Colquitt appoint an impartial investigator—someone unknown to the Rangers or other officers. "If my humiliation and mental anguish should result in awakening the public conscience of the cattle thieving syndicate of the Rio Grande I will feel my suffering fully paid for." Caracristi hastened to assure the governor that the "reputable people" of Laredo had nothing to do with his banishment and it would be "an insult to those honest people to impute it to them, for it would hurt that town as I am widely known throughout the United States."[82]

Caracristi certainly did not suffer from low self-esteem. He described himself as a Virginian of Austrian ancestry who had studied law in Washington, had carried out a confidential mission in South America for Secretary of State Blaine, had been a soldier, and was a Ph.D. geologist of international reputation who had represented large corporations on four continents. He said that prior to the Mexican Revolution he had been a business associate of the oligarchs who controlled the state of Chihuahua, had made Texas his home for the past fourteen years, and was friends with the rich and powerful. Caracristi didn't just drop names; he fired salvos of names of influential personages whose wrath he could call down on those who crossed him. That he had been around was indisputable. In 1905, for instance, the El Paso press described him as a " noted mineralogist and an Italian count" who claimed to have discovered immense sulphur deposits near Toyah.[83] In 1910, he was again in El Paso, the reporter describing him as "one of the most prominent mining men of the United States" who was en route to Chihuahua and then to South America, "where he has very large coal and petroleum interests."[84] And when the Mexican Revolution erupted, he claimed to be one of Madero's advisors in San Antonio: "Dr. Caracristi is a member of the revolutionary junta, and is a lawyer, physician and world traveler." Caracristi then joined the maderista junta in El Paso as diplomatic agent and legal counsel. In early 1911 he suborned the Mexican consul in El Paso, who gave the rebels information on Díaz's troop movements in Chihuahua and a copy of the government's code in exchange for a payoff of $3,000, in weekly installments of $300. Caracristi quit giving Madero advice but announced that he was to receive an important government post when Madero became president. Not only did Madero's intimates deny the allegation, but as president, Madero expelled Caracristi from Mexico in October, 1912, as a "pernicious foreigner."[85] Caracristi claimed he had been authorized by Senator Albert B. Fall of New Mexico to investigate revolutionary conditions in Mexico.

Caracristi ended up in Laredo, making the Hotel Hamilton his home for the next eighteen months. He had no visible means of support but lived very well. He let it be known he was a Huerta spy and was a close friend and advisor of General Félix Díaz, and indeed he was in contact with Díaz.[86] He made it his business to pry into other people's business, doing everything he could to discomfit the Constitutionalists and developing close ties with Sheriff Sánchez. Eventually he made himself so obnoxious that a vigilante committee ran him out of town. Yet they did so in a most gentlemanly fashion, avoiding any violence or even the use of vile language. Because Caracristi was flat broke, they bought his train ticket to San Antonio and even took up a collection so he would have spending money for a few days. In San Antonio he made the elegant Hotel Bender his headquarters and began deluging Governor Colquitt with demands for justice.

Colquitt replied that he was assigning Captain Sanders to investigate Caracristi's charges and make a report but explained that as governor there wasn't much he personally could do, and he recommended that Caracristi seek redress through the courts.[87] Sanders, who was stationed in Laredo, informed the governor that he had already begun an investigation of Caracristi's expulsion from Laredo and that he had been soliciting the opinions of a number of local officials and businessmen regarding Caracristi. The Ranger captain reported that the almost universal view was—good riddance. As for the allegations of cattle stealing, which Caracristi claimed to have been investigating merely "to serve a friend," Sanders found no evidence against those cattlemen who were accused, and whom he personally knew to be honorable men. To substantiate his conclusions, the Ranger captain secured statements from the deputy collector of Customs, a prominent rancher, the assistant United States attorney, the Immigration inspector in charge, and two leading businessmen. The statements varied only in the writers' degree of dislike for Caracristi. Several even suggested that he was demented.[88]

Caracristi indignantly denied their portrayal of him, stressed that he was in mortal danger, and requested that Colquitt issue him a Ranger commission so that he could arm himself for protection. He also said he "had charges to make against Captain Sanders," whose Rangers had allegedly cooperated in his expulsion. Furthermore,

> . . . in view of the fact that Captain Sanders was angry at my sending you my first message regarding stolen cattle and treated me with a lack of courtesy, his present recommendations can logically be on the same line. The Captain

is unquestionably an honest man but his lack of education and the fact that he is the constant associate of the very men who are responsible for present border conditions—men who have become rich over the despoiling of Mexican ranches—leads me to foreshadow the terms of his report to you.[89]

Yet he admitted that "I am a nervous and mental wreck over the treatment received at Laredo." And his letters became more belligerent. He demanded, for instance, that Colquitt write him a letter—for publication—specifying what Colquitt was doing to answer Caracristi's allegations, things such as his assertion that Captain Sanders and two of his Rangers "went looking for" Caracristi when they learned of his original appeal to Colquitt, or that Sanders's report had been made to discredit Caracristi.[90] Colquitt had grown weary of Caracristi's constant complaints, so he did the sensible thing and turned the whole matter over to Hutchings. But the governor wanted no whitewash of Sanders, instructing Hutchings that:

> I request you to make thorough investigation of any insinuation against the Rangers, and that this investigation be free from partiality on their account. If the Rangers are standing in with any body, I will not consent to their standing in after proof of this fact is made known to me.[91]

Hutchings asked Caracristi to make specific, concrete charges rather than constantly dealing in generalities. Instead, Caracristi replied that he was leaving for Boston to lecture on border conditions and then to Washington to testify before the Senate Foreign Relations Committee. He implied that unless Colquitt issued the statement he had demanded, he would go public regarding the governor and the "cattle mafia." He reminded the adjutant general that he was a man of considerable influence. Hutchings replied coldly that the governor would not be intimidated, and that Caracristi could publicize whatever he chose.[92] Still, correspondence continued to flow between Caracristi, Colquitt, and Hutchings, culminating in Caracristi's informing Colquitt that he was leaving for an extended cruise on his yacht, and then he was going to England. Whether he returned as an American or an Englishman was entirely up to Colquitt and his acceding to Caracristi's demands.[93] How Colquitt discharged this awesome responsibility is unknown. In early 1916, however, Caracristi was in El Paso saying he was representing a syndicate of United States and English capitalists prepared to invest $10,000,000 in Mexico on his recommendation.[94]

The available documents do not indicate whether Caracristi ever presented concrete proof of his allegations. In all probability he did not. Yet, as we shall see, it was reliably alleged that some cattlemen were not above making a fast buck out of the conditions produced by the Revolution. Significantly, in July Colquitt transferred Captain Sanders's Company B from Laredo back to Del Rio. The local newspaper was at a loss to explain why, commending the Rangers for conducting themselves in a gentlemanly manner. The newspaper speculated that the transfer "was perhaps at the instigation of some law violators that representations made to the governor resulted in his recalling the rangers from Laredo."[95] Perhaps so, but some Hispanic residents of Laredo were not sorry to see them go, for they had been the particular objects of the Rangers' attention. Back on April 23, the Huerta garrison had evacuated Nuevo Laredo, setting fire to the town before they left. The largely Hispanic population of Laredo, overwhelmingly sympathetic to the Constitutionalists, reacted to the evacuation of Nuevo Laredo with jubilation, but "on Saturday the 25th, the Mexicans became so disorderly and unruly that it became necessary for the Rangers to whip seven, pistols being used, but no shots fired."[96]

Company B left Laredo for their new station at Del Rio on July 17, but Captain Sanders wasn't with them. He was indisposed, but not from his usual ailments—he had been shot, but not in the line of duty, and as he hastened to assure the adjutant general, "was not shot by a Mexican." It seems that Mrs. Sanders had come for a visit, and she had brought their young grandson along. The lad was presumably thrilled to see his famous grandpa at a real Ranger camp. Unfortunately, the inquisitive youngster began examining Sanders's six-shooter and accidently shot his grandfather in the right calf. The soft-nosed bullet ripped through the calf, severely damaging the tissues. The wound became infected, requiring several operations. For more than a month Sanders experienced a great deal of what the medical profession refers to as "discomfort," that is, excruciating pain. Not until July 22 was he able to leave his bed in Mercy Hospital and join his men in Del Rio. Soon thereafter, though, he decided to go home to Lockhart to be treated by his family physician.[97] It again fell to Sergeant Grimes to run the eight-man Company B.

At the other end of the Texas border, tensions hadn't been as high following the American seizure of Veracruz. True, on April 21 detachments of cavalry and infantry had patrolled the streets of south El Paso, the Hispanic *barrio* known as Chihuahuita. The city had also added ten men to the police force, and deputy sheriffs were deployed in Smeltertown. Moreover, the next day Ranger O. W. Goodwin went to the printing office of *México Libre*, a radical newspaper, seized all the circulars, and destroyed the type. But there were no disturbances in El Paso, and 600 Hispanics offered their services to their country. For their part, hundreds of Anglos swarmed the courthouse to enlist in the sheriff's posse; fifty were selected.[98] All this while newspapers as far away as San Francisco were engaging in an orgy of yellow journalism, reporting that Villa had captured El Paso and that a massacre had ensued. The mayor of El Paso issued a formal protest against this kind of hysterical and irresponsible reporting.[99]

Ranger activities in the El Paso area were thus of a more routine nature, assisting the local authorities. But on occasion these activities could become exciting, as occurred on April 25 at Ysleta. A posse made up of Texas Ranger Grover C. Webb, Deputy Sheriff Cecil C. Crechet, Mounted Customs inspectors (and ex-Rangers) H. A. Carnes and J. D. White, Special Deputy George Spencer, and (future Special Ranger) Deputy Constable Paul Wuerschmidt went looking for a dangerous fugitive, one Luz Pedraza, "a Mexican-Indian half breed" who was not only wanted for the murder of an Indian woman but was suspected of being one of the two men who had tried to assassinate Constable Wuerschmidt a few nights earlier as he made his rounds; the shooters emptied their pistols without effect and fled into the darkness. As if all this weren't bad enough, "it is reported that he has been trying to incite the Indians and Mexicans of Ysleta against the Americans." When the lawmen surrounded the adobe hut where Pedraza was staying with his confederates Carlos Tapia and Antonio Bustamante, Pedraza barricaded himself and invited the officers to come and get him. They were happy to oblige. Pedraza managed to get off two rounds before Ranger Webb shot him in the head, killing him instantly. His companions were arrested for trying to help Pedraza escape. Ranger Goodwin took them to jail in El Paso.[100] This incident illustrates a pattern regarding posses: They were often composed of various kinds of peace officers, as in this case—local, state, and federal. There was but one Ranger in this six-man posse. Two of the others, however, were ex-Rangers. And there's no indication of who, if anyone, was in command of the posse. Thus, had anything untoward happened, it's difficult to determine who was responsible. What can be determined is that Ranger Webb stated that "Pedraza was known as one of the bad men of this section and will not be mourned."[101]

Rangers more often operated in pairs, as when Captain Sanders and Private Speed tracked down a vicious murderer near Shafter. One Pedro Posado, a Mexican refugee at Shafter, became insanely jealous of a fellow refugee, Conchita Ramírez, and threw a bomb into her house one night. The victim's legs were shredded and one of her hands was blown off. Posado lit out for the Rio Grande, but the two Rangers ran him to earth halfway to the border and brought him back for trial.[102] A more deadly encounter involved another pair of Rangers, Private Ira Cline and Sergeant H. L. Roberson. They went to serve a warrant in Marfa on Carlos Morales Wood, who for several months had been editor of the Spanish-language newspaper *Patria Mexicana*, published in Valentine. Wood was charged with "inciting riot" by publishing articles attacking "the rangers, soldiers and Americans stationed and residing on this side of the Rio Grande of being murderers, cut throats and thieves, charging them with doing many heinous crimes, and informing the Mexican people that it was time for them to put a stop to same and give the Americans what they deserve." The Rangers located Wood in front of the Palace Drug Store, and when they tried to serve the warrant he reportedly pulled a gun on them; they shot him five times, and he died a few hours later. The newspaper account of the incident was headlined "Rangers Kill Bad Mexican at Marfa."[103] Yet another pair of Rangers investigated rustling around the hamlet of Lobo, in Culberson County only some twenty miles from the Rio Grande. Sheriff Peyton Edwards received reports by wire at El Paso that Mexicans had crossed the river at Pilares and were driving off horses and cattle. He dispatched Ranger O. W. "Doc" Goodwin, who had been detailed to the sheriff's office, and Ranger Grover Webb, stationed at Ysleta, to handle the case. The Rangers had orders to organize a posse at Lobo and try to head off the thieves before they could drive the stolen stock across the river.[104] They were too late. Captain Hughes later declared that it would take months of effort to rid the area of undesirables and bring robberies under control.[105]

These raids against ranches in West Texas were a source of continual frustration to the Rangers—as well as to the army—since they were forbidden to pursue the raiders into their privileged sanctuary across the Rio Grande. On occasion, however, ordinary citizens ignored the diplomatic niceties. In September there occurred a running fight between Mexican cattle rustlers and a group of cowboys. The rustlers crossed the Rio Grande near the foothills of the Quitman Mountains and began rounding up horses from ranches near Sierra Blanca. Gathering about 100 head of horses, they herded them to the river. But cowboys from the affected ranches were searching for the stock and spotted them going into Mexico. The cowboys went, too, and a running battle ensued. The rustlers abandoned the animals and tried to escape. Four of them were killed, and the fifth was wounded but eluded his pursuers, who returned in triumph to Texas with the horses.[106]

This is not to imply that the Rangers were ineffectual, however. Captain Hughes and his men were able to get the upper hand, at least temporarily, on rustlers in the Sierra Blanca area by dint of several weeks of intensive effort. They recovered a large number of stolen cattle and captured one Mexican rustler, who was jailed at Marfa. Not all the rustlers were Mexicans by any means—Rangers also arrested one Amos Marlowe, who was suspected of belonging to a gang operating back and forth across the border—stealing livestock on one side and selling it on the other.[107] Furthermore, back in April, an irate rancher at Allamore, west of Van Horn, had complained to the governor that "there are a lot of white men that are suspected of being into the business with the Mexicans."[108] With the Rangers concentrated on the border, the campaign against rustling turned a corner by September; both Captains Sanders and Hughes reported the situation essentially under control.[109]

The same could not be said for the financial situation of the Ranger Force. It was precarious, as always. The appropriation was $20,000, of which $13,704.36 had been spent by May 23. Hutchings calculated that the remaining $6,295.64

should barely last until the next fiscal year began on September 1, although the recent addition of three new Rangers would probably cause a modest deficit.[110] However, by August 7 the situation had become critical. Hutchings wrote to Hughes and Sanders that:

> The Ranger appropriation is so nearly exhausted that it is not practicable to approve the subsistence and expense accounts for July and August out of this appropriation. If a deficiency is incurred, warrants could not issue for thirty days, and these warrants could not probably be cashed prior to March 15. Company commanders are requested to try to arrange with local banks to carry the July and August subsistence and expense accounts until about September 15, at which time it is believed vouchers can be approved that will be paid out of the next year's appropriation. There is just about enough left in the appropriation to pay the August pay rolls promptly. Should a vacancy occur in your company do not enlist a new man until after August 31.[111]

And even when the new fiscal year began, finances remained tight, with Hutchings assuring Governor Colquitt in early October that ". . . this department will not incur any expenses which can be avoided between now and January 1 next."[112] Colquitt thanked him for his cooperation in keeping the state treasury on a cash basis by curtailing expenses down to those absolutely necessary until January 1, by which time taxes would begin to flow into the treasury.[113]

In an ironic turn of events, toward the end of his term Colquitt used the Rangers to enforce the liquor laws—the very practice for which he had excoriated Governor Campbell back in 1910 when he was campaigning to succeed Campbell.[114] In June, 1914, the governor received a confidential request from Eagle Pass for "a bunch of Rangers" to arrest army officers for gambling and rowdy soldiers for drinking. The writer said the liquor laws were being blatantly violated, and the local peace officers were doing nothing for fear of offending voters, while the local businessmen were keeping silent because they feared losing money.[115] Colquitt instructed Hutchings to inquire if the comptroller would send a man to Eagle Pass; if not, the adjutant general was to have Captain Sanders investigate.[116] The comptroller agreed to send an agent to Eagle Pass.[117] Hutchings sent Captain Hughes and Ranger Jefferson Eagle Vaughan, who had been doing similar work in Marfa, to cooperate with the comptroller's man. The latter and Vaughan systematically visited the town's four saloons; for the most part, Vaughan drank lemonade, although he did break down and join his companion in a beer at one of the establishments. Yet Captain Hughes reported that three days' investigation had revealed no flagrant violations of the law, nor any soldiers staggering drunkenly through the streets. There were, however, violations of the closing law.[118] Several months later, Colquitt again ordered the Rangers to assist the comptroller's department in enforcing the liquor laws, this time in response to a complaint that the gambling and liquor laws were being flouted in San Diego, the county seat of Archie Parr's fiefdom of Duval County. Colquitt directed that a Ranger be sent to investigate.[119] And in another part of the state, at San Angelo, Ranger Jeff Vaughan had been conducting a similar investigation.[120]

Not only was Colquitt following his predecessor's liquor enforcement policy, but he was also receiving some of the hostility that it generated. It was one thing for the Rangers to be down on the border rousting Mexicans; it was something else again when they interfered with decent, hard-working, law-abiding, God-fearing Anglo citizens of Texas. This was the view most emphatically expressed by the residents of Calvert, a small farming community northeast of Austin. They scheduled a local option liquor election for August 5, 1914. To their dismay, the day before the election two Rangers, "fully armed," appeared in town and informed the folks that "they were there to keep down expected riots" as a result of the election. The townspeople were outraged—they didn't need Rangers, hadn't requested Rangers, and didn't want Rangers. The mayor telephoned Colquitt to protest, and the governor promised to withdraw the Rangers. But he didn't do so until after the election, prompting the citizens to hold an angry mass meeting in the Baptist church and pass resolutions condemning Colquitt and "any other person instrumental in sending said Rangers to the city of Calvert. . . ."[121] Shades of 1910!

John R. Hughes, who had had an outstanding twenty-seven-year career in the Rangers, twenty-one of them as a captain, began to explore his options in the summer of 1914. He arrived in Brownsville on June 7, checked into the San Carlos Hotel, announced that he wouldd be in town for a few days, and began holding discussions with prominent residents of Cameron County. It turned out that some of these influential citizens were urging him to run for sheriff in the forthcoming Democratic primary on July 25 as a compromise candidate. Hughes initially consented and his name was included on the list of candidates, but within a couple of days he changed his mind, and by June 17 he had withdrawn. The winner in the primary and next sheriff of Cameron County was W. T. Vann, deputy U.S. marshal for the Southern District of Texas for the last six months, having resigned as Lea County sheriff, a position he had held for twelve years. Vann, by the way, had been rated as one of the best sheriffs in Texas.[122]

The 1914 municipal election marked yet another step in Brownsville's shedding of its violent past. In matters political, compromise was seemingly replacing confrontation. Although Captain Fox and two Rangers were sent to Brownsville at election time in November, their presence proved superfluous—the election was the quietest the town had experienced for at least the past eight years.[123]

The reason Captain Hughes had been open to suggestion regarding the office of Cameron County sheriff was because James E. Ferguson emerged as the

Democratic gubernatorial candidate, and Hughes was evaluating what effect Ferguson as governor would have on his own career. Whatever misgivings Hughes may have had came true. Governor Ferguson announced the reappointment as adjutant general of Henry Hutchings, who had shrewdly been the Secretary of the Travis County Ferguson Club.[124] Ferguson also reappointed Ranger Captains Fox and Sanders. The governor did not, however, reappoint Captain Hughes, and it was announced that Hughes would retire about January 15, 1915.[125]

Depriving the underpaid sixteen-man[126] Ranger Force of its respected senior captain was a portent of Ferguson's policy regarding the Rangers. That organization was about to enter its most controversial period, a time when outstanding leadership would be desperately needed.

Part Two

The Ferguson
Years, 1915—1917

CHAPTER SEVEN

FERGUSON RANGERS

THE year 1915 began eventfully for the Texas Rangers. There was a new administration in Austin, and James E. Ferguson was inaugurated on January 19. Unfortunately, he proved to be the crookedest governor in Texas history.[1] The advent of Ferguson was a disaster for the Rangers. Ferguson had political debts to pay, and Ranger commissions to bestow. Because the Rangers served at the pleasure of the governor, there were twenty-odd positions that could be filled by deserving Ferguson supporters.

Since Ranger captains commanding companies in the field traditionally selected their own men, the first item on Ferguson's agenda was to fire Captain Hughes and replace him with someone more pliant. Because Hughes was non-political he was an easy target. On January 31, 1915, he resigned.[2] Captain Sanders, who had been a big Ferguson supporter, was Hughes's replacement as captain of Company A. Captain Fox, who'd been serving as a one-man Company C in Austin, replaced Sanders as commander of Company B in February.[3] There was one more captain, Edward H. Smith, who headed a one-man Company D. In February, Smith received a paper transfer to Fox's old position as commander of the one-man Company C.

Captain Edward H. Smith, not to be confused with former Captain William "Australian Billy" Smith, who had earlier served as the Ranger detective, was new to the Force. Born in Pulaski, Tennessee, Smith had been a peace officer since 1901 and was serving as such in Waco when on January 19, 1915, he received his Ranger commission. From what little is known about him, he had nothing in particular to recommend him except his political connections.[4]

As of April, 1915, the breakdown of the Ranger Force was:

Company A
Captain J. J. Sanders   1 sergeant, 9 privates   11

Company B
Captain J. M. Fox   1 sergeant, 12 privates   14

Company C
Captain E. H. Smith   1
                                                             _____
                                                                     26

Not only was Hughes fired, but by May, 1915, more than half of the Ranger Force had been discharged or had quit in disgust. Several Rangers were immediately hired by U.S. Customs, while others joined local law enforcement agencies. Their replacements were at best a pretty mediocre crew.[5] It has even been alleged that Ferguson Rangers weren't "real Rangers," which of course is absurd.[6] But the Ferguson Rangers did have their troubles.

In the Big Bend there had developed a vendetta between mounted Customs Inspector Joe Sitter and the wily Mexican bandit and horse thief Chico Cano. Sitter, the grizzled former Ranger who had twice been wounded in gun battles, most recently in a shootout with Cano along the river, was determined to get the Mexican, and he was not too particular as to how he went about it. Hearing a rumor that Cano was stealing horses on the Texas side of the river, Sitter and a rookie Ranger, Eugene Hulen, captured a man whom Sitter suspected could tell him Cano's whereabouts, and the two officers "roped, dragged and put through the 3rd degree a Mexican. . . . It is said that from him they obtained certain information desired." They then released the brutalized but unidentified prisoner.[7] Sitter immediately organized a posse, on May 24, consisting of himself, Customs inspector (and ex-Ranger) Charles Craighead, and three of Captain Fox's Rangers: a veteran, Harris C. "Harry" Trollinger, and two brand-new Rangers. One was Eugene Hulen, a brother of former Texas Adjutant General and National Guard Brigadier General John A. Hulen, who was now a railroad executive.[8] Obviously General Hulen had a certain amount of influence, and on February 27 he had written to Hutchings requesting a Ranger commission for his brother. He noted that his brother Eugene was thirty-six years of age, "sober, steady and reliable," although he "has never served as a peace officer." Notwithstanding his total lack of experience, Eugene Hulen was enlisted as a Ranger on March 29, 1915, on Governor Ferguson's explicit order. The other new Ranger was A. P. "Sugg" Cummings, appointed on February 1.[9] The party set out with high hopes but soon blundered into a deadly ambush.

The accounts of the ambush are all based on various versions given by the survivors, who ran and left their colleagues to die. According to Cummings, Craighead, and Trollinger, they were tracking the bandits and there was a disagreement among the five officers as to whether they should enter Pilares Canyon, a deep box canyon on the north bank of the Rio Grande eight miles east of Pilares. The officers from a distance were able to see the stolen horses. The written and oral testimony of the three survivors varies as to what happened next. Several said it was a trap to draw them into the canyon. However, Sitter, both as a former Ranger and the senior law enforcement officer among the five, apparently forced the issue and convinced his companions to follow him on horseback into the canyon.

Once inside the canyon, the men divided into two groups: Sitter and Hulen turned right and the other three turned left into a ravine within the canyon. When Cummings, Trollinger, and Craighead reached the bank of the ravine they were fired on by Cano's men from a distance of approximately forty yards. Under what they described as "heavy fire," they retreated into the ravine, dismounted, and sought cover. They said they could see Sitter and Hulen on a small hill. According to the survivors, Sitter motioned them to "go down the ravine the way they had come," while Sitter and Hulen provided covering fire, which enabled them to retreat because they were cut off from their horses. The survivors claimed they attempted five times to reach Sitter and Hulen but were unsuccessful. They also stated that Sitter and Hulen changed their position during the prolonged gun-battle and they lost sight of them. The three officers claimed that Chico Cano had between thirty and thirty-five men, though it can be speculated that the bandits were actually fewer. Being out of drinking water and still under heavy fire, the lawmen retreated. They stated for the record that "the firing ceased and we knew Sitter and Hulen were either dead or had made their escape."

Cummings, Trollinger, and Craighead walked to a water hole approximately four miles away where their pack mules had been left, stripped off the pack saddles and rode the animals to a nearby ranch from where they sent a message for help. At daybreak the next day, an eleven-man posse arrived from Marfa and with the three survivors cautiously rode to the site of the ambush. There they found Sitter's and Hulen's bodies, stripped naked. Their faces were unrecognizable, for they had been pounded into pulp by large rocks, according to the eyewitnesses. Captain Fox later reported that Sitter's body had ten bullet holes and Hulen's eight. Not only had the Mexicans stripped the bodies of clothing, they had taken Hulen's boots, had killed Sitter's horse, and had stolen the dead officers' guns. The survivors stated that there were some sixty empty bullet casings around Sitter's body, attesting to the fact that he had gone down shooting. According to their account, "Hulen was wounded early in the fight and was able to fire only one shot." How they knew Hulen had been wounded early in the gunbattle is open to question. This statement was probably made to cover up the fact that Hulen had performed poorly and might have "frozen from fear" in what was his first and last shootout. The survivors undoubtedly knew that the adjutant general would send their account to Hulen's brother, which probably explains what they said.

The task of removing the bodies from the canyon proved gruesome. The corpses were lashed to pack saddles and carried out on mules. Given the intense summer heat in the Big Bend, the bloated corpses had rapidly decomposed and in Captain Fox's words, "had already bursted." The stench from the decaying bodies was so pungent it caused the mule hauling Sitter's body to vomit. Both bodies were quickly buried on a nearby ranch, although Hulen's body was subsequently disinterred and shipped to Houston for burial. In a final ignominious note on the engagement, Fox in his report to the adjutant general stated that Rangers Trollinger and Cummings had their horses and saddles stolen by Cano's bandits.[10] Adjutant General Hutchings considered sending the entire Ranger Force after Cano and his associates. On June 2 he wrote to Fox, "Do you believe . . . the body of Mexicans could be led to return; if so, I should like to concentrate all of the Rangers at that point to meet them. . . ."[11] Chico Cano, however, was not that obliging.

The bottom line was that two Texas Rangers and a U.S. Customs inspector (and ex-Ranger) had left their comrades to die—conduct most unbecoming. As a result, the Rangers who ran, Trollinger and Cummings, were summarily fired by an outraged adjutant general.[12] According to Trollinger, people who had talked with the other two survivors immediately after the gun battle stated that Cummings and Craighead admitted that Trollinger had wanted to stay and fight, but they had refused. One source is Ranger W. F. Bates, who was in the process of being fired at the time and is perhaps not the best source, but his account does coincide with other statements. Governor Ferguson, who met with Trollinger, noted that he "seems to be laboring under great humiliation at being called a coward." Trollinger petitioned for reinstatement. Ferguson believed his story and ordered his reenlistment, which Fox endorsed.[13] On October 16 he was permitted to reenlist in Company B. In January, 1917, he was promoted to sergeant. Trollinger, however, did have a drinking problem and when in his cups became mean and disorderly. On March 1, 1918, he was again fired, for drunkenness, this time for good. As for Cummings, after he was fired he became a stockman at San Angelo. He again enlisted in the Rangers on January 29, 1924, and was assigned to Company E. He was subsequently transferred to Headquarters Company, then to Company B. He was discharged on May 14, 1927, finally ending his career as a Ranger.

Nor was Hulen the last Ranger killed in Fox's Company B. Only thirteen days after the Big Bend ambush, another Ranger died in the line of duty, on the night of June 7. Ranger Lee Burdett and a new Ranger recruit, Charles Beall, were in Fabens, downriver from El Paso. They attempted to search five Mexicans who, drunk and disorderly, had been driving through the streets. The revelers disappeared into an alley, and when the Rangers attempted to disarm them a gun battle broke out and Burdett was shot just below the throat. Beall reported that he thought he had wounded one of the Mexicans, but the killers succeeded in escaping across the Rio Grande. Three of them were executed several weeks later by Villa officials for crimes they had committed in Mexico.[14]

The purging of the Rangers and the employment for political reasons of inept gunmen crippled the Rangers' ability to respond to crises. There simply were not enough Rangers to go around, and many of those available were not first-rate lawmen. The ambush that cost Sitter and Hulen their lives was evidence of a deteriorating Ranger Force, but it also reflected the inability of the army and peace officers in the Big Bend to work together in order to rid the area of Chico Cano. For example, by early May, 1915, Cano's band had created such havoc that Customs inspectors requested assistance from the commanding officer of the Big Bend District. As a result, on May 7 a twenty-man detachment complete with pack train was sent to Candelaria, where they were to link up with the inspectors. But the inspectors unaccountably informed the troops that they were not wanted.[15] For four days the cavalrymen patrolled the river from Candelaria to Pilares, being mocked by some twenty-five of Cano's men, who kept pace with them on the Mexican bank. Under the rules of engagement, American troops were forbidden to cross the river without specific orders from the secretary of war.

Then on the morning of May 13, Cano and his men attacked a detachment of some thirty villista troops at Pilares, capturing forty of their horses and effectively reducing them from cavalry to infantry. A subsequent attempt by a U.S. cavalry patrol to synchronize patrols on the Rio Grande with these villistas was unsuccessful, and the troopers returned to Marfa "without having accomplished anything."[16] And then a week later Cano carried out his ambush of the Customs inspectors and Rangers. When Sergeant Ira Cline of Fox's Company B learned of the attack he immediately telephoned the army camp at Marfa requesting assistance. The army detachment at Candelaria was ordered to the site of the ambush. When they arrived to meet Sergeant Cline, no one was there—neither bandits nor Rangers. J. J. Kilpatrick, Sr., the unsavory Candelaria businessman, wrote to his congressman following the ambush to appeal for additional troops on the river, saying that "This border for eighty miles up the river is now in the hands of 41 bandits, and no man's life or property is now safe . . . in the upper part of the Big Bend country."[17]

The killing of Sitter and Hulen caused Major General Frederick Funston, the Southern Department commander, to respond with outrage. He ordered the commanders of the Fabens and Big Bend districts to "make every effort to break up [Cano's] band of outlaws . . . whether requested to do so by Customs or State authorities or not. . . . It is important that Big Bend be rid as soon as possible of these bands of outlaws. . . . You will take the necessary steps to do so." However,

Funston's superiors in Washington feared an international incident and ordered him to modify his instructions to his subordinates, prohibiting the crossing of the Rio Grande.[18] Funston did the best he could within these constraints and in the knowledge of just how effective Cano's intelligence network was, for he reported resignedly, "No information could be obtained from any of the people on or near the border."[19]

The general deployed several cavalry detachments supported by a pack train. One of these units patrolled the vicinity of the ambush accompanied by ten Rangers and river guards. Despite extensive patrols by 117 cavalrymen, plus a dozen Rangers and Customs inspectors, no trace of the outlaw band was found. The Rangers were in a vengeful mood. An army report for early June stated:

> The ranger force under Captain Fox which visited Pilares in company with twelve of Lieut. Overton's party reported nothing there. The rangers used energetic methods to convince the women remaining that the [Chico Cano] band could not return to the U.S. Any activity now on the American side at Pilares will indicate a return of suspects, as the place was cleaned out at that time.[20]

Several days later, the army reported that Rangers A. P. "Sugg" Cummings and S. M. Jester, together with a six-man detachment of Troop A, 15th Cavalry, visited Pilares to arrest one Anastacio Segura, allegedly a member of Cano's gang who had been indicted for rustling. According to Jester, when Cummings placed Segura under arrest Segura tried to stab him, whereupon the Rangers shot Segura dead. The troopers weren't involved in this incident. Although Jester claimed that Segura was a bandit, "Captain Cole and Mr. Jiménez talked to Segura during their stay in Pilares and thought him otherwise."[21]

Captain Fox's Rangers returned to Valentine. On June 1, the War Department ordered the 15th Cavalry, based in the Big Bend, transferred to the Philippines. Funston pointed out that operations against Cano would have to be suspended, and the incoming 13th Cavalry would require some time to become acclimated before it could contemplate launching operations against the outlaw. Only a handful of Customs inspectors now patrolled the river. Yet Major George T. Langhorne, commanding the Big Bend District, was still gamely trying to organize an effective defense. On June 12 he conferred with Captain Fox, the sheriffs of the Big Bend counties, and a representative of the Mexican Army. Unfortunately, no feasible plan emerged. A major problem for the authorities was the attitude of the American cattlemen in the area. One of the lawmen at the conference declared: "I have been 30 years as an officer in this county and if you can show me one cattle man on this border of any means who has not and does not buy and handle stolen and smuggled stock, then I will show you a white blackbird."[22]

Funston also commented on the reason for lawlessness in the Big Bend, explaining that army officers stationed there believed that "nearly all of the people living along the river are in league . . . with the band of outlaws. These outlaws operate on both sides of the river, bringing over cattle and horses from the Mexican side, and selling them cheap to men on the American side who grow rich on the trade." The general quoted one of his officers, who reported that:

> There are a great number of citizens on this side of the border who make it a business to buy horses and cattle stolen in Mexico and smuggled across the border. It is believed that this traffic constitutes the sole business of some men, while with others it is an adjunct to their ranch business. It is believed that this traffic is carried on by both Americans and Mexicans all the way from El Paso down along the Rio Grande. These dealers naturally encourage the smuggling of stock and withhold any information as to the guilty persons.

Funston concluded his dispatch with an attack on the Texas Rangers: "The problem is a civil and not a military one, and should be solved by the State of Texas. The ranger force . . . is entirely inadequate, consisting at the present time of only twelve men. These men are stationed at Marfa, and as far as can be ascertained they visit the border only when they hear of some impending trouble, and by the time they reach the district where the trouble occurs, the outlaws have disappeared."[23]

Funston's comments were accurate insofar as they pertained to Captain Fox's company of Rangers, but unfortunately in Washington Adjutant General Tasker Bliss misread Funston's report and thought that the entire Ranger Force consisted of only twelve men, and this was the figure he reported to the army chief of staff and the secretary of war, leaving them with the impression that Texas was doing very little to protect her border and expected the federal government to shoulder the burden.[24] Bliss stated that:

> My experience while in Texas was that the most insistent appeals for protection by the Army came from sections which notoriously and since long prior to the outbreak of Mexican disorders had been infested with lawless men. The laws of the State of Texas authorize the maintenance of a force of four companies of Rangers to give protection against this lawless class. For reasons of economy the force was reduced (or was so when I was in the State) to less than one company. I think the total number was sixteen men. A reasonable increase in this force, to do what the Army cannot lawfully do, would probably meet all requirements.[25]

In point of fact there were actually thirty-three Rangers by June 7, but they were still not nearly enough.

Particularly in the counties along the Rio Grande, 1915 saw a resurgence of goat rustling and cattle and horse stealing, which in part can be blamed on the Mexican Revolution. As contending armies marched back and forth, law and order in the adjacent states of Tamaulipas, Nuevo Leon, Coahuila, and Chihuahua collapsed, and banditry became endemic. As economic conditions continued to deteriorate with the prolongation of the Revolution, increasing numbers of bandits crossed the Rio Grande to steal livestock. And there was a plentiful supply of local thieves both in the Texas counties along the Rio Grande and just off the river who were stealing horses, cattle, and goats and taking them to Mexico to be sold. In early February, Captain Sanders reported that he was headed for the Brownsville area with Rangers Reneau and Cardwell because "there is more horse and cattle stealing being carried on than ever before."[26] A week later Sanders declared that, "I have never heard of as much stealing in a country in all my life, all the way from the King Ranch to Jim Hogg County."[27] And in the midst of trying to stop the cattle thieves in the Lower Valley, the governor ordered that all available Rangers be rushed to Laredo. An outbreak of an estimated 150 cases of smallpox had hit Laredo, and the Rangers were reluctantly dragooned into enforcing the unpopular quarantine regulations.[28]

In February, the legislature was in session, and Hutchings felt confident that the lawmakers would add sufficient money to the Ranger appropriation to enable him to hire ten additional men. He notified Sanders and Fox to begin looking for five men for each company.[29] Newspaper accounts of the contemplated augmentation of the Ranger Force drew a flood of applications.

But Governor Ferguson was at the front of the line with a recommendation for enlistment. In a letter to the adjutant general dated February 26, he stated that:

> I am in receipt of a letter from . . . Byron B. Parrish . . . asking for a place on the Ranger Force. In my opinion he is one of the best qualified men in Texas for this service. He would make an excellent Ranger Captain. Captain Sanders knows him and I shall very much appreciate it, if you can give him a place. He would be exceedingly valuable to us for special work. He knows the Spanish language and has served many years on the Border.[30]

Needless to say, Parrish was offered one of the ten open positions, but Hutchings deftly evaded the governor's virtual order to make Parrish a Ranger captain. In a letter to the governor Hutchings noted that under current law, ". . . the Governor may appoint four captains. . . ." He reminded Ferguson, who had a request pending in Washington for federal funds to pay for additional Rangers, "Should [the federal government] agree to furnish funds for thirty additional men,

I would then suggest that Captains Sanders, Fox and Smith be each given the Maximum Statutory command of twenty men and that . . . Parrish then be commissioned captain." The adjutant general then obsequiously added, "I await further direction from Your Excellency."[31]

In March Captain Sanders, who was finally able to return from San Benito to his camp at Del Rio, continued to complain about the wholesale stealing of cattle and horses in the Lower Valley. And rustling was hardly confined to the Valley. In mid-March Sanders ruefully reported to the adjutant general that "one of the best horses . . . in my command . . . [had been] stolen from the [Ranger] corral" in Del Rio. Sanders explained that he had sent his sergeant and a veteran Ranger to try to recover the animal, but after a futile two-day search he concluded that the horse "has been taken across into Mexico."[32] If a horse thief could steal an animal literally from under the noses of a Ranger company, then ranchers didn't stand much of a chance.

But Sanders's Rangers were having to deal with more serious crimes such as murder. For example, Rangers Reneau and Cardwell were summoned to Edinburg by Sheriff Baker "to assist him in quieting a riot at Monte Christo in which W. C. Warmick [sic-Warnock] had killed Frank Lamb. . . ." The Rangers arrested Warnock on a charge of murder and one P. E. Montgomery for carrying a pistol and threw both of them in the Hidalgo County jail.[33]

Meanwhile, Captain J. M. Fox's Company B in West Texas operated from its base at Valentine. Fox wanted a camp (really a house) at Marfa but was unable to find one he could rent. In a letter to the adjutant general he complained that the weather was so cold that it was impossible to do anything. Hutchings did send Fox four additional blankets so that his men would not freeze to death. In case they became engaged in a firefight, the adjutant general also shipped Captain Fox five carbines and 1,000 rounds of .45 caliber ammunition. Unfortunately 900 rounds were black powder ammunition and only 100 rounds were smokeless ammunition. As is well known, black powder ammunition when fired gives off a puff of smoke that discloses the location of the shooter, which is somewhat disadvantageous in a gun battle.[34]

Captain Sanders continued to have problems, with more requests pouring in to assign Rangers to specific locations in the Lower Valley than he had Rangers. A petition from the elected officials and prominent merchants in Starr County, upriver from Brownsville, requesting that two Rangers be based in the county had been sitting on Governor Ferguson's desk since mid-February. In mid-March the governor finally got around to sending it to the adjutant general, with the instruction that he respond to the petition if additional Rangers were hired. Ferguson pointed out that state Representative L. H. Bates, a strong ally of the Ferguson administration and one of the lieutenant colonels on the governor's staff, "is much interested in the matter."[35]

In addition, Sanders was having to deal with a delicate political situation involving a recently hired Ranger, James D. Dunaway, who had been a Ranger sergeant back in 1906 and later became chief special agent at Houston for the Santa Fe railroad. When Sheriff L. A. Clark of Edwards County (one county north of Del Rio) learned that Dunaway was about to be given a Ranger commission, he telegraphed the governor requesting that he not be appointed. Edwards followed up with a letter informing Ferguson that he had earlier fired Dunaway as one of his deputies because he "is a troublemaker. . . ." The governor asked the adjutant general to find out from Captain Sanders if he found Dunaway to be "personally objectionable" and, if so, he "does not intend to force him on you. . . ." However, Hutchings explained in a letter to Sanders that the governor said that Dunaway's "recommendations are so strong that . . . [Ferguson] wishes at least to give them serious consideration." The bottom line for the governor was that state Senator Claude B. Hudspeth of El Paso, a strong supporter of the Ferguson administration, insisted that Dunaway and the future Ranger legend Frank Hamer be commissioned. They were. Hutchings, who by March had learned to read the governor, managed this personnel problem by assigning Dunaway and Hamer to Captain Smith, the Ranger detective based in Austin.[36]

Dunaway proved to be an embarrassment. In September he was in Fredericksburg when he walked by a nineteen-year-old named Taliaferro, who was seated in a local business establishment. Dunaway said, "You little son of a bitch don't look at me so mean." Taliaferro leaped to his feet saying, "I cannot take this off any man." They argued, then got into a fistfight, which Dunaway ended by fracturing Taliaferro's skull (presumably by "bending" his pistol over Taliaferro's head). The grand jury investigated and indicted Dunaway. A Fredericksburg attorney who wrote to Ferguson requesting Dunaway's expulsion from the Rangers pointed out that if he weren't removed he would eventually kill some good men. The governor ordered Hutchings to investigate and if the allegations were true to get rid of Dunaway. They were, and Hutchings fired Dunaway as of October 31.[37]

While Sanders was having to deal with politicians demanding the appointment of either incompetent or inexperienced individuals as Rangers, the adjutant general and the governor were also having to deal with politicians who did not want the Rangers anywhere near their counties. In late March, the sheriff of Montgomery County, north of Houston, along with the county judge, the county attorney, the state senator, and a group of prominent citizens from Conroe, sent telegrams to the governor's secretary urging the governor not to send Rangers to the county to monitor elections.[38] The Rangers were not sent.

Political direction of the Rangers by Governor Ferguson had become a pattern by the end of March. Sheriffs, state senators, and influential businessmen throughout the state had gotten the word that whether Rangers were needed or not, the person to communicate with was not a Ranger captain or even the adjutant general, but the governor, who decided where and when they would be deployed. This situation was not unique, for the governor had statutory authority over the Rangers, but what was unique was Ferguson's extraordinary micromanagement of the Rangers for political purposes.

Captain Sanders grappled with the various instructions he had received both from the adjutant general and the governor—instructions which sometimes differed as to which men should be commissioned in Company A. For example, Sanders explained in a letter to the adjutant general that he had been ordered to enlist three individuals. He had enlisted two men, and the governor (who prevailed in these matters) wanted him to bring Byron B. Parrish on board. However, state Representative Lawrence Bates, one of the governor's most influential political advisors, informed Sanders that the governor also wanted his brother, W. F. Bates, commissioned in Sanders's company. Thus the governor wanted two men to fill one slot. Sanders also reported to Hutchings that he had been unable to locate either Parrish or Bates. Sanders wrote somewhat plaintively, ". . . please advise me."[39]

By early April the Lower Valley was, to use Sanders's words, "reasonably quiet," but to make sure, he had deployed eight members of his company from Rio Grande City to San Benito.[40] In fact, Sanders had returned to Company A's camp at Del Rio and things seemed peaceful enough for Sergeant Grimes to take a few days' leave.[41]

It should have been comparatively easy to recruit ten additional Rangers, but inevitably there were problems. For example, one of Captain Sanders's newly recruited Rangers, Will T. Lott, came down with an arm ailment that put him in a San Antonio hospital for treatment. Sanders tried to explain to the adjutant general that Lott had been healthy when he enlisted.[42] Hutchings was unsure as to what to do about Lott since he had not been wounded or injured in the line of duty. He asked Sanders for additional information on Lott's medical condition. On April 30, Private Lott finally resigned, apparently because his arm ailment had not improved.[43] In addition, Byron B. Parrish had not shown up to receive his commission and report for duty. Sanders prudently attempted to station two-man teams in the volatile Lower Valley. Since Ranger Felps was alone at San Benito, Sanders requested permission to enlist someone else, since Parrish apparently was not going to report. However, Parrish finally wrote the adjutant general that his mother was seriously ill and he had been staying with her. Hutchings assured Parrish that his slot would be held for him but requested that he report as soon as possible. Parrish kept the adjutant general and Sanders on the hook for more than a week, and finally on April 21 he sent a letter explaining that he must decline the Ranger commission. Captain Sanders moved swiftly and recruited Charles Price to fill the position.[44]

Nor were problems confined to Company A. Captain Fox had to leave his company in Marfa for two weeks in order to travel to Richmond, near Houston, to bury his father-in-law and settle his affairs. While Captain Fox was absent, one of the newest members of his company, Charles Brooks, who had enlisted on April 1, suffered a serious gunshot wound on April 13. He had left his .45 revolver in camp and someone had used it for target practice, reloading all six chambers. Brooks accidentally dropped the weapon, which fired, putting a round in his knee, the slug ranging upward into his hip. He was rushed from the Ranger camp at Valentine some 165 miles to an El Paso hospital. Although he recovered, he faced months of rehabilitation.[45] Another personnel problem in Company B involved Ranger W. F. Bates, the brother of former Ranger and state Representative L. E. Bates. W. F. Bates could not get along with anyone. By contrast, his brother, who was very close to Governor Ferguson, had been a popular and respected Ranger. Fox's sergeant, S. M. Jester, reported in April that Bates refused to go on scouts along the Rio Grande, announcing that he did not join the Rangers to ride up and down the river. Fox, painfully aware of Bates's brother's influence with the governor, attempted to smooth over the controversy, but Bates continued to be a major headache for Company B.[46]

In addition, the pressure to assign men to assist various sheriffs along the border further depleted the ranks of available Rangers. The sheriff of Dimmit County, W. T. Gardner, used both his district attorney and local congressman, John Nance "Cactus Jack" Garner, to put pressure on Governor Ferguson to loan Ranger Willis, a member of Captain Sanders's company, to Gardner for an extended period of time. Hutchings ordered Sanders to send Willis (a future Ranger captain) to assist the sheriff.[47] Nor was this the only allocation of Rangers on semi-permanent assignment to local law enforcement entities. At virtually the same time, at Del Rio, the sheriff of Val Verde County, John W. Almond, was able to harness the political power of state Senator Claude Hudspeth to have two Rangers assigned to Val Verde, Edwards, and Kinney Counties in an effort to stop wholesale goat stealing.[48] In addition, the sheep and goat ranchers raised funds to hire an additional deputy, ex-Ranger Nat B. Jones. Senator Hudspeth asked the governor to issue a Special Ranger commission to Jones, and Ferguson promptly ordered it done.[49]

Meanwhile, Company B was of necessity being dispersed to three separate locations. At Captain Fox's direction, four Rangers were to be based at Valentine; another four would be stationed at Fabens, downriver from El Paso; the remaining five Rangers—Captain Fox, Sergeant Jester, and three Ranger privates—were based at Marfa.

There was plenty for them to do. Mexican rustlers had made off with nearly 1,000 head of cattle from Big Bend ranches during the previous months. Hoping to put an end to these depredations, Captain Fox and Sheriff Walton planned a raid against the outlaws' hideout on the river near Boquillas. In mid-May a party of Rangers, mounted Customs inspectors, and a brand inspector for the Cattle Raisers Association swept down on the Mexicans. In the desperate fight that followed, Ranger Bates and the Customs inspectors killed a lieutenant colonel in the Carranza army and the brand inspector killed another Mexican. The Americans suffered no casualties, and the officers recovered quite a number of stolen cattle. Interestingly, several well-known citizens of Marathon were later arrested because they were implicated in the thefts.[50]

There was authorized nepotism in the Rangers. In May, Hutchings authorized Captain Sanders to enroll his son Jesse and would subsequently do the same for Captain Fox, whose son was also signed on.[51] In addition, Hutchings, who thought well of Sanders, authorized him to come to Austin so that he could buy a brand new hack for Company A.[52] Unfortunately Captain Sanders was accident prone. He managed to break one finger and severely bruise another when a train window fell on his hand. Dr. E. S. McCain suggested that Sanders be hospitalized in San Antonio, because "of his depressed condition." The physician believed that he needed both a nurse's attention and rest and that he could obtain them in San Antonio. Sanders, however, was treated by two physicians in his hometown of Lockhart. In any case, Sanders's constant medical problems reduced his effectiveness as a Ranger captain.[53]

By May 23, Sanders was back at Company A headquarters in Del Rio with his men scattered downriver: Ranger Willis was at Carrizo Springs assisting the local sheriff; Craighead was stationed at Hebronville; Brooks and Price were in Alice; Reneau and Cardwell were at Pharr; Felps and Edwards were at San Benito; Aldrich and Davenport were at Rio Grande City; and Sergeant Grimes kept Sanders company at Del Rio.

In early June the greatest difficulties were in West Texas with Fox's snakebit company. The problems with Ranger W. F. Bates refused to go away. As mentioned earlier, his brother L. E. Bates was an influential state representative and much admired ex-Ranger, but his brother was cut from a different bolt of cloth. W. F. Bates openly sparred with veteran Rangers in his company and refused to take orders.[54] Bates apparently believed that because of his brother's influence with Governor Ferguson he could get away with anything. However, his arrogance finally tipped the scales and Bates realized that he was going to be asked to resign his Ranger commission. He did so on June 8 in a telegram to Fox.[55] Before he left the Rangers, Bates wrote a spiteful letter to Governor Ferguson damning the members of Fox's company, including his sergeant whom Bates claimed was both a drunk and a border bootlegger. Bates also denounced his colleagues who he said had run away and left Hulen and Sitter to die. He noted that the previous month he himself had been involved in a gun battle in which he had killed a Mexican. He reported that in this incident two Customs river guards "had run off and left me to fight it out. Had there been any more Mexicans . . . I would have been murdered."[56] There must have been a sigh of relief, both among his long-suffering colleagues in Company B and in the adjutant general's office, when Bates was no longer around to create problems.

And in the Big Bend there was an unprecedented situation—bad blood between the Rangers and mounted Customs inspectors. As we have seen, these two groups traditionally enjoyed cordial relations, not only because they worked closely together but also because so many Customs inspectors were ex-Rangers. What had brought on this animosity is not known. We do know that something had occurred three months earlier during a scout along the Rio Grande in which Ranger W. A. Roberts had accompanied Customs inspectors. Subsequently a Customs investigator asked Roberts to answer a written questionnaire that indicated illegal activity.[57] Another contributing factor to this turn of events may have been the circumstances surrounding the Pilares ambush in which Customs inspector Sitter and Ranger Hulen were killed. Because Sitter was the senior officer and knew the border like the back of his hand, he was at least nominally in command of the five men who were scouting the river. Survivors of the ambush asserted that it was Sitter who had insisted on entering the box canyon where he and Hulen were killed. Apparently the surviving Rangers and their colleagues felt that Sitter was thus responsible for leading the Rangers into a trap, and although two Rangers had fled, so had a mounted Customs inspector. Some Rangers felt that they had received the wrong end of the stick as a result of Sitter's blunder.

Not only were relations between the Rangers and the Customs inspectors strained, but Fox's company continued to have its problems. In his Monthly Return for June, Fox enumerated in the "Remarks" section the following changes that had occurred during the month: out of fourteen men, one Ranger killed—Burdett (Hulen had been killed the previous month)—three Rangers fired, one Ranger transferred out of the company, four Rangers recruited, and one Ranger who had managed to shoot himself and was convalescing in the hospital.[58] Yet whatever Fox's problems, his job was secure as long as he remained loyal to Governor Ferguson.

Speaking of Ferguson, his reputation among Texas political historians is that of a crooked politician, which he unquestionably was—he would be impeached and removed from office in 1917. But he was also a governor who has not been given his due by historians regarding his efforts to keep the peace along the Mexican border. This is not to imply that he sympathized with the Mexican Revolution. As he informed one of his correspondents: "I like you am tired of these Mexican outlaws, calling themselves statesmen, constantly fomenting revolutions upon our borders for their personal gain."[59] In his Mexican policy Ferguson was quite prepared to cooperate with Washington, unlike his predecessor. Unfortunately, Governor Colquitt had fouled the nest for Ferguson. Colquitt had been something of a wild man in dealing with the impact of the Mexican Revolution on Texas. He had acted as if he were the president of the Republic of Texas who upon occasion would call upon a friendly neighboring country (the United States) for help. As we have seen, in 1911 Colquitt issued his own neutrality proclamation, wanted to send the Rangers into Mexico to arrest fugitives, persuaded President Taft to subsidize a threefold increase in the Rangers so they could better patrol the border, and then condoned the Reyes conspiracy, employing the Rangers only when the federal authorities had moved against Reyes. In 1912 during the Orozco rebellion Colquitt planned to utilize the Dallas field artillery battery of the Texas National Guard to shell Ciudad Juárez if shots were fired into El Paso. On several occasions he thwarted the State Department by refusing to permit the movement of Mexican troops across Texas soil. In 1914, he tried to have Clemente Vergara's murderers kidnaped from Mexico, and that same year he ordered elements of the Texas National Guard to Brownsville, raising fears in the War Department that he might invade Mexico. And he had consistently called for intervention, deriding Wilson's Mexican policy. This track record had created in Washington a tremendous amount of animosity against Colquitt in particular and Texas in general, and Ferguson now became the target of that animosity.

When he took office, Ferguson realized that Texas faced enormous problems in protecting her 1,200-mile meandering river boundary with Mexico. There were only twenty-six Rangers (although the legislature in February passed a bill introduced by Senator Claude Hudspeth providing $10,000 to hire ten more).[60] Moreover, the State of Texas was living on the ragged edge financially in the early twentieth century, often being forced to issue scrip—essentially I.O.U.s—which could not be redeemed until there was money in the comptroller's office.[61]

Ferguson decided to appeal to President Wilson in February for help. On its face this was logical. President Taft, a Republican, had provided funds in 1911–1912 so a Democratic governor of Texas could increase the Rangers. And in 1912, Texas Democrats had played a pivotal role in securing the presidential nomination for Wilson. As a result, three members of Wilson's cabinet—Attorney General Thomas Watt Gregory, Secretary of Agriculture David Houston, and Postmaster General Albert Sidney Burleson—were Texans, as was Wilson's principal foreign policy advisor, Colonel Edward House. Although Wilson had intervened in the 1914 Texas Democratic gubernatorial primary, backing Ferguson's opponent, the President and Ferguson had met in Washington in October, 1914, and had papered over their differences.[62]

Given what would transpire in the coming months, the governor's appeal to Wilson was prescient and yet naive. He pointed out that ". . . information . . . reaching my office [indicates] . . . there is almost a reign of terror [along the Texas border]. The local officers in each county have not the means and admit their inability to cope with the situation, and are appealing to me for assistance." Ferguson explained that the Rangers had been expanded ". . . to full capacity, and our State is making special and liberal appropriation to maintain our increased force. . . . It seems however that conditions are growing worse . . . [and] our Ranger Force will have to be . . . increased." Ferguson requested $30,000 so that thirty additional Rangers could be hired for one year—a repeat of Colquitt's successful request to President Taft four years earlier. He ended by stating that "only the gravity of the situation impels me to make this appeal."[63]

Unfortunately, Ferguson did not begin to understand the extent to which the army brass were predisposed against Texas in general and the Rangers in particular. The resentment went all the way back to 1906 when black troops in Brownsville had been involved in a disturbance and Captain Bill McDonald had forced his way into Fort Brown to arrest the guilty. Although McDonald had failed, from the army's point of view his grandstanding was humiliating. And the military resented the way Colquitt had tried to claim credit for the Rangers in the 1911 dismantling of the Reyes conspiracy, the army having played a much more important role. And now here was Ferguson begging for money for the Rangers. Wilson consulted with Secretary of War Lindley Garrison, and the result was that Wilson politely rejected the governor's request for $30,000. The President did give instructions for the army to cooperate with Ferguson and redouble its efforts in patrolling the border.[64]

As was customary, the secretary of war had submitted Ferguson's letter to the chief of staff and his subordinates for comment. Their responses were revealing. General Frederick Funston was ordered by the secretary of war to communicate with the governor as to how the army might assist him. Funston reported that he had had a "long talk" by telephone with Ferguson and that the governor had asked him to urge his superiors to support the $30,000 request for the Rangers. Funston also commented that Ferguson had naively wanted the army to assign troops to the Rangers to "act in the capacity of rangers to assist the civil authorities of the state." The governor, according to Funston, stated that some 30,000 goats, cattle and horses (principally goats, constituting approximately 10 percent of the goat population of Edwards County) had been stolen, and the state desperately needed help to stop these massive thefts.

Funston ordered Colonel F. W. Sibley, the commanding officer at Fort Clark, to investigate the livestock thefts in Edwards County. Sibley reported that it was a local matter and none of the army's affair. He quoted a former resident of Edwards County who had served on a grand jury several times: "there is [an] organized band of . . . rustlers who . . . have been operating in Edwards County . . . for the past 10 or 12 years. He believes that this stolen stock is rarely taken to the border. . . . The grand jury has . . . found indictments against these parties only to have witnesses run out of the county by these bandits. The people of Edwards

County could stop this if they wished to. . . . I can find no reliable evidence that stolen stock, especially goats, in any quantity have been crossed into Mexico . . . during the past year."[65] This report delineating goat thefts on the Edwards Plateau of Texas was passed up to the President.[66] Rarely has goat theft reached such an exalted level in the councils of government.

Funston did reassure the governor that the army would of course cooperate with the State of Texas "with a view to preventing marauding bands from crossing from Mexico into the United States and of aiding in the capture of those who did cross and in the recovery of stolen property." The general informed Ferguson that he had ordered the commanders of the cavalry patrol districts in the Big Bend to "Redouble vigilance to prevent . . . acts of lawlessness and continue to do everything possible to capture thieves, recover stolen property . . . and cooperate with state and county authorities." Funston informed the adjutant general that "Reports from the Big Bend District indicate that ranchers on the river are terrorized through fear of marauders, and extraordinary efforts are being made . . . to give protection along the border."[67]

Not only was Governor Ferguson turned down by the President, but in late April he was faced with yet another problem with the federal government—a huge scandal that was not of his making, but one with which he would have to deal. On April 14, Captain Collin H. Ball, the army officer assigned as Instructor/Inspector of the Texas National Guard, submitted a confidential report to the Division of Militia Affairs in the War Department reporting what the secretary of war would delicately call "certain irregularities" regarding the illegal sale of rifles, ammunition, uniforms, tents, saddles, etc., which had been furnished to the TNG by the War Department.[68]

Captain Ball's report worked its way through the War Department bureaucracy, and on April 23, Army Chief of Staff Major General Hugh L. Scott ordered the Southern Department to send an inspector general to investigate the missing arms and equipment.[69] Interestingly, seventy-two hours later the secretary of war directed General Scott to notify the inspector general of the Southern Department "to suspend until further orders" the investigation.[70] However, on April 28, 1915, General Mills notified the adjutant general that the investigation which had been "temporarily suspended" was to move forward.[71] It is unclear from the available documentation why the investigation was briefly suspended, but it can be speculated that certain Texas politicians in Washington were notified and their advice solicited before resuming the investigation.

Secretary of War Garrison formally notified Governor Ferguson of the investigation in the first week of May. On May 5 a worried Ferguson responded: "Like you I have only just received information about this matter and I shall use every effort to develop the facts . . . bringing the guilty parties to speedy justice."[72] The principal guilty party the governor alluded to was Lieutenant Colonel

Emmet E. Walker, the veteran assistant quartermaster general of the Texas National Guard. Walker's partner in crime was Captain George J. Head, commanding the national guard company in Brownsville. Ironically, Walker had been relieved on February 1, at the beginning of the Ferguson administration, not because of malfeasance but presumably because he had not supported Ferguson during the gubernatorial campaign. Walker was demoted to the rank of major and reassigned as Subsistence Officer on February 1. Then, as a result of the unfolding scandal, he received a dishonorable discharge effective on April 15. He did the intelligent thing and fled to Mexico. Adjutant General Hutchings employed the Pinkerton Detective Agency to track Walker down. Head not only fled to Mexico but got himself a commission as a major in the Carranza army. But both fugitives eventually returned to Texas. In June, 1916, they were tried in Austin. They pleaded not guilty but were convicted on all counts and were sentenced to three years and one day in the federal penitentiary at Leavenworth.[73]

When the scandal surfaced in Texas newspapers, former governor Colquitt was also embarrassed by the flap, which could well have implications for his political future. He wrote to Hutchings: "If the federal government ever complained about the state militia selling their equipment to the Mexicans during my administration I did not hear of it." He asked Hutchings if he were aware of the theft and stated the obvious—"the statement from Washington is a serious reflection on the Texas National Guard . . ." if it were true.[74] It was all too true. Colquitt asked Hutchings to write to him at once. Hutchings prudently did not commit his response to paper but saw his former boss and explained in person the extent of the thefts.[75]

During the Colquitt administration Colonel Walker, with the enthusiastic assistance of Captain Head, had sold off an estimated $30,000 worth of rifles, small arms ammunition, uniforms, saddles, tents, beds, and mess gear both to Mexican revolutionaries and to St. Louis and New York City arms dealers.[76] For example, on December 21, 1914, Walker shipped two boxcar loads of military hardware to Cal Hirsch and Son of St. Louis, Missouri, a major army surplus dealer.[77] Earlier in the year he had sent the Hirsch firm thirteen crates of rifles, fifty-four crates of small arms ammunition, "one bundle" of tents, and assorted cots.[78] It should be noted that not all of the equipment Walker attempted to sell was usable. Six crates of unidentified "military supplies" were shipped on November 14, 1914, to Isaac Lehmann, an army surplus dealer in New York City. In January, 1915, Lehmann shipped them back to Walker, apparently because they were worthless.[79] The resourceful Colonel Walker also shipped a boxcar load of uniforms to Captain Head in Brownsville. Head moved them across the river to Matamoros where General Lucio Blanco's Constitutionalist troops were soon splendidly attired in Texas National Guard uniforms.[80] Colonel Walker and Captain Head received an estimated total of $7,300, which was a respectable sum in 1915, from the sale of the stolen military equipment.[81]

Walker had been able to conceal his thefts by a perfectly legitimate technique known to every military quartermaster—"surveying," or stipulating on the appropriate army form that the items were no longer usable and were declared surplus. This equipment was usually destroyed and was so certified by an officer. Since the good colonel was personally responsible for this equipment, he knew how to manipulate the system. By "surveying" he effectively covered his tracks. Only after Walker was fired did his fraud come to light, probably as a result of someone on the adjutant general's staff tipping off Captain Ball, who immediately initiated an inventory of all army equipment that had been furnished to the Texas National Guard.[82]

On its face the scandal should have had little or no impact on the Rangers, but the attention of the governor, the adjutant general, all three Ranger captains, and several Rangers was focused on investigating the massive thefts at the very time when every Ranger was desperately needed in the Lower Valley. A few examples will suffice. In April, Hutchings sent Captain Fox to St. Louis to obtain an itemized list of the equipment Walker had sold to Cal Hirsch.[83] In May, Captain Edward H. Smith was ordered to Appleby to locate stolen national guard equipment.[84] In July, Hutchings ordered Captain Sanders to travel to Eagle Pass to recover some national guard equipment that Colonel Walker had consigned to himself.[85] That same month Captain Henry Lee Ransom, commanding a newly created company in South Texas, was ordered by the adjutant general to go to the Brownsville national guard rifle range to remove all the equipment, box it up, and ship it to Austin.[86] Ranger O. D. Cardwell spent approximately six months traveling throughout the state during the period April–September, 1915, attempting to recover missing equipment.[87] He made his most startling discovery when he located a tent belonging to the national guard unit at Corpus Christi. The tent had been "loaned" to a group of enterprising prostitutes, who were using it as a portable brothel on a beach south of town.[88]

While the Rangers were attempting to retrieve the stolen equipment, Secretary of War Garrison sent Ferguson in early July the results of the inspector general's investigation. It was as damning a report as one could imagine. Insofar as the Rangers were concerned, it noted that whenever there were thefts at national guard armories, the Rangers were called in to investigate. The report observed, however, that as a result of these Ranger investigations, "Nothing seems to have been accomplished. . . ." Furthermore, the report seemingly called for the removal of Adjutant General Hutchings, noting that had he been "active in the performance of his duties . . . he would have discovered many of the irregularities and illegal practices going on in his office. From all I can gather . . . , he is very weak and seems to be afraid to take any action against any members of the Organized Militia on account of the political effect it would probably have against him."[89] The secretary of war's final comment was: "In conclusion, my dear

Governor, I take the liberty to say candidly . . . that the general efficiency of the National Guard of Texas has reached a very low point. I know that you are anxious to put an end to this unfortunate condition and I therefore beg to offer you the hearty assistance and cooperation of the War Department in any measures that you may undertake to rehabilitate the military establishment of the State."[90]

As a result of the scandal, Ferguson wanted to replace Hutchings but was apparently unable to find a suitable candidate. He explained that the

> Question of an adjutant general has concerned me no little. With alleged shortage and recheck of Federal property and the indictment of former officers of the Texas National Guard for misappropriation of federal property pending, the question of a change of Adjutant General has been one of serious expediency. In addition, the matter of finding an Adjutant General of necessary qualifications has been a matter of considerable difficulty.[91]

But it was the potential financial liability that the state faced which most worried the governor. In his letter to Ferguson, the secretary of war had quoted the inspector general's recommendation that $91,136.44 be charged against the State of Texas's annual national guard allotment of $100,000.[92] This caused Ferguson to cancel the national guard summer camp because if the state were forced to repay the War Department there was not enough money for the encampment.[93] For the governor to cancel summer camp was unprecedented. National guard units nationwide spent fourteen days every summer under the eyes of army officers, and this was literally the only time they received any real training. Furthermore, the cancellation would have consequences less than a year later when in early May, 1916, President Wilson activated the entire Texas National Guard (along with the Arizona and New Mexico National Guards) and sent them to the border. Because it had been almost two years since the TNG had received any specialized instruction, the troops performed miserably when they were called up. Furthermore, as noted earlier, the State of Texas was perpetually in arrears in paying its bills. One hundred thousand dollars, or any significant part thereof, would put a severe strain on the treasury.

Therefore Ferguson had his adjutant general, the Rangers, and national guard officers scrambling to locate blankets, shoes, tents, and rifles which over the years had been loaned to citizens, including Governor Colquitt's brother, had been misplaced, or had been stolen by someone other than Colonel Walker and Captain Head. As the inspector general's report noted, "Property has evidently been loaned to civilians not authorized to receive it," and "rifles had been loaned to some Shriners at Fort Worth and were badly abused by them." Moreover, "tentage was used by officers for pleasure trips," and "the use of the issue shoe [shoes issued with uniforms] for general purposes seems quite common."[94]

What happened as a result of the discovery of Colonel Walker's theft was an exhaustive inventory of all national guard equipment. Since a significant portion of the missing equipment had been lost, misplaced, or stolen as early as 1900, Ferguson was understandably irate that his administration was being blamed for incidents that had occurred under previous governors.95 Yet he soldiered on, grumbling privately to political friends but publicly and privately continuing to support the Wilson administration.96

Hutchings, who unquestionably realized that his job was at stake, used all of the resources at his command—particularly the Rangers—to try to locate as much missing equipment as possible. Given the paltry Ranger appropriation, the cost of the statewide search quickly depleted the Ranger budget. By July, Hutchings was ordering Ranger captains not to spend a cent that was not absolutely necessary. He even suggested that each Ranger company might have to carry over expenses into the next fiscal year, which began on September 1, because there simply was not enough money remaining in the budget, in large part because of costs associated with the national guard scandal.97

It was under these inauspicious circumstances that in the summer of 1915 the Ranger Force had to confront the greatest challenge in the history of the organization, when the Plan de San Diego caused South Texas to explode in violence.

CHAPTER EIGHT

THE PLAN DE SAN DIEGO

T HE Plan de San Diego embodied the most bizarre irredentist conspiracy in American history, and it led to the bloodiest and most controversial episode in the history of the Texas Rangers. The "Plan," or manifesto, reflected the practice in Mexico of any self-respecting revolutionary movement being accompanied by a manifesto denouncing those in power and setting forth the aims of the rebels. Such a "plan" was named for the locality where it was first promulgated. The Plan de San Diego was purportedly signed on January 6, 1915, in the small South Texas town of San Diego, population 1,900.

The provisions of the document were truly breathtaking.[1] It established a Provisional Directorate and designated one Agustín S. Garza as the military chief of the revolutionary movement. The document then laid out the movement's specific objectives:

1. On February 20, 1915, at 2:00 a.m. there would occur an uprising against the United States government to proclaim the liberty of blacks from the "Yankee tyranny" that had held them in "iniquitous slavery since remote times," and to proclaim the independence of Texas, New Mexico, Arizona, Colorado, and California, "of which States the REPUBLIC OF MEXICO was robbed in a most perfidious manner by North American imperialism."

2. To achieve these objectives an army would be formed under the leadership of commanders named by the Supreme Revolutionary Congress of San Diego, Texas. This army, known as the "Liberating Army for Races and Peoples," would fight under a red and white banner bearing the inscription "Equality and Independence."

3. Each commander was assigned certain cities to capture; once he had done so, he would amass their weaponry and funds in order to provide the necessary resources to continue the struggle. Commanders would account for everything to their superiors.

4. Upon capturing a city, especially a state capital, commanders must immediately appoint municipal authorities to preserve order and assist the revolutionary cause.

5. "It is strictly forbidden to hold prisoners, either special prisoners (civilians) or soldiers; and the only time that should be spent in dealing with them is that which is absolutely necessary to demand funds (loans) of them; and whether these demands be successful or not, they shall be shot immediately without any pretext."

6. "Every foreigner who shall be found armed and cannot prove his right to carry arms, shall be summarily executed, regardless of his race or nationality."

7. "Every North American over sixteen years of age shall be put to death; and only the aged men, the women, and the children shall be respected; and on no account shall the traitors to our race be spared or respected."

8. "The Apaches of Arizona, as well as the INDIANS (Redskins) of the territory" would have their lands returned, so that they would assist the revolutionary cause.

9. All appointments and ranks of subordinate officers in the revolutionary army, as well as those of other conspirators who might wish to cooperate with the cause, would be reviewed by their superiors.

10. "The movement having gathered force, and once having possessed ourselves of the States above alluded to, we shall proclaim them an INDEPENDENT REPUBLIC, later requesting (if it be thought expedient) annexation to MEXICO, without concerning ourselves at that time about the form of government which may control the destinies of the common mother country."

11. When the revolutionary movement had obtained independence for the blacks, the revolutionists would grant them a banner, "which they themselves shall be permitted to select," and the revolutionists would aid them in obtaining "six States of the American Union, which states border upon those already mentioned," so the blacks could form an independent republic of their own.

12. "None of the leaders shall have power to make terms with the enemy, without first communicating with the superior officers of the army, bearing in mind that this is a war without quarter; nor shall any leader enroll in his ranks any foreigner unless said foreigner belong to the Latin, the Negro, or the Japanese race."

13. It is understood that upon the triumph of the cause, no member of this conspiracy would fail to recognize his superior, nor to aid others seeking to destroy "what has been accomplished by such great work."

14. As soon as possible, each local junta would select delegates who would elect a Permanent Directorate of the Revolutionary Congress. At this meeting the powers and duties of the Permanent Directorate would be determined, and the Revolutionary Plan could be amended or revised.

15. It was understood that the revolutionists would achieve the independence of the blacks, and that "on no account will we accept aid, either moral or pecuniary, from the Government of Mexico; and it need not consider itself under any obligations in this, our movement."

The Plan de San Diego could, without exaggeration, be termed visionary. But as so often happens, what one is dealing with insofar as the Plan is concerned, is a question of just whose ox is being gored. Militant Hispanics were outraged that the Americans stole Texas from the Mexicans—who stole it from the Spaniards, who stole it from the Indians, who stole it from each other. The social justice envisioned in the Plan took little notice of Indian claims; there was a nod toward the Apaches of Arizona, but no specific reference to other tribes whose claims to the Southwest presumably had equal merit. As for blacks, their future lay not in a Hispanic-ruled Southwest but in an independent South, and they would graciously be permitted to select their very own flag. Most intriguing of all was the reference to the Japanese. Why? It certainly reflects no concern for Asians in general, since only the Japanese were mentioned. Perhaps it was because Mexican factions such as the carrancistas were anxious to secure Japanese support, both diplomatic and as a source of armaments.

There is much about this conspiracy that remains obscure, including the authorship of the Plan itself. Speculation about who wrote it has produced considerable literature, and the candidates cover a wide spectrum. The suggested authors range all the way from William Martin Hanson, a former U.S. marshal and future Ranger captain who had been expelled from Mexico in 1914, to the Germans, the huertistas, the magonistas, or the carrancistas.[2] Yet the leader of the magonistas, Ricardo Flores Magón, denied there was a Plan de San Diego, describing the conflict in Texas as a Hispanic struggle for social justice.[3] A possible author is one Francisco Alvarez Tostado, a radical journalist who wrote a precursor document in 1914.[4] Several Chicano historians have uncritically accepted the Plan at face value, as a clarion call for the liberation of downtrodden Hispanics.[5] Rodolfo Acuña even attempts to justify the racist and genocidal provisions of the Plan:

> Clearly the most controversial section in the plan called for the murder of all white males over 16. The sensationalism surrounding this statement has muddled a discussion of the merits of or need for an uprising. Extremism must be understood in the prevailing conditions and differences must be drawn between normal circumstances and the violence suffered by Mexicans in Texas. Few, for instance, would have considered it extreme if Europeans had published a similar plan against the Germans during World War II. But a different standard seems to exist for Third World people.[6]

He is evidently an admirer of Barry Goldwater, who famously declared that "extremism in the defense of liberty is no vice."

No one knows for certain who wrote the Plan de San Diego. Nor is it known with certainty where it was written.[7] Almost certainly it was not produced in San Diego, Texas, as claimed, and for a very simple reason. The Plan was not conceived in a vacuum, but little attention has been paid to the context within which it appeared. As for San Diego, previous writers have not considered the fact that San Diego was the county seat of Duval County, which was ruled with an iron hand by the political boss Archie Parr, "the Duke of Duval," and in Duval County not a sparrow fell without Parr knowing about it. Thus it is highly unlikely that such a conspiracy could have flourished under his nose. It was also asserted at the time that the Plan was signed in a Monterrey, Nuevo León, prison, but as will be discussed shortly, this too is improbable. So, not only do we not know the Plan's author, we are uncertain as to its place of origin. The definitive study of the Plan de San Diego has yet to be written. Yet in the final analysis, what is important about the Plan is not who wrote it or where it was written but rather the use to which it was put and who benefited by that use.

The circumstances that created the Plan occurred on both sides of the Rio Grande. By the fall of 1914, the Constitutionalists had triumphed and had driven General Victoriano Huerta into exile. The victorious revolutionists soon began fighting among themselves, unleashing what has been called "The War of the Winners." Pancho Villa's Division of the North was aligned with Emiliano Zapata's guerrillas from Morelos. The villistas and *zapatistas* were fighting Venustiano Carranza who had installed himself as de facto president of Mexico. Carranza's forces were led by General Alvaro Obregón, who proved to be the most successful general of the Revolution.

By December, 1914, Villa's and Zapata's troops had captured Mexico City and outnumbered Carranza and Obregón's soldiers by a margin of more than three to one. Because it seemed certain that Villa and Zapata were going to win, there was a significant shift in sentiment toward the villistas in the northern tier of states— particularly in northeastern Mexico, which had previously been loyal to Carranza. Across the Rio Grande in the Lower Valley, both Hispanics and Anglos linked up with villista organizers who were recruiting guerrilla raiders to attack Carranza strongholds along the river. This was particularly true in Hidalgo County upriver from Brownsville where the political boss, Deodoro Guerra, was an enthusiastic supporter of Villa, loaning $3,500 to Villa's principal organizer in the Lower Valley, Dr. Andrés Villarreal.[8] More importantly, Guerra utilized his sheriff, A. Y. Baker, the redoubtable ex-Ranger, and his deputies, along with McAllen Town Marshal Everett Anglin, a former Ranger and mounted Customs inspector, to pro- tect villista raiding parties from United States officers investigating neutrality vio- lations. Guerra's minions also arrested carrancista spies, and according to a Bureau of Investigation agent, may have even been involved in the murder of one who "disappeared."[9] Guerra's people hauled guns and ammunition to the river for Villarreal, and beginning in late 1914 and accelerating into January, 1915, Guerra and his associates assisted Villarreal in recruiting local Hispanics and refugees from the Revolution. As a result of their cooperation, Villarreal successfully recruited, equipped, and dispatched from Hidalgo County at least five armed expeditions, each numbering from seventeen to fifty men, across the river to attack carrancista units attempting to defend Matamoros against an approaching villista army.[10] Since the defenders of Matamoros were outnumbered at least five to one, car- rancista commanders were desperate to relieve pressure on their troops by stop- ping the harassing raids that were attacking their rear from across the river. They needed a diversion, something that would force the American authorities to crack down on the intrigues of villista sympathizers in South Texas.

To understand the situation in January, 1915, a bit of Lower Valley history is necessary. From Texas independence in 1836 through 1900, the population of the region was predominantly Hispanic (at least 95 percent), and isolated from the rest of Texas; the closest ties were with Mexican communities across the Rio Grande, and traffic back and forth was largely unhampered. But beginning in 1904 with the arrival of the railroad in Brownsville, the area was now linked by rail to the rest of the nation. This meant that the rich soil of the region, when supple- mented by gravity and pump irrigation from the Rio Grande, could produce huge quantities of truck crops for a national market. People poured in, determined to make the desert bloom. Developers in the Valley brought "homeseekers" by the trainload to buy fertile farmland. Land that had sold for only $1 to $2 per acre in 1900 was selling for as much as $300 per acre by 1914. As of 1915, the Lower Valley had approximately 140,000 acres that had been cleared of brush, planted in crops, and watered by an enormously expensive network of some 1,200 miles of canals distributing water pumped from the Rio Grande. This extraordinary land boom inevitably created problems. As the historian of South Texas Evan Anders has noted, the few Anglo settlers who had arrived in the nineteenth century had melded into the society and culture of the region. They learned Spanish, joined the Roman Catholic Church, married into the leading Hispanic families, socialized and did business with the local elites. Furthermore, they often assumed responsibility for their employees, assisting them in a variety of ways. By so doing these Anglo elites won the personal loyalty of their employees.[11]

By contrast, the multitude who arrived after the railroad was completed refused to learn Spanish and despised Hispanics, whom they viewed as ignorant and lazy. Furthermore, they paid the prevailing low wage scales, but unlike the predecessor Anglos they would not deign to assist their employees. They even refused to associate with the Hispanic elite, viewing them as social inferiors. What occurred was a monumental clash of cultures, not unlike the one that had produced the independence of Texas in 1836. The Plan de San Diego was the spark that produced a violent explosion.

The Plan first surfaced on January 24, 1915, in Hidalgo County, at the town of McAllen. A Plan de San Diego organizer, Basilio Ramos, Jr., approached Dr. Andrés Villarreal, the principal villista representative in the Lower Valley, and attempted to persuade him to support the Plan de San Diego. Villarreal asked Ramos to come back and see him again. Villarreal immediately went to Deodoro Guerra, explained what Ramos was doing, and requested that he be arrested.

Guerra notified Hidalgo County Deputy Sheriff Tom Mayfield, a tough hatchet-faced officer, who waited for Ramos to show up for an appointment with Villarreal. When Ramos appeared, Mayfield arrested him and took him off to jail in Edinburg, the county seat. Mayfield seized a variety of documents that Ramos carried.[12] When Mayfield and Guerra examined these papers they were astonished. They immediately telephoned Brownsville and urgently requested Captain T. B. Bishop, the deputy United States marshal for the Southern District of Texas, to come to Edinburg to interrogate Ramos.

When Bishop, accompanied by federal Bureau of Investigation Special Agent Frank McDevitt, arrived in Edinburg, Sheriff Baker informed the federal officials that he wanted them to take Ramos off his hands immediately. Baker said he believed that an attempt would be made by Plan de San Diego militants in the Matamoros area to rescue Ramos. For Baker, who was a gunman of renown, to express apprehension regarding one of his prisoners was extraordinary.

The documents seized from Ramos stunned Bishop and McDevitt. They included a carbon copy of the Plan with its declaration of a genocidal war without quarter against Anglos. The Plan was full of big talk, but of course implementing it was going to prove rather difficult. It has been claimed that the Plan de San Diego insurgents numbered as many as 5,000.[13] This is a figure plucked from the stratosphere. A generous estimate of the insurgents in 1915 is in the 200 to 250 range. But in a region where Anglos were outnumbered ten to one, even half-baked plans caused nervousness among these minority residents of the Lower Valley, and if there was one thing they cared about it was minority rights. While there was skepticism and even some mirth among federal, state, and local law enforcement authorities concerning the seriousness of the Plan, other documents seized from Ramos bore evidence of a plot of some magnitude.

Ramos had both a small codebook with him and a coded letter, not the usual pocket litter which most Mexican revolutionaries carried.[14] Ramos underwent a series of interrogations, first by local officials and then by Bishop and McDevitt, before being transported to Brownsville where Immigration officials questioned him. The veteran head of the Immigration district office in Brownsville, E. P. Reynolds, who spoke fluent Spanish, after interrogating Ramos in his native language described him as a ". . . fanatic of anarchical tendencies and dangerous."[15]

Among the various federal officers who were aware of Ramos's arrest, there was considerable confusion as to which agency would be responsible for formally arresting Ramos and charging him with a specific offense. Robert Barnes, the special agent in charge of the Bureau of Investigation regional office in San Antonio, ordered McDevitt not to arrest Ramos. Consideration was given to turning him over to the army to hold for a period of time, until federal officials could sort out who was going to be responsible for Ramos. The Immigration Service came to the rescue and held a deportation hearing, in case that was the only alternative available. But after considering the matter for several days, Barnes finally decided to file charges against Ramos.

While federal agencies were sorting out their responsibilities, considerable effort was also being expended on locating the other Plan de San Diego organizers named in Ramos's document, but without success.[16] Federal authorities in Brownsville attempted to suppress information concerning Ramos's arrest and the Plan de San Diego so that his confederates could be located and arrested before they learned of his incarceration. However, on February 2 the Associated Press broke the story of Ramos's arrest. The AP dispatch created a sensation in the border press, with newspaper accounts obviously focused on the scheduled date of the uprising (February 20) and proposed massacre of Anglo males.[17]

Meanwhile, Immigration inspectors were attempting to obtain solid information about Ramos. He told his interrogators he was twenty-four years of age, single, and never married. The Immigration inspectors noted that he was 5'11" tall and weighed 140 pounds—he was tall and slim and appeared to be intelligent. He said he had been born in Nuevo Laredo and had completed primary school, after which he enrolled in a "Catholic school" in Norman, Oklahoma, which he attended for several months, which was unusual for Mexican males of his generation. He said he spoke a little English, which he had learned at the Catholic school. He stated that he was a Mexican citizen and that he had served as a clerk/secretary at the Customs house in Nuevo Laredo for approximately two years—apparently 1912–1914.[18]

But his subsequent movements remain murky. Ramos declared that he was a supporter of General Victoriano Huerta, and as a result had been arrested twice in Mexico after Huerta had fled the country. One arrest, he said, was in Nuevo Laredo where in 1914 he was jailed for a month and, in his words, "was ordered to leave Mexico and never return." According to Ramos, he left Nuevo Laredo, crossing to Laredo in the summer of 1914, where he remained for two months seeking employment before traveling to San Diego, Texas, where he worked for five months selling beer. On December 28, 1914, according to his account, he left San Diego en route to Monterrey. He told his interrogators that it was in Monterrey that he was arrested and jailed for five days because he was a huertista. And, according to Ramos, it was in prison in Monterrey that he joined the Plan de San Diego.[19]

Ramos's account of the Plan being smuggled into the jail "by a friend," to be signed by members of the Provisional Directorate, is not only mysterious, it borders on the absurd. And Ramos's statements must be viewed against the backdrop of events in northeastern Mexico. In early January, 1915, villista armies were on the march and Carranza's forces were falling back on Nuevo Laredo and Matamoros, where they planned to make their final stand with their backs to the Rio Grande. Less than a week after Ramos said he was released from prison in Monterrey, the city fell to a villista army. Significantly, Ramos did not say why or by whom he had been released from prison.

We know that Ramos arrived in Matamoros and there obtained a "safe conduct" document and a pass allowing him to cross from Matamoros to Brownsville at will from the carrancista commander, General Emiliano Nafarrate, a capable officer who in April had repulsed a determined villista assault and siege. Nafarrate personally signed, dated, and addressed the pass to Ramos. Suggestions that the Plan de San Diego was a huertista conspiracy, mainly because Ramos said he was a follower of Huerta, must explain these papers that unequivocally link a ranking Carranza general with Ramos, the self-proclaimed huertista.[20] It has been asserted that Ramos's "claim that he and other followers of Victoriano Huerta drafted the document [the Plan de San Diego] while imprisoned in Monterrey convinced nobody."[21] To the contrary, Ramos convinced some American historians, who have accepted his huertista cover story at face value.

Ramos crossed the river to Brownsville between January 13–15—he could not remember the precise date. Following his arrest, Ramos was given an "in camera" (closed) hearing in Brownsville on February 4 before United States Commissioner E. H. Goodrich who ordered him to be bound over for the May, 1915, federal grand jury under a $5,000 bond, which Ramos could not post; he was remanded to the Cameron County jail.[22] Given the preposterous nature of the Plan de San

Diego, there were those who felt Ramos should be committed, not indicted. But on May 13, a federal grand jury in Brownsville indeed indicted him. The indictment had an air of unreality, for Ramos and the other eight signatories were charged with conspiring "to steal certain property of the United States of America, contrary to the authority thereof, to wit, the states of Texas, Oklahoma, New Mexico, Arizona, Colorado, and California. . . ."[23] Indicating how lightly the Plan was by then regarded, federal Judge Waller T. Burns reduced Ramos's bond from $5,000 to $100, commenting that Ramos needed a "hospital rather than a jail." Ramos posted bond and promptly fled across the river to Matamoros, where the Carranza officials entertained him lavishly.[24] This kind of reception was hardly what would be expected were Ramos actually the huertista he professed to be.

In late January the Rangers had been notified of Ramos's arrest, and federal law enforcement officers provided Captain Sanders with translated copies of the Plan de San Diego. The Rangers were asked if they knew any of the individuals named in the document. Copies of the Plan were forwarded to the adjutant general in Austin more as a curiosity than as a serious law enforcement matter.[25]

Federal officers, however, continued to be troubled by additional portents of future activities by Plan de San Diego conspirators who were not in custody. For example, Deputy U.S. Marshal Bishop reported from Brownsville, "It seems as if the Mexicans here are all arming themselves in secret," commenting that they were purchasing new Winchester rifle scabbards. But he was most concerned about a letter mailed from Laredo which Ramos received from a certain "F.H.U." A jailer at the Cameron County jail opened the letter and turned it over to Bishop who had it translated. It read as follows:

> Your letter was given to me . . . and after having carefully studied the matter of which you speak in your letter we . . . Pedro and I fully understand and applaud the enterprise. In view of the fact that we cannot go to Mexico to be more efficient in the great result which this enterprise will produce, our friends left for the Center of the U.S. to procure partners [probably recruits for the Plan de San Diego] and fixtures . . . [presumably weapons and ammunition]. They have not written me. If you know anything of them tell me: also tell me how you are.[26]

The idea that other unidentified Plan de San Diego organizers were recruiting men and procuring weapons was most worrisome. Ramos, who up to a point had been forthcoming with Immigration inspectors who were conducting his interrogations, flatly refused to identify either his friend "F.H.U." or Pedro, when the letter was read to him. A note appended to the transcript of the Immigration hearing for Ramos read as follows: "This alien is rather stubborn and evasive in his answers, and gives the impression of not desiring to tell all that he knows. . . ."[27]

As the scheduled date for the uprising approached, nervousness swept through the Anglo communities in the Lower Valley. At Pharr, population 770, the chairman of the townsite committee sent a telegram to Governor Ferguson urging him to return two Rangers who had been assigned to Laredo for the smallpox quarantine. As tension rose in the Valley, Adjutant General Hutchings telegraphed Captain Sanders ordering him to enlist two additional Rangers immediately. He also directed him "At the earliest practical minute you will detail two men to be stationed at San Benito."[28]

Because the Rangers were stretched so thinly, local officials began appealing to federal officials for help. Specifically the county attorney of Starr County, writing from Rio Grande City to the United States Attorney for the Southern District of Texas, J. E. Green, Jr., reported that "an armed band of Mexicans, probably belonging to the Carranza faction, crossed into American territory, cutting telephone lines. . . ." Bureau of Investigation Agent Barnes reported to his superior in Washington that the Mexicans had also stolen a horse at gunpoint before a posse succeeded in capturing several of the raiders. There were no Rangers stationed in Starr County at the time of this raid, in late January or early February.[29] It may well have been the opening foray of the Plan de San Diego.

On February 20, Hutchings was scrambling to reassure residents in South Texas that there were sufficient Rangers to handle any problems. He explained in response to an inquiry from a Valley resident who had written the governor, that one Ranger was at Hebbronville, two were at Pharr, and two more were scheduled to be sent immediately to San Benito.[30]

While Sanders was en route to San Benito, Sheriff J. P. Osborn of Jim Wells County had called the adjutant general requesting at least two Rangers, pointing out that local citizens had raised enough private money to enable him to hire two additional deputies. Osborn explained that with two Rangers, two more deputy sheriffs in addition to himself and his one deputy, "I think we can handle the situation." The sheriff did explain that he needed the Rangers for a period of one to two months.[31]

February 20—the announced date for the Plan de San Diego uprising—came and went without incident. The only thing that *may* have occurred was the appearance of a revised Plan de San Diego—a manifesto "To the Oppressed Peoples of America." It was purportedly issued at San Diego on February 20, but again this is highly unlikely. The manifesto was issued in the name of the Revolutionary Congress and was signed by nine individuals—the General in Chief, León Caballo, and eight evidently fictitious signatories. The manifesto reaffirmed the original Plan de San Diego but also proclaimed a social revolution in the United States and the formation of the Social Republic of Texas, from which base the revolution would encompass New Mexico, Arizona, California, Colorado, Utah, and Nevada.[32] Whether this manifesto was even written by the authors of the Plan de

San Diego, or was signed at San Diego, or on February 20, remains unproven.

Benjamin Johnson, who portrays the rebels in a heroic light, attempts by indirection to explain away the genocidal clause in the Plan de San Diego. Since genocide is politically incorrect, if the rebels were running around advocating genocide it would tarnish their heroic image. Thus Johnson states:

> Indeed, the origins of the manifestos and the influence of their authors were so unclear as to allow some to speculate that the Plan itself was a forgery, altered, or even wholly fabricated by Texas Rangers or South Texas Anglos to justify their oppression against Tejanos. The Spanish original of the first version of the Plan did not survive, affording Ramos's captors the opportunity to doctor it. The clause for killing all Anglo males over age sixteen seemed particularly well suited to create mass hysteria, and beginning the document with a call for black rebellion would have had much the same effect.[33]

This improbable speculative scenario rests on several assumptions. The first is that the English version of the Plan was somehow fabricated or altered and, by extension, that the Immigration officials who interrogated Ramos and translated the Plan were part of some racist conspiracy aimed at Hispanics and blacks. Both assumptions, to put it mildly, are unproven.

The Anglos in the Lower Valley must have uttered a heartfelt sigh of relief as February 20 passed. Still, there remained a feeling of apprehension. Captain Sanders, for instance, reported that Hispanics were holding meetings "and are causing considerable uneasiness among the White people."[34] To reassure the elites in the Lower Valley (and the governor and the adjutant general) Sanders had deployed six members of Company A's thin ranks in two-man detachments:

Pharr:	Reneau and Cardwell (Reneau in charge)
San Benito:	Felps and Davenport (Felps in charge)
Alice:	Craighead and Brooks (Craighead in charge)

Sanders had Ranger Willis on permanent assignment at Carrizo Springs, and Sergeant Grimes kept Sanders company at the Del Rio Ranger camp.[35] The legislature, in session in Austin, did its bit to reassure Lower Valley residents when it authorized the addition of ten more men to the Ranger Force.

Some historians have ascribed the origins of the Plan to General Victoriano Huerta and/or followers of the Mexican anarchist Ricardo Flores Magón. More recent scholarship has pointed to the Carranza government as being the principal sponsor of the Plan.[36] Documents in the Federal Bureau of Investigation archive on the Mexican Revolution definitively deposit the Plan at the feet of the carrancistas. Ironically these documents are translated telegrams from a ranking huertista operative in San Antonio, "Rogelio" [no last name given], to Severino Herrera Moreno, a member of Huerta's personal staff in New York where the general was planning to launch a counterrevolution in Mexico. A key telegram, dated April 29, 1915, from Rogelio reads in part: "I spoke personally with Carranzista [sic] J. S. Pedrosa who is agitating negroes and Mexico-Texans favor Venustiano. He offered to pay me well to aid him. . . . He continues agitation has agents various towns. . . ."[37] This telegram and hundreds of others were secured in San Antonio from the Western Union telegraph office via a subpoena *duces tecum*. Another telegram from Rogelio on April 25, 1915, to Herrera Moreno at the Ansonia Hotel, New York City, reads in part: "Be Tranquil. Keep absolutely secret. Carranzistas [sic] agitating with secrecy. Negroes and Texans in their favor. . . ." (Rogelio's address in San Antonio is given as Sam Houston Place #11c, P.O. Box 110, San Antonio.) The assertion that Herrera Moreno was a ranking huertista operative is based on telegrams from Herrera Moreno to General Huerta and subsequent telegrams from Rogelio to Herrera Moreno after the latter had traveled to New York City to confer with Huerta.[38] These telegrams make much more intelligible why carrancista general Nafarrate provided aid and comfort to Basilio Ramos, an agent who was passing himself off as a follower of Huerta.

The Plan de San Diego continued to simmer during the spring of 1915, and that summer it boiled over. The exchange of two cryptic telegrams was the first indication that raiders under the banner of the Plan de San Diego had made their appearance in the Lower Valley. The adjutant general in a June 19 telegram to Ranger L. W. Edwards at San Benito inquired: "Are the bandits on Texas or Mexican territory. How is situation today?" Edwards responded, "Bandits on American soil situation unchanged."[39]

In June, Sanders had gone to San Benito, and with a couple of his Rangers and some local officers he had "flushed and scattered" a gang who were probably Plan de San Diego raiders crossing the Rio Grande. He boasted that although they had not succeeded in arresting anyone due to what he called "bad luck," the Rangers had "done lots of good" and "it will be some time before they give us trouble again." Pointing out that he had the full cooperation of sheriff's officers and Customs river guards, Sanders said that having cleared everything up, he and his men were headed back to their respective stations on the first train.[40] Sanders could not have been more wrong.

Figure 26. Of all the Rangers of this period, the most famous was unquestionably Frank
Hamer. This photo of Hamer is undated but apparently was taken around 1910. Hamer would
serve off and on as a Ranger until the 1920's when he was selected as a Ranger captain. He
made his reputation when he led the team of law enforcement officers who tracked down and
killed Bonnie Parker and Clyde Barrow in 1934. However, as often happens, his reputation was
inflated. It would be interesting to see documentation for the fifty-three men his biographers
claimed he killed. Recently even Robert Caro in *The Years of Lyndon Johnson: Means of Ascent*
fell for the Hamer legend. *Photo courtesy of Texas Ranger Hall of Fame and Museum.*

Figure 27. Some of Company B Texas Rangers are shown in this 1909 photograph taken in the Texas Panhandle at Amarillo. Left to right are Rangers W. F. Sallis, C. P. Middleton, A. W. Brown, Captain Tom Ross, Sergeant Roscoe Redus, and Ranger James L. Seale. *Photo courtesy of Texas Ranger Hall of Fame and Museum.*

Figure 28. Gus T. "Buster" Jones enlisted as a private in Captain Frank Johnson's Company A in 1908. Although rather short for a Ranger, Buster could handle himself. Like some other ex-Rangers of his era, he signed on as a U.S. Immigration inspector. By 1916, he was a special agent of the federal Bureau of Investigation. Jones's career with the Bureau was quite successful. He would become special agent in charge of the El Paso, Texas, office. He subsequently was named as the first legal attaché (FBI agent in residence—technically the civil attaché) at the United States embassy in Mexico City. During World War II, he served as the Bureau's liaison officer with British Intelligence in the Caribbean. From *Trails and Trials of a Texas Ranger* by William Warren Sterling. Copyright © 1959 by William Warren Sterling. Assigned 1968 to the University of Oklahoma Press. *Reprinted by permission of the publisher.*

CAPTAIN
J. EAGLE VAUGHAN

COMPANY A. RANGERS TEXAS

Figure 29. Jefferson Eagle Vaughan was big, tall, and tough looking. The cocked hat over his eye and his paint horse were typical of his flamboyant style. Vaughan was also lucky—a useful trait for a Ranger. In 1915, one account has him scheduled to accompany the ill-fated contingent ambushed by the notorious Chico Cano and his gang. Vaughan, for whatever reason, did not go. *Photo courtesy of Texas Ranger Hall of Fame and Museum.*

Figure 30. Following the Norias raid, Captain Sanders's Company A were assigned as virtual night watchmen for the King Ranch. Photographed at Norias were left to right George B. Hurst, C. J. Hanson, C. W. Price, Ben T. Tumlinson, Earl R. Wright, John A. Moran, John E. Hensley, Daniel Hinojosa, W. E. Holmes, Leonard Walker, Elmo D. Reed, W. Alonzo Taylor, and Captain Sanders. *Photo courtesy of Texas Rangers Hall of Fame and Museum.*

Figure 31. Ranger Nat B. "Kiowa" Jones was a veteran Ranger who had served in Captain McDonald's company and subsequently under several Ranger captains. He was an inspector for the sheep and goat association during part of the decade. With piercing eyes, Jones was not a man to be trifled with. *Photo courtesy of Texas Ranger Hall of Fame and Museum.*

Figure 32. Ranger Bert Clinton Veale is shown armed to the teeth in 1917 as a member of Company D. But in February 1919, Veale and several of his fellow Rangers got drunk in Austin and Veale decided to shoot one of his colleagues. Unfortunately his colleague was a better shot than Veale and killed him. Since there was a sensational legislative investigation of the Rangers going on at the time, the killing created a small problem for the Adjutant General and the defenders of the Rangers. *Photo courtesy of Texas Ranger Hall of Fame and Museum.*

Figure 33. Captain Will Davis's Company L, Texas Rangers poses in 1918 on the north bank of the Rio Grande at Ysleta, Texas, downriver from El Paso. From left to right are Sergeant J. G. Perkins, A. J. Robertson, Edd Hallebeke, J. D. McClellan, S. R. Ikard, Frank Black, R. E. Hunt, W. R. Holland, Santos Durán, B. L. Pennington, T. E. Perkins, and Captain Will W. Davis. Indicative of the coming change from horse to automobile in Ranger transportation was Company L's trusty Ford Model T. Note the placard hung over the radiator, "Co. L Rangers." *Photo courtesy of Art Robertson, Jr., Las Cruces, New Mexico.*

Black. R.E. Hunt.   W.R. Holland   Santos Duran.

angers   B.F. Pennington. T.E. Perkins. Captain Will D...

Figure 34. Cradling their hardware, Ranger Captain William Martin Hanson and the members of Headquarters Company pose for the camera in the summer of 1919. In front, sitting on the ground, Ranger S. O. Durst; Second row left to right: Ranger Private John R. McMillan, Colonel H. C. Smith, Captain Hanson, Sergeant Joe Brooks. Standing left to right: Rangers Frank Matthews, George Millard, C. J. Blackwell, J. R. Hunnicutt, Samuel Clay Blackwell. *Photo courtesy of Texas Ranger Hall of Fame and Museum.*

Figure 35. Although a number of Rangers were big and tall, there were Rangers who had significant physical handicaps. One of these was Ranger Arch Miller, second from right in this photograph, taken in the Big Bend. Although it is not indicated in the photograph, Miller had only one arm. However, as one observer put it, Miller was better than a whole lot of two-armed Rangers. From left to right are Pete Crawford, a state game warden, Ray Miller (Arch Miller's brother), John Pool, Arch Miller, and Steve Bernett, Justice of the Peace. *Photo courtesy of Texas Ranger Hall of Fame and Museum.*

Figure 36. Another Ranger who was handicapped was Ranger Pat Craighead whose leg was amputated after he was shot accidentally following a gun battle near Brownsville in 1910 in which a Ranger was killed in an ambush. Craighead remained a Ranger for several years after he lost his leg. From left to right, Ranger H. A. Carnes and Craighead. *Photo courtesy of Texas Ranger Hall of Fame and Museum.*

Figure 37. Although there were very few Hispanic Texas Rangers during the decade 1910–1920, there were more in some Ranger companies than in others. For example, in Captain Will Wright's Company D, three of the thirteen members were Hispanic. Front row left to right are Sid Hutchison and Stanley Morton. Second row left to right: Sanders Peterson, Robert Sutton, Captain Wright, John Hensley and Sam Chesshir. Back row left to right Robert D. Brown, Jesse Pérez, Sr., Roy L. Hearn, D. C. "Jack" Webb, Sergeant John Edds (whose mother was Hispanic), and Juan González. *Photo courtesy of Texas Rangers Hall of Fame and Museum.*

Figure 38. By the early 1920's, most of the Rangers of the previous decade had retired, been
fired, were cattle inspectors, worked for various federal law enforcement agencies, or were
dead. This is illustrated in a comparatively rare photograph (for the period) of the entire
forty-one-man Ranger force. In the front row (sixth from left and following) are Captain
Frank Hamer, Governor Pat Neff, Adjutant General T. D. Barton, Captains Will Wright,
R. W. Aldrich and Jerry Gray. Although there is a sprinkling of Rangers who had served in
the earlier decade in the back rows, most were new Rangers. *Photo courtesy of Texas Ranger
Hall of Fame and Museum.*

Figure 39., Luis de la Rosa, a native of Cameron County, was nominally the leader of the Plan de San Diego militants. This photograph of a button worn by some raiders is found in the archives of the Huntington Library. Interestingly the photograph of the button reads "Cap. Luis de la Rosa" with the note "taken in 1914." This is some evidence that de la Rosa had been a captain in the Carranza Army in 1914. There is also a hole in the photograph, which appears to be a bullet hole. *Photo courtesy of the Huntington Library.*

Figure 40. On November 30, 1915, the de facto President of Mexico, Venustiano Carranza, met on the international bridge linking Matamoros and Brownsville with Colonel A. P. Blocksom, the commander of U.S. Army troops in the Lower Valley. Carranza is in the center with a long beard. Colonel Blocksom is to Carranza's left. On Carranza's right wearing a suit is General de División Emiliano A. P. Nafarrate, who had organized and directed the raids for Carranza. Presumably Carranza and Nafarrate were privately laughing at having repeatedly raided the Lower Valley and yet achieving their objective—diplomatic recognition of the Carranza regime by the United States. *Photo courtesy of Robert Runyon Collection, Center for American History, University of Texas at Austin.*

Figure 41. The most notorious Mexican bandit on the border during this decade was the infamous Chico Cano shown here somewhere in the Big Bend. This photograph was taken several years after Cano's 1915 ambush slaying of Ranger Eugene Hulen and Customs inspector Joe Sitter. Left to right are Army Major Considine, Cano, and Army Captain Leonard Matlack. The U.S. Army's position on Cano was at best ambivalent as indicated by this picture. *Photo courtesy of Ransom Humanities Center, University of Texas at Austin.*

Figure 42. The Norias subheadquarters of the King Ranch was the target of the Plan de San Diego raid of August 8, 1915. Behind the five Rangers is the building housing the offices for the Norias division of the huge million-acre ranch. The tracks of the St. Louis, Brownsville, and Mexico Railroad were only a few dozen feet from the two-story house. From left to right, the Rangers are Howard C. Cragg, Ira J. Heard, Sam P. Chessher, Joe B. Brooks, and Lloyd A. David. *Photo courtesy of Texas Ranger Hall of Fame and Museum.*

Figure 43. The heroes of the Norias battle of August 8, 1915, were not the Texas Rangers, who never even sighted the raiders. They were an eight-man detachment from Troop C, 12th Cavalry, Corporal Allen Mercer and seven privates, who were sent from Brownsville seventy miles north to the King Ranch subheadquarters. Corporal Mercer is standing (third from left) with five of his men. Two of his privates were wounded during the gun battle. *Photo courtesy of Robert Runyon Collection, Center for American History, University Texas at Austin.*

Figure 44. *(Following spread)* The most famous photograph of the "bandit war" was taken the day following the Norias raid. On the left is Ranger Captain Monroe Fox, the horseman in the center is unidentified, and Tom Tate, Norias foreman and former Ranger, is on the right. Fox and the other two men had roped the bodies of four of the dead raiders and were dragging the bodies back to Norias. During the 1919 Ranger investigation there was much ado about the Rangers's disrespect for the dead bandits. Ironically, not a single Ranger participated in the defense of Norias. *Photo courtesy of Robert Runyon Collection, Center for American History, University of Texas at Austin.*

Figure 45. Texas Ranger D. C. "Jack" Webb could have obviously used sensitivity training. Webb is shown playing with what is reportedly the skull of one of the dead Norias raiders. The photograph is undated. Webb would later serve as a member of Captain Will L. Wright's Company D, which was based in the lower Rio Grande Valley. *Photo courtesy of Dogie Wright Collection, Center for American History, University of Texas at Austin.*

Figure 46. A young, unidentified man in early October, 1915, looks at the remains of four visible bodies hidden in the brush at Ebenezer's Crossroads on the road to Donna in south-central Hidalgo County, one county upriver from Brownsville. Although only four bodies are in the photograph, there was a total of fourteen bodies found, apparently by U.S. Army troops patrolling the area. This was the single largest atrocity reported during the "bandit war." The Texas Rangers were credited with killing all of them. *Photo courtesy of Museum of South Texas History, Edinburg, Texas.*

Figure 47. Fighting along the Rio Grande between U.S. Army troops and Carrancista units during September/October 1915 reached such a level, particularly around Progreso on the Rio Grande in Hidalgo County, that cavalry units were forced to dig trenches. This photograph shows one U.S. Army entrenchment with a cavalryman running and keeping low as he sprinted to the trench. *Photo courtesy of Museum of South Texas History, Edinburg, Texas.*

Figure 48. The Plan de San Diego raiders carried out their most spectacular raid on the night of October 18, 1915. They derailed a St. Louis, Brownsville, and Mexico Railroad passenger train less than seven miles north of Brownsville. The photograph was taken the following day and shows a U.S. Army detachment guarding the train. Led by Luis de la Rosa, the raiders killed three passengers (including a U.S. Army enlisted man and a physician who was a State of Texas quarantine officer) and wounded three others. They robbed the passengers and fled back across the border. Anglo Texans were outraged and demanded that the United States government send additional troops to the border. *Photo courtesy of Robert Runyon Collection, Center for American History, University of Texas at Austin.*

CHAPTER NINE

THE BANDIT WAR (July–August)

THE principal targets of the Plan de San Diego's announced war without quarter—Anglo males over sixteen—were too obtuse to realize that their deaths would be both legitimate and necessary, as Rodolfo Acuña would have us believe, and they obstinately refused to be massacred. In fact, their attitude was that since the Mexicans were so anxious to wage a war without quarter they would show them what a war without quarter was all about. What ensued was what Anglos in South Texas called the "Bandit War," a savage struggle involving a lot of racial profiling, with bullets raining on the just and the unjust alike.

When the shooting began in early July, Captain Sanders's Company A, which had responsibility for the middle and lower Rio Grande, was spread all over South Texas. Sanders only had twelve men, and they were responsible for the territory from Del Rio to Corpus Christi, the Rio Grande Valley to Brownsville, and everything in between—16,500 square miles, or about the size of the states of Massachusetts, Delaware, Rhode Island, and Connecticut combined, with 865 square miles left over.

To cover this impossibly vast territory, the company was deployed as follows: Ranger Willis on permanent assignment to the sheriff of Dimmit County at Carrizo Springs; Captain Sanders and Ranger Craighead at Hebbronville in Jim Hogg County; Rangers Brooks and Price at Alice; Cardwell and Davenport at Rio Grande City; Felps and Edwards at San Benito; Sergeant W. T. Grimes held the fort at Del Rio, where the company was headquartered, leaving only two Rangers, Reneau and Aldrich (a recent Ranger recruit), to respond immediately to the crisis.[1]

The outbreak of the Bandit War is usually given as the evening of July 2, 1915, although it actually began some two weeks earlier. On July 2, a "band of outlaws" was reported near the small community of Sebastian, some thirty miles north of the Rio Grande in Cameron County. Ranger Roy W. Aldrich accompanied a tough mounted Customs inspector, Joseph A. "Pinkie" Taylor,[2] Cameron County Deputy Sheriff Leon Gill, and a group of local ranchers to scout the area. "A man supposed to know about the gang" was arrested that night and turned over to local officers at Lyford, near Sebastian.[3] The raiders eluded the posse around Sebastian on July 2 and surfaced three days later ten miles north at Raymondville, a small ranching community in Willacy County. Ranger Aldrich accompanied two veteran Cameron County deputy sheriffs, José Longoria and Mike Monahan, to Raymondville where they spent the night fruitlessly lying in wait along a road for the outlaws to make their appearance.[4]

By July 6, a thirty-five-man posse was assembled by Cameron County Sheriff W. T. Vann forty miles north of Brownsville at Los Indios Ranch. Only two Rangers (an indication of how thin their ranks were and how stretched were their resources in the Lower Valley) were members of the posse with the majority being local ranchers augmenting sheriff's deputies and mounted Customs inspectors.[5] Seven large ranches were scoured without success. The following day the posse was reinforced by twenty-six members of Troop B, 12th Cavalry, and by additional civilians who volunteered their services to Vann, increasing the size of his posse to almost fifty.[6]

Sheriff Vann early on expressed frustration in coping with these outlaws: "Who they are we have no idea. They are Mexicans, and they must be raiders from the other side. . . . We only know there are from twenty to thirty in number." The sheriff also reported rumors that the bandits planned to rob the bank at Lyford. Vann decided to station a deputy at the bank in case the rumors were correct.[7] And on July 8, Vann informed the local newspaper that he had received an unsigned letter in Spanish warning him that a 100-man force was being organized in Matamoros to attack Brownsville. The attack never materialized, but the threat forced the sheriff to take precautions, further fragmenting his manpower.

The search for the raiders meanwhile continued and was concentrated around a large pasture near Raymondville, but once again the posse came up empty-handed. By July 8, they were reduced to staking out wells, springs, and stock tanks the raiders might use. Although the posse's ranks increased when Hidalgo County Sheriff A. Y. Baker and his deputies joined the hunt,[8] the raiders managed to elude the lawmen, abandoning saddle-sore horses, stealing fresh mounts, and feeding themselves by butchering local ranchers' cattle and goats. The terrain favored the marauders, for despite the large tracts cleared for commercial agriculture most of Cameron and Hidalgo Counties had an abundance of chaparral, mesquite thickets, prickly pear and giant cactus.[9] As Brigadier General James Parker put it, "the terrain lends itself very effectively to raids from across the river."[10] The Rio Grande was a meandering river with banks covered by heavy underbrush, and at the time South Texas was suffering from a severe drought; the flow of the Rio

Grande was much reduced, and attackers could pick and choose where to cross into Texas.

By July 10, Governor Ferguson had become sufficiently exercised over the reports he was receiving from the area that he ordered W. T. Grimes, Sanders's sergeant, to travel to San Benito to investigate conditions in the Lower Valley and report.[11] Sanders soon followed Grimes to San Benito.[12] Although it's unclear when he was ordered to the Lower Valley, Captain Fox was there by July 9. On the 10th he reported that he had visited a ranch three miles from Sebastian. He stated, somewhat illiterately: "We heard of 3 Mex going to this Ranch. And no doubt belongs to the bandit bunch. We got up to a Mex house and 2 ran but got stoped [sic] and their names I do not know. So just left them there."[13]

The tactics of the Plan de San Diego raiders baffled the local lawmen. Sheriff Vann in a newspaper interview "expressed puzzlement as to why the raiders attacked the extreme northern portion of the county which was not only thinly populated but had little property that could be stolen."[14] What also bothered Vann was the fact that the raiders were operating not only in northern Cameron County, but simultaneously on the Rio Grande. During the first week of the raids, a cavalry patrol was fired on near the river as they returned to Brownsville from Port Isabel.

The initial death in the Bandit War occurred July 9, on the line between Cameron and Hidalgo Counties—a foreman on the huge King Ranch, Frank Martin, killed one raider and wounded another. The tempo picked up three days later at a Sunday baile (an open air dance) near Brownsville. Two Cameron County officers—a deputy sheriff and a deputy constable, both Hispanics—were shot to death. The two killers, one of whom was seriously wounded and subsequently died, fled across the river to Matamoros. To be sure, shootings at bailes were not infrequent, but Bureau of Investigation Special Agent J. H. Rogers attributed the killing of Deputy Constable Pablo Falcón and Deputy Sheriff Encarnación Cuéllar to Plan de San Diego conspirators: "the Mexican officers knew of the [Plan de San Diego] before the real beginning of the operations and this was the cause of several efforts to assassinate them."[15]

On July 12, eleven raiders (they had apparently separated into two parties) robbed Nils Peterson's store near Lyford. Holding Peterson at gunpoint, they proceeded to steal a dozen boxes of 30-30 ammunition, six dozen buckshot shotgun shells, tobacco, crackers, bacon, and canned goods. An elderly Hispanic on horseback whom the raiders encountered after robbing the store was kidnaped and forced to act as a guide—suggesting that the Plan de San Diego horsemen were not natives of the area. That night the reluctant guide succeeded in escaping from his captors. Sheriff Vann assembled yet another posse to resume the pursuit but once again failed to apprehend the raiders.[16] Things became so desperate that Vann hired a "human blood-hound"—an aged Mexican Indian whom he described as being of "pure aboriginal stock"—to track the bandits who had robbed Peterson's store. However, neither the human bloodhound nor the sheriff's officers nor the Rangers succeeded in locating the raiders.[17]

The bandits' pattern of operations increasingly worried the authorities. For example, the raiders cut telephone wires after robbing Peterson's store, which was more characteristic of guerrilla warfare than of mere banditry.[18] And at the same time, upriver at Mission, somebody attempted to set fire to the Rio Grande Hardware and Machinery Company by breaking out a window and pouring several gallons of gasoline on the floor, but a night watchman succeeded in putting out the fire.[19] Then on the night of July 13, a prominent Mercedes farmer, F. Carlman, narrowly escaped assassination. He was sitting in his residence when a bullet grazed his nose. Carlman quickly ran out of the back door of his residence and escaped the five-shot fusillade that followed. Although Carlman blamed the shooting on a disgruntled former employee whom a posse failed to apprehend, federal law enforcement officers would later attribute the incident to the Plan de San Diego.[20] A caveat is in order here. In all probability some of the violent incidents had nothing to do with the Plan de San Diego, but the Bureau of Investigation and other agencies were quick to blame Plan militants. It should be emphasized that the Plan de San Diego provided a convenient umbrella for both Anglos and Hispanics to settle scores and seize opportunities.

Five days later Plan de San Diego raiders killed their first victim. He was eighteen-year-old Bryan K. "Red" Boley, who had recently moved from Tampa, Florida, to a ranch eighteen miles east of Raymondville. Boley was working with two Hispanic ranch hands when they spotted a Mexican on horseback carrying a rifle. The three men ran to a nearby ranch house to retrieve their firearms. When they returned to the pasture where they had spotted the horseman, he opened fire on Boley, who was shot twice and killed. A twenty-man posse assembled by three sheriffs—Baker of Hidalgo County, Vann of Cameron County, and Clint Atkins of Willacy County—set out in pursuit of the assassin, whom they failed to locate.[21]

As if things weren't bad enough, the Rangers were facing a financial crisis. At the very time (July 17) that half of the Ranger Force was scouring the Lower Valley in pursuit of Plan de San Diego raiders, Captains Sanders and Fox received an order from Adjutant General Hutchings to keep:

> . . . expenses for . . . July and August . . . at a minimum. No scouts will be made . . . except where actually necessary. It is possible that arrangements will have to be made to carry the subsistence accounts for July and August over to next September. . . . Should a vacancy occur . . . no enlistment will be made to fill such vacancy. This will also obtain for next year, as it has been found that one thousand dollars a year will no longer meet the expenses of a Ranger. . . .[22]

The killing of Boley set off panic in the Valley and caused Governor Ferguson to take drastic action in response to the raids. Neither local sheriffs, backed up by the Customs river guards, nor a company of Rangers had made a dent in the operations of the raiders, and conditions were obviously worsening. Sergeant Grimes reported that "conditions are so bad that many ranchmen are moving their families into town."[23] Two factors influenced Ferguson to act as he did. One was a demand that the governor restore order forthwith made by the wealthy and influential manager of the King Ranch, Caesar Kleberg, who had entertained the governor at the ranch some two months earlier. The second factor had to do with the sale of land in the Lower Valley. The development of irrigation agriculture along the Rio Grande had caused real estate prices to skyrocket. The raids threatened the livelihood of almost every influential politician and landowner from Laredo to Brownsville and fifty to one hundred miles inland from the Rio Grande. If the raids could not be ended quickly, not an acre of land could be sold to "homeseekers" from the Midwest. Furthermore, since many of the Valley elite had speculated in land and were in hock up to their eyeballs with local banks, those financial institutions would probably go under. Thus the entire financial structure of the Lower Valley was in imminent peril if something were not done and done quickly.[24]

The State of Texas appealed to the government for help, but the view from Washington was that it was just another case of Texas crying wolf. In late June, General Frederick Funston went public with a statement given to the press in San Antonio regarding requests for additional troops for the border. He explained that he would not request reinforcements because some Texas cattlemen—by implication suggesting that *many* cattlemen on the border—were in league with Mexican cattle thieves. The Southern Department commander suggested that this criminal behavior was partly responsible for the bandit activity in the lower Rio Grande Valley. He also stated that the army was legally limited in its ability to intervene along the border, noting that there were only two circumstances in which he could use troops: One was when armed bands were recruited in the United States to invade Mexico in violation of the neutrality statutes. Significantly, the other circumstance was "where raids are made by armed bands from across the border."[25]

It was carrancista support that enabled the raids to continue. Why would Carranza sponsor raids into Texas? Because he desperately needed United States diplomatic recognition. At first glance this seems a counterproductive policy, but in reality it was brilliant. Carranza was emerging as the winner in the latest round of civil war in Mexico, but he couldn't feel secure unless and until the United States formally recognized him as president of that country. Otherwise the United States retained the option of supporting rival revolutionary factions; Carranza himself had profited enormously from the refusal of the United States to recognize Victoriano Huerta as the legitimate ruler of Mexico. Given the imperative,

Carranza could foment raids in the Rio Grande Valley but control their intensity, ensuring that they didn't become serious enough to provoke American intervention. He could, and did, argue that Mexican exiles and other malefactors were causing all the trouble and suggest strongly that were he recognized as president he would quickly put a stop to these incursions.

General Funston had figuratively revealed his playbook to the Plan de San Diego raiders. By announcing that he would not reinforce the limited number of troops in the Valley, he made life easier for the raiders. In addition, bands of raiders, composed of both Hispanic residents of the Valley and Carranza troops in mufti, would be exempt from army retaliation as long as they appeared to be ordinary bandits stealing horses and cattle. It would be virtually impossible to determine whether they were U.S. or Mexican citizens—only that they were Mexican. As long as they were able to conceal the fact that Carranza troops in civilian clothing were involved, they would only have to contend with the small number of sheriffs' deputies, Texas Rangers, and Customs river guards.

We can only speculate as to whether General Emiliano Nafarrate, the Carranza commander in Matamoros, and the leaders of the Plan de San Diego who reported to him were aware of the legal strictures under which General Funston was operating, but copies of the Brownsville *Daily Herald* went across the river and were read in Matamoros. We can assume that Nafarrate and company read Funston's public statements and acted on them. It should be noted that for more than six weeks the raiders succeeded in concealing the sponsorship of the raids and the fact that troops in Nafarrate's command provided the cadre for the raiders. Although there was evidence that the attacks originated in Mexico, there was no solid proof. The fact that the raiders often fled across the river was in itself not conclusive evidence, for it was common practice for fugitives to escape into Mexico.

Ferguson on June 11 again requested funds from President Wilson to hire an additional thirty Rangers. The governor informed Wilson that "conditions grow worse—Marauding bands from Mexico make raids almost daily. My people appeal to me for aid which I am unable to give." He also requested that fifty soldiers be detailed to the Rangers, something that he should have realized was legally impossible. Ferguson concluded by saying that "I assure you that it is with a degree of reluctance that I make this request but I feel the gravity of the situation makes such action on my part imperative."[26]

Ferguson was not believed. When the President sent Ferguson's letter to the secretary of war, the latter said that it "is really an attempt to get the Government of the United States to furnish Texas with men or money that it should furnish itself." He also suggested that the conditions that caused the governor to appeal for help had "nothing whatever to do with the situation in Mexico; . . . they are local to places entirely removed from the border . . . and . . . are matters which are within State jurisdiction and should be handled by the State."[27]

The governor persisted. In a June 25 letter to General Funston, he requested that additional troops be sent to the Lower Valley and to the Big Bend to calm the fears of the residents.[28] And he also sent the secretary of war correspondence from border residents expressing alarm at the situation along the Rio Grande.[29] Secretary Garrison politely informed the governor that he could not comply with his request. He did note that he had asked General Funston whether he needed additional troops but had not yet heard from him.[30]

Ferguson's persistence finally paid off, at least with General Funston. On July 1, Funston responded to the governor's letter with a reasoned and quite candid reply delineating the nature of the problem. He cited two "great handicaps" that hampered his ability to pacify the border region. First, he did not have sufficient cavalry, but the reasons for that were beyond the ability of the army to solve. Funston pointed out that the army was stretched extraordinarily thinly given its responsibilities in the Philippines, Hawaii, and the Panama Canal Zone, and almost all of the cavalry in the United States were already stationed on the Mexican border.[31]

The second reason Funston cited was one that has received almost no attention but had a significant impact on the border throughout the course of the Mexican Revolution. It had to do with the application of a statute passed by Congress in 1878, the so-called "posse comitatus" law, which essentially forbade the military from engaging in law enforcement except for certain precisely defined situations such as martial law.[32] Funston explained that the War Department had issued very explicit orders based on the posse comitatus statute specifying when troops could be utilized.[33] He gave an example, saying that he was restricted from "using troops to deal with merely local disturbers and 'bad men' as distinguished from armed raiders from Mexico crossing the border." What Funston did not comment on was the extraordinary difficulty of differentiating one from the other. Since uniformed troops were often the exception rather than the rule during much of the Revolution, it was often impossible to determine if an individual were a bandit or an irregular Carranza soldier. What complicated the problem even more was the presence of substantial numbers of Mexican refugees (we do not know the precise number, but estimates range into the thousands) in the lower Rio Grande Valley during this period. Furthermore, Funston noted, "if the state authorities were willing to waive the legal restrictions on the troops assuming the police powers of the state, we could scarcely afford to take chances on allowing our officers and men to run the risk of involving themselves in damage suits or of facing criminal charges in the local courts for possible killing or wounding of people who were resisting arrest."[34] The general could scarcely have been more candid, but this exchange of letters caused his and Ferguson's relationship to warm, to the benefit of both the State of Texas and the Wilson administration.

Governor Ferguson liked Funston's letter so much that he sent a copy to President Wilson, and for the third time in less than five months he requested funds to hire additional Rangers. He apologized to Wilson, explaining that "but for the gravity of the situation I would not intrude upon your valuable time."[35] Ferguson's pleas did produce some action from the Wilson administration; Secretary of War Garrison ordered the adjutant general to communicate with Funston requesting "at the earliest practicable date . . . whether additional troops are needed."[36] But Funston replied that no more troops were needed, for he ascribed most of the troubles to Hispanics and to Mexican exiles; to local Anglo officials who controlled Hispanic voting blocs; and to Texas cattlemen buying stolen stock from Mexican brigands at bargain prices. As for Ferguson's repeated requests, "he has been imposed upon by being led to believe that the depredations . . . are committed by raiders from Mexico. The governor . . . is being constantly harassed by appeals for protection by persons who do not know the legal restrictions on the use of troops or who ignore them." He also noted, rather cynically, that "the money spent by the War Department and by the troops wherever these are stationed is highly appreciated," inferring that chamber of commerce types were crying wolf to pump up the local economy.[37] Funston believed that 50,000 troops would be required to seal off the Texas border, which was simply not possible. But in a significant change of mind, he recommended that the government reimburse Texas for "a very considerable increase in its ranger force," noting that Rangers were not hampered by legal restrictions (!), knew the country, and spoke Spanish.[38] Washington declined to adopt Funston's recommendation, and the pressure on Ferguson continued to mount.

On July 8, the Cameron County judge sent Secretary Garrison a request for 1,500 troops to protect that county. Funston received a copy of the telegram and responded that the "fears on the part of the citizens are entirely without foundation, and from my knowledge of conditions there I believe that band [of] marauders was organized on this side . . . . I am confident that there are sufficient troops in Brownsville . . . to meet any emergency. . . . The people of Brownsville . . . have been making persistent efforts to obtain more troops even going [to] the length of memorializing the Government of Texas with that end in view."[39]

Since border residents were clamoring for protection, and no more troops were coming, and more Rangers were urgently needed, and the government had no intention of paying for them, Ferguson reluctantly decided to increase the Ranger Force from his own slender resources, using a deficiency appropriation. He established a new Ranger company—Company D—to deal with the troubles in the Valley. Company D included Texas State Prison guards—in a word, "shooters." To command Company D, Ferguson commissioned one of the toughest law enforcement officers in Texas—Henry Lee Ransom, who would be the most controversial captain in the history of the Ranger Force.

Ransom was a piece of work. Born on December 29, 1870, at Brenham, he moved to Richmond in 1889. During the Spanish-American War he joined the army, serving in Troop B, 1st Texas Cavalry in the Philippines from 1899 to 1901. He returned home to Richmond after being discharged and became a Fort Bend County deputy sheriff, from 1902 to 1905. He then joined the Rangers, serving in Company A from February to December, 1905. He resigned for a better paying job as city marshal of Colorado City, holding that position until 1907, when he resigned to become manager of the H. S. Ranch in Mitchell County. The restless Ransom tired of ranch life by 1909 and reenlisted in the Rangers, again in Company A, but served only six weeks, in May and June, 1909. He resigned for more lucrative employment as a Waller County deputy sheriff at Hempstead. By 1910, however, he was playing on a larger stage, as a special officer for Mayor Horace B. Rice of Houston. It was in this capacity that he became notorious.

Houston was experiencing an epidemic of killings, including the murder on April 1, 1910, of Night Chief of Police William Murphy by a recently fired policeman, Earl McFarlane. Mayor Rice was determined to put an end to this state of affairs. He hired four special officers, including Ransom and another ex-Ranger, Jules J. Baker (and from 1911 to 1913, Frank Hamer), commissioned them as special detectives, and instituted a crackdown encompassing not only criminals but the widespread practice of pistol toting. As it happened, the most prominent criminal attorney in the city, James B. Brockman, was defending Earl McFarlane, the cop killer cop. At 11:45 p.m. on October 25, 1910, Brockman was standing at the corner of Franklin Avenue and San Jacinto Street waiting to take a streetcar to his home. Ransom and Baker, who had been gathering evidence against McFarlane, strolled up to Brockman, who said he greeted them with "Good evening, gentlemen." Without a word Ransom pulled out a .45 caliber pistol and fired five times, pumping three slugs at point blank range into the attorney. Men were tougher in those days—Brockman lived for twelve hours, remaining lucid almost to the end. Although Ransom's marksmanship left something to be desired, he did get the job done. Immediately after he gunned down Brockman, Ransom surrendered to the authorities and was charged with murder.

His defense was that as an officer in the performance of his duty he had acted in self-defense, a case of kill or be killed. Brockman was indeed carrying a pistol but never used it. Ransom's defense was handled by one of the best lawyers in Texas—a partner in the Houston firm of Lane, Wolters, and Storey. Jacob F. "Jake" Wolters was not only a formidable attorney, he was also one of the most powerful politicians in Texas. Ransom's lawyers secured his release on a $10,000 bond, the newspaper commenting that "the sureties on the bond represent wealth totaling in the millions." His trial took place in April, 1911. "Ransom, a shrewd faced little man, appears in court quiet and complacent."[40] The state admitted that attorney Brockman had a reputation for being violent and dangerous and habitually carried a pistol, whereas Ransom was a lawman of good character. In his summation, defense attorney Wolters eulogized the defendant and stressed that a guilty verdict would be welcomed ecstatically by the criminal element, and he depicted Brockman as "the acknowledged guardian angel of the criminal class." The district attorney argued that Ransom could have disarmed Brockman without killing him. Several witnesses testified that Brockman made the first move, trying to draw his gun. The jury was out for twenty-three hours before returning a verdict of "not guilty."[41]

The level of apprehension among both Houston criminals and law-abiding citizens must have increased markedly when in 1912 Mayor Rice appointed Ransom as chief of police. Ransom's first act was to bring in a group of his ex-Ranger friends, commission them as policemen, and put them to work cleaning up Houston. Their tactics proved a bit rough, and the mayor was deluged with complaints from the citizens who were getting beaten up. The public outcry against Ransom's special officers finally became so great that the mayor replaced him as chief but kept him on as a special officer, along with men such as Jules Baker and Frank Hamer. The chief of police informed the press that he couldn't run the department with so many special officers constantly interfering with and intimidating his regular policemen. The very next day there was gunplay in the chief's office, and two reporters from a newspaper, presumably the *Houston Chronicle*, that had printed the chief's interview were pistol-whipped. This occurred on the eve of Mayor Ben Campbell taking office. He had promised to rid the city of all these special officers, and his first act in office was to fire the lot. Ransom and Baker subsequently encountered Robert Higgins, a *Houston Chronicle* reporter, in a downtown restaurant. Higgins had written a number of articles critical of Ransom while the latter was police chief. The two assaulted Higgins and beat him over the head. Ransom and Baker went to the police station and surrendered but started to leave without posting a bond. Policeman C. E. Horton asked several fellow officers to bring the men back, but they all lacked the nerve to do so. Horton grabbed his gun and ran after the pair. Baker shot him through the neck (Baker was tried at Bryan for assault to murder but was acquitted). As the *Houston Chronicle* expressed it, "That was their last appearance in the role of trouble makers in Houston, although they often visited here."[42]

Ransom became the manager of a Texas State Prison farm for a time before returning to Houston as a peace officer. And on July 20, 1915, he was commissioned as captain of Company D, Ranger Force. Attorney Jake Wolters negotiated his hiring for Governor Ferguson. On July 19, Wolters sent the governor a telegram notifying him that Ransom would report to the adjutant general the following day.[43] Ransom moved quickly, meeting in Austin with both the governor and the adjutant general before heading to San Antonio to confer with Captain Sanders. By July 24, Ransom had set up camp for his Ranger company in Harlingen.[44]

The next day the raiders struck again in the boldest guerrilla attack yet. In the predawn hours of July 25, several of them set fire to a forty-two-foot bridge on the St. Louis, Brownsville & Mexico Railroad near Sebastian. The bridge was destroyed. In addition, the raiders cut the telephone and telegraph lines adjacent to the bridge and removed spikes from the rails, effectively isolating Brownsville for a time. Captains Sanders and Ransom, Sergeant Grimes, and Ranger Felps rushed to the scene and proceeded to trail the raiders throughout the day and into that night but were unable to catch up with them. The following day Sanders and his two subordinates proceeded to San Benito where they learned the identity of one of the guerrillas and rode to the ranch where he lived. The alleged raider, according to Sanders, confessed to being implicated in the bridge burning and provided the Rangers with the names of four other Hispanics who were also involved. The Rangers arrested three of those alleged guerrillas and turned them over to local authorities.[45]

The railroad bridge burning seemed to up the ante and Caesar Kleberg wired Hutchings on July 26: "How soon can we expect [the Ranger] company? Conditions no better." Hutchings immediately ordered Captain Sanders to "run up to Kingsville" to consult Kleberg.[46] Sanders's job was obviously to smooth Kleberg's feathers, but he was immediately confronted by Ransom as to which Ranger company was to patrol which territory. In an attempt to solve the problem, Sanders wired to Hutchings: "Ransom and I differ as to our territory. He thinks he was assigned all counties south of Webb. If so shall I change stations of my men which was directed by the Governor. If so where shall I place them?" Hutchings immediately wired back: "Ransom has Duval, Jim Wells, Nueces, Kleberg, Zapata, Jim Hogg, Brooks, Willacy, Starr, Hidalgo and Cameron. Remove men remaining in your company out of these counties when Ransom enlists his men and locates them at points which he deems best. Then locate your men in your territory to best advantage."[47] It undoubtedly was a bitter pill for Sanders, who had done his best, to be summarily kicked out of the area for which he was responsible. Two days later Captain Sanders notified Hutchings that he was leaving for Laredo to set up a camp for Company A. Seventy-two hours later he wrote to the adjutant general that he would ". . . have my entire command . . . removed from Captain Ransom's territory by 12 o'clock tonight."[48] The new arrangement left Ransom in charge of the territory from the Webb County line to Point Isabel at the mouth of the Rio Grande. Sanders's jurisdiction was from the Webb County line upriver to Del Rio, with a camp in Laredo.[49]

Ransom would soon become notorious because of his ruthless approach to counterinsurgency—when in doubt, shoot. This reflected his method of problem solving, as when he had shot down attorney Brockman back in 1910. According to one who worked with him in the Bandit War:

> Ransom's early life around the Brazos bottom prison farms and his service in the Philippines had caused him to place small value on the life of a lawbreaker. On one occasion I guided his company on a scout through western Hidalgo and eastern Starr Counties. We met a troop of Cavalry from Fort Ringgold who were also looking for bandits, and made a night camp together. The Army captain had served in the Philippines, and after supper he invited Captain Ransom to his tent for a visit. I went along and listened to their conversation. The tales they told about executing Filipinos made the Bandit War look like a minor purge.[50]

Ransom felt that not only should bandits be summarily killed, but even those who *looked* like bandits, as well as anyone who had guilty knowledge of crimes or who sheltered bandits. He certainly conforms to the Hispanic stereotype of the brutal Ranger captain. But there was more to it than just Ransom's "shoot first" mentality. He believed he was an instrument of justice who had a definite mission to perform, reportedly saying that "A bad disease calls for bitter medicine. The Governor sent me down here to stop this trouble, and I am going to carry out his orders."[51] But just what were those orders? Governor Ferguson had given Ransom specific instructions, and they entailed drastic measures. These instructions have been available to historians for decades but have received little attention. As will be described below, there was in 1919 an investigation of the Rangers by the Texas legislature. Testimony was taken and a full transcript is on the record.

One of those who testified was Edward A. Sterling, a rancher from Monte Christo, Hidalgo County who described a meeting with Governor Ferguson:

Q. . . . were you a friend of Governor Ferguson's?

A. Yes, sir.

Q. Did you have interviews with Governor Ferguson regarding the conditions there . . . ?

A. I did.

Q. What was Governor Ferguson's policy . . . as indicated to you and the Ranger captains, about what to do down there in extending protection to those people? Tell the committee.

A. I understood there was a move on foot to remove [Captain] Ransom, and I jumped on the train and came up here and saw Governor Ferguson and told him I was afraid they were going to try to get Ransom out of there, and he was doing some good work and what I thought was actually necessary under the conditions then existing, and that they would probably put in—make complaint against Ransom. Do you want me to go further?

Q. Yes, sir, we would be glad to hear it.

A. He said—we were in his private office down there (indicating)—he said he had been receiving these kicks for some time, but *that he had given Ransom instructions to go down there and clean it up if he had to kill every damned man connected with it*; and I complimented him on it, I told him I thought there would likely be some trouble, but—

Q. What did he say about standing by him, and having the pardoning power?

A. And he said—"I firmly told Ransom that if he didn't do it—if he didn't clean that nest up down there that I would put a man down there that would," and he said, "You can go on back," and I told him about our location and how necessary it was for us to have protection there, and about what we were looking for from above, and he says, "You can go on back and rest assured we are going to take care of you if we can get men enough in the State of Texas—" something like that; and of course I immediately went back.

Q. What did he remark about having the pardoning power and standing by them?

A. He said, "I have the pardoning power and we will stand by those men, and I want that bunch—that gang cleaned up."[52]

Captain Ransom had his marching orders, and they did not come any too soon. In addition to their operations fifty miles north of Brownsville, the Plan de San Diego guerrillas on July 24 robbed S. Saenz's store at the tiny community of Progreso on the north bank of the Rio Grande some fifty miles west of Brownsville. Cameron County Deputy Sheriff Stokes Chaddick shot and killed one of the raiders and Customs Inspector (and former Texas Ranger) John Dudley White killed another raider "resisting arrest."[53] And on the same day at a baile outside Brownsville a Cameron County constable and his deputy were both stabbed. This second unprovoked attack on Hispanic officers was obviously a deliberate tactic.[54]

Before Captain Ransom could carry out his orders, he had to finish recruiting his company. On July 30, he traveled to Houston to do so before returning to his camp at Harlingen.[55] Meanwhile, local officials were conducting their own operations. On the night of July 29, San Benito city marshal Frank Carr and Constable and Deputy Sheriff (and ex- and future Ranger) Daniel Hinojosa,[56] took a prisoner, a man named Adolfo Muñoz, who was accused of murdering an Anglo merchant and of stealing cattle, from the jail, put him in an automobile, and began driving to Brownsville. According to Carr, he and Hinojosa were ambushed near San Benito and their prisoner was kidnaped at gunpoint by eight masked men brandishing Winchester .30-30s. The two officers were ordered to "beat it." The following morning Muñoz was found hanging from a large mesquite. Both Carr and Hinojosa were feared lawmen in the Lower Valley and the idea that a group of men would kidnap one of their prisoners was improbable. What seems quite likely is that Carr and Hinojosa hanged Muñoz and concocted the story about the eight gunmen.[57]

The following week the pace picked up again. On August 2, a party of surveyors some fourteen miles from Point Isabel was fired on by a band of fifteen Mexicans. One of the surveyors was grazed by a bullet but they all managed to escape. At the same time on the outskirts of Brownsville two separate bands of raiders took thirteen horses and five saddles at gunpoint from two ranchers. Eyewitnesses reported that the bandits had crossed the Rio Grande from Mexico.[58]

But the biggest clash to date in the Bandit War occurred the following day. On August 3, twenty-six cavalrymen of Troop A, 12th Cavalry, were summoned before dawn to a point eighteen miles north of Brownsville where a group of raiders had been spotted on the Scrivner Ranch. Rancher Jeff Scrivner, who allegedly bore a grudge against his neighbor, Aniceto Pizaña, informed the authorities that Pizaña was hiding the raiders at his ranch, Los Tulitos, home of the respected Pizaña clan. Aniceto Pizaña would soon become notorious as one of the leaders of the Plan de San Diego uprising. For an hour the Pizañas and the raiders succeeded in holding off the soldiers and some assorted law enforcement officers, but interestingly no Texas Rangers. The 12th Cavalry soldiers were reinforced by three other troops of cavalry and additional federal and local law enforcement personnel plus local citizens, and they succeeded in driving the raiders out of the Pizaña residence, but the raiders, estimated at from twenty-five to fifty, managed to elude posses that numbered into the hundreds of men by nightfall. In the firefight one cavalry private had been killed and two wounded, along with Cameron County Deputy Sheriff C. A. Monahan, who received a leg wound. Aniceto Pizaña evaded capture, but his twelve-year-old son was seriously wounded, and doctors were forced to amputate the boy's leg.[59] Pizaña had been a supporter of Ricardo Flores Magón for some years.[60] One account has Pizaña not participating in the raids until his son was wounded and his home was attacked.[61]

The pitched battle at the Tulitos Ranch raised the level of combat to a new high. And it was quickly followed by several disquieting incidents. At midnight on August 4, telephone and telegraph lines were cut and a seventeen-bent trestle on the St. Louis, Brownsville & Mexico Railroad, thirty-three miles north of Brownsville, was set on fire, isolating the border town.[62]

Immediately following the Tulitos Ranch fight, General Nafarrate issued a statement through an American businessman, one W. R. Jones, denying any complicity in the raids. He did note that unknown parties had distributed inflammatory pamphlets in Matamoros but declared that he had issued orders to jail anyone engaged in such activity.[63] Nafarrate was lying through his teeth and was probably laughing at American officials who had not yet realized his connection with Plan de San Diego operations. "Even Aniceto Pizaña was unsure why Nafarrate gave his forces tacit support." The Mexican general called Pizaña in for a chat and offered arms and ammunition to support the uprising in Texas. Nafarrate's motives for doing so have been the subject of speculation. It has been suggested that he viewed the rebels in Texas as a vehicle for expressing Mexican anger at the United States, or that Nafarrate resented the United States having permitted wounded villistas to receive medical treatment in Brownsville after their failed assault on Matamoros.[64] It may be suggested that Nafarrate was just implementing carrancista policy.

Because of the Tulitos Ranch affair, a group of the leading political, law enforcement, and business figures in the Lower Valley convened an emergency meeting in San Benito on the afternoon of August 5. Sam Robertson and Lon C. Hill, two of the most prominent businessmen in the Valley, called the meeting, from which the press was specifically excluded.[65] We do not know who else attended except for Sheriff Vann and Captain George Head, commander of the Brownsville Rifles, who was currently under indictment for selling Texas National Guard uniforms to the Carranza government, nor do we have any minutes of the meeting. It would appear, however, that the movers and shakers compared notes and came to the chilling realization that the ongoing violence was not just an intensified form of South Texas political feuding but was something infinitely more dangerous—a campaign of guerrilla warfare being waged by Hispanics and Mexicans.

Others were less perceptive. Less than a week after the San Benito meeting, General Funston wrote:

> From best information obtainable situation in Cameron, Hidalgo and Starr counties Texas appears to be due to a political feud with headquarters in Brownsville both parties having organized bands of more or less lawless men to intimidate the other by means of robbery and murderous attacks on ranches belonging to the other. The activities of these bands of cut-throats have now gotten beyond control of leaders and bands have inaugurated a campaign of vengeance against enemies who have incurred their enmity. It is now established beyond a doubt that most of the men concerned in these outrages are residents of Texas only a few being Americans [Anglos].[66]

Fourteen bandits swept into the hamlet of Sebastian in northern Cameron County on August 6. They looted a store, then moved on to a corn sheller being operated by a pair of farmers, A. L. Austin, the president of the local vigilante Law and Order League, and his son, Charles. The marauders seized the defenseless Austins. When one Elmer Millard drove up in a wagon, the bandits forced him to drive the Austins to a spot near their home. They then executed the Austins, but they released Millard because he had once loaned money to one of the band, who interceded for him. During the next couple of days, bandits fired on an automobile near Los Fresnos, wounding one person; they also wounded the night watchman of the town of Lyford.[67] The level of fear in Cameron County rose appreciably.

But the Rangers and local officers were able to learn the identities of some of those who were terrorizing the Lower Valley. When the raiders robbed T. J. Alexander's store at Sebastian before they left to murder the Austins, some residents of the small town recognized several of them. As a result, a posse of more than twenty officers including Adjutant General Henry Hutchings, who had come to the Valley to get a first-hand impression of the troubles, Sheriff Vann of Cameron County, the ubiquitous Captain George Head, Ranger Captain Henry Ransom and four members of Ransom's company, and assorted other federal and local law enforcement officers was assembled to track down the Austins' killers. They were able to locate three members of the Guzmán family who were allegedly involved in the murder of the two Austins.

On the night of August 6, the posse surrounded the Guzmán residence located at the Paso Real, the main crossing of the Arroyo Colorado approximately thirty miles north of Brownsville, and killed the elder Guzmán and one of his sons. The Brownsville *Daily Herald* reported that one of the Guzmáns' bodies was riddled by some seventeen bullets. Sheriff Vann would later testify under oath that neither of the Guzmáns was armed. The next morning the lawmen searched the house again. Ranger Joe Anders was slightly wounded when the surviving Guzmán son, who had been wounded but had managed to slip out of the house the night before, was discovered hiding under a bed. He fired at point blank range—Anders received powder burns on his nose from Guzmán's shot. Anders's shot killed Guzmán.[68]

While South Texas was in turmoil, the Carranza intelligence chief in San Antonio, Teódulo R. Beltrán, revealed that he had sent a letter to the Carranza representative in Washington, Eliseo Arredondo, saying: "Allow me to suggest that you make it clear that bandits operating near Brownsville do not belong to any Mexican faction and possibly are American citizens." He also explained that military officials at Matamoros had taken steps to prevent raids into Texas from Mexico by irresponsible bands.[69] Beltrán was lying, but it was not yet obvious that the Carranza government was playing a double game.

But an incident at the Norias Ranch would soon shock General Funston into a new perception of what was happening in South Texas. On August 8, the manager of the King Ranch, Caesar Kleberg, learned that raiders had been sighted on the Sauz Ranch, one of the five divisions of the ranching empire, south of

Kingsville. Kleberg was in Brownsville at the time, and he immediately requested assistance from the army and the Rangers. A detachment from Troop C, 12th Cavalry—Corporal Allen Mercer and seven privates—was dispatched from Brownsville.[70] Joining the army contingent were Adjutant General Hutchings, Captains Ransom and Fox, and Rangers from their two companies; they all left Brownsville by special train for the seventy-mile trip to the Norias subheadquarters of the King Ranch.[71] As it happened, their departure was witnessed by Cameron County Deputy Sheriff Gordon Hill,[72] two Customs inspectors—ex-Ranger Joe Taylor and Marcus Hines, former Ranger sergeant and a giant of a man weighing 300 pounds—and Immigration inspector David Portus Gay, Jr. Sensing the possibility of some real action, they took the next train from Brownsville and arrived about 5:30 p.m. at the two-story frame ranch house at Norias located next to the tracks. They learned that Hutchings and the Rangers had been furnished with horses and together with foreman Tom R. Tate[73] and several King Ranch cowboys had ridden off to the southeast in search of the raiders, who it was later learned hid in the brush as the Rangers went by.

The soldiers, inspectors, and deputy sheriff remained at Norias, awaiting word on the marauders' location. They ate dinner with some King Ranch employees, and as they prepared to smoke a companionable cigarette or two, Hines at about 6 p.m. noticed riders coming across the plain from the east. He assumed they were the Rangers returning, but a second glance shocked him—they were not Rangers; their big Mexican hats identified them as raiders, some sixty of them galloping toward the ranch house at a dead run. At least one of them was a carrancista officer.[74] The guerrillas carried a white flag and a red one; the defenders of Norias assumed the red was for "no quarter" while the white was for a parley or truce, to get close enough to effect the surrender of the ranch house. The guerrillas dismounted and opened fire with their 7mm Mauser rifles at 250 yards. The sixteen defenders, outnumbered four to one, raced to the railroad embankment for cover and returned fire across the flat terrain.[75] In the initial exchange of gunfire two soldiers were wounded, as was Frank Martin, the King Ranch employee and ex-Ranger who a month earlier had killed one of the Plan de San Diego raiders.[76] The defenders were now reduced to thirteen rifles, then to twelve when George Forbes, the ranch carpenter, took a rifle bullet in the lung. The defenders were hard pressed to cover the ranch house, for the raiders kept attacking from three sides. One charge stalled when a King Ranch cowboy, Lauro Cavazos, shot the guerrilla leader's horse from under him. But it looked as though the defenders would eventually be overwhelmed.

The raiders committed a major tactical blunder—they failed to cut the telephone line, and the defenders put in a frantic telephone call to Caesar Kleberg, who was in Kingsville, requesting ammunition and reinforcements, but to no avail. Kleberg explained that no locomotive engineer was willing to take the risk of running a relief train down to Norias. All the defenders knew was that Kleberg did not help them, and this remained a sore point for years afterward.[77] The battle raged on, with the defenders' ammunition supply constantly diminishing. Things looked bleak. After two and a half hours of fighting and with darkness approaching—at about 8:30 p.m.—the raiders, "yelling like Indians," mounted a determined charge at the headquarters building, but "Pinkie" Taylor shot and killed the bandit leader at forty yards, which halted the charge. Having lost their chief and five more of their companions, the surviving guerrillas decided they had had enough. They strapped their wounded on horses and rode off to the south, abandoning their white flag. A couple of miles south of Norias, one of the leaders of the raid, a captain named "Miguel," killed one of their wounded, an "American-Mexican" who had been badly wounded and "could go no further."[78] Ironically, "If the bandits had stayed a little longer, they would have won," for the defenders were nearly out of ammunition.[79]

The only fatality the Norias contingent suffered was a Hispanic woman whose husband was a section hand on the railroad. The raiders seized her and demanded that she tell them how many gringos were at Norias. According to her son, when she cursed the bandit chieftain for a coward and told him to go find out for himself he courageously shot her in the mouth.[80] It should be noted that the soldiers were the bedrock of the Norias defense. Starting with ninety rounds each, the troops displayed admirable fire discipline, hoarding their limited supply of ammunition. They fired carefully and steadily, playing the key role in holding the raiders at bay. Immigration Inspector Gay in his account of the fight paid tribute to their steadfastness.[81]

The Rangers thus missed out on what proved to be the biggest battle of the Bandit War. The closest they got to the guerrillas was when they had passed near the raiders hidden in the brush prior to the attack on Norias.[82] Adjutant General Hutchings and the Rangers, together with Tom Tate and his men, arrived back at Norias at about 10 p.m., after the bandits were long gone, unaware that there had even been a fight. The lawmen were dumfounded by what the relieved defenders related to them. Embarrassed and frustrated, the Rangers began offering gratuitous advice about what they would have done had they been there. After listening to this, and in particular listening to Captain Ransom pontificate, "Pinkie" Taylor had a bellyful and angrily declared: "Listen, we were here—we did not get a man killed—we were here when they came, we were here when they left, and we are still here, and I don't know what you all would have done if you had been here, but I do know THERE WAS NOT A GODDAM SON OF A BITCH OF YOU HERE."[83]

The one thing the Rangers apparently did was to participate in the interrogation of a wounded raider who was captured that night. Judging from the account by Gay, this guerrilla was interrogated to death. Gay wrote cryptically: "Just after making this statement, he died. I will not state just how or why he died—there were several present at the time—I will let them tell that part of the story."[84] Before he died the prisoner told his captors that the attackers expected to find only three or four cowboys at Norias, and they planned to loot the ranch store, obtain money, rifles, and ammunition, foodstuffs, saddles—and burn the ranch headquarters down, stop the next train, rob the passengers, and burn the train.[85]

Not only did the Rangers miss the Norias fight but they were in no great hurry to pursue the raiders, prudently being concerned about riding into an ambush in the darkness. That night one of the defenders, deputy Gordon Hill, taunted them with "If you all are such hell-roaring fighters, why don't you go after them? They can't be so very far away, as they have not been gone very long."[86] But the Rangers waited until the next morning to begin their pursuit of the guerrillas. The latter managed to elude both the Rangers and the six troops of cavalry scouring the countryside for them and covered the seventy miles back to the safety of the Rio Grande.[87]

Norias now bustled with activity as reinforcements from both Kingsville and Brownsville began arriving, along with abundant ammunition and doctors to care for the wounded. Gay, along with other defenders, was bitter after the raid. He said afterward that none of them "ever received one word of thanks" from the Kings and the Klebergs.[88]

The bodies of the guerrillas killed at Norias were lassoed and dragged into a pile for burial. Photos were taken of Captain Fox, an unidentified man, and Tom Tate posing on horseback with lassos attached to four dead raiders. This was ironic, since Fox and the rest of the Rangers had missed the Norias fight altogether. The photos were widely published and became a source of controversy. The Hispanic politician José T. Canales would in 1919 profess indignation at this lack of respect for the dead.[89] Other photos appeared showing Rangers posing with the skulls of alleged guerrillas found after the Norias raid. Richard Ribb discusses these incidents at length, stressing that the photos were designed to advertise the Rangers' tactics of terror and revealed a callous attitude toward Hispanics.[90] No doubt the Rangers could have used some sensitivity training, but then so could the guerrillas. As we shall see, on September 24, guerrillas and Carranza soldiers attacked the riverside hamlet of Progreso. They captured Private Richard J. Johnson, who was taken across the river, shot to death, had his ears cut off as souvenirs, was decapitated, and had his head displayed on a pole for his comrades across the Rio Grande to see. The Rangers had no monopoly on callousness.

If the Anglo residents of the Valley had been frightened before the Norias raid, they now felt sheer terror upon learning details of the Norias raid. Cameron County Judge H. L. Yates telegraphed the Secretary of War the next day to express his outrage: "Was last night enough to bring adequate protection to the lower Rio Grande Valley, or are we still to be sacrificed again. I implore you to send us adequate protection." And seventeen Brownsville businessmen also telegraphed the Secretary begging him to dispatch at least 1,500 additional troops, with artillery.[91]

Shortly after the Norias raid some thirty bandits complete with flag rode into western Hidalgo County, crossing at Los Ebanos. Sheriff A. Y. Baker quickly formed a posse that included Tom Mayfield and Alf Truitt, future city marshal of Mission, who acted as trailer. For the next three days the posse pursued the bandits, who rode forty miles into Texas, turned east, circling the county seat of Edinburg, then raced back to the Rio Grande, abandoning their flag on the bank of the river.[92]

As a result of Norias and its aftermath, Governor Ferguson ordered Adjutant General Hutchings to concentrate almost the entire Ranger Force, which numbered thirty-nine by early August, in South Texas.[93] On August 9, Captain Sanders, whom Hutchings had summarily ejected from the Lower Valley the previous month, returned, one suspects a bit smugly, to Brownsville with eight members of Company A. At the same time the rest of Captain Fox's Company B was ordered to Brownsville; seven of his men left Marfa for the border city on August 8. The two companies reinforced Ransom's Company D, which had a total of fourteen men at the time of the Norias raid. By August 10, at least thirty of the thirty-nine Rangers were in the Lower Valley.[94] The assistant adjutant general telegraphed all the railroads in Texas: "Please recognize Ranger Warrant of Authority signed by the Adjutant General as temporary pass over your line, must have men on ground this is an emergency."[95] At least nine additional Rangers were enlisted and sent to the Valley.[96] Even ex-Ranger H. C. Trollinger, who had been fired two months earlier because of the Big Bend ambush debacle, wired the adjutant general's department for transportation authorization so that he could reenlist, and "Australian Billy" Smith, the former Ranger detective, offered his services. They were both rejected.[97] Rush orders for ten Ranger rifles to be shipped to Brownsville, pack saddle bags for Captain Ransom, cots for the new Rangers, "horse equipment," ammunition bandoliers, and 1,200 rounds of .30-30 ammunition for Captain Fox poured into headquarters in Austin.[98] Although it had always been standard operating procedure for each Ranger to provide his own horse and saddle at the time he enlisted, this requirement was evidently waived.

The fallout for the army from the Norias fight was enormous. The mere fact that a serious raid had occurred seventy miles north of the border stunned General Funston and his superiors in Washington. Two days after the raid, Governor Ferguson informed Funston in an hour-long telephone conversation that the "situation is beyond our control."[99] The Southern Department commander was supportive of the Texas governor and of how Ferguson had responded to the crisis. Funston now reported that Ferguson had indeed increased the size of the Ranger Force by 50 percent and "is anxious not to do anything that would embarrass the administration." The general raised the possibility of either the governor of Texas or President Wilson declaring martial law in four counties, stating that this was the only way to control the situation. Funston declared that both he and Ferguson "are up against it," adding that "I do not recommend declaration of martial law by the President . . . without the consent of the Governor of Texas," but he also made it crystal clear that should the President declare martial law, "it must be understood that I . . . shall not hesitate to inflict the penalty of death upon persons who have been properly tried by Military Commission and whose cases have come before me officially."[100]

What had astonished Funston was the information provided by a seventy-five-year-old King Ranch employee, Manuel Rincones, who had been kidnaped by the guerrillas and forced to act as their guide to Norias. The raiders later released Rincones who was interrogated by army officers. He told them that about half of the raiders came from Mexico.[101] It finally dawned on Funston that he had been completely wrong about the troubles arising from the Plan de San Diego. What he faced was something outside his experience—a guerrilla insurgency coupled with an irredentist movement. But Funston still did not comprehend that the Carranza commander in Matamoros, General Nafarrate, was directing the operations of the raiders, for he reported that "It is now established beyond doubt that considerable portion of band of outlaws come from Mexico and were officers and soldiers of Carranza forces, doubtless acting without authority of their chiefs."[102] It had also dawned on Bureau of Investigation Special Agent in Charge Robert Barnes in San Antonio that the raids in the Lower Valley were not just South Texas political disputes. In a telegram to Bruce Bielaski, the Director of the Bureau, Barnes tied the raids to the Plan de San Diego.[103]

Because of political pressure placed on the army by U.S. senators and congressmen from Texas (and indeed by congressmen and senators from other states who had constituents who owned property in the Valley), the Southern Department was forced to station forty small detachments on ranches and in towns from the Rio Grande inland for seventy miles or more.[104] Senator James A. Reed requested that a small detachment of troops "be stationed on the ranch of Mr. A. C. Stuever, located about 17 miles from Brownsville . . . in order to protect that ranch." In response Funston sent a four-man detachment to the ranch. In mid-October, Reed forwarded another letter from Stuever requesting that the detachment not be removed.[105] The policy meant that the army, even with 2,500 men now assigned to the Valley, did not begin to have enough troops to prevent raids from coming across the river. Although almost all of the cavalry units in the United States were deployed along the border, there simply were not enough cavalrymen to go around. As a result the War Department sent infantry to guard towns, with the cavalry assigned to patrol the Rio Grande.

Overshadowing the augmented Texas Ranger force were the masses of troops pouring into the Lower Valley. On August 8, Funston sent a battalion of the 9th

Infantry from Fort McIntosh at Laredo to deploy into detachments at Lyford, Sebastian, Raymondville, San Benito, and Harlingen. Skirmishing continued along the river; on the night of August 10, a private in the 12th Cavalry was killed near Mercedes in a clash with Plan de San Diego guerrillas. The next morning Funston ordered a second battalion of the 9th Infantry to Kingsville and Brownsville at the urgent request of Colonel Blocksom, commander of the Brownsville Cavalry Patrol District.[106] On August 14, Funston telegraphed the War Department that he had "received information within last twelve hours [that] . . . convinced me that . . . disorders in vicinity of Brownsville originated with and are being backed by General Nafarrate . . . and that in event of . . . attack on Vera Cruz . . . or other point on border, Nafarrate proposed to attack and loot Brownsville. . . . Present situation . . . appears to me fraught with such grave possibilities that I no longer dare to refuse to meet appeals for more troops . . . made by Governor of Texas."[107] The dime had finally dropped.

The War Department ordered two batteries of 4.7-inch guns from the 5th Field Artillery and two airplanes (which at the time probably constituted about ten percent of the army air force) from the 1st Aero Squadron at Fort Sill, Oklahoma, to Brownsville. The airplanes would serve as spotters for the artillery.[108] The artillery was sent to Brownsville to overawe General Nafarrate—the guns were pointed directly at his headquarters in Matamoros. The Mexican general protested about their placement, to no avail. And the entire 26th Infantry was dispatched from Texas City to garrison Brownsville, Harlingen, and Kingsville. In ordering the move, Acting Secretary of War Henry Breckenridge telegraphed: "Above is urgent and admits no delay."[109] Remarkably, Secretary of War Lindley M. Garrison still did not get the picture. Although the report quoting Manuel Rincones had not yet arrived at the War Department, it should have been obvious after the Norias raid that something more serious than rough South Texas politics was involved. Nevertheless, Garrison telegraphed Funston on August 12 regarding the possibility of martial law and instructing the general not to use his troops to solve Texas's problems.[110]

By August 13, Governor Ferguson and General Funston, having conferred by telephone, were hopeful that "the trouble is over," to use Funston's words. In a telegram to the War Department, Funston noted that most of the Norias raiders had been driven across the Rio Grande.[111] And Funston, now aware that he had been badly misled by his sources of information in Texas who had been adamantly insisting that Lower Valley politics was the sole source of the raids, took matters into his own hands. He requested that Captain W. E. W. MacKinley, one of a handful of veteran intelligence officers who spoke Spanish and had extensive experience along the border, "be directed to report without delay to me [to carry out] . . . secret service investigation" of the cause of the raids. For a change, the army moved with alacrity—the adjutant general ordered the Commandant of Schools to "send MacKinley to Fort Sam Houston at once."[112] The army also hired civilian scouts who were familiar with the area to assist in the counterinsurgency campaign. One of them served under Captain (and future major general) Frank R. McCoy, 3rd Cavalry, who was based at Mission. He was twenty-four-year-old William Warren Sterling, from a ranching family at Monte Christo in Hidalgo County.[113]

Sterling would in later years become rather famous, serving as a Ranger captain and as adjutant general of Texas (1931–1933). In his memoirs he makes much of the fact that as a Ranger he never shot anybody, or even pistol-whipped a man.[114] Moreover, "My reputation for harmonious relations with Mexicans was gained by according fair treatment to people of all classes."[115] And "Throughout my lifetime, I have held a high regard and deep esteem for Latin Americans. Some of my best friends are members of that important segment of our citizenship."[116] All this was certainly admirable, but it had not always been the case. Sterling refers, obliquely, to the fact that "Before reaching the age of twenty-five, I had been called on to do a great deal more than my share of shooting."[117] One of the shootings he was "called on" to do involved a Hispanic, as described in the reminiscences of Roland A. Warnock:

> He killed an innocent Mexican boy [It is unclear whether he was a youth or a grown man, since the term "boy" sometimes applied to adult Hispanic males, as well as to adult black males] there at Monte Christo over that little sister of his. She was like a tomboy, out there all the time around the lots and pens, and there was a little Mexican boy that played with her. She didn't have enough clothes on to cover her skin and she hollered out there one day, claimed the boy was trying to rape her. I knew this Mexican boy and he wouldn't have harmed anybody, but Sterling went out there and shot him just like a dog.[118]

Warnock's allegations might be dismissed as merely sour grapes by somebody who did not like Sterling. However, the Brownsville *Daily Herald* reported:

OFFICERS [sic] KILLS MAN AT MISSION

Killing Occurred on Main Business Street of Mission at 2 O'clock This Afternoon

(Special to the *Herald*)

Mission, Texas, April 22 [1914]. Melchor Aguirre, a resident of Monte Christo, this county, was shot and killed on the main business street at 2:30 o'clock this afternoon. He received five shots in the breast and death was instantaneous.

Will Sterling, a deputy sheriff of Hidalgo county, and a resident of Monte Christo, surrendered to Deputy Sheriff Taylor immediately after the shooting. No charge has been filed against him. The shooting is alleged to have been the outgrowth of an alleged assault Monday of an eight-year-old sister of Sterling's. No undue excitement was caused by the shooting.

From what can be determined, Sterling suffered no legal consequences for this killing.

Warnock also describes the death of his father at the hands of Sterling. The elder Warnock got into a dispute with a couple of the Sterlings' employees and killed one of them with his Winchester. The Sterlings took umbrage. Seven months later, Warnock was chatting with some acquaintances on a business street in Mission at 6 p.m. when Will Sterling and his brother Ed suddenly appeared from around the corner of a store and without saying a word, put nine bullets into Warnock. Captain Ransom arrested the Sterlings on October 1 at Mission and turned them over to Sheriff Baker at Edinburg. Not that it was intimidating or anything, but five Rangers attended their examining trial the next day.[119] The Sterlings were charged with murder, then released on $2,500 bond each. They were defended by Judge James B. Wells. At their trial several eyewitnesses testified that not only had Warnock been unarmed, but the Sterlings had shot him in the back. Their defense was—what else?—self-defense. Warnock habitually tucked his hands in his armpits when he was standing and chatting, and the Sterlings claimed they saw him pulling a gun from beneath his shirt, even though he was facing away from them and never even knew they were there. Ranger Paul West, a friend of Will Sterling's, testified that he saw a gun. Although no gun was found on Warnock, the ruling was that it had been a clear case of self-defense. The Sterlings were acquitted.[120] In South Texas life remained cheap and justice remained problematical.

Later that month rancher Edward A. Sterling wrote to the adjutant general requesting Special Ranger commissions for his sons William Warren Sterling and Edward A. Sterling, Jr. Hutchings inquired of Captain Ransom, whose territory included the Sterling Ranch at Monte Christo, whether there was any special reason why they should be appointed.[121] Ransom replied:

I don't know of any special reason why they should or should not be appointed. Any more than that Mexicans hate them, and I believe would kill either of them first opportunity. And they recently killed a white man by name of Frank Warnock, whom I personally know to be a bad character. And W. W. Sterling killed a Mexican a short time before this bandit trouble began. W. W. & Ed. both assisted the boys and myself in doing some good work in surrounding country of Sterling Ranch. Those boys are both sober, intelligent young men. I would be glad to see them appointed.[122]

For whatever reason, William Warren Sterling didn't receive a Special Ranger commission until July 12, 1918; it expired on January 15, 1919. This leads one to question Sterling's assertion about the 1915 Bandit War "when I was a ranchman commissioned as a Ranger."[123]

Besides establishing an intelligence service in the Valley, Funston kept pouring in more reinforcements. By mid-August there were approximately 2,500 soldiers between Rio Grande City and Brownsville.[124] The Rangers were as a matter of policy keeping quiet about their operations.[125] Stories were published in the Brownsville *Daily Herald*[126] that bandits had been killed. For example, on August 12 the newspaper reported that three raiders had been killed in Hidalgo County between Mercedes and Donna but could provide no details, nor whether local officers or "state rangers" were responsible. The *Daily Herald* reported a death toll of eleven bandits (six during the previous week) in Hidalgo County but cautioned that their story lacked official confirmation.[127]

Given the fact that both the Rangers and the local officers refused to comment publicly about killing bandits, the *Daily Herald* had to use second- and third-hand sources. The August 12 report of three Plan de San Diego raiders being killed in Hidalgo County was probably the same incident reported four days later. According to the newspaper's unnamed source (a lady who had been visiting her daughter in Mercedes), a man identified as "a Mexican" consulted a Mercedes physician on the night of August 14 for treatment of "a bad sore." The doctor immediately recognized that the bad sore was really a bullet wound. After treating the man the doctor notified the authorities, who interrogated the wounded man. He was persuaded to reveal the identity and location of two of his fellow raiders. All three were executed that night.[128] It is not known whether the Rangers played any part in these events.

The Rangers were involved, however, along with vigilante groups, in ordering numerous Mexicans who had fled the Revolution and had sought refuge in the Lower Valley to leave under threat of death and return to Mexico.[129] This phenomenon was first observed on August 12, when more than twenty-five families in carts and wagons loaded with household goods were counted crossing the international bridge at Brownsville. Thereafter, Immigration officers in Brownsville reported a "slow but steady exodus" of four or five families daily crossing into Mexico.[130] In addition, the Rangers and local officers began a campaign to disarm all Mexicans, without regard to whether or not they were United States citizens. Possession of firearms would, in the words of the Brownsville *Daily Herald*, "mean serious consequences."[131]

By mid-August the Rangers and local officers on the one hand and the army on the other had by default worked out their respective roles. Obviously the Rangers, who had only thirty-odd men in the Valley, were limited by their numbers. In August Rangers were at times even guarding passenger trains on the St.

Louis, Brownsville & Mexico Railroad between Harlingen and Raymondville.[132] But their principal role would be to track down and kill Plan de San Diego militants and raiders who managed to evade the army. (The Israeli analogy again comes to mind.) The army would defend the bank of the Rio Grande and provide small garrisons for towns and ranches. With the augmentation of army units in the Lower Valley this system, which was initially ad hoc, generally worked well. It should be noted that the military, who frequently criticized the Rangers, were quietly envious of the Rangers' extermination program, since they were not officially permitted to do likewise. As one Valley resident succinctly put it, "The soldiers did the guarding and the Rangers did the hunting."[133]

It appeared that because of the efforts of the army, the Rangers, and the local officers the authorities were once more in control. One reason for this was that the campaign of extermination by the Rangers, local officers, and vigilantes was gaining momentum. For instance, two individuals who had allegedly been involved in killing the Austins on August 5 and were in the San Benito jail were "taken out during a few minutes absence by the guards and were later found dead. The two bodies were seen alongside the railroad yesterday, and were being burned."[134] Four days later, Captain Fox reported that his Company B had

> caught a Mexican by name of Tomas Aguilar—one of the 3 that robed [sic] the Depot at Combs and set the R. R. Bridge on fire to which he admitted and was also in the killing of Mr. Austin & son of course he tried to make his escape but we killed him. Everything very quite [sic] here. Don't know whether Captain Ransom's boys caught the other two last night or not they had them located near Harlingen where they have gone.[135]

Captain Fox had wired the adjutant general on August 20 requesting permission to return to Marfa with his men because the peace officers there urgently needed them back.[136] Hutchings had actually ordered Fox and his company on August 23 to return "at your earliest discretion to the Big Bend District," for state Senator Claude Hudspeth and Sheriff Almond at Del Rio desired "to round up some stock thieves about August 31."[137] However, there were influential people who wanted Fox and his men to remain in the Lower Valley. When Robert J. Kleberg of the King Ranch learned of Fox's impending transfer, he wired Hutchings: "Late information indicates that Capt. Fox and men should remain at Raymondville if possible. Hope you can see your way clear to leave them for the present."[138] Hutchings immediately responded to Kleberg's request, informing him: "Countermanded order to Fox this morning. He will remain pending conference Governor and General Funston."[139] Fox, who yearned to return to the wide open spaces of West Texas, expressed some thinly veiled irritation at the on-again–off-again nature of his orders, wiring: "If we stay will have to stop at Hotel have torn up camp there is nothing doing here very quite [sic]."[140] Fox's company remained at Raymondville for three more days, but Governor Ferguson, who had to get along with Senator Hudspeth, on August 28 ordered Company B back to the Big Bend.[141]

Fox could be transferred because it appeared that the crisis in the Lower Valley was over. Adjutant General Hutchings had toured the area from Brownsville to Rio Grande City and reported to Governor Ferguson.[142] The governor wrote President Wilson praising General Funston and commenting that "it now appears the situation is well in hand."[143] He also thanked Congressman John Nance Garner, who represented the Lower Valley, for his assistance and expressed hope that "everything has quieted down on the border, and that we will have no more trouble."[144]

While Captain Fox's company was being sent back to West Texas, Captain Sanders's Company A had been guarding the King Ranch ever since the Norias raid. Sanders and thirteen of his men were based at Norias. The two remaining Company A Rangers were stationed at Del Rio and San Angelo. Sanders wrote that all was quiet at Norias, and he made certain that Hutchings understood that he was keeping in close contact with Caesar Kleberg.[145]

The Brownsville *Daily Herald* also suggested that peace had been restored on the border and praised the Rangers in an editorial titled "Don't Forget the Rangers." While praising the troops on the border, the editorial noted that

> we would not forget the brave Texas ranger boys, who have been beating the brush looking for the outlaws so industriously ever since the fight at Las Norias. If there is anything the ranger excels in, it is hunting stock raiders and outlaws in the brush. They are fearless, good shots, untiring and when they get bush [sic] with their Winchesters, the outlaw would better seek shelter if he can get to it."[146]

But the feeling that peace had arrived proved premature. If there was any doubt that the Carranza government supported the Plan de San Diego, it should have been dispelled when the Matamoros newspaper, funded and controlled by the Carranza regime, published a story on August 19 that Mercedes had been briefly captured by Plan de San Diego raiders.[147] And upriver from Brownsville, the Brownsville Cavalry Patrol District, the administrative unit the army established under the Southern Department, would have its hands full by the end of August. Significantly, General Nafarrate continued his efforts to conceal his involvement in the raids. He informed the United States consul in Matamoros that it was American troops who were firing on Mexican soldiers across the river, and when Mexican army units crossed the river to attack, Nafarrate issued statements to the press asserting that these men had "deserted."[148]

Ten of these alleged Carranza "deserters" crossed the river on August 21 south of McAllen and headed north. Hidalgo County Sheriff A. Y. Baker requested the Rangers' help in chasing them. Four of Captain Ransom's men[149] joined Baker's posse along with a detachment of the 3rd Cavalry. And at the sheriff of Willacy County's request, Captain Sanders sent three of his men to track the same band, who had been spotted west of Sarita. The raiders used hit-and-run tactics, but they were much better at running than at hitting. For four days they eluded the Americans, cutting a wide swath through Hidalgo County but accomplishing nothing and crossing the Rio Grande back to the sanctuary of Mexico ninety minutes ahead of their pursuers.[150]

The next day a firefight occurred at the Progreso crossing of the Rio Grande, one of the flashpoints along the river. There had already been three separate incidents on August 16 and 17, when some seventy-five to one-hundred Mexican troops fired on detachments of the 12th Cavalry, killing one trooper and wounding two others.[151] On August 26, Mexican troops dug in along the river and fired hundreds of rounds at an American cavalry detachment on the north bank. Fortunately there were no casualties, but two of the cavalrymen's horses were killed.[152]

Also on August 26 about twenty raiders crossed into Texas near Progreso but quickly retreated back into Mexico when they encountered more opposition than they had anticipated.[153] But two Rangers—L. W. Edwards and Frank Baker—succeeded in capturing a raider who had documents on his person implicating certain residents of Hidalgo County. The Rangers took him to their camp at Pharr for interrogation.[154]

At the same time, there were clashes with Plan de San Diego militants around Falfurrias, the county seat of Brooks County. This was disquieting because heretofore Brooks County (one county north of Hidalgo County) had been unaffected by the raids. Furthermore, Falfurrias was located in the extreme northern part of the county, close to the Jim Wells County line. Near Falfurrias a posse shot it out with four heavily armed raiders. One was wounded and later died in custody. He was later identified as Alberto Cabrera, who had been convicted of killing Judge Stanley Welch at Rio Grande City nine years earlier. Cabrera had received a life sentence but escaped from a prison farm and fled to Mexico, surfacing years later as an officer in the Carranza army. He had reportedly killed a Carranza captain at Guerrero two months earlier but had been released on bond in Matamoros. He next appeared leading a band of some fifteen Plan de San Diego raiders north of Edinburg.[155] Near Raymondville, the residence of an alleged Norias raider was staked out, and when he returned home, "He attempted to resist arrest and was shot and killed."[156] Whether Rangers were involved in these actions is unknown.

Plan de San Diego raiders repeatedly attacked army detachments but they never had the temerity to attack a Ranger company, despite the fact that the locations of the three companies in the Lower Valley were well known. However, at 4:15 a.m. on August 29, a Mexican who was seen "slipping around in the dark" near Sanders's camp at Norias was shot and wounded by a Ranger and a soldier who were on guard. As a result of his wounds this unnamed individual had to have his right arm amputated.[157]

An interesting situation developed in San Diego, the alleged birthplace of the Plan de San Diego. On August 25, Captain Sanders reported that "The citizens of San Diego are very much alarmed and I am told Americans have all sent their families away."[158] Yet that same day the Duval County officials sent a rather unusual message to Colonel Robert Bullard, the Brownsville Cavalry Patrol District commander. While every other town in South Texas was clamoring for troops, the Duval County officials complained about the presence of a six-man army detachment and requested that they be removed forthwith. The officials, led by political boss state Senator Archie Parr, declared that the troops were not necessary and indeed that their presence was objectionable.[159] Regardless of the apprehensions of the Anglo minority, Parr was supremely confident of his control over the majority Hispanic population. So much for the claim that San Diego was the center of a Hispanic liberation movement.

Reaction to the Rangers' "hunting" operations began to draw fire in broadsides in Spanish produced by Plan de San Diego leaders Aniceto Pizaña and Luis de la Rosa. The latter had been a shopkeeper and a Cameron County deputy sheriff in Rio Hondo, a small farming community near San Benito. As of 1914, he was a captain in one of the Mexican revolutionary armies. The broadsides were distributed on both sides of the Rio Grande. One of them began with: "A cry of veritable indignation and anger has burst forth from the innermost depths of our soul upon seeing the crimes and outrages perpetrated upon defenseless women, old men and children of our race by the bandits and despicable Rangers who are guarding the shores of the Rio Grande." The broadside appeared over the names of Luis de la Rosa, "First Chief of Operations," and Aniceto Pizaña, "Second Chief of the General Staff." In an exercise in wishful thinking, it was purportedly issued at "General Headquarters in San Antonio, Texas."[160] In an effort to boost the morale of the militants, the official Carranza organ in Matamoros, *El Demócrata*, reported at the same time that the army of liberation was advancing on Harlingen.[161] Other official Carranza newspapers in Monterrey, Tampico, Veracruz, Mexico City, and elsewhere published the broadside verbatim and carried stirring accounts of the triumphant progress of the revolution in Texas.

> *El Demócrata* of Monterrey reported that the Texas revolutionists, numbering 5,000 well-armed men, had captured Brownsville and had the American army reeling in headlong retreat. Yet the laurels for imagination must go to *El Dictamen* of Veracruz, which announced that the Indians of the Southwest

had joined the revolutionary movement and were committing all manner of depredations. Besides proving that the pen is indeed mightier than the sword, the press campaign clearly demonstrated the Carranza regime's support for the rebellion in Texas.[162]

By the end of August the tempo of the raids seemed to have lessened, and Governor Ferguson once more micromanaged the Rangers. Captain Ransom was in Austin on August 31 and presumably convinced Ferguson and Hutchings how to divide the territory between him and Captain Sanders.[163] Ransom's Company D, numbering fourteen men, was now responsible for Cameron, Hidalgo, Starr, Zapata, Jim Hogg, and Brooks Counties, with Sanders's sixteen Company A Rangers assigned to cover Willacy, Kleberg, Nueces, Jim Wells, Duval, and Webb Counties, essentially the second tier of counties north of the Rio Grande. But Sanders was hardly mobile, having spent the last three weeks at Norias guarding the King Ranch, where all was quiet.[164]

Hutchings stated the obvious in a memorandum to Sanders on August 31. He observed that since the Rangers had not yet been relieved from their assignment to guard the King Ranch, "If Company A is held down to garrison duty at Norias it would seem impossible for you to do much in the other counties mentioned, which I fear need attention." The adjutant general's solution was to obtain more soldiers to garrison Norias.[165] But it was not at Norias that trouble erupted.

CHAPTER TEN

THE BANDIT WAR (September–October)

R AIDERS ushered in September by burning a trestle on the St. Louis,
Brownsville & Mexico Railroad only fourteen miles from Brownsville.
Officers investigating the blaze found dynamite, machetes, and two pistols at
the trestle. Additionally, raiders cut telephone and telegraph lines and set fire
to several houses in the vicinity.[1] And they tried to assassinate Cameron County
Deputy Sheriff Daniel Hinojosa and three companions as they drove in two automobiles on the road between Brownsville and San Benito. No one was hit in the
fusillade of gunfire from the brush along the road.

Another attack occurred outside Harlingen, when S. S. Dodds, Earl Donaldson,
J. T. Smith, and a crew of Mexican laborers who were working on an irrigation
canal were captured by some thirty Plan de San Diego guerrillas. Their leader was
reportedly Aniceto Pizaña, who spared Dodd's life when a Mexican crew member
declared that Dodd had helped him after he had been wounded fighting as a villista across the river. Donaldson and Smith were asked if they were Germans. When
they said no, Pizaña had them marched into the brush and shot. Dodd and two of
his laborers escaped when a posse caught up with the raiders near the Rio Grande
and killed six of them in a running gun battle.[2]

This incident sent shivers of fear up the spines of Anglo farmers throughout
the Valley, but it was just one in the renewed wave of attacks. A second railroad
bridge between San Benito and Brownsville was burned. American troops
transported in civilian automobiles began patrolling the railroad. No more bridges
were burned, but under cover of darkness telegraph wires between Harlingen and
San Benito and between San Benito and Brownsville were cut.[3] Moreover, two
fierce skirmishes took place along the river between the army and Carranza forces.[4]
The raiders were becoming bolder along the Rio Grande. On the night of

September 2, a contingent attacked the village of Ojo de Agua, near the Cavazos Crossing. After looting the settlement they withdrew across the river. The residents of Ojo de Agua were too terrified to report the incident until the next morning.[5]

The situation in the Valley quickly became so critical that Sheriff Baker, who was not an alarmist, telegraphed the adjutant general requesting that the four Rangers who had been assisting him in fighting the raiders on the river be retained in Hidalgo County. They were not, because they had been ordered to Rio Grande City to protect a district judge who was holding court. In addition, a prominent Valley businessman, Gordon Hill, wired Hutchings: "Can you come down if necessary? Some action must be taken to break up bandit organization."[6]

There was, however, one bright spot. The drought had broken, and with the torrential rains now drenching South Texas, the Rio Grande in places was a hundred yards wide with high water pouring downriver. The high water prevented horsemen who previously could easily ride across the river from crossing. Yet it was still possible to cross using small boats.[7] High water, though, did not prevent clashes between Mexican and American troops along the river.

Between September 3 and 5, Texas Rangers led by Sheriff Baker and 3rd Cavalry troopers under Captain Frank McCoy engaged in a series of firefights at the Madero and Cavazos Crossings. One trooper was wounded and an estimated seven Mexican soldiers were killed. A boat used by the raiders was sunk, and Mexican troops were finally driven from the riverbank by intense rifle fire.[8] In this case and in some others, Mexican casualties seem so one-sided as to raise questions of accuracy.

While the cavalry did most of this fighting, Sheriff Baker and several deputies teamed up with four Rangers at the Madero Crossing on September 4 and killed four Mexican soldiers in a firefight. Captain McCoy reported that some forty Mexican soldiers had engaged Baker and the Rangers.[9]

It was during this series of firefights along the river that the most spectacular incident of the Bandit War occurred. At the Cavazos Crossing on September 6, Sheriff Baker, the ex-Ranger, was fired on from across the river. Knowing that Mexicans habitually shot high, Baker showed his contempt for Mexican marksmanship by calmly strolling out from cover onto a sandbar. When the Mexicans blasted away at him, he pretended to fall down dead, evidently giving a most convincing performance, for the Mexicans celebrated by standing up from the tall grass where they had been hidden and cheering at the demise of *El Panadero*. Baker's deputies, who were deployed in the brush, unleashed a barrage of deadly rifle fire, reportedly killing at least four and putting an abrupt end to the celebration. While they were doing so Baker got up and strolled back under cover.[10] Baker had his faults—among them that of shooting Hispanics out of hand—[11], but lack of nerve was not one of them.

Not unnaturally, the renewed wave of fighting made the authorities quite apprehensive. The mayor of Mercedes called a meeting of all mayors in the Lower Valley in order to present a united front in appealing to President Wilson for more protection.[12] Besides worrying about the fighting in South Texas, the authorities were quite concerned that the Plan de San Diego might spread throughout the state's Hispanics. Funston reported that the "Situation appears to be gradually growing worse and unrest is extending all along border up to and including Del Rio."[13] There were certainly agitators at work. For instance, one Miguel Saiz was arrested in Cameron County on a charge of inciting a rebellion against the United States government. He had spoken at a baile outside of Brownsville, urging his listeners to "rise up in arms and retake all the lands the Americans have taken from us." A red flag was found in his luggage. Saiz, unable to post his $2,000 bond, languished in the Cameron County jail awaiting the action of the grand jury.[14] More disturbingly, three Mexicans addressed a huge crowd, estimated at 1,000 people, in San Antonio. They were arrested and sentenced to 200 days in the Bexar County jail for blocking street traffic, an expedient until federal charges could be prepared.[15]

Meanwhile, the Carranza government continued its efforts to conceal its sponsorship of the Plan de San Diego. For example, the United States vice consul in Matamoros, E. J. Puig, reported that General Nafarrate "assured me that he had given strict orders to his men to retire some distance from the river front and was disposed to assist in every way possible to prevent further trouble."[16]

General Funston, for one, was no longer fooled by the Carranza deception operation. He described the situation rather vividly in a telegram to the War Department:

Information received in last twenty four hours . . . has made it clear to me that conditions are and have been worse than I believed them to be and I felt . . . that I could no longer take the responsibility for failure to provide sufficient troops to adequately protect the people in the disturbed district against a possible uprising among Mexican population. If an uprising should occur without sufficient troops to put it down it will mean the murder of hundreds of defenseless people the destruction of millions of property and a further loss of prestige. These things we cannot afford to risk. . . . If there is an adequate force on the ground no uprising will occur. . . . If I do not have an adequate force ready for instant use, a single act of indiscretion by a subordinate commander on either side may start a conflagration that will extend along the entire border and result in an International crisis. Owing to the great preponderance of the Mexican over the American population all along the border, to the excitable character of the Mexicans and to the vengeful feeling that exists among Americans due to the recent outrages committed by Mexican band of raiders well known to have been composed partly of Mexican soldiers that situation . . . is likely to give rise to such serious consequences that further delay is dangerous. . . . I have heretofore been very conservative in regard to calling for more troops . . . because I wished to avoid unnecessary expense. The time for economy has passed, more troops should be supplied regardless of expense . . ."[17]

Funston specifically requested that two additional regiments—one cavalry, one infantry—and two infantry battalions be rushed to Fort Sam Houston in San Antonio; the two regiments would then be stationed in Harlingen.[18]

General Nafarrate, who was secretly running the raids, complained bitterly in Matamoros to an Associated Press reporter, H. W. Blakeslee, that his troops were observing a strict neutrality and were not involved in the incursions. Further, he charged that the Texas Rangers and Sheriff Baker and his men had killed two civilians and wounded a Carranza officer at the Cavazos Crossing. He declared that he had no problem working with the U.S. Army, "but if the rangers work on the river front . . . they will be causing trouble all of the time." He also told the reporter that the Rangers were indiscriminate in shooting at his troops on the river and that Mexican women had been "roughly treated" by the Rangers, who had killed some of their husbands.[19]

Meanwhile, most of Captain Sanders's Company A continued their vigil at Norias. Ranger Roy Aldrich noted in a letter to the adjutant general that there were only five soldiers at Norias, and if the Rangers left to go scouting that would leave Norias inadequately protected. He also reported that on the Stillman Ranch, southwest of Norias, cowboys branding calves had recently been frightened by gunfire nearby and were now refusing to go into the brush to round up cattle.[20]

Plan de San Diego militants on September 9 assassinated near Lyford a Hispanic, Francisco Guerra, who had been employed by Fred Deyo, a prominent local merchant. Efforts by the cavalry to locate the murderers were in vain.[21] That same day Carranza troops on the south bank of the river yelled to American soldiers that they would not shoot at them, but they would target Texas Rangers and local officers. In an ominous development, the Mexican troops dug entrenchments at the Progreso Crossing.[22]

Despite massive army reinforcements and the extermination campaign by the Rangers and local lawmen and vigilantes, the raiders backed up by Carranza troops accelerated the tempo of combat. On September 13, an estimated twenty to thirty insurgents surrounded a ten-man 12th Cavalry outpost at Los Indios (the Galveston Ranch) at daybreak. In a thirty-minute exchange of gunfire, the sergeant in command of the outpost was wounded, as were two of his men, both of whom subsequently died. Army reinforcements captured five men believed to have been involved and turned them over to the civil authorities.[23]

The five prisoners were jailed in San Benito. Less than seventy-two hours later, three of them were taken from that facility and put in automobiles for transport to the Harlingen jail. According to the newspaper account, down the road they tried to escape by jumping out of the autos but were shot and killed. Almost certainly the ley fuga was applied. The perpetrators were never identified, and the three bodies were left by the roadside. Soldiers later located the bodies, which were then buried.[24]

The owner of the Galveston Ranch, Josiah Turner, bitterly denounced the killing of the three men (one was his employee, one was a tenant on the ranch, and the third just happened to be visiting the ranch, where his mother and sister worked) in a Letter to the Editor of the *Herald*: ". . . who is responsible for the killing of these innocent men? Who is responsible for them being taken from the San Benito jail to their deaths without trial? It is true innocent Americans have been murdered by the bandits, but should Americans as enlightened people be guilty of the same acts?"[25] Whether these three unfortunates were killed by Rangers, local or county officers, or vigilantes is unknown.

With the situation in the Lower Valley threatening to spin out of control, General Funston, who had been working closely with Governor Ferguson, proposed a radical solution to handle the firefights along the Rio Grande. Funston suggested that the Rangers and sheriffs' posses stay away from the river "except in cases where they may actually be in pursuit of marauding bands." Furthermore, he proposed that whenever troops, Rangers, and local officers were engaged in firefights on the river, "the senior military officer . . . will assume absolute control."[26] The secretary of war and the army chief of staff, Major General Hugh Scott, approved Funston's plan, although Scott ordered Funston to "Work with civilian authorities and keep within the law."[27] Funston noted that "It is well established that . . . individuals composing bandit bands . . . have been made up of persons crossing from Mexican side and getting arms from concealed stores on American side; have then started on prearranged raid. When pursued and hard pressed . . . the bands have broken up [and] recrossed into Mexico." To tighten security, Funston decided to have Customs prohibit the crossing of livestock from Mexico except at customs houses; to prohibit individuals from crossing into the United States except at licensed ferries and international bridges; and for the army to seize and turn over to Immigration authorities all persons caught crossing elsewhere. Finally, he ordered that military examining posts be established and manned by officers (nominally cooperating with Immigration officials) to prevent "all male persons capable of bearing arms who cannot satisfy the officer in charge" that they had a legitimate reason for entering the United States from entering.[28]

Governor Ferguson heartily agreed with Funston's plan. He informed the general that he was issuing orders in consonance with Funston's proposal and "you will not only have my official co-operation, but my personal thanks."[29]

Ferguson was beginning to get a handle on the Plan de San Diego problem—he ordered the Ranger captains to make a special effort to capture the Plan's leaders, Luis de la Rosa and Aniceto Pizaña.[30] A letter from Sam Robertson on September 10 was the obvious source of Ferguson's information. Robertson's letter is not in the Ferguson papers, but Ferguson's reply to Robertson is indicative of its contents. Robertson had apparently suggested that the governor offer $1,000 for the arrest of Pizaña and de la Rosa. Funston favored the idea but stated that he did not have the funds to offer such a reward.[31] Six weeks later Ferguson came up with the reward money. But Ferguson still didn't realize that General Nafarrate was orchestrating the raids, acting under Carranza's orders. In a letter to Funston, the governor suggested that "If there are no legal objections to your making demand upon General Nafarrate, I am sure he could capture and deliver them to us."[32]

At Fort Sam Houston, General Funston's chief of staff, Major W. H. Hay, formally issued instructions that had been agreed upon a week earlier by General Funston and Governor Ferguson. The role of cattle-smuggling rings along the border was keynoted in the instructions: ". . . in Hidalgo and Starr Counties, the . . . situation is greatly complicated by the operations of smuggling, especially of livestock, which have been going on in these counties for years. This has led to the organization of powerful bands of smugglers along the river. . . ."[33]

While the governor was urging the Rangers to arrest Pizaña and de la Rosa, he was forced to react to an uproar in Brownsville, where conditions along the river were extraordinarily tense. On September 17, fighting reached the outskirts of Brownsville; American troops reported that Carranza soldiers opened fire on them from across the river, and elements of the Brownsville garrison returned fire.[34] Exacerbating the situation, American soldiers discovered four Cameron County deputy sheriffs and a Brownsville policeman firing across the river, apparently at nothing in particular but simply trying to provoke a reaction from Carranza troops. When General Funston learned of the incident, he was outraged and promptly telegraphed a protest to Ferguson:

> I am sure that you are no more disposed than I am to tolerate such malicious deviltry and so flagrant an attempt to make a bad matter worse. . . . I hope that some sort of punishment [will be administered] . . . to the extent of depriving these men of their positions. . . . It is impossible for the Army in its dangerous and arduous work to cooperate with peace officers who are such scoundrels. There have been accusations . . . [that] civilians have opened fire across the border with the apparent intention of drawing a return fire and then involving the troops in the fight, but this is the first time they have been caught. . . . Such conduct could easily involve us in a long and bloody war. . . ."[35]

Funston thanked the governor, stating that "You have . . . given me the most splendid support but I realize that under the civil law you are as helpless as I am to deal with such outrages. . . . The interests of Texas [and] . . . the whole Nation are involved and [I] consider the situation so fraught with danger that unless these incidents can be at once stopped I shall feel compelled to recommend [that] . . . the President of the United States place the Counties on the lower river under martial law in its severest form."[36]

Reacting to Funston's threat, the governor practically ordered Sheriff Vann to fire the deputies, pointing out that "If you keep these men . . . it will be but one step in the direction of having martial law declared by the Federal Authorities, and then you and the State Authorities will be entirely superseded and we will have no voice in the enforcement of the law."[37] Ferguson also wrote in the same vein to the Cameron County judge and to the state representative from the Brownsville district, Lawrence Bates, who was a lieutenant colonel on the governor's staff.[38] Sheriff Vann, who did not report either to General Funston or to Governor Ferguson, resented the governor's interference and refused to fire the deputies.[39]

At approximately the same time, the First Chief of the Constitutionalists, Venustiano Carranza, complained to Secretary of State Robert Lansing through the Constitutionalists' confidential agent in Washington, Eliseo Arredondo, that the garrison in Brownsville had trained its artillery on General Nafarrate's barracks in Matamoros. Lansing forwarded Carranza's complaint to the War Department, which presumably was pleased that they had gotten Nafarrate's attention. It should be noted that Carranza quoted Nafarrate's accusation that American troops had wounded several of his soldiers, who he said had not fired on the Americans.[40] But this explanation was wearing thin.

The approach of September 16, Mexican independence day, produced increased nervousness, particularly around San Benito. Two companies of the 4th Infantry were rushed to the town by chartered train to augment a public safety committee that had been organized to defend the community. Local citizens contributed several hundred dollars to buy additional ammunition for the committee. In addition, residents provided ten automobiles that were filled with infantrymen who slept in the vehicles, ready to dash into the countryside at a moment's notice. Fears of an imminent attack were taken so seriously that "plans were made to seize some school houses on the outskirts of town and use them as blockhouses."[41]

For several days following the September 18 gun battle at Los Indios between U.S. and Carranza troops, conditions were relatively peaceful along the Rio Grande. One of the reasons was the contemplated transfer of General Nafarrate away from the border. In addition, U.S. Immigration Service and state health officers had begun screening all Mexican males capable of bearing arms who sought to enter along the Lower Texas border. Those who could not give a good account of themselves were barred. Governor Ferguson ordered state health officers manning crossings in the Lower Valley to deny entry to any Mexican male capable of bearing arms "and who may also be infected with disease."[42] In what must have given General Nafarrate a good laugh, U.S. military authorities requested that he arrest Aniceto Pizaña and Luis de la Rosa. Nafarrate replied through diplomatic channels that he had ordered their arrest—if they could be located. Of course they were never found, although they were figuratively under his nose. Pizaña, for instance, was openly strolling around the plaza in Matamoros.[43]

Meanwhile the exodus of Mexican families from the Lower Valley accelerated. The Brownsville *Daily Herald* commented that many were "good Mexicans" who had fled leaving standing crops in the field. The newspaper quoted figures from the local Immigration office to the effect that some 500 families (with average family size of five) or approximately 2,500 persons moved to Mexico during the month of August.[44] This was a sizeable exodus, and it would continue.

Fighting between Carranza troops and the U.S. Army resumed on September 17 only two miles upriver from Brownsville. In a fifteen-minute skirmish during which an estimated 400 to 500 shots were fired, it was reported that one Carranza soldier was killed and another five were wounded before the fighting was stopped.[45] Another clash occurred the following afternoon along the river south of Donna. Two Mexican soldiers initiated the festivities by firing on two American troopers. Before the shooting stopped, twenty U.S. cavalrymen engaged an estimated fifty Mexican troops for approximately one hour.[46]

The continued combat along the river during September continued to draw attention in Washington. Inevitably, Texans in high administrative positions in the Wilson administration received correspondence from their friends in the Lower Valley. Attorney General T. W. Gregory forwarded one such communication to Secretary of War Lindley Garrison. Although Gregory did not identify the writer, it may well have been Sam Robertson of San Benito. Gregory described his unnamed correspondent as "one man who is . . . prominent at San Benito. . . . I have known this man for twenty-five years and he has my absolute confidence. He is not hysterical, but of judicial temperament, and has taken an impartial stand in regard to the different Mexican factions. . . . I send you herewith a verbatim copy of his letter. . . ." A few passages of the letter are worth quoting:

> Beginning . . . eight and ten days ago [probably early September] and increasing in numbers daily, there has been a most remarkable exodus of our Mexicans, many of them American citizens, to Matamoros, taking with them their household goods and in many instances their cattle and horses. Their explanation of this movement was that . . . pardon was offered to all who would cross over before the sixteenth and work promised at attractive wages.

Many of them left crops in the field and other property of value. This explanation did not appeal to us as reasonable and was a source of disquietude. . . . San Benito people have been . . . helpful to the officers and in some instances . . . apprehended bandits have indiscreetly attempted to escape and thus come to an untimely end. . . . The state rangers . . . are acting independently of embarrassing influences, . . . and doing their best to cooperate with the military authorities.[47]

The sporadic pattern of raids declined in late September, and by September 23 both newspaper reporters and motion picture cameramen were leaving the Lower Valley, for it seemed that peace was returning. The reporters, who had spent almost three weeks in the Lower Valley, included Floyd Gibbons of the *Chicago Tribune*, H. W. Blakeslee of the Associated Press, Junius Brutus Woods of the *Chicago News*, and John W. Roberts of the International News Service.[48] But the following morning the raiders struck once again.

This time they attacked the tiny riverside settlement of Progreso, southwest of Mercedes in Hidalgo County. United States cavalry patrolled the area, but because of very heavy vegetation and a number of swampy *resacas*—bends in the river that had been cut off when the Rio Grande changed its course—it was difficult to maintain vigilance along an eight-mile stretch of river above and below Progreso. The village consisted largely of a combination post office and store and was guarded by a three-man outpost of 12th Cavalry troopers. The attackers consisted of about eighty Plan de San Diego guerrillas augmented by Carranza soldiers. The Mexicans crossed by boats in the predawn hours of September 24 and proceeded to loot the store and torch it. Two of the cavalrymen manning the observation trench managed to escape, but Private Richard J. Johnson was captured and taken across the river.[49] American reinforcements arrived on the scene as the raiders were looting and burning the post office, and there ensued a firefight lasting over two hours, in which one United States trooper was killed and two were wounded. By 9 a.m. the Mexicans had withdrawn across the river by boat or by swimming. Significantly, an estimated 100 Carranza troops provided covering fire from entrenchments along their bank of the river. The American commander on the scene estimated that during the engagement the Mexicans had fired some 2,000 rounds and his men had replied with about 1,000.[50]

The repercussions from the Progreso fight would reverberate during the coming weeks. Hidalgo County officials were so frightened by the attack that they appealed for help to Cameron County Sheriff W. T. Vann, who responded by sending a dozen deputies by chartered train to Santa María.[51] More significantly, though, the clash caused General Funston to raise the military ante. He ordered a battery (four mountain howitzers) of the 4th Field Artillery from Fort Bliss to Progreso, where it arrived on October 2 and dug in.[52] There were no objections from Washington to this escalation of the conflict along the border, and, interestingly, there were no further attacks in the Progreso area.

One factor that undoubtedly caused Funston to react as he did was the fate of Private Johnson. Captured during the Progreso attack, Johnson was simply listed as "missing" for several days, the army hoping he was a prisoner of war who would eventually be released.[53] On September 29, Captain McCoy, General Parker's intelligence chief along the river, learned from Tom S. Mayfield, the Hidalgo County deputy sheriff, that he had a source who knew what had become of Johnson. The source, a certain Guadalupe Cuéllar who was in jail on a civil charge, said that Johnson had been shot "four or five times" by Carranza troops, was decapitated, and had his ears sliced off as souvenirs for two Carranza commanders. His remains were then tossed into the river, from where the army was able to recover them. According to Mayfield, Private Johnson's head was stuck on a pole and paraded along the south bank of the river so that Johnson's fellow soldiers could see it.[54]

The day of the Progreso engagement, September 24, a contingent of eight bandits went for what they considered easy pickings—a raid on the McAllen Ranch near Monte Christo in Hidalgo County. The single-story ranch house was occupied only by its wealthy and elderly owner, James B. McAllen, and his housekeeper, a Mexican woman who was a refugee from the Revolution. The bandits rode up to the front of the house, and when the housekeeper asked what they wanted, the leader instructed her to tell McAllen to come out. Realizing that they meant to kill him, she roused McAllen from his afternoon nap, gave him a shot of whiskey, handed him a loaded shotgun, and informed him that he would have to fight for his life. The front of the house had four windows covered by thick green wooden shutters. McAllen fired both barrels of the ten-gauge shotgun loaded with buckshot through one of the blinds. The blast killed not only the leader of the raiders but his horse as well. The astonished bandits scattered behind the outbuildings and laid siege to the ranch house. For twenty minutes gunfire raged between the marauders and McAllen, who moved from one window to another to fire while the housekeeper reloaded his rifles. The rancher managed to kill another bandit and wound three more. The surviving bandits evidently decided that if McAllen was going to act that way, then to hell with him—they rode off, firing a final volley of bloodcurdling threats. McAllen took to the brush in case they came back.

Help arrived in the form of Captain Ransom and two of his Rangers, driven to the McAllen Ranch by Will Sterling in his family's brand new Dodge automobile.[55] After assuring themselves that McAllen was safe, the Rangers regrouped and went after the bandits. According to one account, the latter had stopped at a Hispanic farm, whose residents dressed their wounds and fed their horses. The Rangers tracked the fleeing Mexicans, killing two of the wounded who had been unable to keep up with their companions to reach the Rio Grande. The Rangers then returned and shot the two Hispanic farmers who had helped the bandits. "What had happened was the Rangers had found some bloody rags at their place and they killed them for lying to them. These Mexicans were afraid that if they told the Rangers anything, the bandits would kill them, but if they hadn't helped the bandits, then the bandits would have killed them. They were right in the middle of it and didn't know what to do. You felt sorry for them."[56] This tragic incident was certainly not unique to the Bandit War; it illustrates the plight of civilians caught in the middle of any counterinsurgency campaign.

The impact of the Progreso and McAllen Ranch raids was enormous. A Bureau of Investigation agent based in Brownsville, J. H. Rogers, wired Attorney General Gregory on September 30: "Conditions serious. Trip along river yesterday . . . convinces me present forces inadequate to cope . . . with situation. Danger increased by presence on other side of several thousand Mexicans who recently went from this side. . . . Outlying districts almost depopulated. This section being ruined. . . . My opinion martial law with increased forces justifiable. . . ."[57] In light of the raids, additional measures would obviously have to be taken.

The Rangers, who numbered thirty-eight at the time, could provide only limited help, for they were stretched to the limit. Captain Ransom of Company D, whose principal responsibility was killing as many Plan de San Diego raiders and sympathizers as he could, had a grand total of fourteen men in September. And of these, his sergeant, T. N. Reneau, had been in and out of the hospital for several weeks, finally being diagnosed with tuberculosis. In addition, Reneau urgently needed an operation for hemorrhoids, a condition which obviously made it quite painful to ride a horse.[58] Ransom, like the other captains, frequently had to detail some of his men for court duty, further reducing his effective strength; four Rangers were ordered to Rio Grande City to protect the district judge who was holding court there.[59] Ransom currently had five privates with him at his headquarters camp in Harlingen,[60] Ranger Paul West stationed at the E. A. Sterling Ranch near Monte Christo, Pat Craighead at Hebbronville, where he had been for a considerable time, Reneau in the Kingsville hospital, and John J. Edds, for reasons that are unclear, assigned to Floresville in Wilson County, which was not even in Ransom's area of responsibility. Ransom did not indicate where the four remaining Company D Rangers[61] were stationed. The omission was not that unusual, for Ransom was not only a very poor speller, but he frequently had to get assistance from his sergeant, or borrow a sergeant from another company, to fill out the required monthly paperwork.

With regard to Captain Sanders's Company A, for the better part of two months—since the Norias raid—most of that unit had been stationed at Norias, to protect the King Ranch. The mere fact that almost one-third of the entire Ranger Force was stationed at Norias indicates the political and economic clout of the King and Kleberg families. With the resurgence of fighting in September, it became difficult to argue that Sanders's Company A should still be kept on duty at Norias. Caesar Kleberg would of course have disagreed. However, the army was finally persuaded to reinforce the five soldiers stationed at Norias, thus freeing Sanders's command from static defense to do what the Rangers did best—scouting in the back country.[62] Captain Sanders was not at his best, for he was suffering from one of his frequent bouts of illness. While expressing his sympathy for Sanders's condition, the adjutant general nevertheless ordered him to move his company, explaining that the "Governor directs your company to take station at Alice." Hutchings also ordered Sanders to "go out scouting" and to reassign the men he had at Del Rio and Laredo to the new base at Alice.

Governor Ferguson ordered Sanders's company to leave Norias, but evidence of the Klebergs' influence with the governor and adjutant general is quite apparent in the correspondence that passed between them. Caesar Kleberg wrote to Hutchings after the latter had notified him that the Rangers would have to move. He thanked Hutchings for having guarded the King Ranch and asked Hutchings to "leave several of your boys with mine—after they finish the work they now are on." Kleberg praised the Rangers, saying "I want to thank your department and the Governor for the splendid work and assistance you have so generously given our section of the country."[63] Kleberg even equipped Company A before they left Norias, furnishing them with a "complete outfit, horses, wagon–cook–provisions, etc—so they can make a good scout."[64] Besides passing along Kleberg's praise to the governor, Hutchings, who had developed bootlicking into a fine art, responded to the rancher's letter: "I am glad . . . that you approved of Alice as the station for Captain Sanders's men. . . . I trust that you will keep me fully advised of the conditions in the lower Rio Grande valley, in order that the most effective work may be met."[65]

On October 1, one week after the Progreso and McAllen Ranch raids, there occurred the discovery of the single most horrific recorded slaughter of the entire Bandit War. Eleven Mexican bodies arranged in a row were discovered, apparently by the army, at Ebenezer's Crossroads on the road to Donna in south-central Hidalgo County. The next day three more Mexican corpses were found in the brush nearby. They had all been killed sometime between September 24 and 27, allegedly by Rangers.[66] According to press reports, friends and relatives of the deceased were so frightened of retribution that they were afraid to bury the dead. And the county coroner wouldn't even go to the scene to conduct an inquest until he had an armed escort.[67]

Writers have tended to broad-brush the killings of Hispanics during the Bandit War by blaming everything on the Rangers.[68] But except for a brief period in August, Fox's company was in West Texas, and Sanders's men spent much of their time guarding Norias. As for Ransom, he never had more than sixteen men, and effectively seldom more than twelve. So, even for the Regular Rangers it would have been quite a feat to have been responsible for most of the deaths during the Bandit War. An unknown factor in all this was the actions of the Special Rangers in the area, sometimes acting not in their capacity as Special Rangers but as vigilantes belonging to organizations such as the Law and Order League. And city and county officers also killed people. It is thus impossible to state with any precision how many killings were attributable to each of these categories.

Ironically, following the McAllen Ranch and Progreso raids peace returned to the Lower Valley. The principal reason had to do with international politics. Carranza was well on the way to crushing his rivals, Pancho Villa and Emiliano Zapata, and as he emerged the winner in the latest round of vicious civil war devastating Mexico, the Wilson administration was in the process of deciding to confer diplomatic recognition on Carranza as the de facto president of Mexico. Evidencing this, on October 14 Washington granted Carranza's request to transport some 5,000 Mexican troops over American railroads from Eagle Pass to Sonora to reinforce General Obregón's forces fighting Villa, who was besieging Agua Prieta. (Governor Ferguson, unlike his predecessor, was a team player when it came to the Wilson administration, and he raised no objection to the passage of Mexican soldiers across Texas soil.) This was a triumph for the Mexican leader's policy regarding the Plan de San Diego, which he had used effectively as a way of exerting pressure on the United States. Carranza was evidently prepared to fight to the last Hispanic in order to achieve diplomatic recognition.

Among the elites in the Lower Valley there was the expectation that diplomatic recognition might produce a cessation of the raids, although most people thought it was just General Nafarrate who was responsible for the incursions. They still didn't realize that Nafarrate was merely carrying out the Carranza regime's orders. Making a show of acceding to American demands, Carranza ordered the transfer of Nafarrate and his command away from the border on October 1. On September 26, Carranza had rewarded Nafarrate for a job well done by promoting him to general of division, the highest rank in the Mexican Army.[69]

To replace the controversial Nafarrate, Carranza assigned General Eugenio López to command in Matamoros. López immediately announced plans to restore peace to the lower border. On October 9, Captain Sanders, who had just returned to Alice from Brownsville and Norias, reported "everything apparently quiet."[70] And on October 13 a relieved General Funston reported that it had been ten days since the last hostile shot had been fired.[71]

Carranza received American diplomatic recognition on October 19, 1915.[72] Ironically, the previous night there occurred perhaps the most brazen attack of the Bandit War. Almost certainly it took place despite Carranza's orders, for it would have been the height of stupidity for him to have jeopardized the vital American recognition. On the night of October 18, at approximately 10:45 p.m., raiders boldly struck the lifeline of the Lower Valley—the St. Louis, Brownsville & Mexico

Railroad. The southbound passenger train was less than seven miles north of Brownsville, near Olmito and Tandy Station, when an estimated sixty Plan de San Diego raiders, principally from Matamoros and led by Luis de la Rosa, derailed the train.[73]

The raiders had pulled up the spikes holding a rail in place, and when the locomotive approached they yanked the rail away. The engine overturned, killing the engineer and severely scalding the fireman with steam. The engine, tender, baggage, and express cars left the track, while the smoking car and first-class coach remained upright. Half a dozen masked raiders swarmed into the passenger cars yelling "Viva Carranza, Viva Luis de la Rosa, Viva Aniceto Pizaña" and robbing and shooting Anglo passengers. Hispanics were not molested. Three soldiers in uniform were shot immediately; one died and the other two were wounded. Ex-Ranger Harry J. Wallis and Dr. E. S. McCain, a State of Texas quarantine officer, tried to hide in the lavatory but a Hispanic youngster revealed their hiding place to the raiders, who fired through the door. McCain died of his wounds the next day, but Wallis, who had a finger shot off and was hit in the shoulder, survived. The local district attorney, John Kleiber, who was returning to Brownsville from court in Corpus Christi, also survived, because he was covered in blood from one of the soldiers who'd been shot, and the raiders thought Kleiber was dying. Kleiber later stated that there was blood from one end of the coach to the other.[74] Besides shooting Anglos—three killed and three wounded—the raiders were busy looting. They took from the passengers $325 in cash in addition to diamonds and watches, and even the sample cases from traveling salesmen. The raiders even stole shoes, favoring regulation U.S. Army footwear, which they stripped from two of the soldiers they had shot. District Attorney Kleiber, who had had his own shoes ripped off by a raider, would exact a measure of revenge, for he would later prosecute several men alleged to have participated in the attack on the train. As for Luis de la Rosa, the wounded Harry Wallis said he positively identified the guerrilla leader, whom he knew, despite de la Rosa's wearing a mask.[75]

What disturbed the authorities was not just the attack, carried out within a few miles of Brownsville, but the fact that in less than twenty-four hours de la Rosa had learned that the army had removed the detachment guarding Tandy Station, a detachment that had been stationed there for almost two months, and had planned the raid.[76] The guerrillas had spent only about ten minutes aboard the train before retreating across the Rio Grande, eluding the army patrols being deployed to cover crossings along the river. The raiders had burned a railroad trestle south of Tandy Station, and when troops from Fort Brown were rushed by rail to the scene of the attack, they had to get off the train and walk the last mile.[77] In addition to the troops at the site of the wreck, Sheriff Vann and his deputies arrived from Brownsville, as did Captain Ransom and some of his Company D Rangers from their camp in Harlingen.[78] Joining them were approximately 1,000

Brownsville residents who flocked to the scene the following day. According to the local press, hundreds of women were among the sightseers, and "a large number had to be carried from the scene because of fainting spells."[79] Railroad workmen replaced the 185-foot trestle with cribbing, and train service to Brownsville resumed within forty-eight hours.

The train wreck produced another wave of Anglo hatred for Hispanics and Mexicans, and demands for revenge were commonplace. Colonel Augustus Blocksom at Fort Brown informed his superiors that "about fifty percent of the Mexican male population [in the Lower Valley] are disloyal in thought and possibly ten percent of these disloyal in action when opportunity offers. Even loyal Mexicans are now so timid and secretive as to make it hard for officers . . . to get information of value from them."[80] Governor Ferguson expressed a similar sentiment in a letter to Secretary of State Robert Lansing responding to an inquiry regarding the alleged killing of Hispanics by Texas Rangers. According to Ferguson, "The great trouble with the Texas-Mexican population is that their sympathies are with Mexico, and never extend any cooperation to our authorities, but are continually aiding and abetting the lawless element overrunning our country from Mexico and this accounts for a great deal of their trouble."[81]

Hispanics certainly had trouble. Captain Ransom engaged in a small-scale rinchada upon his arrival at the scene of the train wreck. Sheriff Vann later testified that Ransom's men seized four Hispanics the day after the train wreck and "carried them out in the woods and shot them."[82] One account alleges that ten were executed, but the most credible evidence would indicate that only four were killed.[83] Vann had earlier attempted to persuade Governor Ferguson not to station Ransom in the Lower Valley, but it was the killings after the train wreck that caused an open breach between the two lawmen. Vann further testified that "we came out there and arrested those four men. Captain Ransom had them and walked over to me and says, I am going to kill those fellows, are you going with me? I says no. . . . He says, if you haven't got the guts . . . to do it, I will go myself. I says, that takes a whole lot of guts, four fellows with their hands tied behind them, it takes a whole lot of guts to do that." Vann went off to investigate several Hispanics and arrested two whom he believed were involved in the train wreck. When the sheriff returned to the scene he learned that Ransom had indeed executed the four prisoners. One of Vann's deputies informed him that Ransom also wanted to kill the two Hispanics that Vann had arrested, but "I says, no they are my two, he hasn't enough Rangers here to kill my two . . . and we . . . put them in jail and they proved to be innocent."[84] The local newspaper reported on October 21 that the bodies of the four men had been found. It noted that "no inquest will be held over the bodies."[85]

Anglo fury escalated as a result of an attack on October 21 by some twenty-five guerrillas on an army outpost at the village of Ojo de Agua, seven miles south of Mission on the Rio Grande. The fifteen-man Signal Corps detachment at Ojo de Agua was there to provide radio communication for the cavalry units deployed along the river. The raiders surprised the detachment, killing three and wounding eight of the soldiers. But the fight was not one-sided, for after the engagement the bodies of five raiders were found at the scene.[86] Interestingly, one of these was a Japanese who had on his person his commission in the Carranza army.[87] The Ojo de Agua raid so infuriated General Funston that he requested of the War Department that he be allowed to issue "no quarter" orders to his troops in the Lower Valley—in other words that he be authorized to order the execution of captured raiders.[88] Funston also requested twenty bloodhounds and fifty Apache Scouts from Fort Huachuca, Arizona, to use as trackers.

Funston explained why he had proposed the "no quarter" order, noting that his suggestion "will doubtless startle [the] War Department." The general stated that "The American inhabitants of the lower border have about reached the limits of their patience in the matter of the border raids and it will not take many more outrages like the recent wreck of a train and the murder of its defenseless passengers to send them over the border . . . they will do a thorough job. . . . Since the raids began [they have] summarily executed more than one hundred fifty suspected Mexicans." Funston ended his telegram by suggesting that "there is but only one way to end it and that is to make it almost certain death to engage in one of these raids."[89] Funston's "no quarter" request coupled with his request for bloodhounds and Apache Scouts generated an immediate response from Secretary of War Garrison. He explained that he couldn't approve the proposal, pointing out that it could result in sensational charges that the army was "reverting to methods of barbarism." He was, however, sympathetic to Funston's problem, informing him that he stood ready to send as many troops as Funston needed.[90]

Three days after Ojo de Agua, on October 24, an estimated twenty-five raiders attempted once again to burn the Tandy Station railroad trestle. The army, however, had resumed guarding this strategic installation, and in a five-minute skirmish the troops drove off the attackers, with only one soldier being wounded.[91] What no one realized at the time was that this was the last raid of the Bandit War.

However, the combination of these last three attacks generated a significant response from both the federal government and the State of Texas. The day after the Ojo de Agua raid the 28th Infantry Regiment, 800 strong, was dispatched from Dallas to augment the 5,000 troops already stationed in the Lower Valley. Four days later they were garrisoning the towns of Mission, Donna, and Pharr, which freed up cavalry units to patrol the river.[92] Moreover, immediately after the train wreck General Funston requested $5,000 from the War Department to establish a "well paid secret service . . . to get hold of Mexican ringleaders and others behind them."[93] The Secretary of War immediately forwarded the request to Attorney General T. W. Gregory, who replied that he could not give the army the $5,000 but that he would have the head of the federal Bureau of Investigation in San Antonio, Robert Barnes, confer with General Funston and proceed immediately to the Lower Valley to establish a secret service and assist the army.[94]

Barnes hurried to Brownsville and called in Special Agent E. B. Stone from El Paso to help formulate a plan for stopping the raids. Stone soon located some individuals who might be willing to arrange the assassination of de la Rosa and Pizaña. Barnes approved of Stone's plan to offer a $1,000 reward each for the killing of the two Plan de San Diego leaders. One of the men the Bureau agents contacted believed he could arrange the assassinations for the agreed sum. Proof of the killings would be the delivery of de la Rosa and Pizaña's heads in a gunny sack on the American bank of the Rio Grande. Barnes sent the proposal to the Director of the Bureau of Investigation, A. Bruce Bielaski, who sent it to Attorney General Gregory for approval. The latter approved the plan but reduced the reward to $250 for each man. Unfortunately for Barnes and Stone, the U.S. Attorney for the Southern District of Texas, John E. Green, Jr., (who was receiving copies of Barnes's correspondence) was outraged that the United States government would be party to assassinations and protested to the Attorney General. Gregory responded that he had only approved a plan to *capture* Pizaña and de la Rosa. The upshot was that Green's protestations effectively ended the plan to kill the fugitives.[95]

While the federal Bureau of Investigation was trying to assassinate de la Rosa and Pizaña in their sanctuary across the Rio Grande, the Texas Rangers were reduced to more mundane activities. Captain Sanders and his company once again became in effect night watchmen for the King Ranch. They were sent to protect Norias for a week. Captain Ransom's Company D were assigned as guards on passenger trains in the Lower Valley.[96] Despite criticism of Ransom's methods of dealing with suspected raiders, he was viewed as a necessary evil, by San Benito attorney Sam Spears for one. Following the train attack, Spears wrote to Adjutant General Hutchings that "Ransom is yet necessary for a time, otherwise our people will take matters in hand and that is a situation to be avoided by all means."[97]

By October 29, the elites in the Lower Valley had appointed a committee to go to Austin and meet with Governor Ferguson. Following that meeting they sent U.S. Senator Charles Culberson a telegram to be presented to Secretary of War Garrison. Given the fact that despite the best efforts of the Rangers, county officers, and vigilante groups in killing a respectable number of Hispanics, most of whom were innocent and which undoubtedly caused some Hispanics to assist Plan de San Diego militants, and despite the presence of some 6,000 soldiers in the Lower Valley, the raids had continued. Therefore the committee had reluctantly concluded that the federal government should "take exclusive charge . . . of the situation." This of course meant martial law.[98]

Yet by the time this request was being seriously considered in Washington, the raids had ceased, and conditions in the Lower Valley rapidly improved.[99] And at General Funston's suggestion, Governor Ferguson had on October 27 offered a reward of $1,000 each for Luis de la Rosa and Aniceto Pizaña dead or alive.[100] On October 29 the Brownsville *Daily Herald* published the text of the proclamation. The newspaper's opening paragraph introducing the proclamation read, "Governor . . . Ferguson offering a reward . . . for the heads of Aniceto Pizaña and Luis de la Rosa. . . ." Reports out of Austin at the same time suggested that the governor might increase the size of the Ranger Force to its full statutory strength of eighty, although Ferguson had rejected a suggestion for 500 volunteer Rangers as being too expensive.[101]

Prominent Hispanics opposed the Plan de San Diego. Deodoro Guerra, the political boss of Hidalgo County, had led posses against the raiders, and another initiative was launched by the Brownsville attorney and politician J. T. Canales.[102] Canales's biographer, Richard H. Ribb, asserts that "No one individual did more to end the horrific violence of the Border War of 1915–16 than J. T. Canales."[103] This claim cannot be substantiated, as a quick look at chronology demonstrates. On October 19, 1915, Carranza achieved his goal of securing diplomatic recognition from the United States; the raids ended five days later, not weeks later as Ribb asserts. The evidence Ribb adduces consists first of the formation of the Canales Scouts, a group of local Hispanics that Canales organized to serve as scouts and spies for the army in the Lower Valley. Canales formed the Scouts on October 21. He later boasted that once this happened the raids ended. They did indeed end three days later, on October 24, though not because of Canales but because Carranza now wanted them to end. The last three incidents—the train wreck, the attack at Ojo de Agua, and the attempt to burn the railroad trestle— were in all probability manifestations of the frustration felt by Plan de San Diego militants when they realized Carranza was about to pull the rug out from under them. Second, Ribb describes how Canales met with Carranza in Matamoros in late October and, according to Canales's account, requested that the First Chief transfer Nafarrate away from Matamoros.[104] Carranza must have been amused, for he had weeks earlier promoted Nafarrate and transferred him away from the border. Canales, like many others in Brownsville, just never realized that Carranza, not Nafarrate, had been the prime mover in the raids. No one single individual did more to end the violence than President Venustiano Carranza. And if, as has been claimed, the Plan de San Diego represented a genuine Hispanic liberation movement, then J. T. Canales was a traitor to his people by virtue of his enthusiastic collaboration with the Anglo oppressor.

Once Carranza withdrew his support, the insurrection in Texas collapsed like a punctured balloon. Carranza ordered that the rebellion be crushed, and almost overnight the guerrillas "were too busy avoiding the Constitutionalist regulars to continue their campaign in Texas." Some guerrillas were arrested and a few were shot, but "repeated attempts to arrest De la Rosa and Pizaña failed, probably because of the significant local support that the two men enjoyed."[105] Perhaps, but it seems highly unlikely that the regime that assassinated Emiliano Zapata was intimidated by the likes of Aniceto Pizaña and Luis de la Rosa. While assuring the United States that he was trying to have the fugitive guerrilla leaders arrested, Carranza merely kept them available in case he should need them in the future.

Peace returned to the Lower Valley, but the cost had been high. The raiders had caused a great deal of turmoil but had inflicted surprisingly few Anglo casualties: six civilians killed (not "dozens of Anglo farmers" as has been claimed[106]) and eight wounded, eleven soldiers killed and seventeen wounded.[107] But the raids had triggered a massive backlash. The Anglo minority had taken the Plan very seriously, believing they were in a struggle for their very survival. And even General Funston called for "no quarter" for the raiders, an aspect of the Bandit War that has been ignored. Anglo fear had manifested itself in a wave of summary executions by Texas Rangers, local officers, and vigilante organizations. The number of Hispanics and Mexicans killed will never be known.[108] The death toll has been estimated at anywhere from 102 to 5,000. The 102 figure was compiled by the unofficial historian of the Lower Valley, attorney Frank Pierce, and Pierce himself noted that the number was incomplete.[109] The historian of the Texas Rangers, Walter Prescott Webb, stated that the "number killed in the entire valley has been estimated at five hundred and at five thousand. . . ."[110] But no credible source for these numbers has appeared. U.S. Secret Service Agent Edward Tyrrell in late November, 1915, reported, "There has been over 300 or more Mexicans killed in this vicinity [Brownsville] most of them shot down in cold blood. . . ."[111] General Funston reported in the summer of 1916 that state and local officers "did execute by hanging or shooting approximately three hundred suspected Mexicans on [the] American side of [the] river."[112] About three hundred seems a reasonable estimate of Hispanic and Mexican deaths.

Two of these can be amply documented. Thirty-four Hispanics were indicted in connection with the raids, most on multiple counts of murder. Of this number, the authorities were able to arrest twelve, and they were tried for murder. Only four were convicted. Two of them were sentenced to fifteen years in prison, and one of these convictions was overturned on appeal. Amid intense public excitement, the other two were hanged in Brownsville. Considering the temper of the times, the group could have fared much worse.[113]

Regarding the Plan de San Diego and the Bandit War, it has been said that

the thread running through the Plan's operational phases is the Carrancista connection. Carranza emerges as a master manipulator, as in his use of Mexican-Americans as pawns. The only times the Plan functioned were when it received support from Mexico, and such support was forthcoming only when it suited Carranza's purposes. Viewing Mexican-Americans as a useful fifth column, Carranza skillfully played on their hopes and fears as a means of exerting pressure on the United States. When his policies shifted, they were cynically abandoned. Unfortunately, the Anglos also viewed Mexican-Americans as a fifth column, with the results that we have seen. The Plan left a legacy of racial tension in south Texas that has endured to the present.[114]

THE PLAN DE SAN DIEGO RESURFACES

WHILE the Bandit War raged in South Texas, the Rangers were also busy elsewhere. In the summer of 1915 there was an upsurge in revolutionary intrigue in El Paso. General Victoriano Huerta, the exiled Mexican strongman, was planning an armed comeback, with German support, and he had enlisted the aid of his former subordinate and fellow exile, General Pascual Orozco. The focal point of their conspiracy was El Paso, where arms were being stockpiled and men recruited. On June 27, 1915, the two Mexican generals were arrested at the train station in Newman, New Mexico, on their way to El Paso to launch their revolution. They were taken to El Paso and charged with conspiracy to violate the neutrality laws. Subsequently released on bond, they remained under house arrest. Nevertheless, Orozco managed to escape on the evening of July 3. He was reportedly driven from El Paso to Fabens by Sabino Guaderrama. This seems quite probable, since Sabino's brother Jesús was one of those indicted along with Huerta and Orozco.[1] Huerta was transferred to Fort Bliss for safekeeping.[2] An intensive search by American authorities failed to apprehend Orozco. He was finally located on August 30, when he and four companions were shot to death near Sierra Blanca by a posse which spotted the Mexicans encamped in Green River Canyon, opened fire, and mowed them down.[3] Being a professional revolutionist was a hazardous occupation.

The posse that killed Orozco claimed they thought he and his companions were rustlers since they had stolen their mounts from the Dick Love ranch. It has been stated that the posse was composed of "federal marshals, deputy sheriffs, Texas Rangers, and troops of the Thirteenth Cavalry."[4] One Mexican historian even asserts that the men who killed Orozco were officers of the 13th Cavalry disguised as Rangers, and he goes on to give a delightfully fanciful account of

Orozco's death.[5] Upon examination, Orozco's death proves to be one of those cases where the Rangers are blamed—or credited, depending on one's point of view—for something they didn't do. Federal marshals, Rangers, deputy sheriffs, and patrols of the 13th Cavalry had indeed been searching for Orozco, but on August 26, the six Rangers operating along the river east of El Paso were reassigned to that city to work under Sheriff Peyton Edwards until further notice.[6] The posse that killed Orozco contained neither Rangers nor soldiers. The army reported that "The actual extermination of the red flaggers, however, was due principally to the energy, determination and trailing ability of the civilian posse."[7] The group did include two ex-Rangers: Herff A. Carnes, who had resigned in 1911 and was a mounted Customs inspector, and David William "Dave" Allison, the constable at Sierra Blanca. Allison was a gunslinger with a colorful past. He'd been sheriff of Midland County (1888–89), Texas Ranger (1899–1903), Arizona Ranger (1903–06), and city marshal of Roswell, New Mexico (1911). He despised Mexicans; as Sierra Blanca constable "he kills several Mexicans each month," according to a young army lieutenant stationed there named George S. Patton, Jr.[8] Allison, who led the posse,[9] would become a brand inspector for the cattlemen's association in 1917, and as such received a Special Ranger commission (1917–1919). There was another future Ranger in the posse, rancher Robert C. Love, who would serve for several months in 1918. At the request of Sheriff John A. Morine, he and his fellow posse members were indicted for murder by the Culberson County grand jury. Their trial the next day resulted in the entire posse being acquitted.[10] Thus there were no legal loose ends to worry about.

The size of the Ranger Force fluctuated wildly in 1915–1916. Because of the Bandit War, Ferguson in 1915 had increased the strength of the Force to fifty men, although the $30,000 appropriated would support only thirty; he planned to make up the difference with a deficiency appropriation of $20,000. But as that conflict ended following Carranza's diplomatic recognition, it became possible to reduce the Rangers accordingly. In mid-December, 1915, the force numbered thirty-nine:

Company A (Sanders)	15
Company B (Fox)	12
Company C (Smith)	1
Company D (Ransom)	11[11]

Hutchings hoped to continue making reductions by attrition until the Ranger Force approximated the thirty men that, at about $1,000 per Ranger per year, the appropriation would support.[12] As of February 10, 1916, the organization had been trimmed to thirty-six: four captains and thirty-two enlisted men. The total monthly expenditure for the Rangers was about $3,500, or $100 per month per man. After paying January's bills, there remained exactly $8,700.07 in the Ranger account, meaning that the appropriation would be exhausted in April. Hutchings inquired whether Ferguson would approve a deficiency appropriation of some $17,500 to get through the rest of the fiscal year. Ferguson said he would and instructed Hutchings to prepare the necessary paperwork.[13] As of late March, though, the Rangers had been further reduced to thirty-four men, and the probable deficiency to $15,000. Hutchings's goal was a thirty-man force, to be achieved by attrition, unless "border conditions should become so very much worse as to justify the increase in the force, and consequent greater deficiency."[14] Border conditions indeed became much worse.

In the predawn hours of March 9, 1916, Pancho Villa unleashed some 485 of his irregulars in a surprise attack on the little border town of Columbus, New Mexico, burning down part of the village and killing eighteen soldiers and civilians before troopers of the 13th Cavalry drove the raiders off, pursuing them several miles across the international boundary, killing a number of villistas, and forcing them to abandon most of their loot. In reaction to the raid the United States once again intervened militarily in Mexico; a reluctant President Wilson dispatched Brigadier General John J. Pershing and a Punitive Expedition that eventually numbered more than 10,000 men into Chihuahua after Villa.

This poor man's Pearl Harbor naturally caused a sensation, especially in nearby El Paso. After conferring with Sheriff Peyton Edwards, state Senator Claude Hudspeth advised Hutchings by telephone that conditions in that city were very serious, with a threatened "uprising of Mexicans in New Mexico in vicinity of El Paso and from El Paso to the New Mexico line." The sheriff and senator asked for two companies of Rangers and for the governor to come in person. Hutchings asked Captain Fox for a situation report.[15] Fox, who was already in El Paso with some of his men, replied that the seriousness of the situation in El Paso depended on the attitude of the Carranza government—whether it would fight to expel General Pershing and the Punitive Expedition. El Paso was as well protected as possible, but there was cause for concern in the county, due to the many villista sympathizers and the low level of the Rio Grande. Also, Fox had "reliable information as to an organized band of Mexicans in New Mexico across from La Tuna Texas." And he passed along the sheriff's plea that the Rangers be immediately increased to their full statutory strength.[16] Rangers patrolled the streets of El Paso, helping to maintain order. No ammunition was sold to Hispanics since the city contained many Villa sympathizers, and the police suppressed six Spanish-language newspapers. Telephone communications were established between the sheriff's department, Ranger camps, and army units.[17] On March 21, Captain Fox and a party of Rangers, along with the chief of El Paso detectives and several of his men, and two members of the army provost guard, arrested six suspected villistas at the smelter.[18]

On March 27 there was a report of Mexican raiders trying to steal 100 cattle from the ranch near Fabens of C. E. Kelly, former El Paso mayor. Cavalry detachments from Ysleta and Fabens and four Texas Rangers rushed to the scene, but it turned out that this was just another of the false alarms that plagued the peace officers and the military.[19] Nervous citizens were seeing villista hordes everywhere. But there was also no lack of men eager to fight the Mexicans. One was forty-eight-year-old Walter "Dad" Rushin, a recently discharged Ranger who wrote to Hutchings from Sierra Blanca the day after Villa's raid: "I hereby offer you my service if there is any chance to fight those copper collored [sic] chillies. As you know I resigned my position as a Ranger of Company B State Rangers Jan 15 this year but am still raring to go if there is a chance for a fight."[20]

Villa's raid on Columbus also set in motion a chain of events that by the summer of 1916 brought the United States and Mexico literally to the brink of war. It developed that Pershing's Punitive Expedition was based on a false assumption—because Villa was the enemy of Venustiano Carranza as well as of the United States, the Wilson administration had naively believed that Carranza would welcome American help in crushing Villa. Washington was disconcerted when Carranza, a staunch nationalist, forcefully denounced the Punitive Expedition as a violation of Mexican sovereignty and demanded its immediate withdrawal. The United States had no intention of complying, and relations between the two countries rapidly deteriorated.

As a ploy to force the withdrawal of the Punitive Expedition, Carranza dusted off the Plan de San Diego—unless the American troops were withdrawn, serious trouble would again break out in South Texas.[21] The Mexican president had ended the raids in October, 1915, when he secured American diplomatic recognition, but he had prudently retained the Plan de San Diego cadre. Luis de la Rosa and Aniceto Pizaña were available to launch a new wave of raids. By April there were confirmed reports that de la Rosa was openly recruiting in northeastern Mexico. Apprehension swept through Texas border towns, and Washington was deluged with pleas for military protection. General Funston announced that there simply weren't enough troops available and suggested that towns form local defense companies, which a number of them did.

While the lower Texas border braced for attacks, in Chihuahua the Punitive Expedition enjoyed success against Villa's guerrillas but found itself on a collision course with Carranza's army; a clash occurred in the city of Parral on April 12. In the Big Bend, a band of Mexican irregulars raided the hamlet of Glenn Springs on May 5, and a small American punitive expedition crossed the Rio Grande in pursuit. With the international situation becoming increasingly threatening, President Wilson on May 9 imposed an arms embargo on Mexico and mobilized the national guard of Arizona, New Mexico, and Texas.

Adding to the tension, the American authorities learned that de la Rosa planned a wave of raids between May 10 and 15 coupled with some kind of Hispanic uprising in Texas. On May 8, Governor Ferguson announced that the Ranger Force would immediately be increased to fifty men.[22] Although these dates passed uneventfully, the American government developed information that the Carranza administration entertained a grand design—an invasion of South Texas by units of the Carranza army coupled with a Plan de San Diego rebellion, all this to occur on June 10.[23] Toward that end, Carranza began massing troops near Nuevo Laredo. And this time the carrancista commander on the Rio Grande was not Emiliano P. Nafarrate as in 1915—he was General Alfredo Ricaut, who just happened to be Carranza's nephew. Besides the concentration of regular carrancista units, a special Plan de San Diego brigade was organized. Its commander, significantly enough, was not Luis de la Rosa but Colonel Esteban E. Fierros, a native of Laredo and a regular carrancista officer. In May, Fierros was promoted to brevet general and given command of the Brigada Fierros, a 450-man unit being assembled at Monterrey. As was common during the Mexican Revolution, the unit was top-heavy—Fierros commanded three subordinate generals—one of them was Luis de la Rosa himself. And, to lend Plan de San Diego credibility to the operation, Fierros was commissioned as a brigadier general in the "Liberating Army of Races and Peoples in America," which was the military arm of the putative Revolutionary Congress of San Diego. Fierros's commission was purportedly issued at San Diego, Texas, on May 30, 1916, by General in Chief León Caballo. It was Fierros who controlled the unit's funds, thereby ensuring that de la Rosa would have to operate under strict carrancista direction.[24]

Regarding the grand design, the Mexican generals really believed that the United States was so militarily unprepared that Mexico stood a reasonable chance of winning a war. The Mexican high command seemed oblivious to the fact that the last time Mexico had fought the United States, the United States had ended up with nearly half of Mexico. However feasible the plan may have seemed on paper, when the Mexicans realized that the United States had discovered it they quietly abandoned the scheme at the last minute. But Carranza was still determined to continue exerting pressure, so he reverted to his successful 1915 strategy—a wave of raids, none of which by itself would be serious enough to provoke massive American retaliation. The Brigada Fierros conducted the raids with the assistance of Plan de San Diego militants. A small unit cut telegraph lines and tried to burn a railroad trestle north of Laredo, another group attacked an army outpost on the river at San Ignacio, while still another band tried to ambush an army patrol near Brownsville.[25] And some militants tried to incite Hispanics around San Antonio. But as the carrancistas discovered to their sorrow, the United States Army's rules of engagement had changed—on June 17, hundreds of American troops crossed the Rio Grande in pursuit of the raiders near Brownsville, and they skirmished with Carranza soldiers before withdrawing. On June 18, President

Wilson mobilized the remainder of the national guard and deployed some 112,000 men for border duty as a show of force and to free the regular army for an invasion of Mexico. On June 21, a small unit of Pershing's Punitive Expedition was defeated by Carranza troops at Carrizal.

Peace and war were balanced on a knife edge, but in the event both countries pulled back from confrontation and tried to settle their differences through diplomacy. Once again Carranza shut down Plan de San Diego operations and kept de la Rosa and Pizaña on a short leash.[26] Throughout the June crisis, General Pablo González, commanding the Army Corps of the East, had supervised the raids into Texas, forwarding to Carranza reports from Fierros and others asking Carranza for additional funds for the campaign. However, on June 23, Carranza ordered de la Rosa's arrest and prohibited armed bands from crossing into Texas. General Ricaut arrested de la Rosa. On June 24, a disappointed González wired Carranza: "Please tell me if this was Your Excellency's order and if said individual could be liberated so that he can proceed into the interior of the United States to continue carrying out the mission that he has in conjunction with Fierros. . . ."[27] De la Rosa remained in custody in Monterrey, but his detention was quite comfortable. He was lodged in a hotel at the expense of the Mexican government, which also paid for his meals, liquor, and cigarettes, besides providing him with an allowance for expenses.[28]

Four carrancistas captured in the San Ignacio clash were tried as bandits for the death of an American soldier in that attack. They were quickly convicted of murder and sentenced to hang.[29] However, in 1918 the Texas Court of Criminal Appeals overturned the lower court's ruling on the ground that a state of undeclared war between the United States and Mexico had existed in the summer of 1916. The men were therefore prisoners of war, not bandits. They were freed and returned to Mexico.[30]

It has been asserted that "Most important, no further raids into Texas occurred. Although the Sediciosos had proven their ability to gather large numbers of men in coordinated attacks—and apparently to convince some local Constitutionalist officers to join their efforts—their new strategy failed."[31] This is clearly a case of trying to make the tail wag the dog.

Ranger involvement in these tumultuous events was modest but quite memorable, consisting as it did largely of the Morín affair. In late April and early May, a Mexican named José M. Morín, using the alias of J. M. Leal, was busily organizing Hispanics and Mexicans from San Antonio south to the border. He professed to be a villista, but he was urging his listeners to participate in an uprising planned for May 10—the very uprising the Carranza government was sponsoring. And in fact Morín subsequently admitted that he had become a Carranza general in 1914.[32] As part of his activities Morín issued commissions to the men who would lead the envisioned army of liberation. Unfortunately for Morín, one of his associates, Colonel B. Salvador Cervantes, was a Bureau of Investigation informant, and Morín's plot began to unravel. The process accelerated because in addition to the information Cervantes was providing, others had become aware of Morín. They included Caesar Kleberg, manager of the King Ranch, and William Martin Hanson, chief special agent of the San Antonio, Uvalde, and Gulf Railroad (and future Texas Ranger captain). Kleberg was worried about unrest among the King Ranch's Hispanic employees, and he hired D. E. "Cap" Hamer, who had been a soldier of fortune in Mexico, as a private investigator on the Morín case.[33] (D. E. Hamer was a Special Ranger in 1916–1917, and in 1933–1935 was captain of Headquarters Company.) Hanson, who had considerable experience in Mexico, furnished the Bureau of Investigation's San Antonio office with a steady stream of intelligence about the activities of Mexican exiles.[34] Kleberg and Hanson even went to Austin to discuss the Morín plot with Governor Ferguson, who expressed great interest in the matter and offered his cooperation. The governor also had Hanson write him a report on the case.[35]

The Bureau agents and Hanson, who was working closely with them, faced the classic dilemma of counterintelligence officers—whether to keep the subject under surveillance and identify more of his contacts, or whether to arrest him before he can escape or cause more damage. It was decided to neutralize Morín on May 10. The Mexican took the night train for Kingsville to confer with one of his key associates, Victorino Ponce, who operated a bakery in that town. The informer Colonel Cervantes saw Morín off at the station. Hanson assisted Bureau agent Howard P. Wright to arrest the general just before he got off the train at a way station. Morín offered no resistance, to the relief of the Bureau agent who had been told that the Mexican was a dangerous character. Agent Wright arranged to have Morín taken to the county jail in Kingsville, and he also had Sheriff J. B. Scarborough arrest Victorino Ponce.[36] They were left to stew overnight in the jail before Wright interrogated them the next day at his room in the Casa Ricardo Hotel, with Hanson helping to interpret. Both Morín and Ponce of course denied participating in any plot, but the officers had incriminating documents seized from both men. The result of several prolonged interrogation sessions was partial confessions by the prisoners.[37] They were left in the Kingsville jail while Wright went back to San Antonio to help prepare the case for presentation to the federal grand jury. Captain Sanders and his men assisted in a roundup of Hispanic suspects in Kingsville and vicinity, and the jail was soon overflowing.[38]

On May 23, 24, and 29, the *San Antonio Express* ran articles reporting the deaths of Morín and Ponce, the article on the 24th including a photograph of Morín. A surprised Agent Wright immediately tried to determine whether this were true. He telephoned Sheriff Scarborough at Kingsville, who informed him that the sheriff of Willacy County had taken Morín and Ponce away for identification, Morín as an alleged murderer and Ponce as an alleged participant in wrecking the train near Brownsville in 1915. Wright then telephoned Sheriff Clint Atkins of Willacy County, only to be told that he had turned the prisoners over to the Texas Rangers for transport to Brownsville. The sheriff claimed he didn't know the names of the Rangers to whom he had delivered the prisoners.[39] The Bureau agent in Brownsville checked around and reported that "Inquiry of soldiers and civilians about Morin and Ponce failed to elicit any information. No one seemed to know what has become of them and no one seemed to care to discuss the matter."[40] He added that

> The official class here are as close mouthed as those at Kingsville, which leads to the fear that Morin and Ponce are dead.
>
> This may not be true. It is possible, if not probable, that these prisoners were taken to some place of safety where there will be no knowledge of their whereabouts to prevent any effort being made to rescue them. Of the three theories: that they escaped, that they were killed, and that they were spirited away to some unknown place of safety, I believe the latter is the most probable.
>
> But this is only an opinion and is not worth much. All that is definitely known to me is that Morin and Ponce were delivered to the Rangers of Capt. Saunder's [sic] Company. Mr. Scarborough himself told me this last Tuesday night at Kingsville as I was en route to San Antonio. It has been reported that the men were seen tied to a tree at Norias. This is likely true as the men were to be identified at Norias and there is no jail there. It is reported that while the men were being taken to some place in Willacy county to be identified they were killed while trying to make their escape. I do not believe this because I do not believe they would have tried to escape from Saunders [sic] Rangers. And if the Rangers did kill them while they were trying to escape, I do not believe they would object to telling it.[41]

When the Bureau telegraphed Captain Sanders asking whether or not Morín and Ponce had been killed as the press claimed and, if not, their whereabouts, Sanders replied: "I have no knowledge of Morin and Ponce being killed. Do not know their whereabouts."[42] While the authorities proceeded to dismantle the rest of Morín's revolutionary network the central question remained unanswered: Where were Morín and Ponce?

The United States attorney in San Antonio finally suggested that Agent Wright call on Adjutant General Hutchings for enlightenment. Wright did so. Hutchings told him he hadn't received any official report from the Rangers but he would try to get Wright an answer by the following day. When Wright returned, Hutchings said he had talked with Sanders on the telephone but Sanders denied any knowledge of the missing pair. Hutchings said, however, that he had also telephoned the Willacy County sheriff, who stated that he had turned the prisoners over to Rangers [Joe B.] Brooks and [W. T.] Moseley (Brooks, of Company A, was a future Ranger captain; Moseley, a brand inspector at Kingsville for the Cattle Raisers Association of Texas, was a Special Ranger attached to Company C) "and that he heard that Morin and Ponce got away from the rangers."[43] Hutchings added that he too thought the prisoners were alive and at large but stressed that that was just his opinion. He did mention that Sanders was due in Austin shortly and he would take the matter up with him.

The frustrated Bureau agent reported, "I formed the impression, while talking to Gen. Hutchings, that this matter has been treated lightly by the State and that Capt. Sanders report, whatever it may contain, will be accepted; the authority of the rangers appears to be unlimited in matters of this character." Hutchings promised to send the Bureau a copy of Sanders's report just as soon as he received it.[44]

When more than a month passed without the Bureau receiving the report, Agent Wright again went to see Hutchings. The adjutant general happened to be out of the office, and when Wright explained his purpose, the clerk obligingly let him read Sanders's report. While he was doing so, Hutchings came in, and he reprimanded the clerk for having shown Wright the report. The clerk replied that in Hutchings's absence, the assistant quartermaster general, Colonel James T. Stockton, had told him to give Agent Wright whatever information he needed since Wright was working on the Morín case. Hutchings then explained that he wasn't trying to keep the report from Wright but was just concerned about the legality of granting him access to it. Wright promptly offered to get an opinion from Assistant Attorney General C. M. Cureton. Hutchings agreed, and Cureton declared it was entirely proper for Wright to get a copy of the report, the relevant parts of which are:

SCOUT REPORT OF CAPT. J. J. SANDERS FOR MAY 1916

May 21st: Went to Alice and returned. This morning Ponce was identified by a member of the train crew as being one of the men who wrecked the Gulf Coast train near Brownsville last Fall and murdered Dr. McCane [sic] and others. He was picked out of a bunch of 17 Mexicans in the Kingsville jail and positively identified. In evening, Brooks, Sheriff Scarborough, Special Ranger Moseley and I left Kingsville with two prisoners, Morin and Ponce, who were charged with horse stealing and murder, for Sarita. At Sarita, Morin was identified as the leader of the band of outlaws which attacked the Norias Ranch, Aug. 8, 1915.

May 22nd: By consent of Sheriff of Willacy County, Brooks, Moseley, myself left from Sarita with the prisoners for Norias for further identification. From

Norias, Brooks and Moseley left in auto with the prisoners for Raymondville via the Sauz Ranch where they were being taken for further identification. Between Norias and Sauz while Brooks and Moseley were trying to get auto out of sand bed, the prisoners, Morin and Ponce, made a quick dash and escaped through the bush, it being dark at the time. Brooks and Moseley proceeded to Raymondville and reported the occurrence to me.

May 23rd: Brooks and I returned to Alice and Moseley and other officers remained and made a search for the escaped prisoners but failed to apprehend them. Sergt. Grimes with a posse then made a careful search without result.[45]

Rangers Brooks and Moseley had engaged in what the politically correct would call "inappropriate behavior"—they shot their prisoners. This was emphatically the opinion of Assistant Attorney General Cureton, for Wright reported: "Mr. Cureton remarked to me: 'You know, Wright, from this report they killed them.'"[46] The Rangers had evidently used the same variant of the *ley fuga* that the Huerta soldiers had employed in 1914 in the Clemente Vergara case— "the prisoner wasn't shot while trying to escape, he did escape, and we have no idea where he is." Those who knew where the bodies were buried never talked. Morín and Ponce just "evaporated." Not surprisingly, Sanders's incriminating Scout Report is not found in the Adjutant General's Correspondence. The only copy is in the microfilmed records of the federal Bureau of Investigation.

While this was certainly not the first time the Rangers had saved the state the expense of a trial by summarily eliminating the accused, two things made the Morín affair noteworthy. First, a crusading attorney in Kingsville named Thomas Wesley Hook generated a good deal of publicity about the case. He wrote to President Wilson on June 4 enclosing a petition originating in Kingsville protesting the treatment of Morín and Ponce specifically and of Hispanics in general. The newspapers quickly picked up the story.[47] In fact, Hook caused so much trouble for the Rangers that when Captain Sanders encountered Hook in the courthouse in Falfurrias, he cursed the attorney and tried to pistol-whip him, which of course gave the case even more publicity.[48]

The second factor making the Morín case noteworthy was that Hook's letter and petition to the president were referred to Attorney General T. W. Gregory who, being a Texan himself, was presumably embarrassed by the whole thing. Gregory sent the file to Secretary of War Lindley Garrison, who replied that he would have General Funston investigate. In the meantime, suggested Garrison, it would be a good idea for both the military and the Bureau of Investigation to be instructed "to turn all prisoners arrested by them on Federal complaints of any kind over to the military authorities rather than to the local civil authorities." He further suggested that the president wire Governor Ferguson to send the Texas attorney general to Washington to confer with Gregory so that "cooperating relations can be worked out between the State of Texas and the United States in all of these matters. I realize of course, that Governor Ferguson is entirely independent of Federal control in the operation of the local constabulary, but in such a situation as this the interests of Texas and of the United States are identical and it would be to the interest of both if a common understanding could be reached so that the authorities in Texas would cooperate with rather than antagonize the Federal authorities in their efforts to preserve order."[49] The federal government did not take kindly to its prisoners being killed before they could be brought to trial.

The Morín affair overshadowed some of the Rangers' other activities. On May 14, 1916, Ranger Gustave "George" Snyder, a German who claimed to have been a secret agent for the Chinese and Canadian governments, received his baptism by fire. He was stationed at Company B's Ysleta camp under Sergeant W. A. Roberts, who sent Snyder and three other Rangers to arrest drunken 8th Cavalry troopers who were "taking in the town." One of the soldiers backed up against a fence and pulled out his .45 automatic, jabbing it into another soldier's stomach and threatening to kill him. Ranger Earl Langford remonstrated with him, telling him to put the gun away. The soldier then cursed Langford and stuck the gun in Langford's abdomen. The Ranger knocked it aside just as the soldier fired, hitting Snyder, who was some fifteen feet away, about two inches above the heart. He was rushed to Hotel Dieu hospital in El Paso in critical condition, with the state defraying his expenses. Snyder, age forty two, had enlisted in the Rangers only the day before.[50] Although he eventually recovered from his wound, Snyder resigned on July 20. Evidently a career where you got shot the second day on the job was not for him.

Also in May an unusual Ranger detachment was created, at Del Rio. Sheriff John W. Almond proposed to the adjutant general that four Regular Rangers be enlisted and a camp established, with Almond in charge of the whole operation.[51] Hutchings reacted favorably, sending enlistment blanks, copies of the law governing the Ranger Force, and informing Almond that "the character of the camp to be established will depend on the character of the work you propose to do. Submit your plans and suggestions."[52] Almond duly enlisted the four privates and requested the necessary weapons and equipment for them. He proposed to keep at least three men scouting up the Rio Grande to the mouth of the Pecos River, a section that was currently unprotected: "The soldiers apparently only seem interested in protecting the railroad bridges." The Ranger camp would be in Del Rio itself—a vacant lot and a barn belonging to the mother of one of the Rangers and located a block from the courthouse.[53] Hutchings approved these arrangements, informing the sheriff that "These men are enlisted in Company C, but under your jurisdiction."[54]

In July, union streetcar workers in El Paso went on strike. The company hired non-union crews to keep the streetcars running, and things soon got ugly. Strikers rode the cars to the end of the lines, which were outside the city limits and thus beyond the jurisdiction of the local police. They then attacked the crews. On July 3, six such attacks took place. The Rangers were increasingly visible in combating these assaults, on one occasion rescuing a kidnapped motorman. But their most spectacular operation occurred at the end of the Manhattan Heights line, when ten strikers beat and kicked a crew, sending a motorman to the hospital. Tipped off that something like this might happen, an automobile load of Rangers raced to the scene. As soon as they spotted the approaching lawmen the strikers scattered, with Rangers in hot pursuit. One athletic striker started running up the slope of Mount Franklin. The pursuing Ranger yelled for him to halt. He didn't. The Ranger fired a warning shot from his carbine, but the striker just ran faster. The exasperated Ranger then unhitched a horse from a nearby buggy, rode it bareback, and ran the miscreant to earth.[55]

That same month Rangers J. B. Swift and William B. Sands were called from the camp at Fabens to investigate a burglary. A homeowner had discovered three Mexicans in his house on the Island near Fabens. He and the Rangers went to the house, and the Rangers called for those inside to come to the door. One of them, Silverio Madrid, allegedly grabbed the end of Swift's carbine and refused to release it, whereupon Swift forcefully thrust the weapon into Madrid's abdomen to make him let go. He did. The Rangers took him to their camp for identification and released him. Unfortunately, Madrid died that night at his home in San Elizario from internal injuries. Captain Fox filed a complaint against his two men and took them to El Paso, where the justice of the peace charged them with negligent homicide and released them on $500 bond each.[56]

Several weeks later the same two Rangers were involved in a firefight near Fabens. White, Sands, a constable, and a deputy sheriff had captured a Mexican horse thief. The Mexican managed to escape and fled toward the river in a hail of gunfire, being hit twice. As he ran a dozen or so Mexicans concealed on the opposite bank opened fire on the officers, who took cover and shot back. A number of rounds were exchanged, and under cover of the Mexican fire the prisoner reached the other bank of the Rio Grande, although he was believed to have died later of his wounds.[57]

And there was the perennial problem of finances. In July, Ferguson approved a $10,000 deficiency appropriation to tide the expanded Ranger Force over until the new fiscal year began on September 1. The Rangers entered the new fiscal year 1916–1917 numbering:

4	captains
4	sergeants
56	privates
64	total

Yet the appropriation for the new year was only $30,000, and problems were inevitable. In an effort to lessen them Ferguson approved Hutchings's recommendation that the Force be gradually reduced.[58] Captains were ordered to effect an immediate reduction of sixteen privates, which still left the Force underfunded.[59]

There occurred a regrettable incident in Austin on the afternoon of Labor Day, 1915. People had thronged the shore of Lake Austin to celebrate the holiday. As it happened, Mrs. Edwin R. Huck, whose husband owned the Lake Austin Navigation Company, tried to use the telephone party line but was cursed at by someone also using the line at the nearby Lake View Cafe. She informed her husband, who stormed up to the cafe to demand satisfaction. He learned that three Rangers were being boisterous and disorderly in the establishment, and that the one who had cursed his wife was the senior member of the trio, Captain Edward H. Smith. When Huck demanded an apology from Smith, the latter slapped him. Huck suggested they take their quarrel outside, to which Smith agreed, but he then slugged Huck and kicked him when he was down; but according to some eyewitnesses it was Ranger Steve Henrich who knocked Huck down and kicked him. When a crowd of bystanders tried to intervene, Henrich started to draw his pistol but was restrained by his colleague Ranger P. A. Cardwell. The crowd fell back. Both the Austin police commissioner and the chief of police were on the premises but the police did not arrest Smith, whereupon the crowd expressed their disgust with both the Rangers and the city police. Captain Smith ranted against the commissioner for interfering, but the police chief eventually managed to calm him down. Smith, who had been drinking, subsequently appeared contrite and apologized for his unseemly behavior. The incident of course caused a furor, and Huck complained to the adjutant general. Hutchings investigated, taking testimony from a number of eyewitnesses, and his final determination was that Ranger Cardwell, whom one witness had described as the only one who had acted as a gentleman, was guiltless, and that Henrich should be fired—as indeed he was on September 8. As for Captain Smith, Hutchings left his fate up to Governor Ferguson. As far as can be determined, nothing was done to Captain Smith.[60]

Political winds continued to buffet the Ranger Force. Take the case of Henry Felps. He served in Companies B and A from 1913 to 1915, when he resigned and settled in San Benito. Then in 1916 he considered applying for reenlistment, and in so doing unknowingly brought down on himself the wrath of Judge James B. Wells, the formidable South Texas political boss. Wells wrote a personal letter to his friend Adjutant General Henry Hutchings saying that two prominent Democrats in San Benito had just telephoned him that Felps was hoping to reenlist and be stationed in San Benito, and they begged Wells to take the matter up with Hutchings—to prevent Felps's enlistment, and if by some mischance he did become a Ranger again, at least to keep him away from San Benito. Wells complained that Felps was unfit to be a Ranger, had constantly abused his authority as a peace officer, and, getting to what the letter was really about, had dabbled in local politics. He had "made trouble for all our Democratic friends in San Benito, and is really a 'tool' in connection with some of our enemies, the Republican and Independent local politicians."[61] Felps was not reenlisted.

Another South Texas political boss, state Senator Archie Parr, likewise influenced Ranger appointments. In October, 1915, at the request of Caesar Kleberg, the governor appointed Paul McAlister, at the time a Duval County deputy sheriff, as a Special Ranger.[62] McAlister, it will be recalled, had killed Brownsville police chief José Crixell in 1912. The adjutant general didn't hold that against him, for in notifying Kleberg of the appointment Hutchings said that "McAlister was in the Ranger Service before, and I know that he is a good man."[63] McAlister's Special Ranger appointment did not set well with either the Duval County sheriff, A. W. Tobin, or Tobin's boss Archie Parr, apparently because McAlister had dealings with those malcontents disputing Parr's power—the Republicans and Independents who, according to Parr, "want to try and get in these Special Rangers to harass our people." Parr complained that McAlister was always drunk. When Hutchings asked Kleberg what he knew of the charges against McAlister, Kleberg replied that he had contacted "some of the substantial citizens" of San Diego and the letters they had written him back supported McAlister. Kleberg's judgment was that "McAlister is crowding some of them [Parr's partisans] just a little too close. No doubt he takes a drink, but I doubt seriously if he permits himself to get under the influence of it because it would put him before his enemies as a target."[64] Hutchings forwarded Kleberg's letter and its accompanying endorsements of McAlister to the governor. Ferguson had himself a dilemma: one politically powerful supporter—Kleberg—wanted McAlister to keep his Ranger commission while another political powerhouse—Parr—wanted it revoked. Parr was not known for his subtlety: "If he's a Special Ranger please cancel his commission. We have absolute control of this county and no Republican need apply for any office as long as we control the county."[65] Two days later McAlister's commission was canceled by order of Governor Ferguson.[66]

Parr did not want Rangers in his domain any more than he wanted soldiers, but he couldn't keep the Regular Rangers out. His Republican and Independent enemies in Duval County had the gall to demand an audit of the county's finances, and they were prepared to take Parr to court. When the grand jury met to examine the county's books, Parr and Sheriff Tobin barged in and demanded that the audit be stopped or they would seize the books. The jury foreman refused, whereupon they seized the books and stormed out. This outrageous action so infuriated Parr's opponents that the district judge and the district attorney called for Rangers to protect the grand jury and the court and to keep the peace, fearing a gun battle between the pro- and anti-Parr factions. And the district judge needed Rangers to enforce his contempt of court ruling against Parr and the sheriff. The job fell to a disgusted Captain Sanders, who had been looking forward to a two-week leave in order to be with his sick wife. He went to San Diego "with all available men" and on the judge's order arrested the sheriff and Archie Parr, placing them in the Duval County jail. The pair stayed in jail only about an hour, the judge instructing Sanders to release them when they paid a fine of $100 each. Parr's reaction may be imagined. At the judge's request Sanders stationed Rangers in San Diego for the next three weeks until the court session ended.[67] Parr fumed at the indignity he had suffered but he had his revenge—the whole question of auditing the county's finances became moot when the courthouse mysteriously burned down and all the records went up in flames.

Local politics also figured in a case at the other end of the Texas border, in Ysleta, and therein, as the saying goes, lies a tale. On April 28, John Dudley White asked Hutchings to order Captain Fox to enlist White in his company. White had been a Ranger in Company A in 1913 and had resigned to become a mounted Customs inspector, and in this capacity he had recently assisted Fox's Rangers and a Bureau of Investigation agent. They had arrested at Ysleta a certain Juan Mendoza, who was allegedly a villista agent recruiting men on the American side of the river. In assisting the other officers, White "came very near connecting one old Mexican politician into all of this so they began to howl," accusing White of overstepping his authority. White was already controversial, for he explained that "in Jan. I had to kill a Mexican from Mexico with a smuggled horse a pistol and a pocket full of pistol shells. This was while I was performing my duty as a customs Inspector. I was tried for murder just to please some Mexicans in and around El Paso but thank god was acquitted. The jury was out just 10 minutes." But because of the recent flap the collector of customs in El Paso intended to transfer White to Brownsville. White stated that "I don't think it is right for me to have to leave just because I have caught some political crook and it is for this reason I appeal to you my life long friend for a place on your Ranger force." White referred the adjutant general to Captain Fox and his men, who would corroborate his account. Furthermore, ex-Ranger captain John Hughes and the other Anglo residents of Ysleta would sign a petition on White's behalf if it were needed.[68] White's family had political clout in Austin, which may well have been a factor in his being enlisted in Company B on May 10.

White was stationed in Ysleta. A certain Mrs. A. Alderete, who owned the Central Ice Cream Parlor in Ysleta wrote to Governor Ferguson on August 28 a scathing denunciation of the local Ranger detachment. Her litany of their abuses ranged from their lack of decency in the presence of women and children to the allegation that "thuggery and murder is a pastime with them." She pointed out that their actions reflected directly on the governor and implored him to have them removed. Then Mrs. Alderete got to the crux of her complaint—Ranger

John Dudley White: "Mr. White is a bad dangerous killing man" who was "possessed with very satanical spirits" besides being "a deliberate fiend and blood thirsty villain." Her animus against White stemmed from her husband being the Hispanic politician who had clashed with White while the latter was still a Customs inspector. The Alderetes were a family politically active and involved in revolutionary intrigue in El Paso and vicinity.[69] Mrs. Alderete claimed that White now lurked around their house wanting to harm Alderete. But in addition to White, the other Rangers were nearly as bad, according to Mrs. Alderete: "on election day a big bully by name of Clint Holman attacked Mr. Alderete." Ferguson directed Hutchings to investigate the matter.[70]

A few days later, Hutchings telegraphed Captain Fox to transfer the Ysleta detachment elsewhere. If Fox thought it necessary to maintain a camp at Ysleta, then assign different men.[71] The adjutant general followed up with a letter to Fox enclosing a copy of Mrs. Alderete's complaint to the governor and instructing the Ranger captain to investigate the matter thoroughly and report the results in writing. Hutchings explained that his telegram ordering the transfer of the Ysleta detachment "is not to be considered as accepting or not accepting the truth of the charges made in the letter of Mrs. Alderete."[72] When Sheriff Peyton J. Edwards of El Paso County learned that the Ysleta Rangers were to be transferred, he wired a strenuous protest to Hutchings, emphasizing that they were experienced officers who were well acquainted with conditions in the area and adding that "am satisfied that should new ones be placed there you would receive some protest about them as soon as they begin to perform their duty. Those asking their removal do not represent the law abiding citizens." He begged Hutchings to rescind the transfer.[73] Hutchings was unmoved, wiring back that "I regret that you and other responsible citizens should be indignant at change of station of enlisted men in Ranger Force. The order will not be rescinded."[74] Furthermore, Hutchings followed up on his own Mrs. Alderete's charge that a Ranger had pistol-whipped a sergeant in the Massachusetts National Guard stationed in Ysleta, requesting the commander of the Massachusetts troops in El Paso to furnish any information he might have.[75]

As ordered, Captain Fox went to Ysleta to investigate. He was pleased to report that he had interviewed the local businessmen and "all citizens say her statement is false and without foundation":

> She charges Clint Holden with assaulting her husband on election day July 22, when she [sic] refused to stay behind the 100 ft mark; several times he was called down and asked by Holden to keep back of the mark. He then began to abuse and curse Holden and Holden knocked him down and made him stay at the proper place. The J. P. tells me he saw it all and Holden did the right thing and as the Election Judges had asked the Rangers to assist

them on that day, and everybody says that it was the first election that was ever held here on the square. She also charges that the Rangers forget all decency on the streets which is also untrue; every man and woman here disputes her on that charge. She further charges that White came and stood in front of her place and called her vile names. Alderete who she calls her husband came to the door while White was passing by and tried to start trouble and White ask [sic] him to come out if he was after him. She also charges that one of the Rangers, without calling his name, struck a sgt. over the head with a gun without provocation. The man she speaks of was Smith. Mrs. Alderete got the soldiers to go out and blockade the sts. Autos, [sic] women and children could not get by the streets and when Smith ask them to let the people pass this Sergeant informed him that his Capt. was the only one could move them and started to pull his gun and Smith beat him to it. The Judge says that it happened just that way, and that the soldiers then opened up so the people could get by. General I could tell you just who this woman is but don't think it necessary.[76]

Hutchings sent a copy of Captain Fox's report to the governor.[77] That was the end of the matter, but the Ysleta Ranger detachment was gone. Captain Fox's report exonerated them, but they were his own men after all. The Ranger Force had no inspector to conduct presumably more impartial investigations.

There was a need for greater impartiality, at least where Captain Fox was concerned, and especially regarding his relationship with George Holmes. The federal authorities were gathering evidence against Holmes, who was an influential and notorious El Paso cattle dealer/lawyer/cattleman whose ranch was near Fabens. The Bureau of Investigation office in El Paso was closely scrutinizing his activities, on occasion using ex-Ranger captain "Australian Billy" Smith to keep Holmes under surveillance.[78] Holmes was an ardent villista, and in October, 1916, was indicted for having recruited men for a villista filibustering expedition.[79] Holmes also made a fortune as the agent for selling Villa's loot to American buyers. His accomplices included Hipólito Villa, Pancho's brother, and Belén Anaya, whose family owned a ranch near Fabens. According to a 1916 investigation by the intelligence officer at Fort Bliss, "His associates in his enterprises scale from that of high officials of banking institutions in this city [El Paso] down to the lowest criminals and crooks."[80] There were also close ties between Holmes and Captain Fox, whose Ranger company covered the El Paso area. In June, 1916, Fox had written a glowing letter of recommendation for Holmes to General Pershing, "vouching for his reliability and integrity." This was something akin to Eliot Ness writing a letter of recommendation for Al Capone. The intelligence officer investigating Holmes stated that:

In investigating this case I soon found an answer to the question as to why the state rangers of Texas never succeeded in detecting violations of neutrality and never were instrumental in bringing violators of neutrality to justice. Ranger headquarters [at Fabens] have been made the rendezvous for Holmes and his confederates while in the very act of violating neutrality. Holmes has stated, and I have confirmed it indirectly though not personally, that he furnishes the rangers with arms and mounts and that they are his friends. He told a party of his co-confederates in the hearing of an informant of mine that they could meet at his ranch at any time without fear of being molested by the rangers because the rangers were his friends. This circumstance is narrated to show that both the rangers and local authorities are either implicated or indifferent and that about the only recourse left is that of the Federal courts to prevent this form of exploitation of Mexicans.[81]

In August, Rangers were dispatched to the town of Teague, forty miles east of Waco. The state commissioner of insurance and banking, John S. Patterson, and bank examiner J. E. McKinnon had been investigating the condition of the Farmers and Merchants Bank, and Patterson was posting a notice that the bank would be closed because of irregularities. The distraught bank president, T. R. Watson, took exception and gunned Patterson down in the lobby; he also fired three times at McKinnon but missed. Following the shooting, Watson and his two sons barricaded themselves in the bank. The shooting shocked the Ferguson administration, and the governor promptly informed the local authorities that if they were unable to arrest the Watsons he would send the Rangers to do the job. The Watsons surrendered. Rangers were dispatched to guard the Watsons and the bank. Commissioner Patterson died of his wound, and Watson was tried for murder, receiving ninety-nine years in the penitentiary.[82]

There occurred some unpleasantness on September 9 in Del Rio involving troops of the black 24th Infantry. Sheriff John Almond called on Rangers W. L. Barler and Delbert Timberlake to accompany him to a brothel where he had been summoned because drunken and boisterous black soldiers were trying to break in and gang rape the whores, who were mainly Hispanic. When the lawmen arrived they found that the troops were gone. The sheriff left the two Rangers on guard while he went to investigate an attack by blacks on another bordello. About an hour later, the Rangers got a frantic telephone call for help from yet a third whorehouse where black soldiers were trying to break in. But as they started to answer that call they found their present location suddenly surrounded by blacks showering the house with rocks, some soldiers climbing over the fence and others coming through the front gate. Timberlake confronted the former and Barler the latter. Barler reported that all stopped except one soldier who kept on coming even though Barler, pistol in hand, ordered him back. Instead, as Barler started out the gate the soldier leaped on him and they rolled on the ground, with Barler fighting for his life. The Ranger finally managed to shoot his adversary between the shoulder blades. Pushing him away, Barler fired three more times, hitting the man in the arm, abdomen, and groin. The soldier died at the scene. His comrades fell back and regrouped about 200 yards from the house. Barler telephoned the army camp and urgently requested that white troops be sent to restore order. Since the two Rangers were armed only with their six-shooters, they drove to the sheriff's office, secured their carbines, and returned to the scene.

When they arrived they were disconcerted to find the brothel surrounded by black guards. As Barler and Timberlake were offering their services to the army officer in command, firing broke out, and it developed that some of the black guards were deliberately shooting into the brothel. This was later established by the testimony of Sheriff Almond's Hispanic deputy, whom the blacks had seized and disarmed, and who witnessed the fusillade, consisting of more than 100 rounds before the officer regained control over his men. Sheriff Almond returned to the scene, and he and the two Rangers evacuated the terrified prostitutes, driving them to the courthouse for safety. White troops were assigned to patrol the town and calm was restored.

The citizens of Del Rio were furious at this rampage by black soldiers, whose presence they had resented all along. The army was embarrassed by the breakdown in discipline and bowed to the clamor of demands that the blacks be withdrawn. Soldiers of the 24th Infantry were transferred to duty with General Pershing's Punitive Expedition in Mexico. The regiment would be based at that isolated and godforsaken border town, Columbus, New Mexico.[83]

A much more serious incident further poisoned the relations between the Rangers and the army. On the afternoon of September 21, the popular Coney Island Saloon in downtown El Paso was crowded with a thirsty clientele, predominantly military.[84] One of the soldiers, a corporal, got into a drunken brawl with another customer, Ranger William B. Sands. Eyewitnesses gave conflicting accounts of what happened. Some said the corporal disarmed Sands, others asserted that the corporal hit Sands across the forehead. In any case the police were summoned and another Ranger, Charles Beall, took Sands in tow. But as the Rangers were making their way to the door, a member of the provost guard, Sergeant Owen Bierne, accosted Sands. Again, eyewitness accounts conflicted. Some said Bierne clubbed Sands over the head; others maintained that Bierne asked Sands about his fight with the corporal and Sands cursed Bierne, who then advanced raising his club. Sands shot and killed Bierne. Some bystanders stated that he pumped a second bullet into Bierne when the sergeant was already on the floor; others denied this, claiming the sergeant was still standing when the second slug took effect.

Sands was arrested on the spot, was charged with murder, and then was temporarily spirited away to Van Horn in the custody of a deputy sheriff to preclude any retaliation by soldiers. Bierne, a member of the 23rd Infantry, had been a twenty-eight-year veteran quite popular with his comrades, who now thirsted for Sands's blood. Bierne received a hero's funeral. Streets were blocked off to accommodate the crowd of more than 1,000 soldiers, in addition to many civilians. An army band led the funeral procession to Fort Bliss, where Bierne was buried. Outrage against Ranger Sands extended all the way up to the slain sergeant's divisional commander, Brigadier General George Bell, Jr. He not only denounced Bierne's killing as a "dastardly deed," but also attended, with his aide, Sands's arraignment and trial. And to honor the late sergeant, Bell named the camp of the 10th Provisional Division "Camp Owen Bierne."[85]

Sands was initially denied bail, but his lawyer convinced the Court of Criminal Appeals to grant him $10,000 bond, and he was released from the county jail. Sands's attorney was able to postpone his trial by securing a continuance.[86] When the trial was finally held in El Paso in May, 1917, there was so much conflicting eyewitness testimony that the jury gave Sands, who of course pleaded self-defense, the benefit of the doubt. The trial ended in a hung jury. Sands was fired from the Rangers.[87]

The fallout from the Sands affair went beyond just the military. Dr. J. D. McGregor, a wealthy and influential West Texas cattleman and former legislator who was friendly to the Rangers, wrote to Governor Ferguson about the Sands case, pointing out that too much emphasis was being placed on a Ranger's bravery; bravery was of course essential, but the criterion for bravery seemed to be the man's record for killing. He strongly suggested that Ferguson instruct the adjutant general to avoid enlisting those who'd been unfortunate enough to have killed their fellow man, and especially to avoid those who drank to excess. Ferguson so instructed Hutchings, who quickly issued a letter to the Ranger captains incorporating much of McGregor's language and demanding they exercise tighter discipline, in order to lessen the "considerable adverse criticism of the Ranger Force" which the governor had been receiving recently.[88]

In December, Rangers were dispatched to Snyder, where a tense situation had developed, one that involved Frank Hamer and one about which Hamer's biographers maintain a discreet silence as, for that matter, does Walter Prescott Webb in his laudatory chapter on Hamer as the very model of the Texas Ranger. On December 16, Edward Sims, a prominent cattleman, was shot and killed by a brother and sister team: Gladys Johnson Sims, his ex-wife, who fired several shots from a small-caliber revolver, inflicting two flesh wounds, and her brother Sydney Johnson, who finished Sims off with a shotgun blast. The motive for the murder was said to be Sims's attempt to take their two daughters away from his ex-wife. The killers surrendered to the sheriff, and at their examining trial Johnson was released on $20,000 bond, his sister on $8,000.[89]

The problem was that the Johnsons were a wealthy and powerful ranching family in Scurry County whereas the Sims were a wealthy and powerful ranching family in adjoining Garza County. Retaliation for Ed Sims's murder was a distinct possibility, as the Scurry County sheriff informed Governor Ferguson in a telegram requesting him to send "two good experienced Rangers to Snyder to remain until after the Holidays." The sheriff explained that there were in Snyder two men claiming to be Rangers who were acting as bodyguards for the Johnsons, and "that is the trouble and are only agitating the trouble more." Ferguson ordered Hutchings to investigate and report.[90] The adjutant general learned from the sheriff and the county attorney that Frank Hamer, who had resigned from Company B to become a brand inspector for the Cattle Raisers Association of Texas, and who thus had a Special Ranger commission,[91] his brother Harrison Hamer, who was a deputy game warden, and a man named Hallman were acting as Johnson bodyguards, "carrying six shooters but claiming to be State rangers; these men stay with Johnsons, ride around with Johnsons in their automobiles with big cartridge belts and guns, making rather a display of their arms," according to the county attorney.[92] He added that "These extra guards and gun displays are only agitating trouble, rather than keeping it down. These men, the Hamers are antagonistic to the local officials of this County. Harrison Hamer has had to pay two fines in this County recently for drunkenness and disturbing the peace, and on which account he unnecessarily displayed his pistol, and made threats against the local officials, or that is stated that the sheriff, nor no other man could arrest him." The attorney asked the governor to have these men removed and that "sober, fair and impartial men be sent to preserve the peace and dignity of this State between all men fairly and impartially." His request was seconded by the sheriff, the first deputy sheriff, the city marshal, the deputy marshal, and the constable.[93] Hoping to prevent bloodshed between the Sims and Johnson factions, the governor ordered Hutchings to send two Rangers to Snyder at once and take steps to have the commission of Harrison Hamer canceled.[94] At the request of the sheriff and the city marshal the Rangers sent to Snyder, John D. White and A. G. Beard, remained until after the Roundup Ball on New Year's Eve in order to prevent any trouble.[95] Although nothing serious happened at New Year's, the sheriff was able to have the Rangers stay until after the March, 1917, term of the district court.[96]

As for Frank Hamer, he resigned as a brand inspector in January, 1917 but asked to retain his Special Ranger commission. Hutchings, who liked Hamer and had stated that "Personally and officially I think very highly of Mr. Hamer...,"[97] reluctantly refused, assuring Hamer that it was just departmental policy and in no way a reflection on him.[98] Hamer continued to make news. He killed Gee McMeans, a former sheriff and ex-Ranger, in a shooting scrape in Sweetwater. And being a hired gun bodyguard for the Johnsons acting under color of his Special Ranger commission really paid off—on May 12, 1917, Hamer married Gladys Johnson Sims.

Part Three

The Hobby Years, 1917—1921

CHAPTER TWELVE

WORLD WAR

THE year 1917 opened with a blizzard of applications for Ranger commissions. War with Germany was looming, and giving impetus to this flood of applications was the publication in the newspapers on March 1 of the sensational Zimmermann Telegram. This telegram from German Foreign Secretary Arthur Zimmermann to the German minister in Mexico had been sent on January 16 in code, a code that the British had broken. The communication was intercepted and decrypted in London, then shared with the American government. Its contents were explosive: Germany would begin unrestricted submarine warfare on February 1; Germany would try to keep the United States neutral, but if this failed, Germany offered Mexico an alliance to make war together against the United States. The inducement for Mexico was generous financial support together with assistance in recovering Texas, New Mexico, and Arizona.[1] Mexico prudently declined the alliance, yet the revelation of Germany's offer intensified in Texas the specter of the "Brown Menace" and got Texans once again remembering the Alamo. When the United States entered World War I on April 6, 1917, Mexican President Venustiano Carranza declared his country's neutrality, but it proved to be very much a pro-German, or better said anti-American, neutrality.[2] The Rangers' principal mission now was to protect the Texas border against Mexican incursions, to suppress subversion, and to combat German activities emanating from Mexico. The adjutant general would declare that:

> the Texas Ranger is an officer of peculiar and varied duties and besides doing State service he is also doing an additional service in providing peace along the border. His duty is not only that of a State peace officer but he differs from State peace officers in that part of his work is a work that should be

done by the Federal Government, for his principal duty is to protect the international border between Texas and Mexico.[3]

One might think that in these troubled times the Plan de San Diego militants, who had caused such an upheaval in South Texas in 1915 and 1916, would again figure prominently in border intrigue, but such was not the case, for the Carranza regime was now anxious not to provoke the United States. The federal Bureau of Investigation had sent an agent to Mexico in December, 1916, and among other things he investigated the status of the Plan de San Diego. He reported that it had petered out. Luis de la Rosa had recently been released from confinement to barracks in Monterrey for quarreling with General Alfredo Ricaut. The agent talked with a dejected Basilio Ramos, who said the movement was falling apart because the leaders were broke and thus could not hold their men together. Colonel Esteban Fierros was in Mexico City, where he had been for some time; although he kept promising to bring funds with which to revitalize the movement, no one believed him. The agent also talked with some of Pizaña's men in Matamoros, and they too were completely disillusioned with a movement that had been held together largely by promises.[4] In January, 1917, de la Rosa was reportedly arrested in Monterrey for plotting with disaffected officers to seize the city. A subsequent report, however, stated that he had a job with the Mexican government. And in 1918, de la Rosa was confined to Monterrey and Pizaña to Matamoros, both closely watched by Carranza military authorities.[5] In October, 1917, Colonel Fierros was reportedly being held under arrest in a Saltillo hotel awaiting transfer to Mexico City to be tried for treason; in December he had gotten as far as Tampico.[6]

The Plan de San Diego had passed into history. These developments merely served to underline that the only time the Plan had amounted to anything was when the Carranza regime wanted it to. Once that government decided that the Plan had served its purpose, it cut off money and support, and the Plan ceased to matter. Those who advance a different interpretation have to deal with this inescapable fact.

Having a hostile, revolutionary, and pro-German Mexico next door during World War I would produce the greatest expansion in the history of the Ranger Force. Most of those applying for Ranger commissions, many of them former Rangers, were men anxious to serve their country by enlisting in that legendary organization, whether as privates or, more ambitiously, seeking appointments as captains in the expectation that the number of Ranger companies would soon be increased. The governor was reminded that "in case of war one ranger will be worth forty soldiers on the border, as the average Mexican fears the ranger, while he has very little fear of a soldier."[7]

The Rangers had been more thoroughly politicized during the Ferguson administration. As one attorney now observed, "I understand that everybody who has a poll tax and can rake up a Ferguson button is an applicant for Ranger service."[8] The usual procedure was for a man to buttress his application by securing as many endorsements as possible from the most influential people he knew. Yet, as a rather cynical editor commented, "letters of recommendation are usually easily obtained and, as a rule, carry little weight."[9] Some letters carried more weight than others. For example, Captain Fox and Sheriff D. M. Daugherty of Culberson County recommended Dr. J. D. McGregor of Lobo for a Special Ranger commission, Fox mentioning that the doctor "owns nearly all the land from Lobo to Hot Wells and Van Horn the biggest ranch I suppose there is on the Border." McGregor's commission was issued forthwith.[10]

Much weightier missives were those from Claude B. Hudspeth of El Paso. Though born in Arkansas, Hudspeth was raised in West Texas and had been a cowboy and a Ranger in his youth. He had become a successful stockraiser, owning three ranches, and an equally successful politician, currently serving as state senator for the 25th district. Besides being an important politician, Hudspeth was on the executive committee of the Panhandle & Southwestern Stockmen's Association, whose other members included prominent cattlemen like L. C. Brite, T. D. Love, E. E. Townsend, and Luis Terrazas.[11] Hudspeth's recommendations were generally approved.[12] A notable exception was the case of his colleague on the executive committee, E. E. Townsend (an ex-Ranger). Despite recommendations to the governor by Hudspeth and a number of other notables, Townsend was denied both a Ranger captaincy and a Special Ranger commission, evidently for political reasons. Besides Hudspeth, another heavy hitter was Caesar Kleberg, manager of the King Ranch, who, along with his cousins Richard Mifflin Kleberg and Robert Justus Kleberg, Jr., was commissioned as a Special Ranger. He maintained extremely cordial relations with the adjutant general's office, and his requests were given respectful attention.[13] Not only that, but detachments of the 3rd Texas Infantry were stationed at Norias and Santa Gertrudis to protect those headquarters of the King Ranch.[14]

At the other extreme, some applicants were pathetic, like Bill Connally at San Marcos. He was an old-time ex-Ranger, who'd been fired for getting drunk—the only time, as he assured Hutchings. Connally was now fifty-nine years old and was trying to feed a family of twelve by chopping cotton at $1 an acre. He found he just couldn't do it, although "Captain Sanders is older, and I do not believe he could chop an acre of cotton in *two* days." Connally applied for a Ranger captaincy, not surprisingly to no avail.[15]

Run-of-the-mill applicants had to rely on whatever endorsements they could secure, generally from city and county officials, businessmen, and politicians, as the adjutant general's correspondence for 1917 amply demonstrates. There was another side to the wave of applications, though, as evidenced by a letter to Ferguson from a young attorney from Temple:

Dear Governor:

In a few weeks I will be called for military service, and I am trying to head this call by making application for service with the Texas ranger force. And I am kindly asking you to assist me in that line . . . I am twenty-five years old and the head of a family.[16]

Trying to enlist in the Texas Rangers as a way of dodging the draft is an aspect of the organization's history that has not been touched on. Furthermore, there were allegations that influential fathers were trying to secure Ranger commissions for their sons to avoid their conscription.[17]

If a man worked as a brand inspector for one of the livestock raisers' associations—The Texas Cattle Raisers Association, the Panhandle & Southwestern Stockmen's Association, or the Sheep and Goat Raisers Association of Texas—he had little difficulty in securing a Special Ranger commission. The same held true for railroad special officers, and for a range of other railroad employees, from superintendents down to a sprinkling of conductors, brakemen, and watchmen. Then there were those who wanted a Ranger commission for other reasons, such as James O. Winborn, first assistant county attorney for Madison County, who explained that "I am not caring so much for the little bit of money that I would receive as compensation for my services, but more so for the honor and distinguishment [sic] that it will give me among my friends here."[18] Others wanted to make a visual impression, sporting "big high-top brass-toed boots, two six shooters and a big white hat."[19]

It took months to get the application situation under some measure of control, but a policy gradually developed: the applicant had to get the endorsement of the sheriff of his county. On occasion, though, a sheriff's endorsement was a joke; Sheriff John R. Banister of Coleman County recommended a man partly because he was "a typical ranger in appearance"—tall, slender, active.[20] Any other endorsements were nice but theoretically not essential. Furthermore, the applications of men subject to the draft would simply not be considered unless they had secured an exemption. Lastly, the Ranger Force would be purged of any draftable men who had already been commissioned. Thus, during World War I the Rangers as a whole tended to be older, for the military siphoned off the adventurous young men who had traditionally constituted the majority of the enlistees. And more married men served in the Rangers.

At the beginning of 1917, that organization was operating at its usual precarious financial level. In fact things were so bad that Captain Edward H. Smith, who constituted Company D, was transferred on January 21, 1917—to the Game, Fish, and Oyster Department as an economy measure. His salary would now be paid by the state game warden; Smith was given Special Ranger status.[21] By

February, lack of appropriation made further steps necessary. Hutchings said that "I regret that in the interest of economy it has been found necessary to reduce the Ranger Force and it seemed the best policy to muster out the men in Captain Ransom's Company, and this has or will be done."[22] In March, Hutchings lamented that "I am compelled to try to maintain the Ranger Force at its minimum on account of lack of funds," but he hoped that the forthcoming special session of the legislature might increase the Ranger appropriation.[23] The Ranger Force currently consisted of Captain Sanders's Company A at Alice, Captain Fox's Company B at Marfa, and Captain Ransom, who constituted Company C, at Austin.

The United States' declaration of war changed everything. Ferguson immediately began considering an increase in the Rangers, and Adjutant General Hutchings did his best to move things along. He reminded the chairman of the senate finance committee that the state Democratic platform called for, and conditions certainly required, that the Ranger Force be increased to its statutory maximum strength. To that end, he requested an appropriation of $40,000 for the period April 1–September 1, 1917.[24] The legislature was way out ahead of both Ferguson and Hutchings, sending the governor a resolution asking him to submit legislation for an appropriation of not less than $1,000,000 for border protection.[25] There were of course those who argued that protection of the Mexican border was the duty of the federal government, not of Texas, and the government was already performing that duty adequately. Thus the proposed appropriation by the legislature would be an extravagant waste of money.[26] Nevertheless there was strong support for the measure. For instance, an impressive delegation of lawmen and prominent ranchers led by Joe D. Jackson of Alpine, ex-Ranger and former president of the Texas Cattle Raisers Association, descended on Austin to lobby for an adequate force of Rangers to protect the border from bandit raids.[27]

State Senator Claude Hudspeth introduced a bill that passed the Senate on May 9 and the House on May 14. It authorized increasing the Rangers to 1,000 men, and a Ranger appropriation of $250,000 over the next two years. The Ranger Force figuratively resembled a man accustomed to subsisting on tuna casserole but who could now feast on chateaubriand. Ferguson signed the new law on May 25, but it did not become effective for ninety days—until August 17. One of its most welcome provisions was that it included a long-sought pay raise: captains from $100 to $125 a month, sergeants from $50 to $60, and privates from $40 to $50.[28] (A Ranger private now earned every bit as much as the elevator operator in the federal building in Brownsville.) By increasing the Rangers' pay it was hoped that the new law would upgrade Rangers themselves, attracting men who were courageous, discreet, honest, of temperate habits, and from reputable families. Further, on pain of immediate dismissal, Rangers were forbidden to participate directly or indirectly in the election of any candidate for public office. Captains would promptly discharge any man who abused his authority, or who might use "abusive language to or be guilty of unnecessarily harsh treatment toward those with whom he comes in contact in his line of duty." Other provisions dealt with captains promptly reporting and explaining discharges to the adjutant general, inspecting the horses of their men, and reporting in writing any absence of their men lasting more than twenty-four hours, so the adjutant general could remain abreast of the Rangers' locations and be able to deploy them effectively. Finally, captains must acknowledge by telegraph the receipt of telegraphic orders.[29]

The law had one immediate effect—it accelerated the exodus of Hispanics and Mexicans from the state, especially from the Rio Grande Valley. After what had happened in South Texas in 1915 and 1916, the Hispanic population was, to say the least, apprehensive as to what a vastly increased Ranger Force would mean. A report was being circulated among Hispanics that Governor Ferguson planned to station 800 Rangers on the border within a few weeks.[30] Mexicans were fleeing to Mexico in droves, fearing not only the Rangers but mainly the prospect of being drafted into the American Army. Their fears were fed by propagandists, some of them working for Germany, and by those eager to drive out Hispanics in order to acquire their property at bargain prices. Farmers in particular were frantic, since the economy of South Texas depended on cheap Mexican labor. Moreover, the Mexican government launched a campaign urging its citizens to return to Mexico. The situation became so alarming that Governor Ferguson had to issue a proclamation on May 16 reassuring Mexicans about conscription. Similar assurances were forthcoming from Washington, from county and local officials, and from the Mexican government itself. The exodus began to slow.[31]

The Rangers were primarily focused on the Mexican border, but several counties in northwest Texas were also trouble spots in the spring of 1917. The Farmers' and Laborers' Protective Association, organized in 1915, had several thousand members in this area. Members had to take an oath of secrecy under threat of death. The FLPA became a problem when the United States entered World War I, for its members allegedly mobilized to oppose the draft, by force if necessary, and they were accused of intimidating officials and prominent citizens. Local officials appealed to Governor Ferguson for help. From Abilene, Sheriff J. T. Dodson of Taylor County requested the immediate appointment of twenty-seven Special Rangers. His colleague, Sheriff E. K. Register of neighboring Jones County, wrote that he had only ten deputies and petitioned the governor to appoint twenty-nine Special Rangers. Ferguson promptly complied, instructing Hutchings to commission all of the fifty-six men the two sheriffs had listed.[32] In addition, many Special Ranger commissions were issued later not just in Jones and Taylor Counties but also in nearby Kent and Scurry Counties, where unrest was also present. Not only were all these solid citizens empowered to enforce the law, but several Regular Rangers were also assigned to the troubled area. Their efforts helped the federal authorities smash the FLPA in May and June, 1917; some seventy members were arrested and indicted for seditious conspiracy. At their trial in U.S. district court in Abilene in September, the prosecution argued that FLPA leaders advocated widespread sabotage and sought to ally the organization with the radical Industrial Workers of the World. But testimony at the widely publicized trial brought out that the whole affair was much ado about very little. The prosecution failed to substantiate its charges, and all defendants except three of the leaders were acquitted.[33] Nevertheless, some public officials and businessmen feared the FLPA's revenge. In December, Captain Ransom's Company C would be stationed in Abilene to keep the peace.[34]

The Ranger buildup began with the appointment of additional captains, and it would be they who would determine the organization's effectiveness. Thirty-three-year-old Jerry Gray was the first, perhaps because he was from Temple, Governor Ferguson's hometown. Between 1910 and 1917 Gray had been a policeman in Temple and a constable in Bell County. He was at present a Bell County deputy sheriff, and Sheriff Hugh Smith recommended him.[35] On May 28, 1917, Gray was appointed as captain of Company D at Austin. (His son Jerry Cope Gray would also become a Ranger.) The next selection was thirty-five-year-old Carroll Bates, who had been sergeant of Company F, Frontier Battalion. Thereafter he had been a deputy sheriff in Tom Green County, deputy city marshal of San Angelo (1907–1909), and since 1909 had been serving as San Angelo city marshal. In his application Bates stressed that he understood Mexicans and spoke their language.[36] Bates had considerable support, among others from state Senator Claude B. Hudspeth, who reminded Ferguson that Bates had been one of the governor's original supporters. Another endorser said Bates had enormous influence with voters in Tom Green County and had enthusiastically supported Ferguson.[37] On August 22, 1917, Bates was appointed captain of Company F. Two days later, Ferguson made another selection, this time a serving Ranger. W. L. Barler, age forty-three, also enjoyed Hudspeth's support as well as that of Sheriff John Robinson of Val Verde County at Del Rio, where Barler was stationed. Barler had been a Llano County deputy sheriff for four years, then had spent the last seventeen along the border, three of them in Chihuahua and Coahuila, besides being a rancher in El Paso County. On April 9, 1915, he had enlisted in Company C. On August 24, 1917, he was promoted to captain of Company E.[38]

Ferguson had signed the new Ranger law into being, but neither he nor Hutchings got to implement much of it. The governor's stormy political career was rapidly moving to a climax in the summer of 1917. He had certainly made his fair share of enemies, through actions such as vetoing the appropriation for the University of Texas. In July he was indicted by a Travis County grand jury, and in August the legislature convened to consider impeaching him. Adjutant General Hutchings was one of those called to testify before the House and had some interesting things to say. At the request of the governor's wife, Hutchings had had a Ranger guarding Ferguson and the governor's mansion since May 15, because of threatening letters the governor had received. Moreover, Hutchings had suggested to the Speaker of the House that at least two Rangers be stationed in the gallery while the governor was sitting in that chamber—in case some crank took a shot at him. The Speaker emphatically declined the offer. With regard to the Rangers, Hutchings said that it had always been customary to keep six Rangers at the capitol. Whereas the detail had heretofore consisted of one captain and five privates, at the present time two captains, two sergeants, and two privates were stationed there. Upon further questioning, Hutchings declared that it cost the state $1,000 per Ranger annually. But as for Special Rangers not paid by the state, Hutchings was unable to give a precise number, saying "probably there were not 100."[39]

The next act in the drama was the House drawing up twenty-one articles of impeachment against Ferguson, who spent much of his time issuing pardons—400 since July, nineteen in one day—a new record. On August 24, Ferguson was suspended when the House voted for his trial. The lieutenant governor, William Pettus Hobby, automatically became acting governor. The axe fell on September 25 when the Senate removed Ferguson from office for things such as misapplication of public funds, failure to enforce the banking laws, and receiving $156,500 in cash from a source he refused to reveal. Ferguson vowed to seek vindication by running for reelection in 1918.[40] He issued a lengthy statement alleging he hadn't been tried by an impartial body: "The governor of Texas did not have the same chance of securing an impartial jury as is given to a nigger crap shooter or a nigger bootlegger."[41] The Brownsville *Daily Herald* published perhaps the best judgment on Ferguson:

> The legislature of the state of Texas had done its duty by James E. Ferguson. Texas made a monumental mistake when it elected this man governor. The legislature has rectified the mistake. Texas can only thank those members of the legislature who stood boldly by the state and did their duty fearlessly, in purging the state of this disgrace.
>
> The people of Texas feel ashamed of the Ferguson scandal. They regret that such a man was given the opportunity to bring this disgrace upon their state. But, since the mistake has been remedied so far as the state can do it, the people of the state can only promise that they will never do such a thing again.
>
> And so exit Ferguson.[42]

Governor Hobby, like his predecessors, wanted his own man directing the Ranger Force, but he refrained from doing anything until Ferguson had been formally removed from office.[43] He then replaced Henry Hutchings as adjutant general. Hutchings went on to command the 71st Infantry Brigade of the 36th Division.[44] Hutchings's replacement was Brigadier General James A. Harley who had resigned effective September 29 as state senator from the 21st district upon his new appointment. Harley's assistant, as of October 15, was Major Walter F. Woodul, former state representative from Laredo.[45] It would be Woodul who would direct most of the Rangers' day-to-day activities.

When Harley took over on September 29, the Ranger Force had expanded to consist of Companies A, B, C, D, E, and F, each with a captain and a sergeant. There was also a total of sixty-one privates, making the grand total seventy-three men. In addition, some 300 individuals held Special Ranger commissions. Captains Sanders (A), Fox (B), and Ransom (C) were ordered immediately to recruit their companies up to the statutory maximum.[46] Governor Hobby announced his determination to "select for the Texas Ranger Service men of the best type and best character."[47] The 1917 law enabled Hobby to appoint the vast majority of the Ranger captains. Like Ferguson before him, Hobby selected most of them from outside the Rangers. His most unusual choice was Harry M. Johnston, a newspaper reporter from Houston whose main qualification was that his father, Rienzi Johnston, had advanced Hobby's earlier career at the *Houston Post*. On November 5, 1917, at the age of thirty-three, Johnston was appointed captain of Headquarters Company and quartermaster of the Ranger Force. The assistant quartermaster was Ranger Sergeant P. A. Cardwell. Johnston and Cardwell worked out of Camp Mabry. Soon thereafter, the governor appointed perhaps the most interesting of the new captains, Charles F. Stevens of San Antonio, son of Edward A. Stevens, who had been a Ranger in the 1840's and who served two terms as Bexar County sheriff in the early 1880's. In his forty-seven years Charles F. Stevens had built a solid law enforcement career, serving five years as a deputy constable in Bexar County, seven years as a constable, six years as chief deputy sheriff, and two years as a deputy U.S. marshal for the Western District of Texas. In addition, he was fluent in Spanish and was familiar with both sides of the border. In 1913 he was an informant in San Antonio for the federal Bureau of Investigation, covering the movement of Mexican exiles. Stevens was highly recommended by F. A. Chapa, who was still a lieutenant colonel on the governor's staff, and by the U.S. Marshal for the Western District of Texas (and ex-Ranger captain) John H. Rogers.[48] On November 27, 1917, Stevens was commissioned as captain of Company G. What made Stevens unique among the Ranger captains was that from 1914 to 1916 he had been a secret agent for the Constitutionalists.[49]

By contrast, Captain William M. Ryan, appointed on November 28, 1917, to command Company I, was pretty dull. He'd been born in Gonzales, was thirty-six, and had been a peace officer in Luling. Ryan took his time assembling his command, rejecting a number of applicants trying to join the Rangers to avoid military service.[50] Another rather undistinguished appointment was Captain Will W. Davis. He was forty-seven, had been born in Brazos County, and was a peace officer when on December 8, 1917, he became the captain of Company L. A much more colorful captain was Roy Wilkinson Aldrich. Unlike the other captains, Aldrich (whose brother J. W. Aldrich also became a Ranger) had a military background. During the Spanish-American War he had been a second lieutenant in the 2nd Missouri Volunteers. He had served during the Philippine insurrection, and in the Boer War he had been a member of the British army remount service. Aldrich then tried law enforcement, as deputy sheriff of Kiowa County, Oklahoma, from 1903 to 1907. He next turned his hand to the real estate business in San Antonio and Corpus Christi from 1907 to 1915. In March, 1915, he enlisted in the Texas Rangers, as a private in Company A. In July, 1917, he became the sergeant in Captain Gray's company. Now, at the age of forty-eight, he was promoted to captain of Company H, on December 1, 1917. The last captain appointed was K. F. Cunningham, a forty-three-year-old former state prison farm manager and peace officer. He became captain of Company M on December 10, 1917. Then there was Frank Holoday, an attorney who acted as special agent for the adjutant general's department. He held a commission as a Regular Ranger captain from April 13 to July 31, 1918, then was made a Special Ranger from August 1, 1918, to January 15, 1919. And James P. Flynt of Ballinger, who had been sheriff of Runnels County for six years, received a captain's commission on April 13, 1918, at a salary of $50 a month, serving until August 30, 1918. There were getting to be more Ranger captains than you could shake a stick at—with more to come.

Adjutant General Harley approached his challenging assignment in a work-manlike manner. One of the first policies he implemented was also one of the most important—the new law's temperance requirement. Harley announced zero tolerance regarding drinking: any man who took a drink was to be summarily fired. Demon rum had been a continuing problem in the Rangers; as Sheriff Dudley S. Barker of Pecos County (himself an ex-Ranger) put it: "I am a ranger friend as long as they let whiskey alone."[51] Furthermore, even as new Ranger companies were being organized, Harley was trying to assess the qualifications of their prospective personnel. He wrote to several district attorneys requesting any knowledge they might have as to the honesty, sobriety, and integrity of some men whose appointments were pending. Harley also asked if any of these men had ever been indicted, and if so, what for. He assured the district attorneys that whatever information they furnished would be regarded as strictly confidential.[52] Harley was also interested in learning about those men already serving as Rangers. He issued a directive to Captains Sanders, Fox, and Barler:

You are advised that this Department would like to have a personal record of every member of your company pertaining to his honesty, sobriety, integrity, if any previous service as a peace officer prior to his enlistment in the Ranger Force, his efficiency as a peace officer, in fact, all pertinent data that pertains [sic] to the above subject. Kindly comply with the above directions at your earliest convenience.[53]

Sanders replied that he could not comply fully with the directive until he'd had a personal interview with each of his men, most of whom were away from headquarters at present. Nevertheless, each of his men came highly recommended and he was prepared to vouch for them since they had been in his command. Private E. M. Dubose, an efficient and experienced peace officer on the border for years, at one time did have a drinking problem but hadn't taken a drink in more than a year, and Sanders had enlisted him with the understanding that if he ever took a drink he would have to resign. Sanders sent in the personnel information a week later.[54] Captain Barler promptly sent in the information for his men, mentioning that he had been taking his time in assembling his Company because he was trying to get "good, honest, and sober men." He had specifically ordered his command to stay out of saloons unless on official business, and anybody caught taking a drink would be immediately discharged.[55]

Further tightening the adjutant general's control over Ranger personnel, Harley informed the captains:

> You are hereby directed that in the future before you enlist any other men in your company you should first send in their name, address, occupation, and personal record for the information and approval of this Department. The applications will be given due consideration and you will be notified of the result.[56]

Increasingly, the important criteria for Regular Ranger commissions were being a Texas resident, experience as a peace officer, knowledge of border conditions, and the ability to speak Spanish.[57] Plus, of course, a physique strong enough to endure the rigors of border life. To anticipate for a moment, experience, often bitter, would show that tight control over enlistments by the adjutant general was not really a good idea, and the captains were again empowered to select their own men.

Regarding the critical matter of railroad transportation, Regular Rangers continued to enjoy the free passes the railroads provided; these passes were not extended to Special Rangers as a rule. There was, however, a special category of Special Ranger—the brand inspectors for the livestock associations. The adjutant general secured free rail transportation for these individuals, who numbered more than twenty for the Cattle Raisers Association of Texas alone. In 1918, six of them stationed in the Panhandle would be reclassified as Regular Rangers without pay.[58]

As for the sometimes stormy relations between Austin and Washington, Hobby's (and Harley's) policy was one of cooperation. Harley notified the Ranger captains that:

> It is the intention of this Department to co-operate with the National Government in the execution of the selective service law in Texas.
>
> TO THIS END, you are instructed that no claim for exemption will be made in behalf of members of the Ranger Force who registered on June 5th, and have enlisted as Rangers since the 1st day of April, A.D., 1917.
>
> Such men will be discharged from the Ranger Force when they are ordered to report for entrainment to Camp Travis.[59]

Clarifying this directive, the adjutant general subsequently worked out an agreement with the War Department "which exempts Rangers who were in the service before June 5, 1917."[60]

While the new captains were being appointed during November, Adjutant General Harley, and perhaps the governor, had second thoughts about Captain Carroll Bates, who'd been appointed back in August. Bates, after all, had been a strong supporter of deposed governor Ferguson, and Ferguson intended to challenge Hobby for the governorship in 1918. Harley directed his assistant, Major Walter F. Woodul, to write to the mayor of San Angelo, Bates's home town: "We would like to know anything pertaining to him that would be of benefit to us in the new re-organization of the Ranger Force. It is our understanding that for some time he was a peace officer in your city." Woodul assured the mayor that this information would be held in strictest confidence "and your letter destroyed after receiving the [Adjutant] General's consideration." The mayor contented himself with writing at the bottom of Woodul's letter: "If he is controlled by a strong enough power to make him amenable to strict discipline think that he could be made a good ranger."[61] Bates, worried about his job, inquired of Woodul whether the ongoing reorganization of the Rangers would eliminate serving captains and, if so, whether the captains would have to reapply for their commissions. He ended by assuring Woodul that "if at any time I can ever be of service to you politically or otherwise all you have to do is command me."[62] Bates's protestations of loyalty apparently did the trick. He kept his job. Harley was not implementing the prohibition against Rangers participating in politics with the same zeal as the prohibition against drinking.

The adjutant general was, however, doing everything possible to implement Hobby's policy of building and maintaining good relations with county and local officers:

We are obliged to look to local peace officers over the state for cooperation with our Ranger force . . . we do not want to but [sic] into local police conditions, as our business must assume a wider and more state-wide scope, such as border conditions and assisting local officers where they desire it, but if we conflict with local peace officers we will be courting our own destruction and injuring the ranger force. This is a policy which must be general.[63]

Shortly after Hobby became acting governor, J. C. Rawlings, a prominent cattleman in the Panhandle, and Fred Pearce, an attorney from Plainview, discussed with him in Austin the idea of a company of Special Rangers in the Panhandle. Hobby was receptive to the idea and referred them to Harley. They proposed organizing in Plainview a twenty-man company with Rawlings, who was thirty-two and described as educated and cultured, possessing great ability, very knowledgeable about conditions in the area, and not least, a strong Hobby supporter, as captain. Pearce and Rawlings would be happy to select the members.[64] On November 22, 1917, Rawlings duly received his commission as captain of Company B Volunteers, which by December numbered nine men, mainly cattlemen, including Rawlings, who was eager to root out any pro-German sentiment in the area.[65]

Besides this type of Special Ranger company, there were the home guards. On October 15, Hobby signed into law—effective on December 28—a bill providing for the organization of home guards in the various counties as a precautionary war measure. Unlike Governor Colquitt's proposed home guard in 1914, Hobby's version was not to be directed and controlled by the Rangers. Rather, home guards were to be organized by the county commissioners and directed by the sheriffs, and the locals would be responsible for all expenses.[66] Reaction among the sheriffs was mixed. The sheriff of Mason County, in the Hill Country of Central Texas, didn't think it necessary, as "we have very few Mexicans in the county," most of "our German citizens" were loyal, the IWW wasn't causing trouble, and there were very few socialists.[67] At Fort Stockton in West Texas, the crusty and longtime sheriff of Pecos County, Dudley S. Barker, was more forthright: "I wouldn't give two Texas rangers for four dozen home guards."[68] In sharp contrast, J. S. Scarborough, sheriff of Kleberg County in South Texas, had anticipated the new law. As he informed Harley:

More than a year ago I saw the need for a Home Guard. I called together a few good friends and instructed them—all was done in secrecy. When Senate Bill No. 8 was passed, creating the Home Guards, we came to light with this organization and started to recruit a Company of six squad strength. We have now about three squads of pretty well trained men and expect to be recruited up in a very short time to the desired strength.[69]

As might be expected, the home guard concept was most popular in those counties within striking distance of the Mexican border.

As Harley became more comfortable with his job of directing the Rangers, he turned to the matter of the Special Rangers, of whom there were some 300, not the less than 100 that Hutchings had claimed. He decided to make a clean sweep and on December 15 revoked all of these commissions issued before October 1, 1917; this move enabled him to weed out draftable men as well as unwanted Ferguson supporters. He informed the sheriffs, railroad chief special agents, and local draft boards of this directive and asked their assistance in collecting the warrants of authority and reporting anyone passing himself off as a Ranger.[70] Since the number of Special Rangers was not limited by law, Harley began issuing what would become another 300 or so Special commissions. In many cases—especially those of brand inspectors and railroad special agents—commissions were merely renewed.[71] For new men, the criteria were that they be "good substantial citizens, men who will not embarrass the service by drinking, etc."[72] Those whose applications tended to be approved quickly were ranchers along the border, especially if they lived in the Big Bend.[73] But these new Special Rangers had to be acceptable to the local authorities, specifically the sheriff.[74] This lent itself, unavoidably, to the injection of local politics into the process, especially when it was the sheriff himself who recommended someone.[75] The adjutant general touched on this point when he wrote to the sheriff of Mason County regarding two applicants: "You will appreciate that we do not know these two men and are acting solely upon your recommendation."[76]

By December, 1917, the expanded Regular Ranger Force was deployed as follows:

Company:	Captain:	Station:
A	Sanders	Alice
B	Fox	Marfa
C	Ransom	Abilene
D	Gray	Austin
E	Barler	Del Rio
F	Bates	Marathon
G	Stevens	Edinburg
H	Aldrich	Austin
I	Ryan	Laredo
L	Davis	Ysleta
M	Cunningham	Eagle Pass

And in December, 1917, there was a sharp increase in violence along the border, especially in the Big Bend. That region had remained a sore spot for the Rangers not only because of raids from Mexico but more specifically because Chico Cano was still at large. The Rangers desperately wanted to avenge the deaths of Ranger Hulen and Customs Inspectors Howard and Sitter, but the wily Cano remained out of reach in Mexico and in fact flourished. He progressed from being an ordinary bandit to becoming a captain in the Carranza army. In January, 1917, he commanded a twenty-six man garrison at San Antonio, southeast of Ojinaga, but when a sizeable villista force approached Ojinaga, Cano adroitly switched sides and took his men with him.[77] As a newly minted villista, Cano clashed with some of his colleagues, notably José Inés Salazar. The latter's career had declined precipitously, from being a leading general under Pascual Orozco in 1912 to his current status as a minor villista chieftain. Cano and Salazar quarreled and Cano reportedly disarmed Salazar and forced him to take to the hills with but four followers. And when the Villa forces finally captured Ojinaga on May 30 and drove the garrison into Texas, it was Chico Cano who led the triumphant villistas into the border town.[78] In the event, the villistas soon had to abandon Ojinaga as Carranza columns converged on the town. But the villistas returned and captured Ojinaga again on the night of November 14, and again the Carranza army had to drive them out. Chico Cano continued to be a regional menace. On one occasion his death was reported, but to the Rangers' bitter disappointment the report proved false.[79]

There's little doubt but that Chico Cano would have received summary execution at the hands of the Rangers. Captain Fox informed the adjutant general from Marfa in May:

> I have just arrived from the River. We have been expecting a battle near Ruidoso [sic] between the Carrancistas and Salazar and Chico Cano. Salazar and Cano has [sic] about 90 men. I was in hopes they would put Chico across where I could get him. Carranza has about 400 after them but the country is so rough its hard to find them.[80]

The adjutant general replied: "I should very much like to get hold of Chico Cano. Hope you will get him ultimately."[81] More to the point, the assistant adjutant general, Walter Woodul, wrote in December: "I went all over the Big Bend country but did not run into that criminal Cano. Believe me those Rangers will give him his whenever they get him."[82] The trouble was, they never got him. To the Rangers' enormous frustration, Cano continued his successful career as bandit and sometime revolutionist. And he continued to deal out misery. On one occasion he and his drinking buddy encountered a boy at a Rio Grande crossing. Cano was drunk on *sotol*, and to impress his friend he forced the boy to stand with an empty sotol bottle on his head, which Cano, who fancied himself the Mexican William Tell, proposed to shoot off. Not surprisingly, he missed, and blew the terrified child's brains out. Cano was remorseful for a while but he managed to get over it. In 1920 he finally retired to his little ranch in Chihuahua. He died peacefully on August 28, 1943.[83]

The 1917 raids in the Big Bend up to December were minor incursions.[84] In December, however, the tempo quickened. On December 1, the ranch of J. F. Tigner was raided, and some cattle were driven into Mexico. A detachment from Troop K, 8th Cavalry led by Captain Leonard Matlack, accompanied by Tigner and his foreman, crossed the Rio Grande the next day in pursuit of the raiders. The troopers ran into an ambush at a hamlet called Buenavista, losing one man killed, one wounded, and five horses, but they drove the Mexicans out of the town. The American commander counted nineteen dead Mexicans, but it was later learned from Mexican sources that thirty-five were killed and nine wounded. The Americans found the carcasses of Tigner's cattle and also found Tigner—he had gotten separated during the engagement and hid in the brush until Matlack rescued him the following morning. They also found the corpse of Tigner's foreman, Justo González. The raiders had captured him, tied his hands, and crushed his head with a rock.

On December 3, Mexicans from the village of Los Mimbres fired across the Rio Grande at a patrol of the 8th Cavalry, wounding a trooper. The cavalry mounted an attack, routed the snipers, inflicting twelve casualties, and burned both Los Mimbres and Buenavista, well known to the Rangers and mounted Customs inspectors as nests of bandits.

On December 17, a Mexican soldier fired across the river at Captain Matlack. The captain returned fire, shooting the man off his horse, which then crossed to the American side. The horse was identified as belonging to the murdered Tigner foreman Justo González.[85]

Then on Christmas morning, a large-scale raid by thirty to forty-five bandits occurred at the Brite Ranch some eighteen miles south of Valentine and about twenty-five miles from the Rio Grande. One of the defenders, Sam Neill (a once and future Ranger and a lay Baptist preacher), later related that the leader "hollered to his men—that was the first I knew there were any others there—and jerked his horse up, and he hollered at his men to kill all the Americans. And as he said it, I shot and he didn't, of course, holler no more."[86] What followed was something out of a John Wayne movie. Neill and his son, T. T. "Van" Neill (a future Special Ranger), who was the ranch foreman, fought the raiders to a standstill—Neill racing back and forth firing out of the windows of five rooms of the ranch house while his son covered the other three and Mrs. Neill reloaded their rifles. The Neills rejected both demands for surrender and threats to bomb the house, making it plain they were prepared to fight to the finish. After half an hour of shooting, the attackers sent word that all they wanted were the saddle horses and the contents of the store. On this basis a tense truce resulted. As luck would have it, while the bandits were looting the store, a mail hack making its scheduled run drove onto the scene. The raiders shot the two Hispanic passengers out of hand, but for the driver, Mickey Welsh, they had something more imaginative in mind. They dragged Welsh into the store, hung him by his feet from a rafter, cut his throat, and watched him bleed to death. After five and a half hours the raiders finally withdrew, no doubt frustrated because the twenty-odd horses they stole weren't enough to carry all the goods they'd looted from the store.

In the aftermath, the dead bandit leader was identified as a carrancista captain, one of hundreds of carrancistas who had composed the garrison at Ojinaga and had been driven across the river into the Big Bend when villistas captured the town in November. As soon as news of the raid reached Marfa, cavalry with a civilian guide, ex-Ranger Grover C. Webb, raced to the Brite Ranch and took up the pursuit.[87] They sighted the retreating marauders in the distance and followed them across the Rio Grande. They caught up with the Mexicans, and in the ensuing running fight reportedly killed eighteen of them.[88]

On the night of December 26, bandits struck Raymond Fitzgerald's ranch. A band of ten Mexicans, some of them allegedly Brite Ranch raiders, tied his foreman hand and foot and made off with ten mules, two horses, a quantity of groceries and bedding, and a government rifle.[89]

Along the entire border the main problem was the theft of livestock which was driven across the Rio Grande. All the Rangers could do was scout along the river, often in conjunction with mounted Customs inspectors. Since the initiative lay with the rustlers, the peace officers were at a significant disadvantage. It should be noted, though, that the illicit trade in livestock crossed the Rio Grande in both directions. Some American ranchers brought over stock either from ranches they owned in Mexico or had purchased there and evaded paying the carrancista export tax, sometimes in collusion with local Mexican officials.[90]

More often the local Mexican officials were in collusion with the rustlers, as in the case of the Indio Ranch, located eighteen miles south of Eagle Pass on the Rio Grande. Fearing confiscation, ranchers had shipped thousands of cattle across to the United States; the price of meat in Coahuila had soared beyond the means of most people. But they had only to look across the river where American ranchers were prospering. Thieves soon worked out an effective procedure: when cattle came to the riverbank for water in the late afternoon, they struck. The American bank had been cleared of brush, while the Mexican side had thick undergrowth. Mexican rustlers shot the cattle, then rowed across at night and butchered the carcasses, selling the meat at a tidy profit. And there were strong indications that mounted Mexican river guards were being systematically bribed to absent themselves on these occasions. One of the American ranches suffering the greatest losses was the Indio Cattle Company, which was raided on June 27, August 10 and 15.[91] Another raid occurred on November 28, when sixty head of cattle were stolen. And on December 3, a cavalry patrol was fired on from the Mexican bank of the river five miles from Indio. One trooper was wounded. Cavalry stationed at Indio crossed the river and pursued the attackers, killing twelve. Predictably, the Mexican authorities protested this incursion into Mexican territory but did little to control the raids.[92]

With the situation worsening, Rangers were sent to work with the cavalry. Captain Barler and four of his men from Company E were dispatched on December 1 from Del Rio to the Indio Ranch, as were four additional Rangers from Austin.[93] This was but a temporary move, for later that month they were replaced by Captain Cunningham's Company M, stationed permanently in Eagle Pass.

Cunningham took an aggressive approach to the problem of raids on the Indio Ranch. On December 28, he telegraphed the adjutant general: "Have corralled bunch of Indio Ranch goats across Rio Grande river. Think we can recover stolen property if you will grant permission to cross river. Answer."[94] Headquarters wired back: "Cannot give you authority to cross river."[95]

Cunningham crossed anyway. He took his available men and rushed to the Indio Ranch, where he joined the manager, A. H. Allen. The latter stated that he was going across the river to retrieve the stolen goats and would be supported by his six men, four of whom were Special Rangers. Together with Cunningham's men they made a total of twelve. In addition, there arrived a most welcome reinforcement of three troops of the 14th Cavalry and a machine gun troop—some 150 men commanded by Major E. C. Wells. The combined force splashed across the Rio Grande at 1 p.m. on December 30; about a mile inland they came to the settlement of San José. The Rangers were at the head of the column with Cunningham in the lead, and as they entered the village they were fired on. Cunningham was the first to return fire, dismounting his men and engaging the enemy for fifteen minutes before the cavalry could dismount and deploy. The Mexicans, whom Cunningham estimated to be forty to sixty men, were in a semicircular line about 800 yards long in the chaparral and cactus. For the next half hour a furious gun battle raged, the Mexicans using Mausers and .30-30s, the Rangers blasting away with their regulation Winchesters, and the cavalrymen firing toward the flanks. The American troops finally got a machine gun into action, and when it began hosing the Mexican line the latter broke and retreated, contenting themselves with only an occasional shot from long range. The Americans searched the settlement, finding evidence of Indio Ranch livestock.

It was now after 3 p.m., the temperature was below freezing, the cavalry were in summer uniforms, the Rangers had been on their feet for thirty-six hours and hadn't eaten for twenty-four, and there was no food for the men nor feed for the horses. It was time to return to Texas. The Rangers were the rear guard as the column recrossed the river. Cunningham reported that he'd made only a cursory examination of Mexican casualties, counting at least six dead. The Americans suffered no casualties either to men or to horses.[96] Amplifying Cunningham's report was one by the American vice consul. It added that accounts circulating in Piedras Negras gave the number of Mexican dead at twelve, including a woman, "which may be true, for those who keep bad company ofttimes suffer." The consul related that the morning of the American incursion he had notified the Mexican commander in Piedras Negras, General Fernando Peraldi, of the imminent American operation and suggested that the general keep his troops out of the way if he didn't want them to get hurt. Peraldi grudgingly did so but was not happy about it. The consul's conclusion was that cattle-stealing had become a profession, "a revival of the older days and can only be stopped by killing the guilty culprits, which was done heretofore by the famous rurales of Don Porfirio Diaz, but who are now a thing of the past. They must be revived, or the Mexican Government must be more energetic, for this molestation is growing, at least it has been growing."[97] In a supplemental report a month later, Cunningham wrote that he had learned from reliable sources that as a result of the firefight there had been seventeen burials at Piedras Negras and three at San José—all men. There were reportedly still a few wounded. Cunningham had also been informed that the governor of Coahuila had formed a company of rangers. They had killed a few bandits and jailed others, evidently making some effort to clean up the border in the vicinity of Piedras Negras.[98]

Because the incursion at San José had been so successful, the adjutant general overlooked Cunningham's clear violation of his orders. Because the cavalry had followed War Department policy on crossing into Mexico, Washington couldn't complain about the Rangers crossing the river as scouts and guides for the cavalry. Things had changed considerably since Colquitt's day.

CHAPTER THIRTEEN

WARTIME RANGERS

T HE new year opened on an embarrassing note. At the end of December, 1917, some 200 citizens met at Marfa in response to a call from Colonel George T. Langhorne, 8th Cavalry, commander of the Big Bend Cavalry Patrol District, to organize closer cooperation for border protection. They sent Adjutant General Harley a telegram urging the immediate organization of a regiment of cavalry and an increase in the Ranger Force. The telegram, signed by Joe D. Jackson, the prominent Alpine cattleman, happened to reach Austin when both Harley and his assistant Woodul were out of town. Whoever read the telegram misconstrued the message and telephoned Harley that Mexicans were raising unshirted hell in Alpine and 100 Rangers were needed. The adjutant general immediately dispatched two companies—Captain Davis's from Ysleta and Captain Gray's from Austin to the relief of the beleaguered town. When the Rangers arrived on January 1, they reported to Jackson for duty. He had no idea why they were there, and they were dumbfounded to find that there was no emergency. The local newspaper, which Jackson owned, found the whole incident hilarious. The discomfited Rangers returned to their stations.[1] Captain Davis later explained to the adjutant general that what Jackson and the others at Alpine wanted was to raise a company of 100 Rangers from Brewster, Presidio, Jeff Davis, and Hudspeth counties, claiming that strange Rangers would do them no good as they would be unfamiliar with the Mexicans in that part of the state. Davis added: "I do not think the people of Alpine want any Rangers but their own boys."[2] The people also wanted to form a regiment of national guard cavalry from these same counties.

While the false alarm at Alpine was taking place, there occurred one of the most positive developments in the history of the Ranger Force—William Lee

Wright was commissioned as a Ranger captain. He came from one of the law enforcement clans: His father, L. B., had been Karnes County sheriff in the 1860's, his brother Milam H. and his sons Charles H. and Emanuel A. all served in the Rangers, as did his father-in-law Sanford Brown and his brother-in-law Charles Brown, as well as his cousins Ben Tumlinson, Jr., Eugene Tumlinson, and Alonzo Taylor. Wright was born on February 19, 1868, at Yorktown, and while a young man worked as a cowboy. He then became a deputy sheriff in Wilson County in 1892, serving until 1898. Wright enlisted in Company E, Frontier Battalion on January 1, 1899, and when he resigned on September 1, 1902, he had attained the rank of lieutenant. Like some other ex-Rangers, he ran for sheriff, and from 1902 to 1917 he was sheriff of Wilson County, earning an enviable reputation. The bespectacled and avuncular Wright left his home in Floresville to become captain of Company K, Ranger Force, on January 1, 1918. He was without question the most capable captain appointed during the entire decade and was of the caliber of the four captains of the original Ranger Force.

Wright served on the border, as did most of the other Rangers. As of January 3, 1918, the force was deployed as follows:

Captain		**Company**		**Station**	
J. J. Sanders		A		Alice	
J. M. Fox		B		Marfa	
H. L. Ransom		C		Sweetwater	
Jerry Gray		D		Austin	
W. L. Barler		E		Del Rio	
Carroll Bates		F		Marathon	
Charles F. Stevens		G		Edinburg	
Roy W. Aldrich		H		Austin	
W. M. Ryan		I		Laredo	
W. L. Wright		K		Laredo	
W. W. Davis		L		Ysleta	
K. F. Cunningham		M		Eagle Pass	

Captain Harry M. Johnston was the Ranger Quartermaster, and Captain Roy W. Aldrich (who constituted Company H) was loaned to the federal government as inspector of draft boards throughout Texas.[3] Assistant Adjutant General Woodul commented on January 8 that "we have already appointed about 18 more Rangers than our appropriation is going to allow us."[4] Still, the Rangers were under continual pressure from politicians regarding appointments. A state senator who recommended one of his constituents wrote to Harley that "Of course,

I know you think you have plenty of Rangers, but there is always room enough for one more. . . ."[5] As of February 13, there were 165 Regular Rangers; the adjutant general was contemplating increasing the force to 200.[6] This even though "we have more Rangers on the Force now than the Appropriation Bill is going to stand up under and we may have to let out some later on."[7] Nevertheless, one more Ranger company was formed, presumably as a result of the pressure from citizens in the Big Bend. On April 16, 1918, Company N (the Hudspeth Scouts) was activated, its captain being Dan G. Knight. He was born in San Antonio in 1858, served as sheriff of Presidio County for fourteen years, enlisted in Company A in 1912 and was discharged in 1914. The next year he became a Customs inspector in the Big Bend, then a rancher near Valentine.

Although the Rangers' main duty was to protect the border, Governor Hobby wanted much more firepower along the international boundary. He sent Harley to Washington in January, 1918, to discuss the matter with the War Department. On August 5, 1917, the Texas National Guard had been mustered into the army; Hobby now wanted to raise two new brigades of cavalry—16,000 men (later increased to a full division of 30,000 men)—strictly for border duty. The federal government refused to authorize the recruitment of these troops, ostensibly because of a critical shortage of equipment.[8]

Furthermore, the government dealt the Rangers a body blow by putting an end to their free rail transportation. On January 1, 1918, as a wartime measure the government forcibly leased all the Class 1 railroads in the country; the United States Railroad Administration was created to operate them. On January 28, William McAdoo, Director General of Railroads, issued General Order No. 6, canceling all railroad passes in the United States.[9] As one can imagine, this caused panic in Austin. Governor Hobby spearheaded a campaign to use every bit of political influence Texas could muster in Washington to get McAdoo's order modified to exempt the Rangers. Among those enlisted were Senator Morris Sheppard, Congressman John Nance Garner, and Attorney General T. W. Gregory.[10] Members of the Texas delegation in Washington also received appeals from prominent ranchers such as L. C. Brite and Caesar Kleberg.[11]

Harley laid out the argument: Rangers were doing the work of the federal government in protecting the border, that being their principal duty; to do so they were frequently moved from one point to another by rail; moreover, they often rode trains to prevent them from being attacked; besides their work on the border, Rangers assisted the federal authorities in suppressing disloyalty and in enforcing the draft law; lastly, since the legislature had not appropriated money for transportation, the cancellation of railroad passes would materially hamper the Rangers' operations and thus handicap both the state and federal authorities in preventing bandit raids along the border.[12]

Hobby sent a telegram on February 19 to the Interstate Commerce

Commission putting the matter in perspective. Those Texas peace officers affected by the anti-pass ruling were:

165 Rangers
246 sheriffs
592 deputies
1,968 constables

The governor urged that at least the Rangers and sheriffs be permitted free transportation.[13]

In a bit of hyperbole, the assistant adjutant general told a friend that "If the Director General of the Railroads continues on his present plan all the Rangers will have to walk."[14] McAdoo remained unmoved, and by late February the adjutant general accepted defeat and notified all the Rangers to send in their railroad passes.[15]

It was beginning to seem like old times, with the Ranger Force in increasing financial difficulty. Revocation of the railroad passes was unquestionably a calamity, but its impact was somewhat lessened by the fact that there were now many more Ranger companies, so personnel didn't have to be shifted as often as in the past. In keeping with their principal mission of border protection, most Ranger companies were stationed along the Rio Grande. Special Ranger Y. P. Garrett was discharged because he refused to report for border duty, the condition on which he had been commissioned.[16] The adjutant general stated that "in inland counties we feel that the local officers are perfectly able to cope with conditions unless we are advised to the contrary."[17]

Regarding the deployment of the Rangers, the El Paso area was the responsibility of Company L, stationed at Ysleta. Captain Davis got off to a rather shaky start in organizing his command, prompting some citizens of Ysleta to petition Hobby for the return of Davis's predecessor, Captain Ransom.[18] Davis seemed uncertain as to just what his duties were, for he had merely been instructed to relieve Ransom, to follow his advice as much as possible, and to take over Ransom's state property at Ysleta.[19] Davis requested more specific guidance from headquarters. The adjutant general's office replied that:

Your orders will be to stay out of El Paso unless we order you there.

The duties of State Rangers are not those of local police officers, but are for border protection and we cannot clean up any cities.

You should be ever diligent along the border, using your eyes and ears for raids, cattle stealing and such kindred troubles.

Keep your men out of town and have them ride the border. Of course, if any matters pertaining to the local misdemeanors come to your attention, you might give the information to the proper local authorities. . . .

You will make reports to this office from time to time as to your activities.[20]

This is not to imply that Davis was devoid of ideas. He favored a direct approach in dealing with crime along the Rio Grande: "I would like to make all strange Mexicans leave this side who can not give a good account of themselves. I can get the justice of the peace here to fine them for vags [vagrants]. If this meets with your approval I will do so."[21] The adjutant general didn't think this was such a good idea.

The level of criminal activity in the Ysleta area was actually rather modest. Some horses were stolen; the Rangers recovered three but the thieves of course fled across the river. Davis reported that there were plenty of villistas on the other bank but they hadn't tried anything so far. Still, there was no lack of rumors. Davis was soon reporting that a raid was expected at Clint. Against that possibility he had organized posses at Ysleta and Clint, and the army had dispatched troops to the area. His command had been issued no ammunition, however, and he urgently requested permission to purchase a supply at state expense. Permission was granted, along with a reminder to order ammunition well in advance.[22]

Part of Davis's problem was that his company was understrength: he had only seven men—four at Ysleta and three at Fabens. He assured the adjutant general's office that he was keeping his men out of El Paso except on business and forbade them to take a drink under penalty of dismissal, for "I do not believe in peace officers drinking." He and his men patrolled the river every day. There had been no incidents, but "people are more or less alarmed as there are plenty of Villistas all along the border and they have no food and sooner or later will come across to get it. We work with the River Guards all the time and investigate all rumors but they are not very definite." Although he was beginning to settle in, Davis was still somewhat uncertain about his duties, and he requested permission to go to Austin "and find out more definitely just what to do." Permission was granted.[23]

Paperwork was not Davis's strong suit. It was pointed out to him that one of his men was "A. J. Robertson," not "A. J. Robinson," as Davis had him listed on the payroll. But what was aging Davis prematurely was having to compile his Subsistence and Forage Returns. The assistant Ranger quartermaster kept sending them back, explaining that if they weren't correct the comptroller wouldn't issue the corresponding treasury warrants. Gradually Davis got better at it, but not much.[24]

Then there was the problem of trying to weld together a company whose personnel were constantly changing. Private James Lowenstein resigned to take a better job with the government; Davis enlisted "an old cowpuncher," J. E. Faubion, to replace him; Private L. D. Oden then resigned to become an El Paso mounted policeman. But when Private J. L. Wade deserted, Davis was told not to enlist a replacement—one would be sent to him from Headquarters Company in Austin, which was overstocked. Davis got another man, who transferred in from Captain Fox's Company B—Ben L. Pennington. He was such a drunk that, Fox reported, "the boys are all afraid to work with him." The trouble was, Pennington was the nephew of the influential cattleman Joe D. Jackson. So, instead of just firing Pennington, Fox got approval to dump him on Captain Davis.[25] But Pennington would not stay sober and he was driving Davis, who was painfully aware of the J. D. Jackson connection, to distraction. Davis was of the opinion that Pennington would make a good Ranger if he had just left the booze alone.[26]

To add to Davis's troubles, at the request of the district attorney in El Paso, he and three of his men went there every day for several weeks to keep order at the sensational murder trial of one Felix Jones, daily searching for weapons the turbulent throng attending court. Yet Davis still had to patrol his sector of the border. To this end he shifted all but one of his men to Fabens and downriver from that town, for Mexicans were crossing and butchering cattle quite often, but he ruefully reported that "I have not enough men to do much good."[27]

Conditions continued to deteriorate, with Davis informing the adjutant general that "the Mexicans are sniping across the river nearly every day at soldiers but so far have not bothered my boys." The adjutant general did not let Davis enlist six more men as requested, but he sent him two—one from Captain Ransom's company on temporary duty and—a most welcome addition—Private Reno Eickenroht, whom he could use as a company clerk to handle the paperwork.[28] Offsetting this good news, Harley ordered Davis to detail two or three of his Rangers to protect some government reclamation engineers who would be working on the Island.[29] Davis assigned three men to this duty. Captain Davis must have hoped that no emergencies occurred after 5 p.m., because the telegraph office at Ysleta was closed after that. And trouble did occur at night. He advised that "The soldiers have been giving us some trouble lately. Last Saturday night two of them got drunk and shot up the town and held up a man. We were called up and we caught them."[30] The adjutant general evidently approved of Davis's performance, for he offered "If you need any further assistance, please write at your earliest convenience." Davis did so the next day, requesting 200 .45 Colt pistol cartridges and 500 .30 cartridges for the Government rifle.[31]

The adjutant general also instructed Davis not to take orders too literally:

There seems to be too close a construction being placed on paragraph 3, G.O. No. 2, of the 13th of February, 1918.

That paragraph is for the purpose of cutting down as much as possible needless traveling on the part of the Rangers. Whenever possible I want Captains to co-operate with one another as much as they can, and when their good judgment deems it advisable to send a man into another Captain's territory, such move will have my sanction. In cases of raids or threatened raids I want the Captains and their men to back each other up. Best results can be obtained by co-operation.[32]

Davis certainly could have used a little cooperation, for he reported that on March 23:

Ranger Perkins & River Guard Griffith were on river below Fabens on a scout when they heard firing above. They returned and saw 8 U.S. Cavalry patrolmen [of the 5th Cavalry] running and 14 or 15 Mexican River Guards shooting at them. They got between the parties and dismounted and opened fire on the Mexicans who retreated to cover. Perkins sent Griffith back to get the Patrol who had run. He succeeded in getting three of them to return. They charged the Mexicans and drove them across the river, where they were reinforced by about three hundred Carranza troops. Perkins took charge and kept them from crossing the river again. In about forty minutes Rangers Black & Pennington & River Guard O. Neil [sic] from Fabens got there. In an hour soldiers from Fabens arrived. He [their commanding officer] had great difficulty in doing anything with his men. Could only [get] five or six up to the river bank where the fighting was. I understand that about twenty are in the Guard House for cowardice.

We from Ysleta did not get the news until too late to get in the fight. It lasted about three hours.

I do not know exactly how many Mexicans were killed. Reports say from eight to twelve. I know that eight were killed for they were in plain sight. About fifteen Mexicans' horses were killed and one U.S. horse. The Mexican commander sent a flag of truce and took away his dead & wounded and asked for a peace talk the next morning at 9 o'clock but he never showed up. I think Ranger Perkins killed at least five of them. The other Rangers and River Guards probably got the rest. The soldiers acted mighty badly and their Captain "who is a brave man" says he is going to send a bunch to Leavenworth. This is the only fight that the Rangers have been in. But hardly a day or night passes without Mexicans shooting across at soldiers or civilians. They seem to let the Rangers alone as they are out all the time on the river, sometimes day often night [sic].

There is possibly eight hundred soldiers and river guards between Juarez and Guadalupe and a good number of Villaistas [sic] on both sides of the river. The feeling is very bitter out here. The Americans hate the Mex. and visa versa. People are looking for raids at any time, and I think they are right.[33]

In the aftermath of the engagement, Davis's first priority was a resupply of ammunition; he requested 1,000 rifle cartridges "as we are about out after yesterday's fight." Second was manpower. Davis still wanted to enlist six more men. Harley authorized him to enlist three men at once, besides which Davis sent in applications for four Special Rangers, all ex-peace officers recommended by the sheriff and the mayor. Davis was especially pleased with the performance of the black-sheep Ranger, Ben Pennington: "Ranger Pennington showed good nerve & judgment and as he promised never to take another drink would you please give him another showing."[34] Woodul replied: "As to Pennington, if he ever so much as touches another drop you will immediately dismiss him from service, and this goes for any of your men." Woodul also informed the captain that the four Special Ranger commissions would be issued.[35] Sergeant Cardwell was even helpful in preparing Davis's payroll, because the latter had enlisted four new men since the last payroll.[36] Davis's stock in Austin was rising.

An increasingly confident Davis established an additional camp, at Clint "as they needed & wanted Rangers very badly and the reclamation people, who are going to work on the Island are working out of Clint—in that way I can kill 2 birds with one stone, as that will protect Clint at night. I have four men there, four at Fabens including the sergeant and myself, and three at Ysleta." Significantly, he added "I have my automobile here and one at Fabens at my disposal. It looks like conditions are growing worse here."[37] Davis's auto represented yet another step in the motor vehicle replacing the Ranger's horse.

Davis might be more mobile, but he remained short of manpower. Because of the appropriation crisis, Harley limited Company L to twelve men including Davis. This made it impossible for Davis to accede to a request from Captain John H. Rogers, the U.S. Marshal for the Western District of Texas, that he station some men north of El Paso at Canutillo and Vinton, which had reputations as tough little towns.

Davis was largely on his own:

> The sheriff has informed me that I need not expect any assistance from him in case of raids or trouble as he had been asked to keep away by Military officers. I told him it was all wrong as it took too long for the Army to get any place but he still hold [sic] to their view. The newspapers are so sensational that they keep the people all worked up and if they [see] two or three mounted Mexicans or hear a few shots they immediately call the Rangers.[38]

To add to Davis's worries, one of his new recruits, Charlie Hyde, a cowboy who had enlisted on March 25, was dying at Clint of amoebic dysentery. Davis inquired of headquarters whether there was any provision for medical and funeral expenses. There was, "but they must be reasonable."[39] Hyde died on May 1, as did his baby daughter; his wife and two of the other Rangers contracted dysentery but survived. Davis said that "the rest of us had diarrhea and it looked like a general die up might occur but we are all well now." Ranger Hyde, like some other Rangers, among them "Doc" Goodwin,[40] was destitute when he died. His comrades and his captain took up a collection from their own meager funds to pay for the baby's medical bills and funeral expenses and to send Hyde's widow to her relatives in Kerrville.[41] The dysentery was traced to a contaminated well at the Clint camp. Davis had the well destroyed and relocated his men in another house.[42]

Captain Davis also had problems with the army. The commanding general of the Southern Department, Major General W. A. Holbrook, wrote to Captain W. M. Hanson of the Rangers in May quoting an extract from a report by the commanding general at El Paso:

> The Rangers have indefinite orders and my conference with Captain Davis was brought about by my getting wind of a plan that he was intending to post his men at two fords near Ysleta Friday night and open fire upon all Mexicans in the vicinity, whether on our side or the Mexican side, on the plea that by that method he would stop what he characterizes as wholesale horse and cattle stealing by draft evaders. He admitted that he might kill a few innocent Mexicans, but he proposed to stop stock stealing at the cost of innocent lives, if necessary. Davis's plan was with the understanding that our patrols were to be near-by. Of course, I stopped that kind of nonsense, for the time being at least.

General Holbrook requested that Davis be reined in, so as to avoid international incidents, and to maintain good relations between the army and the Rangers.[43]

At Hanson's suggestion Woodul wrote to Captain Davis giving him the gist of Holbrook's letter and strongly cautioning him against taking "heroic measures." Woodul reminded Davis that "in the past, some Rangers have assumed the attitude of court and jury in addition to their duties as peace officers. This is the wrong attitude absolutely."[44] Woodul sent General Holbrook a copy and assured him that the adjutant general always welcomed any suggestions Holbrook might make.[45]

Davis replied that the whole thing had been blown way out of all proportion, and he gave a detailed account of his dealings with Captain Galway, stationed at Ysleta, and General Hamilton Howze at El Paso. He stated that if Woodul didn't believe him, Woodul should request the notes that Howze's stenographer took at their meeting. Davis said he told Howze he was going to put an end to stealing on the border if he could. Howze then said something about killing innocents.

"I told him there was no danger of that, but we might kill some of the thieves if we had to." Davis assured Woodul that "you need never fear of my pulling off any bad stunts as I am not the least bit blood thirsty, and I have no desire to get that kind of a reputation." Woodul replied that he had been sure that a mistake had been made by Davis's accuser.[46]

The area between Davis's company and the Big Bend was the responsibility of the newest, and arguably one of the best-run Ranger companies—Company N, the "Hudspeth Scouts." This was a rather unusual company. It was formed as a result of a mass meeting of Big Bend citizens, who appointed Claude Hudspeth, now a congressman, and his successor as state senator for the 25th district, R. M. Dudley, to go to Austin and lobby the governor. The result was the formation of a sixteen-man company whose captain, Dan G. Knight, had been a long-time sheriff of Presidio County. Knight was commissioned and the company was activated on April 16. The Hudspeth Scouts were deployed along the Rio Grande and worked closely with Colonel Langhorne, who even established a field telephone network so they could report to him nightly. The men drew a monthly salary of $100, plus $2 a day for subsistence, while Captain Knight received $225 per month. Not until May did the adjutant general's office get around to issuing the company's warrants of authority. Interestingly, the warrants were sent not directly to Knight at Valentine but rather to Dr. J. D. McGregor at Lobo, who with his sons owned the huge Bar M Ranch. As we have seen, McGregor had received a Special Ranger commission in 1917. General Harley had assured Hudspeth that the men would be paid from the 16th of April. Harley instructed Dr. McGregor to have Captain Knight "write in here at least twice a month stating the nature of the work done and results accomplished, telling us where his men are stationed, arrests made and situation generally in his sector of the country. Please have him make this report at once."[47]

McGregor proudly reported that:

> The scouts are working in conjunction with Col. Langhorne's soldiers on the river and are doing very effective work, as we have had no raids since they have been put on; a few cattle have been stole [sic] from this side and they have made it so hot for them that most of the Mexicans have gone back into the interior, and they report they have seen none along the river in the last few days.[48]

McGregor extended his thanks to the adjutant general and the governor for the protection afforded, "as conditions had got almost unbearable in this part of the country." Company N personnel may also have been involved in disarming Hispanics. Captain Gray mentioned that "the boys at Lobo got two shot guns 5 Winchesters 5 pistols away from Mexicans at Van Horn."[49]

Captain Knight certainly had the support of state Senator R. M. Dudley, whose 25th district covered much of West Texas. Dudley wrote to Harley:

I have just returned from a trip to the border, where Captain Knight and his men are located, and I want to tell you that I am writing you very seriously and earnestly and honestly, he is the right man in the right place, and you will never have any un-necessary killings or scandals with Captain Knight on the ground. His modesty may prevent him from telling you some facts that I am going to tell you. He is not afraid to use his gun, but he is a diplomat, and almost daily, he is in conversation and communication, not only with the Mexican soldiers, but the bandits themselves, and they fear him and they respect him, and the way he has his force distributed and the high regard in which Col. Langhorn [sic] and the other American officers hold Captain Knight makes him most useful. Of course he is not getting any results in dead men and news-paper notoriety, but not a man has been killed, nor a head of stock stolen in his territory since he went to work.[50]

In August, though, there was an upsurge of cattle stealing along the Rio Grande, which a low water level facilitated.[51]

Documentation about Company N is sparse, but evidently the unit was formed in large measure because of political pressure from Senator Hudspeth, it was controlled by ranchers, and the members were mainly cowboys. But by August, Company N was a luxury the adjutant general could no longer afford because the Ranger appropriation was inadequate, and the company was disbanded on August 31, 1918.[52] Knight anticipated that most of his men would seek employment on ranches.

In the Big Bend the principal Ranger station was at Marfa, headquarters for Captain J. M. Fox and Company B. There was no headquarters camp; Fox and his men operated out of a rented room.[53] In January and February, Fox reported that things were relatively quiet along the 140 miles of riverfront in his sector, but he requested more Winchester cartridges, "as we might run out. Have been using a good many lately. Making a run to night look [sic] a little bad on River at present."[54] Still, Fox reported no major engagements: Private A. J. Woelber arrested J. J. Kilpatrick, Sr., at Candelaria for three misdemeanors and a felony, jailing him at Marfa. Woelber on January 28 also killed an alleged raider. The next month Fox's men arrested two draft dodgers and one man suspected of spying.[55]

As an experienced officer, Fox knew that trouble would probably erupt again in the near future, and he was concerned to get his company in fighting trim. He had a hack and a mule to pull it, as well as equipment for three camps. He also received a shipment of sixteen new rifles. Each Ranger had to purchase a rifle out of his salary. The Rangers used the army .30 Winchester because in an emergency they could request ammunition from the army. And the Rangers got their rifles at a discount—the Ranger Force had a contract with the Walter Tips Co. in Austin to pay only $28.50 per rifle, which represented a 17.5 percent reduction in the price.[56] This arrangement, incidentally, occasionally led a Ranger to sell his rifle for a few dollars more than he had paid but still below the retail price, and then order another one.[57]

As to personnel, we have seen that Fox managed to rid himself of Ben L. Pennington, but the sergeant of Company B, Harris C. "Harry" Trollinger, remained a major problem. Trollinger, it will be recalled, was one of the survivors of Chico Cano's ambush in 1915. He was fired, appealed his dismissal, and was reinstated, but in October, 1917, he was reportedly drunk, mean, and disorderly in El Paso and tried to pick a fight with the district attorney.[58] Trollinger managed to keep his job, but by February, 1918, Fox had had a bellyful of Trollinger's drinking bouts—he fired him on March 1.[59] And in an unrelated development, another of Fox's men, Clyde Ellison, resigned on March 1. As one replacement, Fox thought "it important to enlist a man here who stands well and . . . is over the draft age."[60] He chose Sam H. Neill, the former Ranger who had been a mounted Customs inspector from 1912 to 1916 and who with his son had defended the Brite Ranch against raiders in December, 1917. Neill enlisted in Company B on March 1, 1918.

Captain Fox also enjoyed temporary assistance from an unlikely source—a Ranger groupie. Harry Scullin, age fifty-two, was president of his own firm, Scullin Steel Company of Saint Louis. He was fascinated by the Rangers, and in 1915 got himself attached to Captain Ransom's company in South Texas. In 1916 and 1918, he spent his vacation riding with Rangers in the Big Bend. Captain Fox met him in September, 1917, and they became fast friends. In requesting a renewal of the Special Ranger commission Scullin had held in 1916, Fox explained to the adjutant general that "He has been trying to get down here for several months but they are so busy making big shells for the Government he could not get off. He only wants a Special commission from you, more to show his people than anything else. Would like to get [it] as early as possible as he can't stay long."[61] Strange things went on in Captain Fox's company.

The strangest event occurred on January 28. According to Fox's Monthly Return for January, all that had happened on the 28th was that "Guadalupe Foris [sic] (Raider) killed by [Ranger] A. H. Woelber on Butes [sic] Ranch." But there had also occurred on the night of the 28th an incident that Fox neglected to mention. Apparently Colonel Langhorne, the hard-bitten commander of the Big Bend District, urged Fox to clean out a nest of bandits at the riverfront settlement of Porvenir/Pilares, across from the Mexican hamlet of Pilares. It was commonly believed that the inhabitants of Porvenir acted as spies and informants for bandits across the Rio Grande, casing ranches on the pretext of looking for work. The men spent their days across the river, returning to visit their families only at night. At least some of them were suspected of having participated in the Brite Ranch raid in 1917.

Whether at the suggestion of Colonel Langhorne or not, Fox assigned eight of his men—Bud Weaver, J. B. Oliphant, A. C. Barker, Clint Holden, Allen Cole, W. K. Duncan, Max Newman, and J. H. McCampbell—to the Porvenir operation. Fox also enlisted the help of four area ranchers—Buck Pool, John Pool, Tom Snider, and Raymond Fitzgerald, who said Fox asked them to act as guides for his Rangers because Porvenir could only be reached by trails through very rough and mountainous country. This even though Rangers had already visited Porvenir and had noticed people wearing new shoes, suspiciously like shoes stolen from the Brite Ranch store.

According to the accounts of the participants, the party reached Porvenir about 2 a.m. and fanned out through the settlement rounding up all the men, some twenty or twenty-five in all. They also began searching the houses, finding soap, shoes, and pocket knives later identified as coming from the Brite store, as well as a saddle said to belong to Ranger H. C. Trollinger, stolen when Chico Cano ambushed Trollinger and his companions in 1915.

The participants further stated that as they were searching their prisoners and the houses, they suddenly came under fire from the right rear. In the melee their horses stampeded, while they themselves dove for cover and began shooting back. Ranger Weaver stated that they fired about sixty rounds at their attackers, who broke off the engagement. The ranchers and Rangers retrieved their horses and left, arriving back at Fitzgerald's ranch at daylight. Rancher John Pool later stated that "I do not know whether we killed any one or not, but it was reported that there were about fifteen dead Mexicans there next morning."[62] And that was that—another deadly clash between lawmen and Mexican bandits in the Big Bend. Governor Hobby reported it as such in response to a State Department inquiry.[63]

Yet since the Porvenir affair involved half of Fox's Company B, it surely merited being mentioned in his Monthly Return. The reason why it wasn't gradually emerged. As Kenneth C. Miller, an attorney in Marfa, informed his friend Adjutant General Harley, "I understand Harry Warren, who was a school teacher near Pilares, is attempting to stir up trouble about the killing of fifteen Mexicans at or near Pilares." Warren had been in Marfa on March 2 and had spoken with Miller, saying he'd investigated the killings and had spoken with the families of the dead, who told him they didn't know who had done the killing. Attorney Miller added: "I do not suppose there is any doubt but that the Rangers killed the fifteen Mexicans at Pilares and Warren may have been trying to throw me off when he stated they did not know who did it. If the Mexicans were bad citizens the Government should not be troubled with any such claims."[64]

With questions being raised about Porvenir, some of the participants gave sworn statements concerning the incident. And on March 15, Colonel Langhorne sent a memorandum to Ranger headquarters recounting his experiences since his arrival in West Texas in 1915 and specifically since becoming commander of the Big Bend District in October, 1917. His account of the Porvenir incident essentially supported that of the participants. Regarding the schoolteacher, Harry Warren, Langhorne dismissed him as a troublemaker who had "gone native":

There was only one white man living at Porvenir, a school teacher, who was getting $85 per month from the County, and his only pupil was his son. He married a Mexican woman and divorced her, took another woman, and then employed the divorced wife as a nurse for the child. He is said to have stated that "The Rangers killed the patrons of his school, the wolves killed his goats, the hawks killed his chickens, and a Mexican ran off with his wife." What I have heard of this man is that he was well educated, but lost his position of trust through drink. That in the community of Porvenir, he lived like the Mexicans and urged upon them the advisability of keeping all other white men out of the community. He is one of the three white men in this County that has failed to work with the others for the preservation of order.

Captain Fox, since last November, has been loyally co-operating with the troops and the civil authorities in the Big Bend, and has rendered excellent service.[65]

Harry Warren (1859–c. 1930) was something more than a troublemaker who had "gone native." He was well educated, having graduated in 1881 with a B.A. in philosophy from the University of Mississippi. He taught school at various places in West Texas and Arizona, became an attorney in 1890, Inspector of Customs at Eagle Pass in 1905, and deputy collector in 1906, resigning in 1909. He settled in Presidio County, serving as justice of the peace, ranching and farming at Pilares until 1918. In 1920, he was employed as a cotton picker in Gadsden, Arizona. Between 1920 and 1929 he taught school in several small West Texas towns.[66]

The Porvenir investigation was soon overshadowed by another incident—a raid on the Nevill Ranch on March 25. Rancher E. W. Nevill later estimated that some fifty Mexicans attacked at dusk, riddling the ranch house with gunfire. Nevill and his son Glenn grabbed their Winchesters and returned fire, hitting several of the raiders, but they quickly realized their situation was untenable—bullets were coming through the walls. The Nevills decided to make a run for the safety of a ditch some 200 to 300 yards away. Nevill made it but then had to elude three of the attackers who trailed him for several hours. Glenn Nevill was not so lucky. He was shot several times as he ran from the house, one slug smashing through his forehead. The marauders then proceeded to pound his face and head with rifle butts and a stick. The raiders demonstrated their *machismo* by shooting the Hispanic cook three times, leaving her dead in the kitchen in front of her three small children. They ransacked the premises, ran off nine horses, then returned and killed the cattle. Nevill soon thereafter sold out and moved to Marfa. The purchaser quickly learned that ranching was impossible, so he abandoned the place.[67]

Captain Fox reported that some of the raiders were from this side of the Rio Grande.[68] He also ordered a resupply of ammunition for his company—1,500 steel-point Winchester cartridges and 800 rounds of Colt .45 smokeless, adding "Please rush as we are likely to have lots of trouble. Send by express."[69] Fox also needed replacements to bring his company back up to the authorized sixteen men: Clint Holden had resigned to care for his widowed mother, and W. K. Duncan had also resigned: "He is just a young boy and I guess thought it too tough. You know it takes a man with hair in his nose to stand the gaff here and it looks as though the whole of Mexico is going to get on us now." Fox also mentioned that "the Mex are raising cain across the river. The American soldiers had a fight with them and without letting anything out the Americans got cleaned to a finish and whipt back to Texas. It look [sic] awfully bad here at this time."[70]

Adding to the tension in the Big Bend were the wartime restrictions on food-stuffs. Fox complained that the War Department had ordered merchants not to sell flour to anyone unless they agreed to buy an equal amount of cornmeal. Fox's men on their scouts couldn't use cornmeal, and he had some 500 pounds of the stuff on hand getting musty. He asked the adjutant general's office to contact the proper authorities and resolve the matter.[71] More importantly, the government had prohibited the export of food, and with northern Mexico ravaged by years of revolution, the supply of food there was inadequate, and people were becoming frantic. This situation was especially acute in the Big Bend, where Mexicans had traditionally imported many of their commodities from the United States. In anticipation of desperate Mexicans intensifying the raids against area ranches, the citizens of Alpine held a mass meeting and passed a resolution asking for increased protection.[72]

Fox would be unable to provide it, for his time was rapidly running out. The Porvenir investigation concluded that the fifteen Mexicans were farmers who had been killed by the Rangers and ranchers after they had been disarmed and were helpless prisoners. It had been a massacre. Captain William M. Hanson, who conducted the investigation for the Ranger Force, went to Marfa and secured affidavits from some of the Porvenir widows and from participants.[73] In an undated and unsigned letter Harry Warren informed Governor Hobby that the men killed at Porvenir were innocent farmers, not bandits. He also stated that Captain Anderson, commanding Troop G, 8th Cavalry, at Camp Evitt, in Valentine, had sent a twelve-man detachment with the Rangers to Porvenir. Anderson evidently thought the Rangers were only going to arrest the men. The soldiers helped to seal off Porvenir and waited while the Rangers went in to make the arrests, not knowing that the Rangers and ranchers were bent on murder. Furthermore, Warren alleged that: "Some days ago two Rangers started to Marfa in an auto with a Mexican prisoner, Guadalupe Torres by name, and killed him near one of Brite's gates, they claiming that he tried to escape. His body was found there. The Mexican consul had found out these facts." Warren asked the governor to "Please remove these Rangers regardless of whatever whitewashed report may have been made to you or the adjutant general."[74]

The adjutant general had a real crisis on his hands. Fox was summoned to Austin on May 16, and there ensued what must have been an intense meeting with Harley. Fox returned to Marfa on the 21st, by which time matters were rapidly moving to a climax. The army was conducting its own investigation of Porvenir, and Hanson forwarded to Woodul a letter from Colonel Langhorne written on May 22 concerning the army's inquiries, adding: "This is for your information. I think some action must be taken to keep our Department from getting the worst of it from the U.S. Government. If this was possible it would ruin the Ranger force and the General [Harley] if he does not take action. Call his attention to it."[75] Fox was again summoned to Austin on May 27. Harley evidently did not subscribe to the idea that a commander was responsible for everything his men did or failed to do, the stern standard that had been applied to Captain Tom Ross back in 1910. Harley's solution was to fire those Rangers involved in the Porvenir massacre, disband Fox's company, and transfer Fox to a desk job in Austin. Fox refused to take this way out, insisting that his men had done nothing wrong. On May 31 he wrote to Harley: "I am leaving for Marfa and will mail you or the governor my resignation as I don't feel that I am getting a fair deal."[76]

General Orders No. 5, issued on June 4, disbanded Fox's Company B effective June 8. Rangers A. C. Barker, Max Newman, Bud Weaver, Allen Cole, and J. Boone Oliphant were fired. The other three Rangers involved in the Porvenir raid—J. H. McCampbell, Clint Holden, and W. K. Duncan—had already resigned. The seven remaining members of Company B were transferred to Captain Jerry Gray's Company D. Gray assumed command of the Marfa District. Woodul sent Fox the General Order on June 4 and informed him that he would be stationed in Austin.[77] Fox would have none of it—on June 11 he published in the Marfa newspaper his resignation in a blistering open letter attacking Hobby, claiming that the governor had acted from base political motives.[78] As far as the administration was concerned, Fox had resigned on May 31, and on June 17, Governor Hobby telegraphed Woodul to accept the resignation.[79] Woodul did so, informing Fox that "We're not keeping men on the border to murder and kill, but to prevent innocent people from being murdered and their property stolen and destroyed. The good Mexican citizens of this State and of Mexico will receive our entire protection, if they conduct themselves lawfully, the Rangers will protect them."[80] In the final analysis, Fox had been brought down by an obscure school-teacher with a drinking problem.

The Porvenir Rangers were of course subject to criminal prosecution, and Woodul informed Fox that the adjutant general would take action if the unlawful acts were true, for he desired to punish the offending parties. But he also added that "I'm reliably informed that the Presidio County grand jury has the facts but doesn't find it necessary to take any action for the unlawful killings."[81] The grand jury at Marfa didn't get too excited over the elimination of what was considered a bunch of undesirable Mexicans.

This was certainly the view of Dudley S. Barker, the sheriff of Pecos County for the last fourteen years. He wrote an impassioned letter to Hobby protesting the firing of the Porvenir Rangers. Barker asserted that some of the Mexicans killed were part of Chico Cano's gang, and he recounted Cano's crimes. "Those are the Mexicans the Rangers killed, and for those sort of greasers you have seen fit to fire the rangers. I do not deem it a crime to kill those kind of sneaking thieves, especially when they are resisting arrest." Barker praised Fox and his men, and warned of the dire consequences "when the Mexicans of this part of the Country find out that the Governor of Texas is with them, and fires the State's peace officers who have had to kill some sneaking, thieving out-laws, that conditions will become desperate, and it would be well for you to notify those people living in the thinly settled River section of the Big Bend to get out, for the Mexicans will taken [sic] them in when they find out that the Rangers have been disposed of."[82] The governor's secretary thanked Barker for his "kindly interest in reviewing the facts" and turned his letter over to Harley. The latter sent Barker a firm reply laying out the facts, the crux of which was "Governor Hobby is not responsible for the discharge of these men. They are responsible for their own discharge and Captain Fox who had charge of them, while he did not admit the facts in the beginning, now says that he ordered the wholesale slaughter of these men."[83]

Captain Gray was quite pleased with his new assignment at Marfa. Up until then he had been based in Austin as captain of Company D, and his function had been as the Ranger Force's utility outfielder. He and his men investigated everything from liquor law violations in Texarkana and in St. Hedwig, near San Antonio, to cases of desertion from Camp Travis.[84] He announced his arrival at Marfa: "We arrived here all O.K. and like the looks of things fine. Capt. Fox has been very nice to us." Among the first things Gray asked for was another man for his company, cautioning headquarters: "Don't send a boy for this is a man's job out here."[85] When he heard nothing, Gray notified headquarters that he had found a candidate in Marfa—La Fetra Trimble "who is 23 years of age. But has been turned down by Local Board acct. one bad eye. He is a good rider, speaks Spanish and knows the country. And I think he would make a good man." Gray requested permission to enlist Trimble, and the adjutant general's office authorized the enlistment.[86] (Trimble was not the only handicapped man enlisted in the Rangers during 1918. John Arch Miller, who "had the distinction of being the only one-armed Ranger,"[87] joined Captain Stevens's Company G on November 25, 1918. The one-armed Miller proved to be better than a lot of men with two arms. He served from 1918 to 1920, then from 1923 to 1933, rising to the rank of sergeant.)

A second Ranger company operated in the Big Bend—Captain Carroll Bates's Company F, based at Marathon. Bates's men spent most of their time on the river. Besides the headquarters camp, Bates maintained camps at Rio Grande Canyon, Santa Elena, and Lajitas. Each detachment patrolled the river nine miles each way from its camp on a daily basis. In February Bates's command arrested three Mexicans and relieved them of their Winchesters, for smuggling sugar, flour, other provisions, and clothing to Mexican soldiers across the Rio Grande, and also arrested two Anglos for burglary of a business in Sanderson. The burglars and the recovered property were delivered to the sheriff at Sanderson, while the smugglers were turned over to the federal authorities.[88] The Rangers kept the confiscated goods. Private J. R. Hunnicutt at Lajitas informed Captain Johnston, the Ranger quartermaster, that "we have a regular store in our camp. You should come out and see our stock."[89]

But sometimes things got ugly, as Bates reported on April 6:

On the evening of the 2nd the ranch of John Daniels was raided and his horses were driven across the river. We were notified about 10 o'clock the same night. Went out among the Mex on this side and learned it was Pablo Dominguez who did the work. I was short of men so I borrowed eight soldiers from a nearby camp and at day-light we crossed the river and followed the trail into the interior to where Pablo and his gang make their headquarters. We surrounded the village and Pablo opened fire on us. [Ranger Bill] Stillwell was killed early in the fight[90] as was Pablo and ___ [an unidentified Mexican]. I think we have broken up his band. Most of the guns used were the same as we have, all new and plenty of ammunition. Pablo Dominguez was the terror of this side and the other. He was neither Carrancista nor Villasta [sic] but furnished both with beef and horses. He has figured in most of the raids and all of the stealing, was a commander at the Glenn Springs Raid where the soldiers were killed, and at one time a price was on his head of 500.00 by the Govt. The price we paid was too dear but certainly did do away with one of the hardest gangs along the river. We carried Stillwell out horse-back and I brought him into Alpine by auto where he was buried by the K. of P. [Knights of Pythias] and W.O.W. [Woodmen of the World] Lodges with Rangers as Pall Bearers. All business houses closed and [it] was one of the largest attended funerals ever attended in Alpine, his friends were numbered by his acquaintance. Jim Wilson and Joe Jackson looked after the funeral expenses. I asked them to give him an average man's burial which I think they did and for which I enclose statement of expense over their signature.[91]

Continuing his report, Bates advised that "your man J. C. Palmer[92] has turned out bad." Palmer was one of the Rangers enlisted in Austin and then assigned to a company. He had deserted, had sold his saddle and rifle, for which he owed, and had been writing hot checks on the banks in Alpine. "He told the soldiers he was going to Mex. as he was offered a Captain command." The good news was that Captain Bates had just closed a deal for a small ranch for $25,000. On the other hand,

> Conditions are sure bad here now and no prospect of them getting better, as the Mex. are worse then poverty stricken and everything has been destroyed across the river that would sustain life, in many places they are eating burro meat and go for days without meal or flour, under these conditions I don't see much chance for the raids to cease.
>
> I am badly in need of some steel point bullets as the soft point don't work good in the guns we have and I don't want any of my men killed without a fighting chance.[93]

Just the following day Company F had another clash with Mexicans on the river. Bates wired the adjutant general that "Another fight this morning at Santa Helena. Fifteen Villistas. Two Mexicans left on ground. Wounded carried away. No Rangers wounded."[94] Bates continually worried about personnel; he had only twelve men rather than the usual fifteen per company. And things weren't getting any better, Bates reporting that "The situation here is still bad. Some sniping going on between Rangers, soldiers and Mexicans but nothing serious. It may become serious at any time, as there is [sic] lots of Mexicans all along the line, and the feeling is very bad on both sides. Col. Langhorne's troops had quite a little fight below Ft. Hancock the other day, killed seven or eight Mexicans."[95]

The adjutant general was becoming a bit nervous about the possibility of clashes along the Rio Grande leading to some international incident, for he wrote to Bates: "Replying to your report on the killing of Mexicans recently, advise that I appreciate your competent handling of the situation and congratulate you on your work in that section of the country. However, I would advise caution in a probable violation of the International Law—for as you know we are not looking for any international complications."[96] On May 14, a band of Mexicans crossed the Rio Grande and drove off thirty head of cattle from a ranch on the river. Captain Bates and his men, together with a troop of the 8th Cavalry, pursued the raiders into Mexico.[97]

This latest incursion heightened Harley's apprehension regarding international incidents and resulted in an order to all Ranger captains that pursuit of Mexican bandits would terminate at the border, except in cases involving the rescue of American citizens who had been captured by bandits. Even so, the pursuit should not extend beyond twenty miles from the border, and it should not be undertaken at all unless the trail were hot. Moreover, there was to be no shooting across the border unless fired on first, Mexicans entering the United States illegally should be captured, not shot at, and unarmed Mexicans who crossed from the United States into Mexico [presumably referring to filibustering expeditions] would not be fired on. The guiding rule in all cases was to use the assistance of the Mexican authorities whenever possible, "and to avoid the appearance of infringing upon the sovereign rights of the Mexican Government when other means of protecting American citizens are available."[98] What this meant in practice was that Mexican bandits could operate from a privileged sanctuary.

The adjutant general was concerned not only about international incidents but also about Captain Bates's leadership qualities. In June, Harley sent a man out to Marathon to investigate Bates,[99] who seemed to be losing control over his men. The breakdown in discipline was graphically illustrated by an incident in June. Rangers J. R. Hunnicutt, Joe Bratton, Will Bevill, A. A. Sanders, and J. D. Hall were stationed at Mariposa, with Hall in charge of the camp. Hall became insufferable, constantly harassing his comrades and taking an especial dislike to Hunnicutt. When not being disagreeable, Hall spent much of his time drinking and gambling. On June 26, Bratton, Bevill, Hunnicutt, and Hall started on a scout up the Rio Grande. Hall had been drinking heavily and had a gallon and a half of the potent liquor sotol with him. After camping for the night they resumed their patrol. Hall wanted to spend the day drinking at a candelaria wax factory, so the others left him behind. After they had gone a couple of miles Hall overtook them, drunk and shooting repeatedly into the air as he galloped between his companions. Hall resumed berating Hunnicutt, who announced that he was going to report him. Realizing that Hall was drunk and dangerous, Bratton told Hunnicutt to stay away from him. Hall not only threatened to beat up Hunnicutt, who told him to try whenever he was ready, but he actually took a shot at Hunnicutt with his six-gun. Hall's horse wheeled as he fired, and when he turned back around to take another shot, Hunnicutt had him covered. Bratton rushed over and disarmed Hall; Hunnicutt gave Bratton his own pistol. Hall was still blustering about wanting to thrash Hunnicutt, who offered to fight him there and then. Hall declined and left. He soon returned with his Winchester, told Hunnicutt to get his, as they were going to settle things right there. Once again Bratton disarmed Hall. The patrol made it back to camp, and Hunnicutt promptly reported the incident by phone to Captain Bates, who promised to come and resolve matters. He didn't, and Hunnicutt finally had to go to the Santa Helena camp to see Bates and make his report. Hunnicutt requested a transfer to another company, and Bates promised to approve the transfer, fearing that otherwise serious trouble would result.

Hunnicutt applied to the adjutant general's department for a transfer on July 5, enclosing a detailed account of the trouble.[100] Hall had already been fired for drunkenness on July 1.[101] Hunnicutt was transferred to Captain Gray's Company D. And despite a ringing endorsement from the sheriff of Brewster County, Bates was through. As the adjutant general put it, "Captain Bates signified a desire to resign because he was unable to hold his men together in that section of the country. Owing to this fact we found it necessary to disband his company and accept his resignation."[102] Bates resigned on August 31, 1918. Besides Bates's personal failings, his resignation and the demise of Company F were due to retrenchment. ·

Bates thereafter devoted himself to operating his Santa Elena ranch near Marathon. In October, 1918, Colonel Langhorne asserted that Bates was involved with a pair of Anglo smugglers who made his ranch their headquarters. This allegation was vigorously disputed by the Bureau of Investigation agent at El Paso, Gus T. Jones (himself a former Ranger and currently a Special Ranger) who had known Bates well for the past twenty years. Jones characterized Bates as being "exemplary," and pointed out that Colonel Langhorne was unaware that Bates was acting as a confidential informant for Jones. Bates had volunteered to provide information about the smugglers, and he had been following Jones's instructions. It would appear that Bates was sincerely trying to assist Jones and the Bureau of Investigation, although there remains the possibility—every counterintelligence officer's nightmare—that Bates was playing a sophisticated double game and was in league with the smugglers after all. As of June, 1919, Colonel Langhorne was still convinced of Bates's involvement with smugglers.[103]

A new captain arrived in Marathon on August 20, 1918, to conduct the mustering out of Company F—Joseph Lee Anders. He was born in January, 1871, in Bainbridge, Georgia. After working as a convict guard and as a merchant, he enlisted in Company C on July 19, 1909, resigning on September 30, 1910, with the rank of sergeant. From 1911 to 1913 he was one of Mayor Rice's special officers in Houston. On September 9, 1913, he again enlisted in the Rangers, serving in Company B until January 31, 1915, when he was discharged as part of Governor Ferguson's purge of the Ranger Force. But on July 30, 1915, he was back in the Rangers, serving until March 31, 1916, when he resigned. After a brief stint as a Wells Fargo guard in Houston, he reenlisted on September 30, 1916 as sergeant of Company D. And on August 20, 1918, Anders was promoted to captain of Company F. He represented something increasingly rare in the Ranger Force—promotion from within.

CHAPTER FOURTEEN

MORE WARTIME RANGERS

D OWNRIVER at Del Rio was stationed Captain W. L. Barler's Company E. As in the case of the Hudspeth Scouts, there is little documentation concerning Company E. The use of Monthly Returns was going out of style, and captains simply kept the adjutant general apprized through correspondence. Either Barler didn't correspond much or few of his reports are extant; the adjutant general's correspondence contains only three letters from him for 1918. In January he had detachments scouting near the towns of Comstock and Langtry, whose citizens were uneasy because groups of men had been sighted on the Mexican side of the Rio Grande.[1] A volunteer company of Special Rangers (Company A Volunteers) under Captain James B. Murrah was organized at Comstock, but the adjutant general rejected some of the applicants, informing Murrah that "hereafter Special Rangers in your territory will only be appointed on the recommendation of your county sheriff and Captain Barler."[2] Barler had rancher Ernest F. Hamilton enlisted as a Special Ranger on January 5, explaining that "The thing of it is he don't want to be under some one else [sic] orders and wants to serve with me with out pay and go at any time I need him which I know he will do as he has been tryed [sic]."[3] In February, Barler was making extended scouts along the river in his sector, apparently without incident. He also informed Austin of a conversation he had had on the train with one Jose Fuentes, a "high class, highly educated Mexican" from Monterrey who had traveled over much of the world. Fuentes was greatly alarmed about German influence in Mexico.[4]

Whereas there's little documentation concerning Barler, the opposite is the case for Captain K. F. Cunningham and his Company M at Eagle Pass. Like other captains, Cunningham did not have full control over the composition of his company. He was permitted to enlist his own sergeant, but at least two of his men were enlisted in Austin and assigned to him, while two others were transferred in from Company E. Soon thereafter, the adjutant general transferred Private C. P. Engelking out of Company M for temporary duty with Captain Hanson in San Antonio.[5] And Cunningham had to fire Private W. H. Martin because he disobeyed orders and conducted himself in an unspecified manner unbecoming a Texas Ranger. The military authorities had complained to Cunningham, and when the latter investigated he found the complaints against Martin to be well founded.[6] It was difficult for Cunningham to forge an effective company while presiding over a revolving door, but he did the best he could.

Cunningham probably would have preferred, like the other captains, to shoot it out with some bandit gang rather than have to fill out the required paperwork. He'd send in his Subsistence and Forage Returns and his company's expense accounts, and they were routinely returned with comments and requests for explanations.[7] These problems were in addition to those involved in securing rifles and ammunition and cots for the men and arranging for the delivery of the pack mules which were indispensable on scouts.[8]

Company M was responsible for some ninety miles of the Rio Grande, about equally divided above and below Eagle Pass. The company operated in three detachments: five men north of Eagle Pass, seven downriver, and two men in Eagle Pass itself. Cunningham reported a few minor incidents of cattle stealing north of town, and his men in this area arrested five suspicious characters, presumed to be draft dodgers, whom they turned over to the military authorities. Some of what Cunningham's men did was to combat the smuggling of foodstuffs and ammunition into Mexico. He sent the adjutant general as a souvenir a "smuggler's sack" worn by a woman caught smuggling sugar.[9]

South of Eagle Pass, Cunningham's men on occasion made scouts into Dimmit and Zavala Counties[10] but their main concern was protecting the Indio Ranch. The joint army-Ranger incursion into Mexico in December, 1917, had discouraged raids on that ranch, several of whose employees had received Special Ranger commissions.[11] The secretary of the Indio Cattle Company advised Harley that Cunningham, the military, and the Indio personnel were working together harmoniously. He anticipated no further attacks on the ranch in the near future, although the Rangers and the army were less optimistic.[12]

A prominent rancher, Thomas Atlee Coleman, urged Governor Hobby to recommend to the Rangers and the military patrolling the border that they be "more conservative." Coleman certainly had Ferguson's ear, for he had been commissioned as a lieutenant colonel on the governor's staff in 1915. In September, 1917, Coleman was appointed collector of customs for the new San Antonio district (the old Laredo and Eagle Pass districts). Between 1916 and 1919 he was a Special Ranger. Assuring Hobby that he very much liked both Cunningham and the army commander at Eagle Pass, Coleman nevertheless devoutly hoped there would not be a repetition of the San José incursion, for this would result in serious consequences. He stated that the Mexican authorities were doing their best to patrol the border and protect American interests, but it was impossible to prevent occasional cattle thefts from American ranches. Coleman's solicitude for the Mexican authorities was perhaps due to the fact that he was a partner in the Coleman and Keeran Ranch across the Rio Grande in Coahuila.[13] Nor was this all; Captain Cunningham was able to shed considerable light on the machinations of Coleman and his cronies in Laredo. In March, the Ranger captain sent a "strictly confidential" report to Harley. In it he enclosed a memorandum he had received at the Indio Ranch from Captain C. H. Strong, 14th Cavalry, stationed at Camp Eagle Pass. Strong stated that on February 10, while on duty at the Blocker Ranch some sixty miles south of Eagle Pass he met two Texas Rangers from Laredo, Charles B. Burwell[14] and Robert H. Johnson. In the course of their conversation Johnson talked quite confidentially. The Ranger cursed the cattlemen along the Rio Grande as "a band of Smugglers and Grafters," especially Tom Coleman and F. L. Jordan, two of the largest ranchers in Texas, who owned a spread some hundred miles below Eagle Pass on both sides of the river. "He said he knew for a fact that Coleman and Jourdan [sic] were 'standing in' with the American authorities, both Military, Civil, and Ranger," and that with the knowledge and even help of said authorities were smuggling cattle across the border where and when they wanted. The Ranger said he personally knew that Coleman had unlawfully crossed 500 head of cattle into Mexico the previous week. Furthermore, the Ranger asserted that Coleman had instructed him as to who were the good Mexicans and who the bad and who to let across the river.[15] "He said he promised Coleman to follow instructions, but that he was not that kind of a boy and he knew God Damned well what to do to any Mexican he caught breaking the law around the River. Johnson seemed an honest, good natured sort of man, but death on Mexicans and Smugglers and a very loyal American." Captain Strong swore that his memorandum was a true report of the substance of what the Ranger had said.

Cunningham stated:

Allow me to further inform you that this report only tends to bear out rumors which have come to my ear frequently of late. In fact, it is frequently mentioned in official circles that some of the "Higher Ups" are not always inclined to apply the laws to all persons alike, at least they do not enforce them as rigidly in some cases as in others, and the result is that many try their luck to see whether or not they are among the favored ones. Such naturally brings about a sad state of affairs and at times things look gloomy.

I am informed that F. L. Jordan, Tom A. Coleman and R. W. Dowe are partners in a ranching project in Mexico. The first two named have big holdings on both sides of the Rio Grande and R. W. Dowe is shaping the affairs and managing the business. Coleman is the present Collector of Customs of this district; R. W. Dowe was formerly the Collector of Customs here and also sheriff of Maverick County for some time. His brother, Luke Dowe, is for all purposes and intents the present Collector of Customs. Jordan is a personal friend of Carranza and stands "aces high" in Mexico. Jordan, Coleman, and R. W. Dowe had planned to ship 27000 head of cattle into Mexico under bond to return same to the United States on April 1, 1918, the bond providing that on every head not returned, the owners have to pay 20% of the value of the animal to the Government. 5000 head actually crossed under the superintendence of R. W. Dowe, acting as live stock agent for the I. & GN Railway Co., but for some reason they have not undertaken to cross the balance. I understand that Mexican bandits have lately operated in the vicinity to which these cattle were shipped, and a serious predicament has arisen. Rumors reached me that cattle are being crossed from the Coleman Ranch on this side of the River to his ranch on the other side to take place of the cattle lost in the raids by Mexican bandits. However, these ranches are below the district assigned to my company and I therefore have not investigated these rumors closely.

The military authorities seem to be awakening to a full realization of the situation and are apparently becoming more alert. The Rio Grande can be crossed almost anywhere and we positively know that some of the ranchmen sanction the crossing and recrossing by their employees. The families of many of the employees live in Mexico.[16]

It was precisely this sort of thing that General Funston, commander of the Southern Department, had decried in 1915, saying that "certain cattlemen" were profiting greatly from herds driven into Texas and sold at about half the market price. These cattlemen knew the herds were stolen but they didn't hesitate to buy the cattle and even to aid the desperados' escape back into Mexico. To Funston's great frustration, when thieves rustled cattle from Texas ranches, these cattlemen refused to provide information even though they knew the thieves and their whereabouts. "It is to their financial interest to protect the cattle thieves. And so they do." Funston made a point, however, of saying that these cattlemen weren't typical.[17] It will be recalled that Dr. C. F. Z. Caracristi had denounced the "cattle mafia" at Laredo in 1914.

By March, Cunningham's company was fully operational, its personnel totaling the prescribed fifteen men. And Cunningham had a reserve, for in April the adjutant general sent him a list of the Special Rangers under Cunningham's jurisdiction on whom the captain could call whenever needed.[18] Cunningham stationed five of his Regular Rangers at his upper camp on the land of the Val Verde Irrigation Company, which owned some forty-five miles of riverfront. South of

Eagle Pass, the camp on the Indio Cattle Company's land was staffed by six men, while four Rangers were in town with Cunningham. There continued to be minor instances of rustling, and this kind of irritant sometimes caused Cunningham to lose his temper: "A Mexican reported three of his horses stolen and taken across. The thieves were notified to return the horses within 24 hours or suffer for the theft and they return [sic] some time the following night."[19]

Cunningham's men in Eagle Pass managed to keep busy. They worked in conjunction with Military Intelligence, Immigration, Customs, Justice, and representatives of the War Trade Board. The Rangers made thirty-eight arrests in March, including two Industrial Workers of the World, two violators of the Mann Act, two for unlawful possession of high-powered rifles, five slackers, and a number of smugglers of ammunition and sugar. "One of the arrests led to the discovery that one of the leading business houses here is over 1,000,000 rounds short on high powered ammunition which they are supposed to have accounted for to the Federal authorities." The Ranger captain mentioned that all persons arrested for violating federal laws were promptly turned over to federal authorities, but he complained that "The county officials would not assist in this work as they did not consider it their business and as they expressed it, 'IT INTERFERED WITH LOCAL BUSINESS INTERESTS.'"[20] Cunningham also commented on something that applied all along the Rio Grande—the breaking of traditional patterns of traffic back and forth across the river: "Crossing the River at Indio and other points and also illegally selling to people on the other side of the River has continued for so long that some people think they have an inherent right to continue that kind of business and think they are doing no wrong to do so. Enforcement of the laws resulted in considerable friction but things are gradually coming our way."[21]

Increasingly, food was the main topic of conversation. As conditions in Mexico became more desperate,

> smuggling is the employment and business of a large portion of the inhabitants of Piedras Negras, Coah., Mexico and quite a few Americans on this side of the river. Many who are not actively assisting, loan their moral support by sanctioning it in a passive way. In the latter class may be included some of the officials and leading citizens of Maverick County. Many of the rich and influential men here own land and other interests in Mexico. . . . The County Officials naturally do not care to seek the enmity of the Mexicans. Some told me that they had to buy the Mexican votes to get their office.[22]

Besides identifying the worst offenders, Cunningham described in detail the methods of smuggling used by speculators, who were getting rich. An average of 2,500 people crossed the international bridge daily, many of them carrying smuggled provisions. And many Mexicans were swimming the river to the Texas side, frankly admitting that they preferred being imprisoned rather than starve. To add to the misery, there was an epidemic of smallpox in the area.[23]

What Cunningham neglected to mention in his report to the adjutant general was that he was up to his Stetson in Mexican revolutionary intrigue. And he was not too subtle about it, either. It was common knowledge in Eagle Pass that Cunningham was on intimate terms with anti-Carranza exile leaders in Eagle Pass and the surrounding area, to the point of attending their meetings, both in Eagle Pass and in San Antonio. It was of course possible that Cunningham was cultivating them in order to secure information, but such was not the case. Not only did the Ranger captain boast that when the exiles seized control of Piedras Negras he would be a general in Coahuila and would have all the money and property he wanted, but when in his cups he also tried to bribe the resident Bureau of Investigation agent in Eagle Pass to ignore the activities of the exiles, assuring the agent that he would be very well paid for doing so. The Bureau agent of course strung Cunningham along, thus securing a great deal of valuable information from him about the activities of the Mexican exiles. Moreover, according to both the Bureau of Investigation and military intelligence, the sergeant of Cunningham's Ranger company, W. H. Claiborne, was also enthusiastically supporting the exile plotters.[24]

In mid-March, the detachment of the 14th Cavalry at Eagle Pass was transferred, leaving only infantry to patrol that sector of the border. Colonel Day, the commander at Camp Eagle Pass, asked Cunningham to loan him some men to act as scouts along the river. Since the army had provided valuable assistance to Cunningham he readily agreed to the request but, he assured the adjutant general, the Rangers would remain under his absolute command.[25]

Cunningham was a hard taskmaster, and this caused some dissension in Company M. There were problems at the upper camp, the men disliking the Ranger whom Cunningham had put in charge. One of them, E. Hornsby, resigned in a huff. Another man wanted to go complain personally to Harley. A third requested a transfer, receiving an unsympathetic reply from Austin: "We are sorry that conditions are not satisfactory to you, but we have no desire to transfer you; and if conditions are as you say, your resignation will be accepted by General Harley upon your presenting it."[26]

In his own defense, Cunningham wrote to Harley: "As to the men who are dissatisfied, I will ask you to remember that some of the men in my company have been transferred from other companies. Some of them are from towns and are not used to country service and it naturally strikes them pretty hard. And I probably do run my company a little different from the way that some of the other companies have been managed in the past."[27] Then there was the problem that some of the men were married, and when difficulties developed at home and they were given leave they did not always return on time.[28] This concern for family even extended to Cunningham himself; he couldn't report to Austin as ordered because his wife was ill with smallpox.[29] Cunningham explained to Harley why he had fired Private W. D. Hale, the man who had wanted a transfer: "there has been quite a lot of contrariness among the members of this Company, and it seems there is no other way to get them straight, except by the weeding process."[30]

The adjutant general agreed—in June, he weeded Cunningham, relieving him of command and assigning him to a desk job in Austin. This despite Cunningham's being on very friendly terms with Governor Hobby "and is likewise said to be the personal political representative in Eagle Pass of Governor Hobby." Harley's decision to relieve Cunningham may have resulted from information provided by the Bureau of Investigation. A Bureau agent overheard Cunningham and his sergeant talking in the Western Union office in Eagle Pass and reported that Cunningham said "he was damned tired of livestock being run across into Mexico. He intended to combine his company of fifteen with another Ranger company of fifteen, and the thirty of them would cross the river and kill thirty or forty of those _____ Mexicans and show the Mexicans who in the hell the Rangers were and a lot of other stuff of the same kind."[31] Cunningham's proposed raid would cause an international incident and risk heavy casualties among the Rangers, for according to the Bureau agent Cunningham had badly underestimated the number of Mexican troops across the river—there were not 150–200 as he thought but rather 800. The Bureau agent ascribed much of the Ranger captain's enthusiasm for the proposed raid as being designed to show his Mexican exile friends that he was doing everything he could against the Carranza regime. The agent also reported that only two of Cunningham's men could be trusted to cooperate with the Bureau and other federal agencies.

Sergeant Lon L. Willis, whom Tom Coleman had warmly recommended, was assigned to take temporary command of Cunningham's Company M.[32] He was a seasoned veteran of the service. Born in Odem, San Patricio County, in February, 1888, Willis was a stockman when he enlisted in the Rangers on November 1, 1912. He served in Company B until February 1, 1915, when he was reassigned to Company A. On January 1, 1918, Willis was transferred to Company I and promoted to sergeant. He performed capably as temporary commander of Company M, and on September 10 was promoted to captain of Company M.[33]

As sergeant, Willis had provided stability to the newly formed Company I, stationed downriver at Laredo and commanded by Captain William M. Ryan. In January the unit totaled only eleven men.[34] The logistical support Ryan received was somewhat whimsical; in March his men were having to pay for cartridges out of their own pockets because they hadn't received any from Austin.[35] There was also disagreement as to how well Ryan was performing. The district attorney in Laredo complained in July that "as yet I have received no assistance whatever from the rangers."[36] This despite the positive report Captain Hanson had sent to Harley from Laredo in February: "Capt. Ryan is here and he and his men are very active, and giving satisfaction to the people. He is very popular, and his showing good judgment in his work. All his men that I have seen so far look good to me, and I believe will prove an honor to the force."[37] On February 16, Ryan, Hanson, and Sergeant Willis met the Mexican commander at Nuevo Laredo, General Bernardo de la Garza, at the middle of the international bridge, conveyed Governor Hobby's and Adjutant General Harley's compliments, and discussed border issues of mutual interest, exchanging information about bandits. De la Garza complained that American soldiers firing across the river had killed a horse on the Mexican bank. He was also upset because he had been told that Texas lawmen had crossed into Mexico looking for stolen livestock. The general asked that this not happen again. The Rangers assured him it would not. The meeting became a veritable love feast.[38]

During the first few months that Ryan was in command, headquarters kept an eye on him. Major Walter Woodul, the assistant adjutant general, conferred with him in Laredo in January, as did Captain Hanson in February. That month Ryan was called to Austin for discussions.[39] The visits to Laredo from headquarters personnel were not solely to confer with Ryan. Laredo enjoyed the temporary distinction of having two Ranger companies stationed there—Ryan's Company I and Company K, commanded by Captain Will Wright, who was a much more experienced officer than Ryan and had a more impressive reputation. Wright was an outstanding peace officer, and he was also a man of unswerving integrity. When he became a Ranger captain he refused to participate in a longstanding practice of petty graft practiced by captains: claiming subsistence and forage allowances for their men when in fact grateful ranchers had furnished some of the feed and board. Wright's display of moral courage resulted in an end to this practice.[40] Not only did Wright's men respect him, but they liked him as well, because he was thoughtful of them. This was shown even in little things, such as the company's stationery. Each captain had stationery printed with the company's designation, station, the captain's name and that of the sergeant. Wright, however, had stationery that included not only the above but also listed the names of his men.

Ryan held the fort in Laredo while Wright conducted scouts downriver as far as Rio Grande City. This arrangement posed logistical problems; Wright appealed to Woodul to "please have Capt. Johnston [the Ranger quartermaster] rush my accounts and pay roll as all the men are broke and in a strange country." Wright also mentioned that "I have had lots of callers this morning. They are tickled to death about me being sent to their country."[41]

Captain Hanson, the adjutant general's representative, gave a glowing report about Wright: "Capt. Wright has been down the River as far as Rio Grande City and has stationed his force at the most advantageous points. He has a fine lot of men, the best I have seen, and they are under perfect control, and discipline, and I believe will prove a great honor to our force. Such men are hard to get and but for his personality think it would be impossible to get together such a force of men. He is in full accord in everything with your ideas as to the management of the border and her people."[42]

Wright's mettle would soon be tested. He and six of his men left Laredo on March 3 on a scout, arriving in Hebbronville the evening of the 4th. Wright said: "I found that grass was good, so I decided to rest ourselves and horses a day or so. Mr. Henry Edds furnished me a place to camp and a room over his office to sleep in." Wright already liked rancher Edds, having described him as being "all right in every way and is a Ranger friend from top to bottom." The adjutant general had issued Edds a Special Ranger commission, advising that he had been assigned to no company but left with a free hand for "I know you are going to assist Captain Wright whenever needed."[43]

About 4:30 a.m. on March 7, Wright was awakened with the news that bandits had attacked and robbed the East Ranch, about thirty miles from Hebbronville. Tom East was one of the largest ranchers in South Texas, as his letterhead attested: "T. T. East, All Classes of Cattle, Ranches in Jim Hogg, Starr, and Hidalgo Counties, San Antonio Viejo, Headquarters Ranch, Hebbronville." All this in addition to being the son-in-law of R. J. Kleberg, Sr., of the King Ranch. Wright immediately assembled a posse and notified (ex-Ranger) Sheriff Pat Craighead and ex-sheriff Oscar Thompson. But the posse didn't just gallop off in a cloud of dust—they rode in automobiles, while Oscar Thompson furnished a truck to haul their saddles. On reaching San Antonio Viejo, the posse, composed of Wright, his six Rangers, Tom Moseley, who was a cattlemen's association brand inspector and Special Ranger, Special Ranger Dudley V. "Bud" Stillwell, who was an employee of Tom East, John C. Draper, who had been a Special Ranger in 1916–1917, and Special Ranger Steve Franklin, who was one of East's foremen, mounted up and followed the bandits' trail. The latter were heading for the riverside village of Roma, about fifteen miles above Rio Grande City, but the marauders left the Roma road and plunged into brush so dense that the posse had to proceed in single file, their Winchesters at the ready.

Suddenly, at a distance of only twenty feet, the posse sighted the raiders, who were dismounted and resting their horses. In a flash the bandits leaped on their horses and fled, the posse on their heels. The Mexicans quickly scattered, and the posse scattered after them. Wright and four men pursued a group of eight for about three miles, the bandits shooting over their shoulders and the officers firing back. Wright wasn't certain how many they killed, but they put a dent in the bandit gang—he thought they'd killed at least two; they buried one later but couldn't locate another who had also been shot off his horse. Moreover, they wounded several more, evidenced by the blood on the saddles of horses the officers recovered. "We crowded them so close that they threw away everything. They lost pistols, Winchesters, five of them lost their hats, and also their booty they had taken from the store on the East Ranch," Wright reported. The fine horse, stolen from the East Ranch, that the bandit leader was riding was recovered, and there was evidence that the leader had been wounded. Four of this group made it across the Rio Grande. The posse's horses were worn out.

Incredibly, Tom East did not follow with fresh horses as he had promised. While the Rangers were risking their lives to recover his property, Wright later learned, East had his men dip several hundred head of cattle before he let them start out with remounts for the posse. "Consequently, their horses never reached us in time to do us any good," Wright wrote. "If Mr. East would have followed us with his horses, as I instructed him to do, I am almost certain that we would have been able to have captured or killed every last one of these bandits. They would not surrender at all, as I holloaed at them to throw up their hands, and the other boys did too, to surrender, but they paid no attention to our request. It seemed that they would rather die than surrender." Henry Edds had one of his Hispanic employees drive along in an auto behind the posse to relay messages, and Captain Wright was fulsome in his praise of this man, who after the chase took a message to Roma, returning with reinforcements and provisions, "as there wasn't a living thing in that whole country but the brush and prickle pear, not even a rabbit."

Wright ended his after-action report by generously sharing the credit:

> The next morning after the chase, we all had fresh mounts, so we trailed the other six to the Rio Grande. We captured seven horses, and two mules, also the same amount of saddles, bridles, spurs, some Winchesters and pistols. I wish to say in conclusion, that the State of Texas owes to Mr. Henry Edds and Mr. Oscar Thompson many, many thanks in this chase alone, for the services they rendered in running down these bandits. Had they gotten away with this booty it would have encouraged many, many others to do likewise. And I am certain that this will teach these that got away an everlasting lesson. I also want to mention to you the gallant services that Mr. Tom Moseley, John Droeper [sic], Dudley Stillwell, and Mr. Franklin rendered us. They showed skill and bravery in running these bandits through the thick brush. Several of the boys, after the chase, didn't have enough clothes on to hide themselves.[44]

The adjutant general warmly commended Wright and those who had assisted him.[45]

Tom East wrote an enlightening account of the raid, which was certainly an atypical attack on a South Texas ranch. The morning of the raid, an automobile with the curtains drawn and containing two Mexican men and a woman drove up to the ranch. The men "had coats drawn up over their faces, so as to disguise themselves, but one of the fellows did pull the cover off his face enough" to ask East's wife for directions to Hebbronville. She gave him directions, and later mentioned to East that "it looked awful suspicious," but he thought nothing of it at the time.

Having cased the ranch headquarters, the bandits struck that night and quickly took over the complex. They captured Will Franklin, his son, and their wives, and when Claude McGill of Alice and Special Ranger Steve Franklin, East's ranch foreman in Hidalgo County, drove up, the bandits fired about a dozen shots at them. The two men surrendered, were stripped of valuables, and were taken to the ranch house to join the other captives. Half an hour later, at about 8 p.m., East's chauffeur drove him and his wife to the ranch. East got out to shut a barn door while the car drove on. He was shocked to see four men run out to the car and point pistols at his wife and driver. The bandits relieved their latest prisoners of the three rifles and one pistol that were in the car. The attackers didn't spot East, as the car's headlights were shining in their faces. He ran about a hundred yards, jumped a fence, stopped and listened, and tried to figure out what to do. He decided to go for help. It took him an hour of walking to reach a group of his cowboys camped for the night. They mounted up and went to several nearby ranches for assistance, bringing back Dudley Stillwell and Tom Moseley.

Meanwhile, back at the ranch the Mexicans were busy ransacking the place, taking what they could carry, including seven guns and a good deal of merchandise. Some of them then remained guarding the prisoners while the rest got into two autos and drove off toward Hebbronville, announcing they were going after whiskey and were planning to rob the bank. Within a few miles of Hebbronville, though, they got scared and returned to the ranch. The women captives were made to cook them a meal, while the bandits went back through the store, taking everything they missed the first time around.

East was later told that the reason the Mexicans stayed as long as they did was because they expected him to arrive. They reassured the captives that they only wanted East and Stillwell. Finally giving up, the bandits left about 3 a.m., passing close to East, who had gotten his horse and had returned to a spot about a hundred yards from the house, had tied his horse, and was crawling through the brush toward the ranch house.

The bandits made off with some $1,200 worth of loot, including two horses and saddles. East's wife identified one of them as the man who had asked for directions that morning. East related that:

> The Mexicans could all talk English and said they were Texas Mexicans. We recognized three men in the bunch. They were all young men from 21 to 30 years old. They were very polite to the ladies and did not hurt them in any way, but punched the men around with their guns and talked of killing Will Franklin Jr., as they thought he was Stilwell [sic], and did put a rope around his neck. They also said they were going to take Mrs. East away if I did not

come. When they left they made them all tell them "Good-bye," and said if they sent after the Rangers, they would come back and kill them all. . . . It is true some of these fellows talked English and claimed they were all from this side [of the river], but I think some of them might have been from the other side.[46]

East's friend Woodul wrote to him that after reading East's account of the raid he had talked with Caesar Kleberg and "I believe it will not be amiss to send a couple of men down on your ranch for a while at least."[47] For good measure, Woodul issued Special Ranger commissions to Tom East and his brothers Roy E. and Arthur L.[48] The latter was a member of a Home Guard company whose captain was Oscar Thompson. The company's nineteen men, two of them Hispanics, would be directly under Captain Wright in case of need.[49] And the district and county clerk of Jim Hogg County wrote to his friend Woodul from Hebbronville that "since we have just recently had a bandit raid, and not knowing at what time each man (American) in this town will be called upon to assist the State and County officials in putting down disorder" he would like a Special Ranger commission.[50] He got it.

This practice of promiscuously appointing Special Rangers troubled Captain Wright. In a letter recommending D. N. Cobb for Special Ranger status, Wright stressed that he had known Cobb for years and he was a good, reliable man. He went on to advise the adjutant general that "I would consider it a special favor if you would not appoint any more Special Rangers from here without my passing on them, as there are some in the service now, who should not be."[51] One of those who should not have been in the service was Tom East's employee Dudley V. "Bud" Stillwell, who had been a Regular Ranger in 1916 and was currently a Special Ranger. Woodul wrote to East that "Reports coming to this office seem to indicate that Bud Stillwell is a little inclined to be rough and to exert too much authority under a Special Ranger's commission. General Harley has directed me to write you to have Stillwell send in his commission and that if you want a man in his place to confer with Captain Wright at Laredo. Now, Tom, I talked to Mr. Caesar [Kleberg] about this and I think he has some suggestions to make to you before you say anything about this matter. You might move Stillwell away from your territory."[52]

East replied:

Walter I want you to reconsider Stillwell's ranger commission and let him keep it. If you do, I will see that he don't do anything that will conflict in any way with the policy of the regular ranger force, or with your office, and he will not mix in any affairs outside of looking after the Jenson Ranch, which he has always done. Now Walter, I have just got to keep a man in that country, because I can't depend on the Mexicans, and I can't find a good reliable man that can speak Mexican to take his place, for up until Capt. Wright got that country in his district, there was not an officer down there but about two or three times. Our sheriff [Pat Craighead] is crippled and can't get around as much as he would otherwise, and Stillwell has done practically all of his outside work for him down in that section, and has done him lots of good, which he will confirm. There never has been but two Mexicans that he has beaten up, in one case, I think he was wrong and [I] got after him, but in the other case he was justified. Now I ask you as a *SPECIAL FAVOR* to me, to let this man keep his commission, and I will see that he attends strictly to his ranch business, and nothing else.[53]

Woodul then wrote: "Please talk to Mr. Caesar [Kleberg] again about the matter as I suggested a way out and he will tell you what it is. I think everything can be fixed up. Now, Tom, please caution Stillwell to be a little more careful and not quite as rough as he has been reported to be."[54] Despite Woodul's efforts, Stillwell's warrant of authority was canceled in June.[55] Since Stillwell was "a little inclined to be rough," this may explain the odd nature of the raid on the East Ranch, where the perpetrators were primarily interested in getting Stillwell and Tom East rather than looting, although they were certainly not averse to stealing everything that was not nailed down. Yet Captain W. M. Hanson, who investigated the affair for Harley, was absolutely certain that the band was composed entirely of Mexicans for the express purpose of robbing the Hebbronville bank, and that they were supposed to be joined by another band from San Diego, "and from there they were to rob other banks and ranches in Texas." Hanson identified the bandits by name, noting that the Rangers had killed one of them in the running fight after the raid. An investigation by the Mexican consul general determined that the raid had originated in Mexico.[56]

In the lower border, the job of protecting the volatile area of Cameron and Hidalgo Counties was the responsibility of Captain Charles F. Stevens and Company G. Unlike his counterpart in Ysleta, Captain Davis, who initially was rather tentative about discharging his duties, Stevens hit the ground running. He was commissioned on November 27, 1917, and by the end of December the fourteen men of his company, including several Hispanics, had assembled at their assigned station, Edinburg, and were ready for duty despite the usual logistical delays. And like his fellow captains, Stevens despised paperwork: "I'd like to enlist a young man who'd keep my books & payroll correctly, as the keeping of those are the most of my troubles."[57]

Unlike some of the other captains, Stevens had an eye for public relations. Upon arriving in the Lower Valley on December 11, he had made a point of calling on Sheriff Vann of Cameron County, Sheriff Baker of Hidalgo County, and Sheriff

Guerra of Starr County, as well as all the other peace officers he could find, introduced himself, asked for their cooperation and offered that of himself and his men. Sheriff A. Y. Baker was especially pleased with Stevens, who had arranged to rent one of Baker's houses in Edinburg as his headquarters.[58]

The Ranger captain didn't limit himself to establishing good relations with the local peace officers. He called on the Mexican consul in Brownsville, who escorted him across the river to Matamoros, where Stevens conferred with the military commander and the collector of customs. They agreed to cooperate in returning stolen property and each other's fugitives. Lastly, Stevens called on the American consul, who was flabbergasted to see a Ranger in Matamoros. After they had talked, the consul said Stevens's visit to Matamoros would have a salutary effect, lessening the hard feelings that existed there against the Rangers.[59]

Stevens was of a progressive cast of mind. Pointing out that his company had no wagon as yet, he suggested that "on account of condition of surrounding country mostly sand hills away from river, that a Ford Truck would much better answer our purpose. Feed is also very high here and with a truck we would only need two mules for pack saddles. The roads along river are good and when we go in the sand hills we can use pack mules. Our out lying camps are all situated on good roads so can be reached quickly by truck."[60] The adjutant general's department instructed Stevens to purchase a wagon; they would consider the matter of the truck later.[61] Initially Stevens deployed some of his men in detachments at Harlingen and Raymondville and on the river at El Ebano and Hidalgo, the company's headquarters remaining at Edinburg. On December 26, Stevens and Sheriff Baker made a tour of the Lower Valley "and called on some of the influential people both Americans and Mexicans and explained to them that men and myself were down here to treat all the people well and to protect them against Bandits and Outlaws."[62]

As usual the region seethed with intrigue. For example, the Mexican consul in Brownsville informed Stevens that General Juan Andreu Almazán, who had fought in the ranks of several factions, was now a felicista, had recently led a filibustering expedition, had been defeated by Carranza troops, and was currently in McAllen being protected by Deodoro Guerra and sons. The consul urged Stevens to arrest the general.[63] Stevens left it to the federal authorities, for it was they who handled neutrality violations. He went to McAllen and informed the army commander, adding that "these Guerras are merchants at McAllen and have stores in different parts along the border and are connected with a smooth bunch of men on both sides of the river. One of these Guerras is sheriff of Starr County."[64]

In order to keep abreast of events in his sector, Stevens wanted to move his headquarters. He explained that "Edinburg is the county seat but is a dead town." It was located at the end of an eight-mile branch railroad line over which there was but one train daily, in the morning, and no train at all on Sunday. Moreover, the place had a very poor telephone system and the telegraph office was closed at night. He was considering moving either to Mission or Mercedes, both being on a main railroad line. He inclined toward Mercedes, for a delegation from there had just asked him to station Rangers in Mercedes. He had agreed to detail two men, and the overjoyed delegation promised to furnish free of charge automobiles and whatever else the Rangers needed. The adjutant general's office approved moving Stevens's headquarters wherever he chose.[65] He decided on Mercedes.

In many respects Stevens was an excellent officer, but he had a significant blind spot—he saw German influence everywhere. In his view "the various Mexican Revolutionary parties—Felicistas, Villistas, etc., are nothing more than a German Sympathizers Party and promoted by German Agents to cause trouble, both here and in Mexico."[66] And "The way I figure things out here, it seems that some of the Germans want intervention, knowing that it would take between three and four hundred thousand soldiers to go into Mexico and police that country which would take so much of our army away from the European War."[67] Accordingly, Stevens spent a good deal of his time combating what he considered German subversion.[68]

Of course there were other kinds of problems for him to deal with, not the least being personnel issues, and these usually had to do with liquor. Early on, Stevens had to fire Private William M. Scott, one of the Rangers stationed at Harlingen and who had been in the company less than a month, for drinking.[69] This was particularly painful because the young man's father, William Scott, had been a respected Ranger captain, commanding Company F from 1885 to 1888. Stevens discharged four more of his men. One was Private A. B. Hardin, who got drunk at Los Ebanos and created quite a disturbance. Evidently he made unwanted advances toward two young Anglo schoolmarms. Stevens reported the incident to Harley but managed to hush it up locally. The schoolteachers agreed not to go public as did the county school superintendent.[70] As a result of these incidents Stevens changed his personnel policy: "It is my intention never to enlist another man unless I see and talk with him personally as it seems some people get recommendations and in many instances from local politicians, and the party they recommend is absolutely worthless.[71]

Most of Stevens's men did their jobs. The army captain commanding the cavalry troop stationed at Hidalgo wrote to Stevens praising the work of Rangers W. E. Hodge and J. M. Gentry in the seizure of arms and ammunition from Hispanics along the river. He added: "I would say that we are always glad to make use of the rangers and will surely call upon you again should the occasion require it."[72] Two of Stevens's men not only arrested a pair of rustlers but secured the evidence to break up a gang of cattle thieves who'd been operating for more than two years.[73] In fact, Company G was so effective that the commander at Fort Brown, Colonel Herbert J. Slocum, 13th Cavalry, who had been in command at

Columbus, New Mexico when Villa raided the town in 1916, was quite complimentary. This was remarkable, for Slocum stated that heretofore he had despised
the Rangers, basing his dislike on reports of brutalities and other excesses. Slocum
candidly admitted that Stevens's men had done what the army had failed to accomplish in suppressing rustling. Slocum sent Harley his compliments and requested
that an additional company of Rangers be stationed in the Brownsville area.[74]

Yet rustling, like smuggling, was a time-honored occupation on the border,
and cattle thieves were soon back in evidence, this time at the Piper Plantation,
ten miles downriver from Brownsville. The manager called on Stevens for help,
saying the soldiers were useless and the sheriff couldn't cope. Stevens replied that
Sheriff Vann didn't want Rangers around; in fact, Vann had recently informed
Stevens that his Rangers were guilty of robbery with firearms for having gone to
the homes of some suspected cattle thieves and confiscated their rifles. But the
manager insisted that the sheriff had changed his tune and now wanted Ranger
help. Stevens detailed three men to the Piper Plantation with orders to stay there
until they had broken up the gang of rustlers. They arrested two of the Mexicans
implicated in the thefts and located the stolen cattle, which unfortunately were
already in Mexico.[75]

Stevens commented that:

There is quite a bit of cattle stealing going along on this Border now, and I
have been trying to apprehend some of these thiefs [sic]. This country is a
very brushy country and it is not such an easy matter to apprehend these thiefs,
and especially when there are so many on our side of the River who are looking
to make a dollar, no matter what way they get it. The other day I was down
on the River and was talking with some Mexicans who had been on the other
side of the River, and they stated that there was a good many slackers who
had crossed over to the Mexican Side and that they could not obtain work
over there and that they were doing quite a bit of this cattle stealing.[76]

In response to this situation, the adjutant general revised Stevens's sector of
the border. The four men Stevens had in Rio Grande City were now deployed
between Brownsville and Point Isabel. Stevens himself inspected the Piper
Plantation. The Mexican consul had informed him that when certain Mexican customs officials were on duty something was always stolen on the American side of
the river. The Ranger captain hoped to capture them if they crossed to steal anything.

Increasingly, though, Stevens was concerned with German subversion; he was
eager to assist the federal authorities in every way possible, at their request. He
had been keeping an eye on a certain Dr. Richard Lindner, a German working a
farm north of Mercedes. Stevens had speculated on how easily Germans could

introduce something like the boll weevil to devastate the cotton industry in Texas. When Stevens received word that Lindner had left his farm and was heading for the Rio Grande, he immediately notified the military, who sent out patrols and captured Lindner as he was about to cross the river. Stevens later learned that Lindner was a lieutenant in the German army, an escaped prisoner of war who had made his way from Canada to Mercedes, Texas. Stevens searched Lindner's farm, seized all his papers, and arrested an associate of Lindner's, a Reverend Rooper, a onetime Lutheran pastor in the area. The Ranger captain delivered the documents and Rooper to the army. Stevens was certain the Germans were part of a spy ring.[77] He subsequently arrested two German-Americans for treason, as they had allegedly helped Lindner in his attempt to reach Mexico. According to Stevens, "this section of the country is a hotbed of German spies and propaganda." Stevens was not paranoid, however, for "Harley was well pleased with our work down here and he instructed me to go after all these parties, and to keep a close watch on all this German propaganda."[78] Stevens did so, in cooperation with agents of the Bureau of Investigation and the postal authorities. They were following the money trail regarding some funds sent to Mexico ostensibly for missionary work.[79]

Trouble began brewing for Stevens over the case of one Florencio García. Sheriff Vann wrote asking about García and several other Mexicans with whom the Rangers had recently had dealings. Stevens declined to answer the sheriff, explaining to Woodul that "In regard to me answering and explaining in letters to Sheriff Vann—I do not think it my duty to make reports to Sheriff Vann. In the first place, I do not consider him a safe officer."[80] Stevens informed Woodul that when some of his Rangers were operating near Brownsville they arrested ten men on different charges, "and I asked them in regard to this García. They stated that two of the men whom they arrested, they investigated and released them and they do not know where they went after being released." He went on to relate that another of this group, reputed to be a professional rustler, was now in the Hidalgo County jail; another smuggler had been turned over to the army at Fort Brown. Regarding another aspect of Vann's inquiries, one of Stevens's Rangers, a Ranger Sadler, had indeed confiscated several weapons from a certain Pedro Lerma and had sent them to Stevens's headquarters. Lerma lived on the bank of the Rio Grande, "and in my judgment, these people have these guns to give to any bandit along the river on either the American or the Mexican side. Saddler [sic] took these guns for the safety of the people in this Valley."[81]

Matters became more serious. The adjutant general ordered Stevens to meet Captain Hanson in Brownsville. Together they conferred with Sheriff Vann and Judge James B. Wells, the longtime political boss and friend of the Rangers. Wells complained because Rangers were disarming Hispanics, who were becoming angry and apprehensive. Stevens said suspicious individuals were being disarmed for the public safety. Wells insisted that these people were "good Mexicans." Stevens replied that all the serious border raids were made by Hispanics, mostly residents of Cameron County, and that most of these bandit leaders "were at one time either deputy sheriffs, policemen or some other kind of officer of Cameron County or Brownsville." Furthermore, Stevens stressed that German agents and sympathizers were hard at work, and Sheriff Vann should be going after them. Stevens then expounded on why he and Vann didn't get along.[82] Local politics was a major reason. Vann was tied to Brownsville politicos, whereas, Stevens said, "the majority of the people in this valley are now mostly prosperous farmers from the northern states and are intelligent people and most all of them are with the [Hobby] Administration and for the Rangers."[83]

The Florencio García case began to take on sinister overtones. The Mexican consul inquired about his disappearance:

> The only data available that we have is that he was arrested about three weeks ago at "Las Trasquilas," (The Piper Plantation) by rangers Saddler [sic] and Locke, and that since that date, his people have not had any word of him, and that I have made every effort in my power to locate him, my efforts reached as far as Edinburg but Mr. Baker, the Sheriff, says that he never was taken there. After he was arrested at Piper Plantation, the Rangers were seen with Garcia at Point Isabel for the last time. As far as I have been able to investigate, Garcia never has been guilty of any crimes or misdemeanors in [sic] the Mexican side and there is no reason for him to remain in hiding if he were there now. We have made every effort to locate him.[84]

Then in May, Florencio García's clothing, his hat with bullet holes in it, and some bones were discovered near Point Isabel. Some Hispanics in Brownsville filed a complaint charging Rangers Sadler, Sittre, and Lock with his murder. The trio stoutly insisted that after they had arrested García they released him and that was the last they had seen of him. Stevens stood by his men: "These Rangers are all good men, and I do not think that they are guilty."[85] Moreover, he stated that "It seems to me that it is not so much in finding a dead Mexican, but ever since I have been active in breaking up some of this German spy work and German propaganda in this valley, there has been a kind of underhand work being done against my Company, either to hurt my Company, or to hurt Gov. Hobby's candidacy for Governor, for having Rangers breaking up and interfering with this German propaganda." He suggested that the adjutant general send a lawyer to represent the three accused Rangers, for the local attorneys were tied up in local politics.[86]

On May 31, the Mexican consul made an official protest to the authorities and to Governor Hobby over the disappearance and subsequent death of García, a Mexican citizen. He stated

I do not wish to be misunderstood as making or even implying a general protest against Captain Chas. Stevens and all his Company of Texas Rangers; my action is intended to cover only the three men under suspicion, to wit: Rangers Locke, Saddler and Setter [sic]. I always found Capt. Stevens willing and ready to co-operate with my office and have no cause to complain about him personally or the rest of his Company. I have known Capt. Stevens for a number of years and I consider him too honorable to protect or acquiesce any criminal or dishonorable conduct in [sic] the part of his men. He is persona grata to my Government and his choice to this section of the Border, was a source of satisfaction to us, feeling that we can rely on his sense of justice, for that is all we are asking in this matter, justice to our Citizens.[87]

Sittre, Sadler, and Lock waived examination before a justice of the peace; their bond was set at $3,000 each. Stevens was confident that there was not a shred of evidence against them, and he was most gratified because a number of citizens were ready to post bond for them regardless of the amount. In addition, people throughout the Valley were preparing to contribute money for their defense. In Stevens's view "There are only a few men around Brownsville who are against these Rangers, and they are men who stand for nothing that is good for the interest of the country." Furthermore, he blamed Sheriff Vann for the filing of the complaints against the Rangers.[88] When the Cameron County grand jury met, it returned no bill against the Rangers, citing a lack of evidence to tie them to the supposed remains of García.

In the meantime, Stevens had work to do. He reported in June that a band of twenty-four filibusters had been organized in Starr County and had crossed the river near Roma. Their leader was said to be from Rio Grande City.[89] When headquarters asked what attitude federal agents took regarding this kind of neutrality violation, Stevens replied that there was a Bureau of Investigation agent at Rio Grande City, at Mission, and at Brownsville. When the army got word of filibustering activity, strong patrols went out to try to prevent their crossing the Rio Grande. Whenever Stevens got such information he immediately notified the military and coordinated the deployment of his Rangers with that of the troops to prevent any friendly fire mishaps.[90]

Whatever notions of Mexican treachery Stevens might have had were reinforced by an incident that occurred on June 9. Stevens, his sergeant Joseph E. Baker,[91] and (ex-Ranger) Customs inspector Marcus Hines were watching some fifteen soldiers swimming their horses in the Rio Grande. One of the cavalrymen, a nonswimmer, slipped off his horse and drowned. While his comrades were trying to recover the body, a five-man patrol of the Carranza army led by a captain arrived on the scene. The captain gave permission for the Americans to come over to the Mexican side to continue the search. The Mexican patrol then went off inland.

Taking the captain at his word, a Lieutenant Schole and four soldiers crossed the river. For whatever reason they proceeded about half a mile inland, where they were confronted by the Mexican patrol, whose captain placed the Americans under arrest. The Mexicans later claimed that Schole tried to escape, and they killed him, shooting him in the back six or seven times and leaving the body lying there for a day until it was recovered. The Americans were convinced that the killing was a cold-blooded assassination by the Carranza patrol.[92]

One aspect of Stevens's work in enforcing federal laws was apprehending draft dodgers and delivering them to the military authorities so that the local registration board could conscript them: "Most all these young Mexicans who are born on the American side try to evade Registration, on the ground of being Mexican citizens. The custom of Mexicans who are born on the American side, most all are baptized on the Mexican side of the river, and they try to claim exemption from the draft, by getting a certificate from the church of their baptism, stating they were baptized."[93] But Stevens's principal mission was to keep "a close watch on the river," his territory extending from forty miles above Mercedes to Point Isabel.[94]

These nine Ranger companies, most of them stationed along the Rio Grande, constituted the State of Texas's first line of defense against trouble from Mexico. There was, in addition, Captain Sanders's Company A based at Alice, which represented a reserve source of protection for South Texas. Granted, most of the action was along or at least near the Rio Grande, but even so the available documentation leads one to suspect that by 1918 Sanders was a burned-out case, just going through the motions. This was probably due in large measure to his perennial health problems, for Sanders was a competent enough officer. Captain Hanson informed the adjutant general that a group of influential citizens of Brownsville "were very free to confess that in the past they did not like Capt. Sanders for the reason that he drank some, but when I assured them that they had a new Adjutant General, and that your policy was to fire any one from the service that drank, they said, 'Under that condition we had rather have Capt. Sanders and his men than any other Companies you could send here.'" They were adamant in that they did not want Captain Ransom.[95]

Sanders commanded a fifteen-man company with a first-rate sergeant, W. T. Grimes. Yet Grimes, who had been a Ranger in Company A for five years, the last four as sergeant, was becoming frustrated. He aspired to a captaincy, considering himself better qualified than someone with no Ranger or border experience.[96] He was right of course but oftentimes merit is not enough. Grimes finally had enough, and on May 15 he resigned for more lucrative employment as a city detective in Port Arthur.[97] Besides losing his sergeant, Captain Sanders lost his most experienced man when Edwin M. Dubose resigned on March 10. Dubose had been a deputy U.S. marshal in the 1890's, served in the Rangers under Captains Rogers and Hughes, was a mounted Customs inspector from 1903 to 1911, resigned, then reentered the Customs service in 1913. On September 1, 1917, he enlisted in Company A.[98] And Private Charles W. Price, who had been a Ranger in 1911–1912 and reenlisted on April 27, 1915, resigned on June 11, 1918, to run, successfully as it turned out, for sheriff of Jim Wells County, a position he would hold for the next 26 years. Furthermore, on December 12, Private John A. Moran died of pneumonia.[99] On top of all this, the adjutant general's department frequently borrowed some of Sanders's men for temporary assignments elsewhere.[100]

Sanders was successful in running to earth several rustlers. In cooperation with the sheriff of Nueces County, Sanders's men recovered sixteen head of cattle and arrested three cow thieves—two Hispanics and one Anglo, "a noted cow thief here for years," taking them to jail in Alice. Several weeks later, Company A Rangers arrested three Hispanics who had stolen a bunch of horses from the King Ranch; they took the prisoners to jail in Falfurrias. And in Jim Wells County the Rangers' activities resulted in eight felony indictments. Sanders was moving with the times—he had an automobile, yet another straw in the wind indicating that the horseback Ranger was gradually fading away. But as for Sanders himself, he was just trying to hang on. As he informed Harley in June, "My health is improving, but not able to do a great deal yet." He would like to go home to Lockhart for a few days.[101]

There was one more Ranger company in the field, the only one not within striking distance of the border: Captain Henry Lee Ransom's Company C at Sweetwater. Ransom was stationed there for two main reasons. First, a big oil strike at the nearby town of Ranger, which virtually overnight became a boomtown where anything went. Second, several feuds and contract killings in the Post, Snyder, and Sweetwater area, conflicts such as the Sims-Johnson feud, and the assassination of District Judge Cullen C. Higgins while he was eating supper. The adjutant general perhaps felt that a hard man like Captain Ransom was needed to keep this volatile situation from getting completely out of hand.

As if he didn't have enough to contend with, Ransom learned that one of his men had been done in by ham and eggs. Ranger W. E. Hodge was eating breakfast at a local hotel and ordered his usual ham and eggs. When informed that it was a meatless day as per the regulations of the federal Food Administration, he threw a fit in the dining room. The proprietor finally agreed to serve him what he wanted. The other diners were scandalized by Hodge's apparent lack of patriotism. Somebody complained to the adjutant general, who was furious, since the incident hardly enhanced the image of the Rangers. He ordered Hodge to be summarily fired, on February 15. The bewildered Hodge appealed for reinstatement, stressing that the incident had been a misunderstanding and professing his patriotism.[102] The adjutant general relented, and Hodge was indeed reinstated, on March 1, but on July 1 he resigned and went home to Brownwood.

The Hodge affair distracted Ransom from his main concern, to solve the murder of Judge Higgins. This he did, arresting three men and jailing them in Sweetwater. The man who actually killed the judge allegedly hanged himself in the jail. Yet Ransom requested two more men to help him with his ongoing investigation of the violence in the area and insisted that it was his right to select them, as he was the one held responsible.[103]

This proved to be Captain Ransom's last case. On the night of April 1, he was in his room on the second floor of the Wright Hotel in Sweetwater when Marion Long and W. C. Miller began arguing in the corridor over family matters and then started shooting at each other. Ransom, who was already in his night clothes, opened his door and stepped into the hall to tell them to cut it out. He took a bullet from Long in the left shoulder that ranged upward through his left jaw. Death was almost instantaneous. Both shooters immediately fled, but Ranger William H. Koon took up the pursuit, firing a shot at Long, who quickly surrendered. Miller made it out of town in his automobile but Koon pursued him and, after a high-speed chase ending when Miller wrecked his car, Koon arrested him as well. Ransom's sergeant, the veteran Sam McKenzie, was keeping order in the town of Post when his captain was killed. He rushed to Sweetwater and very competently took charge. Among other things, he requested an additional couple of Rangers, and he also made the arrangements to ship Ransom's body back to his home in Hempstead.[104] Those who live by the sword . . .

Ransom was barely cold when applications for his job started to flood into Austin. For example, some citizens of Ysleta petitioned Harley on April 3 to promote Sergeant McKenzie, citing his seventeen years of border service. Tom Hickman, who had been bombarding the adjutant general for months with applications for a Ranger captaincy, reapplied on April 2.[105] To the disappointment of a lot of people Harley decided, for budgetary reasons, not to replace Ransom. Instead, Sergeant McKenzie would run Company C, which he did in his usual efficient manner.[106]

Though the captains of the Ranger companies in the field were the ones who were in the public eye and who generated publicity, by far the most powerful captain of all was a man who kept a low profile and often operated behind the scenes—the Ranger most people have never heard of, Captain William Martin Hanson.

CHAPTER FIFTEEN

HANSON'S EMPIRE

WILLIAM Martin Hanson was a phenomenon in the history of the Ranger Force. Whether one liked Hanson or not (and many did not), the man had a positive genius for self-promotion—not the superficial kind exemplified earlier by Captain Bill McDonald, whose pithy sayings were fodder for reporters, but the kind of self-promotion that translated into real power. In a remarkably short time Hanson built himself an empire within the Ranger organization.

He was born in February, 1866, at Rancho, Gonzales County, where in 1888 he began his law enforcement career as a deputy sheriff. He moved up to deputy U.S. marshal for the Southern District of Texas in 1892, serving at Rio Grande City and Laredo. In 1902 he was appointed U.S. marshal for that district. In 1906 Hanson was reappointed, but he resigned and made a major career change—he moved to Mexico and for the next eight years engaged in the oil and land business mainly around Tampico and Veracruz. He was an officer in the Mexico Land Company, the Tamesi Petroleum and Asphalt Company, the Standard Petroleum Company and a multi-state citrus growers association. Hanson also acquired the 3,000-acre Hacienda Guadalupe near Ciudad Victoria, Tamaulipas. The Mexican Revolution devastated all these enterprises. Hanson's misfortunes culminated in 1914, when his hacienda was seized by the carrancistas, who briefly imprisoned him and then expelled him from Mexico as a huertista spy.[1] Hanson claimed that the charge of espionage was merely a pretext for the carrancistas to confiscate his property.

Either version seemed equally credible. Hanson's hacienda could well have been arbitrarily confiscated, for the logistics of the Mexican Revolution consisted largely of seizing other people's property in the name of the cause. On the other hand, Hanson's past and future activities involved close contacts with Mexican conservatives. He had worked for the Díaz administration as a private detective in 1911, directing a group of informants and secret agents monitoring the activities of Mexican revolutionists in San Antonio.[2] Thus, it is entirely likely that in 1914 he was spying on behalf of the Huerta regime. Hanson returned to the United States as a refugee. He soon settled in San Antonio, where his friend, Duval West, who had been one of President Wilson's emissaries to Mexico, appointed Hanson as chief special agent for the San Antonio, Uvalde & Gulf Railroad, of which West was the receiver.[3] But Hanson by no means spent all his energies on his day job. In June, 1915, an informant in San Antonio notified the War Department that:

> I have seen a letter, written by one J. B. Wood, now in El Paso, formerly a resident of Torreon, Mexico, and a personal friend of [U.S. Consul] Geo. B. Carothers, in which he stated that Orozco and Salazar were rendezvousing at Casas Grandes, about 80 miles from Juarez, and that their agents were there in El Paso enlisting men for another revolution, and that recruits were leaving El Paso daily, amounting to several hundred, and were crossing the river at the smelter.
>
> This letter was addressed to one W. M. Hanson of this city, formerly U.S. Marshal for the Southeastern District in Texas, and who is now claim agent for the S.A., U. & G. Ry, urging him to locate and close a deal for a large quantity of 7 m/m ammunition, which was supposed to be in San Antonio, as he had a buyer for it, who would pay for it laid down at El Paso. The quantity of this ammunition is reported to be about 5,000,000 rounds, and was accumulated here some months ago when [Gen. Félix] Diaz [Porfirio Díaz's nephew] was making plans to start a revolution in Mexico.
>
> Knowing my extensive acquaintance with Mexicans of all classes, Hanson endeavored to enlist my services in locating and buying this ammunition. When I declined to assist him, he turned his efforts in other directions, and is now trying to obtain the ammunition, which has been moved from San Antonio to another location. This information is given you in strict confidence, as I cannot afford to have it known that have given same.[4]

Hanson realized that a Texas Ranger commission would be invaluable in both his clandestine and legitimate endeavors. As a railroad special agent, Hanson had obtained a Bexar County deputy sheriff's commission, but like other railroad special agents he wanted a Special Ranger commission, which would give him authority in all the counties where his railroad operated.[5] Hanson's application had powerful support; his friend Colonel F. A. Chapa warmly endorsed him. And the secretary of the Texas State Council of Defense even nominated him for

Ranger captain, citing Hanson's border experience and stating: "I take it that we want to keep and protect the good Mexican even more than we want to throw a scare into the bad one. He will accomplish both ends."[6] Hanson received his Special Ranger commission on December 24, 1917. He requested that if he were to be attached to a company that it be Company A, whose captain was his life-long friend John J. Sanders.[7]

Hanson was no ordinary Special Ranger. He understood that knowledge is power. It will be recalled that he had provided the Bureau of Investigation with valuable information regarding the Plan de San Diego, and he continued to supply that agency with intelligence on Mexico. One can reasonably speculate that his conservative anti-Carranza contacts provided that information. Once the United States entered World War I, Hanson repeatedly furnished the War and Justice Departments with information, expanding his network of informants.[8] Now in his capacity as Special Ranger he began supplying Ranger headquarters with reports on Mexican matters, employing his contacts in that country. Much of the information was based on rumor and hearsay, and some of it proved to be worthless, but it was no more unreliable than the Mexican information the Bureau of Investigation was receiving from its own sources. Hanson used this informal intelligence connection to lobby quietly for appointment as a Ranger captain.[9] His efforts paid off. Explaining that the Ranger appropriation was limited, Woodul nevertheless told Hanson that "I trust that in time we will be able to have you with us."[10] Woodul was an effective advocate. During a visit to San Antonio, Harley met with Hanson at the Gunter Hotel and was favorably impressed. On January 31, 1918, Hanson was commissioned as a Ranger captain and was placed on active duty.[11]

The new Ranger captain was fifty-two years old, married, six feet one-half inches tall, had a fair complexion, gray eyes, and light hair. He was also supremely confident. He used the title of "Special Investigator for the Adjutant General of Texas," and he intended to paint on a very large canvas. The day Hanson was commissioned the adjutant general wrote to Secretary of State Lansing that Hanson was applying for a passport "into Mexico with a request that same be given him with the right to enter at any port of entry on the Texas border." Harley explained that:

> His business in going over into Mexico is that of investigating in a quiet way reports of impending outbreaks by Mexican bandits along the Texas border and to furnish the department with all information relative to border conditions. He is a perfectly reliable man who can be depended upon to get information in an inoffensive way without causing the least friction with any Government officials across the river. In fact he is furnishing us with necessary information which is procured mostly by associating with men of

affairs in Mexico, and we are very desirous of his having a passport that will give him the right to go into Mexico at any place and at any time that his judgment warrants that he should.[12]

Evidently Hanson's better judgment prevailed; since the carrancistas had expelled him as a spy, and since they now controlled northern Mexico, it was barely possible that if he were caught snooping around in that country they just might stand him up against a wall and shoot him full of holes. It would appear that he never crossed the border.

Yet as the Rangers' one-man intelligence service there was plenty for Hanson to do on this side of the Rio Grande. There was, for example, the whole matter of combating disloyalty. The day before he was commissioned, Hanson received a letter denouncing certain German sympathizers, including the Lutheran pastor, at Kenedy. Hanson soon assigned Ranger Conrad P. Engelking to investigate such subversion. Engelking reported that the whole affair was largely a squabble between preachers: The Methodist minister had denounced his Lutheran counterpart. But since many German-Americans lived in the area, they bore watching.[13]

Working out of his office in the Calcasieu Building in San Antonio, Hanson set about learning everything he could about both the Rangers and the anti-Carranza exile community. Since keeping track of the latter was a tall order, Hanson asked Harley whether he should concentrate on exile activity or on trying to prevent raids from Mexico.[14] Harley had him do both—in addition to keeping an eye on subversives.

As yet another additional duty, Hanson carried out confidential assignments. In February Harley dispatched him to Marfa to investigate the political reliability of Captain Fox. The Democratic primary would be held in July, and ex-Governor Ferguson was making a bid to defeat Governor Hobby. Fox was reportedly a Ferguson man, and it was rumored that he had been distributing Ferguson campaign literature. Hanson informed Fox that his was just a good-will visit to present Hobby's compliments. All the while Hanson was having confidential talks with H. M. Fennell of the Marfa State Bank, to whom he explained his mission. Fennell reassured Hanson that Fox had not been working on Ferguson's behalf, and the banker had good things to say about Fox. Hanson also sounded out the leading ranchers, with the same result. Interestingly, Hanson reported that "I finally suggested to Captain Fox that I was of the opinion that it would be very much appreciated if Marfa had a strong 'Hobby Club' but of course he could not have anything to do with it. He caught the cue and said no I can not openly, but I have a friend that can, and within two hours his friend showed up with a list of fifteen signatures of the best men in Presidio County, who are now forming the club, and who absolutely control that county."[15]

While he was, with a wink and a nod, organizing Hobby supporters in Marfa, publicly Hanson stressed to the civic leaders that "I made it strong that at this time, you [Harley] were not paying any attention to politics"— rather, according to Hanson, Harley was helping the president win the war and was keeping Texas safe from "the Bandits of Mexico." They loved it, and asked what they could do to help. In conclusion, Hanson stated that "I believe Capt. Fox is loyal to the core and that he is doing his full duty, and giving entire satisfaction to the good people of that section."[16]

Shortly afterward Hanson made a flying visit to Brownsville to check on conditions there. He informed Harley that he had first stopped over at Norias, where he "met our mutual friend Caesar Kleberg, and discussed all matters with him." Kleberg would see to it that Hobby clubs were formed in all adjoining counties and would get the mayor of Corpus Christi busy on Hobby's behalf. Proceeding on to Brownsville, where "the new comers are trying to put out the crowd that controls the Mexican vote," Hanson met with James B. Wells, who was also using his influence in support of Hobby. Incidentally, Hanson mentioned that Hidalgo County was experiencing a political scandal; the county treasurer and ex-sheriff, John Closner, had come up short $164,000 and was forced to resign.

As for the Rangers, Hanson reported that:

> The friends of the Rangers who are largely in the majority say the exodus of Mexicans to Mexico was on account of the draft, and that but for the Rangers very few Mexicans would be there now, that they are as afraid of the Bandit gangs as the Citizens of this country. I think this is correct and true. You understand that there are two very bitter parties in that section. The Democrats are largely in the majority and represent the best citizenship of that country, the other the Republicans depend on some good citizens and the floating Mexican population, and as a rule they resort to all methods possible to get that vote. This leads them on line that makes it dangerous to the peace and welfare of that section, for in order to secure and hold them, they have to appeal to the prejudices and is [sic] natural with them, against all officers and it is quite easy sometimes to pick glaring flaws where there are in reality none. The Rangers may have made some mistakes in that section in the past, but the conditions were such that any red blooded human would have done just as they did in the great majority of cases. I feel sure that under your administration we will be able to wipe all this out, and make this Ranger service the very best Texas has ever enjoyed.[17]

Back in San Antonio, Hanson turned his attention to Mexican affairs. He informed Harley that a prominent Mexican, A. Elordy, claiming to be a secret representative of President Carranza en route to New York on a secret mission (which could not have been very secret) was registered at the Saint Anthony Hotel. Hanson dispatched a friend of his pretending to be a reporter for the *San Antonio Express* to interview Elordy. Although Elordy was rather cagey in his answers, he "intimated that his Government was in full accord with Germany in all things." Hanson suggested that Elordy be kept under surveillance while in New York, but added "I will also ask that you do not let any one know from whom you received this information, as I KNOW BY EXPERIENCE that there are leaks there, and often Carranza knows about information furnished and by whom from this end of the line. The value of my work in all things will be (of this nature) more valuable if the Federal Government does not know the source of your information."[18]

A few days later Hanson was on the road again, this time to Laredo. There, it will be recalled, he and Captain Ryan met with General Bernardo de la Garza on the international bridge and discussed matters of mutual concern. While in Laredo, Hanson received a letter from his friend M. A. Spellacy, an American oil man in Tampico, commenting on current conditions. Spellacy was a wealthy anti-carrancista, referring to the Carranza government as "the present scum," and Hanson stated that "I can get much valuable information all along from him."[19] The Ranger captain also had long talks with the Mexican consul and with prominent Mexican conservative exiles in Laredo who, according to Hanson, were both anti-Carranza and anti-German. He also interviewed two more Americans doing business in Mexico about conditions there. They wanted only Harley to know their names, for they feared leaks higher up, which would result in their ruin. Hanson ended his report with "I will discuss personally with Major Woodul other matters of which I cannot write with reference to the betterment of the Ranger service and existing conditions."[20]

Hanson spent only short interludes in San Antonio, but he demonstrated an ability to keep many balls in the air. For instance, it was he who asked Marshall Hicks to wire Attorney General Gregory protesting the cancellation of Ranger railroad passes.[21] And Hanson continued to enlarge his network of informants. One of them, Robert Hazelrigg of San Antonio, reported that the anti-Carranza factions had finally agreed on a leader. Instructing Hazelrigg to keep him posted, the peripatetic Hanson was off on another fact-finding trip, this time to Alice and Edinburg to confer with Captains Sanders and Stevens, then to Austin to report to Harley.[22]

On this trip he stopped in at Kingsville to see Robert J. Kleberg, who needed to be soothed. Kleberg was upset because he had been told that Captain Stevens planned to run for sheriff of Hidalgo County against incumbent A. Y. Baker. Kleberg believed that Colonel F. A. Chapa was behind the move, as Chapa "had been booming Stevens very highly in his [news]papers as being a great friend to the Mexicans and to him they were referred to redress all their wrongs." Kleberg told Hanson that his source for this was Tom East. Hanson interviewed East, who told him in strict confidence that ex-sheriff Oscar Thompson and Henry Edds of Hebbronville were his informants, and they had gotten their information from a Ranger that Stevens had fired. Both Edds and Kleberg requested that Stevens be transferred, as they didn't feel confident that he would protect their interests and property. They urged that Captain Wright be assigned to their territory. Kleberg also related how he'd rejected ex-Governor Ferguson's overtures and was actively supporting Hobby. Hanson hastened to assure them that Harley had anticipated their need for protection from bandits and that in fact was the reason for Hanson's trip. He assured them that Stevens had no ambition to be sheriff and that Colonel Chapa knew absolutely nothing about the matter, that Chapa was a friend of the Ranger service and was all in favor of Stevens being transferred to the Big Bend. As Hanson proudly reported, "I left them in good shape and pacified."[23]

Hanson then met Captain Stevens in Brownsville and broached the idea of Stevens transferring to the Big Bend, stressing "that matters were not in good shape there, and that we thought with his acquaintanceship and long service in that region under Carranza, that he would be of more service to the State than where he was." Stevens was unenthusiastic at first but warmed to the idea of a transfer, but he wanted to be stationed at Ysleta and allowed to visit El Paso to gather information. As we have seen, it was finally decided to keep Stevens in the Lower Valley. After talking with Stevens, Hanson concluded that Robert Kleberg's charges about him were untrue. Hanson also talked with several substantial farmers, all of whom praised Stevens, although "some of them do not think he is pursuing the right course in as they say, 'Petting the Mexicans,' but they like him."

On his way back to San Antonio, Hanson rode the train with Caesar Kleberg, explained everything to Kleberg's entire satisfaction, and asked him to inform Robert Kleberg and Tom East. Caesar Kleberg said he liked Captain Stevens but still wanted him transferred. Kleberg did not feel secure about his 40,000 head of cattle with an inexperienced officer like Stevens between him and the Rio Grande. He "strongly suggested" that Captain Wright be assigned to Zapata, Starr, and Hidalgo Counties and Captain Sanders be given Cameron County, and that Sanders station two men at Norias, two at Nopal, two at Raymondville, and two at Harlingen. Further, he suggested that Sanders move his headquarters to Harlingen and that Sanders and Wright get together and work out a plan for mutual assistance. Hanson listened attentively to all these suggestions and reported them to Harley; they were both keenly aware that these powerful ranchers must not be offended.

While in Brownsville Hanson had also met with exiled General F. R. Betancourt, a Díaz and Huerta supporter whom Hanson had known for years. The Ranger captain debriefed Betancourt in company with an army intelligence captain from Fort McIntosh. Betancourt promised that as anti-Carranza forces gained control of Mexico they would hand over all fugitive murderers, including the Plan de San Diego leaders de la Rosa and Pizaña. As Hanson said "I do not vouch for any statement he makes, for he is after all a Mexican, but I think he is true to us."[24]

This time when Hanson returned to San Antonio he had a long discussion with the head of the felicista movement in Texas, the exiled politician Nemesio García Naranjo, who claimed, incorrectly as events proved, that the Carranza government was disintegrating. Hanson passed this information on to the head of the Bureau of Investigation's San Antonio office, Charles Breniman.[25]

More importantly, that same day, February 28, Hanson made his bid for bureaucratic power. He had already convinced Harley that he was a virtually indispensable intelligence chief for the Ranger Force. Reflecting this, Harley had authorized Hanson to use Ranger Engelking for investigations whenever he wanted.[26] But Hanson wanted much more. In a letter to Harley entitled "Investigation Department," Hanson began by hoping that the adjutant general would not think him officious, for his only desire was to add luster to the administration of Harley, and of Governor Hobby. Reminding Harley that the latter had already established an "investigation bureau" with Hanson in charge, the Ranger captain made a series of suggestions designed to make the bureau one of the glories of Hobby's administration. The Ranger Force currently consisted of ten companies of fifteen men each (plus a captain). The law allowed Harley to appoint as many Special Rangers as he deemed necessary, but these unpaid Rangers were of little direct benefit to the department. What was lacking was an organization that could enforce unpopular laws, like Prohibition, which some sheriffs ignored, fearing defeat at the polls, and also deal with an "Anti-American vote that is very strong," nipping disloyalty in the bud.

This being the case, Hanson argued, how about reducing each Ranger company by one man, each man currently costing the state between $80 and $90 a month in salary, rations, and horse feed. Use the money saved to fund the Investigation Department. Every county would benefit in terms of better law enforcement. This would not cost a cent more, and the adjutant general's department would benefit greatly. "The present Ranger force would not be less efficient, would do their same work, and would be a part of this organization (the Investigation Department)." Hanson added:

My idea of this force would be to attach every Special Ranger in the State to this Department, without pay, but in return for this privilege of being a Special Ranger they would be asked to report all violations of law in their sections to us for attention, and hold themselves ready to assist *when necessary* in the execution of the law. I would then invite every Sheriff in Texas to join this organization, and work in connection with us in all things, but especially in the enforcement of the pending laws. Then let your *confidential friends* in each county suggest say ten Special Rangers for appointment.[27]

After discussing the details, Hanson reiterated that "with such a force, and unity of action, in every county in the state, we would have Texas absolutely under perfect control right from the start, and not have to experiment with any phase of it. Most of the work could be done from HQ."[28]

Having made this suggestion, breathtaking in its audacity and scope and with enormous law enforcement and political implications, Hanson presented his wish list: a two-room office, a telephone, a GOOD office man, and one outside helper, preferably a young lawyer. He assured Harley that "I can perfect this organization to your entire satisfaction, and will deliver the goods and make this Department one of your very best efforts. In case we was [sic] short of help or any rush we would always have the Ranger Companies to draw from." And speaking of the Ranger companies, "if we get the passes renewed, so much the better, but if not and it is not against the law, I can get transportation from all Rail Roads by having them name each one of our force as Special Agents." This suggestion was creative but not feasible. What was feasible, however, was Hanson's proposed Investigation Department being a semiautonomous entity: He shrewdly suggested that because of the Mexican troubles the headquarters for the Department be in San Antonio rather than Austin, "for reasons you are familiar with." But he hastened to assure Harley that everything would be done in duplicate, with a copy to the adjutant general, who would direct all the movements of the Department and handle all the finances. He asked Harley to let him know what he thought.[29]

While Harley digested this grandiose proposal, Hanson concentrated on gathering intelligence about Mexico. Since he talked almost exclusively with conservative exiles, he necessarily formed a skewed view of conditions in that country. For example, he informed Harley that not only was he getting good Mexican information, but he had been promised an introduction to the next president.[30] He also called on the head of the Bureau of Investigation's San Antonio office, Breniman, to learn whether "the U.S. would let up on anti-Carranza forces or not." Breniman replied that his department never went on record in such matters and in any case he was busy with more important investigations. Hanson concluded from this that the Bureau was monitoring Mexican exile activity but was taking no action for violations of the neutrality laws.[31] Presumably Hanson informed his exile contacts that they probably had a free hand to plot against Carranza.

Though concentrating on Mexican matters, Hanson did not neglect the Rangers, informing Harley that "Some complaint is being made of the Rangers along the border holding up Mexicans who cross at other than the ports. This is knocking farmers out of labor. Think it would be wise to indicate to them that this is no violation of the state law, and unless called in not to bother them. I can say to them in a round about way without it coming from you that this is the wrong way to do, provided it meets with your approval."[32] Hanson then turned to the food situation, which was very acute on the border—"the people are hungry and will get desperate soon, and we may look for much trouble unless they are allowed to get work and food."[33]

Hanson continued to gather intelligence on Mexico from whatever source he could, whether in San Antonio or along the border. His old friend Porfirio P. García, of the International Livestock Company of San Antonio, gave his views on pro-German sentiment in Mexico and among Hispanics—Germans were liked, gringos were hated, German propagandists were having a field day, and the Carranza regime was pro-German to the core.[34] Hanson also secured a statement from Fernando de la Garza, formerly assistant chief of detectives in Monterrey, who was an ardent pro-American and a rabid anti-carrancista. Ed Watt, manager of the Mexican Petroleum Company at Tampico, spoke with Hanson while on a visit to San Antonio and expressed a willingness to speak freely to Harley provided his name was kept secret. Hanson urged Harley to see him and sent a list of questions to ask Watt.[35] At the request of Agent Breniman, Hanson interviewed a newly arrived exile, General Francisco Coss, at the latter's home in San Antonio.[36] He soon rushed off to El Paso to hear what a villista source had to say. On the way he stopped off in Marfa to investigate the actions of Captain Fox's men and to secure affidavits about the Porvenir massacre.[37] It will be remembered that he urged Harley to go public with the facts in order to forestall the revelations about to appear as a result of the army's investigation of the affair; Colonel Langhorne had furnished Hanson with a memorandum covering the events.[38]

After a brief sojourn in San Antonio, Hanson was again on the move, this time to Laredo. He learned of a German in Nuevo Laredo who was suspected of being a conduit for intelligence gathered in the United States. Hanson assigned a Mexican to ferret out the particulars. As usual, Hanson interviewed Americans working in Mexico, on this occasion two geologists. He also passed along to the Bureau of Investigation information about Dr. Fernando López, an eye specialist in Laredo whom he suspected of carrying documents from German propagandists in the United States to Mexico City and Cuba.[39]

The Ranger captain returned briefly to San Antonio, leaving for Eagle Pass the same day. There he conferred with Lieutenant B. H. Hamby, the intelligence officer at Camp Eagle Pass.[40] The indefatigable Hanson then proceeded to Brownsville, where a Mexican raid was rumored. He received a letter from Woodul that indicates the esteem in which Caesar Kleberg was held: "Be sure to give Mr. Caesar Kleberg my very best regards. In this respect I believe it would not hurt if you were to tell Captain Stephens [sic] that every time he lends a kindly ear to advice from Mr. Caesar it will please the department. I know Mr. Kleberg can be of great assistance to Captain Stephens [sic]."[41]

The rumored raid on Brownsville led by German sympathizers never materialized.[42] On Woodul's instruction Hanson returned to San Antonio and called on Major General John W. Ruckman, commander of the Southern Department. Ruckman allowed as how he hadn't put much stock in the rumor but had nevertheless taken the necessary precautions. Ruckman, Hanson reported, "seems very sanguine that we are to have a lot of trouble along the border, and I told him that every Ranger in Texas was subject to his call on all border raids and Etc. and he was very much pleased. He asked me to call on him every time I returned from the border and to simply state that I had a previous engagement and walk in."[43] Having this kind of access to the commanding general of the Southern Department didn't hurt Hanson's ego one little bit.

The next day Hanson was at Norias. He notified Harley that General Ruckman planned to tour the border, and that Robert Kleberg had asked Hanson to invite the adjutant general as his guest. Furthermore, Governor Hobby himself planned a border tour of inspection "with a view of cutting a half mile wide stretch along the River in order to better guard the river from the marauding Mexicans." Not only that, but some army commanders favored creating a zone along the river under exclusive federal control. Hanson was sure the State of Texas would never agree to this. Caesar Kleberg was in favor not just of clearing brush inland for half a mile along the river; he wanted it cleared for several miles. Kleberg invited Hanson to accompany the dignitaries on their tour. He hoped to do so, with Harley's permission, but first he was heading for Brownsville to investigate the raid on the East Ranch. A Mexican informant would meet him in Brownsville with the particulars.[44] Hanson and Caesar Kleberg traveled together to Brownsville, where Hanson met with James Wells and Colonel Herbert Slocum, commander of the Brownsville Patrol District, as well as a group of leading citizens.[45] He also sent Harley an extensive report on "Mexico matters" that stressed that the anti-Carranza factions had agreed on a plan to overthrow the regime. This information was given to Hanson in strictest confidence by a Bureau of Investigation agent and had been obtained by intercepting a letter written on March 14, 1918, from Mexico City to an address in New York City. Hanson ended his report on a tantalizing note—he'd learned that General Emiliano Nafarrate, who had figured so prominently in the Plan de San Diego affair in 1915, had been assassinated in Tampico.[46]

Hanson later elaborated on Nafarrate's murder:

I also have information, that I consider to be perfectly reliable, that General Naffertte [sic], who was actually at Tampico a few days ago, wired Carranza to recognize Cabellero [sic][47] as Governor of Tamaulipas, and send him to that state immediately, or he would go to Tampico, and furnish the press of that city and the United States Consul copies of Carranza's telegrams, letters, and documents that he, Naffertte [sic], received in 1915, in which he was ordered to invade Texas for the purpose of forcing our Government to recognize him as President of Mexico. It seems that Carranza did not comply with this request and when Nafertte [sic] arrived at Tampico, and before he could carry out his threat, was murdered by Carranza's orders.[48]

This version was corroborated by the Bureau of Investigation's sources. It seems that at around 3 a.m. on the morning of April 12, Nafarrate was foully murdered in Tampico, shot down while taking care of business in a local whorehouse. He was reportedly killed on Carranza's order to prevent him from publicizing that Carranza had instructed him to mount Plan de San Diego raids into Texas in 1915 in order to force United States diplomatic recognition of the Carranza regime.[49] In a classic bit of bureaucratese Agent Van Curtis wrote: "If General Nafarrate has been killed—which I believe to be a fact, it will not be necessary to submit a further report re his activities."

While in Brownsville, Hanson continued to develop information about German activities both in Mexico and in the Lower Valley, reporting his findings to Harley.[50] But some of his time was spent in clandestine political work on Governor Hobby's behalf. He chortled to Woodul that Lawrence Bates had been there three weeks working for Ferguson, and a Ferguson orator had arrived the previous night, but to no avail—Hobby would carry Cameron County decisively. "Don't be uneasy, I will not make any breaks, every track covered and Hobby stock at 'PAR.'"[51]

Illustrating the political crosscurrents in Cameron County, Sheriff Vann wrote to Hanson that two months earlier, in Austin, Governor Hobby had promised Vann to appoint Everett W. Anglin of Harlingen as Ranger captain for that district. Anglin's mother, incidentally, was Hanson's cousin. Vann now pressed for Anglin's appointment as successor to the slain Captain Ransom. Hanson wrote a note to Harley on the letter: "This for your information. Advise no action be taken at this time."[52]

Sheriff Vann also complained to Hanson about the actions of Captain Stevens:

When you were down here some time ago you were in the office to see me and we had an agreement regarding my co-operation with the rangers on the border all of which I am ready and more than willing to do but I would like for them to co-operate with me also; there has not been a single ranger in my office or even called me up or conferred with me on any proposition since before you were here. They have arrested several parties I understand and carried some of them to the Military Guard house and others to County jail in Hidalgo County and there has been several parties here trying to find out the whereabouts of parties that have been arrested by them and I do not know what they are being held for.

Now Captain, some time ago there were Four men arrested by the Rangers up at Lyford for theft and brought down here to my jail and I was asked by the Rangers not to let them out on bond but they had already had an Examining trial and their bond set at $400.00 each so when their friends and people produced the bond I released them, I had to do it as it does not matter what a man is charged with he is entitled to an examining trial and if it is not a Capital felony case, he is entitled to bond and every man under the laws of the great State of Texas, is presumed to be inocent [sic] until his guilt is established in some Court of jurisdiction.

I re-iterate the fact that I want to co-operate with the rangers and [am] perfectly willing to do so but I do not like to be snubbed and have them sneak around and do things like this and not say a word about it to me. You are the last man on the Ranger force that I spoke to; it seems they shun me and I feel awfully hurt about it to a certain extent. I wrote to Captain Stevens two or three times and got no answer and am writing him again today. Do you think this is co-operating?

To which Hanson added:

General Harley:

Think I will go to Brownsville in a day or two and will look into this matter. I think Capt. Stevens does not work with Vann because Van [sic] turns the thieves loose faster than he can catch them. I will straighten this out without any friction when I get there. I will not write Vann but see him in person."[53]

Stevens, for his part, had no use for Sheriff Vann. On July 15, he sent Woodul a clipping from the Brownsville newspaper relating the killing of a prominent farmer, R. A. Cunningham. Stevens indignantly asserted that:

This is one of the results of the interference of Sheriff Vann with the Rangers and of leaving these thiefs [sic] out on straw bonds. Both the American and the Mexican people are very sore at Sheriff Vann for this happening. Sheriff Vann now wants the Rangers, but I think he has changed his notion too late, for the people of Cameron County.

I was at the place of the killing with four Rangers, and I have the names of two of the men who were implicated in the killing. They are on other

Mexican side, and I have seen the Mexican Authorities and they have promised me to apprehend these men.

The Rangers arrested six cattle thiefs [sic] for stealing cattle in the locality of the killing, two days before the killing, and they were released on small bonds the same day that they were arrested. Two of those men are implicated in this murder.

On the day of the killing, I sent my Rangers one way with the officers on a trail, and I had a posse of ten Mexican citizens with me. These Mexicans were very much interested and wanted to assist in the capture of the murderers, and I took them with me, to show them that I had confidence in them and to show them that I did not blame the good Mexicans for the actions of the bad Mexicans.

The good citizens, both the Americans and the Mexicans, are getting stronger every day for Gov. Hobby. I am saying nothing politically for any one locally, just looking out strictly for Gov. Hobby's candidacy.[54]

Hanson maintained his accustomed pace of traveling up and down the border gathering intelligence. In April, there were disturbing indications that Carranza was massing troops on the Rio Grande, causing concern not just to Hanson but to the army and Bureau of Investigation as well. There was also speculation that Carranza had designs on the vital Tampico oilfields, which so far had been protected by the regional strongman General Manuel Peláez.[55] Even though Hanson diligently pursued his duty of monitoring Mexican affairs, a glorious new opportunity had recently presented itself.

Texas took a back seat to no one when it came to patriotism. Accordingly, a bill was introduced in the legislature making any conceivable act of disloyalty a felony, punishable by not less than two years nor more than twenty-five years in the state penitentiary. This draconian measure was passed in both the House and Senate by unanimous vote, and on March 11, 1918, Governor Hobby signed it into law effective immediately.[56] Obviously, some mechanism had to be created to enforce the Hobby Loyalty Act, and someone had to direct that mechanism. The logical choice was Captain William Martin Hanson.

The adjutant general reviewed the proposal that Hanson had submitted on February 28 for a vastly enhanced Investigation Department and implemented significant portions of it. Harley created the Loyalty Secret Service Department, with Hanson as its head. There would be a Loyalty Ranger Force of three picked men per county in Texas. The organization's headquarters were located at 618 Frost Building, San Antonio. Hanson would have a staff of one Ranger sergeant and two assistants. Harley described the duties of this force: "to act as a secret service department for the State and to work in conjunction with all Federal, State, county and municipal officers in the execution of all State laws, especially House bill No. 15, better known as the "Hobby Loyalty Act." Lest there be any doubt about the Loyalty Rangers being "real Rangers," a Loyalty Ranger was a type of Special Ranger and "will have the same authority as a Regular State Ranger but without compensation."[57]

Hanson must have been ecstatic. He got to run his own show, for the Loyalty Secret Service Department was indeed semiautonomous, though Hanson duly kept Harley informed. And Hanson's intelligence empire now encompassed the entire state. As of late September, 1918, Hanson claimed there were "about eight hundred Loyalty Rangers, not less than three in each county."[58] However, only 476 can be identified from the service records, but even so this was a respectable command. Hanson doubtless felt that sitting in his San Antonio office building a statewide intelligence network sure beat leading a Ranger company in the hot sun somewhere along the border.

Hanson spelled out, with Harley's approval, the duties of a Loyalty Ranger:

FIRST Your commission as Special Ranger entitles you to all the rights and privileges given any peace officer in the State of Texas, with reference to the execution of the State laws.

SECOND It is the desire of this Department that you work in harmony, at all times, with your local peace officers, as far as it is possible.

THIRD In case you hear of any violation of House Bill No. 15, better known as the "Hobby Loyalty Act," you will at once get statements from witnesses, sworn to if possible, and forward to this office for further instructions. This also applies to suspects in your county, who you think should be investigated.

FOURTH In case it becomes necessary for an arrest to be made the process will be served by your local peace officers, providing they care to do so. If for any reason they refuse, then you may be called upon to act, after receiving instructions from this office.

FIFTH You are to serve only in your county, and will not be called out, unless something extraordinary happens.

SIXTH Special Ranger appointments are made mainly for the purpose of assisting our local officers in the execution of the "Hobby Loyalty Act," and for the further purpose of assisting our government in every way possible, especially during this war. You are not expected to, in any way, execute local laws unless called upon by your local officers to do so. You are not expected to make arrests, but are supposed to work under cover as much as possible, and in a secret capacity, and report all disloyal occurrences to this office for instructions.[59]

The service records make it possible to reconstruct the composition of the Loyalty Rangers. Reflecting the rural nature of Texas at the time, nearly half were farmers or ranchers: 101 farmers, 56 stock farmers, and 69 ranchers. The next largest categories were merchants (48), followed by peace officers (21), bankers (18), real estate agents (16), lawyers (13), managers (13), bureaucrats (8), druggists (7), doctors (7), salesmen (6), and barbers (6). Many other occupations were represented, but each by five or fewer individuals.

Even for a workaholic like Hanson the task of getting organized was daunting. The Loyalty Rangers were a type of Special Ranger and the policy was to have Special Ranger applicants get their sheriff's endorsement before a commission was issued. Even more complicated was the process of ensuring that only reliable men were nominated. They had to be reliable not only in terms of patriotism and performance of their duties, but at least equally important they had to be politically reliable.[60] The Loyalty Rangers in effect formed a statewide political network, and it was up to Hanson to see to it that only staunch Hobby supporters were recruited.[61] He had to sift through a mass of applications from those eager to do their bit by crushing the least hint of subversion.[62] While the roster of the Loyalty Rangers was taking shape and Hanson was sending out form letters of instructions to the enlistees, he was also investigating reports of pro-German activity.[63] As might be imagined, Captain Stevens was even more zealous in enforcing the Loyalty Act.[64] Hanson, by the way, was now titled "Ranger Inspector."[65] And he now occupied offices 616–618 in the Frost Building.

As the all-important Democratic primary approached, Hanson spent more of his time quietly working for Hobby's election. A particularly touchy issue was that of campaign contributions by Rangers. On June 5, Hanson was notified that:

> After taking up the matter with the Campaign Committee and General Harley, we have decided that an assessment of the Rangers for a contribution to the campaign would not be a good policy. While we recognize their loyalty, still with the limited salary paid them and with the extreme political agitation now existing, we think it possibly best not to accept any contributions from Rangers.
>
> I had already cashed the check for $100.00 sent to General Harley so I am enclosing my draft for that amount, asking that you return same to its source.[66]

Hanson soon had an opportunity to implement this policy. He wrote to Captain Davis at Ysleta:

> I herewith enclose your check for $160.00 same being your contribution to the Hobby Campaign fund.

I quote you paragraph from a letter I am in receipt of, from Austin with reference to this matter:

"I wish you would explain this to contributors and tell them that Gov. Hobby's attention will be called to these contributors, and that you and I both feel sure it will be appreciated just as much as if the contributions had been accepted by the Committee, they have shown very generous spirit, and I know their motive will be heartily appreciated by the Gov." You will please state to the boys who assisted in this matter, that their willingness to contribute to the election was respectfully refused for the reason that the Campaign Committee did not believe that they were able to spare even this small amount from their salaries for this purpose, but that their willingness to give is just as much appreciated by Gov. and Adjt. General, as if it had been for a much larger amount.[67]

Unfortunately Captain Davis's ethics left much to be desired. He did not return each of his men's $10 contribution; rather, he said nothing and used the $160 to make contributions to local politicians whom he was supporting. Davis's chicanery was discovered by accident several years later when one of his men came across Hanson's letter.[68]

Since having Rangers contribute money to the Hobby campaign was deemed a bit crass, Hanson came up with another way for them to contribute. As he informed Harley:

I am herewith inclosing [sic] you original and copy of list of names furnished us so far for Special [Loyalty] Rangers. Those with a small check-mark in front have taken their oath of office and have received their commissions. The names without check-marks have either not accepted or are in the process of doing so. Wherever you see a name that is not checked I have written a letter to the party who recommended them, asking him to have them accept and send in their oath of office at once or to name another man in their stead in order that we may have three in each county.

I will suggest that you at once furnish "Hobby Headquarters" with this copy I am sending in order that they can take such steps as they see fit towards putting these people actively to work. I will further suggest that each one be given a bunch of Hobby literature for distribution and that a letter be addressed to each one of them asking their opinion as to whether Governor Hobby will carry that county and further asking them for a full report of the county and their opinion as to how is the best way to carry it in case it is doubtful. There is nothing like keeping these men actively in the harness for the next thirty days. In case you find any of them that are not all right *kindly let me know.*

If I can ever get the names of the Hobby County Chairmen in the counties we have not heard from I will write them at once. It seems strange that I can not get this list and I again urge you to see that I get it at once for time is getting short.[69]

Not only was time getting short, the campaign was getting nasty. On June 11, Ranger Captain Monroe Fox published a blistering open letter to Governor Hobby in the Marfa newspaper:

I herewith hand you my resignation to take effect today. I am resigning because you have seen fit to discharge five of my men for the killing of fifteen Mexican bandits on the 20th [sic] day of January, 1918. For if there was anything wrong about this matter of killing those Mexicans I was wholly to blame and I so told General Harley on the 30th of May, and that I was the one to be discharged if anyone should be which he refused to do, and I then told him that if you discharged those men I would resign. Do you not think I would be an ingrate to send my men out on a duty and because they unfortunately had to kill any number of Mexican bandits to let them be discharged for the carrying out of my orders? You may be built in that way but I am not. I think more of my men and friends, than any job I ever heard of. Why do you not come clean and say that this is purely politics just to gain some Mexican votes? The five men you have discharged are good men and were the best of officers, and I want to ask you and all State rangers how you expect to hold up the ranger force under such ruling as in this case. It hurts me to have my men treated in this manner. As to myself I care nothing because only a short while ago you sent a man to investigate me as to whether or not I was for you for Governor or a Ferguson man, so you know that there is no use in trying to have me believe that this action was brought about by anything other than your political reasons. We have stood guard to prevent Mexican bandits from murdering the ranchmen, the women and children along this border while you slept on your feather bed of ease, and then to have my men discharged is too much for me. If there was any wrong done why not leave that for the courts of Presidio County to determine? From your wise view of justice you have found it prudent to try those men without evidence or jury. You may consider this my resignation.[70]

A Marfa lawyer who was a Hobby partisan wrote in outrage to Hobby's campaign manager, the Beaumont attorney Walter J. Crawford:

The good friends of Hobby have told him and Harley all the time that Fox was a snake in the grass. This letter from him clearly shows what kind of a man he is. He has been secretly working for Ferguson all the time.

Hobby ought to have fired Fox long ago, and in the present case he ought to have fired Fox in place of the rangers. But it is a good riddance. He is hanging around here abusing Hobby, but he does not have much influence. Every body here knows that these Mexicans were not bandits, and I presume the official reports obtained by the Adjutant General shows [sic] this. Most, if not all of these Mexicans were harmless.

It is no trouble to get good men to be rangers, and Hobby need not worry about Fox's bluff. We would rather have him openly fighting Hobby than to be sneaking around sniping him in the dark, and using his office to help him.

When he talks about letting local courts investigate he very well knows that the grand juries here are picked and controlled by men of his type and who stand in with him. You know something about that, and I certainly do.

I would suggest that you all have Fox watched, and we will do the same. But what[ever] is done do not let him bluff Hobby and Harley into taking back water. He knows that the Mexican vote here, what few will vote, is for Ferguson and has been for him all the time, and it is a joke to claim that firing these rangers was for the purpose of influencing the Mexican vote.[71]

And a lady in Laredo also wrote to Crawford, concerned because the Ferguson people were using Fox's letter to attack Hobby in that city.[72] The longer Fox's charges were unanswered, the more credible they seemed.

The administration struck back decisively. On July 3, 1918, Adjutant General Harley wrote a reply to Fox, one that was published in newspapers throughout the state:

Replying to your letter of June 11, relative to your resignation, in which you assail the governor as playing politics, I take the liberty of answering, knowing, as you know, that the governor had personally nothing to do with your resignation nor any politics being in it.

The evidence disclosed, after a thorough investigation, as you know, that fifteen Mexicans were killed while in the custody of your men after they had been arrested and disarmed. This is verified by all proof, even to admission from the parties and information gathered by this office and by agents of the United States government.

We are not interested in your political views when a question of the honor and decency of the state is involved. As this department has announced heretofore, the troublemaker and lawless ranger has no place on the border, where international complications can be brought on that will involve our nation in trouble; that will hamper its progress in the war in Europe. You know, as all peace officers should know, that every man whether he be white or black, yellow or brown, has the constitutional right to a trial by jury, and that no organized band operating under the laws of this state has the right to constitute itself judge and jury and executioner, and shooting men upon no provocation when they are helpless and disarmed. We are fighting a world war now to overthrow ruthless autocracy and do not propose to tolerate it here at home. You were not forced to resign by the governor for political reasons, but your forced resignation came in the interest of humanity, decency, law and order, and I submit that now and hereafter the laws of the constitution of this state must be superior to the autocratic will of any peace officer, and that vandalism across the border can best be suppressed by suppressing it on the Texas side first.[73]

Harley's open letter pretty well demolished Fox, and it did not do Ferguson's campaign any good.[74]

Fox was discredited. He remained a peace officer, however, serving as chief of police in Brownwood, Corpus Christi, and Wichita Falls. And his connection with the Rangers was not yet at an end. On June 6, 1925, he was commissioned as captain of Company A, a position he held until his resignation on March 31, 1927. He then fell on hard times; as of 1934 he was a watchman in Austin, and on February 19 of that year, he obtained a Special Ranger commission. It was issued by his old boss General Henry Hutchings, who was once again Texas's adjutant general (1933–1935).[75] Fox's commission expired on January 22, 1935. He died in Austin in 1937 at the age of seventy.

Hobby's campaign staff wanted to follow up Harley's letter by attacking Ferguson's patriotism. The campaign chairman wrote to Harley: "It has been reported to me that when Ferguson was Governor, he appointed one thousand Rangers, within the draft age. What do your records show about this?[76] To the chairman's disappointment the records showed that Ferguson had not done that.

As the political pace quickened, Hanson worked feverishly to enhance Hobby's prospects while at the same time enforcing the Loyalty Act. Besides utilizing Regular Rangers on occasion he added several men, and a woman stenographer, to his staff. At least one of the men worked under cover.[77]

The role of the Regular Rangers in the election itself became an issue. Hobby's campaign chairman sent a *Personal and Confidential* letter to Harley: "Some of our friends are resenting the suggestion that has been made to the effect that Rangers be sent to Corpus Christi on election day. They state that while it might be desirable to send Rangers to Mexican communities, like San Diego and other places near the border, yet it is suggested that they are not necessary in a white community like Corpus Christi."[78] Captain Stevens for one favored having Rangers present at the polls in Mercedes. He requested the transfer to his company of Daniel Hinojosa, one of Captain Sanders's men: "I would like to have [him] down here two or three days before the election and on election day have him at one of the Mexican voting poles [sic] to look out for things. He is familiar with the Mexicans and I can instruct him as to what I want him to do." Harley ordered Hinojosa's transfer.[79] What worried Hobby's supporters was the possibility of Ferguson manipulating the Hispanic vote, since along the border electoral fraud was not just a tradition but an art form.[80]

Hanson was a skilled political operator, but he was also an experienced peace officer. He had to use that experience when in mid-July he was suddenly ordered away from his desk job to direct a manhunt. Ranger Sergeant Joseph L. Anders and Privates Lee Saulsbury, John Dudley White and Walter I. Rowe had been dispatched to East Texas, to the piney woods near Broaddus in San Augustine County, to apprehend two army deserters. About 2 a.m. on July 12, Rangers White and Rowe were sitting on the porch of a farmhouse on a stakeout. They were ambushed, both men being cut down in a hail of gunfire. White died at the scene while Rowe, seriously wounded in the leg, was rushed to a hospital in Beaumont, with the state paying his medical expenses.[81]

Besides the usual urgency of bringing a Ranger killer to justice there was in this case an additional consideration, for the slain Ranger White's father was a well-known political figure.[82] Sergeant Anders wired the adjutant general from Broaddus to send four good men immediately. Harley answered that he was sending six or seven, from Sanders's company, with Captain Hanson to take charge of the operation.[83] A formidable force assembled to track down the murderers—Captain Hanson and his Rangers, three Bureau of Investigation agents, and an army captain commanding sixteen picked sharpshooters, in addition to the local sheriff and his posse of some fifty men. They faced a daunting challenge, for the deserters were hiding somewhere in a thicket fifty miles square, protected by kinfolks who had absolutely no use for peace officers of any kind. Hanson rather colorfully described his problem: "It is like hunting a bob tailed squirrel with a nick in his left ear in the Brazos [River] bottoms in comparison to hunting these deserters. They have no horses, go 10 miles to a shindig afoot, don't farm and do nothing but hunt & fish and sell moonshine whiskey."[84] Yet by July 16, Hanson succeeded in persuading the deserters and their rustic protectors to surrender without a fight. The Bureau of Investigation agent in charge made a point of praising the Rangers' role in this case, as did people all over East Texas.[85] The Hobby campaign did not object at all to this favorable publicity.

Things were definitely looking up as far as Hobby's chances were concerned. For instance, J. T. Canales wrote to Woodul that he'd just toured Cameron County, "and every day we are getting stronger for Hobby. . . . Jim Ferguson is going to be surprised when he receives the returns from this part of the State."[86]

There was some last-minute ugliness in the campaign. The Brownwood newspaper published an article under the headline "Hobby Appoints Mexicans

Over White Men in Ranger Service for Political Advantages." The article was about W. E. Hodge of Brownwood (the ham and eggs Ranger), who said he resigned because of "Governor Hobby's new policy of placing full-blood Mexicans in positions of authority over the white men in the Ranger service." After recounting Hodge's rantings, the article concluded with: "The moral of the situation, as revealed through Mr. Hodge's resignation, and the causes leading to it, appear to be that Hobby is once again trading a free man's principles for political spoils, and is making a drive for the Mexican vote."[87] It is doubtful whether this diatribe swayed many voters even in Brownwood.

A more imaginative approach was tried in Mercedes. Captain Stevens reported that: "Railroad bridge on Brownsville line two miles west of Mercedes was burned at an early hour on election day. Supposition some of the Ferguson sympathizers set fire to bridge for purpose of attracting Ranger Force from polling places. Military forces are extinguishing fire. Myself and company are standing for law and order at any post [sic—cost?]."[88]

When the primary election was held on July 26, Hobby won by a landslide. He carried 234 counties, many of them by substantial majorities. The final vote tally was: Hobby, 461,749; Ferguson, 217, 012.[89] Captain Hanson's contribution to this overwhelming victory had not been insignificant.

CHAPTER SIXTEEN

POSTWAR PROBLEMS

ADJUTANT General James A. Harley created a statewide organization to combat disloyalty and gave Captain Hanson that mission, but, in an ironic development, Harley himself was suspected of disloyalty, because of his connections with Reno Eickenroht. The latter came from a well-to-do family in Seguin, Harley's hometown. Eickenroht's father gave Eickenroht a good education, sent him through college, and bought him a small weekly newspaper published in Seguin, the *Guadalupe Gazette*. As owner and editor, Reno Eickenroht was emphatically pro-German in his editorial policy, a policy that he prudently toned down considerably once the United States entered World War I. Yet his sentiments remained pro-German. Because Harley was a close friend of the elder Eickenroht, the adjutant general commissioned Reno as a second lieutenant in the Texas National Guard. When the guard was activated as the 36th Division, at Camp Bowie outside Fort Worth, Eickenroht was serving as an infantry lieutenant. He managed to resign his commission, according to his own account because Harley made a trip to Washington and personally interceded with Secretary of War Newton Baker on Eickenroht's behalf. Among those who knew Eickenroht, the general opinion was that he had gotten out of the army to avoid going to France.[1]

Harley then commissioned Reno Eickenroht as a Regular Texas Ranger, on January 30, 1918, placing him in Headquarters Company. As a Ranger, Eickenroht was now safe from the draft; in January the attorney general of Texas issued a ruling that Regular Rangers were state officers and thus exempt from the draft, being placed in Class 5 D.[2] In March, Harley assigned Eickenroht to Captain Davis's Company L at Ysleta, telling Davis that Eickenroht had been in the army, was a good man, and authorizing Davis to use him as company clerk.[3] Harley explained:

"I sent you Ranger Eickenroht to be used by you if possible as a company clerk, as he is a good clerical man. My reason for wanting him to get that particular experience is that if he makes good as a company clerk we can probably use him some place else in that line of work; so if you can keep him at the camp for that kind of work, we will consider it a favor."[4] Although grateful for the clerical help, Davis viewed Eickenroht's arrival realistically, describing him as a friend of Harley's who was sent to him from Austin.[5] On April 9, however, Harley ordered that Eickenroht report to his office as soon as possible.[6] On July 27, Eickenroht was discharged from the Rangers.

Both military intelligence and the federal Bureau of Investigation had taken a keen interest in Eickenroht. Among those interviewed was ex-Ranger sergeant H. C. Trollinger, who said he knew Eickenroht personally but had never heard him utter anything disloyal, merely that Eickenroht had on occasion said that "he was scared he would be killed in case he had to go to France, and in my opinion, he is a loyal American but is afraid to get in this fight."[7] Captain Davis's opinion was even less flattering. Eickenroht was in his Company for about thirty days, "but I found him to be of no assistance whatever to me as he was a natural born coward and I practically got no service out of him while with me." Further, Eickenroht had boasted that Harley was a personal friend of his father's and had made a special trip to Washington to secure his release from his infantry regiment stationed at Camp Bowie, and he was going to be commissioned in a new Texas National Guard unit that was being organized.[8] Eickenroht was indeed commissioned as a first lieutenant in the Texas National Guard cavalry brigade being formed. Stationed in Houston, Eickenroht's job was to recruit personnel for this brigade, whose mission would be to protect the border, not to go to France. Military intelligence decided to bring the Eickenroht case to Governor Hobby's attention "through a mutual acquaintance."[9] Despite this precaution, Harley learned of the investigation and requested that the government file charges against Eickenroht at once if they had evidence against him. Military Intelligence had its doubts about Harley. The chief of military intelligence wrote to the Southern Department intelligence officer: "we would like to have your opinion as to Adjutant General Harley."[10]

The upshot of this affair was that Eickenroht resigned his commission, and shortly thereafter he was drafted, on August 1, reporting for duty at Camp Mabry on August 3. Still, military intelligence kept him under surveillance. He was discharged from the army during the week of November 25–December 1, 1918.[11] With regard to Harley, the Southern Department intelligence officer reported that:

It appears that the father of Eickenroht was formerly a client of Adjutant General Harley while he lived at Seguin, Texas and they are rather friendly. . . .

It is my opinion that Adjutant General Harley is absolutely loyal as far as that is concerned. The Texas Rangers under his administration have been as a class of a little higher grade than the Texas Rangers of a year or so ago. On the whole I consider Harley a good man but it is just another incident showing to what extent some men will go to repay political obligations. Notwithstanding the fact that this whole matter was laid before the Adjutant General, he has commissioned suspect in the Texas National Guard. He says that it would have been embarrassing for him to have done otherwise for the reason that prior to the time the matter was brought to his attention, suspect had spent possibly $500.00 of his own funds in assisting in the recruiting for this organization.

For your further information it might be well to go into this matter a little further. Governor Hobby was formerly the editor of the "Beaumont Enterprise" at Beaumont, Texas and was elected Lieutenant-Governor on the same ticket with Jas. E. Ferguson on an anti-prohibition platform. Ferguson was eventually impeached and Hobby succeeded him. Hobby has made an excellent Governor and to some extent has broken away from the influences that surrounded the Ferguson administration.[12]

Harley did not limit himself to using the Rangers in order to help an old friend's son dodge the draft. On September 10, 1918, he wrote to Moses and Rowe, the Fort Worth law firm representing the powerful Cattle Raisers Association of Texas:

If you will send me a list of Cattle Inspectors of the Cattle Raisers Assn. who hold Special Ranger Commissions, and who are on your pay roll as Cattle Inspectors, I will place them in the file as Regular Rangers without pay and they will be taken care of in the draft.[13]

Moses and Rowe were amenable to the idea.[14]

Harley had fulsome praise for his wartime creation, the Loyalty Rangers, and by implication for Captain Hanson: "Through the assistance of the loyalty secret service department this office has been kept advised as to Mexican revolutionary activities carried on, principally outside of San Antonio, and in the border counties in Mexico and this state. The loyalty secret service department has been of great assistance in the successful prosecution of the war and in the alleviation of unsettled conditions along the border."[15] Judging from the adjutant general's correspondence, the Loyalty Rangers' most important achievement was helping to elect William P. Hobby as governor; they also provided some intelligence on matters pertaining to the border and to Mexico, as well as to slackers, deserters, and German propaganda.

And with regard to Captain William M. Hanson, he was not merely report-ing on the Mexican Revolution. The Carranza authorities were infuriated by Hanson's dealings with anti-Carranza exiles. For example, the army intercepted and translated a partially encrypted letter from G. M. Seguín, the Mexican consul in San Antonio to his counterpart in Laredo written on July 23, 1918 (the encrypted portions are italicized):

> Confirming one of my recent communications in which I stated that *State Rangers* were helping the revolutionists widely open [sic], in this I will take the liberty to say that I know through good information *that Captain of Rangers, Hanson*, of whom I have already spoken to you about on other occa-sions and who *was exiled from Mexico as an undesirable stranger* [foreigner] fre-quently receives notices which are sent from Tampico related to the move-ments of the revolutionists in that district, which proves the interest he has in those matters.
>
> It has come to my mind that these communications *can be intercepted in Laredo* sufficient with which to set a formal accusation *against the said Hanson*. I await your opinion in regard to this matter so as to send you greater details.[16]

More to the point was a telegram from General Alfredo Ricaut, Carranza's nephew and commander of Mexican troops in the lower Rio Grande Valley, to Carranza's chief of staff, which translated read:

> Please inform the president that between Laredo and Matamoros there are being organized daily parties of fifty or sixty men, mounted and armed, being assisted in this organization, definitively proven, by W. M. Hanson, Chief of Rangers. This individual is the one who most helps the rebels on the other side [of the Rio Grande], having been expelled by General González while the latter was in Matamoros because he is one of the worst enemies of our cause and now of our Government. I await your answer.[17]

Hanson indeed maintained close ties with anti-Carranza exiles, primarily in San Antonio. Besides assuring them of his desire to cooperate with them in every way, he promised that at the proper time he would "shut his eyes to their revolu-tionary activities in and around Brownsville and Laredo, Texas." When Bureau of Investigation agents in the field reported this to their superintendent in San Antonio, they learned that Hanson had been supplying that office with a steady stream of valuable intelligence about these exile groups. Thus the Bureau's posi-tion was that Hanson had been acting from honorable motives—to secure infor-mation—and had not used his position in the Rangers to assist the exiles; Hanson was entirely trustworthy.[18] There continued to be, therefore, an important, if clandestine, international component to the Rangers' activities.

With Governor Hobby's election it turned out that everybody had been his fervent supporters, and now they were clamoring for favors. Some of these favors involved Ranger commissions. Hobby partisans were not hesitant to recommend themselves or their friends for appointments to the Ranger Force, for promotions within that organization, or for captaincies.[19]

But being a Texas Ranger remained a hazardous line of work, especially in South Texas. At 12:30 p.m. on the night of August 21, 1918, Private S. T. Chávez telephoned Captain Stevens from Brownsville that Private Joe Shaw had been killed about 11 o'clock.[20] Stevens rushed from Mercedes down to Brownsville, arriving about 2:30 a.m. and immediately went to the scene, the small farm of Teófilo Solís, two miles east of town. He found the farmer's son, Francisco Solís, wounded in the head by birdshot.

Upon investigating, Stevens learned that Rangers Chávez and Shaw had been scouting along the river that night. They had spotted some Hispanics in a field, and Shaw sent Chávez to go through the brush and head them off from the river while he checked them out. Chávez did so, but he soon heard shooting; he saw three Hispanics running, and he shot at them. Since he couldn't locate Shaw, Chávez rushed to Brownsville for reinforcements; he notified two of the mounted Customs inspectors, and they accompanied him back to search the field.

They soon found Shaw's body. He had been hit by two bullets, one entering under his left nipple and coming out his back on the right side, and a second slug in the back. He was carrying a shotgun, which had been cut nearly in half by a rifle bullet.

Stevens arrested Teófilo Solís, the father of the wounded man, who of course was also arrested. Solís claimed that he was at home, about a hundred yards from the scene of the shooting, when he heard firing. He investigated, finding his son Francisco wounded and a man's body lying about fifty feet away. He carried his son home, then went to Brownsville for a doctor, but he didn't notify anyone about the body. It turned out that another son, Manuel, was in the field with the wounded Francisco. The Customs inspectors had arrested Manuel and had taken him to jail before Stevens's arrival.

Stevens found two pairs of shoes on the riverbank and tracks of bare feet leading to the river. When he searched the Solís premises he found hidden in a hole in the field a shotgun and three rifles, property of the Solís family. Stevens believed that there had been about six Hispanics involved in a smuggling operation. Because of the thick brush along the river, Shaw had used a shotgun the night he died. But he had loaded it with birdshot—birdshot yet. If he'd loaded it with buckshot, as a prudent peace officer would have done, he'd have blown Francisco Solís's head off instead of just wounding him. This was probably due to

Shaw's inexperience. He had no law enforcement background and had been a Ranger less than two months.

The district intelligence officer at Fort Brown shed further light on the Shaw killing by sending Captain Stevens a confidential report from his "Confidential Agent No. 2": "Four brothers and their father, by the names [sic] of Solis, were at the Tomates last night, August 21, 1918, for the purpose of crossing the river to avoid the draft. A Ranger tried to stop them and one of the brothers fired at him and killed him. One of the Solis brothers was wounded, but this is not the one that killed the Ranger. That one got across to the other side."[21]

Captain Stevens commented on conditions around Brownsville. Most of the trouble occurred along the river and up to fifteen miles inland. The army did very little patrolling. Mounted Customs inspectors did, and they had been fired on from the river several times lately; and on the night of August 1, Customs inspector (and former Ranger) Fred Tate had been killed near Brownsville by Mexican smugglers who escaped across the river.[22] Cameron County peace officers were conspicuous by their absence, and that left the Rangers. Stevens had deployed his men in pairs at the Piper Plantation (Chávez and Shaw), at La Paloma, which was fifteen miles west of Brownsville on the river, at Santa María, fifteen miles west of La Paloma, at Harlingen, and at Mission. The remainder of Company G scouted from headquarters at Mercedes. Stevens enclosed "a petition I received from some of the citizens near San Benito asking for Rangers. The people in this Valley depend on the Rangers for every-thing [sic], and of course I try to please them in every way possible."[23]

The Piper Plantation remained the scene of trouble. On August 24, three days after the death of Private Shaw, a detachment of five Company G Rangers— George Sadler, Lenn Sadler, John Sadler (all related and all from Pearsall, Frio County), O. E. Walters, and John Sittre were involved in a gun battle there. When Captain Stevens arrived to investigate, the Rangers stated that they were scouting near the river at dusk when several Mexicans concealed in the brush on the American side opened fire on them "and then it seemed that the firing became general from both sides of the river." The Rangers said they fired about fifty rounds at their attackers and that there were four or five dead Mexicans on a sandbar in the river and on the riverbank. When the firing ceased the Rangers returned to their camp at the Piper Plantation.

Stevens inspected the scene of the engagement, finding on the American bank a wagon with some corn in it, as well as evidence that "a good many horses" had been tethered there. On the Mexican bank he observed several dead horses and several large Mexican hats. As for bodies, Stevens mentioned that when the fight occurred the river was extremely low, barely running. That night, however, there was a ten-foot rise in the water level, which covered the sandbars; if there were any dead Mexicans on the sandbars they were washed downstream.

On his way back to Mercedes, Stevens stopped off in Brownsville to see the Mexican consul and inquire if that official had heard of any trouble on the river. The consul had not. Nevertheless, Stevens was convinced that slackers had fired on his men, and he anticipated more trouble from draft dodgers: "I expect we will have a lot of trouble with these slackers. And since the age limit has been changed [making men eighteen to forty-five eligible for the draft], there will be hundreds of them trying to get across the river, and after once on the Mexican side, and they can not get work and nothing to eat, they will be coming on this side stealing and giving us a lot of trouble."[24]

Trouble of a different kind was brewing for Stevens. Powerful political forces wanted him out of the Valley. This move prompted one of the leading citizens of San Benito to appeal to Governor Hobby. Alba Heywood wrote:

The report has gained credence here that you have ordered our Ranger Force, headed by Captain Stephens [sic], away from here.

We are circulating petitions this morning asking his retention and this communication is to personally urge upon you that he be allowed to remain, together with the force with which he has surrounded himself. I do not hesitate to say that as the general proposition, I am opposed to the principal [sic] of Rangers in towns and communities like San Benito with a city government, with seven churches, and with a Court House only twenty miles distant [in Brownsville].

It is my belief that the Rangers have been, in the past, in the wild and wooly parts of Texas, when under good captains of great use and benefit to communities where lawlessness could not be reached otherwise, but I have on general principles been opposed to this in the Lower Rio Grande Valley not actively, however, but passively opposed to this.

But the conditions in our Valley and especially in Cameron County, notwithstanding the churches and the courthouse and city government, verge so closely to the wild and wooly that I am forced to believe that certain rangers such as Captain Stephens [sic] and his party are really beneficial and needful. He is, without question, the most efficient and best Captain we have had in the Valley, he does not make a practice of constituting himself detective, peace officer, judge, jury and hangman all in one. He has done more to dignify the Ranger Service than any man I know of and we need him here. I do not wish to be foolsome [sic] in my praise of the captain for I have never met him personally, but I am speaking of what I know of him and his methods.

I don't have to go into details with you regarding the corruption and fraud of the politics of our county, for I know that you are in close touch with the conditions here. I voted and worked for you to the very best of my ability.

We rolled you up a tremendous majority [2,245 to 192],[25] but I am sorry to say that a disgraceful number of that majority was polled through corruption.

In another polling place judges were appointed who could neither read nor write English, but who could and did mark tickets. In still another polling place one of the Candidates officiated and marked tickets. In several polling places there were twice as many votes polled as were entitled to vote according to registration, poll tax, etc.

In other words the same tactics that were employed in Duval county in the Parr-Glasscock election were employed in Cameron County.

It is our belief that the influence that worked to have Captain Stephens [sic] and his party removed from the Valley is the same influence that is responsible for the dirty politics in Cameron county.

We believe it because we know that these people have made threats, did make threats, on election day that they would bring this removal about. That they would have Stephens [sic] removed and we find that this removal would be taken as a victory for the Jim Wells Ring and as a blow to clean politics.

Personally, I am not interested in politics as an office seeker, but I believe that one of the essentials to the success of this Valley, is to clean up this Ring, and I don't hesitate to assure you that the next two years will clean it up.[26]

But a different picture of Stevens was painted by state Representative J. T. Canales. Writing to Harley from Brownsville, he stressed that if Stevens were not transferred immediately "it will cause a great exodus of Mexican laborers from here. We have stopped the trouble by assuring them Captain Stevens was going to be transferred but if this is not true I am afraid we will not have many laborers left inside ten days. Captain Hanson is working with me to keep the Mexican laborers from going across but if Captain Stevens is going to remain here I will refuse to help in keeping the Mexican laborers here."[27] Hanson presented a somewhat different view: "Exodus of laborers on account of draft and other conditions very serious this section. Am requested to attend meetings over county to reassure Mexican laborers of protection by Rangers and that no drastic treatment so long as they are right. Everything here perfectly harmonious. Urge Colonel Chapa to come tonight."[28] As he did whenever an administration called on him to reassure Hispanics, Chapa complied, leaving immediately for Brownsville.[29]

So, unlike the impression Canales's letter left, Stevens was not the sole cause of the exodus of Mexican laborers from the Valley. Fear of the draft, with its age limit raised to forty-five, was a major—probably *the* major—reason for the exodus.[30] Governor Hobby reassured the citizenry regarding both the draft law and the Rangers, and he authorized Colonel Chapa to speak on his behalf.[31] And it will be remembered that a similar exodus had occurred for fear of the draft in the spring of 1917, long before Stevens's arrival on the scene. Still, the "other conditions" Hanson referred to must have included the disappearance of Florencio García, which raised strong suspicions that three of Stevens's men had administered summary justice.

Captain Hanson investigated the matter and his official report ran as follows. At the Piper Plantation, Stevens's men detained several Hispanics who had been in charge of a herd of registered Jersey cows. Thirty-seven of the valuable animals had been stolen and taken into Mexico. Suspicion fell on Florencio García, who was in charge of the herd, and on several of his helpers. The Rangers arrested the lot, took them to the guardhouse at Fort Brown, and secured a confession from one of the helpers naming García as the principal culprit. But several days later, after consulting a lawyer, the helper recanted his confession. Rangers George Sadler, Lock, and Sittre interrogated García for about a day, and they later told Captain Hanson that García had confessed and had implicated a gang of Mexican bandits. The Rangers claimed they had released García on his promise to contact the bandits and inform the Rangers about their next raid.

About three weeks later, skeletal remains were discovered near where the Rangers said they had released García—there were three bullet holes in the coat. Family and friends identified the clothing and hat as being those García was wearing when he was arrested. A criminal complaint was filed against the three Rangers. Sheriff Vann arrested them, and they were released on a $3,000 bond each for their appearance before the grand jury. That body made an exhaustive investigation and exonerated the Rangers because the evidence failed to prove conclusively that the remains were García or that the Rangers had killed him. Hanson concluded his report by stating that the general opinion among good citizens was that García's "bandit partners" had seen the Rangers release him and had killed García to silence him.[32]

Yet there was a lot more to the García case. The Mexican consul in Brownsville launched his own investigation, which convinced him that the Rangers had killed García.[33] Captain Stevens steadfastly maintained that his men were innocent. The Rangers involved gave an account somewhat different from that in Hanson's report. George Sadler, for instance, said that although they had arrested García on suspicion at the Piper Plantation, only four or five miles from Brownsville, they took him to Point Isabel, twenty-five miles away, in order to interrogate him in an unfamiliar setting. According to Sadler, before they turned him loose García promised to get information for the Rangers. But neither Sadler nor his colleague John Sittre could give a reasonable explanation as to why they'd had to take García all the way to Point Isabel for interrogation.[34] Although Rangers Sadler, Sittre, and Lock were no billed by two successive grand juries for lack of evidence they were the last people known to have seen García alive.

Besides the García affair there were complaints about the mistreatment of Mexican laborers, especially at the town of Donna in Hidalgo County. One Pedro

Támez gave an affidavit that on August 7 he was arrested by two Anglos—a Thomas Herter and a lawman whose name he didn't know—and was taken to the local jail, where another Hispanic, Arturo García, was confined. About 9 p.m., "three officers supposed to belong to the Ranger Force" asked the prisoners if they were ready to leave town, which of course they were. The trio put Támez and García in an automobile, drove several miles in the direction of Mercedes, stopped, and attempted to apply the ley fuga. They told the prisoners to run, which they declined to do as they had committed no crime. But as they began to walk away, the Anglos opened fire, hitting García in the leg. Támez hid in the brush, made his way back to Donna, and on the advice of a Hispanic merchant went to Brownsville and told his story to the Mexican consul. García was seriously wounded but managed to reach Mercedes, where he owned some property.[35]

The Mexican consul's investigator, H. N. Gray, an Anglo who had been working as an intelligence agent for Mexican administrations as far back as 1911, visited several Valley towns but focused on Donna, where "I found very good grounds for the complaint of Arturo García, there being here many cases of Mexicans who have been detained by the authorities and compelled to work for much smaller wages than they pay in the neighboring towns. All these men have been compelled to flee by night through the woods as if they were criminals." Gray stated that Támez and García were locked in a small room lacking ventilation or sanitary facilities for more than a day without food or water. In the evening "three men, all members of the Civil Authorities, one Sam Heard of the township of Donna, and the others, M. G. Lubbock and Robert Holliday of the County, took García and his companion, Pedro Támez, marched them to a distance of about three miles from Donna and ordered them to [go] off on a run." They fired about eight shots at the Mexicans, one of which shattered the bone in García's leg. García played dead until the Anglos left, then hid near the road. The next day he managed to flag down a passing motorist, a Mr. Busby for whom García had worked, and Busby took him to the hospital in Mercedes. Gray added that he "did not stay longer in Donna feeling sure that if the authorities had realized the errand I was on, I would have had the same fate as Támez and García, or worse."[36]

To some extent the role of the Rangers in these events can be determined. The "Thomas Herter" to whom Támez referred was actually Thomas I. Hester, whose father, A. F. Hester, was the bank president in Donna. Thomas I. Hester was a druggist and labor contractor there. He was not a member of Stevens's company, but he was indeed a Ranger. Hester received a Loyalty Ranger commission on May 31, 1918, which he held until February, 1919. Regarding the three "members of the Civil Authorities," Sam Heard, M. G. Lubbock, and Robert Holliday, whom Támez "supposed to belong to the Ranger Force," none of them appears in the Ranger service records. This points up the problem that to many Hispanics in the Valley, any lawman was a Ranger.

For example, the consul's investigator "heard that the Rangers had horse-whipped a laborer named José Hernández." Gray visited the ranch where Hernández lived, about ten miles from Donna. Hernández stated that "Rangers, whose names he doesn't know," came to his house, seized him and his ten-year-old son, and said that if Hernández didn't confess to stealing a burro they'd hang the both of them. When Hernández professed his innocence, they tied a lariat around his neck, tossed it over the limb of a tree, and jerked him up so his feet barely touched the ground. They whipped him with another lariat until he fainted. The boy was not harmed. When the investigator interviewed Hernández, six days after the flogging, " black and yellow stripes could still be seen from his belt down to his knees." The Mexican ambassador later filed a formal complaint.[37] Obviously some people brutalized Hernández, but whether they were in fact Rangers remains unclear.

Thomas I. Hester strongly denied the allegations of mistreatment of Mexicans at Donna, attributing the trouble to the fact that Arturo García and others were recruiting laborers for work in Louisiana, which of course infuriated local farmers. Hester stated that Captain Stevens had come to Donna and had arrested the two men who had jailed García. They were later released on $5,000 bond each, but when their trial was held no one appeared against them and the charges were dismissed. Hester admitted that he had helped detain Pedro Támez but again stressed it was because Támez was shipping laborers to Louisiana. He denied having anything to do with the wounding of García or the whipping of Hernández and emphasized that the Rangers had nothing to do with either offense. Hester added that:

> It is a well known fact that when anything of this nature happens in this Valley it is laid on the Rangers, especially by the Mexicans, as they think that every man who wears a ducking suit, as most of the farmers and ranchmen do in this country, or carry arms, which most of the citizens do for the protection of their families, lives and property from such men like Hernandez, are Texas Rangers. They do this, also, for the reason that they know by taking it up through the Mexican Government they can be further protected in their meanness. This class of outlaws are afraid of the Rangers, and they do not fear any other class of officers, and they try on all occasions, to make it as hard as possible for the Rangers.[38]

This was all well and good, but the fact remained that Thomas Hester was a Loyalty Ranger, and the G. M. Abney whom García had identified as one of his attackers and whom Captain Stevens had then arrested was Glenn Maurice Abney, a farmer and a Special Ranger. Abney had previously served in Company A in 1917–1918.

Captain Hanson investigated the matter, securing statements from Thomas Hester and others. Hanson reported that Captain Stevens had arrested Sam Bernard and G. M. Abney.[39] As Hester mentioned, they were freed when no one appeared at their trial. Hanson observed that "I do not believe that any one could be convicted in that country for preventing outsiders from coming in and disturbing their laborers." He also doubted that even if the unknown parties who had whipped Hernández were brought to trial they would be convicted, for the locals had suffered greatly from the "depredations on their lives and property from people who live on both sides of the river in Texas and Mexico." His conclusion was that "the Rangers had absolutely nothing to do with the arrest, detention, or release of García and Támez, but on the other hand, took prompt action and bound over Bernard and Abney, who were identified by García as being his assailants to await the action of the grand jury for shooting García."[40] Hanson was lying, for in a letter to Harley on November 8, only two weeks after submitting the above report, he referred to "Special Rangers Abney and Hester."[41]

Another incident involving Rangers occurred in September. This was a particularly ugly affair, at El Barroso Ranch in Starr County. Two Anglos—one said to be a Ranger named David and the other a certain Franklin, manager of El Rincón ranch of which El Barroso was a subdivision—arrived about 9 p.m. and ordered a goatherd, Antonio Pérez, to prepare them something to eat. Pérez at once killed a kid. While Pérez and another goatherd were preparing the meal, the Anglo named David, who had been drinking, went to Pérez's shack and attempted to rape his wife. Hearing her screams, Pérez rushed to her defense, armed only with the small knife he had used to kill the kid, and inflicted a cut on the would-be rapist, who then shot Pérez three times, killing him. The two Anglos fled, leaving behind a bottle of *pulque* and one of whiskey. Pérez's body lay where he fell for two days until a couple of Hispanics sent by Franklin arrived to bury it. But no one bothered to report the murder to the authorities. The distraught widow was finally befriended by rancher Macario Solís of La Grulla Ranch. The Mexican consul was contacted and took her deposition, in which she not only described her husband's murder but entered a claim for her meager possessions and for his back wages of 50 cents a day for the eight months he had worked and had never been paid.[42]

Captain Hanson investigated the murder of Antonio Pérez and reported to Harley rather cynically: "I am herewith enclosing you result of investigation of W. Stillwell who killed Antonio Perez in Starr County some time ago. There is no question but that he murdered this man but the Mexican was fortunate enough to inflict a wound from which Stillwell died about two weeks ago, so this settles the case in the Stillwell matter."[43] (Special Ranger) W. Stillwell died in the hospital in Kingsville around November 1 and was an employee of Tom East, to whom Hanson wrote regarding the murdered Pérez's back wages and his widow's belongings.[44]

While Captain Hanson was investigating these cases, Captain Stevens was increasingly becoming the center of controversy. Given the byzantine nature of Cameron County politics, Stevens's problems may well have arisen not because he wasn't doing his job but because he was trying to do his job too well. Stevens's efforts to combat what he perceived as German influence offended some important people. Furthermore, he had no use for Sheriff Vann of Cameron County, refusing even to communicate with Vann, whom he considered just a lackey of Jim Wells. Stevens complained that criminals jailed in Brownsville were quickly freed on what were called "straw bonds"—when a public official acted as an accused's bondsman—in effect, a bogus bond.[45] Many of those thus free on bond promptly fled across the river. So Stevens adopted the practice of having his men take those they arrested to jail in Hidalgo County, where Sheriff A. Y. Baker could be counted on to keep them locked up. Sheriff Vann protested, pointing out that by law people were entitled to bail, and it was not his fault if they absconded thereafter. More significantly, Stevens also clashed with Jim Wells himself, especially over the practice of disarming Hispanics along the river, something that not only the Rangers but the army did on a systematic basis.[46] Wells protested that some of those being disarmed were "good Mexicans" who had been his friends and clients for years. Stevens reminded Wells that there was a war on, and extraordinary measures were necessary. Periodically, Captain Hanson had to go to Brownsville to try to keep the peace among these strong-willed individuals. State Representative J. T. Canales also got into the act, criticizing Stevens, in part because one of Canales's relatives had a run-in with Stevens's men, and he began to demand Stevens's transfer out of the Valley, alleging that, as we have seen, the Ranger captain was causing the exodus of Mexican laborers, on which the Valley's economy depended. Stevens had become so controversial that his masters in Austin decided that he had to go. He and his company were transferred to Sanderson on August 29, 1918. But Harley had Stevens return to the Valley temporarily in September to make a tour and reassure all those who had been clamoring for his retention that his transfer had not been politically motivated but had occurred only because Harley needed his services in the Big Bend.[47]

While he was back in the Valley, Stevens left Sergeant P. A. Cardwell in charge at Company G's headquarters in Sanderson. Cardwell thoroughly enjoyed his work, writing to Captain Harry Johnston, the Ranger quartermaster, that:

> You sure ought to come out to see us. This is the best country in the world and talk about WILD WOMEN. I went to a dance last night and believe me there were some women there. All the real men have gone to war and of course even slackers are in demand here and the women are good looking too. There were no real women here, all of them were white; however, I guess after I associate with them for awhile I will get used to white women.

Everything has been turned over to me and I practically run the company. The captain instructed all the men to obey my orders. The captain wants you to come out and stay for awhile. Of course we will have some *mescal* on hand.[48]

But during Stevens's absence some of his men got a little too rambunctious. At the Ranger camp on the Devil's River, some horseplay on September 15 resulted in tragedy. Ranger A. P. Lock was sitting on the ground cleaning his weapons, which were spread out on a canvas in front of him. Ranger Lenn Sadler walked up behind him and playfully grabbed Lock by the ears. Lock was evidently in a grumpy mood because without looking back he picked up his six-gun and fired over his shoulder, the bullet hitting Sadler in the abdomen and ranging upward to exit near his shoulder. The wounded Ranger was rushed to Del Rio for medical treatment but died the next morning. Sadler's comrades attended his funeral in San Antonio.[49]

There was also bad news from the El Paso area. On the night of November 7, Ranger T. E. Perkins of Company L, whose sergeant was his brother James C. Perkins, and Special Ranger Joe Place, a farmer who lived a hundred yards from the international boundary on the Island, were ambushed while scouting there.[50] Captain Davis reported that for the last two weeks his Rangers had been working nights trying to intercept a large shipment of arms and ammunition that the villistas were trying to cross. Villa's brother, Hipólito, was known to be waiting somewhere between Fort Quitman and Guadalupe, a stretch of more than sixty miles of border, with a considerable amount of silver bullion to pay for the munitions. Two nights earlier the Rangers had searched the house of Belén Anaya, a rancher who was a prominent villista, a close associate of the notorious George Holmes, and the head of the ammunition smuggling ring, but had found nothing. Nevertheless they kept Anaya's place under surveillance.

On the evening of November 7, Perkins and Place had left the Ranger camp at Fabens in an auto. Place later claimed that their car had run out of water near the Anaya Ranch, and they stopped to fill the radiator and repair a hose. Whether in fact they had car trouble or were simply using it as a pretext to observe the Anaya Ranch is unclear. In any case, according to Place, they were working on the car when Perkins shouted a warning: Riflemen began firing on them from a canal, and Anaya himself approached the car, drawing his pistol. Perkins was faster, putting three slugs in Anaya's heart. But almost immediately Perkins was shot in the stomach. Armed only with his pistol which now had only two bullets left, the wounded Perkins staggered off into the darkness. Place was captured, disarmed, put on a horse, and sent off to Fabens, where he arrived at 8:30 p.m.

He gave the alarm, and posses soon fanned out searching for the missing Ranger. He wasn't found until the next morning, when a posse noticed a dog barking at a clump of bushes on an alkali flat 200 yards from the road and a mile from the Anaya Ranch. Anaya's father had trailed Perkins there and had clubbed the wounded man to death. The elder Anaya had fled across the Island boundary into Mexico. Captain Davis contacted the Mexican river guards, offering them $100 if they captured the elder Anaya and turned him over to Davis.[51] The slain T. E. Perkins had been a cowboy before enlisting in Company L on September 1, 1918. He was a Ranger for a little over two months.

The Rangers had also taken casualties at Brownsville. To replace Stevens's Company G, the adjutant general reconstituted Company F, commissioning as its captain William W. Taylor, born in June, 1869, in Yorktown, De Witt County. Taylor too had Ranger familial connections: His uncle, Thomas Carney "Creed" Taylor, had belonged to Companies E and B from 1899 to 1900 and to Company B, 1902–1904, besides serving as sheriff of Kimble County from 1900 to 1902 and in 1911. Creed Taylor was also a Special Ranger in 1917. Captain Taylor's grandmother, Elizabeth Tumlinson Taylor, counted a number of Rangers among her descendants. As for Captain Taylor, he had been Kimble County sheriff in 1898–1900, and 1902–1910, thereafter becoming a rancher. On February 18, 1918, he was commissioned as a Special Ranger and on August 16, 1918, went on active duty as a Regular, becoming captain of Company F in Brownsville. Among the members of his company were Frank Hamer and Delbert Timberlake.

Timberlake was another Wilson County Ranger, born in Floresville in September, 1882. His brother Edgar served in Company A from 1904 to 1906, rising to the rank of sergeant. Delbert Timberlake himself served in Company A in 1904–1905, then spent two years as a Galveston County deputy sheriff. After that he became a rancher in Del Rio, holding a Special Ranger commission (March–May) in 1916. Timberlake was not one to turn the other cheek. While living in Del Rio, he and his friend George Newberry crossed the river to Las Vacas (today Ciudad Acuña), where they ran afoul of the collector of customs, a Señor Rivera, who threw them in jail and confiscated their horses. Subsequently, on the evening of October 8, 1916, Rivera decided to visit Del Rio. Timberlake and Newberry spotted him and gave him a world-class beating. The unfortunate Rivera couldn't even complain to the Del Rio city marshal because Timberlake *was* the city marshal. Newberry, who was a cowboy, was also a Special Ranger, enlisted by Sheriff Almond and working under the latter's direction. The sheriff promptly arrested Timberlake and Newberry, who just as promptly secured bail. On October 10, Newberry was dismissed from the Rangers, but Timberlake remained as city marshal despite the complaints of the Mexican authorities.[52] After serving as city marshal of Del Rio from 1916 to 1918, Timberlake became a peace officer in Laredo. On June 27, 1918, he enlisted in Company I, being transferred to Company F in September, 1918, and promoted to sergeant.

Captain Taylor and Sheriff Vann mounted an operation to break up a gang of dangerous Mexican smugglers led by a certain Encarnación Delgado. Learning that the smugglers were planning to cross the river just below Fort Brown on the night of October 10, Sheriff Vann and his deputy Fred Winn, Captain Taylor and two of his Rangers—Frank Hamer and Sergeant Timberlake—and two Customs officers prepared an ambush, guarding the two paths the smugglers would use from the river. About 9:30 p.m., after being on stakeout for a couple of hours, Vann and Hamer saw a man cautiously coming up the path. They let him pass, and when he was some thirty feet away they rose and Vann ordered him to halt. The Mexican, who turned out to be Encarnación Delgado himself, spun around and fired his pistol. Vann and Hamer immediately returned fire, hitting him five times. Delgado staggered a few feet and toppled over dead, clutching his pistol in his right hand and spare bullets in his left. But the one shot he had gotten off had struck Timberlake above the left hip, ranged through his stomach, and lodged against his watch in the watch pocket of his trousers on the right side. Timberlake's watch stopped at exactly 9:27 p.m. The gut-shot Ranger was rushed to the hospital in Brownsville, where exploratory surgery revealed that he was mortally wounded. The best the doctors could do was to keep him comfortable. He remained conscious until he died at 7 a.m. Timberlake's death may well have occurred because he was more conspicuous than his companions, being dressed in a light khaki-colored suit, not the best choice for a night operation. Captain Taylor bought a nice coffin, and he and two of his men escorted the body to Timberlake's father's home in Uvalde.[53]

Besides reporting on Timberlake's death, Captain Hanson commented on the general situation at Brownsville. He noted that Harley had ordered Captain Wright and some of his men to support Taylor; they would be stationed temporarily at Santa María, thirty miles upriver from Brownsville. And both Taylor and Wright would have telephone connections with their various detachments, for the army had graciously invited the Rangers to tie into the military telephone network.

Coordination between the Rangers and the army was badly needed, for the level of depredations had increased. Several nights earlier, bandits had crossed somewhere above Rio Grande City and were raiding ranches thirty miles south of Hebbronville in Jim Hogg County. The sheriff and a detachment of Captain Wright's Rangers were on their trail, and Wright had arranged a joint operation with the military to guard the river above Rio Grande City and to intercept the bandits as they raced back to Mexico. Besides this raid, Wright reported that the riverside store at Salineño, just above Roma, was robbed by a group of men armed and uniformed like Mexican soldiers, which presumably they were. This was the second or third time the store had been robbed in the last several months.

Hanson also reported on a problem that would increasingly occupy the Ranger Force—the smuggling of liquor. With Prohibition making liquor scarce in Texas, there had sprung up a flourishing trade in *mescal*. The fiery liquor was dirt cheap in Mexico, costing two or three dollars a gallon. In Texas it sold for up to ten dollars a quart. The economic incentive was irresistible and underlined the fact that smuggling had existed as long as there had been an international border, the only change being the commodities smuggled and the direction they were going; as with drugs today, if there were no demand there would be no supply. Hanson ended his comments on smuggling by expounding on the lack of cooperation by the Mexican authorities.[54] He also mentioned that "I had a long talk yesterday with our mutual friend, Representative Canales, and I find that he is rather bitter, and seems a little bit unreasonable, as usual, and that he, as well as all other Mexicans believe the Mexicans should not be killed regardless of the facts of justification in the case."[55]

Hanson was correct in that Canales tended to be a bit obsessive, but Canales did have reason to deplore some of the Rangers' actions. One focus of his indignation was Sergeant John J. Edds of Captain Wright's Company K. Sergeant Edds, by the way, would have qualified as Hispanic under today's ethnic guidelines, for his mother was Hispanic. But reflecting the tenor of the times, he bristled when she was referred to as "Mexican," which had a lower-class connotation, insisting that she was "Spanish."[56] Sergeant Edds, who was one of two Rangers stationed in Rio Grande City, the seat of Starr County, was involved in several controversial incidents.

On September 2, 1918, a noted horse thief, one José María Gómez, was captured by cowboys working for rancher Eduardo Yzaguirre, from whom Gómez had stolen thirteen head in the preceding ten months. Sergeant Edds and Ranger S. S. Hutchison questioned the prisoner at Yzaguirre's ranch, but they were unable to transport him to jail in Hebbronville because they had to be back in court in Rio Grande City the next day. Yzaguirre offered to have two of his cowboys take Gómez to jail, an offer that Edds gratefully accepted. The sergeant wrote a letter to Ranger Paul Perkins in Hebbronville, outlining the case and instructing Perkins to put Gómez "in jail and file a case against him immediately, so that he won't get out on a writ of Habeas Corpus as Judge [James B.] Wells asked me about him yesterday." Edds explained that he didn't want to take the prisoner to Rio Grande City because he "was afraid Judge Wells would get him out on a writ of Habeas Corpus" before Edds could assemble the evidence against Gómez. Edds also wrote a note "To Whom It May Concern—These two men are authorized to convey Jose Ma. Gomez from Agua Nueva to Hebbronville (to jail). Any courtesies shown them will be appreciated by me."[57] The prisoner and his cowboy escorts, Sabás Osuna and Federico López, set out on horseback for Hebbronville, but about four miles from that town the cowboys shot and killed Gómez. They claimed he had suddenly made a break into the brush and had refused to halt when so ordered. Gómez's body, however, was found in the middle of the road, handcuffed and shot in the back. Rangers arrested the two cowboys, who were released on a $500 bond each.[58] This incident would cause Edds considerable grief, for it would be alleged that he had engineered the killing, despite the two cowboys' statements that he had nothing to do with it.

A month later Sergeant Edds was again the center of controversy. An army deserter, Alonzo Sánchez, was said to be hiding at Los Saenz Ranch near Roma. Edds and Privates R. W. Lorenz and M. M. Wells were assigned to capture him. About dawn on October 6, 1918, they arrived at the ranch. Edds posted the other Rangers to cover the house while he quietly slipped into the yard where two men were sleeping on cots. One seemed to fit the deserter's description, and Edds, Winchester in hand, awakened him. According to Edds, he told the man he wanted to talk with him but instead the man lunged at him, grabbing the rifle by the barrel and attempting to jerk it away. They scuffled for a few minutes. The assailant, who was bigger than Edds, was about to gain the upper hand when Edds fired, the bullet severing his adversary's femoral artery. The man quickly bled to death. Tragically, it turned out that the dead man was not the deserter but his cousin, Lisandro Muñoz. The other man in the yard, Zaragoza Sánchez, said he was asleep until the shot awakened him and was thus unable either to corroborate or to contradict Edds's account.[59]

Interestingly, though, Captain Hanson wrote to Harley:

Sergeant Edds killed a Mexican by name of Lebrado [sic-Lisandro] Munoz some days ago, twelve miles west of Raymondville and Mr. Guerra, banker of Rio Grande City, wired Colonel Chapa that he was one of their best citizens. I wired Fred Marks for a confidential report and he wired me that he thought the matter should be investigated. Captain Wright wired as per enclosed telegram. I do not believe Sgt. Edds would take chances especially so soon after his last escapade near Hebbronville but after we get straightened out it might be a good idea for me to make an investigation as the people along the border look to you to stand between them and the Rangers. Would be pleased to have your orders with reference to this matter.[60]

The Fred Marks referred to had been a deputy sheriff and deputy U.S. marshal and was currently a druggist in Rio Grande City. He was also a Loyalty Ranger who on October 20, 1918, went on active duty as a Regular, on detached service in San Antonio under Captain Hanson. The banker Fred Guerra was a member of the Guerra clan who controlled Starr County politically. He was not exactly a disinterested and concerned citizen, for the Guerras resented having Rangers stationed in Rio Grande City cramping their style. On the other hand, Captain Wright reported that "the good citizens in this county and that community view the case as I do, and several of them had voluntarily come to me and told me in case the local officers decided to have Sgt. Edds arrested, that they wanted to go on his bond, these people were Mexicans but of a very high class.[61] And the commander at Fort Ringgold in Rio Grande City was most complimentary about Edds and his cooperation with the army.[62] In the event, the Starr County attorney, along with the sheriff and justice of the peace, investigated the Muñoz killing and ruled it "justifiable homicide," throwing in a glowing tribute to the Ranger Force for good measure.[63] Hanson, in his capacity as Ranger inspector, subsequently notified Harley that "I am positive from what Capt. Wright tells me, that Sgt. Edds was perfectly justifiable, yet, I think it necessary to fortify your Department with sworn facts from both sides of the question."[64]

Hanson was called on to investigate another instance of alleged Ranger misconduct, one involving W. V. Bentley, who had been a salesman before enlisting in Company M on April 8, 1918. On the night of October 2, Bentley and two friends were having supper at the San Francisco Cafe in San Antonio. When they were paying the bill, one of his companions declared that he shouldn't be charged for the oyster stew he'd just eaten because the milk was sour. The waiter told him it was because the customer had put catsup in the oyster stew, whereupon Bentley, who was drunk, called the waiter a son of a bitch and pistol-whipped him for his impertinence in disputing the word of Bentley's friend. Bentley paid the bill and covered the astonished patrons with his pistol as he backed out of the restaurant. He then staggered into F. A. Chapa's nearby drugstore and identified himself as a Ranger, showing Chapa his warrant of authority. Chapa immediately got on the phone and advised Harley of the incident. Since Bentley's outrageous behavior had occurred in front of numerous witnesses, it caused a considerable flap. But to the great relief of the adjutant general, and of Hanson, it appeared that Bentley had been dismissed from the Rangers on October 1, the day before the incident. Hanson reported to Harley that since Bentley hadn't been a Ranger when the assault occurred, the Ranger Force had no further interest in the matter.[65] The Rangers thus narrowly escaped responsibility, but the incident showed the kind of man Bentley was, and evidenced the fact that there were some pretty undesirable characters on the force. So Canales had justification for his anger at Ranger excesses. It would appear, however, that most of his anger against the Rangers was politically motivated, and a good deal of it stemmed from their role in the Parr-Glasscock senate race.

As a generalization, it can be asserted without much fear of contradiction that everyone elected to public office in South Texas during this period—Representative Canales included—benefitted from electoral fraud, but the 1918 Parr-Glasscock race for the state senate showed South Texas politics at their worst. In the July 27 Democratic primary, state Senator Archie Parr supported Ferguson while Jim Wells reluctantly backed Hobby and persuaded other political bosses—A. Y. Baker in Hidalgo County and the Guerra family in Starr County—to do the same. Hobby carried every county in the region except Duval. It was Parr's support for Ferguson that nearly cost him his senate seat.

Running for reelection, Parr faced the opposition of Governor Hobby, the state Democratic party, progressive voters, and—the Texas Rangers. In the ensuing political battle his chief ally was Jim Wells. His support proved invaluable as Parr used electoral fraud, manipulation of the district convention, and a friendly judge to overturn his apparent defeat and retain his senate seat.

Parr's opponent was D. W. Glasscock, a lawyer and former legislator from McAllen recruited by anti-Parr insurgents. In an attempt to break the grip of Parr's corrupt political machine that relied on bloc voting by Hispanics, the Rangers were ordered to assist Glasscock. Captain Hanson, for instance, helped Glasscock activists discourage Hispanics in Corpus Christi from voting; the Rangers allegedly told Hispanics they would go to prison if they were illiterate and still tried to cast a ballot. Hanson also dispatched several Rangers to Duval County to monitor the voting. In Cameron County the day before the primary Stevens's men arrested a county commissioner for bootlegging, seizing the liquor they were convinced he planned to distribute gratis to the voters in his precinct. They kept his arrest secret from Sheriff Vann and moved the prisoner around until after the election so that Jim Wells could not arrange bail for him. And when Stevens learned of an effort in Mercedes to prevent the local Ladies Hobby Club from voting, he quite properly assigned men to the polls so the good ladies could cast their ballots without intimidation.

Glasscock won an upset victory, building a lead of 1,200 votes, without those from Duval County, which Parr refused to release. Glasscock feared that Parr would steal the primary with inflated returns from Duval County, and he persuaded Hobby to order a Ranger investigation in Duval County and Hispanic-majority precincts in Cameron and Hidalgo Counties. To no one's great surprise the Rangers uncovered a pattern of massive electoral fraud. When Parr submitted the Duval returns—1,303 votes for him and 23 for Glasscock—it gave him a 118-vote majority for the senatorial district. With Jim Wells's considerable help, the district convention declared Parr the winner and Democratic nominee. Glasscock filed suit, but the case was decided in Parr's favor by a less-than-impartial judge.

Refusing to admit defeat, Glasscock launched a write-in campaign for the November general election. In September, Hobby ordered a further Ranger investigation of electoral fraud in Starr and Hidalgo Counties, and Captain Hanson publicly conferred with Glasscock's campaign managers. Furthermore, Hanson had Rangers supervise the voting in Hispanic precincts in Duval, Cameron, Hidalgo, Nueces, and Starr Counties.[66] Parr's supporters charged that the mere presence of the Rangers intimidated Hispanic voters. Although the Rangers' presence did sharply reduce the Parr vote in Duval County—from 1,303 in the primary to 226 in the general election—the political boss and his allies controlled the electoral machinery in several counties, allowing ineligible

Hispanics to vote and throwing out hundreds of Glasscock ballots on technicalities. Parr was declared the winner by 624 votes. He was duly seated as the senator for the 23rd district and retained his seat until 1934.[67]

As historian Evan Anders has observed, "The Rangers had conducted their investigation in a partisan spirit, but the corruption that they had uncovered was undeniably real."[68] So was the animosity toward the Rangers by South Texas politicians such as Archie Parr and J. T. Canales.

It might be mentioned in passing that politics in South Texas didn't get much cleaner as time went on. Archie Parr's stealing the 1918 state senatorial election was vastly overshadowed when Lyndon Johnson stole the U.S. senatorial election in 1948. Almost a million votes were cast, and Johnson managed to defeat Coke Stevenson by eighty-seven, winning the derisive nickname of "Landslide Lyndon." Johnson's biographer, Robert Caro, characterizes Johnson's opponent, former governor Coke Stevenson, as a legend: "Known as the 'Cowboy Governor,' not only was he a true cowboy, his whole life, it seemed, was a Western epic, right down to the 1948 campaign, when, in an almost incredible confrontation on the main street of a dusty little South Texas town, Stevenson and his old ally, the renowned Texas Ranger Captain Frank Hamer, faced a band of Mexican *pistoleros* who had been ordered to prevent Stevenson from inspecting the disputed ballots that had taken victory from him and given it to his despised foe, Lyndon Johnson."[69] Caro adds that "It wasn't eighty-seven votes that Lyndon Johnson stole to win in 1948, but thousands of votes—many thousands, in fact."[70] The eighty-seven-vote margin was delivered by precinct thirteen in Alice, the county seat of—fittingly enough—Jim Wells County, which was then part of the domain ruled by political boss George Parr, Archie Parr's son and heir. Archie Parr and Jim Wells would have been proud. Caro presents a masterful account of the whole sordid episode.[71]

A new area of concern for the Rangers was developing during 1918. Oil had been discovered in the vicinity of towns such as Ranger, which attracted the disreputable element rushing to capitalize on every oil boom. The Rangers were called on to keep this turbulent throng of parasites under control.

Sergeant Sam McKenzie, who had been running the late Captain Ransom's Company C in the area, informed headquarters from Snyder on December 20 that Private John Bloxom had just telephoned him from Ranger saying that he and Private J. Berry Nalls had raided a gambling den the previous night; in the course of the raid a man had resisted arrest and they had had to kill him, but everything was now under control and quiet. McKenzie went to Ranger to investigate personally.[72] At the same time, Governor Hobby received a petition from outraged citizens of Ranger calling the death of Ernest W. Richburg a murder and demanding a full investigation.[73] Both Harley and Captain Hanson went to Ranger and took statements from various people.[74] Mounting evidence indicated that indeed Rangers Bloxom and Nalls had murdered Richburg. They were dismissed from the Ranger Force on January 10, 1919, by order of Governor Hobby.[75] Nalls and Bloxom were quickly tried for murder. Nalls was tried at Eastland and found guilty on January 29, 1919. He was sentenced to three years in the state penitentiary. Bloxom, who was also found guilty, was tried at Abilene on February 20, receiving a sentence of two years in the penitentiary.[76]

Obviously this was not the kind of publicity the Ranger Force needed, especially because in the first months of 1919 the organization faced the gravest crisis in its history, with Representative J. T. Canales acting as the Rangers' nemesis.

CHAPTER SEVENTEEN

The Investigation

THE Texas State Ranger Force reached its greatest size by the end of World War I. According to Captain Hanson, who was presumably in a position to know, there were

150 Regular Rangers [in actuality, ten companies of fifteen men each, plus eleven captains]

400 Special Rangers

ca.800 Loyalty Rangers.[1]

This total, however, far exceeds the statutory limit of 1,000 Rangers. Even if there were in fact only 476 Loyalty Rangers, this was still an impressive aggregation. But the end of the war necessarily produced a significant reduction in the Ranger Force.[2] The perceived threat along the Mexican border had decreased considerably, for Carranza's wartime policy of pro-German neutrality had backfired. Since he had bet wrongly on the war's outcome, Carranza was keeping a low profile, and the last thing he wanted was a clash with a victorious and militarily powerful United States. Moreover, the heavy financial burden on the Texas state treasury had to be reduced as quickly as possible, and as of September 1, 1918, the appropriation for the Ranger Force during the forthcoming fiscal year 1918–1919 was slashed to just $50,000.

The reduction encompassed all three types of Rangers. The Loyalty Rangers were now of course superfluous, and they were abolished in February, 1919; Hanson's empire was no more. The adjutant general also decided there were too many Special Rangers—some 460—and it was time to start over. He revoked all

Special Ranger commissions, mainly on January 14, 1919, with only brand inspectors and a favored few such as Hobby's campaign manager Walter J. Crawford receiving new ones.[3] But since neither of these two categories of Ranger was paid, the savings were negligible. The real effect of the reduction was on the Regular Rangers. Adjutant General Harley announced that the cuts would take effect on December 31, 1918. As the dreaded day approached, a lot of Rangers began maneuvering to keep their jobs, soliciting letters of recommendation from everyone they could think of.

The first to go, on December 31, was William W. Taylor, who had received his commission as captain of Company F on August 16, giving him the distinction of having the shortest tenure of any Ranger captain. He had been last hired and was first fired. He returned to Junction, and in 1920 was again elected sheriff of Kimble County.[4] Taylor's Company F was disbanded on December 31; five of the men were discharged, and seven were transferred to Captain Wright's company.[5] One of them was Sergeant Frank Hamer, for whom Captain Hanson had secured special privileges, writing to the Ranger quartermaster: "He is a good man and his expenses are more than he gets out of the service. Help him all you can as he is the best Ranger in Texas."[6]

One who most emphatically didn't share that opinion was the state representative for the 77th district, José T. Canales. The forty-one-year-old Canales came from a wealthy ranching family and was well educated, having graduated from the University of Michigan. He had been practicing law in Brownsville for years while pursuing a political career. Canales had been a faithful supporter of Jim Wells in the legislature from 1905 through 1908. The following year he broke with his patron over the issue of Prohibition and in 1910 ran as the Independent candidate for county judge. It will be recalled that he wrote a plaintive letter to the governor denouncing the "bossism and dictation of Judge Wells." The latter saw to it that Canales was defeated at the polls. Having learned his lesson, by 1912 Canales had returned to the Wells fold and was elected Cameron County school superintendent. His most sweeping policy was one that many people today would denounce as a blatant instance of racism—he decreed that only English would be spoken in the schools and schoolyards of Cameron County.[7] During the troubles in 1915 he had organized Hispanics to gather intelligence for the army. At the same time, he was virtually the only local Democratic politician denouncing the atrocities of the Rangers and vigilantes against Hispanics. In 1916, Canales was again elected to the state legislature, with the backing of Jim Wells.[8]

Although Canales had been instrumental in getting Captain Stevens transferred out of the Valley, the politician continued having trouble with the Rangers, on a personal level. It has been stated that in October 1918:

While following the trail of some stolen cattle, one of Canales's relatives, Santavo Tijerino [sic- Santiago Tijerina], encountered a posse of Rangers, who accused him of participating in a smuggling operation but never pressed formal charges. The lawmen cursed Tijerino [sic] repeatedly and made insulting remarks about his family. The relative believed that the Rangers were trying to provoke a fight so that they could shoot him for resisting arrest.[9]

Upon examination this account proves to be both incomplete and biased. First of all, Tijerina never claimed that "a posse of Rangers" was involved, saying only that "some officers and Rangers" had abused him. The "posse of Rangers" turns out to have been composed of the following officers, according to the testimony of federal Bureau of Investigation Special Agent E. H. Parker, who was there: "[Ranger Frank] Hamer, myself, Customs officer Atkins and Ranger Lee Rosser and another Customs officer" and Deputy Sheriff Fred Winn. So, instead of a "posse of Rangers" we have a party of six county, state, and federal officers, only two of whom were Rangers. Moreover, the business of Tijerina trailing some stolen cattle was only Tijerina's story. Again, according to Agent Parker's testimony, the officers had information that mescal smuggling was taking place on Tijerina's property on the river. They mounted a sting operation in which they would establish a stakeout there while two soldiers were sent to buy the illegal liquor from smugglers. But Tijerina was spotted creeping down to the river; he alerted the smugglers and blew the stakeout. The officers were upset. Hamer told Rosser, who spoke Spanish, to tell Tijerina that they knew what he had done and that if they were to come again he had better not interfere. Agent Parker commented that at the time Tijerina had said nothing about any stolen cattle. He added that Tijerina was not abused or mistreated, although he "might have been cursed at."[10] This incident is worthy of comment because it illustrates how stereotypes get perpetuated. The Rangers had enough to answer for without historians accusing them of things they didn't do.

Something a Ranger did do, however, was to threaten J. T. Canales. Frank Hamer warned Canales that he was "going to get hurt" if he continued criticizing the Rangers over the Tijerina matter. Being a lawyer, Canales wanted Hamer to admit making that threat in front of a witness. Hamer, who wasn't the sharpest tool in the shed, obligingly did so.[11] But, even if he could now substantiate Hamer's threat, having Hamer for an enemy would have terrified a braver man than Canales. That worthy appealed to Sheriff Vann for protection. Vann, that paragon of law and order, replied, "My advice to you is, take a double-barreled shot-gun and I will give you a man and go over there and kill that man. . . . No jury would ever convict you for that."[12] Luckily for Hamer, Canales was a Christian, as he later informed the committee investigating the Rangers, and his religion forbade his taking human life.[13] Hamer was thus spared having to shoot it out with Representative Canales.

Instead, Canales wrote to Governor Hobby on December 12 appealing for protection. He complained bitterly that Captain Hanson had done nothing about the Tijerina incident but instead had notified the Rangers in Brownsville about Canales's complaint and had apparently instructed them to threaten Canales into silence.[14] He focused on the threats against him by "this ruffian Haymer [sic]" but saved his best invective for Captain Hanson: "This corrupt Republican intriguer, Hanson, and his gang of ruffians, who are called State Rangers. . . ."[15]

As was his custom when he received correspondence regarding the Rangers, Hobby referred the letter to AdjutantGeneral Harley. The latter wrote to Canales on December 19, regretting the situation, promising to straighten things out, pointing out that Rangers, like anyone else, sometimes made mistakes, and stating that Hanson had assured him that he had given no instructions for threats to be made against Canales.[16] Two days later Canales wrote back that Hamer's threat against him had been no mistake, that Colonel Chapa had recommended Hanson to the adjutant general's department in the first place, and that Hanson hadn't reprimanded any of the Rangers but rather had whitewashed their misdeeds. He added sarcastically that "Judging from that I am sure Hanson will reprimand this fellow Haymer [sic] by making him Captain of the Rangers." Canales reiterated that his life was in danger and closed melodramatically with "I shall be glad, if I live that long, to see you in Austin in January."[17] Harley telegraphed Canales on December 23 that on the governor's orders he had ordered Hamer to make no threats against Canales, whom Hamer was instructed to protect.[18]

While appealing to Governor Hobby, Canales also appealed to Congressman John Nance Garner, referring to the Rangers as "American bandits," denouncing Hanson, who he said was appointed through the influence of Colonel Chapa, explaining that Chapa was a member of Hobby's staff who had been convicted of conspiracy with General Reyes and who had continued to support right-wing Mexican factions and who was using Hanson to bring about U.S. intervention in Mexico. Canales enclosed a copy of his December 12 letter to Hobby. Garner sent the letter to President Wilson's secretary asking whether the matter could be investigated, adding that Canales was a reputable citizen and a state legislator.[19]

Military Intelligence got the assignment. The intelligence officer in Brownsville was ordered to report on the advisability of Canales's request to have the Rangers withdrawn from that vicinity. The War Department, which had no particular axe to grind, was well aware that the most that could result from such an investigation would be a recommendation to the governor of Texas. The acting director of Military Intelligence commented that: "The previous impression of this office has been that the Texas Rangers, since the force was reorganized by Adjutant General Harley, are now of a much better type of men than heretofore and that there had not been a great deal of cause for complaint. It is also possible that the Governor has already taken appropriate action in the premises."[20]

The district intelligence officer in Brownsville's investigation included interviewing Canales at length. The officer reported that Captain Taylor's Ranger company stationed in Brownsville had taken a very active role in the primary and general elections in that district, thereby incurring the enmity of the politicians of one party. He concluded:

> It is the opinion of this office that the Rangers are needed on the Border and should by no means be removed, but that they should be required to refrain from using their authority for political gains; that about one third of the Rangers [sic] force in this section are not the proper men for the positions they hold and are of the type that shoot first and investigate afterwards.
>
> The salary paid the Ranger is very small and therefore the position is not desired by men of education and proper qualifications.
>
> The people in this section of the country are either for or against the Rangers, depending entirely upon what side they are politically, and for that reason it is very hard to make an impartial investigation by interviewing the citizens of this District.[21]

Military Intelligence headquarters incorporated these findings in its formal report to the adjutant general of the army, commenting about the Rangers:

> This organization has served a very useful purpose in suppressing lawlessness in the State and along the border, and while it is true that their methods are not always in conformity with strict judicial procedure, they are never-the-less effective.
>
> Normally it would appear that the matter is one for the State of Texas to pass upon and unless the conduct of the Texas Rangers was such as to seriously menace the peaceful and friendly relations between the United States and Mexico, it is not believed that we would be justified in recommending their withdrawal from Brownsville or any other border point. The complaint of Mr. Canales appears to have been inspired to some extent by personal animosity and political differences.[22]

As for "political differences," one longtime Brownsville resident stated that the fights in Brownsville were not so much between Democrats and Republicans as between the local Democratic machine (Jim Wells) and an independent faction. There were some Republicans in both factions, but most Republicans lined up with the Independents.[23]

Canales adopted a different strategy. He informed Harley that he did not think Harley was taking the matter seriously, and thus his only recourse was to appeal to the citizens of Texas and solicit their support. Any Canales-Harley correspondence was at an end.[24] Since neither Hobby nor Harley had complied with Canales's demands, especially with regard to summarily firing Hanson and Hamer, Canales decided to attack the Ranger Force through the legislature.

His political ally Sheriff Vann was also attacking the Rangers. On January 14, Vann wrote to the president of the Sheriff's Association of Texas urging him to have the legislature take up the matter of eliminating the appropriation for the Ranger Force. Vann stressed that the Rangers were not needed, especially on the border. He ended with "Now, Sheriff, I want you to take this matter up with the Legislative Committee as you know who they are, and insist upon their immediate action before the present Legislature."[25]

Vann sent a copy of the letter to Canales, who responded on January 17:

I received the copy of your letter of January 14 to Sheriff Hollingsworth and I thank you for sending me that copy and for the interest that you are taking in the matter of abolishing the State Ranger force, especially when we have had such a sad experience with them in the last three years. Permit me to suggest, Captain, that when the next Grand Jury meets on next Monday, that they should take up the matter of indicting Ranger Saddler [sic] for the murder of that man Garcia near Point Isabel, and also the Rangers that kidnapped County Commissioner Eddie Edwards and, if possible, get the Grand Jury to petition the Legislature for a law requiring that the Rangers should be under the civil authorities of the counties and not to override them; or to abolish the Ranger force entirely as a menace to our democratic idea of local self government.

I have a bill now pending regulating the Ranger service so that when any sheriff, county judge or commission court petitions the Governor for their removal, that they should be removed within ten days, otherwise they shall cease to be peace officers in that county. This is known as House Bill No. 5, and I will send you a copy just as soon as I can get it copied. I had a conference with the Adjutant General, and he is inclined to support my bill, but it will help get it passed quicker by getting our Grand Juries to petition the Legislature for relief along those lines. See Judge Timon and Mr. Kleiber with regard to this matter of the Grand Jury petitioning the Legislature for this relief.[26]

Canales's bill, introduced in the regular legislative session in January, 1919, was designed to gut the Ranger Force while purporting to reform that organization. It would eliminate the Loyalty Rangers (who were no longer needed anyway since the war was over), limit the Regular Rangers to twenty-four men "in time of peace" and eighty during an emergency, limit enlistees to U.S. citizens over twenty-five years old with two years' peace officer experience, and require applicants to present evidence from their county commission that they were peaceful and law-abiding. Moreover, the bill also contained provisions that reflected the historic clash between state and local authorities regarding control of the Rangers: Rangers would be required to deliver their prisoners without delay to the sheriff of the county where the arrest was made; any complaint from the sheriff, county judge, and county commissioners that a Ranger had abused a prisoner would automatically result in his dismissal. And these local officials would be empowered to petition the governor to have Rangers removed from their county. Should Austin fail to comply within ten days, the Rangers would automatically cease to be peace officers in that county. In addition, the Rangers, like sheriffs and their deputies, would be subject to civil damages for any abuse of authority, and they would be required to post surety bonds—from $5,000 for privates up to $15,000 for captains.[27]

Canales thus went after the Rangers with a legislative meat ax; should his bill become law, the Ranger Force would be at the mercy of corrupt local officials. As we have seen, these were not in short supply in South Texas. When the bill was being debated in the House, Canales was not at all reticent in stating his case. He informed his colleagues that "my life is threatened by a Ranger now in the service of the State of Texas because I have dared to insist on reform measures," and he charged dramatically that "The Rangers of Texas have committed crimes equal to those of the Germans in Belgium . . . , by spilling the blood of innocent men who were accorded no right under the law while in their hands."[28] Canales was terrified that they would spill his innocent blood as well. On January 30, Canales sent *his wife* to tell the Speaker of the House that he was afraid to go to the capitol because of the Rangers' threatening attitude. The Speaker sternly warned the Rangers that he would tolerate no intimidation of a member of the House. The Rangers vehemently denied that they had in any way attempted to interfere with Canales and even offered to furnish him with a bodyguard.[29] But the Rangers were presumably vastly amused to learn that their tormentor barely registered on the machismo scale.

Canales's virulent hatred of the Rangers was rather ironic, for one of his best friends was a Ranger. Though Canales claimed that ever since the Ranger atrocities of 1915 he had considered the force a disgrace to Texas, he had been willing to make one exception. On July 22, 1918, he had written to the assistant adjutant general, Walter Woodul:

Major: I wish you would do me the favor to get my brother A. T. Canales of Premont, appointed special ranger. Captain Hanson's boy knows him well; you can also get information as to his character and as to the fact that he goes out with the rangers whenever they call on him, and renders them all kind of assistance, from Captain Saunders [sic] who is stationed at Alice. My brother has in charge 3 ranches belonging to my father, one located in Jim Wells County, one in Duval County and the other in Jim Hogg, and he has to travel often from one ranch to another to protect our interest, and everybody there knows that my brother is friendly to the rangers and helps them in making arrests, and I am afraid that some one might do him an injury unless he is permitted to carry arms, and for this reason I would appreciate it if he is appointed special ranger. Captain Hanson told me, when he was here, that he would be glad to do so in case I thought this necessary.[30]

Woodul replied: "It is a pleasure to us to take care of your brother."[31] A. T. Canales was duly commissioned as a Loyalty Ranger on July 25, 1918. Evidently Representative J. T. Canales did not consider the Rangers at all despicable when they could be used to protect his family's interests.

Predictably, Canales's bill and his accompanying rhetoric created a firestorm of controversy. People began lining up either in support of the Rangers or in support of Canales, except for Jim Wells, who tried to have it both ways: He reiterated his longstanding practice of representing the Rangers without cost in legal matters while at the same time supporting Canales's bill, and he referred contemptuously to Captain Hanson as "a so-called Ranger."[32] Someone who would not have grieved at the abolition of the Rangers was Archie Parr, who was at this time fighting for his senate seat and who argued that the Rangers' tactics of intimidation had kept hundreds of Hispanics from voting (for Parr). But there was also a groundswell of support for the Rangers. Much of it came from South Texas, from Anglo farmers and political opponents of Canales, Wells, and Parr; the Brownsville chamber of commerce also expressed its support. These people held mass meetings and deluged the House with protests, for they feared that the Rangers might be withdrawn from the Lower Valley, and in their view it was the Rangers alone who had maintained order and had tried to enforce the election laws. Others, such as ex-captain Tom Ross, just generally supported the Rangers. And not a few people suspected that Canales was really acting on behalf of Wells and Parr, a perception strengthened by the fact that Canales welcomed the support of those political bosses.[33] Yet with his usual bluster, Canales declared that "I don't care about Wells, he doesn't control my conscience."[34] Perhaps not, but Wells sure as hell controlled most of the votes that got Canales elected, so the representative's declaration of independence should be taken with several large grains of salt. Another aspect of the opposition to Canales was the view that he was, after all, an "uppity Meskin" who was attacking one of the most venerated institutions in Texas. Illustrating what Canales was up against is the following quotation from Representative Stewart of Reeves County, who declared to his colleagues in the House that:

There are three great monuments to Texas liberty in this wonderful State: One is the Alamo—that sacred place where Texans proved to the world that liberty was to be prized more dearly than life. The second is the battleground of San Jacinto, where Texas won her lasting independence—where the "Napoleon of the West" was beaten and overthrown, while his palsied followers fell prone on their faces with the cry "Me no Alamo, me no Goliad!" The third monument, continued Mr. Stewart, is a living monument so far as Mexican banditry is concerned, and it is none other than the brave, gallant, dashing and courageous Ranger organization.[35]

Governor Hobby's supporters in the House attached crippling amendments to the bill, and Canales reluctantly agreed to send it back to the Committee on Military Affairs for further study. But Canales won a major victory in that he brought about the formation of a joint House-Senate committee to investigate the Rangers. This occurred because the Rangers' defenders were quite eager for an inquiry in order to clear the organization's name.[36]

On January 26, Adjutant General Harley requested that the legislature appoint a committee to investigate charges against the Rangers "and to determine the causes of complaint and the motives of those making said complaints." He referred to his difficulties in trying to maintain high standards for personnel who were receiving "starvation wages," and he asked the committee to support better pay for Rangers. Harley maintained that neither he nor Hanson had ever condoned or approved misconduct in the force and that he had tried to eliminate "the bad element from the force which is evidenced by the fact that he [the adjutant general] has discharged approximately 108 men during his term of office which is 100% of the actual number of men now on the force." Harley also pointed out that many of the acts complained of antedated his tenure as adjutant general. He ascribed "base political motives" to those casting aspersions on the Ranger Force.[37]

The "Joint Committee of the Senate and the House in the Investigation of the Texas State Ranger Force" was composed of two senators and three representatives. Its chairman was Representative W. H. Bledsoe of Lubbock, and the committee's stated purpose was to "investigate the activities and necessities for a continuance of the force." Not only were witnesses subpoenaed but notices were published in the newspapers that anyone who knew anything about specific charges regarding the conduct of the Rangers could appear before the committee and testify. The committee held its hearings in the capitol beginning on January 31, 1919, and the ensuing testimony would run to 1,605 typed pages. As the Military Intelligence officer in Brownsville had observed, people were either for or against the Rangers depending on their politics, and it was most difficult to conduct an impartial investigation. Various witnesses from the army and the Treasury Department spoke well of the Rangers and praised their cooperation.[38] Canales acted as the prosecuting attorney, introducing a laundry list of nineteen charges against the Rangers, plus one more at the behest of Representative John J. Ford. Canales's accusations dealt with alleged offenses committed during the Hobby administration, that is since September 25, 1917, but in his examination of witnesses he ensured that the Rangers' controversial actions as far back as 1912 were covered at length. And throughout his questioning he often manipulated the evidence to place the Rangers in the worst possible light.[39]

What enabled Canales to conduct a freewheeling examination was the committee's decision to give wide latitude to the introduction of hearsay evidence. Perhaps the best way to deal with the committee's investigation is to discuss each one of Canales's charges.

1. On or about November 16, 1918, Rangers George B. Hurst and Daniel Hinojosa were drunk and disorderly on the streets of San Diego, fired their pistols, and threatened the life of a constable should he attempt to arrest them.

The adjutant general replied that the charge was untrue, but if it were true Canales never brought the conduct of Hurst and Hinojosa to the adjutant general's attention and thus was derelict in his duty as a citizen. Canales's rejoinder was that although it was true he had not called the matter to Harley's attention, it was because he had become convinced of the incapacity of the adjutant general to give relief for outrages by Rangers, or his unwillingness to do so.

Canales introduced two witnesses, the constable in question, one Ventura Sánchez, and Mrs. Virginia Yeager, a resident of San Diego. The constable repeated the charge, adding that he had been told the best place to get a drink was at the Ranger camp. He declared that Hurst and Hinojosa not only drove around in a car shooting up the town on November 16, but on December 24 he'd seen Rangers Hurst and Blackwell drunk. Hurst had threatened to shoot him; then on December 30, Sánchez was warned that Hurst was looking for him with murder on his mind. The constable secured warrants, went to Alice, and got Sheriff Charles Price (an ex-Ranger) to go to San Diego to serve them. Price came to some kind of arrangement with the justice of the peace, and the Rangers were never arrested. They apologized and promised to behave. Sánchez did not report the incidents to the adjutant general or the governor. The witness admitted that prior to November 16, Hurst had arrested him for gambling, although the Rangers were in San Diego primarily to investigate electoral fraud. Sánchez asked the committee for protection against Hurst, who was now stationed in Austin.[40]

The second witness, Mrs. Virginia Yeager, was considerably less credible. She was the same lady who a couple of years earlier had complained to the governor about Ranger oppression. When the case was investigated, she admitted that she'd been wrong, having misinterpreted the whole thing.[41] And now she was decrying that "lawless breed of highwaymen known as Rangers," who "have abused me and I've complained to the adjutant general," asserting that "I am sure that they are the German propagandists—they keep strife between the United States and Mexico." She declared that they harassed Spanish-speaking citizens; many men went to Mexico "not to avoid the service of the United States but to avoid the inevitable unwarranted assaults and arrest by the Rangers. It was and still is a reign of terror." She further complained about a fellow who abused a young man in a garage—"People said he was a Ranger—he had a gun and wore a stetson." It turned out this was Captain Sanders, who had arrested a deserter, turned him over to the federal authorities, and collected the standing $50 reward. Mrs. Yeager claimed he had used vile language in her presence while making the arrest. Sanders denied abusing her. In short, Mrs. Yeager maintained that "Rangers have always been cruel and unjust to me,"[42] but all she could contribute to illuminating the Hurst-Hinojosa charge was hearsay.

Mrs. Yeager notwithstanding, subsequent testimony revealed that Daniel Hinojosa was among the worst of the serving Rangers. He had been in Companies A and B in 1910–1911, then had at various times been a Cameron County deputy sheriff and constable at San Benito. He and city marshal Frank Carr were suspected of having murdered their prisoner Adolfo Muñoz in 1915. In 1916, at a mass meeting in San Benito, Hinojosa had stated that on Carr's orders he had been collecting ten dollars a week as a payoff from each bar and brothel. They were both arrested and released on $1,000 bond. In 1917, a Cameron County court had dismissed the case because of insufficient evidence. Another witness remarked on Hinojosa's heavy drinking. The consensus among witnesses was that Hinojosa was a disgrace. But despite his track record, Hinojosa had been allowed to reenlist in the Rangers on June 7, 1918, in Captain Sanders's Company A, presumably because of his local knowledge and contacts. Both Harley and Hanson professed to be surprised by the adverse testimony and said that Hinojosa "was engaged in some special work and they would dispose of him immediately."[43] Hinojosa resigned on February 3, 1919. As for Sergeant George B. Hurst of Company A, on March 10, 1919, he was reduced in rank to private and transferred to Company B, not as punishment but just because Company A was disbanded. On March 18, 1919, he resigned.

2.   On or about September 15, 1918, Jesús Villarreal, of Duval County, while in the custody of Sergeant J. J. Edds and other Rangers, was tortured to make him confess to a supposed crime.

The adjutant general replied that the charge was untrue, and even if true the adjutant general had no knowledge of it, and if Canales did he didn't disclose that knowledge to the proper authorities and was thus derelict. Canales's rejoinder was the same as for charge 1.

Villarreal, a Duval County rancher and constable, alleged that on September 4, 1918, Rangers had arrested him, pistol-whipped him, tortured him by suffocation, shoved a cocked pistol in his mouth, and were going to plant a knife on him after they killed him. The reason for all this was because the officers believed he was transporting slackers across the river. The lawmen took him to an army camp; he was then taken to Rio Grande City and released on bond. Again, the question arises as to just who these lawmen were. Villarreal stated that "I don't know what they are but I judge them to be all Rangers." They proved to be two Rangers—John Edds and Sidney S. Hutchison—and two army scouts—Royal Collins and Lee Dickens. Villarreal acknowledged that he was transporting three young men in his car, saying they were going to Roma to buy goats. This story seemed improbable, because the incident occurred at 3 a.m., the men were dressed in their Sunday best, and they had several suitcases filled with clothes. Edds stated that Villarreal had been drinking and was impudent, and that Villarreal said he was a constable, whereupon Edds replied, "Well, you are a pretty son-of-a-bitch to be a constable, taking slackers to the river." Edds said he shoved a pistol in Villarreal's stomach and searched him. Then to preclude Villarreal's escaping, the Ranger made him sit down. "He didn't want to do that." All the officers denied torturing Villarreal in any way, and they declared that when they searched him they found a big knife. The young men arrested with Villarreal confessed to being slackers and said Villarreal had been paid to transport them, but Canales claimed that at the examining trial they told the U.S. commissioner they had confessed to Edds "because you'd given them the same treatment you'd given Villarreal." However, Canales admitted that he had no personal knowledge of the whole affair "except what Villarreal told me."[44] As in so many of these affairs, it all came down to whose version one believed.

3.   On or about October 5, 1918, Sergeant J. J. Edds killed Lisandro Muñoz near Rio Grande City under circumstances amounting to second-degree murder, and despite Captain Hanson's investigation, Edds was still in the Ranger service.

The adjutant general admitted the fact of the killing of Lisandro Muñoz but stated that it was unavoidable. Canales replied that the adjutant general's records showed that the killing constituted second-degree murder and offered as evidence Hanson's investigation. This was a case that particularly upset Canales, who did his best to discredit Edds.

It will be recalled that Edds, mistakenly believing Muñoz to be a deserter, had awakened him, and, according to Edds, Muñoz had tried to take the Ranger's rifle away. They had grappled for possession of the weapon and Edds, believing his life was in danger, had shot Muñoz. Canales introduced the statements that Edds and four others had made on October 18. He also presented Hanson's report to Harley on October 23, in which Hanson stated that the Guerra family in Rio Grande City were very much against the Rangers and Edds in particular because they had customers, kin, and friends engaged in smuggling and helping draft dodgers and deserters. And as Harley had ordered, Edds had been active in assisting the federal authorities, thereby incurring the enmity of the Guerras, who were "the political leaders of the county and backed by Wells, Canales and others" and were trying to give Edds all the trouble they could. Hanson concluded his report by stating that Edds had to kill Muñoz in order to save his own life. What is interesting is that despite the Guerra family's dislike of Edds, when the local authorities investigated the Muñoz killing they filed no charges against the Ranger. The justice of the peace refused to bind him over to the grand jury, ruling that the killing was justified. The grand jury refused to indict Edds. And when Edds took the stand Canales couldn't shake his story. Canales sulkily declared "I believe officers failed to do their duty."[45]

4. On or about September 2, 1918, José María Gómez Salinas was murdered by two Hispanics under circumstances indicating that they acted under Sergeant J. J. Edds's orders.

The adjutant general acknowledged the fact of the killing but denied that they acted under Edds's orders. Edds didn't order the killing and wasn't present at the time.

This charge proved particularly frustrating for Canales. When a member of the committee asked "Have you any evidence Edds had anything to do with that except to authorize those two men to carry those two [sic] fellows to jail?" Canales replied "All I have is hearsay but I have evidence upon which I really believe that he authorized them to kill him." Canales claimed that a relative of the deceased had told him, and that it was a common report on the Yzaguirre Ranch where the relative had been living, but he had to admit this was merely hearsay. He insisted that if the two killers were put on the stand they would admit that Edds gave them the order, pointing out that in their statements they professed too much that Edds had nothing to do with the killing. And he charged that Hanson had whitewashed Edds in his investigation.[46] Although he "really believed" Edds was guilty, being unable to prove it made Canales a little irrational, as illustrated by the following exchange between him and the adjutant general's lawyer, R. L. Knight:

Knight: You have no personal knowledge regarding that?
Canales: No, sir; none at all and no personal animus either.
Knight: That man was killed by two other Mexican cow boys?
Canales: Yes
Knight: And no ranger was present when it occurred, nor is there any claim that there was?

Canales:	Yes, sir; some people are very smart in covering their tracks.
Knight:	I mean by you?
Canales:	I said some people are very smart in covering their tracks.
Knight:	Now, what ranger was there—who had covered their tracks?
Canales:	Well, the facts show that this man was received from two Mexicans who had ample opportunity to kill him before they turned him over to the rangers, and—
Chairman:	Wait a minute—he asked you if you had charged that any ranger was there.
Canales:	Where?
Knight:	At the time of the killing.
Chairman:	All right, answer it yes or no and let's don't argue these matters.
Knight:	Then I understand that you do not charge that there was any ranger present when this man Salinas was killed?
Canales:	No, sir; but those two fellows were protected by rangers afterwards—I charge that.
Knight:	You don't charge it in your indictment.
Canales:	No, sir.
Knight:	By what rangers were they protected?
Canales:	By the rangers in Hebbronville.
Knight:	Who were they?
Canales:	I don't know their names, but you can find that out from Capt. Wright—he will tell you who they were.
Knight:	Isn't it a fact that the rangers arrested those parties and put them in jail?
Canales:	Yes, sir; and it is also a fact that they were given bond for five hundred dollars and turned out.
Knight:	And you say the rangers protected them?
Canales:	Yes, sir.
Knight:	Isn't it a fact that they were arrested by rangers?
Canales:	Yes, sir.
Knight:	And carried to Hebbronville?
Canales:	No, sir; they were arrested in Hebbronville.
Knight:	And carried before the officers of the county?
Canales:	The justice of the peace, and given bond for five hundred dollars.
Knight:	You say they were let out on five hundred dollars bond?
Canales:	Yes.
Knight:	Did the rangers grant them bond?
Canales:	Well, the rangers—
Knight:	Answer the question.

Canales: I don't know who is [sic] their bondsmen; I would like very much to get a copy of the bond, because I think we will get some very valuable information from it—

Knight: Now, Mr. Canales, I'll swear—

Chairman: Don't volunteer statements of that kind, Mr. Canales, because this is cross-examination and when it is completed, then you may make such statements as you desire. I will ask you, as a lawyer of experience, to observe the rules.

Canales: All right, Mr. Chairman.

Knight: They were given bond by the duly constituted local legal authorities?

Canales: I think so.

Knight: Yes. And you don't attempt to say that rangers named the amount of the bond or granted it?

Canales: I don't know anything about it of my own knowledge.[47]

The best thing Edds had going for him was the support of his captain, Will Wright, who declared that he had known Edds since the latter was a boy. Edds had been his chief deputy for four years while Wright was sheriff of Wilson County. Wanting to advance Edds's career, Wright had gotten him a job as a Customs inspector. But after being in the Customs service for two years, Edds had voluntarily resigned and had taken a cut in pay to become Wright's sergeant. Since Wright was widely respected, his endorsement carried a lot of weight.

5.   On or about April 4, 1918, Florencio García was killed while in the custody of Rangers Lock, Sadler, and possibly Sittre under circumstances which according to the adjutant general department's investigation show that it constituted murder, but despite this none of the Rangers was dismissed.

The adjutant general stated that there was no evidence that Rangers killed García. The grand jury investigated and returned no bill of indictment. Moreover, Captain Stevens, "whom said Canales admitted before this Committee was a good officer," had reported that from his investigation he had concluded that the Rangers were not guilty. Besides, Rangers Lock and George Sadler were no longer in the service. Canales maintained that only the Rangers could have killed García, and that Hanson's investigation had been a whitewash. As for no indictment having been returned, Canales claimed that "It is a custom along the border for the Grand Juries to refuse to indict Rangers for unlawful acts," and for this reason he had appealed to the adjutant general for protection. Furthermore, the García killing was being investigated by the present Cameron County grand jury.[48] Canales was being less than truthful; in a number of cases Rangers had been indicted and tried for capital offenses. Often they preferred this procedure, which usually resulted in acquittal, because as long as they weren't indicted, a grand jury could always indict them in the future.[49] In the event, the present Cameron County grand jury also refused to indict Rangers Lock, Sadler, and Sittre, for lack of evidence. These grand juries were predominantly Anglo in composition. Despite a parade of witnesses, including the Mexican consul and his investigator, all Canales could prove was that García had last been seen alive in Ranger custody. However convinced he might be that the Rangers were guilty, he couldn't overcome the fact that two legally constituted grand juries in his home county had failed to indict.

In an unrelated incident involving Sadler and Sittre, witness Octaviano Narváez, who farmed near Sebastian, testified that an ex-Ranger, Harry Wallis, who was at the time a ranch foreman, swore out a complaint against him for stealing and killing a steer. Sadler and Sittre arrested Narváez and jailed him in Harlingen. Four men then removed him from jail, tied his hands, blindfolded him, took him a short distance out of town, and hanged him twice from a tree trying to make him confess to the theft. The second time they hanged him he lost consciousness. Narváez stated that during his ordeal the blindfold slipped and he glimpsed his abusers, who were Rangers. Harry Wallis was with them. Narváez refused to confess, and they returned him to the Harlingen jail. Three or four days later a deputy sheriff transported him to jail in Brownsville.[50]

5a. This charge was made at the behest of Representative John J. Ford of Nolan County, who alleged that Rangers McKenzie and Bills engaged in misconduct in Sweetwater and were guilty of mistreating a prisoner in that jail.

The adjutant general declared that this charge was completely unsubstantiated by anything. Canales said he knew nothing about Ford's charges.

It would appear that at least to some extent Ford was engaged in a bit of payback. He'd been the attorney for FLPA members arrested in 1917; the Rangers had helped to smash that organization. The worst thing that Ford's examination revealed was that according to the witness Filmore C. Decker, a wood hauler in Eastland, about a year ago he had a pint of whiskey, and Rangers confiscated it, knocked him down, handcuffed him to a tree, and telephoned the sheriff to come get him, which took two hours. Decker was in jail for six days. Decker added that "I was told the men who arrested me were Rangers. I just supposed they were Rangers." Decker mentioned that he had been jailed four or five times, once for assault to murder, had broken out of the Eastland jail twice, and a decade earlier was in the penitentiary for some twenty-two months. Ford's efforts also brought to light that Sergeant McKenzie had a temper. He had once thrown a saltshaker at a waiter in a restaurant (this prompted the adjutant general's attorney to ask the witness whether any other man in Sweetwater had ever lost his temper), and

McKenzie had once engaged in a cursing match with a barber who had made an insensitive remark concerning the murder of Ranger John Dudley White by draft dodgers in East Texas. In addition, McKenzie was accused of playing poker, which legally constituted gambling. McKenzie had pleaded guilty.

But the intriguing aspect of Ford's charge was what it revealed about an apparent suicide in the Sweetwater jail. A man named Bostick had been delivered to the jail by Rangers on March 21, 1918, accused of murdering Judge Cullen Higgins, who had been shot through the window of a hotel. The next morning Bostick had been discovered hanged in his cell. There were those who immediately felt the Rangers were somehow involved. To their disappointment, there had been no Rangers in Sweetwater overnight, the closest Ranger presence being Captain Ransom, who had arrived by train at 7 a.m., had been informed of the suicide, and had gone to the jail to investigate. What he found was that Bostick had hanged himself from the bars of his cell with his belt and a bedsheet. And a red cotton bandana had been jammed so far down his throat that the examining physician had difficulty extracting it. Perhaps Bostick had thoughtfully done so in order that whatever noise he made while choking to death would not disturb others, but then perhaps not. He was the only prisoner in the jail, and the only two other people who had spent the night in the building were the sheriff and his deputy the jailer. Since no one could prove that Bostick's death had not been a suicide, it was so ruled.[51]

6.   On or about December 19, 1918, Rangers J. B. Nalls and John Bloxom, Jr., murdered Ernest W. Richburg in his place of business in Ranger.

The adjutant general could not refute this charge, since Rangers Nalls and Bloxom had murdered Richburg on December 19, 1918, in his place of business in Ranger. Harley therefore argued that Canales's allegations that Hanson had not conducted a proper investigation and that the two Rangers had not been immediately dismissed were unfair and misleading and were designed to reflect on the adjutant general. Harley stressed that Nalls and Bloxom were discharged on January 10, 1919, after both he and Hanson had inspected the scene of the crime and had interviewed witnesses. When Harley returned to Austin he had left Hanson to complete the investigation. The evidence was turned over to the district attorney and was also presented to the governor along with the recommendation that Nalls and Bloxom be discharged. And this had been done. But the two Rangers, in response to an appeal by the citizenry, had been left on duty as the only protection against crime until relieved and discharged on January 10. As far as Harley was concerned there was no issue except *when* the pair should have been discharged; they were discharged as soon as the investigation was completed.

Canales said that no further reply was needed, and he directed the committee's attention to Hanson's report of his investigation, which according to Canales clearly showed that Hanson hadn't taken the testimony of any reputable citizens of Ranger except for some barbers and a watchman, when he could have interviewed more knowledgeable and respectable citizens. Canales urged the committee to read Hanson's report and see for themselves how he tried to justify the two Rangers. He also introduced into evidence Special Orders No. 1 of January 9, 1919, by which Hanson and four other Rangers were ordered to Ranger to relieve Bloxom and Nalls, who were to be discharged by order of Governor Hobby effective January 10.[52]

> 7. On or about September 24, 1918, Ranger D. F. [sic] Barnett, at Marfa, unjustifiably shot at two Hispanics, wounding one. Even though the adjutant general's investigation showed that Barnett was guilty of assault with intent to commit murder, or at least aggravated assault and battery, the adjutant general had excused Barnett's action.

The adjutant general claimed the allegation was unfair and misleading, implying that he was encouraging bad conduct. This was just not true. Harley said the evidence would show that the Hispanic had been wounded by Deputy Sheriff W. T. Davis of Presidio County, who assumed all responsibility for the shooting. Barnett had merely shot in an effort to apprehend said Hispanic and was reprimanded for doing so.

Canales reiterated that the charge was made solely on the evidence in Harley's possession and from his own records.[53] Ranger DeWitt T. Barnett had been stationed on W. T. Davis's ranch in Presidio County fifteen miles from the Rio Grande. According to Barnett's affidavit, on September 24, 1918, he went with Davis to the latter's pasture to round up some cattle. About 1 p.m. they saw two Hispanics on horseback in Davis's pasture. When the two Anglos started back with a bunch of cattle they noticed the Hispanics following them. Davis rode over and asked why they were following. One of them replied "We are trailing some mares. What the hell is it to you?" Thereupon Davis hit him with his pistol. The Hispanics rode off and Barnett and Davis each fired three or four rounds over their heads to discourage them from following any more. Barnett said they weren't shooting to hit but just to frighten them and keep them from following. One of the Hispanics was wounded in the arm.

The aftermath is revealing. Captain Jerry Gray took Davis and Barnett to the "local court," presumably in Marfa, but the judge didn't think the matter was "worth fooling with." Gray also suspended Barnett for ten days pending instructions from Austin. Harley sent Hanson to conduct an investigation. On October 9, 1918, the latter sent Harley his report, adding that "I wired Gray to reinstate Barnett, since deputy sheriff of Presidio County [Davis] takes all the blame." On October 18, Harley wrote to Gray that "Barnett perhaps acted indiscreetly but wasn't entirely to blame. Matters will be overlooked this time provided you advise him to be more careful in the future and not be using his gun too promiscuously when not necessary."[54] This hardly constituted a reprimand as Harley claimed. Perhaps the adjutant general was influenced by the fact that Barnett had only been a Ranger for a month, or perhaps it reflected the view of Anglos that you sure didn't want any Mexicans trailing along behind you where you couldn't see what they were up to.

8. On October 2, 1918, Ranger W. V. Bentley without provocation pistol-whipped a waiter in the San Francisco Cafe in San Antonio. Although the adjutant general had discharged Bentley, the assault "shows the notorious character of some of the Rangers in the force today," and was thus worthy of mention.

The adjutant general declared the charge false, adding that Canales knew it was false when he made it, for he was trying to mislead the committee "deliberately and with evil intent" when he said Bentley was a Ranger. He wasn't. He'd been discharged for misconduct (on October 1).

Canales fired back that he had relied on correspondence in the adjutant general's own records, namely, a letter on October 5 from Sergeant C. H. Arnold to Hanson informing him of Bentley's attack on the waiter and Hanson's comment at the bottom of the letter on October 6: "Will suggest you suspend from service Ranger W. V. Bentley pending the investigation. . . ." and Hanson's telegram to Captain Lon L. Willis of the same date: "Will suggest you suspend. . . ." Canales pointed out, reasonably enough, that if Arnold and Hanson were unaware four days after the incident that Bentley was no longer a Ranger, how was he, a member of the legislature, supposed to know better? Furthermore, the adjutant general had submitted no record that Bentley had in fact been discharged prior to the assault. Although Hanson in a letter to Harley on October 9 stated that Bentley was discharged on October 1, Hanson's statements "are thoroughly unreliable. I reiterate the charge." In addition to the above correspondence, Canales introduced statements from the staff of the San Francisco Cafe.[55]

The adjutant general's attorneys also introduced correspondence, notably a letter from Harley to Captain Willis on September 21 informing Willis that he'd been promoted to captain and "As an afterthought, you are directed to discharge Private W. V. Bentley of Company M on October 1st. It appears that he is a trouble-maker so let him out." Willis testified that he had indeed taken up Bentley's commission on October 1 and had so informed the adjutant general that same day; Bentley had been discharged, not merely suspended. But it will be recalled that, according to Captain Hanson's investigation, Bentley still had his warrant of authority on October 2, for Bentley had showed the warrant to Colonel Chapa shortly after he had struck the waiter.[56] Canales failed to notice the discrepancy, as did all the committee members except one, who skeptically asked Captain Willis

"Did you give the true date when you wrote that letter?" Willis blandly replied "I always try to give the true date on every letter I write."[57] Bentley's service record, by the way, shows October 1, 1918, as the date of his discharge from the Rangers. Still, one suspects that some backdating of documents occurred.

9. Captain Hanson, the adjutant general's investigating officer, was unfit for his office because he investigated for the purpose of justifying the Rangers' actions, whitewashing them.

The adjutant general denied the charge, asserting that Hanson had been a diligent and faithful officer, adding that "he has incurred the disfavor of the said Canales because he has been too active in enforcement of law in the said Canales section of the country." The adjutant general requested the committee to call Hanson to testify.

Canales retorted: "When the adjutant general says that Hanson's been a diligent and faithful officer and incurred my disfavor, I take issue—admit that the said W. M. Hanson is a shrewd, smart man, but I deny that he is a diligent and faithful officer," covering up facts to protect desperate characters. "If this is what diligent and faithful means, I concede it; otherwise, I deny it."

Harley questioned Colonel F. A. Chapa as to whether he had ever heard Canales criticize Hanson prior to the time Hanson began investigating electoral fraud committed during the July primary. The colonel said he had not, and he maintained that position despite Canales's intense cross-examination trying to get him to recant. Their exchanges became quite testy, at one point Chapa telling Canales to quit trying to put words in his mouth. Canales argued that Hanson never investigated anything until after the November general election. Chapa replied that "in September you were always full of praise for Hanson. Since [then] he has been stepping on your toes." The issue boiled down to the approximate date when Canales had first realized that Hanson was, as he put it, a "crooked politician." Harley's lawyer emphasized that Canales had delivered speeches reassuring Hispanics in the Valley together with Hanson and Chapa, and at that time Canales had praised Hanson.

In a burst of candor that pretty much encapsulated what Canales was all about, he replied, "Yes, sir, because he had the authority and power to look into cases, and I always like to be on the good side of those in authority," adding that "Discretion is the better part of valor."[58]

The exchanges between Canales and Harley's lawyer became increasingly vituperative. At one point Canales called his adversary a crooked politician, prompting the committee chairman to reprimand Canales for indulging in personalities. The chairman threatened to report him to the House. The adjutant general's attorney brought up the matter of Canales's having written to Hanson in July, 1918, requesting a Special Ranger commission for his brother. Canales answered, "I asked Hanson and the adjutant general to appoint my brother, and he was, and I thank them for it." Canales explained that "We have five ranches, in Jim Wells, Duval, part of Kleberg, and Jim Hogg Counties, and my brother goes from one to another." Getting back to Hanson, Canales explained that "Mr. Hanson captivates a person simply by making those promises, you understand," but Hanson had never deceived him. "I was playing politics like anybody else with him." But Canales also stated that he first realized in mid-October, 1918, that Hanson was whitewashing the investigations he conducted, specifically that of the Muñoz killing.[59]

10. The adjutant general had been using the Rangers "for the purpose of showing special favors to his political friends and political 'pets' of the administration." Canales further charged that this had been a custom of long standing, but had been markedly abused by the present incumbent of the office, and he wished to call attention especially to one among others that could be proven, to wit: "In my district large numbers of Rangers are stationed and have been kept and maintained on ranches at State expense." He cited the King Ranch and its general manager, Caesar Kleberg, who was a member of the Democratic state executive committee and who had been actively lobbying against Canales's bill. The representative charged that Kleberg was one of the administration's political "pets," receiving "undue and unnecessary" protection from the adjutant general. Moreover, Kleberg used the Rangers to deprive people of their legal right to hunt in large pastures of more than 5,000 acres. The same protection was denied to other large cattlemen "chiefly because they did not happen to be politicians."

The adjutant general of course took exception: "This charge is made for the deliberate purpose of reflecting upon the Governor of Texas and upon Mr. Caesar Kleberg because he happens to be friendly to the administration." Harley denied the charge, which he termed a "malicious, unwarranted untruth."[60] He went on to say that the reason for Rangers being stationed on the King Ranch (at Norias) was to protect that section "from Mexican bandits, thieves, and murderers." Harley argued that for the last fifty years the King Ranch, along with others, had been the special target of the bad element from Mexico and from this side of the river, evidenced by the many raids and murders in that section of the state. He also denied that proper protection had been denied to other ranchers, citing specific examples.[61]

One of these ranchers was recently elected Congressman Claude B. Hudspeth, who declared that Canales might as well accuse him. Those pesky goat rustlers had been quite active on his three ranches in Val Verde and Sutton

Counties. He had appealed to the local authorities but they could not cope, so he had asked Harley for help. "He filled that country full of Rangers and stationed two of them on my ranch on Devil's River for about a year, and today there is not a goat thief."[62] Hudspeth gave the Rangers a ringing vote of confidence, which was only to be expected given the close relations between Hudspeth and Harley. In April, 1918, for instance, Hudspeth had written to Harley—"Dear Jim,"— requesting a Special Ranger commission for rancher Will Hill of Christoval because there were Mexicans in Hill's neighborhood. Hudspeth stressed that "you must appoint him. Do it by golly without fail. It will help me."[63] Hill was commissioned. Yet Harley had had to put pressure on Hudspeth to come from El Paso and testify. Initially Hudspeth had begged off, citing cases he was arguing in court and merely offering to wire or write in support of the Rangers. An angry Harley replied: "You remember your promise to me last August when you said you would be here to defend the Rangers. I expect you to keep your promise and come at once."[64] Hudspeth had come.

Canales denied the insinuation that his charge was made in order to reflect on the governor and Caesar Kleberg. He said that on January 25, before the investigating resolution was introduced in the legislature, he had called on Hobby together with Senator J. J. Strickland. Canales had informed the governor that he planned to conduct a thorough investigation but feared it would reflect on Hobby's administration because Canales possessed certain facts, especially with regard to the adjutant general and his department:

> and that as his friend and staunch supporter I did not wish to cast the slightest reflection upon him or his administration, and that all I wanted was the cleaning out from the Ranger Force all desperate characters and gun men who had committed, and were committing, outrages upon the good citizens of this state, and the Governor then, in the presence of Senator Strickland stated that he wanted the investigation, and that if any one of his appointees were [sic] not doing their duty, or were unworthy to discharge the office to which they were appointed, he wished to know it, or words to that effect. I take issue with Harley on this point and deny the reflection made on me and my motives.[65]

Canales was less than truthful about his motives and, as we shall see in connection with his charge 11, his claim to be Hobby's "friend and staunch supporter" was a joke.

Canales kept making the point that Norias was seventy miles north of the border and hence needed no protection from Rangers or anybody else. He studiously avoided any mention of the raid on Norias in 1915. But when he asked Colonel Herbert J. Slocum, commander of the Brownsville Patrol District, why

Rangers were stationed at Norias, Canales was discomfited by the colonel's answer, which was that they were there to prevent raids from Mexico. In fact, continued Slocum, he wanted to station troops on the King Ranch but lacked the manpower to do so. And, for good measure, Slocum declared that he found no evidence of Hanson being biased in his investigations.[66]

A politician can rarely be accused of consistency, and Canales was no exception. At the same time that he was railing against the administration for its favoritism toward Kleberg by maintaining Rangers at Norias, Canales assured the committee that "I am thoroughly acquainted with the Ranger business. I have known the Rangers ever since I was born, in fact my home, La Cabra Ranch, that belonged to my father, has been a haven for the Rangers. They stayed there, were stationed there, came there at all hours, got our horses, got meals there, and they got our services." He described Captains Hughes, Rogers, and Wright, who was then a sergeant under Hughes, as "some of the noblest men I know. . . . At that time they gave us protection."[67]

He then declared that Caesar Kleberg and two of his relatives had Special Ranger commissions during the Great War, and that because Kleberg was a member of the district board of exemption in Houston he had used his influence to secure draft exemptions for his relatives. Harley's lawyer gleefully pounced on this allegation:

Knight: They were both exempted *before* Caesar Kleberg was on the district Exemption Board. Didn't you know that Special Rangers weren't exempted from the draft?

Canales: No, I didn't know.[68]

Unfortunately for Canales he was unaware of certain documents in the adjutant general's correspondence. One was a letter from the Ranger quartermaster: "Brooks was just in and told me that in the deer season of 1917, he and Heard were camped in the King pasture keeping out hunters, when they took two new 30-30 rifles and a shot gun away from three Mexican boys."[69] And had Canales known of the following telegrams it would have made his whole day:

Caesar Kleberg to Adjutant General, October 29, 1918: "If agreeable and consistent would like to have the services of Ranger S. P. Chesshir now stationed at Norias for about twelve days with shipment cattle going to Florida. There will be no expense to the state. Answer."

Sam D. W. Low, Adjutant General's Department, to Caesar Kleberg, October 29, 1918: "With Captain Sanders permission it is satisfactory with this department."

Canales was absolutely correct about favoritism being shown to Caesar Kleberg, and this is a particularly egregious example. The Texas State Ranger Force should have had better things to do than to keep deer hunters off the King Ranch and guard an interstate shipment of Kleberg's cows. In 1921, incidentally, Ranger Sam Chesshir resigned and went to work for Kleberg at Norias, which seems about right.[70]

    11.   On January 28, 1918, fifteen Hispanics arrested at Porvenir by Captain Fox's men on suspicion were murdered by those Rangers. Hanson's investigation tried to justify the Rangers, which Canales said supported his charge number 9.

There was no question but that Fox's men had carried out the Porvenir massacre, so Canales focused his attack on the investigation of the affair. He noted that an army investigation by Lieutenant Patrick Kelly had showed that the Hispanics were killed in cold blood. Canales also stressed that although the adjutant general had fired Fox and the Rangers involved, yet Fox had assumed sole responsibility and had asked that he alone be discharged. The adjutant general had refused. And Fox charged that his subsequent dismissal occurred because he was not supporting Hobby but supported Ferguson. Canales was referring to Fox's self-serving letter of resignation on June 11, 1918, claiming that Hobby's motives were blatantly political and designed to attract the Hispanic vote. Although Fox had been thoroughly discredited, Canales professed to believe that Fox had been right in his diatribe against Hobby—so much for Canales's protestations of being Hobby's "friend and staunch supporter." This incident showed Canales at his most shameless.[71]

Canales hammered away at Hanson's investigation having been conducted in order to justify the Rangers. He introduced a number of documents regarding Porvenir to support this allegation.[72] Harley's attorney, however, asked Canales:

Knight:	Now, as a matter of fact, Fox was fired, wasn't he?
Canales:	Yes, sir.
Knight:	And he was fired on reports made to the Adjutant General's office?
Canales:	But not by Capt. Hanson.
Knight:	You are sure of that?
Canales:	The Adjutant General's records—
Knight:	Mr. Canales, are you not advised that 1st Lieutenant Patrick Kelly, United States Army, who investigated the matter, was under the direction and cooperated with Capt. Hanson?
Canales:	I don't know; I know there were two investigations, one by the United States Army and the other by the Adjutant General's

Knight: Department. It looks to me like that would be a very nice way to get out of the trouble.

Knight: Have you ever asked Capt. Hanson or Lt. Kelly or the Adjutant General if that was a fact?

Canales: No, sir; I don't know—

12. Regarding the Richburg killing, Hanson's investigation tried to justify the Rangers by alleging that the killing occurred in a raid on a gambling den; in fact Richburg was murdered in his place of business. Canales claimed this further supported his charge number 9.

He said that since he had filed his charges with the committee, a jury had found one of the Rangers guilty of murder, and this further supported his charge number 9.[73] The adjutant general's attorney denied that Hanson ever claimed the killing occurred in a raid on a gambling den.

13. In August, 1918, at Donna, Arturo García and Pedro Támez were taken from jail by officers, Stevens's Rangers among them, who then tried to kill the prisoners. Hanson's investigation tried to blame local officers and citizens, in order to shield the Rangers.

Canales introduced copious documentation—from letters by the Mexican ambassador demanding an investigation, through the report by H. N. Gray, the Mexican consul's investigator, to statements by some of the locals involved, such as Sam Bernard, Thomas I. Hester, and G. M. Abney.[74] His object was to prove that Hanson's investigation had sought to protect Stevens's Rangers by blaming "local officers and citizens."[75] There is a certain irony here. Stevens testified that his men had been nowhere near Donna, having been stationed at Mercedes, Harlingen, and the Piper Plantation at the time and in fact had later arrested several of the locals who were involved.[76] Canales was right about Hanson's investigation trying to protect the Rangers, but Canales thought Hanson was trying to protect Stevens's Regular Rangers, which wasn't the case at all. As we have seen, Hanson was protecting Hester and Abney, the two locals who were Special Rangers.

The testimony did reveal something interesting about Canales. When he was asked about Arturo García, the man who had been shot in the leg, Canales replied: "He was a Mexican citizen and I didn't have anything to do with Mexican citizens; I was looking out for American citizens of Mexican descent, that was all I was looking after."[77]

14. At about the same time and place, José Hernández was flogged and horsewhipped by Stevens's Rangers. While investigating, Hanson

had told Canales that Fred Winn, a Cameron County deputy, had admitted the act. Canales knew this to be untrue, for the offense was committed on a ranch south of Donna in Hidalgo County, fifty miles from Brownsville. Winn knew nothing of the incident, and this had awakened Canales to the fact that Hanson was engaged in a coverup.

As with the previous charge, Canales focused on the wrong perpetrators. Stevens's men had nothing to do with this affair. Hanson's report blamed "unknown parties" for having whipped Hernández because they believed he had stolen livestock. The guilty parties were presumably locals; Hanson wrote that he believed they should be punished, "but under the circumstances I don't believe a conviction could be secured."[78] Many of the documents cited for charge 13 also pertain to charge 14. Hanson's report said nothing about Deputy Sheriff Fred Winn.

15. There were, and had been for some time, desperate characters in the Rangers—gunmen, "their only qualification being that they can kill a man first and then investigate afterward." The adjutant general was either negligent or it was his policy to hire these thugs.

Here Canales had considerable justification for his charge. There were, and had been, desperate characters on the Ranger Force—without much effort the names of Daniel Hinojosa, W. V. Bentley, John Bloxom, J. B. Nalls, and H. L. Roberson, who will be discussed in charge 18, come to mind. One can sympathize with Canales when he complained that "As soon as I find the bad men they always say he [sic] has been discharged."[79] But Canales was also upset because Rangers whom he considered "bad men"—such as Hamer and Edds—were still on the force. Canales claimed that 90 percent of Rangers were gunmen, although he never explained how he had arrived at that precise percentage.[80]

One would have thought the Rangers would be on their best behavior during the committee's investigation. On the contrary, they seemed bent on helping Canales to make his case. On February 7, 1919, while the committee was still holding hearings, there occurred in Austin an incident that must have left Harley close to weeping tears of rage, and perhaps considering a different line of work. Chairman Bledsoe told the committee that he mentioned the matter with much reluctance but it related to the activities of some of the Ranger Force:

Bledsoe: This unfortunate occurrence out south of town here the other night. Is there any explanation to be made of it, or what are you going to say in the record about it? I understand that all four of the men involved in that were Rangers.

Knight: Yes, sir.

Bledsoe: And if the press reports are to be judged at all, they were violating practically every provision of our State statutes.[81]

It seems that Ranger Bert C. Veale, who had been a convict guard and then had served two years in Company D, had a bottle of whiskey and an automobile. Being a convivial sort, he invited Captain K. F. Cunningham, who had commanded Company M at Eagle Pass, Captain Harry M. Johnston, the Ranger quartermaster, and Sergeant Walter E. Mayberry[82] to join him in a spot of relaxation. That night the group had dinner at a restaurant and more than a few drinks. As Chairman Bledsoe bluntly put it, "Just to use a common English term, they got pretty well drunk." As the evening progressed and they got drunker, Veale and Cunningham got into an argument. The quarrel intensified, and Veale finally became so angry that he drew his pistol and fired at least twice at Cunningham. The other two Rangers tried to separate them but in the struggle Veale fired again, broke free, and fired several more rounds at Cunningham, who was getting really tired of being shot at; he fired back several times. When the shooting stopped, Cunningham was wounded in the neck and Veale was dead. This disgraceful affair of course made the front page of the newspapers, for it was not just a scandal but a juicy scandal involving two Ranger captains, one of them a killer.[83]

The adjutant general's attorney hastened to assure the committee that the survivors had all been expelled from the Ranger Force. Chairman Bledsoe commented that from the newspaper accounts only one Ranger had been discharged, the other two only suspended. Harley then explained that that had been the immediate action taken, but since then all three had been discharged after he had had time to verify the press accounts. The adjutant general added that witnesses were still being interviewed and so no formal report of the incident had as yet been prepared.[84] Harley disallowed the funeral home's bill for Veale's casket and services.[85] According to the service records, Cunningham was fired on February 7, but Johnston and Mayberry were only suspended on that date. They were fired on February 13.[86]

The loss of Captain Johnston was no great loss. Besides his incredibly poor judgment, he had no law enforcement background and had gotten his job because of familial connections. According to his assistant, Sergeant P. A. Cardwell, it was Cardwell who did most of the work, Johnston not bothering to come to the office for extended periods. Furthermore, Johnston did not pay his debts. An Austin sporting goods company had sued him and had won a judgment against him, but Johnston ignored it. The company wrote a hot letter to Harley, threatening to go public with the fact that Harley employed a deadbeat in a responsible position. Harley, to his great relief, was able to inform the company that Johnston had been discharged. Johnston evidently landed a job with the Texas Department of Insurance and Banking.[87]

Canales was eager to provide the committee with further details of this deplorable Ranger affair. He said that reliable sources had informed him that the

Travis County grand jury was investigating. Although he couldn't name his source, who was connected with the grand jury, that body had learned that "They had poker chips, and they have got them over there; they were playing poker at the time; and they had two women, and that wasn't only a drunken brawl, but also they were gambling at the time, and they had some women. That same information came to me, and I will state that if you can get one of those men—Mayfield or whatever his name is, on the stand he will have to tell you, because he has gone before the Grand Jury and those matters have been revealed in the Grand Jury." Canales also urged that the women be brought to testify before the committee. Harley and Hanson were prepared to take the stand should the committee desire their testimony. Chairman Bledsoe, however, suggested, and the rest of the committee agreed, not to pursue the investigation and to let the criminal justice system take its course.[88] Captain Cunningham was indicted for murder; he pleaded self-defense, which under the circumstances seemed quite reasonable. Ranger Mayberry was quietly reinstated to his rank of sergeant on November 25, 1919, after the dust had settled.

16. Citizens in Canales's and surrounding counties refused to bring charges against Rangers because they were convinced the adjutant general's investigations were just coverups to protect the Rangers. Here Canales recounted his own experience with Frank Hamer.

Canales asserted that he had many unsigned letters from intimidated citizens, but he refused to produce the letters or divulge the names.[89] John I. Kleiber, for the past twenty-five years the district attorney for the 28th Judicial District, encompassing Cameron, Hidalgo, Willacy, Kleberg, and Nueces Counties, testified that occasionally there had been trouble in getting witnesses to testify before the grand jury, whether because of intimidation or not, but these were decidedly the exceptions.[90] Thus Canales did not substantiate his sweeping allegation about citizens being too intimidated to press charges against the Rangers. What really bothered Canales was his experience with Frank Hamer. He was outraged because his complaint against Hamer had been made in secret to the adjutant general, who had then informed Hamer. Canales introduced a telegram from Harley to Hamer on December 23, 1918:

> Under Governor's orders you are instructed not to make any threats against the lives of any citizens especially J. T. Canales and that he is to be given proper protection as a citizen. Complaint has been filed that you have made some threats. Without going into the truth of the matter you are instructed to be careful and courteous at all times and not to make a personal matter of your official duties. Undertake to adjust differences as best you can without causing any trouble. Answer.[91]

Canales evidently thought that Harley should have summarily dismissed Hamer on the basis of the representative's complaint.

It is fairly obvious that Canales had been traumatized by Hamer. In relating Hamer's original threat, Canales stated that "his eyes glistened."[92] Hamer continued to play mind games with Canales. When the latter had come to Austin on January 12 for the legislative session, he saw Hamer in the Driskell Hotel "and his presence was made known to me very marked by passing in front of me, as though he simply wanted me to know that he was here and on the force." Canales later went to the Avenue Hotel, and Hamer again showed himself. "He wanted me to know it and I know it, of course. . . . I took his action as a challenge that I would be intimidated if I would make any charges against those rangers or introduce any law attempting to regulate them." The adjutant general's attorney asked Canales sarcastically "Hamer didn't go into hiding because you were in town?" The sarcasm was lost on Canales, who replied: "No, but he showed himself very markedly, as much as to tell me he was here in Austin." Canales did admit that Hamer had done nothing menacing.[93]

17. The adjutant general should have investigated and eliminated from the Rangers notoriously bad men. Harley was incompetent and the committee should recommend to the governor some proper person to fill the office.

The committee wanted no part of this charge. Chairman Bledsoe declared that it was "beyond our scope." Senator Paul Page, the vice chairman, moved that this charge be stricken. Canales explained that he had included the charge because the House had authorized a wide-ranging investigation. Bledsoe informed Canales that he was bound by the scope of his own resolution and could not make charges against the adjutant general in an investigation of this kind. Representative Dan S. McMillin inquired whether the adjutant general was even a member of the Ranger Force. Harley informed them that the governor was the head of the Ranger Force. Harley merely acted under his orders, so if they investigated Harley they would have to investigate the governor as well. Harley stated that the adjutant general was the governor's chief of staff and had little discretionary power (which was hardly the case), though he allowed as how he and the governor did make appointments to the Rangers. The committee decided that it would be permissible to investigate the adjutant general's department but not the adjutant general himself, and they voted to strike charge 17. Canales protested that the Rangers were absolutely under the adjutant general's control. This was incorrect—they were under the governor's absolute control, although in practice the adjutant general did administer the Ranger Force.[94] Canales's biographer believes that Harley accused Canales of trying to sodomize the Rangers: "Remarkably, the adjutant general managed to characterize Canales's efforts to reform the Rangers as a homosexual assault from behind."[95] How very odd.

> 18. Canales was reliably informed that H. E. [sic—H.L.] Roberson, longtime Ranger, did unjustifiably kill two and one-half years ago the unarmed H. F. Boykin at Sierra Blanca, and also killed a bystander. Canales explained that he did not charge that Roberson was a Ranger at the time, but he had been until shortly before and was again commissioned despite having been tried and convicted of murder.

Canales was absolutely correct. Horace L. "Hod" Roberson was a man who literally got away with murder. Roberson was a hard-bitten border character, soft-spoken, and with a short fuse. Born in November, 1875, at Staples Store in Guadalupe County, Roberson was a cowboy when he enlisted on October 11, 1911, in Company A under Captain Hughes. Roberson soon made his presence felt. On December 2, 1911, he and two other Rangers were returning on horseback from El Paso to Ysleta. At the settlement of Calero, five miles east of El Paso, they saw the saloon proprietor ejecting from his establishment some loudly cursing Hispanic drunks who began fighting among themselves. The Rangers identified themselves and attempted to separate the brawlers. One of them cursed Roberson and attacked him with a knife. Roberson shot him dead. Roberson surrendered to the sheriff, was released on a $500 bond, and was subsequently acquitted on a plea of self-defense.[96] Thereafter Roberson spent much of his time on what amounted to detached duty, based at Dickens in the Panhandle assisting the brand inspectors of the Cattle Raisers Association of Texas.[97] Captain Hughes promoted Roberson to sergeant in June, 1913. In July, 1913, however, Roberson resigned. He reenlisted on April 1, 1914, once again as sergeant, and was once again involved in a shooting scrape. In late June, he and Private Ira Cline tried to serve a warrant in Marfa on a certain Carlos Morales Wood, editor of a Spanish-language newspaper, who reportedly drew a gun. They shot him dead. They were acquitted at their trial.[98] On September 4, 1914, Roberson again resigned from Company A, this time for good.

He left the Rangers to become foreman of the huge T O Ranch across the Rio Grande from Sierra Blanca, Texas. He maintained a force of some twenty-five gunslingers to protect the property from raids by Mexicans. Roberson was a man of violent temper, as exemplified by an incident that occurred on January 16, 1915, at the stock pens in Sierra Blanca. He got into a heated argument with one Foote Boykin over a discrepancy in counting cattle. Roberson pulled a gun; Boykin called Roberson a coward; Roberson slashed Boykin across the head with his lariat; Boykin charged him with a knife; Roberson wheeled his horse, firing over his shoulder. Not being Buffalo Bill, his aim was off—his shot killed his friend Walter

Sitter, who was an innocent bystander; Sitter was the son of Customs inspector Joe Sitter, killed in the 1915 ambush in the Big Bend. But Roberson then put three slugs into Boykin, who fell and was trying to get up when Roberson finished him off with another bullet.[99] Roberson surrendered to Rangers Cline and Craighead and was taken to jail in El Paso. Released on a $7,500 bond, he was tried for murder, entering a plea of self-defense.

Ranchers who did not like Roberson hired state Senator Claude Hudspeth to assist in prosecuting him. Roberson's lawyer brought fifty character witnesses from the Panhandle, but to no avail. Hudspeth did a competent job, for Roberson was found guilty of murder and was sentenced to twenty years. However, one of the jurors later swore that he was a convicted felon, and because of this the judge set aside the verdict. The juror was later indicted for perjury, but the ploy had gotten Roberson a new trial. Hudspeth was again the lead prosecutor, and again Roberson was found guilty, but this time only of manslaughter, and his sentence was but five years. Roberson appealed his conviction and was released on bond while his case went through the appeals process. While the appeal was pending, he went to work at Dickens as a brand inspector for the Cattle Raisers Association of Texas. And because of this on May 8, 1916, he received a commission as a Special Ranger, attached to Company C. In 1918 the guilty verdict against Roberson was reversed.[100] He kept his Special Ranger commission until January 15, 1919, when such commissions were revoked. In 1918, along with other brand inspectors, he had been reclassified as a Regular Ranger without pay.

Roberson remained a brand inspector until April 1, 1923. He and fellow brand inspector Dave Allison, who had led the posse that killed Pascual Orozco in 1915, were in the Panhandle town of Seminole to testify to a grand jury about a rustling case. The night before their scheduled appearance they were seated in the lobby of the Gaines Hotel shooting the breeze when the two rustlers against whom they were going to testify burst in shooting a .38-caliber revolver and an automatic shotgun. Roberson and Allison never had a chance. Allison was killed instantly, toppling from his chair. One of the gunmen walked over and emptied his pistol into the fallen inspector. Roberson also died quickly, from a shotgun blast to the heart. He collapsed in his chair, his head lolling against the wall. Mrs. Roberson was upstairs in their room, and on hearing the shooting ran downstairs and opened fire on the assassins with her ladylike little automatic, hitting both of them. They took a wild shot at her and managed to escape.[101]

> 19. In 1917 [sic—1916], Ranger W. B. Sands, drunk in a notorious resort, the Coney Island saloon in El Paso, killed army Sergeant Owen Bierne, who had arrived to quell a disturbance there.

Ranger William B. Sands was indeed drunk and disorderly in the Coney Island saloon on September 21, 1916, when he shot Sergeant Bierne. Sands was immediately dismissed from the Rangers. When he was tried for murder in El Paso in May, 1917, he had a good lawyer, state Senator Claude Hudspeth, and his trial ended in a hung jury.[102] Sands was hardly a credit to the Ranger Force.

The joint committee ended its investigation on February 13, 1919. In evaluating Canales and his attack on the Rangers, two conclusions seem indicated. First, Canales was a South Texas politician, which in itself speaks volumes. Second, he won the battle but lost the war. Canales proved some of his charges while signally failing to substantiate others, but he brought to the public's attention the dark side of the Ranger Force, characterized by abuse of authority, brutality, killings, drunkenness, racism, and political partisanship. For that he was to be commended.

As one witness testified: "You've got to have safeguards regarding the Rangers. These young men, hot blooded young fellows without much education, men who are willing to go out and risk their lives for forty, fifty, or sixty dollars a month and lead the kind of lives they do, are not the type of men you want to entrust the lives and properties of the citizens to without throwing around them some safeguard."[103]

Furthermore, Canales cast serious doubt on the way Captain Hanson, the Ranger inspector, conducted his investigations. Hanson's approach was indeed to justify the Rangers whenever possible. But this was nothing unique to Hanson. It would appear that any institution, whether it be the Texas Rangers or the Roman Catholic Church, instinctively tries to avoid scandal by covering up the misdeeds of its members. In terms of personalities, Canales's revelations led to the dismissal of Hinojosa and Captain Sanders, but he failed to secure the firing of those Rangers whom he particularly disliked: Hanson, Hamer, and Edds, as well as Adjutant General Harley.

Canales's vendetta against Hanson included denouncing the Ranger captain to the Department of Justice. On February 6, Canales wrote:

> If your department is interested in catching a big intriguer and violator of the neutrality laws between the United States and Mexico, and a man who has through political influence secured a respectable position in the State of Texas as Inspector of Rangers, you had better send one of your best men to watch the investigating proceedings pending in Austin and keep an eye on one W. M. Hanson. I know, and I believe that I can show that he is a crook of the first order and also a man disloyal to our country, for the reason that he was a partisan of Gen. Huerta, that Mexican usurper and human beast, at the very time that our President sent our troops to Vera Cruz, Mexico, to punish him for the indignity done to our flag.
>
> I trust that you will not pursue the same course of our State Department of showing correspondence of this kind and putting the crooked on notice that they are about to be investigated.[104]

On February 12, Bruce Bielaski, Chief of the Bureau of Investigation, wrote to C. E. Breniman, Division Superintendent in charge of the Bureau's San Antonio office, that he had received information from Military Intelligence that they had been reliably informed that Hanson "is implicated in, or at least has criminal knowledge of, the smuggling of ammunition from the United States to Felicista rebels in Mexico," and left it up to Breniman to investigate.[105] The San Antonio office noted that during the Ranger Investigation Canales had produced no evidence to support the charges made against Hanson in his letter, and, further, Canales had had ample opportunity to interrogate Hanson but had declined to do so. Superintendent Breniman characterized Hanson as "the most efficient official with whom I had ever come in contact."[106]

As for the investigating committee, it has been observed that the "conclusions and recommendations of the joint committee represented an awkward attempt to arrange a political compromise."[107] While thanking Canales for his efforts and acknowledging that many abuses had been documented, the committee also recognized the exemplary service of many of the Rangers and the organization's contribution to law enforcement on the border. The committee praised Harley's efforts to upgrade the Ranger Force, and it virtually ignored the provisions of the Canales bill.[108] Harley and Hanson triumphantly telegraphed various supporters that "Committee report all we could ask for. Vindication complete."[109]

Canales was furious, and he urged the House not to accept the committee's report, blasting the committee for refusing to investigate Harley. This produced a counterblast from Chairman Bledsoe, who charged that Canales was just the mouthpiece for an unnamed but more powerful border politician, obviously Jim Wells, who along with others of his ilk was obstructing law enforcement, trying to protect his own selfish interests at the expense of the state's best interests. Canales got clobbered: the House adopted the committee's report by the overwhelming vote of 87 to 10.

With Harley's enthusiastic support, Bledsoe then introduced a substitute bill for Ranger reform. It eliminated the most controversial features of the Canales bill, such as the requirement that Rangers be bonded. It provided for Special Rangers. Dayton Moses, attorney for the Cattle Raisers Association of Texas, had helped to argue the Rangers' case before the committee. He now helped to draft the substitute bill, and despite Bledsoe's reluctance included a provision for Special Rangers, who had to be recommended by district judges and district attorneys. This would lessen the chances of irresponsible parties being appointed while enabling the Association to have its brand inspectors continue to hold Special Ranger commissions. In a nod to local control, the bill provided that Rangers had to deliver their prisoners promptly to the sheriff of the county where the arrest had been made. Regarding charges of abuse of authority, these could result in a hearing before a local magistrate to determine if the offender should be dismissed from the force, but—*only the adjutant general could initiate such a procedure*. In a throwback to the old Frontier Battalion the bill reestablished one lieutenant per company. It also raised salaries, something that both the Rangers' detractors and supporters agreed was necessary. It provided for $200 a month for captains, $150 for lieutenants, $125 for sergeants, and $100 for privates. However, the House eliminated lieutenants and reduced the salaries.[110]

As debate in the House intensified, tempers frayed. In a noteworthy incident, Representative Bledsoe came close to slapping Canales on the floor of the House. Bledsoe apologized to his colleagues but explained that after having to endure Canales's sleazy behavior before the committee for two weeks, his patience was exhausted. Apparently the House had also had enough of Canales. When Bledsoe's substitute bill came up for a vote, it passed by 95 to 5. And in the Senate the bill met scant opposition—only one senator opposed its passage.[111]

As a result of the legislature's having overwhelmingly defeated his attack on the Rangers, the disillusioned Canales decided not to seek reelection in 1920.[112] And despite Canales having dramatically told the House that "If you kill this bill, you had just as well sign an order to send my body home feet first" and predicting that he wouldn't live six months,[113] neither Frank Hamer nor anybody else tried to kill Canales. In fact, he lived until 1976, when he died in Brownsville at the age of ninety-nine.

There is a serious misperception concerning the impact of Canales's 1919 attack on the Rangers. It has been stated that "the result of the Canales investigation was a complete reorganization of the Texas Rangers. They were reduced from twelve to four companies."[114] Even the Texas Department of Public Safety subscribes to this assertion: "A Legislative investigation was launched and caused a cutback in the force to four companies of not more than fifteen men each."[115] The Regular Rangers were indeed reduced to four companies, but not because of Canales. Their numbers were reduced because World War I was over (the U.S. Army was drastically reduced in 1919 for exactly the same reason). The wartime Ranger companies, along with the Loyalty Rangers, were no longer needed, especially since Carranza's attitude was now considerably less hostile. The Rangers' prewar authorized strength was eighty-nine men; the 1919 law reduced this to seventy-five—hardly a drastic reduction. The Canales bill would have reduced the Ranger Force to twenty-four men. One historian even asserts that "Because of their partisan activities, the Rangers were reorganized by the legislature and reduced to a company of special investigators in 1919,"[116] whatever that means. Further, it has been claimed that the Rangers "were weakened by legislative action and discredited in the eyes of the public."[117] The only legislative weakening was a temporary suspension in the issuing of new Special Ranger commissions. Otherwise, as the overwhelming approval of the Bledsoe bill demonstrates, the legislature strongly supported the Rangers. As far as the Rangers being "discred-

ited in the eyes of the public" is concerned, given the times, it is extremely doubtful that most Texans were outraged to learn that the Rangers had committed
excesses against Mexicans. Yet there are still references to "the Canales
reforms,"[118] when even Canales's biographer admits that by the time the legislature got through, "Nothing remained of Canales's original bill."[119] "Despite the
revelations of the Ranger hearings, the victory for both the Hobby administration and the state police was now complete. Bledsoe's revision of the Canales
reform proposal left the governor and his adjutant general with a free hand to run
the Rangers as they saw fit, and the overwhelming majorities in both houses provided the lawmen with a strong vote of confidence."[120]

CHAPTER EIGHTEEN

AFTERMATH

THE law of March 31, 1919, which did not take effect until June 20, in theory meant a kinder, gentler Ranger Force. But as has been observed, "Without structural reform as [Canales] had advocated, however, the Rangers of Gov. William Hobby underwent only cosmetic change."[1] The new law established a peacetime strength of seventy-five men: four field companies, each having a captain, a sergeant, and fifteen privates; a headquarters company of one senior captain, a sergeant, and four privates; and a quartermaster captain. The statute empowered the governor to increase the Ranger Force as he saw fit during emergencies, but there was no provision for commissioning Special Rangers, it being felt that this type of commission had been abused. Although the Cattle Raisers Association lobbied for Special Ranger commissions to be reinstated for its brand inspectors, the lawmakers refused. (The issuance of Special Ranger commissions was resumed in 1920.) The new law also enabled any citizen to complain about any Ranger for any kind of offense, *but it would be the adjutant general who would investigate and initiate legal action if warranted.*[2] This actually was not all that different from the old system. The pay scale was improved in hopes of attracting better men: captains received $150 a month, sergeants $100, and privates $90, and all Rangers got $30 for subsistence. A Ranger had to furnish his own horse, saddle, rifle, and pistol. The state supplied forage and ammunition. Only men, whether single or married, between twenty-three and forty-five years old would be accepted. Captains could select their own men, but the adjutant general had final approval. Unfortunately the new law retained one of the gravest weaknesses of the Ranger Force—men enlisted for two years but could quit or be fired at any time.[3] Thus, the personnel revolving door continued.

So did the battle with penury. Even before the new law was passed the Ranger

Force was being slashed in anticipation that fewer men would be authorized. On March 10, Company A was disbanded. Its commander was the veteran Captain John J. Sanders, whose career thus ended on a sad note, for he was not reappointed. In part this resulted from his chronic ill health; when he testified before the Investigation Committee he began by announcing that he had been sick all night and was still sick. Mainly, though, Harley felt that Sanders had outlived his usefulness. In the investigation, Sanders had admitted that in 1915 he had tried to pistol-whip attorney Thomas W. Hook in the courthouse at Falfurrias.[4] Presumably for this offense Sanders was suspended on February 6, 1919. There were also allegations that he had a drinking problem. Despite this charge being vigorously refuted by reputable people, the committee did not look with favor on Sanders. Harley informed one of Sanders's defenders that "acting under the findings of the Investigation Committee it became necessary for us not to re-appoint Captain Sanders," assuring him that there was nothing personal in this decision.[5] Sanders was discharged on March 4, 1919. Since there was no pension for Rangers, he had to shift for himself. As of October, 1922, he was a railroad special watchman. Sanders died on February 6, 1924.

On the same day Company A was disbanded two of the wartime companies met the same fate. Companies M and L were disbanded, and reductions were made in Companies B, D, and I. In all nineteen Rangers were honorably discharged, including Captain W. W. Davis of Company L. Captain Lon L. Willis of Company M was reduced in rank to sergeant and transferred to Company I. Then on March 19 it was the turn of Company E to be disbanded. Harley wrote its captain, W. L. Barler, a warm letter of appreciation.[6] Later that month Captain Will Wright of Company K was ordered to discharge men until he got his company down to fifteen.[7] It was stipulated that those men honorably discharged could apply for reinstatement when the Ranger Force was reorganized in September.[8] But September was a long way off, and the legislature's appropriation of $50,000 for the 1918–1919 fiscal year was clearly inadequate since it cost over $1,000 to maintain a Ranger for a year. The Rangers had to operate on a shoestring until the next legislative session, when hopefully the lawmakers would be more generous.

The man charged with pinching the pennies was Captain Roy Aldrich, who took over as quartermaster on February 13 when Captain Harry Johnston was fired for conduct unbecoming. Although Aldrich had field experience, his strong suit was administration.[9] But by 1915, he again got the itch for something more exciting, and he enlisted in the Rangers. Now, as quartermaster captain, Aldrich was able to expand the scope of his duties, and consequently his power. In this connection it might be mentioned that Aldrich was an avid collector, and he had Rangers throughout the state acquiring artifacts, animal horns, and pottery for his collections. As he mentioned to one Ranger, "I am a crank about arrow-heads and deer horns, as you know."[10] Hanson remained the senior captain but was focusing on Mexican affairs, so it was Aldrich who administered the Ranger Force on a day-to-day basis, occupying much the same position as had Walter Woodul. Aldrich overshadowed the assistant adjutant general, Colonel W. D. Cope. There was a lot of administering to do, for the Rangers were becoming much more bureaucratic. For instance, instead of the Monthly Returns that captains had submitted earlier in the decade, General Orders No. 4 of March 24 established a new system, which took effect on April 1. Every Regular Ranger was now issued a pocket-sized notebook on each page of which he made his Daily Scout Report in duplicate. Each Monday he tore out the completed pages, sending the yellow copy to his captain and the white copy to the adjutant general's department. Each Monday the captain mailed the reports to the adjutant general together with his report showing the disposition of his men for the ensuing week and whatever other information concerning conditions in his district he considered worthy of comment.[11] This was the theory; in practice, many Rangers sent in their Daily Scout Reports at irregular intervals.

Since Rangers did not wear uniforms, there had always been the problem of enabling them to identify themselves. Now each Regular Ranger received a pocket-sized leather wallet containing his commission, for purposes of identification.[12] These folders cost the state over four dollars each, and captains were financially liable if their men lost their folders. The adjutant general's department still did not furnish Rangers with badges, but a few of the men had badges made privately at jewelry stores.[13]

Aldrich had his hands full reviewing accounts. Sergeant P. A. Cardwell, who as assistant quartermaster had performed this tedious function very competently for several years, resigned from the Rangers in disgust when he was passed over for quartermaster in favor of Aldrich; Cardwell realized he would never be promoted to captain.[14] Paperwork had always been the bane of captains' existence, but now everybody got to share the pain. Aldrich explained the new system: "We have gone on the budget system and so much money is appropriated for this and so much for that and money cannot be used for one thing that was appropriated for another. It used to be all in a lump and could be used for anything considered necessary." Now, there were thirteen separate accounts to which expenditures were to be charged.[15] Aldrich continued: "The state of our finances won't permit the expenditure of a dollar more than is necessary." He also referred to a Special Order of Harley's directing that no railroad fare would be allowed for trips not directly authorized by the captains of companies.[16] There had to be receipts for everything; rank-and-file Rangers suffered agonies trying to fill out their expense accounts properly. And whenever possible, the adjutant general rejected claims. We have seen that he refused to pay for Ranger Bert Veale's funeral, since Veale most emphatically had not died in the line of duty. Harley also refused to pay more than $50 for the medical expenses and medications for Ranger Lenn T. Sadler, who had died in Del Rio of a gunshot wound from a fellow Ranger. The attending physician contemptuously refused to accept what he considered a pittance, which suited the adjutant general just fine.[17] Harley also rejected an $85 claim by Ranger George W. Sadler, who had ridden his horse to death chasing bootleggers. The adjutant general pointed out that the state would pay only for Ranger horses *killed in action*.[18] Sadler should have trotted after the bootleggers.

Not only did the Rangers have to contend with new and improved paperwork but they were also supposed to conform to a new and stricter code of conduct. Back on September 24, 1918, Harley had issued an order prohibiting Rangers from criticizing each other and directing that any complaints be referred to his office.[19] Expanding on that order, Harley now sought legal advice in preparing his *Rules and Regulations Governing State Ranger Force of the State of Texas*.[20] Besides the usual admonition to enforce the law impartially and to work harmoniously with local officers, Rangers were instructed that prisoners must always be accompanied by at least one Ranger. Captains were held accountable for their men's actions, and when detachments were sent out, one man would be placed in charge and be held accountable for the actions of the others. Furthermore, "Rangers must be gentlemen at all times and under all circumstances," including their relations with fellow Rangers. "There must be good fellowship shown, at all times, between Rangers. Heated arguments or dirty or obscene language will not be tolerated." The *Rules* prohibited drinking or gambling even when off duty. There was even a dress code: "While in cities or small towns or riding on trains, narrow belts with cartridges and pistol well hidden must be conformed to." And "Scout clothes that make you conspicuous must not be worn when visiting cities or large towns, and it will be pleasing to this Department if you will dress when off actual scout duty, in cities and small towns, in such manner as not to draw unnecessary attention."

In a further effort to avoid unnecessary attention, Rangers in Austin were relocated to the outskirts of the city, to Camp Mabry, headquarters of the Texas National Guard, where they would be under Captain J. L. Anders. The move was less than popular, especially among the married men.[21] The Rangers' situation was alleviated somewhat when, in a gracious gesture, the 9th Texas Infantry Regiment cordially invited them to spend their leisure time in the regiment's armory, making themselves at home in the lounge and athletic hall.[22] Rangers were adaptable sorts, and soon Aldrich was able to report that "The boys have a fine camp at Camp Mabry and I believe *most* of them are satisfied now."[23]

Aldrich's duties included handling applications for reenlistment when the new law took effect on June 20. Among those reenlisted were, undoubtedly to Representative Canales's intense disgust, Frank Hamer and John J. Edds. Canales evidently had no further dealings with Hamer, who resigned in 1920 to become a federal Prohibition agent, then resigned that position in 1921 to become a Ranger captain, but he went after Edds with a vengeance. Canales not only pressed further charges against Edds but also became the attorney for parties filing civil suits against Edds, who was hard pressed to defend himself on what a Ranger's salary would buy in the way of legal talent. Yet despite Canales's best efforts, Edds emerged from his legal troubles still a Ranger, remaining on the force until December 10, 1921, when he resigned.[24]

While all these changes were taking place in Austin, it had been business as usual out in the field. As a general policy, Rangers were sent into a community only when requested by the sheriff and district or county attorney.[25] But there were exceptions, usually because local officers were unwilling or unable to enforce the law. For instance, on January 13, the county attorney and district judge of Hill County wrote to Governor Hobby urgently requesting that at least six Rangers be dispatched to Hillsboro, some eighty miles north of Austin, because a black man was to be tried in two days, and lynching was a virtual certainty.[26] The sheriff, interestingly enough, had refused to participate in the request, informing the district judge and county attorney that:

> I am just as anxious as you gentlemen to see the law enforced and will do all that's in the power of myself and men to see that same is enforced, but realizing that if a number of good determined citizens of Hill County, Texas, are set on mobbing this negro, my force nor the Rangers you speak of could prevent same without bloodshed and knowing the Rangers have a reputation as gunmen and knowing that they would live up to same if occasion demanded it I will have to refuse your request as I feel that myself and men can handle same as satisfactorily as the Rangers you speak of. . . . I would rather give up my office as Sheriff of Hill County, Texas, than to have a good citizen of Hill County killed or wounded by Texas Rangers ordered here by me.[27]

Governor Hobby did not share the sheriff's tender solicitude for the good citizens—and voters—of Hill County and ordered a detachment of six Rangers, three of them captains, to Hillsboro on January 14.[28] The Rangers overawed the locals during the trial, which resulted in the defendant being convicted. Unfortunately, as soon as the Rangers left town the black man was lynched.[29]

A similar situation arose at Tyler, in East Texas, in early April. The county attorney, district attorney, and sheriff jointly requested that Rangers be dispatched to Smith County immediately to prevent racial violence. Two Rangers were sent.[30] They had a calming effect.

But in July a full-scale race riot broke out elsewhere in East Texas, at Longview, and the local authorities lost control. The adjutant general telephoned Captain Hanson in San Antonio on July 11 to take Sergeant Brooks and Ranger C. J. Blackwell and proceed to Longview immediately.[31] They arrived by train the next day, constituting the advance guard of what became a contingent of ten

Rangers. On July 11, Lieutenant Colonel H. C. Smith of the adjutant general's department also arrived to investigate the situation. On July 13, at the request of the citizens, Governor Hobby proclaimed martial law, and some 300 Texas National Guard troops were sent to Longview. Martial law was lifted on July 18.[32]

Hanson's report recapitulated the events in this disgraceful affair. Several weeks earlier, the sheriff had arrested a black man for insulting an Anglo woman. The sheriff then allowed "certain individuals" to take the prisoner from jail in order to give him a good beating and run him out of town, but they ended up shooting him to death. A black newspaper in Chicago ran a story on the incident, making remarks about the woman in question that the sheriff and Anglo citizens of Longview considered scurrilous.

They suspected that a local black educator had written the article, and on the evening of July 10, two brothers of the Anglo woman beat the educator to a pulp. Blacks began to gather at his house as the news spread. Later that night a mob of some twenty Anglos, including young men from good families, went to the educator's house, supposedly to kill him. But the blacks guarding the house had the effrontery to defend themselves, opening fire and wounding four Anglos, although "the general opinion is that some of the wounds were caused by shooting each other." The mob retreated, regrouped, and grew. The next morning they began burning down black-owned structures, as well as severely beating several black men and an eighty-year-old black woman.

Captain Hanson and Lieutenant Colonel Smith convened a mass meeting of the respectable citizenry and had them appoint a committee, composed of the sheriff, county judge, and mayor, to help restore order. A major step in that direction was the confiscation of "several thousand" firearms. Meanwhile, Hanson's Rangers arrested the leader of the mob, who was persuaded to identify seventeen of his fellows. Hanson filed complaints against them for assault to murder, arrested them, and asked for $1,000 bond for each of them. Several others were later arrested for arson, bringing the total to twenty-six. Hanson learned from the prisoners that twenty-two blacks had been identified as defenders of the educator's house, and the racists had them marked for whippings and, if the blacks remained in Longview, for murder.

After conferring with the local leadership, Hanson decided that the best course was to take these blacks to Austin in order to save their lives, for a leader of the mob reiterated that they would be hunted down. Hanson filed complaints against the twenty-two blacks and, in company with a detachment of the Texas National Guard, took them to Austin, where it was arranged for them to be freed on bond. At the request of the Longview establishment, Hanson left three Rangers there to work with local officials and continue the investigation.[33]

Hanson was soon back in East Texas. At the end of July the district judge telegraphed Governor Hobby from Gilmer, fifteen miles north of Longview, asking for Rangers to investigate the lynching of a black man. The next day Captain Hanson and three Rangers arrived on the scene, and Hanson reported to the judge. The Rangers' mere presence helped to restore order, and Hanson and his men worked with local officers in conducting the investigation, which culminated in the arrest of five Anglo men and their indictment for murder.[34] While he was in Gilmer, Hanson took the opportunity to recruit two men for his Headquarters Company.[35]

With racial tensions increasing in East Texas, Governor Hobby and Adjutant General Harley directed Hanson to organize a meeting of sheriffs in that area to discuss how the Texas National Guard and the Rangers could assist them—not to prevent lynchings but rather to suppress black agitation and demands for equal rights. The meeting took place at the Rice Hotel in Houston on August 23. Hanson presided as chairman and appointed Major Walter F. Woodul, the former assistant adjutant general who was now practicing law in Houston, as secretary. Fourteen sheriffs and the Houston police chief were present; the federal Bureau of Investigation was invited but did not send a representative. The assembled lawmen heard Hanson report on the findings of his operatives and on black publications which "tend to inflame the negroes and which naturally lead to race troubles." Then each sheriff reported on conditions in his county, as did the Houston chief of police. They were particularly concerned about blacks arming themselves, and Hanson had assigned a Ranger exclusively to investigate this matter. The adjutant general had also been investigating black organizations, such as the NAACP. The meeting eloquently reflected how law enforcement viewed the racial problem.[36]

There were numerous other requests for Rangers, but they could not be answered for lack of manpower.[37] The principal focus of the Ranger Force remained where it had always been—on the Mexican border, where the field companies were deployed. On May 19, Governor Hobby formally appointed his captains:

W. M. Hanson	Headquarters Company
W. L. Wright	Company K
W. M. Ryan	Company I
Jerry Gray	Company B
J. L. Anders	Company D
Charles Stevens	Company G
Woody Townsend	Company M
W. W. Davis	Reserve status
Roy Aldrich	Quartermaster

Wright, Ryan, Gray, and Stevens commanded the field companies, while Anders ran the camp at Camp Mabry. Hobby explained to Harley that "Three of these appointments are emergency appointments [Townsend, Davis, and Stevens] and I have made them in order to meet the conditions which exist along the border, of which I have been advised in the last few weeks are more serious than has been the case for sometime, and in order to meet the situation which you and I after personal conference concluded is necessary."[38]

As was inevitable, there were those who objected to some of the appointments. Hanson was reappointed despite opposition but with the strong support of a member of the Investigation Committee, Representative Sam C. Lackey, who told Hobby that "In our investigation there was not one sentence of evidence against Captain Hanson and every witness spoke of him in the very highest terms."[39] Another controversial reappointment was that of Captain Stevens, who had been suspended on February 7, 1919, because of his policy of disarming Hispanics in the Valley. The Investigation Committee was averse to his remaining on the Force. Harley had even hinted to Stevens that it might be a good idea if he were to resign, for the good of the service. Stevens refused, and his supporters deluged Hobby with letters of recommendation. The governor was sympathetic, and Stevens stayed on the force.[40]

Congressman Claude Hudspeth was also miffed by the appointments. He chided Harley for not having reappointed Captains W. Lee Barler and W. W. Taylor, for both of whom he had great admiration. Hudspeth referred to Canales's "abortive attempt to destroy the Ranger force in Texas" and pointed out that even Canales could not produce anything negative against Barler and Taylor. He assured Harley that "I went to your relief once and if you get into any trouble in the future I will go again."[41] Harley replied that he and the governor had been unable to agree on all the appointments, and Hobby had of course made the final decisions. But as to Barler and Taylor, Harley agreed that Barler "is as good a man as I think has ever been in the Ranger service, and I regret very much to see him leave it, but I cannot say as much for Captain Taylor as his services were very unsatisfactory."[42] Hudspeth was relentless. He wrote to Harley asking plaintively: "Why did you take all my ranger captains away? I went to Austin and untangled the fangs of Venustiano Canales from around your neck and yet you fired all of your best captains, which included my friends." He urged Harley to reinstate Captain Will Davis, of El Paso, adding: "Now, my son, get right down and wire Captain Davis that you have reinstated him and you will make me happy and make yourself absolutely secure with the people of El Paso."[43] Such a move wouldn't hurt Hudspeth politically at all, since Captain Davis's cousin, Charles Davis, was mayor of El Paso. Hudspeth was most gratified when a few days later Harley notified him that Captain Davis would be reinstated (because Woody Townsend had declined his appointment). But Hudspeth had yet another request to make. He asked that a Special Ranger commission be issued to Captain B. J. Zabriskie, a former El Paso police chief. Zabriskie had been one of Congressman Hudspeth's campaign managers and "I am deeply interested in him."[44] Although Harley was agreeable, the commission was never issued.

The new Ranger law took effect on June 20, and on the 19th all Rangers other than captains were discharged and had to reapply for enlistment. But by then the organization had been reduced to about fifty men, and as Captain Aldrich dolefully reported, "We are mighty near out of money."[45] The financial situation was so acute that Harley ordered that the use of telegrams be kept to an absolute minimum in order to save money.[46]

Captain Hanson, though senior captain and Headquarters Company commander, operated out of his office at 204 Gunter Building, San Antonio, and was concerned primarily with gathering intelligence on Mexico. A sergeant commanded the four privates in Headquarters Company, which handled calls throughout the interior of Texas.[47] Virtually all the other Rangers were on the border.

Hobby and Harley were deeply worried about conditions along the border. President Venustiano Carranza's administration was becoming increasingly unpopular in Mexico.[48] Among the reasons were widespread corruption and the administration's having engineered the assassination of General Emiliano Zapata in April. Carranza's term would end in 1920, and he was barred by the constitution from seeking reelection. Unrest was intensifying as would-be successors to Carranza began maneuvering for position, and there was also suspicion that Carranza would seek to retain power by imposing a puppet president in 1920. An ominous development for Carranza occurred on June 1 when General Alvaro Obregón, whose military prowess had elevated Carranza to power, announced his candidacy for president in 1920. The popular and powerful Obregón would be a formidable opponent to any puppet Carranza might try to impose. With growing instability in Mexico, residents along the Texas border braced themselves for a new wave of depredations.

The governor and Harley did not rely exclusively on Hanson for intelligence data. In early June, Hobby directed the adjutant general to request the mayors of Brownsville, Laredo, Eagle Pass, Del Rio, and El Paso to keep Austin continually informed about border conditions in their areas, promising that the information would be treated as absolutely confidential. The same request was made of several prominent El Pasoans.[49] Harley had another channel of information in the person of Fred E. Marks, whom we will meet again. Marks had been a deputy sheriff and for three years a deputy U.S. marshal. He was a druggist in Rio Grande City and had been a special employee of the Bureau of Investigation. On July 11, 1918, Marks had become a Loyalty Ranger, and on November 21, 1918, was called to active duty as a Regular Ranger, working on detached service for Captain Hanson. In April and May, 1919, he traveled in Mexico on business and made a confidential report on conditions to Harley.[50]

Evidencing the administration's interest in border issues, when Governor Gustavo Espinosa Mireles of Coahuila visited Piedras Negras on May 22, to discuss with the district commander, General Bruno Neira, how to prevent ammunition smuggling by followers of Pancho Villa, a delegation went from Austin to confer with the governor. It consisted of Adjutant General Harley, Colonel F. A. Chapa, and Colonel Webb, commanding the 8th Texas Infantry. When they met with Espinosa Mireles the next day, the conference was cordial enough, with repeated expressions of mutual esteem, but the parties talked past each other. The governor was mainly interested in stopping munitions smuggling, primarily through the Big Bend, to anti-Carranza elements, suggesting that the Rangers cooperate with the Mexican authorities toward that end. Harley was mainly interested in stopping the smuggling of liquor into Texas and in exploring trans-border commercial possibilities.[51]

The federal Bureau of Investigation was also quite concerned about the Texas border, the division superintendent at San Antonio informing Harley on June 12 that:

> Reports reaching this office during the past few weeks indicate that Mexican revolutionary bands are more than usually active near the border and especially so opposite the Big Bend country and El Paso. . . . We have not a sufficient number of agents of the Department of Justice to properly police the border and must, necessarily, depend upon the Ranger force to take a leading part in preventing raids and the smuggling of arms and ammunition to the bandits. . . . The Ranger force has always been prompt and effective in suppressing violations of the State and Federal laws, and I will appreciate your assigning a considerable force to that territory with instructions to co-operate with our agents who may call upon them for assistance.[52]

Harley assured the Bureau that the Rangers would cooperate to the limit of their ability, but of course the Ranger Force was much smaller than it had been during the war.[53]

When the new law became effective on June 20, 1919, the Ranger Force was reorganized as follows:

Headquarters Co.	Captain W. M. Hanson	1 sgt, 5 pvts.	Austin	7
Company A	Captain Jerry Gray	1 sgt, 13 pvts.	Marfa	15
Company B	Captain C. F. Stevens	10 pvts.	Ysleta	11
Company C	Captain W. M. Ryan	1 sgt, 13 pvts.	Laredo	15
Company D	Captain W. L. Wright	1 sgt, 12 pvts.	Brownsville	14
Company E	Captain J. L. Anders	1 sgt, 12 pvts.	Marathon	14
Company F	Capt. W. W. Davis	1 sgt, 8 pvts.	Del Rio	10
Quartermaster	Captain R. W. Aldrich			1

87[54]

The specific focus of concern was Pancho Villa. As had been the case prior to his raid on Columbus in 1916, Villa was down but certainly not out. He was, in fact, trying to make a comeback by mounting a major military campaign. He financed himself by levying "taxes"—protection money—on business enterprises, both Mexican and foreign. He secured munitions both by having them smuggled across the border and by purchasing them from corrupt members of the Carranza army. As for men, he relied heavily on volunteers. The most prestigious of these volunteers was General Felipe Angeles, who had been the artillery commander during the heyday of Villa's Division of the North but who had gone into exile in the United States when Villa's fortunes declined in 1915. The reappearance of this most capable professional soldier in Villa's ranks was a real morale builder. Although there were some 17,000 Carranza troops in the state of Chihuahua compared to Villa's 3,000, the former were of indifferent fighting quality and enjoyed uncertain popular support. Villa stormed and captured the important mining center of Parral in southern Chihuahua, and his military momentum increased accordingly. He began marching north toward the border. And in a move reminiscent of Governor Oscar B. Colquitt, when the Mexican government requested permission to move troops through Texas in order to reinforce the garrison in Juárez, Governor Hobby adamantly refused, an action that struck a responsive chord among his fellow Texans.[55]

To monitor the situation from the vantage point of El Paso, Harley sent Ranger Walter I. Rowe there in May. Rowe, incidentally, was no longer capable of ordinary field work because he had lost $1^1/_2$ inches of his leg as a result of having been shot by deserters in East Texas in 1918, but there was nothing wrong with his mind. He carried out his assignment in exemplary fashion. Rowe also traveled through the Big Bend and down to the Rio Grande, reporting that ninety percent of people in that region sympathized with Villa, and the same was true for El Paso. One who did not was "the famous Chico Cano," who was once again a carrancista. He had been spotted on the river across from Ruidosa; he and his men were well mounted, riding sixteen horses they had stolen from the mounted Customs inspectors the previous winter. Regarding the smuggling of ammunition, Rowe reported that American soldiers were trading considerable quantities of it for booze. He hoped Military Intelligence would take action to stop this illicit traffic.[56]

Rowe worked at a considerable disadvantage. His expense account was limited by law to $3 a day, but Captain Hanson instructed him to work in conjunction with A. Osterveen, "special representative from [the] Mexican government," who spent money lavishly, expecting Rowe to accompany him on trips and stay in the best hotels.[57] Rowe was having to spend money he could not afford. Nevertheless, he carried out his assignment, working closely not just with Osterveen but also with the El Paso office of the Bureau of Investigation. He informed Harley that the Bureau had the smuggling situation there under such tight control that "they know more about what is going on over in Mexico than Carranza and all his agents does [sic]."[58] Rowe's efforts earned him a warm letter of commendation from the Bureau's El Paso agent in charge, (ex-Ranger) Gus T. Jones, who stated that Rowe "has brought us some information of considerable value to the government, cooperating with us to the fullest extent."[59]

Harley and Hanson were also receiving information from Captain Stevens, who with his men was patrolling the river on a daily basis and was also keeping a close watch on the Island, the scene of so much trouble for the Rangers. Stevens worked closely with the army detachment stationed at Fabens and with Rowe and Osterveen as well as with the Bureau of Investigation. He was able to report that "I have a list of all the men who are under suspicion on the American side of being connected with the Villa movement."[60] On June 14, he gave his assessment of the situation: "I think that this Villa excitement is more of a Villa boom, than any thing else. My idea is that they are trying to get the Federals in Juarez to revolt. There [are] a lot of rumors of all kinds in this country, but you know how these rumors are, they grow as they travel."[61]

The next day Villa attacked Ciudad Juárez. Having captured Parral, the only other two cities in Chihuahua were the state capital and Juárez. Villa decided that the capital was too heavily defended, so he planned to repeat his feat of 1913 by seizing the largest port of entry on the border, which would be a serious blow to the prestige of President Carranza. The assault began at 12:15 a.m. on June 15. Villa entrusted command to one of his lieutenants, who shrewdly attacked from the southeast, so that hopefully his troops could fire without their bullets landing in El Paso. After several hours of bloody fighting, the villistas gained virtual control of the city, the Carranza garrison having taken refuge in nearby Fort Hidalgo. But villista discipline broke down, and the men scattered throughout the city, bent on plunder. A Carranza counterattack drove them out, but a counterattack by Villa's forces drove the garrison once again into Fort Hidalgo. Villa was on the verge of a decisive victory when he was undone by the United States. Inevitably, some villista rounds had landed in El Paso, wounding several people. The United States Army reacted forcefully and decisively, with some 3,600 troops: four batteries of the 82nd Field Artillery began pounding Villa's positions, the 24th Infantry regiment stormed across the Santa Fe Street international bridge into downtown Juárez, and the 2nd Cavalry Brigade crossed at three fords downriver from Juárez. In the face of massive American firepower resistance collapsed, and Villa's demoralized followers fled in disarray. Having dispersed the enemy, all American troops returned to El Paso by the next day.[62] The army had even dispatched eighteen airplanes from Kelly Field in San Antonio and Ellington Field near Houston. Four of them crashed en route, and the remainder didn't arrive at Fort Bliss until June 17, after the battle was over.

Nevertheless, the army grasped the potential of air power for patrolling the border, and in July, Fort Bliss became the headquarters for five squadrons assigned to this duty.[63] Predictably, although American intervention had saved his most important border city, Carranza protested against this latest violation of Mexican territory.

Captain Stevens may have been wrong about whether Villa would attack Ciudad Juárez, but he was right about one thing:

> I find a good many people on the American side, mostly Americans, who are Villa sympathizers, and one of the chief reasons that they are, they were anxiously waiting for Villa to take Juarez or some other little port, so that they could speculate or make gain from the loot which Villa and his followers had gathered on their march through Mexico from their starting place to the American border, from the Mexican people as well as from the American residents and foreigners. . . . In the last few years, there has been millions of dollars worth of cattle, cotton, bullion and other properties of all descriptions which has been pillaged by these Revolutionary Bands in Mexico, property of both American and foreign residents of Mexico, and as these Bands arrive at the Border with this pillage, they find hundreds of speculators with open arms ready to receive it, for the purpose of getting something for nothing. It would be immaterial to these speculators if this pillage was obtained by theft or demand from the Mexican, American and foreign people who have property and interests in Mexico.[64]

The Mexican Revolution continued to be big business along the border, but it also continued to create apprehension. The fear now was that the defeated villistas would disperse into small bands and begin raiding into Texas.

Small-scale raids did occur in August against two ranches near Fabens, resulting in the loss of thirteen horses. Captain Stevens reported that the 7th Cavalry major commanding the detachment at Fabens telephoned him at 2 a.m. on August 23 that he was going into Mexico after the bandits and invited Stevens to accompany him. The Ranger captain immediately rushed from his headquarters in Ysleta, leaving behind one man to inform the adjutant general when the telegraph office opened, to Fabens, assembled his five men stationed there, and joined the major and his sixty troopers. They crossed the international boundary on the Island and arrived at the village of Guadalupe at about 7:30 a.m. There they encountered some fifty Mexican river guards, and the situation became tense. Stevens acted as interpreter, explaining that the American force was in pursuit of bandits who had raided American ranches. "They did not seem to like our presence there, but I explained to him that we would treat all good citizens right, but that they had to treat us right." The

Mexicans decided not to press the issue. The American column continued on through several more villages, at one of them confronting another contingent of thirty Mexican river guards "who seemed to be very much excited." Again Stevens explained the Americans' purpose, and again the river guards gave way. After making inquiries, the column arrested a Mexican riding one of the stolen horses, as well as two other suspicious characters and "brought them prisoners to Fabens Texas." (Apparently nobody considered the possible international repercussions of this action for the American Army now had a much more aggressive policy regarding pursuit across the Rio Grande.) In addition to Stevens acting as interpreter, what may have helped calm the Mexican river guards was that the "The Aero-plane-Scouts kept up a continuous patrol over us, delivering messages to the Army, while we were scouting in Mexico." As Stevens put it, "I was in hopes we would keep going," but the expedition crossed back into Texas in the vicinity of Fort Hancock. It turned out that the culprits were not Villa's men after all. "It seems that every time the Carranza Federal Troops patrol the Mexican side of the Border, something is missing from the American side. If we had been two days earlier we would have ran [sic] into the Carranza Troops, who were supposed to have these stolen horses." Stevens was ahead of his time. As we've seen, the previous year he had strongly recommended that the Rangers begin using trucks to transport personnel along the river; now he suggested that "If the Ranger Force would have an aero-plane or two, they would be of great service to the Ranger Force."[65]

No doubt aircraft would make the Rangers more efficient, but the sad reality was that the organization was broke and could not even meet the payroll. On July 19, Aldrich announced: "We are out of money and until we get an emergency appropriation we are up against it."[66] The legislature in special session did come up with an emergency appropriation to tide the Ranger Force over until the beginning of the fiscal year on September 1. A relieved but harassed Aldrich wrote on August 16 that "None of the boys had been paid since the 19th of June, and I had to get out two sets of vouchers and mail the warrants before I could do anything else. I am not near done yet."[67] This monetary infusion enabled Harley to add another field company, commanded by Captain Will W. Davis and stationed at Del Rio.[68] But frugality remained the watchword. Aldrich commented that "I have the strictest kind of orders not to allow items where the receipts are missing."[69]

The appropriation for the fiscal year beginning on September 1, 1919, was generous (see following table):

APPROPRIATION RANGER FORCE[70]

For the year Ending August 31, 1920

Salaries of	$
Six Captains	10,800
Five Sergeants	6,000
Sixty-four Privates	69,120

Subsistence and forage	
Seventy-five men	27,000
Seventy-six animals, 68 horses, 8 pack mules	16,416
Ammunition	2,500
Railroad fare, not to exceed $500 outside of State	5,500
Telegraph and Telephone	750
Five Camps	1,200
Twelve Detachments	2,000
Fuel 17 Camps	408
Water 17 Camps	204
Horse Shoeing 76 head, 6 times per year	864
Auto upkeep	3,600
Camp equipage, tentage, medical and surgical services, express and freight charges, men's lodging and subsistence when traveling, stationery, stamps and other incidental expenses	9,000

All salaries shall be paid in 12 equal monthly installments, except when otherwise provided herein

TOTALS	**$156,362** [sic]

Exactly the same amount was appropriated for the 1920–1921 fiscal year. What is striking is the $3,600 for auto upkeep, another indication that the traditional horseback Ranger was riding into the sunset.

Except for Headquarters Company in Austin, one man covering the oilfields in North Texas, two men stationed at Norias and two at Alice, the Rangers remained on the border.[71] Of particular concern was the Big Bend, where smuggling was a way of life. Smuggling was by no means limited to the illegal export of arms and ammunition, although this was the most lucrative traffic. Smugglers also did a brisk business in clothing and foodstuffs.[72] In what must have been a gratifying development given the past friction between the army and the Rangers, the commanding general of the Southern Department asked Harley to assign Rangers to assist the military in combating smuggling in the Big Bend. The general wanted six Rangers to be placed under Colonel Langhorne's command and stationed at Lajitas, Terlingua, and Santa Helena, the principal crossing points for smugglers. Langhorne would transport the Rangers in army trucks and would arrange for their rations and horse feed at a reasonable cost. The adjutant general's department telegraphed Langhorne on August 20 that Captain Jerry Gray at Marfa had been instructed to place himself and his men at Langhorne's disposal for scout duty "along the border or in Mexico."[73] Captain Roy Aldrich was dispatched to Marfa to present personally to Langhorne a letter containing the adjutant general's agreement.[74] Besides lending Rangers to the army, the adjutant general could take satisfaction in the fact that Rangers arrested three Anglos who had stolen arms, ammunition, clothing, and equipment from the military at Ruidosa.[75]

Captain Aldrich's trip to Marfa went beyond merely delivering a letter from the adjutant general to Colonel Langhorne. On the way he had stopped over in Del Rio to confer with Captain Davis, and he did the same with Captain Gray in Marfa. While there, Aldrich got in on some excitement. On August 10, two army aviators flying a De Havilland aircraft got lost, crash-landed in Mexico, and were unlucky enough to be captured by some of Chico Cano's gang of bandits, led by Jesús Rentería, one of the most feared killers in the region. "During the raid on the Brite ranch he reportedly had sat on Mickey Welch's body while an accomplice held his hair and slit the man's throat with a pen knife."[76] Rentería held the aviators for ransom, demanding $15,000 by a certain deadline or the pilots would be dead. A public-spirited group of ranchers underwrote the $15,000 in a matter of minutes, authorizing the bank in Marfa to deliver the cash to Captain Leonard F. Matlack. The latter arranged with the bandits to bring the prisoners back across the river one at a time on the night of August 19. Rightly suspecting treachery, when Matlack returned for the second flier he not only avoided an ambush but saved $6,500 of the ransom money.

With the airmen safe in Texas, Colonel Langhorne on August 20 ordered troops to cross into Mexico after Rentería while army aircraft flew overhead coordinating the search. Strafing some horsemen who had fired on them, the crew of one airplane would claim they had killed Rentería, although this claim was disputed. A unit of the expedition did, however, capture three Mexicans wanted in Texas. The troopers turned them over to the expedition's civilian scouts, who marched the captives off into a canyon and shot them.[77] Rentería indeed survived.[78] Captain Aldrich accompanied Langhorne's cavalry but to his great disappointment failed to see any of the Mexican bandits.[79]

Captain Gray investigated a holdup by American bandits that had occurred on July 30 at Marfa. This was a most unusual case because just about everybody involved was an ex-Ranger. A Captain Palma, a Mexican army paymaster, arrived by train in Marfa on July 30 along with four associates. Palma's assignment was to transport $22,600 to Presidio and thence across the river to Ojinaga to pay the garrison.[80] Transportation between Marfa and Presidio was scarce, and when a resident of Marfa, Andrew C. Barker, offered to drive the party to Presidio for a fee, Palma readily accepted.[81] They set out after nightfall, and as they neared Camp Alberts, some two miles from town, a Ford automobile containing three men suddenly blocked their path; the men leaped out and robbed the Mexican paymaster at gunpoint, then sped off into the darkness. The distraught Mexicans were quickly driven back to Marfa, where they gave the alarm. The sheriff set out in pursuit of the highwaymen, later announcing that he had followed the tracks of their car to the gate of Camp Alberts, where tracks showed that one man had gotten out and had entered the camp. The sheriff declared that he was convinced that the malefactors were soldiers, and he planned to ask Colonel Langhorne to have the camp thoroughly searched. Langhorne was certain that no soldier was involved, and he demanded an investigation. The hapless Captain Palma was promptly arrested by the military in Juárez, was accused of faking the robbery, and was facing a court-martial.[82]

Because of the international ramifications—a Mexican official being robbed on American soil—the federal Bureau of Investigation was called in, and its agents uncovered a veritable nest of corruption.[83] The Bureau agent who shed the greatest light on the affair was ex-Ranger Gus T. Jones, who was currently based in El Paso (and who held a Special Ranger commission). He quickly identified several suspects, and they turned out to be men he had known for years: Andy Barker, who had driven the Mexican paymaster, had been a member of Captain Fox's Ranger company but had been fired over the Porvenir massacre. He had then become a mounted Customs inspector at Presidio. About two months before the holdup he'd been discharged from Customs and had been in Marfa for the past month, unemployed and spending his time playing poker. He was the nephew of (ex-Ranger) Sheriff Dudley Barker at Fort Stockton. Charles Craighead had also been a Ranger stationed in the Big Bend, after which he became a deputy U.S. marshal, then a mounted Customs inspector. For the past year or so he had been a brand inspector at Marfa but had been dismissed a month earlier. Since then he had obtained a job as constable and deputy sheriff in Marfa. Jim Beard was a former Ranger who had also been fired for his role in the Porvenir massacre. When the town of Marfa had recently been incorporated, Beard was appointed city marshal.[84] He was said to have been one of the civilian scouts who executed the

Mexican prisoners during the cavalry's last incursion.[85] Boone Oliphant was another ex-Ranger fired over Porvenir. He had then gotten a job working on the Luke Brite Ranch near Valentine, but for the past month he had been in Marfa without visible means of support. He was a close associate of Barker, Craighead, and Beard, as was the sheriff, Ira Cline, another former Ranger. He had been appointed sheriff when his predecessor, Milt Chastain, died in office. Sheriff Cline had a younger brother, Beuf Cline, who was a notorious local bootlegger but who was untouchable because of his relation to the sheriff. The Clines were also on Gus Jones's list of suspects, as was Buck Pool, a local rancher who had been involved in the Porvenir massacre. As the investigation proceeded, the Bureau received valuable information from an informant, ex-Ranger sergeant A. J. Woelber, who was at present a clerk in Wagon Company No. 4 in the Quartermaster detachment at Camp Alberts.[86]

Agent Jones concluded that Andy Barker, tipped off by someone in Juárez or El Paso, had planned the holdup, and this view was also held by the respectable citizenry in Marfa; Jim Beard, Boone Oliphant, and Charlie Craighead had carried it out, combining profit and ideology—they were Villa sympathizers, and thus they were striking a blow against the Carranza regime; Sheriff Cline, who had tried to frame the army for the crime, was protecting them as well as his brother and Buck Pool; and they all shared in the proceeds.[87] Strengthening this theory were reports that Cline and Craighead had lost several hundred dollars at cards, and one of them had given $300 to a Mexican woman of dubious reputation.[88] The Bureau of Investigation informed the State Department that their evidence indicated that Captain Palma was innocent, and State so informed the Mexican government, probably saving the distraught captain from the firing squad.[89] Although the Bureau had investigated the robbery, no federal statutes had been violated, and it was up to the state authorities to act. The district attorney at Marfa was unable to secure an indictment from the grand jury for lack of evidence, so something else had to be tried. Agent Jones advised that because no peace officer in Presidio County could be depended upon, someone might be sent in undercover to gather evidence, but he warned that the suspects were experienced lawmen who might well resort to violence if they felt threatened. Agent V. L. Snyder suggested "that if the arrest is made by the Ranger force the men should not be placed in the Marfa jail."[90] Another agent suggested that Andy Barker's uncle, Sheriff D. S. Barker at Fort Stockton, be contacted and asked to persuade his nephew to confess.[91] Agent Jones disagreed, stating that the sheriff "is as square a man as lives in the West, but he is a *BARKER* and will stand by any one of his name and blood, unless conclusive evidence can be produced to show him beyond the shadow of a doubt that a Barker had committed a dishonorable act. Even then, the proof would have to be sufficiently strong and clear to make a conviction certain."[92]

It was in hopes of obtaining such proof that Captain Gray, whose headquarters were in Marfa, was assigned the case. To assist Gray in his investigation, Captain Hanson gave him a letter of introduction to C. E. Breniman, the Bureau of Investigation's division superintendent at San Antonio, so they could exchange information.[93] Captain Gray sent one of his Rangers to El Paso to work on the case.[94] And Captain Aldrich sent a "private and confidential" letter to Ranger Will Alsobrook at Hebbronville informing him that Captain Gray wanted a report on Charlie Craighead "who is now, or has been, at your town." Had Craighead been spending money, or flashing a roll of bills? Aldrich cautioned Alsobrook to be "very careful to not mention the matter outside, and destroy this after you have read it."[95] Alsobrook was a bit slow on the uptake, reporting that indeed Craighead had recently been in town but Alsobrook hadn't seen him with any money, and Craighead had said he was going back to Marfa. Apparently it did not occur to Alsobrook to investigate whether Craighead had spent money around other people, but he did offer to make further inquiries if Aldrich wanted him to do so.[96] Whether Aldrich asked him to is not known, as is the ultimate outcome of this affair. As far as the present writers can determine, no one was ever convicted for the great Marfa payroll heist. Ranger Alsobrook, by the way, was accidentally shot at Crestonia, a hamlet in southern Duval County, on December 8, 1919. He was rushed to the hospital in Laredo by special train, but he died the next day.[97]

In 1919 there were frequent and urgent calls for Rangers in the North Texas oilfields. Boomtowns such as Ranger (where ex-Ranger Byron B. Parrish was now chief of police) had settled down somewhat, but new oil strikes repeated the pattern of a rapid influx of undesirables bent on relieving the workers of their hard-earned wages as quickly as possible. Compounding the problem was inadequate or corrupt local law enforcement.

This was the case in Desdemona, fifteen miles southeast of Ranger. Today Desdemona is a sleepy little backwater, but in 1919 it was a leading contender for the title of toughest town in Texas.[98] Desdemona had it all—liquor, gambling, painted women, and a whole variety of crimes. A Texas Ranger from Headquarters Company was sent in undercover to begin investigating the numerous and blatant violations of the law. He reported that one establishment, the Sans Souci, had a lunch counter and six pool tables in the front part of the building, and in the rear an area that "is frequented by prostitutes who sing, play the piano and boost for the house." Furthermore, "Prostitutes, scantily clothed, can be seen in large numbers on the streets day or night and ply their trade in the so-called Hotels which are roughly-constructed buildings with canvas or wire screening forming the partitions for rooms."[99] Matters came to a head when the deputy sheriffs at Desdemona, who had not been doing such a great job anyway, resigned. The district judge requested that Rangers be sent to keep order. A contingent of five

Rangers arrived in Desdemona under the command of Sergeant Sam McKenzie. The sheriff soon appointed new deputies, but at the judge's request two Rangers were left there temporarily to back them up.[100]

September, 1919, proved to be a most important month for the Rangers. Adjutant General James A. Harley was replaced on September 30 by Brigadier General W. D. Cope, the assistant adjutant general, who assumed command the next day. The Rangers thus had a new boss. And in September they lost their leader—on September 4, Captain William M. Hanson resigned his position as Senior Captain. He was, however, placed on indefinite leave and was permitted to retain his warrant of authority.[101]

Hanson had found a new arena for his talents, as chief investigator for U.S. Senator Albert B. Fall's committee investigating Mexican affairs. This was a perfect partnership: Hanson had no love for Venustiano Carranza, and Fall, who was a leading advocate of intervention in Mexico, was determined to demonstrate that Carranza was behind most of the trouble the United States had been having with that country. Hanson's new position enabled him to make full use of his abilities as an intriguer. He worked closely with the National Association for the Protection of American Rights in Mexico, an organization whose executive committee represented some of the largest American-owned corporations in Mexico, corporations whose interests had suffered because of the Mexican Revolution and who were enthusiastically supporting Senator Fall's committee. Hanson adopted the alias of "Gus Klumpner" and from San Antonio corresponded with one Arthur Thomson, whose pamphlet *The Conspiracy Against Mexico* was being subsidized and distributed in the United States by the Carranza regime, the Mexican consul general in San Francisco alone distributing 5,000 copies of this propaganda piece. Hanson's object was to have Thomson admit in writing that the Mexican government was sponsoring him, which he did.[102]

Besides acting as *agent provocateur*, Hanson proved adept at acquiring interesting Mexican documents, interesting because as the Carranza regime tottered, Carranza considered bringing out of retirement some of the old Plan de San Diego warhorses, and this immediately set off alarm bells in American intelligence circles.[103] Carranza was quite alarmed that a resolution introduced by Senator Fall to the Foreign Relations Committee for the withdrawal of diplomatic recognition of his regime might be adopted. If it were, the United States would have the option of supporting some anti-Carranza movement. Hanson supplied the Fall committee with photostatic copies of two letters, and in December he forwarded from Laredo "two TELEGRAMS, that look good to me. This is a connection with the two photostatic letters.... I will suggest that Photostatic copies of these telegrams be used and originals filed, for I would not like to have to explain where and how I secured them."[104] A few weeks later from San Antonio he sent the senator more material: "I am herewith enclosing copies of two telegrams that are self-explanatory. I could not get the originals and it was too dangerous for my informer to have photostatic copies made in Laredo, Texas."[105]

Of particular interest were the activities of one Lino Caballo, who with two other men had arrived in Nuevo Laredo from Monterrey on December 14, 1919, and stayed at the same hotel as the labor leader Luis Morones, with whom they had reportedly come to confer. Hanson advised that "Consul Randolph Robertson was asked who this Lino Caballo was that had been in Nuevo Laredo, Mexico, lately, and he replied 'His correct name is Agustin Garza.'" As far as Hanson could determine, Lino Caballo and Agustín S. Garza, "the signer of the Plan of San Diego is one and the same and quite probably he has been known as Leon Caballo also. . . . My information is that Agustin S. Garza was formerly a school teacher in Duval County, Texas; that during the Madero Revolution he took the name of Leon Caballo and went to Mexico and later headed the plan of San Diego. He is described to me as having a glass eye and being a very smart, slippery fellow."[106]

Military Intelligence was also quite interested in Lino Caballo and the Plan de San Diego. Its information was that Lino Caballo a.k.a. Leon Caballo a.k.a. Agustín Garza had been sent with two others to "carry on radical revolutionary propaganda in Texas. His movements should be closely watched and reported to this office with particular reference to establishing his connection with the Mexican government and with leading radicals in this country. . . . Efforts should be made to ascertain the identity and whereabouts of this man."[107] Military Intelligence had obtained in Mexico City and had translated several letters bearing on the matter, the most significant of which was, in translation:

V.C.   Mexico, June 14, 1919.

Señor Lic. Manuel Aguirre Berlanga,
Esteemed Friend:

Señor Lino Caballo bearer of this letter, is the person who, in company with two friends, will bring to you the manifestos and the plan which they desire to put into practice in the State of Texas.

This plan being very favorable for Mexico, please aid them in every way and give the necessary instructions in the frontier states,

I remain your affectionate friend

V. Carranza.[108]

Manuel Aguirre Berlanga was the Secretary of the Interior (*Gobernación*) and one of Carranza's closest associates. Military Intelligence had also obtained several Mexican government telegrams, including one on December 16 from General Juan Barragán, Chief of the Presidential Staff, instructing the commander at Nuevo Laredo to deliver to Agustín Garza and L. C. Caballo the sum of $1,000, charged to special service (intelligence), by order of the president. The reply reporting that the sum had been delivered, however, stated that the money had been given to "Mr. Agustín Garza. Mr. Caballo is not here at present."[109] Thus it appeared that Agustín Garza and Lino Caballo were two different people. Military Intelligence continued to wrestle with the problem of identity.

A subsequent Military Intelligence report shed some light on the matter. Lino Caballo was identified as a confidential agent of Carranza who passed through Laredo en route to New York. "Leon Caballo's right name is Agustin S. Garza one of the signers of the Plan of San Diego, and now supposed to be in Mexico D.F. acting as an agent for the I.W.W. organization there. He was born in San Diego Texas, or reared there and was a School teacher for several years prior to his going to Mexico. He has a glass eye." (Obviously Military Intelligence and Hanson were using the same information.) The most intriguing part of this report, though, is the following passage:

> *Jacobo Villarreal* wrote the "Plan of San Diego." He was formerly from Naco Arizona. He is now in Matamoros Mexico, and holds the position of "Interventor de bienes Confiscados" under appointment of Carranza.[110]

Unfortunately the report does not elaborate on this tantalizing statement, which is the only time that the alleged author of the Plan has been mentioned by name. (The reader will note that Jacobo Villarreal was a Carranza official.) Yet anything pertaining to the Plan de San Diego was of intense interest to the Hobby administration and to the Texas Rangers, as we shall see in the next chapter.

PEACE ON THE BORDER

EVER since 1915 it had been a frustration and an embarrassment to Texas administrations that the leaders of the Plan de San Diego were in Mexico beyond the reach of the law. Aniceto Pizaña was working in the commission business in Matamoros,[1] Basilio Ramos had been elected as an alternate to the Tamaulipas legislature, and Luis de la Rosa had been in Monterrey, alternately plotting against and working for the Carranza administration. But in January, 1920, there suddenly seemed to be a good chance of apprehending de la Rosa, the most wanted fugitive of them all.

Ranger Fred E. Marks resigned from Headquarters Company on December 8, 1919, because he could not be stationed in San Antonio rather than Austin. Most unusually, at the request of Colonel F. A. Chapa the adjutant general held the resignation in abeyance.[2] Meanwhile, Marks returned to his former home in Rio Grande City. From there he wrote a confidential letter on January 5 to Adjutant General Cope saying that "a friend of mine has made me an offer of $500.00 if I get our man across the river, delivered on this side to me." Marks proposed talking with his Mexican contacts and offering them the full $500 if they could deliver de la Rosa, alive, to Marks on the American side of the river. Marks was most anxious to proceed, had formulated a plan, and had asked the adjutant general for instructions but had received no answer, and he reiterated that he "Would like to hear your views in matters hereto referred," promising that "As soon as I can get in touch with parties across the river, I will mail you a full report on matters that I have under investigation. . . ."[3]

Two days later, Marks sent General Cope a more detailed confidential report:

I have been reliable [sic] informed that the bandit de la Rosa is now making Camargo, Mexico, his home and has his family there with him. Camargo is a town opposite this town [Rio Grande City] and about five miles south. I am informed by this same party that de la Rosa is making frequent trips to ranches up and down the river but his mission is unknown. It is known that he spends money freely, buying mescal and for gambling and claims that he is electioneering in behalf of Carlos Ozuna, a candidate for the governorship of Tamaulipas. He is known to carry in his coat pocket several letters from President Carranza, but the contents of these letters is not known to my informant.[4]

Marks stressed that the simple fact that de la Rosa visited riverside ranches and drank mescal while doing so would make it easy to seize him and bring him across the Rio Grande, although "He is feared by the natives as he stands in the good graces of President Carranza." Marks awaited the arrival of his Mexican contact and hoped the latter would take the job of kidnapping de la Rosa and delivering him alive, adding "I am going to offer him the standing offer of $500.00, that I have from a friend of mine, but at the same time I do not want to do anything until I can hear from you in regard to this matter, as I would not do anything to embarrass Governor Hobby or your department." With regard to his Mexican contact, Marks said: "I do not know yet, that I can convince my man to make the delivery, that is, to bring him over alive, but of course, I would not stand for anything else than to have him alive. I would like to hear from you without delay so that I will know what I must do. I just confirmed my information thru other source that de la Rosa is living in Camargo with his family."[5]

The adjutant general was interested. Despite Marks having been careful to put in writing that he "would not stand for anything else than to have him alive," one suspects that Cope would not have been outraged were Marks to secure de la Rosa's corpse, or even his head in a sack. Cope replied: "Referring to your letter of January 7th, regarding de la Rosa, you are requested to continue the investigation as set forth in this letter, and keep in touch with this office regarding this man's movements. I will advise you later about the matter of going after De la Rosa."[6] Frustratingly but understandably, Cope's instructions to Marks are not found in the adjutant general's correspondence.

Cope became more enthusiastic in his next letter to Marks:

From the reports contained in your letters, it occurs to me that you are on the right track and in position to render a valuable service to the State and reflect credit upon yourself as an officer and the Rangers as a whole, and I trust you will procede [sic] with this investigation and succeed in bringing to justice this man who has depredated upon the lives and property of that section of the State, for so many years. I explained to you fully in the phone conversations at the time I detailed you for this particular duty. I feel, with your knowledge of international law, you will be able to handle this situation in a manner becoming a Texas Ranger. With your knowledge of conditions along the border and your acquaintance of the character you are dealing with, places you in a position to obtain these results. Captain Wright has three men at Rio Grande City that will assist you if you need them.[7]

Marks acknowledged receipt of Cope's instructions and his compliance with them. He advised that:

Since the receipt of your letter my party came to see me and I have made all the arrangements to carry out the task of the delivery of De la Rosa to me. I went over the ground very thoroughly with my man, but we encountered certain conditions that I would like very much to discuss with you and our mutual friend Col. Chapa. I consider it very important that you should be aware of certain facts before this delivery takes place. My man returned to Mexico to be back Saturday morning to let me know more as to his future plans. The only delay will be my conference as suggested. Awaiting your authority by wire to return for the conference.[8]

On January 19, the assistant adjutant general wired Marks to report to Austin at once; upon arriving in San Antonio Marks was to notify Colonel Chapa.[9] Marks acknowledged receipt of the telegram and its instructions to confer with Colonel Chapa on the way to Austin. It may be speculated that Chapa was the "friend" of Marks's who offered him the $500 reward. Chapa could certainly afford it. However, Marks would be delayed: "I will leave as instructed as soon as I can again see my man. He was to return last Saturday, but for some reason he did not come. I do not want to leave until I see him."[10] On January 23, Colonel Chapa wired the assistant adjutant general from San Antonio that "Ranger Fred Marks leaving on noon train to confer with you and the governor on important matter. Make appointment with the governor for him."[11] Unfortunately, we do not know the details of this most unusual meeting—the governor of Texas and the adjutant general were hardly in the habit of conferring at the capitol with a rank-and-file Ranger. We do know the outcome of the meeting, however—Hobby gave his approval to the kidnapping operation.[12]

Marks returned to Rio Grande City to continue making his arrangements. His secretiveness greatly irritated Sergeant John J. Edds, in charge of the three-man Ranger detachment in that town: "Mr. Fred Marks has been here several days I presume on official business. He comes here frequently and stays several days at a time but he never takes us into his confidence or consults us on any matters. We naturally form the opinion that he is entrusted on [sic] some case that we are not capable of handling."[13]

Marks wrote to Cope from Rio Grande City on February 12 explaining that he had been ill with the flu, but "Relative to the other matter, I have seen my man and [he] will notify me in due time. The delivery will be made on this side."[14] But Marks's activities increasingly bothered Sergeant Edds, who wrote to Captain Aldrich:

> Capt. I wish you would advise me whether Fred Marks is in the service or not. He has been here for 3 weeks or more and during that time was sick for about three or four days. He comes down here frequently and stays several days at a time, and always trys [sic] to appear mysterious and leave the impression that he is on some special business and to be frank with you I don't like that kind of business. It reflects on the Rangers stationed here, in this manner. We and others would think that he is entrusted with some class of work that we are not capable of doing. Of course that is possible too, but if we are not worthy of his confidence while he is working in our territory I think we should be dismissed from the service. His brother here is bootlegging and violating the law and I like to had serious trouble with him myself. I have heard that he was going to make an application before outer [sic] the service. If he does I hope they will investigate his reputation here before passing on his application.[15]

Aldrich replied that he fully agreed with Edds's opinion.[16]

The affair took a most unexpected turn when on March 13, the adjutant general wrote to Marks that after giving careful consideration to Marks's ultimatum in his letter of resignation that he could not remain in the Rangers unless he were stationed in San Antonio, he had decided to accept Marks's resignation. Moreover, "You will turn over the matter you have in hand to Sergeant Eads [sic] of Captain Wright's company stationed at Rio Grande City, giving him the benefit of all information you have in order that he may intelligently proceed with the matter you now have in hand," adding that "I feel that you have proceeded with this work to the extent that Sergeant Eads [sic] can carry it on to completion." Cope closed with "I regret that the circumstances are such that I am compelled to accept your resignation from the service."[17] The adjutant general sent a copy to Colonel Chapa along with a letter further explaining his position.[18]

Chapa was furious. He telegraphed to Governor Hobby:

> Ranger Fred E. Marks resignation was accepted and recalled from Rio Grande City by adjutant general while on special duty on important matter that you are aware of. The action of Gen. Cope I deeply resent because it

was done when he was absent to render a valuable service to state and your self. In discharging this mission and now returning there to live requires for his protection that you order issued to him a special ranger commission. This is a matter of justice and will consider it special favor to me. Will see you soon and explain fully. Please rush this matter.[19]

Hobby passed the telegram over to Cope to answer. The adjutant general replied to Chapa:

I explained to you fully the last time you were in the office the reasons for accepting Mr. Marks's resignation and thought you fully understood the matter. Under the ruling of the Attorney General's Department, this department has issued no Special Ranger Commissions since I assumed the duties of this office. However, the Attorney General's Department is now considering another phase of this question, and should they advise that the Governor has authority by law to issue these commissions, we will then take up the question of issuing Mr. Marks the Special Ranger Commission.[20]

This is the last reference to Marks's "special duty." Marks himself died in a San Antonio hospital on October 12, 1920, and was buried in Rio Grande City.[21] For whatever reason the extraordinary operation aimed at de la Rosa was canceled. Whether Marks in fact briefed Sergeant Edds and turned the operation over to him is unknown, but even if he did, it is probable that Marks's man in Mexico was leery of working with anyone but Marks. Yet the affair demonstrated once again, as did Colquitt's 1914 scheme to get Vergara's killers and Ferguson's 1915 instructions to Captain Ransom, that Texas governors were not averse to playing hardball.

Other intrigues were occurring along the Rio Grande at the same time as the de la Rosa matter. For example, in January there was discovered at Fort Ringgold, at Rio Grande City, a plot involving both soldiers and civilians to steal machine guns, pistols, and ammunition. The governor of Tamaulipas, through one of his friends living at Camargo, had allegedly made arrangements to purchase the munitions.[22]

Life along the Rio Grande remained exciting. In January, Captain Gray's Company A was based in Presidio, and the captain reported a recent encounter.[23] Two of his men, privates P. F. Dyches and Ben H. Woodland, had fortuitously prevented a murder. They happened to ride up to the Baldwin store on the river just as one Francisco Cacho, leader of a gang that had robbed that establishment on New Year's night, was outside the front door trying to entice Baldwin to come out; Cacho had a man in a nearby ditch waiting to shoot Baldwin as soon as he appeared. The two Rangers immediately arrested Cacho, relieved him of his two pistols, had Baldwin identify him, and started back to their camp at Indio with the handcuffed prisoner in tow. Meanwhile, Cacho's man had alerted the rest of the gang, who lived across the river, and they set out to rescue their leader. When the Rangers had gone about a mile, the six bandits closed to within 400 yards of them and opened fire. The Rangers leaped off their horses to return fire, but Woodland's horse bolted before he could draw his Winchester. Dyches was able to keep the attackers at bay in an encounter in which some fifty shots were fired. He managed to wound two of the Mexicans, but they escaped back across the river. So did Cacho. As soon as the firing began he bolted back into Mexico, where carrancistas reportedly cut off his handcuffs with an axe. Captain Gray was frustrated: "Col. Hornbrook would not let army cross into Mexico, therefore we didn't go over. They sure need cleaning out, and I would like to do it & have stationed Dyches & Woodland at Baldwin's." However, Captain Hanson, who later interviewed the two Rangers for the Fall Committee, declared disdainfully: "I understand that Woodland got very badly excited and later on concluded that the climate in east Texas was better than that of the Big Bend and resigned."[24]

Speaking of Captain Gray, all was not well in Company A. Private Nathan N. Fuller requested a transfer on the grounds that Gray was unfair to him. The captain had ordered him to report to Indio for duty under Ranger Dyches. Fuller complained that Dyches was a new man—he had only been in Company A for two months, while Fuller had been in for over four years. Furthermore, Fuller said, "I told Gray I wouldn't work under Dyches. I will not work under no man who let a few mexicans come to this side and shoot him loose from a prisoner, in broad open daylight, and the prisoner hand cuffed." Fuller's complaint went further. Gray wanted rid of him because Fuller had made it known he would not vote for the man Gray "was running for sheriff." Gray had "done more lectionaring [sic] the last two months than the man he wants to be elected." There was more: Gray was "always harping on the booze question, when he buys as much or more than any man he has under him, this is not hear say I know what I am telling."[25] Furthermore, "It is well known he has brought all the pressure possible to force the rangers to vote for Jeff Vaughn [sic] for sheriff. In fact he publicly stated that all rangers who did not so vote would soon be hunting a job. This is simply mixing in politics and is contrary to the rules and regulations of the service."[26]

The fate of these three men is interesting. Fuller was fired on February 11, 1920, the date of his first letter of complaint. He later became a rancher near Marfa. The adjutant general evidently did not give much weight to Fuller's allegations, for Gray remained a Ranger captain until he resigned on April 30, 1925. He became a rancher and farmer at Presidio, and had a Special Ranger commission in 1925–1928, 1930, and 1932–1933. As of 1935, he was still residing in Presidio. Jefferson Eagle Vaughan, the veteran Ranger whom Gray was allegedly running for sheriff, resigned from Company A on July 1, 1920, to make the race.

He was successful, and was still serving as Presidio County sheriff in 1926. He held a Special Ranger commission in 1926–1927, was a rancher at Marfa as of 1933, and in that year was commissioned as captain of Company A, a post he held until 1935.

Captain Gray also caused some hard feelings when on March 15, 1920, he discharged Ranger Sam H. Neill because of the latter's age. Neill was seventy-four, so Gray had some justification. Yet it will be remembered that in 1917 Neill had been one of the defenders of the Brite Ranch and had given an impressive account of himself, so he could justifiably argue that he was as good as Rangers half his age. But when he protested to Adjutant General Cope, the latter callously replied that captains had the authority to enlist and to discharge, and "I feel sure that Captain Gray would not have relieved you if your service with that company had been satisfactory to him."[27]

Much of what Rangers along the border were now doing was combating the smuggling of liquor from Mexico. One incident occurred near Redford (Polvo) in the Big Bend on March 30, when Ranger Elmer B. McClure was in a stakeout in the brush on the riverbank. According to McClure, in midafternoon he saw a Mexican across the river leave a keg under a tree and start across with the heavy sack. When he was halfway across he suddenly turned back. McClure called on him to halt, but instead the Mexican dropped the sack and splashed toward the far bank. When he neared the bank he turned around, and McClure fired, the bullet striking the man above the left eye. The Mexican fell dead on the bank. There were no other witnesses. The Mexican authorities investigated, along with an American officer, a Captain Berry stationed at Redford. The Mexicans interviewed several people who identified Ranger McClure as the shooter, and the Mexican investigation concluded that "the murder of Ramon Monje by the American citizen, ranger McClure, was perpetrated without any motive at the moment when Monje was drinking water at the edge of the river."[28] According to the Ranger account of the incident, Ramon Monje had fled to Mexico to avoid the draft several years earlier, and his father, who lived in Redford, had been arrested by McClure two weeks earlier for bootlegging and was in jail at Marfa.[29] This does not speak to the issue of whether McClure was justified in killing Ramon Monje, but it does suggest that Monje was at the river not just to take a drink of water.

The smuggling of liquor had become big business. Sergeant Edds at Rio Grande City seized 650 quarts in a single week and filed charges against ten individuals.[30] In the Lower Valley, the smugglers, called *tequileros*, brought across pack trains of liquor and were quite prepared to shoot it out with anyone who got in their way. Captain Wright pursued them aggressively, moving his men by truck, car, and on horseback.[31] The same apparently could not be said for Captain Ryan in Laredo. There were complaints that Ryan and his men spent most of their time in town, where they did no good, and were under constant surveillance by smuggler sympathizers, so that when the Rangers left on one of their infrequent scouts, the smugglers were immediately warned. The adjutant general was urged to order Ryan to operate in the back country, where he might have an impact on the roving bands from across the river.[32]

Across the river the situation was becoming critical. As many had feared, Carranza indeed sought to perpetuate his power by imposing a puppet president in 1920. His choice of candidate was Ignacio Bonillas, the Mexican ambassador to the United States. The colorless Bonillas quickly became the object of popular derision despite desperate efforts by Carranza to inject life into the campaign. Then on April 11, Carranza attempted to have General Obregón arrested in order to neutralize the latter's presidential campaign—exactly the same tactic Porfirio Díaz had employed against Francisco Madero a decade earlier, touching off the Mexican Revolution. Carranza's clumsy ploy likewise touched off a revolution, one which quickly toppled Carranza from power. On April 12, Obregón's native state of Sonora virtually seceded from Carranza's Mexico, and on April 23 the Sonorans issued the obligatory revolutionary manifesto, the Plan de Agua Prieta, thus formally launching the rebellion. The unpopular Carranza regime began to disintegrate as the president's erstwhile supporters deserted him in droves.

The Carranza administration requested permission in April for Generals Juan José Rios and Manuel Gamboa and their staffs, about thirty-five persons, including women, to proceed from Nogales to El Paso en route to their homes in Mexico City. The State Department had no objection, pointing out that this would be distinct from a troop movement, and the Mexicans would be traveling as civilians. The Department asked Hobby to wire his agreement.[33] Hobby made his position quite clear: "I desire to reiterate the protest made by me when a similar request was formerly made to our Government and to say even more emphatically that I am unalterably opposed to the movement of Mexican troops over Texas soil since it would endanger the lives and property of American citizens living on or near the border between Texas and Mexico."[34] Hobby further explained to the secretary of state his opposition to the transportation of Mexican troops "or any military officials thereof across Texas soil," for this would provoke trouble and "put the lives and property of American citizens along the border, to a large extent at the mercy of the bandit forces opposing the forces represented by the Generals referred to in your telegram."[35] Hobby's policy of refusing to assist either Carranza or the rebels fighting to overthrow him met with wide popular approval in Texas.[36] Yet it should be noted that Hobby was not necessarily anti-Carranza. In 1918, at the request of the Mexican government, Hobby had asked the mayor of El Paso to prevent the showing of the film "The Flame" because it presented Mexicans in an offensive manner.[37]

In Del Rio there was considerable excitement among the Hispanic population over events in Mexico. Captain Davis had a car, greatly increasing his company's mobility, and he worked closely with the Bureau of Investigation in monitoring revolutionary activity. Bureau agents showed him some fifty letters addressed to Pancho Villa by people in the United States and seized from a Villa courier at Marfa, and they asked his help in watching for the exiles David de la Fuente and Francisco Vázquez Gómez, who were supposed to be coming from Los Angeles with the intention of slipping across the river near Del Rio.[38]

Hopefully the Rangers at Laredo would not have to engage in any firefights, for they were critically short of ammunition.[39] Incredibly, they could expect little help from Austin. Captain Aldrich wrote on May 4 that:

> I am sending Captain Ryan some 45 cal. ammunition today, and a few boxes of 30-30's. Captain Ryan said that he would rustle the rifle ammunition himself. I am sorry that we cannot send the boys enough ammunition, but the Legislature cut my estimate half in two, and the price has gone up, so that we can supply but little. Have the boys take care of what they have for I can send but a little more this [fiscal] year."[40]

The situation at Brownsville was not much better. Captain Wright's clerk wrote that "When Capt. Wright started out on his scout he told me to write you and ask for some more ammunition; since then I have received the box of pistol ammunition. We were long on this and short on the 30-30."[41]

Fortunately the Rangers at Laredo did not have to expend any ammunition. When the rebels seized Nuevo Laredo on May 9 there was little fighting involved—only five dead. The Carranza commander, General Reynaldo de la Garza, escaped to the American side of the river. Captain Ryan was able to report that conditions in Nuevo Laredo were practically normal.[42]

Still, the Ranger Force remained on alert, waiting for the situation in Mexico to clarify. Every available man was on border duty.[43] The winner in this latest Mexican upheaval was General Obregón, around whom the rebels coalesced. On May 7, Carranza in effect admitted defeat and abandoned Mexico City, heading for Veracruz by rail with a large entourage. But even his military escort mutinied, joining the rebels, and Carrranza was forced to continue his flight on horseback with but a handful of diehard followers. He got as far as the obscure hamlet of Tlaxcalantongo. There on the night of May 20, the local *cacique* had Carranza shot to death while he slept.

Although of course no one realized it at the time, the Mexican Revolution had nearly run its course. There would be military revolts in 1923 and 1929, but 1920 marked the last time the Mexican government would be overthrown by force of arms. General Obregón emerged in 1920 as the new strongman, was promptly elected president, and began the herculean task of imposing order and rebuilding a country shattered by a decade of civil war. Another event made 1920 memorable—Pancho Villa laid down his arms. With Carranza dead, Villa had a face-saving way of surrendering to the new government; he could argue that his quarrel had been with Carranza. Villa accepted a deal whereby he received amnesty, a hacienda in the state of Durango, and a cash settlement in return for retiring from public life. He kept his end of the bargain until 1923, when the government decided he was just too dangerous to have around and had him assassinated.

Border intrigue continued, as exemplified by Captain William M. Hanson. After his work for the Fall Committee, Hanson returned to San Antonio in 1921 and with his friend F. A. Chapa figured prominently in local politics. His efforts bore fruit, for in 1923 Hanson received a patronage appointment as District Director of the Immigration Service, supervising the Texas border.[44] The following year he made news by publicly denying Ranger Captain B. C. Baldwin's testimony regarding irregularities in the enforcement of the neutrality laws along the border, specifically a plot to run guns.[45] In February, 1926, the Agrarian Commission in Tamaulipas reportedly ordered that Hanson's confiscated hacienda be returned to him.[46] Perhaps not coincidentally, Hanson was accused in the United States Senate of using his Immigration position to have Mexican exiles arrested and delivered to the Obregón government, which promptly executed them.[47] As a result of the uproar Hanson resigned, ostensibly to engage in business in the Lower Valley. His business affairs evidently did not prosper, for until his health failed five months before his death he was serving as bailiff of the corporation (municipal) court in San Antonio, where he died on February 20, 1931.[48]

The year 1920 not only ushered in a new era for Mexico, but it also marked the end of an era for the Texas Rangers. They could increasingly shift their focus from defending the border, as they had done for the past decade, to performing law enforcement duties throughout the rest of the state. Back in January, trouble had developed at the other end of Texas, on the Red River, the border with Oklahoma. A bitter dispute raged between Texas and Oklahoma over ownership of land that contained valuable oil deposits, Oklahoma claiming a strip of land on the Texas bank. Several Rangers had been sent to Wichita Falls to back up Texas's claim.[49] Adjutant General Cope ordered Captain Charles Stevens to the area to assume command. Stevens refused, and on February 3, 1920, he wrote to Governor Hobby from San Antonio to explain why. He began by saying that "When, in November 1917, I entered the service as Ranger Captain, it was with the firm determination to do my full duty in enforcing the law and co-operating with all other federal and state officers, to the same end," then recapitulated his career in the Rangers, recounting how on August 28, 1918, he had been transferred from the Lower Valley to Sanderson, then in May, 1919, to Ysleta. There the federal authorities asked his help in suppressing the smuggling of liquor. He gladly cooperated, and doing so antagonized influential El Pasoans involved in the traffic, who mounted a campaign to have him removed, arguing that local lawmen were sufficient.[50] Accordingly, General Cope on January 5, 1920, ordered Stevens's company out of El Paso County. Stevens was ordered to Austin, where Cope told him his next assignment would be in the town of Ranger to enforce the gambling and liquor laws. Stevens told the adjutant general that if sent he intended to enforce the law to the letter, and if Cope were not prepared to back him up he had better not send him to Ranger.

For reasons unknown to Stevens, he was not sent there. Instead, Stevens was ordered to Wichita Falls "to take command of an armed band of men in charge of the disputed oil fields, for the Texas claimants who were holding possession against the Oklahoma claimants." Stevens protested to Hobby, who told him to obey Cope's orders. According to Stevens, Cope "said that he wanted me to displace the two other Ranger Captains then on the ground, take full charge of an armed band of men representing certain claimants to the oil fields in dispute, and repel, by force and arms, any attempt of the Oklahoma claimants to regain possession." Although the issue was in the courts, Cope's strategy was to maintain possession regardless of what the court might rule. At this point Stevens balked: "as a sworn peace officer I would not be a law breaker simply to protect private claimants of valuable oil holdings. . . ." Stevens ended his letter by informing Governor Hobby that "Under the circumstances, I cannot reconcile my conception of duty as an officer with the Adjutant General's conception of his authority over me, and I therefore beg leave to resign my position as Ranger Captain in the service of the State, effective immediately."[51] Three of Stevens's Rangers resigned with him for the same reason.[52] Stevens's Company B was disbanded, and his remaining men and his equipment were transferred to Captain Gray.[53]

A lawman of Stevens's experience and reputation had no difficulty finding employment. On March 26, 1920, he became a Prohibition agent in San Antonio for the Internal Revenue Service. In 1922, he resigned to become supervisor in San Antonio of mounted Customs inspectors. In 1925, he transferred back to Internal Revenue, working as a Prohibition agent in Fort Worth, New Orleans, and San Antonio. Early on the morning of September 25, 1929, Stevens and two other Prohibition agents were driving back to San Antonio after having raided a still in Atascosa County when they were ambushed, rifle and shotgun fire raking their car from both sides of the highway. The officers returned fire, killing one of their attackers, but the rest escaped. Stevens was mortally wounded by shotgun slugs. He was rushed to the hospital in San Antonio, and when word spread of his condition, hundreds of well-wishers, both Anglos and Hispanics, crowded the corridors to pay their respects. Stevens died later that same day. The Bexar County sheriff declared that the motive for Stevens's murder was revenge for the numerous raids he had been conducting against illegal distilleries. Stevens was distinguished from all other Rangers by having a corrido composed in his honor, entitled "Capitán Charles Stevens."[54]

Although Captain Stevens had chosen not to participate, the Red River controversy with Oklahoma raged on. Governor Hobby on January 19 ordered Cope to send as many Rangers as necessary to the area in order to enforce the laws of Texas.[55] Rangers were dispatched to Wichita Falls to protect the interests of the Lone Star Oil and Refining Company. The adjutant general himself even put in an appearance in March.[56] At the height of the dispute more than fifteen Rangers were stationed at Wichita Falls and in a camp on the river, performing a duty of watchful waiting that had rapidly become extremely unpopular.[57] The problem was the inflated cost of living in the oil belt. The statutory $3 a day expense allowance was woefully inadequate, and as the Rangers' monetary losses increased so did their grumbling.[58] As one of them inelegantly put it, "I want the State of Texas to know that if I am on the Ranger Force now that I am a white man and married to a white woman and expect to live as such as not as a Mexican on chile to save the State money."[59] He and several others finally quit in disgust and went to work at a higher salary as guards for Lone Star Oil.[60] The boundary dispute was fought out in the courts, and Aldrich could write on April 30: "The boys are all back from the oil fields, and I am sure glad of it. The expense up there was a fright."[61]

It was fortunate that Rangers were back from the Oklahoma border because they were needed in Desdemona, the oil boomtown they had cleaned up the previous year but which had since reverted to its evil ways. As before, Ranger R. D. Shumate went in first to evaluate conditions; having done so, he called for reinforcements. These included Captain Roy Aldrich, who made several trips to Desdemona. The Rangers' presence emboldened a mob of citizens fed up with corruption to seize the local constable and justice of the peace, compel them to resign their offices, put them in a car and deport them from the county.[62] There was some question as to whether the Rangers should be indicted along with those who had actually deposed and exiled the constituted authorities, but the county attorney informed the district judge that "no one was indicted and that his opinion is that no one would be, as is usual in all instances of mob violence."[63]

The Rangers confiscated a good deal of gambling paraphernalia—craps tables, poker tables, etc. Rangers R. D. Shumate and W. M. Molesworth were in and out of Desdemona and surrounding communities for several months. Their efforts did not entirely stop activities such as gambling—partly because the sheriff was not inclined to arrest gamblers—but they severely curtailed the once-thriving illegal trade.[64] What really made the difference, though, was that the oil boom at Desdemona was largely over by July, and the riffraff moved on in search of juicier pickings. Moreover, the members of the American Legion managed to help elect a slate of more conscientious county and local officials.[65] Shumate resigned from the Rangers on September 1 for a better-paying job as a federal Prohibition agent.[66]

Another Ranger operation involved strike duty at Galveston. On March 19, 1920, some 2,500 longshoremen struck at the Morgan and the Mallory Line docks. The port of Galveston was virtually shut down, and businessmen throughout Texas suffered as a result. The local authorities proved unable to protect temporary workers, or "scabs," whom the shippers desperately wanted to bring in.[67] On May 13, at the request of the mayor and the chief of police, Captain Aldrich and three other Rangers were sent to Galveston to help the police preserve order, "but as time went on it became apparent that even the presence of these rangers, who were acting under orders of the local authorities, was not sufficient to insure [sic] the safety of laborers desiring to work on the docks."[68]

The mayor and the police chief appealed to Governor Hobby for immediate assistance. The governor sent the adjutant general to investigate and take the necessary action. General Cope mobilized units of the Texas National Guard on June 4, and on June 7, Hobby proclaimed martial law and ordered the guard into Galveston. Brigadier General Jacob F. "Jake" Wolters, the prominent Houston attorney, commanded the 1st Cavalry Brigade, which established its headquarters at the newly created Camp Hutchings. The governor issued a supplementary proclamation on July 14, suspending all city officials, so that the commanding general could enforce the penal statutes. At a September 18 meeting between a citizens' committee and Hobby's secretary, the parties reached an agreement whereby martial law would be lifted and the governor would designate a Ranger captain to take charge of the police department, issuing orders through the police chief and replacing the military. On September 21, Hobby ordered the adjutant general to detail Captain Joe B. Brooks, the Headquarters Company commander, to proceed to Galveston with as many men as were necessary to accomplish the mission.[69] Hobby revoked his July 14 proclamation so that local officials could once again enforce the penal laws. The Texas National Guard evacuated the city on October 8.[70] The Militia Bureau warmly congratulated the guard on its performance.[71] This was in sharp contrast to the Bureau's justified criticism of the scandal-ridden Texas National Guard in 1915.

The Rangers established a strong presence in Galveston, and they were prepared to stay for the long haul. Not only were men rushed to the port city, but also equipment such as cots and mattresses from Fort Sam Houston, and even eleven horses—very effective for crowd control—from stations as distant as Marfa and Marathon.[72] To show that the Rangers meant business, Emergency Company No. 1 was created, commanded by Captain C. J. Blackwell, to remain in Galveston as long as necessary.[73] Rangers remained in the city until the following year.[74]

Four of Captain Wright's men were originally scheduled for Galveston in September, but the order was rescinded because of a flare-up of trouble in the Lower Valley. Wright took on a gang of bandits, capturing four and closely pursuing the other five on the Tom East Ranch. Prominent citizens appealed to

Hobby and to Cope that Wright's Company D be allowed to continue this kind of important work. The order regarding Galveston was immediately canceled.[75]

There was also plenty of work for the Rangers in North Texas. They were again called to the Wichita Falls area, this time not to face off against Oklahomans but to suppress a wave of crime in the oilfields and the shanty towns that had mushroomed, seemingly overnight. In August the district attorney explained to Governor Hobby that local law enforcement was both overwhelmed and corrupt; unless the citizenry got some relief "they feel like that the only solution left for them is to apply lynch law and mob violence."[76] In October, three district judges and the district and county attorneys formally requested that Hobby send Rangers to Wichita County.[77]

The adjutant general ordered Captain Aldrich to take six Rangers and clean up that county.[78] Aldrich reported that:

A Special Grand Jury was convened, and a general clean up commenced. The County was overrun with gamblers, pimps, bootleggers, highjackers and prostitutes. Hold-ups were a nightly occurrence and neither life or property was safe. The Deputy Sheriffs were corrupt; one of them being an ex-convict from Oklahoma. Three of them were indicted by the Grand Jury for receiving bribes, etc. We captured three stills with a quantity of mash and arrested two boot-leggers who were selling whiskey at soft-drink stands. Many such places were running and probably are yet, as it takes time to get rid of them all. Many gamblers were arrested as were highjackers [sic] and other undesirables, and nearly all the rest left for [other] parts promptly. The matter of prostitution has not been taken up yet, as it is a very hard matter to handle. Many of these women own their houses and run them as hotels, keeping a register, etc. Others run cold drink stands and have their bed rooms in the rear. The prostitute is the key to the whole situation. If it was not for her presence we would not have the other classes of criminals to contend with, or to a much lesser extent anyway.[79]

Aldrich expanded the scope of his activities. He sent in a man undercover to gather intelligence in several oil towns, for in December the Rangers carried out a general cleanup of the entire oilfield—Eastland, Stephens, and Wichita Counties.[80] Assigned to police this area as a temporary measure was Emergency Company No. 2, under Captain Tom R. Hickman.[81]

Aldrich remained a Ranger captain until January 31, 1931, when the new adjutant general, ex-Ranger captain William W. Sterling, fired him. In his memoirs Sterling makes no effort to disguise his contempt for Aldrich, whom he excoriates for being neither a "real Ranger" nor a "real Texan."[82] In his capacity as adjutant general, Sterling contacted Major General Frank R. McCoy, under whom he had served as an army scout during the 1915 Bandit War. McCoy was currently in command of U.S. forces in Nicaragua combating the guerrilla chieftain/freedom fighter Augusto Sandino. Sterling, who was much given to chauvinistic bombast, offered to take a bunch of Rangers to Nicaragua and go capture that Sandino fella.[83] McCoy politely refused the offer. And while Sterling makes much of his accomplishments in improving the Rangers, some of the Special Ranger commissions he issued were to people such as the humorist Will Rogers and the singer Jimmie Rodgers, or to the movie actor Tom Mix as a reward for the latter's help in organizing the first prison rodeo.[84]

Aldrich had the proverbial last laugh, however. On January 18, 1933, in what Sterling indignantly describes as "a day of infamy," the incoming governor, Miriam "Ma" Ferguson, fired Sterling and the entire Ranger Force, just because they had actively opposed her candidacy.[85] The governor, who acted as her husband ex-Governor James E. Ferguson's surrogate, commissioned a new complement of Rangers, including Captain Roy Aldrich. He remained a captain until 1947, when he retired, having served longer than any other Texas Ranger. He then devoted himself to extending hospitality to the hundreds of people who came to enjoy the gardens and collections at his estate on the outskirts of Austin. Aldrich died on January 29, 1955.[86]

In 1920, the Rangers were "used principally for border guards and in the oil fields to keep order."[87] Increasingly, the oil fields were the principal focus, for in December, Captain Aldrich could report "Everything quiet along the border."[88] Thus by December, 1920, the Rangers were performing regular law enforcement duties, as they had been doing in January, 1910. The Texas State Ranger Force had come full circle.

EPILOGUE

In the early 1920's, suppression of the liquor traffic from Mexico remained one of the Rangers' highest priorities. What was involved was not just the illegal liquor itself but the well-organized bands of smugglers who posed a threat to the lives and property of border residents.[1] As one of his last official acts, Governor Hobby in January, 1921, ordered Adjutant General Cope to have the Rangers clear the border of these criminals.[2] Captain Wright was particularly effective in the ongoing struggle against the tequileros, engaging in several memorable encounters with these smugglers. In September he informed the new adjutant general, Thomas D. Barton, that he, five of his Company D Rangers, a mounted Customs inspector, and a La Salle County deputy sheriff had learned where some heavily armed Mexican smugglers were camped. The lawmen took them by surprise, capturing four at once and another two when they returned to camp from the brush. The leader, however, chose to shoot it out. Sergeant John Edds, Ranger Jesse Pérez, and the deputy wounded him several times, whereupon he chose not to continue shooting. Wright's haul from this operation was 575 quarts of tequila, seven men, six Winchesters, and eleven horses.[3] In November, Wright, five of his men, and two mounted Customs inspectors made a scout that culminated when they struck the trail of sixteen smugglers from Mexico leading thirty-seven loaded horses and mules. Despite being outnumbered, the lawmen attacked the smugglers' camp in the brush. In the ensuing gun battle they wounded several of the Mexicans, but the latter all managed to escape back across the river. Yet it was still a successful scout: "In five days we caught 3800 qts of liquor and 65 horses & 6 men, also [a] world of pack saddles. I am very sorry all these men escaped but they will have something to remember the Rangers by."[4] And in December, 1922, Wright and five men trailed three Mexicans leading a train of fifteen horses.

Wright ambushed them, killing all three and seizing 800 bottles of liquor and all the horses.[5] These firefights and others like them usually took place quite a few miles inland from the Rio Grande. Knowing they themselves were under surveillance by smugglers' sympathizers along the river, officers preferred whenever possible to try to deal with pack trains when the latter were well into the back country.[6]

Captain Wright, the most outstanding of the Ranger captains during the period of the Mexican Revolution, remained in command of Company D until April 1, 1925, when he resigned. He became a peace officer in Robstown until May 15, 1927, when he was appointed captain of Company A, serving in that capacity until discharged on January 18, 1933. Wright then secured employment as a peace officer in Kenedy. On February 14, 1935, he again joined the Rangers, but this time had to suffer the humiliation of enlisting as a private in Company D. He resigned in 1939. As has been aptly stated: "While counterfeit Rangers who were not worthy of blacking his boots were basking in the favors of those in charge, Captain William Lee Wright terminated his service patrolling the docks in Corpus Christi."[7] After his resignation Wright returned to his home in Floresville, where he died on March 7, 1942, at the age of seventy-four. He did receive some posthumous recognition from the service that had treated him so shabbily—a two-foot-high bronze statue of Captain Wright on horseback leading his pack mule is displayed in the office of the Director of the Department of Public Safety.[8]

Wright's case illustrates the extent to which the Ranger Force remained vulnerable to the whims of politicians. "The Ranger captains were always greatly concerned over a change of administration, and were particularly interested in knowing as soon as possible the identity of the new [adjutant] general."[9] And the politicians were their usual tightfisted selves—on July 6, 1921, for example, it was announced that Rangers traveling on state business would have to pay their own expenses until the next fiscal year began on September 1, when they would be reimbursed. The annual transportation allotment had been slashed from $6,000 to $4,000, and it was exhausted.[10]

During the 1920's, maintaining order in the oilfields and cleaning up oil boomtowns was the other high priority for the Rangers. On January, 7, 1922, Adjutant General Barton[11] led two companies of Rangers into Mexia, eighty miles northwest of Austin, where an oil bonanza had produced a state of utter lawlessness. The Rangers conducted a series of surprise raids, gathering information that caused the governor to proclaim martial law on January 11 and send in the national guard. The soldiers and the Rangers succeeded in establishing order to such an extent that on March 1, martial law was lifted.[12]

All these activities were carried out by a shrinking Ranger Force. On June 20, 1919, there were eighty-seven Rangers. As of January 1, 1921, there were sixty-seven. On February 15, the organization was reorganized: Emergency Companies

1 and 2 were disbanded, and the Rangers were reduced to fifty-five men. Then on September 1, 1921, the legislature passed an act further reducing the force to a total of fifty. By August 31, 1922, the Rangers numbered forty-eight. This small force proved inadequate when a major railroad strike broke out in Denison in July, 1922.[13] Therefore the governor used the emergency powers granted him by the 1919 law and quickly had some 450 men commissioned as "Railroad Rangers" for the duration of the strike, with the railroads paying the bill. As for the Regular Rangers, in 1922 the adjutant general urged that the legislature increase the force to at least 100 men and raise their salaries.[14] The legislature had no intention of doing so.

The Texas State Ranger Force remained in existence until 1935. That year the Texas Department of Public Safety was created, composed of the Rangers and the Highway Patrol, and the new agency proved much more professional and much less vulnerable to political interference. Although the Rangers are no longer a separate entity, they have maintained their proud tradition. And they have remained controversial.[15]

CONCLUSION

"One riot, one Ranger?"—hardly.[1] That chestnut can be laid to rest, for there is a considerable gap between the myth of the Texas Rangers and the reality. For the decade 1910–1920, the most important in the organization's history, the conclusion one must inevitably reach is that the Texas State Ranger Force was under-strength, underpaid, and living on its reputation. It was definitely not an elite organization composed of Gary Cooper-like figures. There were crippled Rangers, a visually-impaired Ranger, a one-armed Ranger, two one-legged Rangers, and an aged Ranger. And there were a lot of drunken Rangers; liquor got more Rangers into trouble than any other factor. Furthermore, the low salaries Rangers received were not an inducement for first-rate men to enlist. The State of Texas usually got pretty much what it paid for. Given the wage scale, what is striking is that there were as many first-rate men in the Rangers as there were. This shows that remuneration was not the only consideration, and that being a Ranger conferred a certain cachet. It has been observed more than once that when men became Rangers they did not change, but the public perception of them changed. People might like and support the Rangers or hate and fear them, but in either case they took them very seriously indeed. Relatively few men made the Rangers a career. The pattern was for them to serve intermittent enlistments, an organizational weakness facilitated by a policy of allowing men to resign when-ever they felt like it. If there is a discernible career pattern it is that of cowboys becoming deputy sheriffs, then Rangers, then in a few cases sheriffs, and some sheriffs becoming Ranger captains.

Ranger alumni constituted a significant force multiplier. The popular per-ception of the Rangers as a small but elite force was not the case at all because in addition to the Regular Rangers there were hundreds of Special Rangers as well as hundreds of wartime Loyalty Rangers. The Regulars were but the tip of a sizeable law enforcement pyramid consisting of 1,785 individuals who held Ranger commissions of one type or another during the decade under study, to say nothing of the hundreds who had served earlier. Reinforcing this was the phenomenal number of familial connections among Rangers and former Rangers, and between Rangers and other peace officers, in some cases constituting veritable law enforcement clans. Moreover, some sections of Texas produced a disproportionate number of Rangers, with Wilson County being the extreme example.

It is perhaps worth making a final observation about "real" Rangers. The claim has been made that only those who measured up to some nebulous standard of conduct were "real" Rangers, but as we have seen, this is merely a rationalization. It is also claimed that the only "real" Rangers were the Regulars, for only they made arrests, etc. The trouble with this function-based definition is that it does not always hold true. If Regulars were the only "real" Rangers, then Special and Loyalty Rangers must have been "unreal." But when, as happened in the case of Morín and Ponce for example, a Special Ranger assisted the Regulars, presumably he temporarily became "real" then reverted to being "unreal" when the job was done. And the wartime brand inspectors who were Special Rangers but who were reclassified as Regulars to avoid the draft thus presumably became "real" Rangers even though they continued working as brand inspectors. Since exactly the same warrant of authority was issued for Regular, Special, and Loyalty Rangers, we have adopted a simple criterion: if a man held a commission—of whatever type—in the Texas State Ranger Force, he was a "real" Texas Ranger.

In any discussion of the Ranger Force what is of paramount importance is that the Rangers were answerable to the governor. This single fact explains a great deal of Ranger history, for the organization was shot through with politics. Every time a new governor took office there was a churning of Ranger personnel, from the appointment of captains to would-be enlistees mustering all the political influence they could, and Ranger commissions were often bestowed on the politically faithful. The situation made it difficult for a man to rise through the ranks. Speaking of political influence, men like Jim Wells, F. A. Chapa, Claude Hudspeth, and Caesar Kleberg affected not just Ranger appointments but on repeated occasions how the organization was utilized. Individuals like these represented economic as well as political influence. Yet it was the governor who ultimately determined how the Rangers would function. Oscar B. Colquitt came into office quite antagonistic toward the Rangers and was determined to bring the organization to heel. During his tenure, however, he came to rely heavily on the Rangers as he made strenuous efforts to defend Texas and Texans. James Ferguson thoroughly politicized the Rangers, and he often directed their day-to-day activities. When in 1915 Ferguson was faced with invasion and insurrection in South Texas he authorized a rinchada on an unprecedented scale. The Ferguson Rangers were in a situation analogous to that of the CIA under the Kennedys, when that agency was ordered to get rid of Fidel Castro by whatever means necessary, even if it meant using the Mafia to attempt his assassination. Governor William P. Hobby took a much more hands-off approach toward the Rangers, giving his adjutant general a great deal of latitude in running the organization. Yet Hobby had no objection to the Rangers being used in his gubernatorial campaign or in the unsuccessful attempt to rid the state senate of Archie Parr. Even the 1919 Ranger investigation, which performed a public service by revealing many Ranger abuses, was motivated as much by political considerations as by J. T. Canales's professed desire to reform the Ranger Force. And what tends to be overlooked is that the legislature overwhelmingly exonerated the Rangers. The political dimension to Ranger history, crucial as it was, has been overshadowed by rather simplistic "shoot 'em up" chronicles of Rangers versus outlaws. The Ranger Force continued to be dominated by politics until 1935, when the Department of Public Safety was created, taking the Rangers away from the governor. The hope was to make the Rangers a better law enforcement agency by theoretically removing them from politics.

The supreme irony is that the Mexican Revolution saved the Texas Rangers. By 1910, the Rangers were increasingly viewed as an anachronism. Although they were a revered symbol of Texas, the legislature begrudged spending money on the organization because they were not doing anything that local or county peace officers could not do, and because they were the governor's personal police, often being sent to intrude where they were not wanted and thus fueling resentment that local rights were being trampled. When Rangers went into a community, especially during elections, inevitably one faction hailed them as peacekeepers while the rival faction considered them intimidators.

The Mexican Revolution ushered in a whole new era. The Rangers were of course a state constabulary, but they were now also called on to defend the Texas border against Mexican incursions. The Rangers not only performed a unique role in doing so, but they were once again fulfilling one of their principal original functions—that of fighting Mexicans. The size of the Ranger Force waxed and waned in direct proportion to the perceived menace posed by the Revolution, whether along the border or within Texas by threats such as the Plan de San Diego. The Ranger Force went from a low of thirteen men to a high of 1,000. It could be argued that they reached their maximum strength of 1,000 in 1918 because of World War I, but it is obvious that this buildup occurred because Texas faced a revolutionary, hostile, and pro-German Mexico on its southern border. It was the Mexican Revolution that gave the Ranger Force a new lease on life, enabling it to continue as an independent agency until 1935.

We have tried to specify what incidents are attributable to the Rangers and which ones are not. Regarding the most controversial episode in the history of the Texas State Ranger Force, the so-called Bandit War of 1915, the Rangers unquestionably committed atrocities.[2] This conflict is usually presented in a law enforcement context, with the Rangers violating the civil rights of Hispanics. But by way of explanation—not justification—whether the struggle is called the "Bandit War" or the "Border War," the operative word is "war." Anglos believed they were in a struggle for their very survival, a struggle in which the loyalty of Hispanics was very much in doubt. Not only did the Rangers and the Anglo citizens use ruthless tactics to combat the combination of Hispanic insurrection and Mexican invasion, but also Major General Frederick Funston wanted to declare "no quarter" against the raiders, which puts the Rangers' activities in some perspective. To employ the Israeli analogy, what concerns Israelis today is not getting blown up by suicide bombers. To state the obvious, most Israelis favor doing whatever it takes to ensure their own safety, and are less concerned about the rights of Palestinians.

As for the Plan de San Diego, the evidence shows that the Plan mattered only when the Carranza regime supported it—for its own purposes.[3] Carranza cynically used Hispanics as pawns to help him secure United States diplomatic recognition in 1915. In 1916, Carranza revived the Plan as a ploy to remove the Punitive Expedition from Mexico. And in 1919 he again toyed with the idea of resurrecting the Plan. Those who view the Plan as a genuine Hispanic liberation movement must explain why it collapsed whenever Carranza ceased to support it. *Within five days after Carranza's diplomatic recognition by the United States, the raids in 1915 stopped.* Mere coincidence? We think not.

The principal accomplishment of the Plan de San Diego militants was infinitely to worsen the plight of Hispanics in Texas for generations to come. The massive Anglo backlash not only resulted in some 300 Hispanic and Mexican deaths. The raids also confirmed in the minds of many Anglos that Hispanics were indeed a Fifth Column, whose allegiance was really to Mexico. The Plan's proclamation of a "war without quarter" proved to be a double-edged sword. The Bandit War also served to dispel some of the myths entertained by border Hispanics about the Rangers, such as "If it weren't for the American soldiers, the Rangers wouldn't dare come to the Border. The Ranger always runs and hides behind the soldiers when the real trouble starts."[4] This view may have been comforting to Hispanics, but the facts are otherwise. The Bandit War provided militant Hispanics with their best opportunity to strike back at the hated Rangers, but they prudently declined to do so. Militants repeatedly attacked army units, usually small outposts and patrols, but they never attacked a Ranger company, or even an individual Ranger for that matter. What is extraordinary is that the Rangers killed more Rangers (2) than did the supposed freedom fighters (0).

The Ranger Force was guilty of racism—and of sexism and even ageism—which is hardly surprising since Texas was a racist society. Anglo Texans were convinced that their history demonstrated conclusively that they *were* better than the

Mexicans. The very fact of Texas's independence from Mexico proved that. But some of the discrimination against Hispanics was based more on socioeconomic considerations than on ethnicity alone. Especially along the border a clear distinction was made between upper-class Hispanics, with whom Anglos had business and social dealings and often married, and Hispanics of the lower, or peon, class, who were viewed as being little better than blacks. As was evident during the Bandit War, the Hispanic establishment stood shoulder to shoulder with the Anglos against the militants. Thus the situation was more complex than just Anglos versus Hispanics. Racism was not unique to Anglos, however. Hispanics, like Anglos, were not too fond of blacks in border communities,[5] and the Plan de San Diego had a lot of racist provisions regarding Anglos. Virtually all of the people we have written about would fail today's racism litmus test.

Then there is the matter of stereotypes. Stereotypes usually contain a core of truth: Captain Henry Lee Ransom fits the stereotype of the brutal Ranger captain, while Chico Cano fits the stereotype of the vicious Mexican bandit. As long as people thought in terms of stereotypes it made killing the enemy a lot easier. But upon examination, some of the stereotypes about the Rangers are questionable. For example, the Ranger Force was not exclusively Anglo, as is usually believed. Not only was there a sprinkling of Hispanic Rangers—twenty-three—but a few others, such as Sergeant John J. Edds and Captain Tom Ross, would qualify as Hispanics under current ethnic guidelines. Unfortunately, much of what has been written about the Rangers has reinforced either the positive or the negative stereotype about the organization. Except for the federal Bureau of Investigation archive, which was only declassified in 1977, abundant Ranger materials for the period under study have been available to historians for many decades, but they have been used sparingly and quite selectively. Walter Prescott Webb emphasized the positive, while the authors of *Gunpowder Justice* dwelled almost exclusively on the Rangers' misdeeds. What the present study hopefully demonstrates is that there is a wealth of material to support either version. The trick is to examine all the evidence, not just what supports a preconceived position. In the words of historian Barbara Tuchman: "It is wiser, I believe, to arrive at theory by way of the evidence rather than the other way around, like so many revisionists today."[6]

APPENDIX

The Texas Rangers, 1910–1921

This list of Rangers and their dates of service is derived from the microfilmed Texas Rangers Service Records in the Archives Division, Texas State Library.

NAME	REGULAR	SPECIAL	LOYALTY
Abbot, B. P.			06/06/18–02/00/19
Abernathy, R. H.			07/29/18–02/00/19
Abney, Glenn Maurice	09/19/17–02/28/18	03/01/18–01/15/19	
Acker, Philip			08/27/18–02/00/19
Acosta, Dionicio	12/21/17–03/31/19		
Adams, C. D.		04/29/18–01/15/19	
Adams, Columbus William	12/03/17–01/15/19		
Adams, E. O.	06/07/17–12/00/17		
Adams, Harold W.	01/16/18–12/23/20		
Adams, Roy H.	09/01/09–01/08/11		
Adams, Tom		05/03/18–01/15/19	
Addison, A. K.		07/22/18–01/15/19	
Akens, J. S.		07/04/17–12/00/17	
Albin, G. L.		05/28/17–12/00/17	
Alderman, Stanberry			06/05/18–02/00/19
Aldrich, Roy Wilkinson	03/00/15–01/31/31 00/00/33–00/00/47		
Allbright, James J.		03/30/18–01/15/19	
Allday, William D.	08/06/10–09/30/10		

NAME	REGULAR	SPECIAL	LOYALTY
Allee, Alonzo W.		07/10/16–04/21/17	
Allen, C. J.			07/15/18–02/00/19
Allen, Sam M.		12/05/17–01/15/19	
Allen, Wilbur P.		05/06/18–01/15/19 08/30/19–12/31/19	
Alley, Powell	12/13/17–03/15/19		
Alley, Robert F.		06/13/18–01/15/19	
Alley, William T.	03/15/21–03/20/21		
Allison, David William	00/00/99–00/00/03	04/21/17–12/24/17 01/19/18–01/15/19	
Allman, Ambrus Foster	05/26/16–08/15/16		
Alsobrook, William M.	06/16/19–12/09/19		06/01/18–02/00/19
Ames, L.			06/07/18–02/00/19
Amonett, W. L.		03/11/18–01/15/19	
Anders, Joseph Lee	07/19/09–09/30/10 08/29/11–12/31/11 09/06/13–01/31/15 07/30/15–03/31/16 09/30/16–02/15/21		
Anderson, Herbert H.		05/31/17–12/00/17	
Anderson, J. W.	Sometime before 1906	06/20/18–01/15/19	
Anderson, Ottis Allen		06/20/18–01/15/19	
Anderson, S. R.		07/13/18–01/15/19	
Andrews, Walter William	08/22/19–12/15/21		
Anglin, Everett W.	1905		06/18/18–02/00/19
Apel, Hiram		06/01/18–01/15/19	
Apodaca, Antonio	08/18/19–unknown		
Appleby, John A.		07/25/16–10/01/18	
Appling, John		06/08/18–01/15/19	
Archer, Linton P.	06/05/17–07/31/17 10/06/17–02/25/18		
Armstrong, S. A.		04/30/18–01/15/19	
Armstrong, T. D.	05/18/16–06/01/17		

NAME	REGULAR	SPECIAL	LOYALTY
Arnold, Charles H.	06/29/18–02/01/19		
Arrington, J. M.		10/19/18–01/15/19	
Arrington, M. L.			07/08/18–02/00/19
Asbury, John T.		05/30/17–12/00/17	
Asher, Johnnie H.	02/15/21–04/22/21		
Askew, R. G.	09/01/11–01/31/12		
Askey, W. H.			08/16/18–02/00/19
Aten, C. G.	04/01/88–09/01/90		06/01/18–02/00/19
Attwell, Samuel B.		03/23/17–10/01/18	
Aultman, H. O.	05/17/16–08/15/16		
Austin, V. E.			06/04/18–02/00/19
Avant, A. Mathis		04/25/17–01/15/19 03/15/19–12/31/19	
Avriett, Edd L.	10/05/09–02/01/11		
Avriett, Hall	04/12/09–02/01/11		
Bahr, Jack August		09/30/19–12/31/19	
Bailey, Charles H.	09/28/20–12/17/20		
Bailey, Harry M.		02/13/18–11/08/18	
Bailey, Henry P.		12/27/17–04/00/18	
Bailey, Marvin E.	09/07/05–08/19/06 06/05/08–05/00/11		
Baker, Alfred Randolph	10/03/06–00/00/09 07/24/10–11/00/10 09/12/11–10/23/12		
Baker, Frank P.	08/05/15–11/00/15 05/10/16–11/30/16	08/01/17–01/17/19	
Baker, Joseph Eugene	09/11/15–12/09/15 05/18/16–02/10/17 2/31/17–unknown (still in: 05/01/18)		
Baker, Jules J.	1907 04/11/21–06/09/21		
Baker, Tom		12/21/17–01/15/19	
Ball, Taylor			07/13/18–02/00/19

NAME	REGULAR	SPECIAL	LOYALTY
Ballard, John Houston		02/07/16–12/22/17	
Ballew, Thomas B.		12/11/17–01/15/19	
Barbee, Willis M.	11/11/11–03/25/12 07/14/17–04/30/18		
Barber, John E.			07/09/18–02/00/19
Barder, Aaron	04/03/16–12/31/16		
Bargsley, John L.	09/28/20–02/15/21		
Barker, A. C.	04/01/15–08/00/15 01/00/16–09/00/16 09/06/17–06/08/18	10/21/16–09/05/17	
Barker, George E.		02/12/18–01/15/19	
Barkley, James M.			06/12/18–01/15/19
Barkow, Gus P. H.		08/10/17–01/15/19	
Barler, W. L.	04/09/15–03/19/19 11/01/21–01/03/22		
Barnes, Edward A.		12/28/17–01/15/19 07/06/25–07/06/27 11/07/27–11/07/28 12/05/28–12/05/29 12/18/29–12/18/30 01/08/31–01/07/32 01/15/32–01/18/33 01/25/33–01/22/35 06/01/35–08/10/35	
Barnes, John F.		07/26/17–12/00/17	
Barnett, DeWitt T.	08/21/18–03/15/19 08/24/19–09/16/19		
Barnett, Frank		01/03/18–01/15/19	
Barnett, J. C.		02/12/18–01/15/19	
Barnett, J. G.	05/16/16–01/28/17 11/08/18–unknown		
Barnett, L. B.	05/03/21–07/16/23		
Barnhill, Pink		01/27/16–01/15/19	
Barrett, R. J		05/31/17–12/00/17	
Barrientes, Abel G.		03/21/18–01/15/19	
Barrow, A. B.		06/02/17–12/00/17	

NAME	REGULAR	SPECIAL	LOYALTY
Bartell, Sam E.	05/24/16–08/15/16		
Bartlett, Thomas Edward		06/11/18–01/15/19	
Barton, P. E.			06/12/18–02/00/19
Bass, R. M.		05/23/17–01/00/18	
Bates, Carroll	1900 08/22/17–08/31/18		
Bates, J. R.	10/03/17–06/00/18		
Bates, Lawrence H.	1899–1902	06/15/17–12/00/17	
Bates, Winfred F.	1902–1905 03/29/15–06/15/15		
Batsell, James M.		02/05/18–01/15/19	
Baylor, Albert Searcy			06/17/18–02/00/19
Beakley, J. C.		08/09/17–01/15/19	
Beall, Charles P.	03/01/15–11/30/15 04/12/16–09/00/16	03/09/17–12/00/17	
Beall, T. D.	04/18/18–08/31/18		
Beall, W. E.	04/16/18–08/31/18		
Beall, W. O.		06/04/17–12/00/17	
Bean, Joseph C.	01/01/12–01/31/12		
Bean, J. M.	06/15/15–10/21/15		
Beard, A. G.	05/11/16–03/15/19		
Beard, James I.	00/00/19–unknown		
Beard, Rube Simonton			07/24/18–02/00/19
Beasley, C. S.		04/01/17–01/15/19	
Beasley, H. W. Allen	09/30/20–02/15/21	03/23/18–01/15/19	
Beasley, James M.			06/11/18–01/00/19
Beaty, R. E.		12/26/17–01/15/19	
Beaumier, O. L.	05/12/16–05/31/16		
Beck, John C.			06/19/18–01/00/19
Beckett, Stafford E.	10/04/19–02/02/20		
Bedford, G. E.		05/31/17–12/00/17	
Beezley, C. W.		12/23/16–01/00/18	

NAME	REGULAR	SPECIAL	LOYALTY
Belcher, W. W.	03/01/21–08/31/21	10/29/23–03/05/25 10/01/31–01/20/33	
Bell, C. L.	04/16/18–06/01/18		
Bell, Lee		07/06/17–01/15/19	
Bell, Sie	09/24/17–unknown		
Bell, T. W.		07/24/18–01/15/19	
Bellamy, Oscar		12/12/16–12/12/18 01/11/19–12/31/19	
Bellemy, Raymond	10/22/15–12/06/15		
Benge, T. F.			08/29/18–02/00/19
Bennett, J. E.		08/07/16–12/00/17	
Bennett, J. W.		08/10/16–12/00/17	
Bennis, J. G.		06/24/19–12/31/19	
Benson, F. L.			09/19/18–02/00/19
Benson, Roy H.			07/05/18–02/00/19
Benson, W. W.			07/24/18–02/00/19
Bentley, W. V.	04/08/18–10/01/18		
Berry, H. V.		07/22/16–12/00/17	
Berry, J. T.		06/02/17–12/00/17	
Beverly, Bob		10/05/18–01/15/19	
Beverly, T. H.	12/29/17–03/31/18		
Bevill, W. H.	12/15/17–10/01/18		
Bickler, George W.		11/18/16–01/04/17	
Biggio, William Joseph		07/25/17–01/00/18	
Bilberry, E. M.	06/01/18–08/31/18		
Billings, D. D.			06/01/18–02/00/19
Billings, W. C.		05/07/18–01/15/19	
Billingsley, Albert Walter	11/03/15–12/00/15	01/03/31–07/20/32	
Billingsley, J. P.		10/01/17–01/15/19	
Bills, Lee C.	09/21/15–12/00/15 05/01/18–03/10/19	04/21/17–05/01/18	
Binford, C. B.			06/15/18–02/00/19

NAME	REGULAR	SPECIAL	LOYALTY
Binford, Gene B.			06/08/18–02/00/19
Bingham, Charles T.			06/06/18–02/00/19
Bird, J. W.			06/03/18–02/15/19
Bishop, Leo P.	02/19/14–01/31/15		
Bishop, T. S.		07/12/17–01/15/19	
Black, Augustus L.			06/05/18–02/00/19
Black, E. M.			07/01/18–02/18/19
Black, Frank A.	12/28/17–03/21/19 04/21/19–02/10/21		
Blackwell, Charles J.	07/30/15–07/01/18 11/12/18–02/15/21 04/18/23–02/21/25	07/01/18–11/12/18 11/14/25–01/01/26 11/17/27–03/07/28 01/29/31–01/28/32 02/02/32–01/20/33 06/07/33–01/22/35	
Blackwell, Clell M.	02/01/20–02/02/25		
Blackwell, J. Milton			06/16/18–02/00/19
Blackwell, Samuel Clay	08/01/19–01/30/21		
Blaine, John E.		12/21/17–01/15/19	
Blair, John	06/06/18–07/23/18		
Blair, W. T.			06/06/18–01/00/19
Blocker, A. P.		01/22/19–12/31/19	
Bloxom, John R., Jr.	04/02/18–06/30/18 09/10/18–01/10/19		
Blum, Henry		05/06/18–07/04/18	
Boggs, George E.			07/01/18–02/00/19
Bohart, Charles		08/26/16–12/00/17	
Bohls, A. W.		02/02/18–01/15/19	
Bonner, John S.		01/09/32–01/08/33 03/18/33–01/22/35	07/02/18–02/00/19
Boone, Alfred		05/17/18–01/15/19 01/27/28–01/27/29 01/27/29–01/26/30 01/29/30–01/01/31 02/09/31–/01/18/33	

NAME	REGULAR	SPECIAL	LOYALTY
Boothe, F. H.			06/15/18–02/00/19
Boren, J. M.			06/07/18–02/00/19
Borroum, J. S.		06/25/18–01/15/19	
Bounds, J. E.		05/31/17–12/00/17	
Bowen, Milton L.		06/17/16–12/00/17	
Bowman, J. T.		11/00/17–unknown 01/07/18–unknown 05/11/33–unknown	
Boxley, L. D.			06/05/18–02/00/19
Boyd, Cecil	09/11/17–12/15/17 04/20/18–07/11/18		
Boyd, Robert A.	03/19/21–11/30/22 09/01/23–01/31/24		
Boyd, W. A.		11/22/15–11/01/17 11/18/17–01/15/19	
Boykin, Melvin F.	05/07/18–02/01/19		
Boynton, Alexander		09/23/15–12/00/17	
Boynton, O. P.			06/10/18–02/00/19
Bracewell, James A.	11/18/20–01/18/21	03/29/27–03/29/28 04/17/28–04/17/29 04/19/29–04/19/30 05/01/30–01/01/31 02/05/31–01/20/33	
Bradford, C. A.		10/24/18–01/15/19	
Brady, Hubert P.	05/16/16–11/30/16 10/01/20–06/30/23	05/30/17–12/00/17	
Brahan, R. W.		07/02/18–01/15/19 02/01/19–12/31/19	
Branom, Curt			06/11/18–02/00/19
Bratton, J. O.	05/11/16–07/18/16 01/02/18–09/00/18	02/28/33–02/27/35	
Braziel, J. N.			07/03/18–02/00/19
Brehmer, Oscar C.			06/15/18–02/00/19
Brightman, Oswell Oliver			06/17/18–02/00/19
Brigman, Martin A.			06/08/18–02/18/19

NAME	REGULAR	SPECIAL	LOYALTY
Briscoe, Dolph		05/22/17–12/00/17	
Briscoe, Payne		05/03/18–01/15/19	
Brite, Charles E.		07/16/16–12/00/17 01/29/18–01/15/19	
Brite, John William		12/03/17–12/00/17	
Brooks, Ben Hill, Jr.			06/01/18–02/00/19
Brooks, Charles M.	04/01/15–07/10/16		
Brooks, E. T.		05/03/17–12/00/17	
Brooks, Joe B.	02/20/15–02/15/23	04/18/27–04/16/28 04/10/28–04/10/29 04/17/29–04/16/30 04/16/30–01/01/31 01/31/31–01/20/33 06/24/35–10/01/35	
Brooks, Sam Raymond		08/01/19–12/31/19	
Brophy, J. E.		05/10/18–01/15/19	
Brown, Baylor B.		02/28/17–12/00/17	
Brown, George Calvin	09/27/19–01/31/20 02/28/20–03/31/20 10/30/20–10/31/23	03/02/18–10/01/18	
Brown, George E.			06/05/18–02/00/19
Brown, James A.	07/26/17–09/21/17	05/26/17–07/25/17	
Brown, J. Eugene		05/14/18–01/15/19	
Brown, Robert D.	01/01/20–07/31/20 06/22/25–03/31/26		
Brown, T. T.		02/07/17–12/00/17	
Brownfield, A. R.			06/21/18–02/00/19
Bruni, Louis Henry		08/24/18–01/15/19	
Brunner, Cole K.	08/30/15–10/31/15		
Brunson, Glen S.		06/26/17–12/08/17	
Bruton, W. T.			06/04/18–02/18/19
Bryant, Oscar W.		01/14/17–01/00/18	
Buchanan, J. B.	03/01/21–12/00/21	12/07/17–01/15/19	
Buchanan, M. B.		12/06/17–01/15/19	

NAME	REGULAR	SPECIAL	LOYALTY
Buck, Eugene		12/27/17–01/15/19 09/19/31–01/20/33	
Burdett, Robert Lee	10/06/11–06/30/12 02/01/15–06/07/15		
Burford, W. E.	07/31/18–07/31/18 02/10/23–04/30/25		
Burleson, Stephen M.	05/26/16–11/30/16	01/01/17–06/28/17	
Burns, Cyrus E.			06/08/18–02/00/19
Burns, John P., Jr.			06/08/18–02/18/19
Burns, L. T.		06/22/18–01/15/19	
Burris, Claude Clinton			06/10/18–01/17/19
Burrow, George O.		12/19/16–12/00/17	
Burwell, Charles B., Jr.	09/01/17–04/00/19	12/28/25–02/01/27 05/07/27–05/07/28 05/30/28–05/30/29 06/13/29–06/13/30	
Busby, C. C.		05/12/17–01/15/19	
Buster, Arthur L.		05/31/17–12/00/17	
Buster, J. E.			05/05/18–02/18/19
Butler, Marvin N.	12/28/17–12/01/18		
Butler, Sidney		07/11/16–01/15/19	
Butler, S. C.		01/16/18–01/15/19	
Butler, Thomas B.		01/03/19–01/15/19 06/30/25–01/29/28 01/17/28–01/17/29 01/23/29–01/29/30 01/11/30–01/11/31 02/24/31–01/20/33 01/20/33–01/19/35 05/29/35–08/10/35	
Butler, W. B.	12/22/17–03/17/19		
Buttrill, Clyde		12/28/17–06/07/18	
Bynum, Rufus S.		09/12/17–01/08/18 01/09/18–01/15/19	
Byrd, Steve J.		05/19/17–12/00/17	
Cain, D.C.		12/15/17–02/00/18	

NAME	REGULAR	SPECIAL	LOYALTY
Cain, James Jacob		07/22/16–12/00/17	
Callan, Leo A.		03/01/18–01/15/19	
Campbell, F. R.		01/11/18–01/15/19	
Canales, A. T.			07/25/18–02/00/19
Cardwell, O. D.	04/01/14–01/15/17	01/20/17–05/26/19	
Cardwell, Percy Aubrey	06/18/17–03/24/19		
Cargile, Lee		08/20/17–12/08/17	
Carlisle, J. N.		01/08/18–01/15/19	
Carlson, F. A.		01/12/18–01/14/19	
Carlton, Oswald Snider		06/10/18–01/15/19 09/20/33–00/00/35	
Carnes, Herff A.	02/13/03–08/08/11		
Carnes, Quirl Bailey	00/00/07–07/31/10		
Carnutte, Robert H.			05/31/18–02/00/19
Carothers, G. S.		06/11/18–01/15/19	
Carpenter, S. J.	12/09/19–02/10/21		
Carr, William D.	05/31/16–04/18/17		
Carroll, Ed A., Jr.			06/06/18–02/00/19
Carroll, J.D.			07/25/18–02/00/19
Carson, C. L.	08/21/18–03/08/19		
Carson, F. L.		05/26/17–01/15/19	
Carta, Charles A.	10/18/17–07/31/21	10/21/21–06/30/24	
Carta, John	10/11/17–05/00/18		
Carter, Arthur			06/08/18–02/00/19
Carter, Henry F.		12/06/17–unknown	
Carter, Jim	04/23/18–08/31/18		
Carter, Leonard B.	12/17/17–10/20/21		
Carter, R. C.	05/11/16–11/17/16		
Carter, T. M.			06/21/18–02/18/19
Carver, P. S.	04/10/18–08/00/18		
Carson, R. L.			06/01/18–02/00/19
Cash, W. C.			06/06/18–02/00/19

NAME	REGULAR	SPECIAL	LOYALTY
Cassels, Albert Edward		09/02/18–01/14/19	
Cathey, M. E.	10/03/11–07/00/12		
Causey, T. N.			06/13/18–02/00/19
Cavender, Perry	12/24/17–12/20/18		
Cavitt, J. F.			06/17/18–02/00/19
Chadick, I. Stokes	08/02/15–09/20/15		
Chadick, W. D.			06/01/18–02/00/19
Chamberlain, George E.		03/13/17–12/00/17 03/01/18–01/14/19	
Chandler, J. S.		12/27/17–01/15/19	
Chapman, George Wallace	09/01/17–10/11/17 03/20/20–02/22/21		
Chastain, Richard B.	2yrs 8 mos in 1890s 04/16/18–06/01/18		
Chávez, S. T.	12/18/17–unknown (still in 10/00/18)		
Cherryhomes, Thomas Roy			07/19/18–02/00/19
Chessher, James P.	12/10/17–09/09/18		
Chesshir, Sam P.	03/26/18–08/31/21		
Childers, J. G., Jr.		07/11/17–01/15/19	
Childers, Milas A.		12/27/17–01/15/19	
Childers, Preston A.		07/14/17–12/00/17 04/29/18–01/15/19	
Chilton, Hugh			06/06/18–02/18/19
Chilton, P. H.		02/04/18–01/14/19	
Choate, D. Boone			06/07/18–02/00/19
Claiborne, W. H.	01/10/18–11/01/18		
Clark, Frank B.		04/30/18–01/14/19	
Clark, George W.			06/07/18–02/00/19
Clark, Harvey R.	02/14/18–07/29/18		
Clarke, Rufuio [sic]			07/13/18–02/00/19
Clarkson, William		07/09/18–01/14/19	
Claybrook, J. H.			06/07/18–02/00/19

NAME	REGULAR	SPECIAL	LOYALTY
Clendenin, W. H.			07/09/18–02/00/19
Cleveland, Leroy	09/11/17–12/15/17		
Cline, Ira W.	09/27/12–06/00/15		
Cloud, J. C.			06/08/18–02/00/19
Cobb, Dent N.		05/08/18–01/15/19	
Cochran, John W.			06/04/18–01/00/19
Coffee, W.			06/10/18–02/18/19
Coffee, Walter Douglas			06/05/18–02/00/19
Coffin, A. L.		01/02/17–01/29/18	
Cogdell, D. M.			06/08/18–02/00/19
Coker, L. B.			06/07/18–02/00/19
Coker, R. A.			06/06/18–02/00/19
Cole, Allen	09/06/17–06/18/18		
Cole, J. P.			06/17/18–02/19/19
Cole, L. L.			07/03/18–02/00/19
Cole, S. R.	06/11/15–01/10/16		
Cole, Thomas J.	09/30/20–08/31/21		
Coleman, E. E.		11/02/18–01/15/19	
Coleman, M.			05/31/18–02/00/19
Coleman, Thomas Atlee		06/20/16–12/00/17 02/07/18–01/14/19	
Colley, E. M.	12/15/17–03/15/18		
Colley, G. W.	11/01/11–01/31/12		
Collins, E. I.			06/11/18–02/00/19
Collins, Henry Warren "Rip"	04/02/18–06/29/18 05/01/32–01/18/33	01/24/31–04/30/32	
Collyns, Cecil B.		07/31/18–01/15/19	
Colquitt, R. M.		01/14/18–01/15/19 06/01/32–unknown	
Colquitt, W. Homer		01/02/18–01/14/19 12/26/33–unknown	
Colquitt, Will K.		05/09/17–12/00/17	
Colvert, Carl Lee		07/17/16–12/00/17	

NAME	REGULAR	SPECIAL	LOYALTY
Cone, William Thomas		02/12/18–01/15/19 08/06/25–04/19/27 04/19/27–04/19/28 07/24/28–07/24/29 08/05/29–07/29/30 07/29/30–03/01/31	
Conley, J. T.	12/24/17–04/00/18		
Connally, Thomas	12/22/17–unknown (still in: 09/10/18)		
Conner, J. F.			06/24/18–01/11/19
Conner, W. Max			06/07/18–02/18/19
Connor, George W. "Buck"	05/01/16–05/31/16		
Conro, L. R.			06/10/18–02/19/19
Cook, Charles			06/05/18–02/00/19
Cook, John Cliff	05/27/16–08/31/16		
Cook, L. J.		06/01/17–12/00/17	
Cooper, Herbert Newton		06/11/17–12/17/17	
Cooper, John A.			06/17/18–02/00/19
Cooper, J. M.	08/30/18–11/01/18		
Corder, B. T.		12/14/17–01/15/19	
Corn, G. H.		05/30/17–12/00/17	
Cornett, R. M.			07/08/18–02/00/19
Cotton, D. N.		10/14/16–01/00/18	
Cotulla, Simon			06/05/18–02/19/19
Cousins, F. A.			07/09/18–02/00/19
Covey, J. E.			06/08/18–02/00/19
Cowden, Jax M.			06/14/18–02/19/19
Cox, Bates			06/15/18–02/00/19
Cox, Ben L.		06/15/17–12/00/17	
Cox, Dee W.	09/01/09–09/15/11 12/22/17–02/15/21	02/07/23–03/24/23	
Cox, Walker			06/07/18–02/00/19
Craft, William Bentford			07/22/18–02/19/19
Crager, W. M.			06/03/18–02/00/19

NAME	REGULAR	SPECIAL	LOYALTY
Cragg, Howard	06/12/16–01/15/19		
Craig, Walter A.		05/31/18–01/14/19	
Craighead, Charles A.	00/00/10–03/20/11	01/07/18–05/21/19	
Craighead, J. P. N. "Pat"	03/01/10–05/12/16		
Cravey, Fletcher		05/18/18–01/15/19 06/30/25–10/21/26	
Cravey, James		05/17/18–06/10/18	
Crawford, Charles M.		01/19/21–09/05/24 09/23/27–09/23/28	
Crawford, W. J.		01/27/19–12/31/19	
Crittenden, Frank C.	06/04/18–04/19/19		
Crittenden, W. R.			07/05/18–02/00/19
Crockett, J. E.		06/09/17–12/00/17	
Croft, Ewell Lee		07/17/16–12/00/17	
Cross, H. D.	01/26/18–04/00/18		
Cross, Joe J.			06/01/18–02/14/19
Crosson, John	10/04/19–04/30/21	05/09/17–12/00/17	
Crosson, Thomas C.		01/08/18–01/15/19	
Crow, Emmett M.	09/03/17–09/13/17	12/17/23–12/31/24	
Crow, John Furman	04/16/20–02/15/21 03/19/21–11/31/23 02/15/33–10/31/33		
Crumpler, Henry		01/17/17–03/21/17	
Cullinan, Michael P		04/24/18–01/14/19	
Culp, George C.	08/09/09–10/14/10	09/18/29–09/18/30	
Culpepper, Cornelius V.		12/03/17–01/15/19	
Cummings, A. P. "Sugg"	02/01/15–06/13/15 01/29/24–05/14/27		
Cunningham, Aaron W.	02/15/21–08/31/21		
Cunningham, J. F.		04/23/17–12/00/17	
Cunningham, James F.		08/01/18–11/10/18	
Cunningham, K. F.	12/10/17–02/07/19		
Cunningham, P. A.		01/29/18–01/15/19	

NAME	REGULAR	SPECIAL	LOYALTY
Cunningham, T. B.		03/07/18–01/14/19 01/30/19–12/31/19	
Cunningham, T. M.			06/13/18–02/00/19
Cunningham, W. J.		06/16/17–12/00/17	
Cupples, C. T.	06/17/16–11/01/16		
Curtis, J. R.		06/14/17–12/00/17	
Custer, Ed		04/13/17–12/00/17	
Dannelley, John L.		05/08/18–01/15/19	
Dannelley, W. A.		03/22/18–01/15/19	
Darby, James P.	12/11/17–03/15/19	05/24/17–01/15/19 08/05/33–unknown	
Darlington, Claude	12/11/17–03/15/19 07/01/19–08/15/19 03/28/20–04/30/24 05/05/24–06/27/24		
Davenport, Joseph E.	10/00/11–01/31/12 02/00/15–10/00/15	01/13/17–07/19/17	
David, Loyd A.	11/01/17–01/15/19		
Davidson, Thomas J.	08/21/18–unknown (still in: 06/20/19)		
Davies, Luther			06/04/18–02/00/19
Davis, E. F.			05/31/18–02/00/19
Davis, E. T.		05/19/17–01/15/19 05/26/26–02/01/27 02/24/28–05/13/28	
Davis, Gould		07/23/17–12/00/17	
Davis, Hillsman		05/09/17–12/00/17	
Davis, Howard E.		03/10/17–12/00/17	
Davis, John H., Sr.			06/10/18–02/00/19
Davis, J. B.		07/24/16–12/00/17	
Davis, J. R.		12/26/17–01/15/19	
Davis, Levi	12/15/08–09/30/10 10/03/10–09/12/11		
Davis, W. B.	10/01/17–03/10/19		
Davis, William D.		06/05/18–01/15/19	

NAME	REGULAR	SPECIAL	LOYALTY
Davis, Will W.	12/08/17–03/21/19 07/01/19–02/10/21		
Daws, A. C.			06/14/18–01/15/19
Dawson, James C.			06/05/18–02/19/19
Day, A. R.		05/29/17–12/00/17	
Day, Frank E.		08/26/19–12/31/19	06/05/18–02/00/19
Day, John T.		06/02/17–12/00/17	
Dean, John M.			06/05/18–02/00/19
Dees, M. A.			04/07/18–02/00/19
De la Garza, Miguel			08/02/18–02/00/19
De Mullos, Carlos	08/05/18–08/31/18		
Denalsano, W. L.		02/12/17–12/00/17 02/11/18–01/15/19	
Denison, Frank, Jr.		07/17/17–12/00/17	
Denson, B. F.		03/16/18–01/15/19	
Despain, Duncan L.	07/01/19–09/20/19	03/16/17–07/23/17	
Dial, Jack		05/31/17–12/00/17	
Dial, James L.	11/20/17–03/10/19 12/04/19–02/10/21		
Dillard, E. P.	08/18/15–01/21/16		
Dilworth, J. C.	08/27/18–02/01/19		
Dinwiddie, S. T.			06/28/18–02/00/19
Dissler, John		01/31/18–01/15/19	
Donaldson, John L.		07/15/18–01/15/19 06/21/33–06/20/35	
Dooley, John H.			06/08/18–02/00/19
Dougherty, Marcellus, Jr.	05/18/16–08/31/16	12/18/16–03/31/17	
Dowdy, J. F.		08/14/17–12/00/17	
Dowe, James W.		04/30/18–09/01/18	
Dowe, O. C.	04/12/18–08/00/18	12/15/17–04/12/18	
Downing, S. M.			06/15/18–02/00/19
Downs, J. B.		12/11/17–03/18/18	
Drake, Millard O.	04/16/18–08/31/18		

NAME	REGULAR	SPECIAL	LOYALTY
Draper, Asa		04/30/18–01/15/19	
Draper, John		05/16/16–12/00/17	
Draper, John C.		04/30/17–12/00/17 01/19/18–01/15/19	
Driskill, E. D.		06/01/17–12/00/17	
Driskill, John A.		06/04/17–12/00/17	
Droddy, S. A.			07/10/18–02/00/19
Dubose, Ben B.	08/16/15–10/31/15 05/12/16–12/06/16		
Dubose, Edwin M.	09/01/17–03/10/18	05/03/18–10/21/18 07/01/33–01/22/35	
Dudley, John Lee		07/22/16–12/00/17	
Dunagan, T. M., Jr.	03/28/18–12/31/18		
Dunaway, James D.	07/10/03–03/01/06 04/16/06–00/00/07 03/29/15–10/31/15		
Duncan, J. B.			07/06/18–02/00/19
Duncan, Virgil M.		07/17/16–12/00/17	
Duncan, W. K.	09/28/17–04/00/18		
Duncan, W. T.		01/02/18–01/15/19	
Dunlap, M. L.		01/12/18–06/01/18	
Dunn, George B.			06/07/18–02/00/19
Dunn, Glen	05/30/16–10/14/16		
Dunn, J. B.			06/03/18–02/00/19
Durán, Santos	03/25/18–11/01/18		
Durham, George P., Jr.		06/06/17–01/15/19 01/23/19–12/31/19 10/30/33–01/22/35	
Durst, Sterling O.	09/01/18–03/31/19 08/01/19–02/15/20		
Dustin, Vyvian Glenroy			06/27/18–02/00/19
Dyches, P. F.	12/15/19–01/31/28	11/24/28–12/31/28	
Dycus, Charlie T.			06/06/18–02/00/19
Eads, James T.	03/09/21–08/31/21		

NAME	REGULAR	SPECIAL	LOYALTY
Eads, Ralph		07/20/16–12/00/17	
Early, W. N.			06/05/18–02/00/19
Earnest, D. P.			06/11/18–02/00/19
Eason, Ed P.			06/17/18–02/00/19
East, Arthur Lee		04/30/18–01/15/19 01/24/19–12/31/19	
East, Roy E.		12/22/17–01/15/19	
East, Tom T.		04/18/18–01/15/19 01/24/19–12/31/19	
Easter, J. F.			07/05/18–02/00/19
Easterling, A. C.		02/21/18–01/15/19	
Eckhardt, O. L.		07/02/18–01/15/19 06/12/19–12/31/19	
Eckhardt, Robert J.		06/29/18–01/14/19 05/22/26–02/01/27 02/09/27–04/09/27	
Edds, Henry		02/02/18–01/15/19	
Edds, John J.	09/15/15–03/31/16 01/01/18–12/10/21		
Edwards, L. Walton "Lupe"	05/08/15–10/18/15		
Edwards, Samuel V. "Pete"		11/18/29–11/18/30 12/16/31–unknown	06/14/18–02/00/19
Edwards, W. W.			08/01/18–02/19/19
Eickenroht, Reno A.	01/30/18–07/29/18		
Eidman, Hugh B.			06/10/18–02/00/19
Ellington, F. M.			06/18/18–02/00/19
Elliot, William J.			06/17/18–02/00/19
Elliott, John		06/01/18–09/00/18	
Ellis, Ace		07/24/17–12/00/17	
Ellis, Benjamin S.			06/11/18–02/00/19
Ellis, Jim M.	06/05/19–06/20/20		
Ellis, Louis		08/06/17–12/00/17	
Ellis, W. D.		01/22/18–01/15/19	
Ellison, D. Clyde	09/01/17–03/01/18		

NAME	REGULAR	SPECIAL	LOYALTY
Elmore, G. M.			06/11/18–02/00/19
Elrod, Jesse Lee			06/17/18–02/00/19
Engelking, Carl Phillip	12/11/17–03/25/18		
Engelking, Lucas J.	08/07/15–09/01/15		
Erskine, F. P. G.	08/20/15–09/00/16		
Erwin, Charles D.		08/10/18–01/15/19	
Evans, Arthur		12/27/17–01/15/19	
Evans, A. J.		08/11/16–01/15/19	
Evans, Bob		01/03/18–01/15/19	
Evans, J. R.			06/15/18–02/00/19
Evans, John W.		04/27/18–01/15/19	
Evans, Roger Q.		05/29/17–12/00/17	
Everett, W. J., Jr.		05/21/17–12/00/17	
Ewing, M. B.			06/01/18–02/00/19
Fagan, John Francis		07/18/16–12/00/17	06/17/18–02/00/19
Falls, J. D.			06/08/18–02/00/19
Farrow, John H.		01/12/18–01/15/19	
Fatheree, Ira N.		12/21/17–01/15/19 08/07/25–07/30/27 07/30/27–07/30/28 08/02/28–08/02/29 08/05/29–08/07/30 08/07/30–08/07/31 08/24/31–01/18/33 02/10/33–unknown	
Faubion, J. E.	01/26/18–08/00/18		
Faubion, J. L.	1892 08/13/15–03/31/16 12/13/17–07/28/18		
Faust, Walter			08/05/18–02/00/19
Feagin, J. D.			06/05/18–02/00/19
Feild, Harry			06/08/18–02/00/19
Felps, Henry	06/19/13–08/01/15		
Fenley, Ivy R.	06/08/15–06/30/16	05/25/17–09/01/17	

NAME	REGULAR	SPECIAL	LOYALTY
Ferguson, W. A.			06/12/18–02/00/19
Fields, Charles W.		12/07/18–01/15/19	
Finley, Albert			05/31/18–02/21/19
Finley, I. N.		06/07/17–12/00/17	
Finney, John R.			06/05/18–02/00/19
Fischer, Willie			06/13/18–02/00/19
Fitzgerald, Corea Aquilla			06/05/18–02/00/19
Fitzgerald, Raymond		12/31/17–01/15/19	
Fitzgerald, S. M.	06/26/16–07/17/16		
Fleming, W. A.	12/17/17–02/10/18		
Fletcher, Emmett A.		08/25/19–12/31/19	08/01/18–12/00/19
Fletcher, H. D.		08/14/19–12/31/19	
Fletcher, Lloyd		12/10/17–02/00/18	
Fletcher, Robert R.			06/10/18–02/00/19
Flores, Félix	06/18/18–08/31/18	10/05/18–11/01/18	
Flowers, E. B.		08/03/17–01/15/19	
Flynt, James P.	04/13/18–08/30/18	08/31/18–01/15/19	
Folts, William H.			07/18/18–02/20/19
Ford, Elgin	05/12/16–09/15/16		
Forrest, W. Y.			06/03/18–02/00/19
Fortune, Louis A.		08/05/16–12/00/17	
Fox, J. C.	03/23/18–unknown (still in: 01/00/19)		
Fox, James Leslie	09/30/20–11/04/20		
Fox, James Monroe	10/05/11–05/31/18 06/06/25–03/31/27	02/19/34–01/22/35	
Francis, J. A.	08/12/15–09/12/15		
Franklin, Claude	01/16/18–07/15/20		
Franklin, J. B.	06/10/18–06/19/19		
Franklin, Steve L.		01/23/18–01/15/19 01/30/19–12/31/19	
Franks, Tom C.	1902–1904 04/16/18–05/31/18		

NAME	REGULAR	SPECIAL	LOYALTY
Frazier, Ben		12/31/17–01/15/19	
Frazier, Earl B.			06/05/18–02/00/19
Frye, Roy J.			07/10/18–02/00/19
Fuller, M. A.			06/14/18–02/00/19
Fuller, Nathan N.	05/15/16–02/11/20		
Fuller, R. J.	11/20/18–03/08/19		
Fullerton, J. W.		01/09/18–01/15/19	
Fuqua, Henry Earl		06/25/17–12/00/17	
Furlong, William Harrison			05/31/18–02/00/19
Futch, William Lee		02/16/18–01/15/19 08/08/25–08/08/27 12/06/27–11/26/28 11/26/28–11/26/29 12/19/29–12/18/30 01/08/31–01/07/32 01/25/32–01/20/33 03/31/33–01/22/35 05/29/35–08/10/35	
Gaines, C. M.			06/10/18–02/00/19
Gaines, John Pierce		07/18/19–11/01/19	
Gallagher, D. O.		08/16/18–01/15/19	
Galloway, W. S.			06/03/18–02/00/19
Gamble, J. D.			06/01/18–02/00/19
García, Amador E.		03/05/18–01/15/19	
Gardien, W. L.			06/04/18–02/00/19
Gardner, Charles E.		06/08/18–01/15/19	
Gardner, W. T.			06/07/18–02/00/19
Garlick, Henry Stow		07/01/18–01/15/19	
Garlick, W. Fred	04/16/18–06/01/18		
Garner, H. E.		04/27/18–01/15/19	
Garner, J. R.		01/06/17–01/15/19	
Garner, Lon		12/21/18–01/15/19	
Garrett, A. H.			06/07/18–02/00/19
Garrett, C. C.			06/04/18–02/00/19
Garrett, Joe A.			07/10/18–02/00/19

NAME	REGULAR	SPECIAL	LOYALTY
Garrett, Y. P.		12/29/17–03/05/18	
Garrison, G. Kent		09/14/17–12/17/17 01/10/18–01/15/19	
Gatewood, J. L.		06/27/17–01/15/19	
Gentry, J. M.	01/10/18–08/01/18		
Gentry, Owens E.		07/02/17–12/00/17 08/12/32–01/18/33	
Geron, Frank C.			07/10/18–02/19/19
Gholson, Albert F.	09/01/17–03/31/18		
Gibson, George		04/17/16–12/00/17 06/27/18–01/15/19 01/30/19–12/31/19	
Gibson, James		06/10/18–01/15/19 02/10/31–01/20/33	
Gibson, J. Frank			06/10/18–02/00/19
Gill, S. Lamar		05/31/16–12/00/17 01/24/33–01/22/35	
Gilliam, J. D.		01/03/18–01/15/19	
Gilliland, Carl			06/14/18–02/00/19
Gilliland, J. E.			06/15/18–02/00/19
Gillispie, J. P.	12/19/12–06/09/13		
Gillon, John A.	09/09/21–04/15/23 09/01/23–02/21/25	11/12/17–12/00/17 05/06/19–12/31/19 12/17/25–02/01/27 05/28/27–09/27/28 12/01/31–09/09/32 12/11/33–01/14/35	
Gipson, F. C.			07/02/18–02/00/19
Girdley, B. C.			06/05/18–02/20/19
Glascock, Lee		05/11/17–12/00/17 01/09/18–01/15/19	
Glasscock, Henry D.	09/22/17–02/15/31 09/01/31–01/18/33		
Glick, George Alva	08/21/15–12/00/15	09/30/29–09/30/30 10/09/30–10/09/31 10/02/31–01/18/33 01/23/33–08/10/35	

NAME	REGULAR	SPECIAL	LOYALTY
Gonzáles, Willie		05/06/18–01/15/19	
González, Juan C.	08/11/19–01/31/23 05/05/23–02/28/25 07/31/25–05/15/27		07/12/18–02/19/19
Goodlett, J. B.		06/01/18–10/24/18	
Goodloe, Gail Borden		05/27/17–01/15/19	
Goodwin, F. Epp, Jr.		06/06/17–12/31/19	
Goodwin, O. W. "Doc"	04/06/14–02/10/16		
Goodwin, Richard Lawrence		12/06/17–01/15/19	
Goodwyn, James Dobie		01/10/19–12/31/19	
Goolsby, John Arthur	06/10/18–10/31/18		
Gossett, J. W.		07/10/18–01/15/19	
Gouger, Roland A.	12/12/19–02/10/21	07/15/18–01/15/19	
Graham, Hosea	04/16/18–06/01/18		
Graham, Joe M.		12/27/17–01/15/19	
Graham, John	01/19/18–06/00/18		
Graham, Wade B.			06/04/18–02/00/19
Grantham, R. G.		09/21/18–06/16/19	
Gravis, Charles K.			08/31/18–02/19/19
Gray, Charles N.		05/21/18–01/15/19	
Gray, George W.		06/02/17–12/00/17	
Gray, Jerry	05/28/17–04/30/25	07/25/25–07/25/27 09/12/27–09/12/28 03/04/30–06/01/30 06/14/32–01/18/33	
Gray, John M.		06/21/18–01/15/19	
Gray, J. W.			05/31/18–02/00/19
Gray, W. H.			06/12/18–02/00/19
Gray, W. K.		02/28/18–01/15/19 04/23/30–01/01/31 03/03/31–03/02/32 01/28/33–01/27/35	
Green, J. W. B.			06/12/18–02/00/19
Greer, D. C.			07/25/18–02/00/19

NAME	REGULAR	SPECIAL	LOYALTY
Gridley, B. C.			06/05/18–02/00/19
Griffin, K. W.			09/10/18–02/00/19
Griffin, Ray		09/02/16–12/00/17 05/17/18–01/15/19	
Griffitts, Homer W.	12/21/17–unknown (still in: 01/09/18)	09/04/15–unknown	
Grimes, Frank		06/09/17–09/13/17	
Grimes, J. J.			05/31/18–02/00/19
Grimes, W. Tom	03/08/13–05/15/18		
Grisham, W. J.			05/31/18–02/00/19
Gross, Abe		11/29/17–12/00/17	
Grover, James Edward	06/17/19–10/16/19		
Guilford, H. Boyd		03/16/18–01/15/19 03/04/30–01/01/31	
Guillemette, Louis		07/29/18–01/15/19	
Gunn, Elmer G.			05/31/18–02/00/19
Gustafson, Oscar		07/25/18–01/15/19	
Guynes, W. P., Jr.		12/12/17–01/15/19	
Haby, William			08/29/18–02/00/19
Hagler, C. H.	06/05/18–04/10/19		
Hale, Charles L.	09/29/10–02/01/11		
Hale, George A.		12/31/17–01/15/19	
Hale, Grant		12/31/17–01/15/19	
Hale, Will			06/26/18–02/00/19
Hale, W. Duff	01/03/18–03/31/18		
Hale, W. F.		01/17/18–01/15/19	
Haley, Patrick Daniel		12/18/16–12/00/17	
Hall, Asa D.		06/29/17–12/00/17	
Hall, Horace C.		02/21/18–01/15/19	
Hall, Howard N.	12/13/19–11/22/20 02/24/21–08/05/23		
Hall, Jerrey D.	04/12/18–07/01/18		
Hall, Larry L.	09/01/19–12/31/21		

NAME	REGULAR	SPECIAL	LOYALTY
Hall, Ollie			06/24/18–02/00/19
Hall, William H.		12/20/16–05/18/17	
Hallebeke, Edd	08/20/18–03/10/19		
Hallmark, W. P.			07/01/18–02/00/19
Hamer, D. E.	01/19/33–01/24/35	07/12/16–12/00/17	
Hamer, Francis Augustus "Frank"	04/21/06–11/00/08 03/29/15–11/08/15 10/01/18–06/19/19 11/25/19–05/11/20 09/01/21–06/30/25 02/02/27–02/01/33	11/08/15–01/10/17 07/01/25–02/01/27 02/01/46–01/01/55	
Hamer, Harrison Lester	10/23/18–01/01/19 06/20/19–12/31/19 04/01/32–01/18/33	04/09/27–04/01/28 05/01/28–05/01/29 08/22/29–08/22/30 09/25/30–01/02/31 01/03/31–04/01/32 07/18/35–08/10/35	
Hamilton, Austin Travis	10/12/18–08/17/19		
Hamilton, Ernest F.		01/05/18–01/15/19	
Hamilton, J. D.			06/06/18–02/00/19
Hamilton, J. H.			06/17/18–02/00/19
Hamilton, W. T.		07/07/19–07/07/21 08/29/27–08/21/28 09/20/28–09/20/29	
Hampton, E. G.		06/14/17–12/00/17	
Hamrick, George T.		05/27/18–01/15/19	
Haney, John		10/19/18–01/15/19	
Hanks, M. B.		06/09/17–12/00/17	
Hansen, Ernst C.			07/12/18–02/21/19
Hanson, C. J.	05/15/16–11/30/16 09/11/17–05/26/19		
Hanson, William M.	01/31/18–09/04/19	12/24/17–01/30/18	
Harbison, Pelton Bruce	12/09/19–08/19/21		
Hardesty, Roy W.	05/05/21–03/31/23		
Hardie, J. Gunter		07/03/17–12/00/17	
Hardin, A. B.	01/22/18–03/01/18	01/16/18–01/21/18	

NAME	REGULAR	SPECIAL	LOYALTY
Hardin, A. H.		08/22/16–12/14/16	
Hardin, Mike O.	04/15/18–08/00/18		
Hardin, William Arthur		05/23/18–01/15/19	
Hargis, W. B.			07/04/18–02/00/19
Hargus, Van D.	01/16/19–02/03/20		
Harkey, J. D.	1905		06/12/18–02/00/19
Harper, J. H.			07/01/18–02/00/19
Harrell, Edward Hogan		07/08/18–01/15/19	
Harrell, M. W.			07/15/18–02/00/19
Harrington, Lee		10/28/16–12/00/17 03/20/18–01/15/19	
Harris, H. B.			05/31/18–02/00/19
Harris, Irwin C.	12/14/17–01/22/18		
Harris, J. C.		03/11/18–01/15/19 05/07/19–12/31/19	
Harris, Lon			10/07/18–02/00/19
Harris, T. M.			07/02/18–02/00/19
Harris, Will			06/14/18–02/00/19
Harris, William T.		08/29/17–01/15/19	
Harvey, Jess W.			06/08/18–02/21/19
Harvey, William		07/17/16–12/00/17	
Harvick, J. Ad		01/11/17–01/15/19 04/18/27–04/18/28	
Harvie, Crawford			07/04/18–02/21/19
Harvin, James A.		12/27/17–01/15/19	
Harwell, Oscar		06/01/17–12/00/17	
Haughton, Charles M.			06/06/18–02/28/19
Hawkins, Richard Crews "Red"	11/25/11–03/00/14 02/19/35–08/31/39	01/03/18–01/15/19 05/13/34–01/22/35	
Hawkins, T. T.	09/23/20–02/15/21	11/19/17–01/15/19	
Hay, G. C.			06/12/18–02/00/19
Hayden, Audie T.	12/18/19–01/09/20		
Hayes, Travis			05/31/18–02/00/19

NAME	REGULAR	SPECIAL	LOYALTY
Haynes, B. H.			06/10/18–02/00/19
Haynes, W. H.		12/15/17–03/00/18	
Haysner, C. L.			06/06/18–02/00/19
Head, M. C.			07/30/18–02/00/19
Heard, James I.	09/01/17–03/10/19		
Hearn, Roy L.	12/09/19–08/10/21		
Hedgecoke, Eugene			06/10/18–10/07/18
Helton, H. D.			06/14/18–02/00/19
Henne, Herbert G.		06/10/18–12/31/19	
Henrich, Steve	08/13/15–09/08/15		
Henrichson, H. C.		05/07/18–01/15/19	
Henry, Dempsey F.			06/05/18–02/00/19
Henry, John Quincy		12/08/17–01/15/19	
Henry, Lee W.	08/06/18–unknown (still in: 10/28/18)		
Hensley, John E.	05/27/18–03/10/19 06/20/19–02/21/25		
Heppel, Frank Barrett		01/04/19–12/31/19 10/16/25–10/16/27 12/10/27–11/26/28 11/26/28–01/26/29 12/19/29–04/03/30	
Herbst, A. W.		04/30/17–12/31/19	
Herr, A. W.		10/19/17–06/27/18 07/16/28–06/14/29 06/14/29–06/14/30 06/14/30–06/14/31 06/14/31–01/18/33 01/31/33–01/22/35	
Herrera, Jose		02/05/18–01/15/19	
Herzing, J. F.	09/20/17–unknown (still in: 09/10/18)		
Hester, Thomas I.			05/31/18–02/00/19
Heuermann, Edward Joseph	01/01/16–00/00/16	03/23/31–01/20/33	
Hey, Ben		12/20/17–01/15/19	
Hibbert, Frank H.			06/14/18–02/00/19

NAME	REGULAR	SPECIAL	LOYALTY
Hick, Alexander Lincoln			05/31/18–02/00/19
Hickey, Richard T.	02/23/21–05/31/21		
Hickman, Thomas R.	06/16/19–01/18/33 01/23/35–11/12/35		
Hicks, Stonewall Jackson			05/31/18–02/00/19
Highfill, K. L.		05/05/19–12/31/19	
Hilburn, A. B.	12/14/17–09/10/18 unknown–12/00/18		
Hilburn, Ernest		07/24/16–12/00/17	
Hill, A. W.	12/22/17–03/00/18		
Hill, Charles W.		04/15/18–01/15/19	
Hill, George O.	12/26/17–07/16/18		
Hill, Gordon		09/08/15–12/00/17	
Hill, Jesse J.	12/00/17–12/01/19		
Hill, John A.		01/07/18–12/31/19 02/22/33–02/26/34	
Hill, Lon C.		08/28/15–12/00/17 01/28/18–12/31/19	
Hill, Sam Houston	1881	02/25/18–12/31/19	
Hill, William Hickman		04/26/18–01/15/19 01/23/19–12/31/19	
Hillboldt, Frank W.	06/06/18–05/11/20		
Hilliard, Claude A.	07/01/19–unknown		
Hillyard, D. M.		04/15/18–01/15/19	
Hines, Marcus W.	05/05/11–04/01/14		
Hines, R. E.			06/06/18–02/00/19
Hinojosa, Daniel	09/06/10–02/01/11 06/07/18–02/03/19		
Hitt, John F.			06/03/18–02/00/19
Hodge, W. E.	09/01/17–02/15/18 03/01/18–07/01/18		
Hodge, W. T.		06/10/18–01/15/19	
Hodges, Arthur B.		06/23/17–12/00/17	
Hoerster, Henry		02/16/18–01/15/19	

NAME	REGULAR	SPECIAL	LOYALTY
Hoffman, R. H.		07/10/18–01/15/19	
Hogg, Tom		05/19/17–12/00/17	
Hoggett, L. S.		12/21/17–01/15/19	
Hogren, Samuel	02/20/14–03/01/14 05/13/14–unknown		
Hogue, C. C.			06/05/18–02/00/19
Holbein, Reuben		05/06/18–01/15/19	
Holden, H. Clint	05/16/16–04/01/18	03/19/28–03/13/29 01/31/34–01/22/35	
Hollan, J. G.	04/01/18–02/01/19		
Holland, J. Grady			06/04/18–02/00/19
Holland, Murray		05/27/18–01/15/19	
Holland, W. R.	05/01/18–02/28/19		
Hollis, John Ransom		06/04/17–12/00/17 12/29/17–01/15/19	
Hollis, John Robert	08/22/19–08/31/21 03/31/23–05/15/27		
Hollis, L. W., Jr.		02/06/18–01/15/19	
Holloman, F. E.	12/10/17–12/01/18		
Holman, E. M.		06/27/17–01/15/19	
Holmes, Walter M.			10/10/18–02/00/19
Holmes, W. Eli	05/20/18–02/15/19		
Holoday, Frank	04/13/18–07/31/18	08/01/18–01/15/19	
Honea, R. F.		05/31/17–12/17/17	
Honse, Frank	06/08/18–11/05/18		
Hooks, D. A.		10/01/17–01/15/19	
Hope, Emmett	12/18/17–08/00/18		
Hope, L.			07/04/18–02/00/19
Hopping, R. C.		06/09/19–12/31/19	
Hord, Ed		12/03/17–01/15/19	
Hornsby, Emory	12/19/17–03/15/18		
Hornsby, John W.		10/17/19–12/31/19	
Hornsby, W. W.	06/10/18–01/01/19		

NAME	REGULAR	SPECIAL	LOYALTY
Horton, Fred B.			06/18/18–02/00/19
Houchins, J. F.			05/31/18–02/00/19
Houston, Edwin			08/15/18–02/00/19
Houston, Tom A.			06/07/18–02/00/19
Howard, John B.		09/18/33–01/22/35	06/03/18–02/00/19
Howell, James M.		06/24/18–01/15/19 08/20/19–12/31/19	
Huddleston, Clyde Eugene	12/01/17–09/10/18	07/01/27–07/01/28 07/09/28–07/09/29 10/17/29–10/17/30 10/22/30–01/01/31	
Hudgins, W. O.		06/06/18–01/15/19	
Hudson, R. M. "Duke"	05/08/06–00/00/08 04/01/10–07/15/10		
Hudson, W. W.		05/29/18–10/00/18	
Huff, Lee		02/09/17–12/00/17	
Huffaker, D. Hunter		02/05/18–01/15/19	
Hughes, Covey M.			06/20/18–02/00/19
Hughes, Howard R.		04/22/19–12/31/19	
Hughes, John Reynolds	08/10/87–01/31/15		
Hulen, Eugene B.	03/29/15–05/24/15		
Humphrey, A. A.			07/08/18–02/00/19
Humphreys, Ernest		06/07/17–12/00/17	
Humphreys, Fred		06/06/17–12/00/17	
Hunnicutt, J. R.	11/20/17–03/10/19 07/11/19–08/28/20	02/02/28–02/02/29 03/04/29–03/04/30 04/10/30–01/01/31	
Hunt, Edward L.		10/14/16–01/15/19 06/26/25–01/26/27 01/26/27–01/26/28 01/21/28–01/14/29 01/14/29–01/11/30 01/11/30–01/07/31 01/07/31–01/07/32 01/07/32–01/18/33 01/20/33–01/19/35 05/29/35–08/10/35	

NAME	REGULAR	SPECIAL	LOYALTY
Hunt, John W.		03/30/31–01/20/33	05/30/18–02/00/19
Hunt, Robert E.	06/08/15–04/11/16 08/20/18–10/15/18		
Hunt, T. J.		02/02/18–01/15/19	
Hunter, C. T.	11/03/17–03/10/19		
Hunter, George David		01/09/19–12/31/19	
Hunter, J. L.	12/19/17–unknown (still in: 06/00/18)		
Hunton, George P.	11/30/17–03/01/18	08/16/17–11/30/17	
Huntsucker, W. H.			06/05/18–02/00/19
Hurst, Cleveland C.	11/08/15–unknown 08/08/16–01/06/17 09/12/17–03/31/18		
Hurst, George B.	07/31/15–03/18/19		
Huskey, L. C.			06/13/18–02/00/19
Hutchison, J. W.		03/26/18–01/15/19	
Hutchison, Sidney S.	12/22/17–12/15/20		
Hyatt, S. W.			06/26/18–02/00/19
Hyde, Charlie	03/25/18–05/01/18		
Hyde, James A.	09/03/20–11/29/20 12/06/20–12/21/20		
Iglehart, David T., Jr.		01/07/18–01/15/19	
Ikard, S. R.	08/11/18–03/10/19		
Ingham, A. Y.			06/06/18–02/00/19
Irvin, T. A.		05/31/17–12/00/17	
Isaacs, John C.			06/04/18–02/00/19
Ivey, Curtis L.			06/17/18–02/00/19
Ivy, Josh			06/29/18–02/00/19
Izaguirre, Eduardo		05/01/18–01/15/19 08/06/19–12/31/19	
Jackman, Tom J.	06/28/19–09/20/23		
Jackson, Cecil	09/04/17–unknown		
Jackson, Ford		02/04/18–01/15/19	
Jackson, O. C.			07/24/18–02/00/19
James, C. B.		12/29/17–01/15/19	

NAME	REGULAR	SPECIAL	LOYALTY
James, D. L.		12/18/17–01/15/19	
James, S. A.		08/31/16–12/00/17	
Jameson, L. C.			06/05/18–02/00/19
Jarrett, Thad Johnson		12/03/17–01/15/19	
Jefferies, A. T.		06/26/17–01/15/19 06/12/19–12/31/19 04/22/27–04/01/28 05/15/28–05/15/29 05/23/29–05/15/30 05/15/30–01/18/33 02/01/33–01/22/35 06/07/35–08/10/35	
Jeffries, J. D.		11/06/16–12/00/17	
Jenkins, Joe J.	10/06/11–06/10/13		
Jenkins, W. W.	04/20/18–06/01/18		
Jennings, Clyde	12/14/17–03/31/18		
Jester, Sue M. "Mack"	10/06/11–03/00/12 02/01/15–11/12/15 06/01/24–02/21/25		
Johnson, Adam R., Jr.		05/31/18–01/15/19 11/22/33–unknown	
Johnson, E. E.	03/24/17–01/15/19		
Johnson, Francis Noel "Frank"	01/28/07–09/30/10		
Johnson, J. H.			06/05/18–02/00/19
Johnson, J. W.			09/28/18–10/28/18
Johnson, L. E.			06/08/18–02/00/19
Johnson, L. M.		05/11/18–01/15/19	
Johnson, Robert Hudson	12/15/17–05/01/18		
Johnson, Robert L.		09/28/18–01/15/19	
Johnson, Thomas J.		11/08/17–01/15/19	
Johnson, W. A.		01/11/18–01/15/19	
Johnson, W. E.		05/10/17–01/15/19	
Johnson, W. J.			06/17/18–02/00/19
Johnston, Harry M.	11/05/17–02/13/19		
Johnston, William Scott			06/15/18–02/00/19

NAME	REGULAR	SPECIAL	LOYALTY
Jones, A. C.		05/06/18–01/15/19	
Jones, Fred V.		02/26/18–01/15/19	
Jones, George Lee		05/02/17–12/00/17	
Jones, Gus T. "Buster"	03/00/08–07/01/10	03/01/17–12/00/17 05/15/18–01/15/19	
Jones, H. Worth		02/05/18–01/15/19	
Jones, James H.	06/24/16–08/31/16		
Jones, John R.		02/13/18–01/15/19	
Jones, Nat B. "Kiowa"	09/23/17–07/01/18	05/04/15–09/22/17 06/29/18–01/15/19 02/11/19–12/31/19 05/20/26–02/01/27	
Jones, T. S. "Tony"		07/26/17–01/15/19	
Jones, Walter F.		05/19/17–12/00/17	
Jones, Will C.	12/21/17–08/31/18		
Jones, William Frank		05/02/17–12/00/17	
Jones, William J.			07/30/18–02/00/19
Jordan, Aaron C.		02/15/33–01/08/35	06/07/18–02/00/19
Jordan, T. E.			06/10/18–02/00/19
Jordan, Wiley D.	04/16/18–08/31/18		
Joseph, Lee			06/21/18–02/00/19
Julian, James L.		06/04/18–01/15/19	
Keahey, Thomas E.			06/01/18–02/00/19
Keck, Frank			06/29/18–02/00/19
Keene, Henry	09/04/17–02/15/21		
Keeran, C. A.		07/12/16–12/00/17 04/26/18–01/15/19	
Kellis, J. R.			06/14/18–02/00/19
Kelly, E. L.		12/19/17–06/00/18	
Kelly, O. B.			06/07/18–02/00/19
Kelso, Eber B.		07/18/19–12/31/19	
Kempner, R. Lee			06/12/18–02/00/19
Kendrick, A. E.		06/14/17–12/00/17	

NAME	REGULAR	SPECIAL	LOYALTY
Kennedy, A. V.		08/12/16–12/00/17	
Kennedy, S. R.			06/11/18–02/00/19
Kercheville, Mack		01/15/18–unknown	
Kerr, J. D.		01/21/18–01/15/19	
Kerr, Joseph Perry	08/01/19–08/28/19		
Key, J. G.			07/05/18–02/00/19
Kiefer, E. H.		05/31/17–12/00/17	
Kilborn, O. E.		06/06/18–01/15/19	
Kilgore, F. H.			06/08/18–02/00/19
King, Harold A.	06/10/18–09/31/21	07/10/16–06/09/18	
King, Jacob Luther		07/28/19–12/31/19 10/05/25–12/04/26	
King, Richard, Jr.			06/05/18–02/00/19
King, R. M.			06/13/18–02/00/19
King, W. H.			05/31/18–02/00/19
Kirk, William	07/14/17–11/13/17		
Kirkland, Montie	09/22/17–03/01/19		
Klaerner, Ed H.		12/20/16–12/00/17	
Klaus, Theo C.	11/26/17–01/23/19		
Kleberg, Caesar		11/30/17–12/31/19	
Kleberg, Richard Mifflin		04/04/18–12/31/19 04/10/31–unknown	
Kleberg, Robert Justus, Jr.		08/19/18–12/31/19	
Klemann, Newton R.	04/20/18–07/01/18		
Klinger, Walter J.		07/22/18–01/15/19	
Knight, Dan G.	09/28/12–02/15/14 04/16/18–08/31/18		
Koon, James A.		08/17/18–01/15/19	
Koon, William Henry	09/17/17–04/16/18		
Koonsman, Martin Nic	10/21/20–04/01/25	03/09/27–03/09/28 04/12/28–04/08/29 04/08/29–04/08/30	
Kornegay, C.		04/13/18–01/15/19	

NAME	REGULAR	SPECIAL	LOYALTY
Kothmann, Elgin O.		01/29/18–01/15/19	
Kring, Joseph H.		07/15/18–01/15/19	
Krohn, I. H.	10/10/11–01/31/12		
Kuykendall, W. H.		03/19/17–01/15/19	
Laas, August E.			06/22/18–02/00/19
Lacy, Joe L.	11/18/10–02/01/11		
Lacy, T. H.		03/26/17–01/15/19	
Lamb, Rufus H.			05/31/18–02/00/19
Lamkin, Lem	04/01/21–07/31/25		
Lane, J. C.			06/13/18–02/00/19
Lane, Joe Y.			06/01/18–02/00/19
Langford, Earl	05/13/16–08/20/16		
Langford, I. B.		05/14/18–01/15/19	
Langford, Mark L.	06/01/18–03/03/19 06/13/19–11/04/20		
Lanier, G. T.			07/04/18–02/00/19
Largent, J. S.			06/10/18–02/00/19
Largent, Tom J.		07/19/16–12/00/17	
Larkin, Baker		03/24/17–01/15/19	
Larremore, Ed A.		05/14/19–12/31/19	
Latham, G. Cleve		06/06/17–12/31/19	
Latham, John Barkley		08/08/17–12/00/17	
Lawrence, Ernest			06/10/18–02/00/19
Lay, W. H.	10/17/20–12/31/20 06/01/36–05/31/38		
Laymance, Tom I.	04/06/21–02/28/23		
Layne, George Edgar		05/16/18–01/15/19 01/28/27–01/28/28 01/26/28–01/14/29 01/14/29–01/11/30 01/11/30–01/07/31 01/07/31–01/07/32 01/18/32–01/18/33 01/20/33–01/19/35 05/29/35–08/10/35	

NAME	REGULAR	SPECIAL	LOYALTY
Layne, Hugh			06/01/18–02/00/19
Lazenby, Walter H.		01/26/18–06/00/18	
Leahy, D. P.	05/10/16–08/28/16	04/03/33–unknown	
Leaverton, T. H.			06/04/18–02/24/19
Le Blanc, Arthur J.			06/06/18–02/00/19
Ledbetter, F. W.			07/19/18–02/24/19
Ledbetter, J. J.		09/04/18–01/15/19 04/19/19–01/30/21	
Lee, Flint			06/12/18–02/00/19
Leeman, W. B.			06/06/18–02/00/19
Lefevers, J. M.			06/04/18–02/00/19
Lehr, Fred P.			06/20/18–02/00/19
Leigh, J. S.		06/04/17–01/15/19 01/13/26–10/16/26	
Lenz, Emil R.	03/01/15–unknown (still in: 06/00/15)		
Leslie, Andrew Y.			06/17/18–02/00/19
Lesueur, W. L.	10/18/20–04/30/21		
Levering, Paul C.			06/18/18–02/00/19
Lewis, E. P.		08/08/16–12/00/17	
Lewis, J. B.			07/03/18–02/00/19
Lewis, J. E.			07/10/18–02/24/19
Lieb, Victor E.		08/04/19–12/31/19	
Lincecum, A. L.		08/01/17–06/17/18	
Lindsey, David			07/23/18–02/00/19
Linn, O. M.			07/05/18–02/00/19
Lipscomb, Walker B.			06/24/18–02/00/19
Lipscomb, W. C.			06/08/18–02/00/19
Little, James			06/11/18–02/00/19
Little, John T.		09/24/18–01/15/19	
Livingston, Henry L.		05/16/18–06/14/18	
Lochwitzky, Alexander M.	02/16/21–unknown	08/01/19–12/31/19	
Lock, A. P.	03/18/18–10/01/18		

NAME	REGULAR	SPECIAL	LOYALTY
Locke, Henry W.		10/08/17–07/00/18 05/28/30–unknown	
Lockwood, Thomas S.		04/28/17–12/00/17	
Long, Fred		01/07/19–12/31/19	
Long, F. M.			06/07/18–02/00/19
Long, George		07/17/16–12/00/17	
Long, J. F.			07/09/18–02/00/19
Long, John H.	07/12/18–02/21/19		
Longoria, J. L.	04/26/18–05/00/18		
Lonsford, J. B.			06/29/18–02/00/19
Lorenz, A. Wade	12/21/17–03/03/19		
Lott, Will T.	03/29/15–04/30/15		
Love, R. C.	06/01/18–08/31/18		
Love, Thomas H.		02/13/18–01/15/19	
Low, Sam D. W.		09/17/18–01/15/19	
Lowe, W. A., Jr.			06/08/18–02/00/19
Lowenstein, James L.	12/25/17–01/25/18	03/23/18–07/05/19	
Lubbock, James L.	05/13/16–11/01/16		
Lynch, I. L.			07/17/18–02/00/19
Lynch, William West		08/07/17–12/00/17	
McAlister, Paul	11/22/11–02/01/12	10/05/15–01/14/16	
McAlpine, A. D.			06/05/18–02/00/19
McBee, Charles W.	05/01/18–unknown		
McBride, P.		04/30/18–01/15/19	
McCallum, E. B.	01/09/18–01/00/18		
McCampbell, J. Howell	01/07/18–05/15/18	07/27/18–01/15/19	
McCarthy, Ed, Jr.	09/28/20–09/28/22		
McCauley, William J.	1891–09/23/10		
McClamroch, Robert Sidney			06/13/18–02/26/19
McClanahan, M. R.		05/27/17–12/00/17	
McClellan, James D.	03/12/18–02/21/19		
McCloy, J. B.		01/07/18–01/15/19	

NAME	REGULAR	SPECIAL	LOYALTY
McClure, Elmer B.	08/21/19–11/30/20 03/27/23–08/03/23	11/30/32–11/29/34	
McColloch, William H.		12/17/19–12/31/19	
McCombs, D. I.	05/20/18–07/01/18		
McCormick, James W.	03/27/20–04/23/20 10/18/20–12/31/20 02/15/21–04/18/22 04/13/23–10/07/24 08/03/26–05/31/35	10/07/24–03/06/25	
McCoy, S. M.	12/14/17–01/15/18		
McCracken, William Ross		12/06/17–01/15/19	
McCullum, E. B.	01/00/18–01/31/18		
McCurdy, Frank B.		10/22/18–01/15/19 03/16/34–unknown	
McCutcheon, W. W.		06/23/17–12/00/17 05/13/18–01/15/19	
McDonald, George N.		06/04/18–11/21/18	
McDonald, John Thomas (1)		12/22/17–02/00/18	
McDonald, John Thomas (2)		06/24/18–01/15/19	
McDonald, William D.		06/18/18–10/16/18	
McDowell, Bert J.		05/04/17–12/00/17	
McDowell, H. H.			06/07/18–02/00/19
McElroy, John L.			06/26/18–02/24/19
McElroy, Will A.		01/08/18–01/15/19 12/14/34–01/22/35	
McFarland, T. C.		03/02/18–01/15/19	
McFarland, Van E.		02/07/18–01/15/19	
McFarlane, Samuel J.	12/01/13–02/10/14		
McFarlin, J. L.			06/13/18–02/24/19
McGaffey, A. B.	12/19/17–unknown		
McGee, J. L.		03/22/16–05/25/16	
McGee, Jinks		06/14/17–12/00/17	
McGee, Phil		07/23/17–07/01/18	
McGill, O.		12/08/17–02/14/18	

NAME	REGULAR	SPECIAL	LOYALTY
McGloin, George D.		10/05/18–01/15/19	
McGregor, J. D.		01/18/17–01/15/19	
McIntosh, Pike			06/07/18–02/24/19
McKenzie, Sam	1903–1909 08/03/11–01/01/12 05/15/17–03/31/19 11/29/19–02/15/21		
McKinley, P. M.			06/21/18–02/24/19
McKinney, Allen L.		08/13/18–01/15/19	
McKinney, C. S.		07/01/18–01/15/19 09/02/32–unknown	
McKnight, A. D.	10/22/17–05/00/18		
McLaughlin, A. D.		06/02/17–12/00/17	
McMahon, M. H.		05/11/18–01/15/19	
McMillan, J. A.			06/08/18–02/00/19
McMillan, John R.	09/19/18–07/00/19	08/11/19–12/31/19	
McMillan, Sam J.			06/10/18–02/00/19
McMordie, Edgar B.	02/15/21–08/31/22 11/25/27–11/30/28	12/01/28–12/01/29	
McMurrey, Willie		01/10/18–01/15/19 11/22/29–11/22/30 09/14/31–unknown	
McMurtry, R. L.		06/27/17–01/15/19	
McNamara, Mike		08/28/18–12/31/19 04/11/33–04/10/35	
McQueen, John C.	03/30/20–06/01/20		
Maddox, Guy O.	12/16/10–02/01/11		
Magee, Edgar S.	09/07/05–03/00/06 06/02/16–02/10/17 03/01/17–05/01/18 05/03/18–09/20/18		
Magee, L. B.	05/17/16–unknown		
Magruder, Hamilton		07/03/17–12/00/17	
Mahoney, G. M.			06/06/18–02/00/19
Mallard, A. R.			07/20/18–02/00/19

NAME	REGULAR	SPECIAL	LOYALTY
Malone, Charles A.		12/07/17–03/00/18	
Malone, James Nat	05/10/16–10/31/16 10/23/17–03/10/19 03/01/21–05/20/21	05/31/17–10/22/17	
Malone, John		05/14/17–12/00/17	
Mann, James S.			06/01/18–02/00/19
Manry, A. L.		04/12/18–01/15/19 08/14/19–12/31/19	
Marks, Fred E.	10/21/18–12/08/19		07/11/18–10/20/18
Marshall, John	05/19/20–07/31/20		
Marshall, William F.			05/31/18–02/00/19
Martin, Andrew H.		12/03/17–01/15/19	
Martin, Arch			06/05/18–02/24/19
Martin, C. L.			06/21/18–02/00/19
Martin, E. C.			06/03/18–02/00/19
Martin, Frank		06/06/17–11/25/17	
Martin, G. C.			06/17/18–02/00/19
Martin, J. C.		01/23/19–12/31/19	
Martin, J. F.		11/21/18–01/15/19	
Martin, James T.	08/12/19–08/31/20 09/27/20–04/30/21		
Martin, John G.		10/07/18–01/15/19	
Martin, R. B.		01/03/19–12/31/19	
Martin, T. J.		03/25/18–01/15/19	
Martin, W. H.	10/20/17–02/12/18		
Martin, William E.	06/02/16–01/06/17		
Martínez, Mercurio		02/05/18–01/15/19	
Mason, J. N.		05/23/16–12/00/17	
Masterson, N. T.		02/11/18–01/15/19	
Mathews, Christopher Columbus		02/05/16–12/00/17 03/27/26–02/01/27	
Matthews, Frank W.	07/01/19–03/08/20 03/27/20–04/22/20		

NAME	REGULAR	SPECIAL	LOYALTY
Maxey, J. W.		05/31/17–12/00/17	
Maxwell, J. W.		11/19/18–01/15/19	
May, J. D.			07/15/18–02/00/19
May, W. P.		02/21/18–01/15/19	
Mayberry, Walter E.	12/21/17–02/13/19 11/25/19–06/01/24	12/30/16–12/20/17	
Mayes, Will		11/26/18–01/15/19	
Mayfield, John	08/14/11–10/15/11		
Mayfield, Tom S.			06/06/18–02/00/19
Mayfield, Walter	06/01/18–08/31/18		
Meadows, W.D.		04/13/18–01/15/19	
Meeks, Thomas Houston		08/16/18–01/15/19	
Megee, Robert E.		07/20/17–12/00/17	
Mellard, F. C.		12/08/17–01/15/19	
Melton, George W.			07/27/18–02/00/19
Melton, W. S.		05/29/17–12/00/17	
Mercer, James B.	11/20/11–09/00/12		
Merrem, Edgar J.			05/30/18–02/24/19
Merrick, J. A.		07/24/18–01/15/19	
Merrill, W. T.			06/27/18–02/00/19
Metz, R. H., Jr.		01/25/18–01/15/19	
Middleton, Charles P.	03/02/09–04/15/09 05/30/09–unknown	01/29/17–10/00/18	
Milam, J. W.	09/30/20–02/15/21		
Miles, Bassett R.		08/06/18–01/15/19	
Miles, W. A.	09/01/17–03/01/18 06/06/18–03/10/19		
Miles, William T.	12/15/17–02/21/25	02/11/32–unknown	
Milhoan, Miles			07/15/18–02/00/19
Millard, George M.	06/20/19–01/30/20		
Miller, A. N.			06/11/18–02/15/19
Miller, C. E.		06/04/17–12/00/17	

NAME	REGULAR	SPECIAL	LOYALTY
Miller, Charles Edward	12/10/19–09/08/21 10/01/21–09/30/22 08/06/23–10/31/23 12/23/23–02/21/25	05/09/28–05/08/29 06/03/29–06/03/30 06/14/30–01/20/31 06/14/31–06/14/33 06/16/33–10/18/33 10/03/33–01/22/35 06/21/35–08/10/35	
Miller, Charles R.		03/29/18–unknown 09/21/18–01/15/19	
Miller, Hugh		10/05/16–01/15/19	
Miller, John Arch	11/25/18–02/17/20 03/31/23–01/18/33	11/21/33–11/20/34 06/26/35–10/01/35	
Miller, Robert M. "Bob"	09/01/17–04/08/18	03/03/27–03/03/28 03/05/28–03/05/29 03/07/29–03/07/30 01/24/33–08/25/34	
Miller, William L.	10/14/18–12/03/23	03/30/18–10/14/18	
Millican, Leander R.		07/08/19–12/31/19	
Milsap, J. V.		06/04/17–12/00/17	06/03/18–02/00/19
Mims, R. K.		06/15/18–01/15/19	
Mobley, E. M.		12/31/17–01/15/19	
Molesworth, William M.	03/29/18–05/15/27	10/19/27–07/13/28	
Monkhouse, G. A.			06/13/18–02/00/19
Monroe, J.			06/01/18–02/00/19
Montgomery, J. D.		08/01/18–01/15/19	
Montgomery, John W.		06/02/16–01/15/19	
Montgomery, M. D.		11/27/17–02/00/18	
Moon, R. B.		05/31/17–12/00/17	
Moor, Earl T.		07/18/17–12/00/17	
Moore, Charles R.	00/00/09–03/00/13		
Moore, F. R.		06/13/18–01/15/19	
Moore, Jack	05/12/16–11/31/16		
Moore, Jeff B.		12/08/17–01/15/19	
Moore, John W.		01/09/18–01/15/19	
Moore, J. W.			07/10/18–02/00/19

NAME	REGULAR	SPECIAL	LOYALTY
Moore, Rufus A.		12/21/16–12/00/17	
Moore, W. H. "Harry"	05/01/09–02/28/10 05/03/10–07/05/11		
Mooring, C. E.			06/04/18–02/00/19
Moorman, Cull C.		07/07/19–12/31/19	
Moran, John A.	11/01/17–12/12/18		
Morgan, Thomas I.	12/21/17–08/31/18		
Morley, John L.	02/16/14–unknown (no longer in as of: 05/13/14)		
Morris, Richard L. "Dick"	10/05/11–unknown 12/14/17–04/00/18		
Morris, Roscoe	03/22/21–04/30/21		
Morrison, A. H.		12/14/17–03/00/18	
Morrisset, J. M.		06/04/17–12/00/17	
Morse, Henry DeWitt, Jr.	05/15/16–07/31/16	04/21/33–04/26/34	
Morton, Stanley	12/15/19–05/15/21		
Moseley, L. B.	08/30/11–10/31/11		
Moseley, W. T.		07/23/15–01/15/19	
Moss, E. J.			06/04/18–02/00/19
Motley, R. A.			06/07/18–02/24/19
Moynahan, Thomas	07/29/16–12/00/17		
Muil, Charles G.			08/28/18–02/24/19
Mundine, J. H.			09/23/18–02/00/19
Munn, John S.		06/18/17–12/00/17	
Murchison, Claud		08/30/16–08/31/18	
Murdock, William	05/14/18–03/10/19		
Murphy, Jay G.	12/11/17–04/00/18		
Murrah, Dan		12/27/17–01/15/19	
Murrah, Jake R.		12/03/17–01/15/19	
Murrah, James B.		12/01/17–01/15/19	
Murrah, James E.		12/03/17–01/15/19	
Murray, J. R.		05/27/18–07/18/18	

NAME	REGULAR	SPECIAL	LOYALTY
Murrell, F. E.			07/04/18–02/00/19
Mussey, Hart, Jr.		04/30/18–12/31/19	
Myers, Edwin Clark		10/10/17–01/14/19	
Myers, Graham		06/07/17–12/00/17	
Mynatt, Jeff D.	12/29/17–05/01/18	09/12/18–01/15/19	
Myres, S. D.			06/06/18–02/00/19
Myres, Tom G.	05/15/16–unknown		
Myzell, E. R.		02/21/18–05/00/18	
Nabers, S. A.	04/18/18–08/31/18		
Nalls, J. Berry	09/01/17–01/10/19		
Neil, C. E.			06/15/18–02/00/19
Neill, Samuel H.	03/01/18–04/15/20		
Neill, T. T. (Van)		08/12/18–01/15/19	
Nelson, Floyd S.		08/30/18–01/15/19	
Nesbitt, J. W.			06/01/18–02/00/19
Neumann, Paul			07/13/18–02/00/19
Nevill, Frank			06/04/18–02/00/19
Newberry, George W.		05/30/16–10/10/16	
Newberry, G. W.			06/08/18–02/24/19
Newberry, James H.		06/01/17–01/15/19	
Newman, Max "Mack"	09/26/17–06/08/18		
Newman, Tom B.		07/16/17–12/00/17	
Newsom, James G.	05/10/16–09/15/16		
Newton, T. M.		02/07/18–01/15/19	
Newton, W. R.		02/20/18–01/15/19	
Nichols, D. M.			06/07/18–02/00/19
Nichols, E. E.	10/20/11–01/31/12		
Nichols, M. W.			07/17/18–02/00/19
Nichols, Roy C.	02/15/21–03/31/27		
Nicholson, J. M.		12/10/17–01/15/19	
Norton, William Dale		01/28/18–01/15/19	

NAME	REGULAR	SPECIAL	LOYALTY
Nunnery, James C.	10/13/11–01/31/12		
Nutt, J. W.			06/01/18–02/24/19
Oberste, A. W.		12/20/17–02/00/18	
O'Brien, Thomas Edmund			09/02/18–02/00/19
Odem, David			05/31/18–02/24/19
Oden, Louis D.	12/22/17–01/31/18		
Odom, Dorse		06/02/17–12/00/17	
Odom, J. M.			06/12/18–02/00/19
Ogden, Ralph R.		08/26/18–01/15/19 08/23/27–02/23/28 04/26/33–unknown	
Ogg, Lester	08/26/15–09/08/15		
O'Keefe, Marvin			07/08/18–02/00/19
Oliphant, G. C.	12/24/17–01/13/19		
Oliphant, J. Boone	11/13/15–10/15/17 12/16/17–06/08/18		
Oliver, John Jefferson		12/31/17–01/15/19	
Olson, G. N.		04/29/18–01/15/19	
Orberg, Joe	02/15/21–02/21/25	03/23/27–03/31/27	
Orenbaun, T. A.			06/08/18–02/00/19
Ormand, G.		01/31/18–unknown 07/30/18–01/15/19 03/24/34–01/22/35	
Orth, Leonard A.			05/31/18–02/00/19
Osgood, Jesse G.	12/06/19–09/30/21		
Otting, A.		09/17/18–01/15/19 01/09/33–01/09/34 04/18/34–unknown	
Owen, Ira D.	10/23/11–01/31/12		
Owens, Bevil		04/27/18–01/15/19	
Owens, H. W.			07/01/18–02/00/19
Owens, Troy R.	10/01/17–08/31/21 10/01/21–03/10/22		
Oyervides, Miguel	10/16/11–01/20/12		

NAME	REGULAR	SPECIAL	LOYALTY
Pace, Charles D.	09/15/11–04/09/12 12/17/12–04/18/13		
Palmer, John C.	01/03/18–04/00/18		
Parchman, James Lemuel	05/11/18–08/31/18		
Parker, B. J.			06/06/18–02/00/19
Parker, Clarence Edgar		07/17/16–12/00/17	
Parker, E. S.			06/07/18–02/00/19
Parker, Frank		06/02/17–12/00/17	
Parker, H. C.			07/02/18–02/00/19
Parker, H. R.			07/07/18–02/00/19
Parker, J. F.	09/11/17–12/15/17		
Parker, Oscar		06/08/17–12/00/17	
Parker, T. C.			06/04/18–02/00/19
Parker, William A.		07/24/18–01/15/19	
Parmer, Clint L.		07/22/18–01/15/19	
Parr, Jack		05/31/17–12/00/17	06/01/18–02/00/19
Parrish, Byron B.	06/04/17–02/17/18		
Parsons, R. B.			06/08/18–01/15/19
Patterson, Frank	09/19/17–10/01/18	08/05/22–12/01/22	
Patterson, George B.		05/13/18–01/15/19	
Patton, O.			07/10/18–02/00/19
Patton, R. M.		12/31/17–01/15/19	
Patton, W. B. (1)		07/03/18–01/15/19	
Patton, W. B. (2)	03/01/14–unknown (still in: 07/00/14)		
Patton, W. F.			06/06/18–02/00/19
Payton, Cross		06/06/17–12/00/17	
Pearce, Fred C.		12/10/17–02/00/18 03/27/18–01/15/19	
Pearce, George W.			06/15/18–02/00/19
Peebles, J. J.		06/01/17–12/00/17	
Peek, H. F.			05/31/18–02/00/19
Peevey, L. L.		06/30/17–12/00/17	

NAME	REGULAR	SPECIAL	LOYALTY
Peevey, Tom		06/30/17–12/00/17	
Penick, R. E.		05/31/17–12/00/17	
Penland, R. L.		08/17/34–unknown	06/04/18–02/00/19
Penn, Justo S.			06/04/18–02/00/19
Penningon, Ben L.	10/04/17–10/12/18		
Pérez, Jesse, Sr.	1890–1892 1906–1908 03/16/18–11/10/18 06/20/19–07/31/20 03/19/21–01/31/23		
Perkins, C. F. Dell	09/20/17–unknown (still in: 09/10/18)		
Perkins, James Clarke	08/25/17–03/10/19 04/21/19–05/17/20		
Perkins, J. P.	12/21/17–10/01/18		
Perkins, Lon A.			06/10/18–02/24/19
Perkins, T. E. Paul	09/01/18–11/07/18		
Perrow, H. C.	12/18/17–03/00/18		
Peterson, William Sanders	12/21/17–02/21/25		
Peveto, Alva B.			07/03/18–02/26/19
Peyton, William S.			05/31/18–02/24/19
Phelps, Robert Carrol, Jr.		03/19/17–12/00/17	
Phelps, William Eura	07/01/19–11/03/19		
Phillips, Charles M.		01/03/19–12/31/19	
Pickle, M. L.		01/23/18–01/15/19	
Place, Joe T.		04/22/18–01/15/19	
Pool, J. F. P.		06/02/17–12/00/17	
Porter, C. C.		01/21/18–00/00/18	
Porter, H. A.			06/08/18–02/00/19
Pouncey, J. M.		01/31/18–01/15/19	
Powell, Bob			06/11/18–02/24/19
Powell, Frank			06/21/18–02/00/19
Powers, Pat		02/23/18–01/15/19	

NAME	REGULAR	SPECIAL	LOYALTY
Powers, William E.	08/12/19–01/31/20 03/27/20–04/23/20 10/02/20–12/31/20 03/01/21–04/30/21		
Prather, J. H.		12/27/17–04/00/18	
Premont, Charles		04/14/17–12/00/17	
Price, Charles W.	10/06/11–01/31/12 04/27/15–06/11/18 07/29/19–12/00/19	06/11/18–01/15/19 02/18/31–01/20/34	
Price, George Harley		07/09/18–01/15/19	
Price, W. S.			06/27/18–02/00/19
Pridgen, Oscar F.	1875, 1882	03/28/18–01/15/19 06/03/19–12/31/19	
Prince, Fred E.			06/07/18–02/00/19
Puckett, John B.	1902–1903	03/05/18–01/15/19	
Puckitt, L. W.		08/06/17–12/00/17	
Pullin, Louis		07/19/18–01/15/19	
Pullin, T. N.	12/22/17–05/00/18		
Purvis, Frank Harris	07/19/17–unknown	07/13/17–07/18/17	
Putman, Amzy	12/19/19–10/31/21		
Putnam, Carl		12/14/17–08/00/18	
Pyle, Charles R.		05/01/18–01/15/19	
Pyle, T. M., Jr.		06/24/18–01/15/19	
Quinn, John Olie		03/11/18–01/15/19	
Rabb, Frank		07/25/18–01/15/19	
Ramsey, H. H.		05/29/17–12/00/17	
Ramsey, M. T.		06/23/17–12/00/17	
Ransom, Elmore W.			06/18/18–02/00/19
Ransom, Henry Lee	02/14/05–12/10/05 05/01/09–06/15/09 07/20/15–04/01/18		
Ranson, G. E.		06/26/17–12/00/17	
Rasco, S. L.			07/16/18–02/00/19
Rather, Charles, Jr.			06/05/18–02/00/19

NAME	REGULAR	SPECIAL	LOYALTY
Rawlings, J. C.		11/22/17–02/14/18	
Rawls, T. H.		02/16/17–12/00/17 05/03/18–01/15/19	
Ray, A. L.			06/07/18–02/00/19
Ray, John C.		12/03/17–12/31/19	
Ray, J. J., Jr.			08/26/18–02/25/19
Rea, Jesse D.		07/20/18–01/15/19	
Reagan, J. M., Jr.			06/01/18–02/00/19
Redus, Roscoe	07/25/08–01/12/10		
Reed, Alex H.		04/22/18–01/15/19 08/16/19–12/31/19	
Reed, Elmo D.	12/16/17–04/00/18 05/07/18–01/01/19	01/13/19–12/31/19	
Reed, William G.		09/14/17–12/00/17	07/24/18–02/00/19
Reese, John Walter	01/23/10–07/18/10	03/12/16–12/17/17 03/23/18–01/15/19	
Reeves, Frank		05/31/17–12/00/17	
Reeves, Mills Q.		08/10/18–01/15/19	
Reneau, J. D.			06/11/18–02/00/19
Reneau, T. N.	04/27/14–06/30/16	03/23/18–01/15/19 08/15/19–12/31/19 10/18/34–12/24/34	
Rhew, Austin		06/20/18–01/15/19	
Rhodes, Erskine		07/14/16–12/00/17 04/30/18–01/15/19	
Rich, Newton G.		12/10/17–01/15/19	
Richards, Statford Harrison		04/16/17–01/15/19	
Richards, William Henry			07/08/18–02/00/19
Riden, Jesse J.			06/01/18–01/15/19
Riley, J. R.			07/08/18–02/00/19
Ripley, Ron Stephen	10/11/11–01/31/12		
Riser, W. D.			08/26/18–02/14/19
Robbins, J. M.		10/03/18–01/15/19	
Roberson, B. F.		07/29/18–01/15/19	

NAME	REGULAR	SPECIAL	LOYALTY
Roberson, D. S.		01/09/18–01/15/19	
Roberson, H. L. "Hod"	10/11/11–07/00/13 04/01/14–09/04/14	05/08/16–01/15/19	
Roberts, H. C.			06/12/18–02/00/19
Roberts, J. B.		05/03/18–01/15/19	
Roberts, J. H.			06/05/18–02/00/19
Roberts, L. D.			06/12/18–02/24/19
Roberts, Raymond	04/27/18–08/31/18		
Roberts, Ross L.	03/25/10–05/28/11		
Roberts, Sidney	02/01/18–10/01/18		
Roberts, W. A.	01/30/15–11/07/16		
Roberts, W. F., Jr.			06/06/18–02/00/19
Robertson, A. J.	01/00/18–03/10/19 02/18/21–03/05/21		
Robertson, H. P., Jr.		07/23/17–12/00/17	
Robertson, Wade H.			06/29/18–02/00/19
Robertson, William James T.	07/01/19–08/31/21		
Robinson, A. J.	12/28/17–03/10/19		
Robinson, D. W.	05/29/16–07/23/16		
Robinson, F. M.		09/12/16–12/00/17 12/02/18–02/10/22	
Robinson, George Washington	01/19/20–09/09/20 02/15/21–08/31/21		
Robinson, Harry H.	12/20/17–02/01/19		
Robinson, Thaddeus P.	09/30/20–03/31/21	03/14/34–01/22/35	
Robuck, Robert G.			06/04/18–02/00/19
Rogers, Clarence Aaron			06/05/18–02/00/19
Rogers, C. L.		05/31/17–12/00/17	
Rogers, Duncan W.		01/03/19–12/31/19	
Rogers, John Harris	09/05/82–01/31/11 05/15/27–11/11/30		
Rogers, O. W.	09/25/10–01/13/11		
Rollins, C. E.			06/18/18–02/00/19
Rooker, Lorenza B.			06/07/18–02/24/19

NAME	REGULAR	SPECIAL	LOYALTY
Rooney, John Monroe	12/08/19–02/10/21	08/03/25–08/03/27 12/06/27–11/28/28 11/28/28–11/28/29 12/19/29–12/19/30 01/10/31–01/10/32 01/26/32–01/20/33 04/01/33–01/22/35 05/29/35–08/10/35	
Ross, Clay E.			06/20/18–02/00/19
Ross, Guy G.			06/07/18–02/00/19
Ross, Tom M.	1898–02/28/10	05/08/29–05/08/30 06/06/30–01/01/31 02/19/31–02/18/32	
Rosser, Lee	09/21/18–12/31/18	05/18/18–10/01/18	
Rountree, Edwin Bruce		09/16/18–01/15/19	
Rountree, Lee J.		03/13/18–01/15/19	
Rountree, Mason	10/23/15–04/30/16		
Rountree, Oscar J.	1906–02/00/10		
Routt, H. R.			09/19/18–02/00/19
Rowe, Walter Ivory	09/01/17–02/07/21	04/06/26–01/26/27 01/26/27–01/26/28 02/28/28–02/28/29 03/04/29–03/04/30 03/07/30–03/07/31 03/08/31–01/18/33 01/27/33–01/22/35 05/30/35–08/10/35	
Rowland, J. R.	12/02/11–01/31/12		
Ruby, T. E.		09/16/18–01/15/19	
Rueter, Will		12/12/17–03/00/18	
Rumsey, Charles Stuart	09/01/13–11/27/13		
Runyon, L. G.	12/13/09–05/15/10		
Rushin, Walter "Dad"	06/08/15–01/15/16		
Rushing, F. C.			09/02/18–02/00/19
Russell, C. A.		12/12/17–03/00/18	
Russell, Max		04/17/18–01/15/19	
Russell, R. L.	01/22/19–03/31/19		

NAME	REGULAR	SPECIAL	LOYALTY
Russell, Sam M.	05/11/14–09/30/14		
Russell, Scott	10/01/12–06/23/13		
Russell, William E.		05/01/18–01/15/19	
Rutherford, L. L.			06/03/18–02/00/19
Rutledge, J. E.		08/05/16–12/00/17	
Ryan, Joseph William			06/28/18–02/14/19
Ryan, William M.	11/28/17–02/10/21 06/16/25–02/02/27		
Sackville, H. A.			07/08/18–02/00/19
Sadler, George W.	12/18/17–01/10/19	05/17/35–08/10/35	
Sadler, John W.	05/08/18–10/15/18 01/23/24–01/18/33	07/27/33–01/22/35	
Sadler, Lenn T.	05/27/18–09/15/18		
Sadler, Tom H.	12/18/17–unknown		
Sadler, William	08/29/18–11/10/18		
Sallis, W. F.	04/20/09–unknown (still in: 00/00/10)		
Salmon, R. S.	11/13/18–01/01/19		
Sammons, Charles		05/31/17–12/00/17	
Sammons, Timothy E.		07/11/19–12/31/19	
Sánchez, Dario			06/14/18–02/00/19
Sandel, Henry Luther			06/06/18–02/00/19
Sanders, Albert F.	12/10/17–12/00/18		
Sanders, Jesse C.	06/03/15–09/12/15		
Sanders, John J.	02/01/11–03/04/19		
Sandifer, W. W.			06/05/18–02/00/19
Sandlin, Charles		07/22/16–12/00/17 03/16/18–01/15/19	
Sands, William B.	12/01/15–unknown		
Saner, J. M.			07/16/18–02/00/19
Saulsberry, Lee	11/30/17–05/01/20		
Saunders, J. C.		04/29/18–01/15/19	
Saunders, W. W.		04/29/18–01/15/19	

NAME	REGULAR	SPECIAL	LOYALTY
Savage, Russell			05/31/18–02/00/19
Scannell, Miles J.	04/16/18–06/01/18		
Scarborough, E. B.		07/11/16–11/05/18	
Scarborough, J. S., Sr.		07/11/16–11/05/18 04/27/18–01/15/19 08/10/31–01/20/33 06/10/33–01/22/35	
Scarborough, J. S., Jr.		05/30/17–12/00/17	
Scarborough, W. F.		06/08/18–01/15/19	
Scheultz, R. Alvin		10/13/17–09/23/18	
Schnaubert, Charles O.		12/03/17–01/15/19	
Schnelle, W. G.		08/23/18–01/15/19	
Schuessler, J. H.			06/20/18–02/00/19
Schurman, S. F.	12/14/17–01/31/19		
Schwinn, F. S.		03/22/18–01/15/19	
Scott, Felix C.	01/03/18–02/01/19		
Scott, Fred	05/10/16–unknown		
Scott, George B.		05/31/17–12/00/17	
Scott, G. W.		11/21/17–01/15/19	
Scott, H. V.		07/05/18–02/00/19	
Scott, S. J., Jr.			07/01/18–02/00/19
Scott, William M.	12/13/17–01/01/18		
Scruggs, J. C.			07/27/18–02/00/19
Scullin, Harry		09/14/16–01/01/17 02/10/18–01/15/19	
Seago, Wiley		10/31/16–12/00/17	
Seale, James Lovett	06/02/09–03/01/10 03/26/18–01/01/19 10/09/19–05/12/20	11/13/33–01/22/35	
Seitzler, Thomas L.			07/05/18–02/00/19
Shafer, W.		02/27/17–12/00/17	
Shank, Silas		03/12/18–01/15/19	
Shanklin, J. F.	08/06/18–12/15/18		

NAME	REGULAR	SPECIAL	LOYALTY
Sharp, A. T.			06/08/18–02/00/19
Sharp, J. A.			07/02/18–02/00/19
Sharp, W. R.		01/17/17–02/16/17	
Sharver, A. M.			06/24/18–02/00/19
Shaw, Joe R.	07/05/18–08/21/18		
Sheedy, Pat	09/20/17–03/01/18 04/01/22–08/31/23	02/16/17–09/19/17	
Shelton, R. S.		07/17/16–12/00/17	
Shely, George Rutledge	08/25/19–01/11/21		
Shely, William Almond	12/12/15–unknown		
Shepard, T. L.		08/07/17–12/00/17 06/05/19–12/31/19	
Shepherd, C. M.		02/16/18–01/15/19	
Sheppard, Simeon C.		02/09/17–12/00/17	
Shipley, Aubrey	10/13/11–01/31/12		
Shoemaker, J. L.			06/13/18–02/00/19
Shults, C. E.		05/10/17–01/15/19	
Shumate, R. D.	02/04/19–08/31/20 01/06/22–02/21/25	03/29/18–01/15/19	
Sielski, Henry M.		02/20/18–01/15/19	
Simpson, Albert E.		06/29/18–01/15/19	
Simpson, Alfred R.	03/10/21–08/31/21		
Simpson, William A.		03/23/18–05/10/19 01/30/33–01/22/35	
Singleton, Darwin E.	07/03/19–unknown 11/02/23–12/01/24		
Sittre, John B.	12/18/17–02/28/19		
Skinner, J. F.		12/26/16–12/00/17	
Skinner, Walter Scott		07/19/17–12/00/17	
Skipper, W. P.		07/18/16–09/10/16	
Slack, H. C.		03/15/18–01/15/19	
Sledge, L. W.		03/23/17–01/15/19	
Slough, John W.		06/06/17–01/15/19	

NAME	REGULAR	SPECIAL	LOYALTY
Slover, M. F.			06/29/18–02/00/19
Sluder, E. A.		07/24/17–12/00/17	
Smiley, Sylvanus	10/07/11–01/31/12		
Smith, B. L.		03/16/18–01/15/19	
Smith, C. D.			07/09/18–02/00/19
Smith, Charles K.		05/06/17–12/00/17	
Smith, Claude T.	07/31/09–08/16/10		
Smith, Dick		01/24/18–01/15/19 07/01/25–07/01/27 11/07/27–11/07/28 12/05/28–12/05/29	
Smith, Ed			12/06/17–01/15/19
Smith, Edward H.	01/19/15–01/21/17	01/22/17–01/15/19	
Smith, G. P.			06/18/18–02/00/19
Smith, George R.			08/05/18–02/00/19
Smith, Hugh		03/20/18–01/15/19	
Smith, H. C.		10/01/19–12/31/19	
Smith, James Marcus			06/03/18–02/00/19
Smith, Jesse Lee	03/01/21–09/30/21		
Smith, M. C.		12/03/17–10/00/18	
Smith, Olin Welborn	05/10/16–10/00/16	07/01/25–07/01/27	
Smith, Riley Robert		08/04/19–12/31/19	06/20/18–02/00/19
Smith, R. R.		02/23/18–01/15/19	
Smith, Sledge			06/07/18–02/00/19
Smith, Thomas Richard		12/03/17–01/15/19	
Smith, Walter			06/07/18–02/00/19
Smith, William	09/01/11–08/00/12		
Smyth, Jot		07/02/17–01/15/19	
Snody, Walter F.			06/01/18–02/00/19
Snowden, J. G.			06/08/18–02/00/19
Snyder, Gustave "George"	05/13/16–07/20/16		
Snyder, H. P.		07/31/16–12/00/17	

NAME	REGULAR	SPECIAL	LOYALTY
Snyder, T. W.		12/31/17–01/15/19	
Snyder, V. L.	02/19/21–03/14/21		
Soape, Ralph		11/07/18–01/15/19 10/29/20–unknown	
Somerville, Charles F.		01/02/17–01/15/19 07/02/25–07/02/27 08/18/27–08/18/28 09/19/28–09/19/29 09/18/29–09/18/30 09/18/30–09/18/31 10/10/31–07/20/32	
Southworth, John		06/16/19–12/31/19	06/29/18–02/00/19
Sowell, Andrew Jackson	10/06/11–01/31/12 12/18/17–01/00/18	11/17/25–12/10/27 12/10/27–12/10/28 12/29/28–12/29/29 02/18/30–12/29/30 02/12/31–01/18/33 01/23/33–unknown 06/11/35–08/10/35	
Spang, Frank Armitage		07/26/10–12/00/17	
Spangler, Ross A.		04/19/20–unknown	
Spann, T. T.	05/24/17–09/01/17	04/23/17–05/23/17	
Spears, Walter T.		01/21/18–01/15/19 06/20/27–06/20/28 07/07/28–07/07/29 07/17/29–07/17/30 07/17/30–07/17/31 07/23/31–01/20/33 06/12/33–06/12/35	
Speed, Robert E.	10/31/11–04/01/14 03/16/21–12/10/23		
Speed, William B.		03/21/18–01/15/19	
Speed, W. Robert	01/01/14–unknown (still in: 11/00/14)		
Spivey, Austin	12/22/17–02/01/18		
Spivey, W. E.		02/07/18–01/15/19	
Sprague, George W.		09/26/18–01/15/19	
Sproles, T. A.		01/07/18–01/15/19	

NAME	REGULAR	SPECIAL	LOYALTY
Spruill, Andrew J.	09/01/18–12/08/19	01/19/18–09/01/18	
Stacy, Tom		11/26/17–01/15/19 03/05/27–unknown	
Stagg, Allen			06/01/18–01/15/19
Stagner, W. E.			06/10/18–02/00/19
Stallworth, Frank M.		10/23/18–01/15/19	
Standard, L. T.			06/11/18–02/00/19
Stanford, Joseph W.	10/04/11–11/08/11		
Stanley, J. E.			06/06/18–02/00/19
Stanley, L. N.		06/15/18–01/15/19 11/20/34–00/00/35	
Stark, P. J.		05/25/18–01/15/19	
Stedham, G. W.	06/16/16–09/04/16		
Steele, Charles	10/26/20–11/06/20		
Stelfox, Clarence H.	08/29/17–11/16/17 01/03/18–02/01/18		
Stephenson, J. C.	10/13/11–11/23/11		
Sterling, William Warren	04/15/27–01/00/31	07/12/18–01/15/19	
Stevens, Charles F.	11/27/17–02/03/20		
Stilwell, Dudley V. "Bud"	05/09/16–06/30/16	01/29/16–05/08/16	
Stillwell, W.		02/05/18–11/01/18	
Stillwell, William P.	02/15/18–04/03/18		
Stinson, James P.		05/31/17–12/00/17	
Stockton, James T.	02/01/17–09/01/17	02/24/33–unknown	
Stokes, J. B.			05/31/18–02/00/19
Stone, John W.			06/01/18–02/00/19
Stoner, G. O., Jr.		08/04/19–12/31/19 06/05/26–02/01/27 02/19/27–02/19/28 02/21/28–02/02/29 02/06/29–01/15/30 01/16/30–01/12/31 01/13/31–01/19/32 01/20/32–01/20/33 06/07/35–08/10/35	
Stoops, Clete		05/14/18–11/00/18	
Stoudenmier, C. S.		09/30/15–12/00/17	

NAME	REGULAR	SPECIAL	LOYALTY
Stovall, Elmer J.	03/01/21–09/08/21		
Strait, John S.		05/01/18–01/15/19	
Strait, Y. C.		05/29/18–01/15/19	
Stubbs, T. J.		05/31/17–12/00/17	06/01/18–02/00/19
Stuckler, E. P.			06/03/18–02/00/19
Sturgis, Dawes E.			06/27/18–03/06/19
Sullenger, R. G.		01/02/18–01/15/19 07/13/25–07/13/27 08/18/27–08/18/28 09/13/28–09/13/29 09/16/29–09/16/30 09/16/30–09/16/31 09/23/31–01/18/33 02/15/33–01/22/35	
Sullivan, H. E.		07/00/16–01/15/19	
Sullivan, John		02/01/17–12/00/17	
Sullivan, J. P.		07/19/18–01/15/19	
Sullivan, M. E.		07/03/18–01/15/19	
Sullivan, Ray	09/28/15–01/10/16		
Sulzbacher, Laurence I.	12/12/17–01/01/18		
Summers, J. W.			06/03/18–02/00/19
Sumrall, Robert W.	12/08/19–12/31/28 09/01/31–01/18/33		
Sutton, C. R.		06/06/17–07/09/17	
Sutton, J. F.			06/04/18–02/00/19
Sutton, M. V.			08/03/18–02/00/19
Sutton, Robert Bell	08/01/18–11/15/20		
Sweny, Guy A.			07/20/18–02/00/19
Swift, John Beakley "Beak"		06/05/16–12/00/17	
Swift, O. G.		10/05/18–01/15/19	
Syler, Robert		08/15/16–12/00/17	
Tabor, Horace J.			07/13/18–03/06/19
Tackett, Louis J.		05/03/19–12/31/19	
Tagle, A. P.	06/01/18–08/01/18		

NAME	REGULAR	SPECIAL	LOYALTY
Talbott, E. L.		12/27/17–01/15/19	
Tardy, John T.		10/02/20–10/22/20	
Tate, Fred		04/26/17–12/00/17	
Tate, Tom R.	11/25/10–09/15/11 01/08/26–02/01/27	08/25/15–02/06/19	
Taylor, Albert			06/17/18–02/00/19
Taylor, Alonzo	11/15/17–11/24/17		
Taylor, A. W.		07/13/17–08/15/17	
Taylor, C. A.			06/05/18–03/06/19
Taylor, Drew K.	1874–1878 10/01/20–04/08/21	10/07/33–10/06/35	
Taylor, Elmer J.		02/11/18–01/15/19	
Taylor, Joseph A. "Pinkie"	04/01/14–01/00/15	11/28/16–12/00/17 01/07/18–12/31/19	
Taylor, Milton, Jr.			07/01/18–02/00/19
Taylor, M. D. K.			06/03/18–02/00/19
Taylor, P. C.			06/17/18–02/00/19
Taylor, R. A.		08/11/16–12/00/17 01/10/18–01/15/19	
Taylor, Stephen L.		05/25/17–01/15/19	
Taylor, Thomas Carney "Creed"	1899–1900 1902–1904	04/07/17–12/00/17	
Taylor, Tom J.			06/06/18–02/00/19
Taylor, W. A.	03/01/18–02/01/19		
Taylor, William E.		06/27/18–01/15/19	
Taylor, William Walter	08/16/18–12/31/18 06/08/25–06/30/28 11/03/32–unknown	02/18/18–08/15/18 02/07/31–02/06/32 02/03/32–11/02/32 09/07/33–01/22/35	
Taylor, Woodward O.	09/28/20–unknown		
Taylor, William Riley "Buck"		07/18/17–12/00/17	
Terry, A. L.			06/10/18–02/00/19
Terry, Tom P.	05/25/16–06/14/16		
Tevis, Reid			08/01/18–03/06/19
Tevis, Robert M.		06/26/18–01/15/19	

NAME	REGULAR	SPECIAL	LOYALTY
Thomason, William	03/01/21–08/31/21		
Thompson, C. M.		01/12/18–01/15/19	
Thompson, Guy		05/11/18–01/15/19	
Thompson, J. C.		01/12/18–01/15/19	
Thompson, Lonnie		08/06/17–12/00/17	
Thompson, Oscar		01/30/18–01/15/19	
Thornton, R. H.			07/15/18–02/00/19
Thorp, Tom D.	10/22/17–unknown	08/04/17–10/21/17 09/05/18–12/19/18	
Thrasher, Chester		08/21/18–unknown 05/23/19–12/31/19 10/25/26–02/01/27	
Tibbs, K. P.			07/05/18–03/06/19
Tilley, George W.		12/02/18–01/15/19	
Timberlake, Delbert	1904–1905 06/27/18–10/11/18	03/09/16–05/03/16	
Timmons, Joe			06/10/18–02/00/19
Timmons, R. H.			06/10/18–02/00/19
Tippen, W. W.			06/06/18–02/00/19
Tisdale, Ira			06/26/18–03/06/19
Tisdale, I. M.			07/17/18–02/00/19
Tittle, Charles T.			07/02/18–02/00/19
Tobin, C. E.		01/26/18–01/15/19	
Toncray, A. C.			06/05/18–02/00/19
Townsend, H. H.		06/22/18–09/00/18	
Townsend, S. T.	10/09/11–01/31/12		
Townsend, W. T.			06/17/18–03/06/19
Travis, Edmunds		06/05/18–01/15/19	
Travis, M. T.			06/06/18–02/00/19
Trimble, La Fetra Elisha	10/02/18–12/10/24	11/12/25–02/01/27 01/14/30–01/14/31 01/24/31–01/30/32 01/30/32–01/01/33 10/05/33–08/10/35	

NAME	REGULAR	SPECIAL	LOYALTY
Trollinger, Harris C. "Harry"	10/30/11–01/31/12 04/01/15–06/13/15 10/16/15–03/01/18		
Tucker, B. F.			07/05/18–02/00/19
Tucker, J. S.			07/16/18–02/00/19
Tullis, W. A.			06/13/18–02/00/19
Tully, T. L.	05/18/16–06/18/17		
Tumlinson, Benjamin T., Jr.	09/08/17–04/01/23		
Turman, John C., Jr.		06/07/17–12/00/17	
Turner, H. A.		01/15/17–12/00/17	
Turner, Joe		04/22/18–01/15/19	
Turner, O. A.	11/09/15–11/07/16		
Turner, W. L.			07/06/18–03/06/19
Umscheid, Max		10/29/18–01/15/19	
Ussery, Charles C.			06/04/18–02/00/19
Valle, Calixto		08/05/19–12/31/19	
Van Cleve, Jack	05/16/16–09/20/16	05/24/17–unknown	
Vandergrift, W. E.		09/16/16–unknown (still in: 01/23/19)	
Vanderstucken, Alfred		01/25/18–01/15/19	
Van Haesen, H. M.			06/08/18–03/06/19
Vann, Bishop L.		05/12/17–12/00/17	
Vann, Charles C.	05/01/11–07/00/11		
Vann, John W.		12/02/16–01/15/19	
Vaughan, Jefferson Eagle	08/12/12–12/00/14 09/15/17–07/01/20 01/19/33–01/24/35	12/20/26–02/01/27	
Vaughan, Rufus G.	07/01/16–08/15/17		
Veale, Bert Clinton	07/31/15–unknown 10/24/18–02/07/19		
Villarreal, Ernesto C.		02/05/18–01/15/19	
Vinson, Theodore R.	10/12/17–02/01/19	11/25/19–12/31/19	
Vivion, Otho D.	06/20/16–02/01/19 02/00/19–unknown		

NAME	REGULAR	SPECIAL	LOYALTY
Wade, John L.	12/22/17–02/11/18		
Walker, E. C.		05/29/17–12/00/17	
Walker, George H.		06/29/18–01/13/19	
Walker, J. C.			06/18/18–02/00/19
Walker, John F.			06/12/18–02/00/19
Walker, Leonard	05/25/18–01/15/19		
Walker, Roy M.			06/04/18–02/00/19
Walker, Sam T.	02/10/21–05/20/21		
Wall, Alonzo E.	09/28/20–01/26/21		
Wallace, Ted			06/08/18–02/00/19
Wallace, W. H.			06/04/18–03/06/19
Wallen, James A.	05/28/16–06/11/18		
Walling, W. A.			07/01/18–02/00/19
Wallis, Hays M.	03/21/21–05/31/22 12/01/22–08/17/23	09/05/18–01/15/19 09/15/23–09/15/25 09/23/25–01/26/27 01/26/27–01/26/28 01/17/28–01/15/29 01/15/29–01/14/30 01/14/30–01/14/31 01/26/31–01/26/32 01/27/32–01/18/33 01/20/33–01/19/35 05/30/35–08/10/35	
Wallridge, J. M.		03/23/18–05/07/19	
Walters, G. E.		12/29/17–01/15/19	
Walters, O. E.	08/05/18–08/00/18		
Ware, A. H.		07/05/17–12/00/17	
Ware, Graydon L.	03/25/18–unknown		
Wartenbach, F. C.			07/15/18–02/00/19
Wasson, A. L.			06/08/18–03/06/19
Watkins, Thomas	11/20/13–11/20/15	05/22/16–08/15/17	
Watson, J. A.	01/22/18–02/16/18	01/16/18–01/21/18	
Watts, C. J.			06/12/18–03/06/19
Watts, R. V.			07/04/18–03/06/19

NAME	REGULAR	SPECIAL	LOYALTY
Watts, W. P.			07/09/18–03/06/19
Waugh, Andrew M.		01/21/18–01/15/19	
Way, J. R.		11/06/16–12/00/17	
Way, W. W.		06/05/17–12/00/17	
Wease, D. C.		12/13/17–01/15/19	
Weatherall, J. G.		01/24/18–01/15/19	
Weatherford, W. W.		01/29/18–01/15/19	
Weaver, Bud	09/05/17–06/08/18		
Weaver, Claremore M.	02/23/21–08/31/21		
Webb, Britain R.		11/15/18–01/15/19 02/25/33–02/24/35	
Webb, David Cornelius "Jack"	08/19/15–06/12/17 02/20/20–08/12/23		
Webb, Grover Cleveland	08/01/10–09/30/10 01/19/14–08/31/14		
Webb, J. R.			06/13/18–03/06/19
Webster, Charles H.	01/13/11–07/00/13		
Webster, James S.		06/16/17–01/15/19 04/06/32–01/18/33	
Weir, T. C.	05/24/17–01/01/18	08/25/16–05/23/17	
Welborn, Bowen			07/05/18–03/06/19
Welborn, C. V.			06/08/18–03/06/19
Wells, Munroe	12/21/17–03/01/19		
Wells, Wright C.	12/25/17–02/09/20		
West, Eugene		05/24/18–01/15/19	
West, Ike		01/10/19–12/31/19	
West, L. Earl		06/19/18–01/15/19	
West, Milton Crockett		06/19/18–01/15/19	
West, Milton H. "Leche"	11/01/11–01/31/12	08/06/27–08/06/28 08/11/28–08/11/29	
West, Paul More	08/14/15–10/00/15		
West, R. S.			06/17/18–03/06/19
West, W. R.		06/02/17–12/00/17	

NAME	REGULAR	SPECIAL	LOYALTY
Westbrook, L. C.	07/06/18–unknown		
Weston, A. G.			08/29/18–03/06/19
Whatley, George			06/01/18–03/06/19
Wheat, Allen		09/23/33–01/22/35 07/24/35–10/01/35	07/14/18–03/06/19
Wheatley, J. B.	02/15/21–01/16/33 02/05/35–unknown (still in: 09/01/37)		
Wheeler, Joel Robert		01/07/19–12/31/19 06/20/25–02/08/28 02/23/28–01/23/31 01/27/33–01/22/35 05/29/35–08/10/35	
Whisenant, M.			06/04/18–03/06/19
White, Buck		05/30/17–12/00/17	
White, Goff	09/07/05–03/17/10		
White, Joe		01/11/18–01/15/19	
White, John Dudley	1907–1911 05/15/13–11/03/13 05/10/16–07/12/18		
White, J. Will			06/10/18–03/06/19
White, Thomas Bruce	09/18/06–05/00/09	04/15/16–12/00/17 05/17/18–01/15/19	
Whitefield, Ben W.			06/14/18–03/06/19
Whiteker, B. M.			06/01/18–03/06/19
Whitfield, Robert Wilkins		08/28/16–12/00/17	
Whitley, William E.	07/05/09–02/15/10		
Whitman, W. J.		05/18/18–01/15/19	
Whittington, A. G.		11/07/16–01/15/19	
Wildenthal, B., Jr.			06/14/18–03/06/19
Wilkins, John	05/23/16–03/00/18		
Wilkite, J. T.		03/28/18–01/15/19	
Willett, Frank		07/02/17–12/00/17	
Williams, Ben		06/11/18–12/31/19	

NAME	REGULAR	SPECIAL	LOYALTY
Williams, Caleb Thomas	10/00/17–12/27/18 10/23/20–02/15/21 04/11/27–05/31/27 06/21/27–08/31/28		
Williams, Elvin W.	04/10/18–unknown (still in: 09/00/18)		
Williams, Harry Frank		08/03/17–12/00/17	
Williams, J. J.			06/17/18–03/06/19
Williams, R. D.		05/30/17–12/00/17	
Williams, T. V.	12/22/17–01/00/18		
Williams, T. W.			06/05/18–03/08/19
Williamson, C. E.		09/18/17–12/00/17 08/09/18–01/15/19 09/15/26–01/25/27 01/25/27–01/25/28 01/14/28–01/11/29 01/11/29–01/11/30 01/13/30–01/13/31 01/24/31–01/18/33 01/20/33–unknown	
Williamson, Fuller		09/05/16–01/15/19 06/25/25–01/24/27 01/24/27–01/18/29 01/18/29–01/15/30 01/15/30–01/15/31 01/22/31–01/22/32 01/21/32–01/18/33 01/21/33–01/20/35 05/28/35–08/10/35	
Williamson, J. E.		06/11/17–12/00/17	
Williford, Frank, Jr.		07/02/17–12/00/17	
Willis, Chris C.	09/24/15–09/30/15	06/05/18–03/06/19	
Willis, C. E.			07/06/18–03/06/19
Willis, F. D.		05/16/17–12/00/17	
Willis, Lon L.	11/01/12–04/15/19	06/10/31–unknown	
Wilmoth, John B.			06/08/18–03/05/19
Wilson, Edgar		02/13/18–01/15/19	
Wilson, E. M.			06/04/18–03/06/19

NAME	REGULAR	SPECIAL	LOYALTY
Wilson, Hillsman D.			06/07/18–03/06/19
Wilson, Maple		08/06/17–02/00/18	
Wilson, Thomas F.		02/04/18–01/15/19	
Wilson, W. B.		12/10/17–01/24/18	
Windham, William C.			06/25/18–03/06/19
Winfree, Edwin H.			07/18/18–03/06/19
Winn, Peter B., Jr.	03/14/21–08/31/21		
Winters, Howard			07/01/18–03/06/19
Wisby, Ernest E.		06/11/18–01/15/19	
Woelber, A. H.	11/12/15–03/10/19		
Wofford, D. W.			06/04/18–03/06/19
Wofford, William F.			06/06/18–03/06/19
Wolf, Carl M.		06/21/18–01/15/19	
Wolfe, O. P.		06/11/17–12/00/17	05/31/18–03/06/19
Wood, Carl	11/16/10–12/03/10		
Wood, D. W.			06/07/18–07/23/19
Wood, Fred T.		06/18/17–12/00/17	
Wood, James Gillam		05/15/18–01/15/19 03/03/27–03/03/28 06/01/28–06/01/29 06/01/29–05/03/30 05/31/30–05/31/31 06/20/31–unknown	
Wood, Samuel Mohon		10/03/18–01/15/19	
Woodland, Ben H.	04/16/18–03/10/19 10/01/19–01/31/20		
Woodley, M. B.			05/30/18–03/06/19
Woods, Alva	05/13/16–07/09/16		
Woods, Henry		03/09/18–01/15/19	
Woods, John D.		07/02/17–09/13/18	
Woodworth, W. W.		11/01/17–01/15/19 07/17/19–12/31/19 05/17/21–unknown	
Word, Thomas Stutsman		08/15/17–12/00/17	

NAME	REGULAR	SPECIAL	LOYALTY
Worsham, Joe Boone		06/16/17–12/00/17	
Wren, John K.		05/16/18–01/15/19	
Wren, W. R.			05/31/18–03/06/19
Wright, Charles Hays	05/11/16–11/30/16		
Wright, Earl R.	09/01/17–04/20/19		
Wright, Emanuel Avant "Dogie"	06/10/18–10/00/18 03/25/21–08/31/21		
Wright, Eugene C.		05/19/17–12/00/17	
Wright, Howell J.		02/18/18–01/15/19	
Wright, James B.		06/20/18–12/31/19	
Wright, Milam H.	1899–1901 12/27/04–01/01/10 03/20/11–07/15/12		
Wright, Thomas R.	08/01/20–02/23/21		
Wright, W. J.			06/14/18–03/06/19
Wright, William L.	01/01/99–09/01/02 01/01/18–04/01/25 05/15/27–01/18/33 02/14/35–00/00/39		
Wuerschmidt, Paul		04/22/18–01/15/19	
Wynn, Fred C.	1909–unknown (still in: 08/00/11)		
Yaeger, W. H.			05/06/18–01/15/19
Yarbrough, J. S.		12/27/17–10/00/18	
Yates, O. W.		05/31/17–12/00/17	
Yates, W. J.		03/07/18–01/15/19	
Yeary, Earl R.	1903–1904 10/07/11–12/31/11		
Yeates, John C.		01/24/18–01/15/19	
Yelvington, Henry B.		11/27/17–01/15/19 08/29/19–12/29/19 12/08/27–12/08/28 01/16/29–01/16/30 02/07/30–01/01/31 03/13/31–03/13/32	

NAME	REGULAR	SPECIAL	LOYALTY
Yolton, Frank Louis		04/16/17–01/15/19 01/04/26–02/04/27 02/04/27–02/04/28 02/15/28–02/15/29 07/06/29–07/06/30 11/06/30–11/06/31 03/15/32–01/18/33 01/28/33–unknown 06/11/35–08/10/35	
Young, J. W.			06/05/18–03/06/19
Young, M. Curtis	09/01/17–10/01/18		
Young, Thomas P.	03/10/21–08/31/21		
Young, William E.	11/01/19–05/15/27 07/01/28–01/18/33		

ABBREVIATIONS

AA	*Alpine Avalanche*
ABF	A. B. Fall Papers
AG	Adjutant General
AGO	Adjutant General's Office (U.S. Army)
AGC	Adjutant General's Correspondence (Texas)
AP	Roy Aldrich Papers
AS	*Austin Statesman*
B*DH*	Brownsville *Daily Herald*
BI	Bureau of Investigation
CAH	Center for American History
CP	Governor Oscar B. Colquitt Papers, Texas State Library
EPH	*El Paso Herald*
EPMT	*El Paso Morning Times*
FC	Frederick Funston Collection
FP	Governor James E. Ferguson Papers
FRC-FW	Federal Records Center, Fort Worth, Texas
Handbook	*The New Handbook of Texas*
HC	*Houston Chronicle*

HP	Governor William P. Hobby Papers
IMA	*Investigation of Mexican Affairs*
LWT	*Laredo Weekly Times*
MID	Military Intelligence Division
MR	Monthly Return
NYT	*New York Times*
PGA	General Pablo González Archive
"Proceedings"	"Proceedings . . . in the Investigation of the Texas State Ranger Force"
RDJ	Records of the Department of Justice
RDS	Records of the Department of State
RRM	Ranger Records, Texas National Guard Archive, Camp Mabry
SAE	*San Antonio Express*
SD	Southern Department, United States Army
TMC	Governor Thomas M. Campbell Papers
TRH	Texas Ranger Hall of Fame
VCA	President Venustiano Carranza Archive
WC	Walter Prescott Webb Collection

NOTES

Introduction

1. The statue originally graced the lobby of the Dallas Love Field airport terminal, was moved to the city's Union Station, and is now back at Love Field.
2. *The Economist*, December 21, 2002, 30.
3. In 1935 the Rangers were incorporated into the Texas Department of Public Safety, where they handle major crime cases. See *General and Special Laws of the State of Texas Passed by the Forty-fourth Legislature at the Regular Session Convened at the City of Austin, January 8, 1935 and Adjourned May 11, 1935*, vol. 1 (Austin: The State of Texas, 1935), 444–454, especially 448–449.
4. Walter Prescott Webb, *The Texas Rangers: A Century of Frontier Defense*. 2d ed. (Austin: University of Texas Press, 1965), 345–367; James M. Day, "El Paso's Texas Rangers," *Password*, XXIV, no. 4 (Winter 1979), 158.
5. William Warren Sterling, *Trails and Trials of a Texas Ranger* (Norman: University of Oklahoma Press, 1959), 194–202.
6. W. H. Timmons, *El Paso: A Borderlands History* (El Paso: Texas Western Press, 1990), 165.
7. Webb, *Texas Rangers*, 297–301.
8. In an effort to maintain a Ranger connection for Hamer, his biographers assert that when he resigned in 1933, "His resignation did not require his giving up his actual commission as a Texas Ranger. He merely went on inactive status." H. Gordon Frost and John H. Jenkins, *I'm Frank Hamer: The Life of a Texas Peace Officer* (Austin: Pemberton Press, 1968), 174. However, Hamer's service record says nothing about any "inactive status." It shows that he resigned as a Regular Ranger on February 1, 1933. Thus, even if he had kept his warrant of authority, anything he did under color of that warrant would have been illegal, because he was no longer a Texas Ranger. On February 10, 1934, Hamer was hired as a "special escape investigator" for the Texas prison system. Moreover, Frost and Jenkins state that when Hamer resigned in 1933 he "had held a Ranger commission for twenty-six years" (p. 174). This is demonstrably not the case. Hamer's career had been fairly typical—intermittent enlistments, as his service record indicates: Regular Ranger—04/21/06–11/00/08; 03/29/15–11/08/15; Special Ranger—11/08/15–01/10/17; Regular Ranger—10/01/18–06/19/19; 11/25/19–05/11/20; 09/01/21–06/30/25; Special Ranger—07/01/25–02/01/27; Regular Ranger—02/02/27–02/01/33; Special Ranger—02/01/46–01/01/55. See also Colonel Homer Garrison, Jr., to Stan Redding, July 26, 1955, Ranger Archive, Texas Department of Public Safety, Austin, Texas.

9. Captain Frank Johnson to Adjutant General Newton, August 8, 1910, WC; Maude T. Gilliland, comp. *Wilson County Texas Rangers 1837–1977* (Brownsville: Springman-King Co., 1977), 41–47.

10. Milo Kearney and Anthony Knopp, *Boom and Bust: The Historical Cycles of Matamoros and Brownsville* (Austin: Eakin Press, 1991), 196–197.

11. Gilliland, *Wilson County*, 44; *NYT*, March 15, 1971.

12. As Webb himself relates, the Rangers took him camping, spun him yarns, let him wear a pistol, and issued him a Ranger commission. *Texas Rangers*, 549–567.

13. Llerena B. Friend, "W. P. Webb's Texas Rangers," *Southwestern Historical Quarterly*, 74 (January 1971), 293–323.

14. Walter Prescott Webb, *An Honest Preface and Other Essays* (Boston: Houghton Mifflin; Cambridge: The Riverside Press, 1959), 17.

15. Oxford: Oxford University Press.

16. San Francisco: Canfield Press, 1972. In a later edition Acuña adopted a blander subtitle: *Occupied America: A History of Chicanos* (New York: Longman, 2000).

17. Notre Dame: University of Notre Dame Press, 1979.

18. For example, Charles M. Robinson III, *The Men Who Wear the Star: The Story of the Texas Rangers* (New York: Random House, 2000), devotes out of 288 pages a whole twenty-four to the *entire* twentieth century, fourteen of them to the decade in question.

19. Gilliland, *Wilson County*, 2, 4. See also the biographical sketches in Maude T. Gilliland, *Horsebackers of the Brush Country: A Story of the Texas Rangers and Mexican Liquor Smugglers* ([Brownsville: Springman-King Co.], 1968), 70–146.

20. Gilliland, *Wilson County*, 4–6, 45–49, 51–56, 88–89.

21. O. B. Colquitt, "The Texas Ranger as He Is," *Leslie's Illustrated Weekly Newspaper*, April 16, 1914, 367.

22. T. R. Fehrenbach, *Lone Star: A History of Texas and the Texans* (New York: Macmillan, 1968), xi.

Chapter 1

1. Webb, *Texas Rangers*, 20, 23–24.

2. See, for example, Samuel C. Reid, Jr., *Scouting Expeditions of McCullough's Texas Rangers* (Philadelphia: G. B. Zieber, 1847); Samuel E. Chamberlain, *My Confession* (New York: Harper, 1956), 173–174.

3. Webb, *Texas Rangers*, 127, 307.

4. Ibid., 143, 146, 151.

5. Ibid., 176–193.

6. Ibid., 219, 220–229, 233–238.

7. Ibid., 307, 311, 238–257; George Durham, *Taming the Nueces Strip: The Story of McNelly's Rangers* (Austin: University of Texas Press, 1962); N. A. Jennings, *A Texas Ranger.* (Norman: University of Oklahoma Press, 1997).

8. Webb, *Texas Rangers*, 233–280.

9. Robert Draper, "The Twilight of the Texas Rangers," *Texas Monthly* (February 1994), 82.

10. *Lone Star Justice*, 158.

11. Webb, *Texas Rangers*, 371–391.

12. Ibid., 425–426, 453–457.

13. *General Laws of the State of Texas Passed at the Regular Session of the Twenty-Seventh Legislature Convened at the City of Austin, January 8, 1901, and Adjourned April 9, 1901* (Austin: Von Boeckmann, Schutz & Co., 1901), 41–43. The statute is reprinted in Headquarters Ranger Force, General Orders No. 5, October 2, 1911, AGC.

14. Webb, *Texas Rangers*, 457; Sterling, *Trails and Trials*, 385.

15. See, for example, AG to J. W. Everman, January 3, 1910; same to J. W. Maxwell, January 3, 1910; same to L. S. Thorne, January 10, 1910; L. S. Thorne to Newton, January 13, 1910, AGC.

16. "Statement of Expenditures and Balances on Account of Appropriations Made for the Adjutant General's Department for the Fiscal Year Ending August 31, 1910," AGC.

17. The New Mexico Mounted Police's salaries were: captain—$166 a month, sergeant—$125, privates—$100. *Laws of the State of New Mexico Passed at the First Regular Session . . . 1912* (Albuquerque: Albright and Anderson, Printers, 1912), 206; Even the fifteen-man Austin police force was better paid. In 1910 the chief made $125 a month, the sergeant and detectives $95, mounted policemen $85, and patrolmen $70. And they were asking for a raise. *AS*, November 20, 1910.

18. Webb, *Texas Rangers*, 288.

19. William S. West to Colquitt, March 8, 1912; same to Hutchings, May 2, 1912; Colquitt to Hutchings, March 11, 1912, AGC; *Biennial Report of the Adjutant General of Texas, From January 23, 1911, to December 31, 1912* (Austin: Von Boeckmann-Jones Co., 1913), 9; *SAE*, February 21, 1913.

20. See, for example, "Ranger Ration Returns 1910," for Company B, AGC.

21. See "Pay Roll" for Company B, January 31, 1910, AGC.

22. As an example see MR, Company A, January 31, 1910, AGC.

23. Sterling, *Trails and Trials*, 358, 367; Webb, *Texas Rangers*, 81, 84–86.

24. R. H. Beckham to Colt's Patent Fire Arms Manufacturing Co., February 9, March 11, April 9 and 25, 1910, AGC; Sterling, *Trails and Trials*, 324.

25. [Lieutenant Colonel Emmett E. Walker] to Colt's Patent Fire Arms Mfg. Co., August 7, 1913, AGC.

26. Sterling, *Trails and Trials*, 316–317.

27. The quartermaster appointed in 1901 was Captain L. P. Sieker.

28. Sterling, *Trails and Trials*, 496–511; the standard work on the Cortez affair is Américo Paredes, *"With His Pistol in His Hand:" A Border Ballad and Its Hero* (Austin: University of Texas Press, 1958).

29. For a recent scholarly biography of Captain Rogers, see Paul N. Spellman, *Captain John H. Rogers, Texas Ranger* (Denton: University of North Texas Press, 2003).

30. Sterling, *Trails and Trials*, 363–382; Webb, *Texas Rangers*, 80, 450–451.

31. *The New Handbook of Texas*, 6 vols. (Austin: Texas State Historical Association, 1996), IV, 392.

32. Webb, *Texas Rangers*, 467; as of June, 1914, fewer than twenty blacks lived in Brownsville. *BDH*, June 19, 1914.

33. Webb, *Texas Rangers*, 468–469; For a recent interpretation see John D. Weaver, *The Brownsville Raid*, rev. ed. (College Station: Texas A&M Press, 1992).

34. *Handbook*, VI, 874; Sterling, *Trails and Trials*, 357–358.

35. Albert Bigelow Paine, *Captain Bill McDonald, Texas Ranger*, (New York: Little and Ives, 1909).

36. *EPMT*, November 7, 1912.

37. *AS*, March 22, April 15, 1911; Sterling, *Trails and Trials*, 334–358; Webb, *Texas Rangers*, 458–460; *Handbook*, IV, 393; *EPMT*, January 16, 1918.

38. Sterling, *Trails and Trials*, 305–323.

39. Hughes to Hutchings, report on the operations of Company A, September 1, 1909–June 29, 1911, RRM; James Ganor reports, August 12, 14, 1912, reel 2; Ganor report, August 13, 1912, reel 3, BI. For an account of the meeting, see Charlotte Crawford, "The Border Meeting of Presidents Taft and Diaz," *Password*, III, no. 3 (July 1958), 86–96. Captain Rogers also spent four days in El Paso as part of the security detail. Spellman, *Captain John H. Rogers*, 150–151.

40. Webb, *Texas Rangers*, 460–461; Sterling, *Trails and Trials*, 383–393; Hughes to Colquitt, July 23, 1911, CP; Jack Martin, *Border Boss: Captain John R. Hughes, Texas Ranger*, (Austin: State House Press, 1942).

41. *AS*, January 30, 1907.

42. Maude T. Gilliland, *Rincon (Remote Dwelling Place): A Story of Life on a South Texas Ranch at the Turn of the Century* (Brownsville: Springman-King Lithograph Company, 1964), 40–41.

43. Ibid., January 29, 1907.

44. Robert W. Frazer, *Forts of the West: Military Forts and Presidios and Posts Commonly Called Forts West of the Mississippi River to 1898* (Norman: University of Oklahoma Press, 1965), 9, 29–30, 141–159.

45. For a scholarly treatment of the *Rurales*, see Paul J. Vanderwood, *Disorder and Progress: Bandits, Police, and Mexican Development* (Lincoln: University of Nebraska Press, 1981).

Chapter 2

1. AG to Mrs. R. F. Ives, December 1, 1913, AGC.

2. MR, Company C, January 31, 1910, AGC; Goff White, who'd been a cowboy before enlisting in 1905, resigned from the Rangers on March 17, 1910, to accept a better position as chief deputy sheriff of Waller County. Hall Avriett had been a deputy sheriff prior to enlisting in April, 1909. He was honorably discharged from Company C on February 1, 1911. His brother, Edd L. Avriett, was a lumberman before becoming a Ranger in October, 1909. In October, 1910 he was promoted to sergeant of Company C, and he was honorably discharged on February 1, 1911. The Avrietts came from Milano in Milam County.

3. *AS*, January 17, 18, 1910.

4. *EPMT*, January 19, 1910.

5. Ross to Newton, January 12, 1910, AGC. Redus had been a farmer and rancher before joining Company B in 1908. He was promoted to sergeant the following year. After his firing he lived in El Paso and San Antonio, and in 1911 was a court bailiff in San Antonio. He also worked for the U.S. marshal in San Antonio keeping Mexican revolutionists under surveillance.

6. *EPMT*, January 19, 1910.

7. Newton to Ross, January 29, 1910; Ross to Newton, January 31, 1910, WC; *EPMT*, February 27, 1910.

8. Newton to Ross, February 12 and 22, 1910; Ross to Newton, February 19, 1910, WC.

9. Petition, March, 1910, AGC.

10. W. D. Twichell to Governor T. M. Campbell, February 1, 1910; J. J. Sanders to [AG] J. O. Newton, February 24, 1910; AG to Twichell, March 3, 1910; MR, Company D, March 31, 1910, AGC; *AS*, February 26, 1910.

11. *Biennial Report of the Adjutant General of Texas for the Period Ending December 15, 1910* (Austin: Austin Printing Co., 1911), 8.

12. *EPMT*, April 23, 1910.

13. MR, Company B, March 31, 1910; AG to Bailey, May 3, 1910, AGC.

14. Bailey to Newton, May 5, 1910; same to Colonel R. H. Beckham, May 24, 1910, AGC.

15. Bailey to Newton, June 2, 1910, AGC.

16. AG to Bailey, June 6, 1910, AGC.

17. Bailey to Newton, June 11, 1910, AGC.

18. Ibid.

19. Neill C. Wilson and Frank J. Taylor, *Southern Pacific: The Roaring Story of a Fighting Railroad* (New York : McGraw Hill, 1952), 78–79; Bailey to Newton, June 27, 1910, AGC.

20. Flier enclosed in Bailey to Newton, June 27, 1910, AGC.

21. AG to Bailey, June 13, 1910; Bailey to Newton, June 14, 15, 27, 1910, AGC.

22. Bailey to Newton, July 20, 1910; J. W. Reese to same, July 27, 1910, AGC.

23. J. A. Walton to Bailey, July 19, 1910; E. F. Higgins to D. W. Gourley, July 20, 1910, AGC.

24. Newton to Company B, July 22, 1910; Bailey to Newton, July 22, 1910, AGC.

25. See the MR, Company A, March 31, April 30, May 31, June 30, and July 31, 1910, AGC.

26. AG to Hughes, May 2, 1910, WC.

27. AG to Guerra, March 8, 1910, AGC.

28. MR, Company C, March 31, 1910, AGC.

29. James A. Clark, with Weldon Hart, *The Tactful Texan: A Biography of Governor Will Hobby* (New York: Random House, 1958), 20–22.

30. MR, Company C, April 30 and May 31, 1910, AGC; *AS*, April 30, May 1, 1910.

31. MR, Company C, May 31, June 30, and July 31, 1910, AGC; *AS*, July 2, 10, 1910; on July 15, 1910, R. M. Hudson resigned to accept a better paying position. He would become sheriff of Anderson County.

32. MR, Company C, June 30, 1910, AGC.

33. Hamer had been a private in Company C from April, 1906, to November, 1908.

34. *AS*, July 19, 1910.

35. Ibid., July 20–26, 1910.

36. MR, Company C, July 31 and November 30, 1910, AGC.

37. Ibid.; Assistant AG to Rogers, August 4, 1910; Captain Louis H. Younger to AG, August 10, 1910, AGC; *EPMT*, July 31 and August 1, 2, 17, 1910; *AS*, July 31, August 1–18, 1910.

38. MR, Company C, July 31 and August 31, 1910, AGC; *AS*, August 18, 1910.

39. *BDH*, October 29, 1910, quoting the Denison *Herald*.

40. *AS*, March 14, 15, 17, 1910; *BDH*, March 14, 18, 21, 1910.

41. MR, Company A, March 31, 1910; Judge W. B. Hopkins to AG, April 4, 1910, AGC.

42. Celedonio Garza et al. to AG, April 4, 1910; MR, Company A, April 30, 1910, AGC; Sergeant McCauley had enlisted in Company B in 1891, becoming its sergeant in 1905. In 1907 he had transferred to Company A, as sergeant. He died of natural causes in Marlin on September 9, 1910, and was buried in Wichita Falls.

43. Johnson to Newton, May 30, 1910, and AG to Johnson, June 2, 1910, WC; MR, Company A, May 31, 1910, AGC; *BDH*, May 30, 1910. Ranger Gus T. (Buster) Jones was an interesting character, besides being fast on the draw. His father, W. W. Jones, had been a lieutenant in Company A, Frontier Battalion. Gus Jones was born in San Angelo in August, 1882, became the deputy city marshal of San Angelo in 1903, a Tom Green County deputy sheriff in 1904, and enlisted as a Company A Ranger in March, 1908. He resigned on July 1, 1910, to become a Customs inspector in Brownsville, then in 1912 an Immigration inspector in San Diego, California. In 1916 he resigned to become an agent of the federal Bureau of Investigation (which in 1935 was renamed the Federal Bureau of Investigation). He remained with the FBI until 1944. His distinguished career included being division superintendent for western Louisiana, Texas, New Mexico, and Arizona in 1921, special agent in charge of the San Antonio office in 1922, being sent to Mexico City as civil (legal) attaché in 1939, and serving as liaison officer with British intelligence in the West Indies in 1943. He retired in San Antonio in 1944. In retirement he was a security consultant to corporations. Jones died in San Antonio on September 28, 1963.

44. See the editorial "Authorities Should Act," *BDH*, April 11, 1910.

45. Johnson to Newton, May 30, 1910, WC; *BDH*, May 30, 31, June 1, 2, 6, 1910.

46. Johnson to Newton, May 31, 1910, WC; see also AG to S. A. Robertson et al., May 31, 1910, AGC; AG to Johnson, June 2, 1910, WC.

47. *BDH*, May 27, 1910.

48. Ibid., August 1, 2, 1910; "Proceedings," 1323–1326; Kearney and Knopp, *Boom and Bust*, 196–197, have some inaccuracies in their account of the Darwin murder and the San Benito ambush: Darwin did not beat Jacinto Treviño's younger brother to death, the dead Ranger was Quirl, not George, Carnes, and he was a Ranger private, not a captain—there's a considerable difference.

49. *BDH*, August 4, 1910.

50. Ibid., June 25, 1910; AG to Colquitt, May 11, 1914, CP.

51. AG to Colquitt, August 16 and September 9, 1910, CP.
52. Johnson to Newton, July 31 and August 8, 1910, WC; MR, Company A, June 30, 1910, AGC; Funeral notice, August 2, 1910, WC.
53. Assistant AG to J. L. Seale, August 24, 1910, AGC.
54. Luther Ellsworth to Secretary of State, August 30, 1910, RDJ.
55. Johnson to Colonel R. M. Phelps, August 14, 1910, and Assistant AG to Johnson, August 18, 1910, WC; A. R. Baker to Rogers, August 8, 1910, and MR, Company A, August 31, 1910, AGC; Johnson to Newton, September 5 [1910], WC; *BDH*, September 5, 7, 8, 1910.
56. *Handbook*, V, 290.
57. M. L. Harkey to Gov. T. M. Campbell, August 12, 1910, WC, and August 13, 1910, AGC; Acting AG to Hughes, August 13, 1910 and Hughes to Colonel M. Phelps, August 13, 1910, WC; Phelps to Harkey, August 13, 1910, AGC.
58. *AS*, August 10, 1910.
59. Ibid., August 14, 20, 21, 23, September 2, 1910.
60. MR, Company D, August 31, 1910; letter from citizens of Coahoma to Rogers, September 24, 1910; E. M. Mobley to same, September 27, 1910; MR, Company C, September 30, 1910, AGC.
61. Bailey to Newton, August 13, 1910; same to E. M. Phelps, August 18, 1910; same to Colonel R. H. Beckham, September 10, 1910, AGC.
62. "Estimate of Appropriations Necessary for the Support of the Adjutant General's Department for the Two Years Ending August 31, 1911," August 31, 1910, AGC.
63. Newton to Bailey, September 16 and 21, 1910; Assistant Quartermaster General to same, September 22, 1910, AGC.
64. MR, Company A, September 30, 1910, AGC.
65. Bailey to Newton, October 1, 1910, AGC.
66. AG to Bailey, October 3, 1910, WC; *BDH*, October 3, 20, 21, 1910.
67. Bailey to Newton, October 31, 1910, AGC; *BDH*, October 20, 21, 28, November 3, 5, 1910; Hughes to Newton, November 4, 1910, and MR, Company B, October 31, 1910, WC.
68. *BDH*, October 3, 1910.
69. See, for example, MR, Company C, September 30 and October 31, 1910, AGC.
70. Canales to Governor Campbell, October 25, 1910; same to Newton, October 27, 1910, AGC. See also unsigned to Governor of Texas, October 28, 1910, TMC.
71. *BDH*, August 17, 1910.
72. Ex-Captain Johnson went off to Argentina for two years as a ranch manager. He then returned to Texas and settled in Thurber. On December 12, 1923, he died in Weatherford of diabetes, aged fifty-five. Johnson Vertical File, TRH.
73. Hughes to Newton, November 1, 1910, WC.
74. Hughes to Newton, November 1, 1910; John I. Kleiber to same, November 1, 1910; W. B. Hopkins to same, November 1, 1910; Newton to Hughes, November 2, 1910, WC.
75. Bailey to Newton, November 3, 1910, AGC.
76. MR, Company C, November 30, 1910; AG to Bailey, November 16, 1910, AGC.
77. D. S. Barker to Newton, November 15, 1910; AG to Barker, November 22, 1910; MR, Company C, November 30, 1910, AGC; *SAE*, November 14, 1910; *EPMT*, November 16 and 18, 1910.
78. P. C. Knox to Governor of Texas, November 10, 1910; T. M. Campbell to Secretary of State, November 10, 1910; see also Knox to Governor of Texas, November 16, 1910, CP. In fairness, it should also be noted that in March, 1910, the Mexican ambassador enlisted the good offices of the State Department to ask the Texas governor to protect the Mexican consul at Rio Grande City, who'd been threatened by the friends of one Carlos Molina, to whose extradition the Mexican government had recently agreed. The adjutant general ordered Captain Frank Johnson of Company A to investigate immediately and provide all possible protection. Knox to Governor of Texas, March 9, 1910; Newton to Johnson, March 12, 1910, TMC.

79. John A. Valls to Gov. T. M. Campbell, November 20, 1910; Assistant AG to Captain J. P. Cranke, November 21, 1910, AGC.

80. Sterling, *Trails and Trials*, 355–356, has an interesting description of what he terms the "cactus telegraph"—a system of signals that Hispanic inhabitants along the river used to warn each other of the approach of lawmen.

81. MR, Company C, November 30, 1910, AGC.

82. Ibid.; AG to Rogers, November 25, 1910, AGC.

83. AG to Rogers, November 28, 1910, AGC.

84. *NYT*, November 28, 1910.

85. Hughes to Newton, November 25, 1910. See also MR, Company D, November 30 and December 31, 1910, AGC.

86. Hughes to Newton, December 10, 1910; Colonel Phelps to Hughes, December 12, 1910; Hughes to Gen. R. H. Beckham, December 15 and 16, 1910, WC.

87. AG to Bailey, November 16, 1910, AGC.

88. *BDH*, December 24, 27, 1910.

89. Ibid., October 4, 8–10, 1902.

90. Webb, *Texas Rangers*, 462–465; Sterling, *Trails and Trials*, 321–325; Kearney and Knopp, *Boom and Bust*, 195–196; Samora, Bernal, and Peña, *Gunpowder Justice*, 56–57; Paredes, *With His Pistol*, 29–30.

91. Benjamin Kowalski and George J. Head to Gen. R. H. Beckham, December 25, 1910, AGC.

92. AG to Judge W. B. Hopkins, December 28, 1910, AGC.

93. Hopkins to Beckham, December 31, 1910, AGC.

94. AG to Benjamin Kowalski, December 28, 1910, AGC.

95. AG to Bailey, December 28, 1910, AGC.

96. Bailey to Beckham, December 29, 1910, AGC.

97. Bailey to Beckham, December 31, 1910, AGC.

98. The standard biography of Colquitt is George Portal Huckaby, "Oscar Branch Colquitt: A Political Biography" (Ph.D. diss., University of Texas, 1946). It is inadequate in its treatment of his Mexican policy.

99. *AS*, July 7, 1910. See also *HC*, September 5, 1910, and *EPMT*, October 9, 1910. Colquitt was presumably referring to the clashes between Rangers and the locals in Amarillo in 1909. See Utley, *Lone Star Justice*, 283–284.

100. *AS*, July 10, 1910.

101. Ibid., July 22, 1910.

102. Ibid., September 5, 1910.

103. Reprint of *The Blue Book for Visitors, Tourists and Those Seeking a Good Time While in San Antonio, Texas.* Published annually. San Antonio: n.p., 1911–1912.

104. *AS*, September 13, 14, 15, 23, 1910; *HC*, September 14, 17, 1910.

105. *AS*, December 11, 1910.

Chapter 3

1. Colquitt to Mrs. W. E. Collins, January 11, 1911, CPB. In March, Colquitt approved a bill permitting Mrs. Collins and her children to sue the state for damages growing out of her husband's death at the hands of the Rangers. *AS*, March 25, 1911.

2. H.A. Carnes to Colonel J. T. Rogers, January 16, 1911, AGC.

3. AG to C. B. Rodgers, January 23, 1911; MR, Company B, January 31, 1911, AGC.

4. Bailey to Beckham, January 18, 1911, AGC.

5. Hughes to Beckham, January 5, 1911, AGC.

6. AG to Hughes, January 9, 1911, AGC.

7. *AS*, January 26, 1911; AG to Bailey, January 25, 1911; Assistant Quartermaster General to same, January 31, 1911, AGC.

8. Rogers to Hutchings, February 1, 1911, AGC.

9. As of 1917, Bailey was city marshal of Navasota. Two of Captain Sanders's sons also served in the Rangers: Jesse C. was in Company A in 1901–1902, later becoming a peace officer. On June 3, 1915, he reenlisted in the Rangers, serving in Companies A and B until September 9, 1915, when he was discharged. Son Albert F. had been a peace officer when he enlisted in Ranger Company G on December 10, 1917. He was transferred to Company I, and in December, 1918, was fired.

10. *Handbook*, III, 803; *AS*, July 31, 1910, April 22, 23, 1911.

11. AG to Chief of Staff, Dept. of Texas, February 13, 1911, AGC.

12. MR, Company D, January 31, 1911, AGC.

13. Peyton Edwards to Hutchings, February 15, 1911, AGC.

14. See, for example, Hughes to Hutchings, February 16 and 27, 1911, AGC; F. H. Lancaster report, February 1, 1911, reel 1, BI.

15. MR, Company A, March 31, 1911, AGC; C. L. Sonnichsen, *Pass of the North: Four Centuries on the Rio Grande* (El Paso: Texas Western Press, 1968), 393–394.

16. MR, Company B, March 31, 1911; M. E. Bailey to Colonel L. T. Rogers, March 8, 1911, AGC.

17. Gen. [Hugh L.] Scott to Adjutant General, State of Texas, February 4, 1911, CP; U.S. vs. Francisco I. Madero et al., no. 771, U.S. Commissioner, El Paso, FRC-FW.

18. Proclamation, February 11, 1911, CP. A copy is in RDS, 812.00/809; Joaquín D. Casasús to Colquitt, July 31, 1911, CP. See also file 90755-495, RDJ; G. R. Matthews report, May 7, 1913, reel 3, BI.

19. Colquitt to Taft, February 23, 1911, 812.00/854, RDS; Colquitt did not hesitate to interfere in the daily operations of the Ranger Force. For example, he offered to the sheriff of Bexar County, John Tobin, the services of either of the Ranger captains to help investigate a sensational murder case in San Antonio. Governor to Tobin, April 5, 1911, AGC.

20. Hughes to Colonel Emmett E. Walker, April 13, 1911, AGC.

21. Hughes to Colquitt, April 6, 1911, CP; Hutchings to H. A. Schrock, April 17, 1911; Hughes to Hutchings, April 19, 1911, AGC.

22. Hughes to Hutchings, April 22 and 24, 1911; MR, Company A, April 30, 1911, AGC.

23. MR, Company B, April 30, 1911, AGC; Hutchings to Governor, April 20, 1911, CP.

24. Hughes to Hutchings, May 9, 1911, AGC.

25. Hughes to Colquitt, May 12, 1911, CP.

26. Colquitt to Hughes, May 15, 1911, AGC.

27. Ryan to Hutchings, May 26, 1911; George Head to same, June 1 and 19, 1911, AGC.

28. AG to Hughes, May 26, 1911, AGC.

29. Hughes to Hutchings, May 29, 1911; see also Assistant Quartermaster General to Hughes, June 27, 1911, AGC.

30. *AS*, August 10, 1911.

31. MR, Company A, May 31, 1911, AGC.

32. Hughes to Hutchings, June 16, 1911, AGC.

33. S. J. Isaacks to Colquitt, July 24, 1911; E. R. York to same, July 25, 1911; MR, Company A, July 31, 1911, AGC; *EPMT*, July 24–30, August 1, 3, 7, 25, 29, 30, 31, September 1, 3, 8, 9, 11–14, 18, November 4, 1911; *BDH*, May 11, 1914.

34. *AS*, March 4, 1910.

35. Ibid., June 20–July 7, 1911.

36. Ibid., August 12, 1911.

37. MR, Company B, June 30 and July 31, 1911, AGC.

38. A. J. Bell to AG, July 6, 1911, AGC.

39. *Biennial Report of the Adjutant General* (January 23, 1911, to December 31, 1912), 9.

40. Hughes to Hutchings, July 7, 1911, AGC. Harry Moore's career was not atypical. He'd served in Company D, resigning in 1904. He became a cowboy, then served in Company D again in 1909–1910, continuing in that unit when it was redesignated as Company A in 1911. Moore resigned on July 5, 1911, to be a mounted Customs inspector, remaining in that post through 1915. In 1916 he became sheriff and tax collector of Hudspeth County, serving until 1920. Captain Hughes actually enlisted two men to replace Moore: J. Mayfield on August 14 and Joseph L. Anders (a future Ranger captain) on August 29. These enlistments brought Company A up to a total of eight. See MR, Company A, August 31, 1911, AGC.

41. Carnes to Hutchings, August 7, 1911; Assistant Quartermaster General to Hughes, August 24, 1911, WC.

42. Mrs. E. R. Jenson to Colquitt, August 17, 1911, AGC.

43. Sterling, *Trails and Trials*, 460, 16.

44. Mrs. E. R. Jenson to Mrs. Colquitt, August 17, 1911, AGC.

45. Colquitt to Hutchings, August 22, 1911; Acting Adjutant General to Mrs. E. R. Jenson; same to Sergeant Levi Davis, August 30, 1911, AGC.

46. Sterling, *Trails and Trials*, 333.

47. MR, Company A, August 31, 1911; Hughes to Colquitt, September 24, 1911, CP.

48. Rudolph Foster to Colquitt, September 19, 1911, Colquitt Papers, CAH.

49. Colquitt to W. R. Blaine, September 30, 1911, Colquitt Papers, CAH.

50. *Expense of Patrolling the Boundary in Texas*, Senate Documents, 62nd Cong., 2nd sess. (Serial 6,175) Doc. No. 404. Washington, D.C.: Government Printing Office, 1912.

51. Headquarters Ranger Force, General Orders No. 5, October 2, 1911, AGC.

52. William Smith to Colquitt, October 6, 13, 25, 1911, CP; *EPH*, May 29, June 7, 1911, February 10, 1912. Captain J. Monroe Fox's son, James Leslie, served as a Ranger in Emergency Company No. 1 from September 30 to November 4, 1920, when he resigned.

53. General Orders No. 5; J. J. Sanders to Richard C. Hawkins, November 23, 1911, AGC.

54. Hutchings to [Colquitt], October 3, 1911, CP. On occasion Colquitt intervened in personnel matters. On October 10, the governor forwarded to Hutchings a letter from his friend F. P. Williams of DeKalb, Texas, who wanted to secure a place for his son in the Rangers. Colquitt hoped Hutchings would immediately communicate with Williams if there were still vacancies. Hutchings wrote to Williams, enclosing a blank oath of office and stating that railroad passes would be sent. Colquitt to Hutchings, October 10, 1911, AGC. Williams's son, however, apparently never enlisted.

55. Wilbur reports, July 6, 1911, reel 2, August 28, 1911, reel 1; Thompson reports, July 7, 11, 15, 26, 1911, reel 1, BI.

56. The whole affair is treated in greater detail in Charles H. Harris III and Louis R. Sadler, "The 1911 Reyes Conspiracy: The Texas Side," *Southwestern Historical Quarterly*, LXXXIII, No. 4 (April 1980), 325–348.

57. *San Antonio News*, September 2, 1970.

58. *A Twentieth Century History of Southwest Texas*. 2 vols. (Chicago: Lewis Publishing Co., 1907), I, 439; *SAE*, March 3, 1911; *LWT*, August 21, September 18, 1910; *BDH*, January 6 and 10, 1912.

59. Chapa was a slick political operator. In 1910, while Madero was in San Antonio organizing his revolution, Chapa had worked both sides of the street. His newspaper followed a pro-Díaz line, while at the same time Chapa maintained relations with Madero. David H. Johnson, "Exiles and Intrigue: Francisco I. Madero and the Mexican Revolutionary Junta in San Antonio, 1910–1911," (M.A. thesis, Trinity University, 1975), 118, 168–169.

60. (tel.) Chapa to Colquitt, July 24 and November 14, 1911, Colquitt Papers, CAH.

61. Lewis L. Gould, *Progressives and Prohibitionists: Texas Democrats in the Wilson Era* (Austin: Texas State Historical Association, 1992; originally published by the University of Texas Press, 1973), 28–57, 88; AG to Chapa, February 6, 1911; Headquarters, Texas National Guard, General Orders No. 48, June 24, 1911, AGC.

62. Luther T. Ellsworth to Secretary of State, February 10, 1911, RDS, 812.00/815; *SAE*, March 28, November 4, 1911; Chapa to Colquitt, August 8, 1911; Colquitt to Chapa, September 23, October 7, 1911, CP.

63. *A Twentieth Century History*, II, 78; *LWT*, February 13, 20, March 27, April 3, July 24, August 7, 1910.

64. H. A. Thompson to [Colonel Edgar Z. Steever, September 10, 1912, no. 42099, Adjutant General's Office, Department of Texas, Record Cards, 1909–12, Records of the United States Army Continental Commands, 1821–1920, RG 393, National Archives and Records Service, Washington, D.C.

65. H. A. Thompson to Stanley W. Finch, October 19, 1911, reel 2; F. H. Lancaster reports, October 17, 18, 1911, reel 2, October 19, reel 1, BI.

66. AG to J. H. Winn, October 14, 1911, AGC.

67. *SAE*, November 17, 1911.

68. C. E. Lane to Hutchings, November 19, 1911, AGC.

69. Colquitt to Taft, November 17, 1911, Colquitt Papers, CAH.

70. Colquitt to Taft, November 18, 1911; Taft to Colquitt, November 19, 1911, CP; [Major W. S.] Scott to AG, November 18, 1911, WC.

71. Colquitt to Hutchings, November 22, 1911, AGC.

72. Colquitt to Hutchings, November 21, 1911, AGC; same to Taft, November 22, 1911, CP.

73. Colquitt to Hutchings, November 18, 1911; E. R. York to same, November 13, 1911, AGC.

74. Hutchings to Colquitt, November 19, 1911, CP.

75. *LWT*, December 28, 1913.

76. Ibid.; MR, Company B, November 30, 1911, AGC. Major Charles B. Hagadorn to Adjutant General, Department of Texas, November 20, 1911, 5761-343, MID. See also the following telegrams: Hutchings to Colquitt, November 19, 1911; Colquitt to Hutchings, November 19, 1911, CP; Hutchings to Colquitt, December 1, 1911, WC.

77. Hagadorn to AG, Department of Texas, December 1, 1911, 5761-358, MID. A copy is in F. H. Lancaster report, November 30, 1911, reel 3, BI. For the army's key role in crushing the Reyes conspiracy, see the testimony of S. Fitzhugh Loughborough in *Revolutions in Mexico*, 62nd Cong., 2nd sess. (Washington, D.C.: Government Printing Office, 1913), 82–83. See also José C. Valadés, ed. "Los secretos del reyismo: diez años de intensa lucha," the memoirs of Dr. Samuel Espinosa de los Monteros, published under different subtitles in *La Prensa* (San Antonio) from October 23 to December 11, 1932.

78. (tel.) Hutchings to Colquitt, November 20, 1911, CP.

79. E. R. York to Hutchings, November 20, 1911; same to Carl T. Ryan, November 20, 1911; Ryan to AG, November 20, 1911; Benjamin Kowalski to same, November 20, 1911; George J. Head to Hutchings, November 20, 1911; York to Head, November 20, 1911, AGC; Colquitt to Hutchings, November 20, 1911, CP.

80. Colquitt to Hutchings, November 20, 1911, CP.

81. Fox to Hutchings, November 23 and 24, 1911, AGC.

82. Colquitt to Hutchings, November 23 and 27, 1911; Hutchings to York, November 23, 1911; York to Head, November 23, 1911; Hutchings to Governor, November 26, 1911, AGC. Colquitt recalled Hutchings to Austin on November 27; *BDH*, November 23, 1911.

83. MR, Company A, November 30 and December 31, 1911; Hughes to AG, November 30 and December 1, 1911; Hutchings to Colquitt, December 1, 1911, AGC.

84. MR, Company A, December 31, 1911, AGC; U.S. vs. Rafael L. Molina et al., no. 983, U.S. Commissioner, El Paso, and no. 1564, District Court, El Paso, FRC-FW. See also Hughes to AG, December 24, 1911, WC; *EPMT*, December 3, 1911.

85. U.S. vs. Roque Segura, no. 147, U.S. Commissioner, Marfa, FRC-FW.

86. Captain J. N. Munro to AG, Department of Texas, December 25, 1911, 5761-370, MID. See also Major Charles B. Hagadorn to same, December 25, 1911, 5761-371, MID.

87. Headquarters, Fort McIntosh to Commanding General, Southern Department, April 10,

1913, Southern Department file 16-347. The comment was by Randolph Robinson [sic—Robertson], Clerk of the District Court, Laredo.

88. Memorandum for Huntington Wilson, December 2, 1911, 812.00/2540, RDS.

89. "Cresse" [Charles E. Jones] report, January 31, 1918, reel 19, BI; see also Harris and Sadler, "The 1911 Reyes Conspiracy," 37–46.

90. Rodolfo Reyes, *De mi vida: memorias políticas*, vol. 1 (1899–1913) (Madrid: Biblioteca Nueva, 1929), 168–185.

91. Attorney General to Secretary of State, December 18, 1911, 812.00/2640, RDS.

92. Colquitt to F. Thumm, January 29, 1912, Colquitt Papers, CAH.

93. Hutchings to Colquitt, December 19, 1911, CP; U.S. vs. Bernardo Reyes, et al., no. 93, U.S. Commissioner, and nos. 552, 893, 2060, District Court, Laredo; U.S. vs. Ishmael [sic] Reyes Retana, et al., no. 2060, District Court, Brownsville, FRC-FW; *BDH*, January 2, 1912. See also the list and brief descriptions of the Mexican revolutionists involved, in Headquarters, Fort McIntosh to Commanding General, Southern Department, April 10, 1913, file 16-347, SD.

94. *BDH*, February 5, 1912. An attempt to explain Burns's actions is found in Lock McDaniel to Attorney General, February 14, 1912, 90755-1315, RDJ.

95. Case 27-219-198 (for Chapa) and 27-418-329 (for Sánchez), General Records of the Pardon Attorney's Office, RG 204, National Archives and Records Service, Washington, D.C.

96. *SAE*, February 19, 1924.

Chapter 4

1. Colquitt to Hutchings, January 12, 1912; Hutchings to Colquitt, January 13, 1912, AGC; Randolph Robertson to Gen. Joseph W. Duncan, February 1, 1912, 40749, General Correspondence, Department of Texas, 1870–1913, Records of United States Army Continental Commands, 1821–1920, RG 393, National Archives and Records Service, Washington, D.C. See also Lock McDaniel to Attorney General, March 8, 1912, 90755-1385, RDJ.

2. AG to Hughes, January 13, 1912, AGC.

3. Henry L. Stimson, "Memorandum for the President," January 18, 1912, WC.

4. AG to Colquitt, January 10, 1912, AGC.

5. "Disposition of Ranger Force January 8—1912," CP; AG to Fox, January 8, 1912; Sanders to Hutchings, January 9, 1912; Hutchings to Sanders, January 10, 1912, AGC.

6. Colquitt to Hutchings, January 12, 1912, AGC.

7. Taft to Colquitt, January 22, 1912, WC; AG to Hughes, Sanders, and Fox, January 27, 1912, AGC.

8. Smith to Colquitt, March 4 and 19, 1912, CP.

9. Colquitt to Hutchings, February 2, 1912, WC.

10. Hughes to Governor, February 1, 1912; Same to AG, February 1, 1912, CP. For a scholarly treatment of these events, see Michael C. Meyer, *Mexican Rebel: Pascual Orozco and the Mexican Revolution, 1910–1915* (Lincoln: University of Nebraska Press, 1967), 46–52.

11. Taft to Colquitt, February 2, 1912; Colquitt to President, February 2, 1912, CP.

12. Hughes to Governor, February 7, 1912, CP.

13. Knox to Governor, February 7, 1912, CP.

14. Hutchings referred to Section 99 of the 1905 Militia Law. AG to Colquitt, February 9, 1912, AGC.

15. Colquitt to Hutchings, February 9, 1912, AGC; *El Paso Times* to Secretary of State P. C. Knox, February 9, 1912, WC. Colquitt at the bottom of this telegram stated his refusal to consent and forwarded the message to Washington.

16. Hutchings to Hughes, February 9, 1912, WC.

17. Knox to Governor, February 9, 1912; Huntington Wilson to Governor, February 13, 1912, CP.

18. Hutchings to Colquitt, February 11, 1912, CP.

19. Colquitt to Taft, February 24, 1912, no file number, RDJ.

20. Hutchings to Colquitt (two letters), February 12, 1912 ; see also same to same, February 13, 1912, CP.

21. Colquitt to Hutchings, February 16, 1912; same to Taft, February 16, 1912, WC; General J. W. Duncan to Colquitt, February 17 and 20, 1912, Colquitt Papers, CAH; "Copy of indorsements [sic] on letter of Governor O. B. Colquitt to Brigadier General Duncan . . . ," February 17, 1912; Hutchings to Colquitt, February 19 and March 5, 1912; Duncan to Colquitt, February 26, 1912, CP.

22. AG to Governor (two telegrams), February 15, 1912; same to same (letter and telegram), February 16 and 19, 1912, CP.

23. Hutchings to Governor (telegram and letter), February 17, 1912, CP; Colquitt to Hutchings, February 17, 1912, AGC.

24. Hutchings to Governor, February 18 and 19, 1912; Colquitt to Hutchings, February 18, 1912, AGC; Edwards to Hutchings, February 22, 1912; Hutchings to Edwards, February 22, 1912, CP.

25. Duncan to Governor, February 26, 1912, Colquitt Papers, CAH; Colquitt to Edwards, February 26, 1912; same to Duncan, February 26, 1912, CP.

26. Colquitt to Taft, February 25, 1912; Taft to Colquitt, February 28, 1912, CP.

27. Hughes to Governor (two telegrams), February 27, 1912; see also Captain William Smith to Colquitt, March 4, 1912, CP.

28. Hughes to AG, February 29, 1912, WC; MR, Company A and Company B, February 29, 1912, AGC; Captain Sanders reported very strong anti-Mexican feelings at Del Rio. Sanders to Hutchings, March 20, 1912, CP.

29. Meyer, *Mexican Rebel*, 52–66.

30. Hughes to Governor, March 20 [?], 1912; Hutchings to Colquitt (two letters), March 25, 1912, CP; Francisco [?] Espinosa y Rondero to Colquitt, March 26, 1912, Colquitt Papers, CAH; Hughes to Governor, March 26, 1912, CP; Hughes to Hutchings, March 27, 1912, AGC; M. A. Esteva to Colquitt, March 29, 1912, Colquitt Papers, CAH. For a discussion of munitions smuggling in El Paso, see Charles H. Harris III and Louis R. Sadler, "The 'Underside' of the Mexican Revolution: El Paso, 1912," *The Americas: A Quarterly Review of Inter-American Cultural History*, XXXIX (July 1982), 69–83.

31. Sanders to Hutchings, March 26, 1912, AGC.

32. General J. W. Duncan to Hutchings, March 2, 1912, AGC.

33. Captain J. N. Munro to AG, Department of Texas, March 4, 1912, AGC.

34. Ibid.

35. Fox to Hutchings, March 4, 1912; Hutchings to Fox (two telegrams), March 4, 1912, WC.

36. Captain J. N. Munro to AG, Department of Texas, March 5, 1912, WC; Dr. Samuel Espinoza de los Monteros, who had been involved in the Reyes conspiracy, had been arrested earlier. García claimed he was on the American side of the bridge when arrested; an eyewitness said not. Deposition of José I. García, March 7, 1912; George J. Head to Captain Monroe Fox, March 7, 1912, WC.

37. Captain J. T. Conrad to AG, Department of Texas, WC; J. W. Poole and C. W. Kilgore to Colquitt, March 18, 1912; Hughes to AG, March 20 and 24, 1912; MR, Company A, March 31, 1912, AGC.

38. Hughes to AG, March 6, 1912, WC.

39. Colonel E. Z. Steever to AG, Dept. of Texas, March 7, 1912, AGC.

40. AG to Hughes, April 15, 1912, AGC; Hughes to Governor, April 21, 1912, CP; MR, Company A, April 30, 1912, AGC; L. E. Ross reports, April 22, 27, 1912, reel 1, and August 17, 1912, reel 2, BI.

41. H. P. Cole to AG, April 11, 1912; AG to Cole, April 15, 1912; MR, Company A, April 30, 1912, AGC.

42. Sanders to Hutchings, April 12, 1912, CP; see also same to same, April 21, 1912, with enclosed "Scout Report of April 20, 1912," AGC; E. P. Warren to Eugene Nolte, April 12, 1912, RDJ.

43. Hutchings to Colquitt, April 5, 1912; see also same to same, April 2, 1912, CP. For additional details regarding this disputed election, see State of Texas, *ex rel* Louis Cobolini vs. A. B. Cole, no. 2353, District Court, Cameron County, (November 11 & 22, 1912), AGC.

44. Hutchings to Fox, May 18, 1912; AG to W. A. Hinnant, May 18, 1912; Fox to Hutchings, May 19, 1912; W. B. Hopkins to same, May 31, 1912; AG to Hopkins, June 5, 1912, AGC.

45. Smith to Hutchings, April 15, 1912, AGC; same to same, April 15, 1912, WC; AG to Colquitt, May 4, 1912, AGC.

46. Peyton J. Edwards to Hutchings, May 19, 1912; Colquitt to same, May 19, 1912; Hughes to same, May 19, 1912; MR, Company B, May 31, 1912, AGC; Sanders to Hutchings, June 9, 12, 1912; AG to Sanders, June 11, 1912, WC.

47. C. R. Moore to AG, May 21, 1912, WC; MR, Company A, May 31, 1912, AGC; C. R. Moore to Hughes, June 2, 1912; Lt. Clarence A. Dougherty to same, June 1, 1912; Hughes to AG, June 2, 1912, WC; AG to Colquitt, June 6, 1912; Colquitt to Hutchings, June 10, 1912, AGC.

48. *EPMT*, April 8, 1914.

49. See, for example, L. E. Ross reports, July 9, 1912, reel 4; July 27, 1912, reel 3; July 29, 31, August 29, 31, 1912, reel 2, BI.

50. L. E. Ross report, July 29, 1912, reel 4, BI.

51. Testimony of Adolph Krakauer, *Revolutions in Mexico*, 648–652, 654.

52. Jesse C. Adkins to Secretary of the Treasury, October 14, 1912, 90755–1857, RDJ.

53. *BDH*, January 15, 1913.

54. Edwards to Hutchings, June 17, 1912; Colquitt to same (three telegrams), June 18, 19, and 23, 1912; Hutchings to Edwards, June 18, 1912; same to Colquitt, June 19, 1912; Colquitt to Taft, June 28, 1912; Taft to Colquitt, June 29, 1912, AGC.

55. Hughes to AG, June 25 and 27, 1912, WC; same to same, June 30, 1912, AGC. For a more detailed account of revolutionary intrigue in El Paso, see Harris and Sadler, "The 'Underside.'"

56. MR, Company A, June 30, 1912, AGC.

57. Hughes to AG, July 1, 1912, AGC.

58. Hughes to AG, July 3 and 6, 1912, WC.

59. Hughes to AG, July 7 and 11, 1912, WC; Captain F. A. Logan to AG, July 1, 1912, CP.

60. MR, Company B, July 31, 1912; Smith to Hutchings, July 10 and 23, 1912, AGC.

61. MR, Company A, July 31, 1912, AGC; Captain E. E. Haskell to Adjutant, Patrol District of El Paso, July 26, 1912, 41817, Department of Texas.

62. MR, Company B, June 30, 1912, AGC.

63. Sanders to Hutchings, July 28, 1912; MR, Company B, July 31, 1912; MR, Company A, August 31, 1912, AGC; Nolte to Attorney General, July 27, 1912, 90755–1649, RDJ.

64. Meyer, *Mexican Rebel*, 83.

65. William Smith to Hutchings, August 1, 1912; Edwards to same, August 2, 1912; Sanders to same, August 5, 1912; Hutchings to Smith, August 6, 1912; Smith to Hutchings, August 19, 1912; Hughes to same, August 8, 1912; York to same, August 10, 1912; MR, Company A, August 31, 1912, AGC; Hughes to Governor, August 11 and 13, 1912, CP; L. E. Ross report, August 13, 1912, reel 2, BI.

66. Colquitt to President Madero, August 6, 1912, Colquitt Papers, CAH; Hughes to AG, September 15 and 18, 1912, AGC; same to same, September 28, 1912, WC; Pat Craighead to Hughes, September 2, 1912, CP.

67. Peyton J. Edwards to Hutchings, September 7, 1912, CP; Colquitt to same, September 9 and 28, 1912; York to Edwards, September 11, 1912, AGC; Colquitt to Alvey A. Adee, September 28, 1912, WC; Hutchings to Colquitt, September 30, 1912, AGC and CP; Huntington Wilson to Governor, September 10 and 30, 1912; Hughes to same, September 11 and 12, 1912; Alvey

A. Adee to same, September 28, 1912, CP; Hutchings to Hughes, October 1, 1912; same to Sanders, October 1 and 3, 1912, AGC; Huntington Wilson to Colquitt, October 1, 1912, CP.

68. Colquitt to Taft, October 22, 1912, and Alvey A. Adee to Colquitt, October 31, 1912, 812.00/5372, RDS.

69. Hughes to Governor, September 27, 1912, CP; same to same, September 28, 1912, WC.

70. John Scofield to AG, September 9, 1912; Office of Auditor for the War Department to State of Texas, (September 17, 1912), AGC.

71. Hutchings to Colquitt, October 4, 1912, CP. Captain William Smith was discharged in August as part of the reduction in force.

72. Hutchings to Colquitt, September 13 and 16, 1912, CP. By comparison, the New Mexico Mounted Police, consisting of a captain, a sergeant, and four privates, had an appropriation of $12,000 in 1912. The salaries were considerably higher than those of Texas Rangers: captain, $2,000 per year; sergeant, $1,500 per year; and privates, $1,200. *Laws of the State of New Mexico . . . 1912*, 206.

73. Colquitt to Hutchings, October 16, 1912; [AG] to Sanders, October 17, 1912, AGC.

74. Governor to Ryan, October 14, 1912; Hughes to AG, October 20 and 25, 1912; same to Governor, October 20, 1912, AGC; Colquitt to Hutchings, October 21, 1912, WC.

75. J. M. Hansbro to Colquitt, October 27, 1912; Colquitt to Hutchings, October 28, 1912; same to Hansbro, October 28, 1912; MR, Company A, October 31, 1912, AGC.

76. Colquitt to Hutchings, October 28 and 29, 1912, AGC.

77. [AG] to Sanders, October 17, 1912; Sanders to Hutchings, October 23, 1912; AG to Colquitt, October 29, 1912, AGC and CP. Captain Fox's Monthly Returns, incidentally, are of little value. Unlike Captain Hughes, Fox kept very sloppy records, and his Monthly Returns mainly reflect the number of miles he traveled rather than what he and his men actually did. See, for example, MR, Company C, October 31, 1912, AGC.

78. Colquitt to Hutchings (two letters), October 29, 1912, AGC; Hutchings to Colquitt, October 30, 1912, CP.

79. Colquitt to Hutchings, November 1, 1912; AG to Hughes, November 2, 1912; H. Oberwetter to Hutchings, November 10, 1912, AGC. Calls for Rangers continued. For instance, on November 9, Dudley S. Barker, the sheriff at Fort Stockton, sent Hutchings a telegram: "Had to kill two railroad Mexicans and wounded four more. Send me two men at once." Hughes got the assignment. Barker to Hutchings, November 9, 1912; York to Hughes, November 9, 1912, AGC.

80. *BDH*, November 5, 7, 8, 11, 1913; Fox to Hutchings, August 10, 1912, AGC. McAlister was a farmer in Hidalgo County when he enlisted in Company C on November 22, 1911. He served honorably until February 1, 1912, when he was discharged in the reduction in the Ranger force. He then became a Cameron County deputy until 1915, when he became a deputy sheriff in Duval County.

81. Fox to Hutchings, October 2, 1912, CP.

82. Hutchings to Colquitt, October 4, 1912, CP.

83. Ibid.

84. Sanders to Hutchings, November 10, 1912, WC.

85. Sanders to Hutchings, November 14 and 18, 1912; Hutchings to Sanders (telegram and letter), November 14, 1912, WC.

86. Committee report, November 20, 1912, WC.

87. M. Bell to Colquitt, November 23, 1912; Colquitt to Hutchings, November 25, 1912; AG to Sanders, November 25, 1912, WC.

88. Statement of Captain J. J. Sanders and R. C. Hawkins, November 30, 1912, WC; see also MR, Company B, November 31, 1912, AGC; "Proceedings," 1275–1281, 1283–1298, 1383–1388, 1392–1395, 1495–1501.

89. Grand jury report, "Proceedings," 1407.

90. Ibid.

91. Ibid.
92. Sanders to Hutchings, December 10, 1912, WC, includes a copy of the "Warning."
93. Tucker to AG, December 24, 1912, AGC.
94. Hutchings to Colquitt, December 30, 1912, CP.

Chapter 5

1. Sanders to Hutchings, January 25, 1913, AGC; *BDH*, January 25, 1913.
2. *BDH*, March 10, September 19, 20, 22, October 15, December 9, 10, 1913. The cases were eventually dismissed. "Proceedings," 393.
3. *BDH*, October 4, 1913.
4. M. Díaz report, February 8, 1917, reel 13, BI; it is usually impossible to determine exactly what Fox did, since his Monthly Returns list only places visited, dates, and miles traveled. See, for example, MR, Company C, January 31, February 28, March 31, 1913, AGC; *EPMT*, July 15, 31, 1913.
5. Colquitt to President, January 30, 1913, RDJ.
6. *EPMT*, January 31, 1913.
7. Colquitt to President, February 12, 1913, 90755–1938, RDJ.
8. AG to Colquitt, January 24, 30, 1913; same to Hughes, January 30, 1913; Hughes to AG, January 30, 1913, AGC.
9. Moore to AG, February 5, 1913, AGC.
10. Sanders to Hutchings, January 30, 1913; MR, Company B, January 31, 1913, AGC.
11. He was back in Lockhart from January 30 to February 5, February 15–18, March 8–10, 21–26, April 3–6. MR, Company B, February 28, March 31, April 30, 1913; Coopwood and Ross to Hutchings, February 17, 1913, AGC.
12. Hughes to AG, February 1, 3, 4, 5, 1913; Sanders to Hutchings, February 5, 1913, AGC.
13. Hughes to AG, February 6, 1913, AGC.
14. For Huerta, see Michael C. Meyer, *Huerta: A Political Portrait* (Lincoln: University of Nebraska Press, 1972).
15. Venustiano Carranza to Samuel Belden, May 17, 1913, no. 189; same to Willard L. Simpson, May 17, 1913, no. 190; same to Colquitt, May 17, 1913, no. 200; Colquitt to Carranza, June 6, 1913, no. 394; Carranza to Colquitt, June 16, 1913, no. 478, Venustiano Carranza Archive, Centro de Estudios de Historia de México, Departamento Cultural de Condumex, S. A., Mexico City.
16. AG to Sanders, February 6, 1913; Sanders to Hutchings, February 7, 12, 1913, AGC.
17. Barnes reports, February 15, 17, 18, 20, 24, 1913, and Thompson report, February 17, 1913, reel 3, BI; Lieutenant Claude B. Bullette to AG, February 15, 1913; John A. Valls to same, February 16, 1913, AGC.
18. Lieutenant Edward M. Matson to AG, February 21, 1913, AGC.
19. George Head to Hutchings, February 17, 18, 1913; W. A. Rutledge to same, February 17, 1913, AGC.
20. *BDH*, February 20, 22, 25–28, 1913; Gen. E. Z. Steever to Colquitt, March 17, 1913, AGC; Hutchings to Colquitt, February 27, 1913, CP.
21. *EPMT*, February 25, 1913.
22. Colquitt to Hutchings, February 15, 1913, AGC.
23. *BDH*, April 4, 1913.
24. Sanders to AG, February 19, March 3, 1913; [AG] to Sanders, February 19, 1913; same to Jeff D. Randolph, February 19, 1913; F. L. Kippenbroch to Hutchings, March 10, 1913, AGC.
25. Hutchings to Hughes, February 19, 1913; Hughes to Hutchings (telegram and letter), February 19, 1913; same to same, February 23, 1913; D. G. Knight to Hughes, March 3, 1913, AGC; *EPMT*, February 18, 19, 1913.

26. Hutchings to Hughes, February 22, 1913, AGC.

27. AG to Colquitt, February 10, 1913, RRM.

28. Hughes to AG, February 22, 1913, AGC.

29. Hughes to AG, February 23, 25, 1913; D. G. Knight to Hughes, February 24, 1913, AGC.

30. Sanders to Hutchings, March 11, 1913, AGC.

31. F. L. Kippenbroch to Hutchings, March 17, 1913, AGC.

32. Sanders to Hutchings, March 13, 1913, AGC.

33. Lieutenant E. M. Matson to Hutchings, March 17, 1913, AGC.

34. *LWT*, April 6, May 11, 25, June 6, 8, 22, July 20, 1913; Barnes reports February 19, 26, March 30, 31, April 1, May 17, 1913, reel 3, BI; Lieutenant Edward M. Matson to AG, October 21, 1913, AGC; *EPMT*, June 6, 1913.

35. Assistant AG to Sanders, March 16, 1913; same to Hughes, March 19, 1913, AGC.

36. Captain Henry L. Newbold to Chief of the Texas Rangers, June 17, 1913; Hutchings to Newbold, June 20, 1913; Major J. D. Leitch to AG, June 23, 1913, AGC.

37. J. D. Leitch to AG, June 23, 1913, AGC.

38. Captain James H. Reeves to Hutchings, July 19, 1913, AGC.

39. Hutchings to James H. Reeves, July 25, 1913, AGC.

40. J. E. Vaughan to Hutchings, March 24, 1913, AGC.

41. Hughes to AG, March 30, 1913, AGC.

42. Captain Fox to Hutchings, April 2, 1913; [Captain George] Head to same, April 16, 1913, AGC; A. M. Tinney to Senator Morris Sheppard, March 6, 1913; W. W. Bogel to same, February 25, 1913, in files 656, 663, 679, 680, SD.

43. U.S. Customs Letter Press Book, Saluria District, 1913, 376–384, FRC-FW; see also Captain Joseph S. Herron to Commanding General, Southern Department, June 11, 1913, no. 1497, SD; E. M. Blanford reports, March 3, 1913, reel 13, BI; *EPMT*, February 11, 12, 13, 15, 17, 19, 1913. For an account of this incident sympathetic to Cano, see Tony Cano and Ann Sochat, *Bandido: The True Story of Chico Cano, the Last Western Bandit* (Canutillo, Tex.: Reata Publishing, 1997), 54–59. For efforts to catch Cano and his gang see S. Engleking to Attorney General, March 11, 1913; W. M. Rice to Supervising Agent, Treasury Department, February 20, 1913; J. A. Harvin to Secretary of the Treasury, February 17, 1913, all in 90755-H-3, RDJ.

44. Hughes to AG, April 1, 1913, AGC; *BDH*, April 2, 1913.

45. Ira Cline to Hughes, April 10, 1913, AGC.

46. Colquitt to Hutchings, April 18, 1913; Hutchings to Colquitt, April 22, 1913, AGC.

47. Moore to E. R. York, March 7, 1913, AGC.

48. Moore to Hughes, April __, 1913, AGC; *EPMT*, April 6, 1913, April 8, 9, 1914.

49. E. R. York to Hughes, January 15, 1913; Hughes to AG, January 15, March 10, 16, 30, 1913, AGC. Scott Russell's younger brother, Sam M. Russell, also served in Company A, from May 11 to September 30, 1914.

50. Edwards to Hughes, April 19, 1913; Hughes to AG, April 23, 1913, AGC.

51. *EPMT*, April 20, 23–25, 1913.

52. Ibid., December 20, 1913.

53. Ibid., February 2, 3, 1915, June 20, 1913.

54. Hughes to AG, June 23, 24, 1913, AGC; *EPMT*, June 24–26, 28, 1913; *BDH*, June 24, 1913; *Biennial Report of the Adjutant General of Texas, From January 1, 1913, to December 31, 1914* (Austin: Von Boeckmann-Jones Co., 1915), 10; *EPH*, June 23–26, 30, 1913.

55. Hughes to Hutchings, June 24, 1913, AGC.

56. Hutchings to Hughes, June 24, 1913, AGC.

57. *EPMT*, June 24, 1913.

58. Hughes to AG, June 26, 1913, AGC; *EPMT*, June 29, July 3, 4, 8, 17, 1913.

59. *EPMT*, July 19, October 8, 9, 26, 29, November 8, December 10, 1913.

60. Ibid., January 14–18, 21–27, 1914.

61. Webster to Hughes, January 31, 1914, AGC.

62. Hutchings to Colquitt, February 3, 1914, AGC.
63. Colquitt to Hutchings, February 4, 5, 24, 1914, AGC; same to same, February 13, 1914; same to Hudspeth, February 5, 1914, AGC.
64. *EPMT*, June 9–13, 15, 16, 18, 19, July 3, 1915.
65. Ira Cline to Hughes, April 27, 1913; D. G. Knight to same, April 28, 1913, AGC.
66. Hughes to AG, May 15, 17, 21, 23, 26, June 15, 1913, AGC.
67. Hughes to AG, June 10, 15, 21, 1913, AGC.
68. BI reports, August 14 and 17, October 2, 1913, 812.00/8500, RDS.
69. Sterling, *Trails and Trials*, 515; BI report, August 14, 1913, 812.00/8500, RDS.
70. *BDH*, June 4, 1913; Ciro de la Garza Treviño, *La Revolución Mexicana en el Estado de Tamaulipas* (México: Editorial Porrúa, 1973), 175–179, 407–414.
71. Hughes to AG, June 24, 26, 28, 30, 1913, AGC.
72. Hughes to AG, July 2, 1913, AGC.
73. Hughes to AG, July 5, 1913; AG to Hughes, July 8, 1913, AGC.
74. Sanders to Hutchings, June 16, 1913, AGC; *EPMT*, June 15, 1913.
75. *EPMT*, June 29, 1913.
76. AG to Sanders, July 18, 1913; same to Hughes, July 18, 1913; Sanders to Hutchings, July 20, 21, 1913, AGC.
77. MR, Company B, July 31, 1913; Sanders to Hutchings, July 22, 28, August 3, 1913; Hughes to AG, July 22, 25, 1913; M. B. Chastain to Colquitt, July 26, 1913, AGC.
78. Hughes to AG, July 25, 1913, AGC.
79. Hughes to AG, July 30, 1913, AGC.
80. Hughes to AG, August 4, 6, 1913, AGC.
81. Hughes to Colonel E. R. York, August 15, 20, 21, 27, 1913; same to Hutchings, August 10, September 14, October 5, 10, 1913, AGC.
82. AG to Ernest G. Woodward, June 21, 1913, AGC.
83. [Captain George] Head to AG, July 24, 1913, AGC.
84. See the replies from congressmen and senators to Hutchings, August 12–18, 1913, AGC.
85. AG to Lieutenant W. Y. Allen, November 11, 1913, AGC.
86. Sanders to Hutchings, September 5, 1913, AGC.
87. Captain Edward M. Matson to Hutchings, October 21, 1913, AGC.
88. Ibid.
89. *EPMT*, June 6, 1913.
90. Acting AG to Sanders, October 6, 1913, AGC.
91. Sanders to Col. E. R. York, October 8, 1913; see also same to same, October 14, 1913, AGC.
92. Hughes to AG, November 6, 1913, AGC.
93. Friedrich Katz, *The Life and Times of Pancho Villa* (Stanford: Stanford University Press, 1998), 222–225; Peyton J. Edwards to Hutchings, November 15, 1913; AG to Edwards, November 15, 1913, AGC; *EPMT*, November 15, 16, 17, 1913.
94. "Report of General Conditions Along the Mexican Border . . ." (hereafter cited as "Weekly report"), Headquarters, Southern Department, November 28, 1913, 5761-A-1, MID.
95. Colquitt to Hutchings, November 26, 1913, AGC.
96. Hutchings to Sanders, November 28, 1913, AGC.
97. Hutchings to Sanders, November 28, 1913; same to Colquitt, November 28, 1913, AGC.
98. Sanders to Hutchings, December 2, 1913; Assistant Quartermaster General to Sanders, December 4, 1913, AGC; *LWT*, December 21, 1913.
99. Sanders to Hutchings, December 8, 1913, AGC.
100. AG to Colquitt, December 6, 1913, RRM.
101. Sanders to Hutchings, December 19, 1913; AG to [Sanders], December 22, 1913; J. D. Randolph to Hutchings, December 30, 1913, AGC.
102. John A. Valls to Hutchings, December 22, 1913, AGC.
103. Colquitt to Hutchings, December 23, 1913, RRM.

104. Sanders to Hutchings, September 15, 1913, AGC.
105. Secretary of War to Secretary of State, September 15, 1913, 812.00/8866, RDS.
106. State of Texas vs. J. M. Rangel et al., no. 1032, District Court, La Salle County, October Term, 1913, WC; 2nd Lieutenant Terry Allen to Colonel F. W. Sibley, September 16, 1913; Commanding Officer, Eagle Pass, Texas, to Commanding General, Southern Department, September 20, 1913, 2356–2491, SD; Secretary of War to Secretary of State, September 15, 1913, 5761-A-1, MID; *BDH*, September 12, 13, 1913.
107. *BDH*, September 15, 18, 1913. For a decidedly pro-PLM account, see W. Dirk Raat, *Revoltosos: Mexico's Rebels in the United States, 1903–1923* (College Station: Texas A & M University Press, 1981), 259–260. For an extensive account based on Charles Cline's interrogation, see BI report, September 24, 1913, 812.00/9114, RDS.
108. *EPMT*, October 24, 1913. See also H. A. Thompson report, September 15, 1913, and R. L. Barnes reports, September 24, 25, 1913, reel 4, BI.
109. Petition to Colquitt, November 15, 1913, Colquitt Papers, CAH; *EPMT*, November 18, 1913; *BDH*, November 17, 1913.
110. Governor to J. A. Hernández et al., November 17, 1913, Colquitt Papers, CAH.
111. "Various True Mexicans" to Colquitt, November 18, 1913, Colquitt Papers, CAH; *EPMT*, November 22, 1913; *BDH*, November 21, 1913.
112. W. T. Gardner to Colquitt, November 20, 1913; see also William Davis to same, November 21, 1913, CP.
113. Colquitt to Hutchings, November 24, 1913, AGC.
114. Guy B. Harrison to Colquitt, November 17, 1913, Colquitt Papers, CAH; Captain Dudley Lansing to AG, November 17, 1913, CP; *EPMT*, November 22, 1913; *BDH*, November 22, 1913.
115. Hughes to AG, September 27, 1913; Hutchings to "J. Reynolds," September 29, 1913, AGC.
116. Hughes to Colquitt, November 24, 1913; Sheriff John Tobin to Hughes, November 22, 1913, Colquitt Papers, CAH.
117. "Voluntary Statement of J. A. Hernandez Before the Grand Jury of Bexar County, Texas," November 21, 1913; Hughes to Colquitt, November 24, 1913; same to AG, November 21, 1913, AGC.
118. H. A. Thompson to W. C. Linden, December 2, 1913; W. C. Linden to Colquitt, December 3, 1913; Colquitt to Linden, December 6, 1913, CP; Hughes to Hutchings, November 28, 30, December 2, 6, 1913; AG to [Hughes], December 8, 1913; "List of signers on telegram to Governor Colquitt . . . ," December 14, 1913, AGC; Hughes to Colquitt, December 11, 1913, CP.
119. *Dallas News*, March 10, 1914, WC.

Chapter 6

1. *LWT*, January 4, 11, 1914; *EPMT*, January 2, 1914.
2. *EPMT*, December 8, 10–11, 1913, January 1–11, 14, 16, 1914.
3. *LWT*, March 1, 1914.
4. *EPMT*, December 31, 1913; MR, Company B, January 31, 1914, AGC.
5. Ashton to Colquitt, March 30, 1914, CP.
6. C. P. Bishop to Hughes, April 28, 1914; Colquitt to Hutchings, April 2, 29, 1914, CP.
7. *EPMT*, January 9, 1914.
8. Ibid., April 4, 12, 1914.
9. Ibid., April 4, 1914.
10. Ibid., April 20, 1914.
11. Hutchings to Colquitt, April 4, 1914, CP.
12. Sanders to Colquitt, February 26, 1914; statement by Dolores Vergara, March 11, 1914. See also M. B. Brown, Jr., to W. P. Webb, September 16, 1930, WC.

13. *LWT*, February 15, 1914; Dallas *News*, February 26, 1914. Citations to the Dallas *News* are from WC.
14. Hutchings to Sanders, February 26, 1914, WC.
15. Ibid.
16. Sanders to Colquitt, February 26, 1914, WC; Assistant Attorney General to Secretary of State, March 16, 1914, reel 9, BI.
17. *LWT*, April 28, May 12, June 2, 23, July 21, 28, August 4, 11, 1912.
18. Ibid., April 6, May 11, 25, June 8, 22, July 20, 1913; Barnes reports, February 19, 26, March 30, 31, April 1, May 17, 1913, reel 3, BI; Captain Edward M. Matson to AG, October 21, 1913, AGC.
19. Statement by Marceo Villareal [sic], March 9, 1914; statement by Ignacio Durán, March 13, 1914; Hughes to AG, March 22, 1914, WC; Robert Lansing to Governor, April 7, 1914, CP.
20. Colquitt to R. W. Roberson, March 3, 1914, Colquitt Papers, CAH.
21. See *LWT*, February 22, 1914.
22. Sanders to Hutchings, February 27, 1914, WC.
23. *LWT*, March 1, 1914.
24. C. R. Moore and C. H. Webster to Hutchings, February 27, 1914, AGC.
25. Hutchings to Matson, February 26, March 3, 1914; Matson to Hutchings, February 26, 27, 28, 1914, WC.
26. B. P. Looney to Colquitt, February 27, 1914, WC.
27. Dallas *News*, March 6, 1914, WC; *EPMT*, February 28, March 1, 1914.
28. Dallas *News*, March 1, 2, 1914, WC; *EPMT*, March 1, 1914.
29. Dallas *News*, March 9, 1914, WC.
30. AG to Colquitt, March 6, 1914; "Report of Captain J. J. Sanders of Recovery of Vergara's Body," March 9, 1914; Statement of Jesús Vergara, March 9, 1914, WC.
31. Dallas *News*, March 10, 1914; Report of Drs. O. J. Cook and W. B. McGregor, March 11, 1914, WC.
32. Scout report, March 31, 1914, RRM.
33. Dallas *News*, March 11, 1914, WC.
34. Ibid., March 12, 1914, WC.
35. Sanders to Colquitt, March 16, 1914; Dallas *News*, March 14, 1914, WC; MR, Company B, March 31, 1914, AGC.
36. See file no. 4325, February 27, 1914, SD.
37. Hutchings to E. R. York, March 13, 1914, AGC.
38. Colquitt to Huerta, March 12, 1914; same to Gen. Miguel P. Alvarez, March 17, 1914; same to Hutchings, March 17, 1914, WC.
39. Huerta to Colquitt, March 17, 1914, WC.
40. Colquitt to Hutchings, March 18–20, 1914; same to Gen. J. Maas, March 18, 1914, WC; same to Hutchings, March 21, 1914, CP.
41. Gonzalo de A. Fernández to Hutchings, April 8, 1914; Hutchings to Fernández, March 30, April 9, 18, 20, 1914, AGC; Sanders to Hutchings, March 27, April 14, 18, 1914; AG to Colquitt, April 17, 1914, CP; Colquitt to Hutchings, April 18, 1914, WC.
42. E. R. York to H. N. Gray, March 17, 1914; Gray to York, March 17, 1914; Dallas *News*, March 25, 1914, WC. In September, 1915, Captain Sanders arrested an Apolonio Rodríguez in El Paso, convinced he was one of Vergara's kidnapers. Sanders took the prisoner to Laredo for identification, but he proved to be the wrong man and was released. *LWT*, September 26, 1915.
43. Hughes to Hutchings, April 20, 1914, WC; same to same, April 22, 1914, AGC.
44. *LWT*, March 29, 1914.
45. Griffith to Commanding General, Southern Department, March 25, 1914, file 4325, SD.
46. Colquitt to Hutchings, March 21, 1914, CP. See also Colquitt to Hutchings, March 25, 1914, and AG to Colquitt, March 26, 1914, CP.

47. Bliss to Griffith, March 25, 1914, file 4325, SD.

48. Webb, *Texas Rangers*, 486–495; Don M. Coerver and Linda B. Hall, *Texas and the Mexican Revolution: A Study in State and National Border Policy 1910–1920* (San Antonio: Trinity University Press, 1984), 65–74.

49. See, for example, *BDH*, March 12, 13, 16, 1914.

50. Ibid., March 16–18, 20–23, 26, 1914.

51. Captain Hughes's Scout Report, March 31, 1914, RRM; *BDH*, March 9–11, 1914; *EPMT*, March 14, 1914; Colquitt to Hutchings, March 3, 1914; Governor to D. G. Osborn, March 3, 1914, CP.

52. *BDH*, March 11, 1914.

53. Ibid., March 13, 1914.

54. Ibid., February 9–11, 24, 27, 28, March 3, 6, 7, 9, 16, 28, 30, 31, April 1, 3, 4, 6–8, 1914.

55. Ibid., April 8, 1914.

56. Ibid., April 9–11, 1914; Hughes to Hutchings, April 8, 1914; Colquitt to same, April 8, 1914; Hutchings to Colquitt, April 8, 1914, CP.

57. See file 4897, April 9, 1914, SD.

58. See Robert E. Quirk, *An Affair of Honor: Woodrow Wilson and the Occupation of Veracruz* (New York: W. W. Norton & Co., 1967).

59. *BDH*, April 18, 21, 22, 1914; [Colquitt] to Ft. Worth *Record*, April 21, 1914, Colquitt Papers, CAH.

60. Hutchings to Chief, Division of Militia Affairs, April 23, 1914; Chief, Division of Militia Affairs to Adjutant General, April 24, 1914, AGC; *BDH*, April 23, 1914; Scout Report, Company A, April 30, 1914, RRM.

61. J. J. Allen to Colquitt, April 23, 1914; Colquitt to Hutchings, April 24, 1914; same to J. J. Allen, April 24, 1914; John R. Robinson to T. R. Smith, April 30, 1914, CP; *BDH*, April 28, 1914; *EPMT*, April 23, 25, 26, 1914. See also AG to Sam H. Anderson, May 18, 1914, AGC.

62. Colquitt to Hutchings, April 17, 1914, CP.

63. Ben Bridges Hunt to Colquitt, April 28, 1914; Colquitt to Hutchings, April 29, 1914, CP.

64. Colquitt to H. P. Brelsford, May 2, 1914, Colquitt Papers, CAH. There was in fact an attempt to blow up the San Benito pumping plant. See *BDH*, May 4 and 7, 1914.

65. Hutchings to Governor, May 6, 1914; Colquitt to Hutchings, May 7 and 8, 1914, CP; *BDH*, May 7 and 12, 1914.

66. See, for example, W. H. McGrath to Colquitt, May 10, 1914; Adjutant General to same, May 11, 1914, CP.

67. *BDH*, May 15, 25, 29, June 1, 3, 6, 9, 13, 1914.

68. Ibid., June 4, 1914.

69. Ibid., April 28 and 30, 1914.

70. San Antonio *Light*, April 30, 1914.

71. Virginia Yeager to Colquitt, July 24, 1914; Colquitt to Hutchings, August 5, 1914, CP.

72. Oscar Thompson to Colquitt, May 29, 1914; J. P. Reed to same, May 28, 1914; Fox to AG, August 27, 1914; Hutchings to Colquitt, August 28, 1914, CP.

73. J. J. Kilpatrick to Colquitt, April 26, 1914, CP.

74. Colquitt to Kilpatrick, May 5, 1914, CP; H. A. Thompson report, May 31, 1913, reel 3, BI. On July 15, 1914, Ranger Sergeant Roberson would arrest J. J. Kilpatrick, Jr., for cattle theft. MR, Company A, July 31, 1914, AGC. In 1919, an army officer prepared a report on the Kilpatrick family at Candelaria, giving the "history of this notorious and infamous family." C. E. Breniman to Frank Burke, October 25, 1919, reel 24, BI. For a more sympathetic view of J. J. Kilpatrick see Glenn Justice, *Revolution on the Rio Grande: Mexican Raids and Army Pursuits 1916–1919* (El Paso: Texas Western Press, 1992).

75. Vaughan to Hughes, May 9, 1914, CP.

76. Statement of Joe Sitter, May 15, 1914, CP.

77. L. D. Louthen to Colquitt, May 27, 1914, CP.

78. Hughes to Hutchings, May 28, 1914; Hutchings to Colquitt, June 2, 1914, CP. On December 31, 1914, Vaughan resigned to become a mounted Customs inspector.

79. *EPMT*, July 13, 1914.

80. *LWT*, July 22, 1917.

81. Caracristi to Colquitt, May 2, 1914, CP.

82. Caracristi to Colquitt, May 5, 1914, CP.

83. *EPMT*, September 15, 1905.

84. Ibid., July 10, 1910.

85. William H. Beezley, *Insurgent Governor: Abraham González and the Mexican Revolution in Chihuahua* (Lincoln: University of Nebraska Press, 1973), 47; *AS*, March 24, 25, 27, 1911; *SAE*, March 25, 1911; *EPMT*, October 28, 1911; *LWT*, October 27, 1912; R. L. Barnes report, February 17, 1913, reel 3, BI. Caracristi and Fall did correspond.

86. *LWT*, July 20, 1913.

87. Governor to Caracristi, May 5, 1914, CP.

88. Sanders to Colquitt, May 6, 1914; Ed Cotulla to Sanders, May 7, 1914; H. H. Jefferies to same, May 7, 1914; N. D. Staner to same, May 7, 1914; W. P. May to same, May 7, 1914; C. H. Stowers to same, May 7, 1914; J. E. Trout to same, May 7, 1914, CP.

89. Caracristi to Colquitt, May 6, 1914, CP.

90. Caracristi to Colquitt, May 6, 8, 11, 12, 15, 18, 1914, CP.

91. Colquitt to Hutchings, May 15, 1914; same to same, June 4, 1914, WC.

92. Caracristi to Hutchings, May 16, 19, 1914; AG to Caracristi, May 18, 20, 1914, AGC.

93. Colquitt to Hutchings, May 20, June 4, 1914, CP; same to Caracristi, May 20, 1914, WC; Caracristi to AG, May 29, June 5, 1914, AGC; same to Colquitt, May 31, 1914, WC; same to Colquitt, July 7, 1914, AGC.

94. *EPMT*, January 4, 1916.

95. *LWT*, July 19, 1914.

96. MR, Company B, April 30, 1914; see also Captain E. M. Matson to Hutchings, April 23, 1914, AGC.

97. Sanders to Hutchings, June 18, 1914; Colquitt to Hutchings, June 26, 1914; Hutchings to Colquitt, June 27, 1914, CP; *LWT*, July 19, August 30, 1914; MR, Company B, July 31, 1914, AGC; Sanders to Hutchings, July 8, 15, 21, 24, 1914, WC; Dr. Willis Edwards Lowry to same, July 12, 1914, AGC; Hutchings to Sanders, July 22, 1914; W. T. Grimes to Hutchings, August 3, 1914, WC.

98. *EPMT*, April 21–24, 1914.

99. Ibid., April 24, 25, 1914; O. W. Goodwin to Captain John Hughes, May 1, 1914, RRM.

100. Scout report of G. C. Webb, April 30, 1914, RRM; Sheriff Peyton Edwards to Captain John R. Hughes, April 25, 1914, AGC.

101. Scout report of G. C. Webb, April 30, 1914, RRM.

102. *AA*, April 16, 1914.

103. Ibid., July 2, 1914; MR, Company A, June 30, 1914, AGC.

104. *EPMT*, May 10, 1914; *AA*, May 14, 1914; Colquitt to Hutchings, May 11, 1914; Hutchings to Colquitt, May 12, 1914, AGC.

105. *EPMT*, May 22, 1914.

106. *AA*, September 3, 1914; a similar incursion occurred in November. See *EPMT*, November 6, 1914.

107. *EPMT*, September 22, 27, 1914.

108. L. R. Millican to Colquitt, April 15, 1914, AGC; *BDH*, July 8, 1914.

109. *BDH*, September 21, 1914.

110. Hutchings to Colquitt, May 23, 1914, CP.

111. AG to Commanding Officers, Company A and B, Rangers, August 7, 1914, AGC.

112. AG to Colquitt, October 3, 1914, CP.

113. Colquitt to Hutchings, October 6, 1914, CP.

114. *BDH*, October 15, 1914.

115. H. O. Rawlins to Colquitt, June 10, 1914, CP.

116. Colquitt to Hutchings, June 25, 1914, CP.

117. Hutchings to Colquitt, June 25, 1914, CP.

118. Ike N. Hartsill to Hutchings, July 9, October 30, 1914; Hughes to same, July 9, 1914; Petition to Colquitt, June 22, 1914, CP.

119. AG to Colquitt, December 18, 1914, CP; same to George B. Hufford, December 22, 1914, AGC; Colquitt to Comptroller, December 19, 1914, CP.

120. J. E. Vaughan to Hughes, December 3, 1914; Hughes to Hutchings, December 8, 1914, CP.

121. J. L. Anders to Seth Bennett, August 9, 1914, WC.

122. *BDH*, June 8, 11, 13, 15, 17, July 20, 21, 27, October 10, 26, 1914.

123. Ibid., November 2, 3, 1914.

124. Ibid., November 23, 1914; [Hutchings] to Judge Daniel E. Garrett, July 23, 1914; Rawlins M. Colquitt to Hutchings, August 8, 1914, AGC.

125. *BDH*, December 17, 31, 1914.

126. *Biennial Report of the Adjutant General of Texas, From January 1, 1913, to December 31, 1914* (Austin: Von Boeckmann-Jones Co., 1915), 10.

Chapter 7

1. Gould, *Progressives and Prohibitionists*, 199–221; Sterling, *Trails and Trials*, 93–94, 273. The best account of corruption during Miriam "Ma" Ferguson's later gubernatorial terms as her husband James Ferguson's surrogate is Norman D. Brown, *Hood, Bonnet, and Little Brown Jug: Texas Politics, 1921–1928* (College Station: Texas A&M University Press, 1984), 266–296. Although much of the evidence is circumstantial, it is so overwhelming, particularly in regard to selling pardons, that there seems little doubt that Ferguson and his wife were the most corrupt governors in the history of Texas.

2. Hughes to Hutchings, January 3, 1915; AG to W. F. Solar, January 7, 1915, AGC; Martin, *Border Boss*, passim; *Handbook*, III, 773.

3. See AG to W. C. Wellborn, February 20, 1915, AGC.

4. Sanders to Hutchings, April 11, 1915; S. M. Jester to same, April 14, 1915; Hutchings to J. W. Almond, April 2, 1915, AGC.

5. See, for example, AG to Hughes, January 13, 1915; Sanders to Hutchings, January 15, 1915; T. B. Rice to same, January 20, 1915; Hutchings to Rice, January 28, 1915; Fox to AG, March 6, 1915; AG to Sanders, March 13, April 6, 1915; (tel.) L. A. Clark to Ferguson, March 15, 1915; Sanders to Hutchings, March 15, April 4, 1915; AG to Ferguson, March 19, 1915; AG to J. W. Almond, April 2, 1915; Almond to Hutchings, April 12, 1915; Sanders to same, April 17, 1915; Parrish to same, April 21, 1915, AGC.

6. Sterling, *Trails and Trials*, 269.

7. Major George T. Langhorne to General Frederick Funston, June 13, 1915, 2294479-B, AGO. See also "Weekly report," June 16, 1915, 812.00/15278, RDS.

8. The Secretary of the Texas Cattle Raisers Association, E. B. Spiller, in late March, 1914, ordered Inspector John Bannister to Valentine to meet with Sheriff M. B. Chastain and three mounted Customs inspectors, Joe Sitter, Charles Craighead, and Sam Neill, and decide how to combat cattle theft in the Big Bend. This group arrived at the Rio Grande below Pilares on March 27 and engaged in a gun battle with Lino Baiza, an indicted murderer, and his men. Baiza had been associated with Chico Cano's gang. Baiza was killed by the posse. In his official report to the Texas Cattle Raisers Association, from Candelaria, March 31, 1914, Bannister, an ex-Ranger, recommended that "at least ten Rangers should be stationed there as soon as possible, to co-operate with the three or four River Guards who are at present too

weak a force to cope with the lawless element of this county." Bannister noted prophetically that he "would not be surprised to learn . . . of the extermination of the small force of officers." Leona Bruce, *Bannister Was There* (Fort Worth: Branch-Smith, Inc., 1968), 156–161; There is an uncorroborated report that Jefferson Eagle "Jeff" Vaughan, a former Ranger and U.S. Customs river guard under Sitter, was initially part of the ambushed contingent. See Joyce E. Means, *Pancho Villa Days at Pilares* (El Paso: Guynes Printing Company, 1976), 32.

9. Hulen to Hutchings, February 27, 1915; Ferguson to same, March 29, 1915; General Orders No. 2, April 1, 1915; Fox to Stockton, February 5, 1915, AGC.

10. The two principal written accounts are Fox to AG, May 27, 1915, AGC, and Cummings, Trollinger, and Craighead's written statement which appeared in the *EPMT*, May 31, 1915. Webb, *Texas Rangers*, 498–499, has an excellent account based in part on interviews with members of the posse. See also Cano and Sochat, *Bandido*, 74–81.

11. Hutchings to Fox, June 2, 1915, AGC.

12. MR, Company B, June 30, 1915, AGC.

13. Trollinger to Ferguson, September 16, 1915; Ferguson to Hutchings, September 22, 25, 1915, AGC.

14. MR, Company B, June 30, 1915, AGC; *EPMT*, June 8, 9, 24, 1915; "Weekly report," July 1, 1915, 812.00/15448, RDS.

15. Funston to Adjutant General, May 27, 1915, 2291741 and his report of June 12, 1915, 2294479, AGO.

16. Funston to AG, June 18, 1915, 2294479, AGO.

17. Kilpatrick to W. R. Smith, May 26, 1915, 2294479, AGO.

18. Funston report, June 12, 1915, his telegram no. 494 of June 3, 1915, and Brigadier General Tasker Bliss telegram to Funston, June 3, 1915, 2294479, AGO.

19. Funston report, June 12, 1915, 2294479, AGO.

20. "Weekly report," June 10, 1915, 812.00/15228, RDS.

21. Jester to AG, June 9, 1915, AGC; *BDH*, June 9, 1915; Commanding Officer Fabens Cavalry Patrol District to Commanding General, Southern Department, June 13, 1915, 2294479-B, AGO.

22. Commanding Officer Fabens Cavalry Patrol District to Commanding General, Southern Department, June 13, 1915, 2294479-B, AGO.

23. Funston report, June 12, 1915, 2294479, AGO.

24. Bliss memorandum to Chief of Staff General Hugh Scott, June 22, 1915, quoting Funston's June 12 report, 2264551-C, AGO; see also Lindley M. Garrison to President Wilson, July 22, 1915, 2264551-F, AGO.

25. Bliss memorandum to Scott, June 22, 1915, 2264551-C, AGO.

26. Sanders to Hutchings, February 6, 1915, AGC.

27. Sanders to Hutchings, February 12, 1915, AGC.

28. Hutchings to Sanders, February 16, 1915, AGC.

29. AG to Sanders, February 26, 1915; AG to Fox, February 26, 1915, AGC.

30. Ferguson to Hutchings, February 26, 1915; Hutchings to Ferguson, February 27, 1915, AGC.

31. Hutchings to Ferguson, February 25, 1915, AGC.

32. Sanders to Hutchings, March 17, 1915, AGC.

33. MR, Company A, February 28, 1915, AGC.

34. Fox to AG, March 7, 1915; AG to Fox, March 8, 10, 1915, AGC.

35. Ferguson to Hutchings, March 13, 1915, with attached petition dated February 16, 1915, from Rio Grande City. The first signature on the petition was that of Manuel Guerra, who identified himself as a stockman, but who was also the brother of the political boss of Hidalgo County, Deodoro Guerra.

36. See, for example, Clark to Ferguson, letter and telegram, March 15, 1915; Hutchings to Sanders, March 13, 1915; Sanders to Hutchings, March 15, 1915; Hutchings to Ferguson, March 19, 1915, AGC.

37. Thomas J. Martin to Ferguson, October 1, 1915; Ferguson to Hutchings, October 9, 1915; AG to Thomas J. Martin, October 28, 1915, AGC.

38. J. Wahrenberger, et al. and C. W. Nugent, et al., both March 15, 1915, to John D. McCall, AGC.

39. Sanders to Hutchings, April 4, 1915, AGC.

40. Sanders to Hutchings, April 2, 1915, and (2 letters) April 4, 1915, AGC.

41. Sanders to Hutchings, April 2, 4, 1915, AGC.

42. Sanders to Hutchings, April 10, 11, 1915, AGC.

43. AG to Sanders, April 12, 1915; Sanders to Hutchings, April 17, 27, 1915, AGC.

44. AG to Parrish, April 12, 1915; Sanders to Hutchings, April 11, 27, 1915; Parrish to same, April 21, 1915, AGC.

45. S. M. Jester to AG, April 14, 1915; Ira Cline to same, April 14, 1915; Fox to Hutchings, April 19, 1915, AGC; *EPMT*, April 14, 1915.

46. Jester report, undated, but probably May, 1915, AGC.

47. W. C. Linden, District Attorney, Bexar County, to Ferguson, with a note from Congressman John Nance Garner to the Governor attached, April 12, 1915; AG to Linden, April 19, 1915; same to Sanders, April 19, 1915, AGC.

48. Almond to Hutchings, April 12, 19, 24, 1915; Hutchings to Almond, April 13, 1915, AGC. Senator Hudspeth in a letter to Ferguson dated April 24, 1915, quoted the Sheriff of Sutton County as saying that ten percent of the sheep and goats in his county had been stolen in the past twelve months.

49. Hudspeth to Ferguson, April 24, 1915, with enclosed copy of petition signed by twenty ranchers in Sutton County; AG to Martin, April 28, 1915, AGC.

50. S. M. Jester to AG, April 14, 1915, AGC; *EPMT*, May 16, 1915.

51. Sanders to Hutchings, May 4, 1915, AGC.

52. AG to Sanders, May 6, 1915, AGC.

53. AG to Doctors Coopwood and Ross, May 24, 1915; Dr. E. S. McCain to Hutchings, May 12, 13, 1915; Hutchings to McCain, May 13, 1915, AGC.

54. AG to W. F. Bates, June 4, 1915, AGC.

55. W. F. Bates to Fox, June 8, 1915, with attached expense account and scouting report, and his formal letter of resignation dated June 9, 1915, AGC.

56. W. F. Bates to Ferguson, June 9, 1915, AGC.

57. A. H. Evans, Collector of Customs, Eagle Pass, to Fox, June 30, 1915; AG to Roberts, June 1, 1915, AGC.

58. MR, Company B, June 30, 1915, AGC.

59. Ferguson to W. D. Lewis, July 9, 1915, FP.

60. *General Laws of the State of Texas Passed by the Thirty-fourth Legislature at its Regular Session Convened January 12, 1915, and Adjourned April 20, 1915* (Austin: A. C. Baldwin & Sons, 1915), 151; *EPMT*, February 25, 1915.

61. See, for example, Ferguson to R. Bergfeld, March 20, 1915, FP: "There has been today a deficiency bill, carrying some $50,000, passed the House, and I think it will pass the Senate. I think probably that the script [sic] which you hold will be payable out of this fund."

62. Gould, *Progressives and Prohibitionists*, 142–148.

63. Ferguson to Wilson, February 25, 1915, FP.

64. Ibid.

65. Funston to AG, March 10, 1915, Southern Department no. 10631 in 2264551, AGO.

66. Garrison to Wilson, March 2, 1915, no. 10631 in 2264551, AGO.

67. Funston to AG, March 10, 1915, Southern Department no. 10631, in 2264551, AGO.

68. Brigadier General Anson Mills to AG, April 30, 1915, 5211/Tex, AGO.

69. Scott to AG, April 23, 1915, and to General Peyton C. March, AG, April 24, 1915, 2281258, AGO.

70. Scott to AG, April 26, 1915, and AG to Commanding General, Southern Department, 2281258, AGO.
71. Mills to AG, April 28, 1915, and AG to Commanding General, Southern Department, April 28, 1915, both in AGO.
72. Ferguson to Garrison, May 5, 1915, FP.
73. Ferguson to Garrison, December 28, 1915, FP. In the letter Ferguson does not explain his reason for firing Walker. *Biennial Report of the Adjutant General of Texas From January 1, 1915, to December 31, 1916* (Austin: Von Boeckmann-Jones Co., 1917), 24, 25, 51, 53; *EPMT*, June 17, 22, 1916; W. H. Smith to Hutchings, August 12, 1915, AGC; "Weekly report," March 23, 1916, 812.00/17754, RDS.
74. *Dallas Morning News*, May 3, 1915; O. B. Colquitt to Hutchings, May 3, 1915, AGC.
75. Colquitt to Hutchings, May 3, 1915; Hutchings to Colquitt, May 26, 1915, AGC.
76. *BDH*, July 13, 1915.
77. AG to Cal Hirsch and Son, July 22, 1915, AGC.
78. Ibid.
79. AG to Lehmann, July 22, 1915, AGC.
80. Garrison to Ferguson, July 1, 1915, 52119/Texas, AGO.
81. Ferguson to Garrison, December 28, 1915, FP. Colonel Walker was also guilty of stealing property of the State of Texas. See Attorney General B. F. Looney to Hutchings, July 7, 1915, AGC.
82. Garrison to Ferguson, July 1, 1915, 2281258, AGO.
83. AG to Cal Hirsch & Son, July 22, 1915, AGC.
84. Hutchings to Smith, May 12, 1915, AGC.
85. AG to Sanders, July 22, 1915, AGC.
86. AG to Ransom, July 28, 1915, AGC.
87. AG to Cardwell, July 16, 1915, AGC.
88. *Corpus Christi Democrat*, June 13, 1915; Cardwell to Colonel J. F. Stockton, June 16, 1915, AGC.
89. Garrison to Ferguson, July 1, 1915, 2281259, 52119/Texas, AGO.
90. Ibid.
91. Ferguson to Brigadier General Anson L. Mills, September 25, 1915, FP.
92. Garrison to Ferguson, July 1, 1915, 52119/Texas, AGO.
93. Ferguson to Brigadier General Anson Mills, September 25, 1915, FP.
94. Garrison to Ferguson, July 1, 1915, 52119/Texas, AGO; Hutchings to R. M. Colquitt, July 22, 1915, AGC.
95. Garrison to Ferguson, July 1, 1915, 52119/Texas, AGO; Coerver and Hall, *Texas and the Mexican Revolution*, 96. There was a protracted correspondence between Garrison and Ferguson, who became increasingly exasperated. He informed Garrison that "Your letter was a distinct disappointment to me and is the most concrete argument against preparedness that I have come in contact with . . . you are willing to reward me by unloading debts . . . accumulating within . . . the War Department since 1900, amounting to $102,025.24." Ferguson to Garrison, January 21, 1916, FP.
96. For example see Ferguson to John Southerland, May 18, 1915; same to George D. Armistead, June 5, 1915; same to President Wilson, July 12, 1915, FP.
97. Hutchings to Ferguson, July 8, 1915, FP; same to Captains Sanders and Fox, July 17, 1915; same to Ferguson, July 8, 1915; same to Major Will E. Jackson, July 6, 1915, AGC.

Chapter 8

1. McDevitt report, January 26, 1915, reel 8, BI; Ramos's copy of the Plan de San Diego was translated by Immigration Inspector J. R. Harold in Brownsville. See E. P. Reynolds,

Inspector in Charge, Brownsville, Texas, to Supervising Inspector, Immigration Service, El Paso, Texas, No. 1537/136, January 30, 1915, Exhibit 1, ABF. Numerous copies were provided to various federal and state and local law enforcement agencies. The copy we have utilized is found in the AGC, January, 1915.

2. Michael C. Meyer, "The Mexican-German Conspiracy of 1915," *The Americas: A Quarterly Review of Inter-American Cultural History* 23 (July 1966), 76–89, *Mexican Rebel*, 121, and *Huerta*, 218; Allen Gerlach, "Conditions Along the Border—1915: The Plan de San Diego," *New Mexico Historical Review* 43 (July 1968), 195–212; James A. Sandos, "The Plan of San Diego: War and Diplomacy on the Texas Border, 1915–1916," *Arizona and the West* 14 (Spring 1972), 5–24, and *Rebellion in the Borderlands: Anarchism and the Plan of San Diego, 1904–1923* (Norman: University of Oklahoma Press, 1992); William M. Hager, "The Plan of San Diego: Unrest on the Texas Border in 1915," *Arizona and the West* 5 (Winter 1963), 327–336; Charles Cumberland, "Border Raids in the Lower Rio Grande Valley—1915," *Southwestern Historical Quarterly* 57 (January 1954), 285–311; Hall and Coerver, *Revolution on the Border*, 85–95, 97–103, 106–108, 111, 118–122; Friedrich Katz, *The Secret War in Mexico: Europe, the United States and the Mexican Revolution* (Chicago and London: University of Chicago Press, 1981), 339–344; Charles H. Harris III and Louis R. Sadler, "The Plan de San Diego and the Mexican-United States War Crisis of 1916: A Reexamination," *Hispanic American Historical Review* 58 (August 1978), 381–408; Rodolfo Rocha, "The Influence of the Mexican Revolution on the Mexico-Texas Border, 1910–1916" (Ph.D. dissertation, Texas Tech University, 1981); Webb, *Texas Rangers*, 484–486; Sterling, *Trails and Trials*, 28; Robert J. Rosenbaum, *Mexicano Resistance in the Southwest: "The Sacred Right of Self-Preservation"* (Austin and London: University of Texas Press, 1981), 50–52; Raat, *Revoltosos*, 262–264; Douglas W. Richmond, "La Guerra de Texas se renova: Mexican Insurrection and Carrancista Ambitions, 1900–1920," *Aztlán: Chicano Journal of the Social Sciences and the Arts*, 2: 1 (Spring 1980), 1–32; Benjamin Heber Johnson, *Revolution in Texas: How a Forgotten Rebellion and Its Bloody Suppression Turned Mexicans into Americans* (New Haven and London: Yale University Press, 2003).

3. Armando Bartra, ed., *Regeneración, 1900–1918: La corriente más radical de la Revolución de 1910 a través de su periódico de combate* (México: Hadise, S. A., 1972), 436–439.

4. See Francisco Alvarez Tostado, "A los Hijos de Cuauhtémoc, Hidalgo y Juárez en Tejas," November 26, 1914, Condumex/A, Documentos 1915 [sic] (Mayo 7 a 30). This document was initially uncovered by Michael C. Meyer. Our former graduate student Tyler Ralston obtained a copy for the authors in Mexico City. Alvarez Tostado was a Mexican citizen from Tepic who had entered the United States. in 1900. He was arrested in Arizona in 1911 for neutrality violations but was released. Since about 1908 he lived in San Antonio. In 1916 Bureau of Investigation agents searched his room at 520 South Laredo Street, interrogated him, and arrested him. He was charged with having conspired at Sebastian, Cameron County, to overthrow the U.S. government. He pleaded guilty. R. L. Barnes report, May 20, 1916; Clifford G. Beckham report, June 1, 1916, reel 4, BI; U.S. vs. Francisco Alvarez Tostado, no. 419, U.S. Commissioner, San Antonio, FRC-FW.

5. Acuña, *Occupied America: A History of Chicanos*, 176–177; David Montejano, *Anglos and Mexicans in the Making of Texas, 1836–1986* (Austin: University of Texas Press, 1987), 125; Juan Gómez-Quiñones, "Plan de San Diego Reviewed," *Aztlán: Chicano Journal of the Social Sciences and the Arts* 1 (Spring 1970), 124–132.

6. Acuña, *Occupied America: A History of Chicanos*, 176.

7. Johnson, *Revolution in Texas*, 1, states that the Plan de San Diego "was drafted in South Texas in early 1915." This is unproven.

8. Barnes report, March 3, 1915, reel 7, BI. Deodoro Guerra remained involved in revolutionary intrigue at least as late as 1919, when he was reportedly involved in smuggling ammunition to anti-Carranza rebels. Manuel Sorola reports, November 29 and December 20, 1919, reel 24, BI.

9. Charles E. Breniman report, February 2, 1915, reel 8, BI. Breniman quoted U.S. Army Captain E. C. Johnson, who commanded an Army detachment at nearby Mission, Texas, as suggesting that the carrancista spy "Elloy" had "disappeared mysteriously and may have met with foul play. . . ."; "Weekly report," January 13, 1915, 812.00/14241, RDS; E. Arredondo to William J. Bryan, January 22, 1915, 812.00/14263, RDS.

10. Barnes reports, January 30, March 3, April 18, 19, 1915; Barnes to John E. Green, Jr., April 21, 1915, reel 7, BI.

11. *Boss Rule in South Texas: The Progressive Era* (Austin: University of Texas Press, 1982), 141–142. Anders's monograph has no peer among histories of South Texas for this period.

12. F. J. McDevitt report, January 27, 1915; Charles E. Breniman reports, January 31, February 3, 6, 1915; reel 7, BI. There is a discrepancy among the various sources as to who actually arrested Ramos. Most sources state that Hidalgo County Sheriff A. Y. Baker arrested Ramos. But the preponderance of evidence suggests that it was Mayfield. Presumably Baker wanted the credit for arresting Ramos. Mayfield stated under oath before the Fall Committee that he was the arresting officer, *IMA*, 1295.

13. Manuel G. Gonzales, *Mexicanos: A History of Mexicans in the United States* (Bloomington: Indiana University Press, 2000), 117.

14. Charles Breniman report, January 28, 1915, reel 8, BI.

15. F. J. McDevitt report, January 26, 1915, reel 8, BI.

16. R. L. Barnes report, January 26, 1915, reel 6; McDevitt reports, January 27, 31, 1915, reel 8; Barnes report, January 28, 1915, reel 8; Breniman reports, January 31, February 3, 6, 19, 1915, reel 8, BI.

17. See, for example, the banner headline story in the *BDH*, February 4, 1915, and a less sensational Associated Press story dated February 2, 1915, which appeared in the *EPMT*, February 3, 1915.

18. Statement of Basilio Ramos, Jr., taken by E. P. Reynolds, Inspector in Charge, File No. 1537/136. U.S. Immigration Service, Brownsville, Texas, January 28, 1915, reel 13, ABF. A Basilio Ramos was secretary to the governor of Tamaulipas in 1913. See Clarence A. Miller to Secretary of State, February 17, 1913, 812.00/6242, RDS.

19. Hearing Transcript, March 20, 1915, Exhibits 10 and 11, File No. 1537/136, U.S. Immigration Service, Brownsville, Texas, reel 13, ABF.

20. See Nafarrate safe conduct and pass, reel 13, ABF. It should be noted that the safe conduct and pass cannot be found in the appropriate files of the U.S. Commissioner, Brownsville, nor in the records of the Bureau of Investigation. Apparently William Martin Hanson, who was the chief investigator of the Fall Committee investigating Mexican affairs, obtained the documents from the U.S. Commissioner in Brownsville and turned them over to Senator A. B. Fall; thus their appearance in Fall's papers.

21. Johnson, *Revolution in Texas*, 82.

22. U.S. vs. Basilio Ramos, Jr. et al., U.S. Commissioner, no. 249, Brownsville, FRC-FW; Charles E. Breniman report, February 4, 1915, reel 8, BI.

23. U.S. vs. Basilio Ramos, Jr., et al., U.S. District Court, Brownsville, no. 2152, FRC-FW.

24. *La Prensa* (San Antonio), May 18, 1915; Sandos, "Plan of San Diego," 10–11; *IMA*, 1205; *BDH*, May 9, 1916; J. P. S. Mennet report, January 28, 1917, reel 10, BI. The Ramos case was continued through 1917. See Judge's Bench Dockets, Criminal Cases, vols. 6 and 7, U.S. District Court, Brownsville, FRC-FW.

25. The Immigration Service provided a translated copy of the Plan de San Diego to Captain Sanders who forwarded it to the adjutant general in Austin. Sanders to Hutchings, February 20, 1915; Hutchings to Sanders, February 23, 1915, AGC.

26. F.H.U. to Ramos, February 2, 1915, reel 13, ABF.

27. E. P. Reynolds, Immigration Inspector, Brownsville, Texas, March 20, 1915, reel 13, ABF.

28. (tel) George Thomas to Ferguson, February 17, 1915; Hutchings to Sanders, February 19, 1915; Sanders to Hutchings, February 24, 1915, AGC.

29. R. L. Barnes to Bruce Bielaski, Chief, Bureau of Investigation, February 12, 1915; Barnes to County Attorney Welles [?], February 16, 1915, reel 5, BI; Sheriff J. C. Guerra to Captain David Von Voorhies, March 11, 1915, 90755-2413, RDJ.

30. AG to James Gibson, February 20, 1915, AGC. On February 20 Hutchings ordered Sanders to proceed to Alice as soon as he could to report on conditions there. See AG to Sanders, February 20, 1915, AGC. Two days later Sanders ordered three Rangers to Alice at the request of the sheriff of Jim Wells County. (tel) Sanders to Hutchings, February 22, 1915, AGC. On February 24, Sanders reported that "the citizens [at Alice] . . . are considerably excited over the killing of one and wounding of another Mexican horse thief by the Sheriff and posse." Sanders to Hutchings, February 24, 1915, AGC.

31. Osborn to Hutchings, February 25, 1915, AGC.

32. The manifesto can be found in S. H. Evans to Secretary of the Treasury, January 31, 1916, 812.00/17245, RDS. A translation of the document is in the FC. See also Sandos, "Plan of San Diego," 9–10.

33. Johnson, *Revolution in Texas*, 81–82.

34. Sanders to Hutchings, March 1, 1915, AGC.

35. Ibid.

36. Harris and Sadler, "Plan de San Diego."

37. Telegrams in A. L. Barkley report, November 15, 1915, reel 8, BI.

38. See, for example, telegrams from Rogelio to Herrera Moreno, April 24, 25, 1915; Huerta in New York City to Herrera Moreno in San Antonio, April 14, 1915, reel 8, BI.

39. Hutchings to Edwards and Edwards to Hutchings, both June 19, 1915, AGC. There was obviously an earlier telegram between Hutchings and Edwards, but it currently does not exist in the adjutant general's files in the Texas State Library. Sandos, *Rebellion*, 87, states that the Plan de San Diego raids began July 4 and Bureau of Investigation special agent J. H. Rogers uses the date of July 6 (Rogers report, November 16, 1915, reel 6, BI). Both are incorrect. The raids began at least two weeks earlier.

40. Sanders to Hutchings, June 27, 1915, AGC.

Chapter 9

1. Sanders to Hutchings, July 4, 1915, AGC.

2. Taylor had been a Ranger under Captain Sanders in 1914–1915 and was a Special Ranger from 1916 to 1919. He got his nickname because when he got mad his face flushed pink.

3. Scout Report of Roy Aldrich, July, 1915, RRM. On Taylor, see Sanders to Hutchings, January 15, 1915, AGC. Sanders had a high regard for Taylor, who probably participated in more firefights in 1915 than any other law enforcement officer on the border. He became a mounted Customs inspector, then in 1918 worked for Caesar Kleberg at Norias. He was farming near San Benito in June, 1924, when he was murdered.

4. Ibid.; *BDH*, July 7, 1915.

5. Indicative of the fact that the adjutant general was not yet concerned over the raids was his order on July 6 to Captain Fox to send Ranger S. M. Jester to Manor to chase bootleggers. AG to Fox, July 6, 1915, AGC.

6. *BDH*, July 7, 1915; On July 6 Sheriff Vann informed the newspaper that there were five or six Rangers in the posse. Records of the adjutant general show that there were only two Rangers involved as of this date. This is illustrative of the tendency to exaggerate the Ranger presence during the initial phase of the Bandit War.

7. *BDH*, July 6, 1915.

8. Ibid., July 8, 1915.

9. For a description of the area by a local resident, see Sterling, *Trails and Trials*, 354–355.

10. Parker Memorandum for the Commanding General, SD, January 30, 1917, FC.

11. Sanders to Hutchings, July 11, 1915, AGC.

12. Sanders to Hutchings, July 13, 1915, AGC.

13. Fox to Hutchings, July 13, 1915, AGC.

14. *BDH*, July 19, 1915.

15. Rogers report, November 16, 1915, reel 6, BI.

16. *BDH*, July 13, 1915; Rogers report, November 16, 1915, reel 6, BI.

17. *BDH*, July 15, 1915.

18. Aldrich Scout Report, July, 1915, MR, Company A, AGC.

19. *BDH*, July 13, 1915.

20. Ibid., July 14, 1915; Rogers report, November 16, 1915, reel 6, BI.

21. *BDH*, July 19, 1915; Rogers report, November 16, 1915, reel 6, BI.

22. AG to Fox and Sanders, July 17, 1915, AGC.

23. Sanders to Hutchings, July 22, 1915, AGC.

24. Anders, *Boss Rule*, 228–229. One of the businessmen who went bankrupt was Lon Hill, at one time among the largest landowners in the Valley. See Sam A. Robertson To Whom It May Concern, July 31, 1928, Lon Hill Papers, CAH.

25. *BDH*, July 1, 1915. Widespread smuggling of cattle from Mexico predates the Mexican Revolution. This topic has received little scholarly attention and yet was a signifivant factor in the border economy. Apparently many Texas ranchers on the border engaged in smuggling cattle; by the 1890's this had become a virtual industry, and it continued throughout the Revolution. Efforts by U.S. Treasury Department special agents to thwart smuggling operations were often stymied by politically influential ranchers who succeeded in halting enforcement efforts. One account, which is based on documentary evidence, describes efforts to collect customs duties and why these efforts sometimes failed. Bruce, *Bannister*, 54–75. See also W. D. Smithers, *Early Trail Drives in the Big Bend* (El Paso: Texas Western Press, 1979).

26. Ferguson to Wilson, June 11, 1915, FP.

27. Garrison to Wilson, June 22, 1915, 2264551-C, AGO.

28. Funston to Ferguson, June 25, 1915, enclosing L. H. Bates to Ferguson letter, June 20, 1915, FP.

29. Ferguson to Garrison, June 25, 1915, FP.

30. Garrison to Ferguson, June 30, 1915, 2299906-A, AGO.

31. Funston to Ferguson, July 1, 1915, 2264551-F, AGO.

32. Matthew Carlton Hammond, "The Posse Comitatus Act: A Principle in Need of Renewal," *Washington University Law Quarterly* 75, no. 2 (Summer 1997), 1–32. (The legal citation is: 75 Wash. U.L.Q. 953.)

33. For an excellent example see Henry Breckenridge, Acting Secretary of War, to General Tasker H. Bliss, October 28, 1914, 2223506, AGO. The Department of Justice had asked the War Department to allow a few army sergeants at Laredo to assist the Bureau of Investigation in arresting Mexican nationals for violations of the neutrality statute. Permission was initially granted and then revoked, which upset local commanders who believed they had complied with regulations under the posse comitatus law.

34. Ibid.

35. Ferguson to Wilson, July 7, 1915, FP.

36. AG to Funston, June 30, 1915, 2264551-C, AGO.

37. Funston to AG, July 6, 1915, 226451-C, AGO.

38. Ibid.

39. AG to Funston, July 9, 1915, quoting telegram from Judge H. L. Yates to Secretary of War, July 8, 1915, 2304296, AGO; Army Chief of Staff General Hugh L. Scott to Secretary of War, July 9, 1915, quoting Funston to AG, July 9, 1915, 2304296, AGO. Copy of the Resolution by the Texas House of Representatives, undated but received by the Secretary of War on June 1, 1915, and replied to by Army Chief of Staff Scott in a letter dated June 5, 1915, enclosed in 22664551-F, AGO.

40. *HC*, October 26–30, 1910, April 17, 1911.
41. Ibid., March 6, April 15–23, 1913.
42. Ibid., April 2, 1918.
43. Wolters to Hutchings, July 19, 1915; Captain H. L. Ransom Scout Report, July, 1915, AGC.
44. Ransom Scout Report, July, 1915, AGC.
45. Ibid.; Sanders Scout Report, July, 1915; Sergeant W. T. Grimes Scout Report, July, 1915, AGC. See also *BDH*, July 26, 1915.
46. Kleberg to Hutchings, July 26, 1915; (tel) Hutchings to Kleberg, July 26, 1915; same to Sanders, July 26, 1915, AGC.
47. (tel) Sanders to Hutchings, July 26, 1915; (tel) Hutchings to Sanders, July 26, 1915, AGC.
48. (tel) Sanders to Hutchings, July 28, 1915; same to same, July 31, 1915, AGC.
49. *LWT*, August 1, 1915.
50. Sterling, *Trails and Trials*, 47.
51. Ibid., 47, 48.
52. "Proceedings," 1503–1504.
53. Rogers report, November 16, 1915, reel 6, BI.
54. *BDH*, July 26, 1915; Rogers report, November 16, 1915, reel 6, BI.
55. Ransom Scout Report, July, 1915, AGC.
56. Johnson, *Revolution in Texas*, 86, describes the pair as Texas Rangers at the time of the incident. They weren't.
57. *BDH*, July 29, 1915; Rogers report, November 16, 1915, reel 6, BI.
58. *BDH*, August 2, 1915; Rogers report, November 16, 1915, reel 6, BI.
59. BI agent Barnes, through Collector of Customs Frank Rabb, met with James Werbiske, whom Barnes employed as an informant. According to Werbiske, "at 2:30 a.m. before the attack at Tolitas [sic] a large number of these bandits came to my ranch west of Brownsville. I knew a number of them personally, Luis de la Rosa, Evarista [sic] Ramos, Vicente Davila, and Jose Yvars [sic]. Yvars is and was then a Carrenzista [sic] soldier under Nafarrate. There were a large number of other soldiers among them whom I knew personally as being soldiers in the Matamoros garrison." Robert L. Barnes report, November 5, 1915, reel 8, BI; *BDH*, August 3, 1915; Johnson, *Revolution in Texas*, 88.
60. See Robert Barnes reports, November 12, 13, 1915, with attached translated Pizaña correspondence, reel 6, BI. See particularly R. Flores Magón to Pizaña, September 22 and November 26, 1914, both attached to Barnes's November 12, 1915, report. Further information on Pizaña's background is in State of Texas vs. Ramón Pizaña et al., no. 3657, District Court, Brownsville.
61. Rocha, "The Influence of the Mexican Revolution," 264–265.
62. *BDH*, August 4, 1915.
63. Ibid.
64. Johnson, *Revolution in Texas*, 101–102.
65. *BDH*, August 5, 1915.
66. Acting Secretary of War Henry Breckenridge to Senator Morris Sheppard, August 9, 1915, AGO quoting Funston report to the Adjutant General, August 9, 1915, AGO.
67. Sterling, *Trails and Trials*, 33.
68. "Proceedings," 559–562. See also Ransom Scout Report, August 31, 1915, AGC, and *BDH*, August 7, 1915; Johnson, *Revolution in Texas*, 87, has what is apparently a garbled version of this incident.
69. *BDH*, August 7, 1915.
70. It is unclear how Kleberg learned of the presence of marauders on the Sauz Ranch. Perhaps Tom Tate, ex-Ranger and a King Ranch foreman, found out from one of his cowboys who had spotted them. Tom Lea, *The King Ranch*, 2 vols. (Boston: Little, Brown and Company, 1957), II, 583. See also "Weekly Report of General Conditions Along the Mexican Border," no. 126, August 14, 1915, 542-2-6, Report from Commanding Officer, Harlingen District, August 14, 1915, AGO.

71. Ransom's Scout Report has no entry for August 8 but he was definitely at Norias. See his Scout Report for August, 1915, RRM. Also along was Captain George Head, commander of the Brownsville national guard company. He had been indicted two months earlier by a federal grand jury in Austin on charges of conspiracy to defraud the government and embezzlement, the charges stemming from his role in selling national guard equipment to Mexican revolutionaries. Head had been arrested by Deputy U.S. Marshal E. T. Herring and was released on a $7,500 bond. Cameron County Sheriff W. T. Vann was one of the bondsmen. *BDH*, June 26, 1915.

72. Gordon Hill was the son of Lon C. Hill, one of the most prominent ranchers in the Valley. Father and son would receive Special Ranger commissions in August.

73. Tate had served in the Rangers in 1910–1911 and would again in 1926–1927; from 1915 to 1919 he was a Special Ranger.

74. The number of raiders given is from Lea, *King Ranch*, II, 584. Lea's account is substantially based on the eyewitness testimony of Lauro Cavazos. See Lea, *King Ranch*, II, 787. Sterling, *Trails and Trials*, 33, gives the number as fifty-two. Other estimates range from fifty to seventy-six. For the carrancista officer see Johnson, *Revolution in Texas*, 92.

75. According to participant D. P. Gay, an unidentified individual who had accompanied the officers to Norias refused to fight and hid under the house during the battle. D. P. Gay, "The Amazing Bare-Faced Facts of the Norias Fight," 2, 4, WC.

76. Martin was a King Ranch foreman who became a Special Ranger on June 6, 1917. He was also a deputy sheriff and was killed on November 25, 1917, while trying to make an arrest at a baile in Raymondville.

77. Gay, "Amazing Bare-Faced Facts," 5; Lea, *The King Ranch*, II, 585–586.

78. Manuel Rincones statement in Captain A. V. P. Anderson to Major Edward Anderson, August 11, 1915, found in Funston to AG, August 13, 1915, AGO; Lea, *King Ranch*, II, 586. Lea, based on Cavazos's account, gives the number of dead guerrillas as ten, which includes one who would die later. Gay, however, states that the defenders killed twenty-five raiders and wounded another twenty: twelve killed at Norias, two wounded who died that night, five more found in shallow graves along the retreat route, and six who reportedly died of their wounds after the raiders had crossed back into Mexico. Gay, "Amazing Bare-Faced Facts," 9. (These figures are obviously much too high.)

79. Gay, "Amazing Bare-Faced Facts," 4–5.

80. Ibid., 3.

81. Ibid., 9. For an account of the defense of Norias by one of the soldiers involved see Walter Collier as told to Bill Leftwich, "Germans' 'Plan of San Diego' Worked Good—On End of a Rope," *The Southwesterner* (May, 1963): 6–7.

82. Sterling, *Trails and Trials*, 33–35.

83. Ibid., 7. Gay felt compelled to write his account years later after overhearing a Texas Ranger claim that he'd been at the Norias fight.

84. Ibid., 9; Lea, *King Ranch*, II, 587.

85. Lea, *King Ranch*, II, 587; Gay, "Amazing Bare-Faced Facts," 8, 9.

86. Gay, "Amazing Bare-Faced Facts," 7.

87. (tels) Funston to AG, August 8, 9, 1915, AGO.

88. Gay, "Amazing Bare-Faced Facts," 11.

89. Sterling, *Trails and Trials*, 35.

90. Richard Henry Ribb, "José Tomás Canales and the Texas Rangers: Myth, Identity and Power in South Texas, 1900–1920" (Ph.D. dissertation, University of Texas at Austin, 2001), 9, 314–332.

91. Yates to Secretary of War, August 9, 1915; S. A. Wayne et al. to same, August 10, 1915, AGO.

92. Sterling, *Trails and Trials*, 35–36.

93. T. R. Fehrenbach is incorrect when he states that "the governor of Texas dispatched

approximately a thousand Rangers, most of whom were recruited especially for the mission" (*Lone Star*, 690).

94. MR, Company A, B, C, D, August 31,1915, AGC.
95. (tel) J. A. McCalmont to General Manager, August 12, 1915, AGC.
96. They were Steve Heinrich, C. J. Blackwell, G. B. Hurst, J. L. Faubion, J. A. Francis, George Glick, F. P. G. Erskine, Lester Ogg, and Cole Brunner. Jake Wolters to John C. McKay, August 12, 1915; Sanders to Hutchings, August 14, 16, 25, 1915; AG to Sanders, August 21, 1915; Ransom to Hutchings, August 22, 28, 1915; unnamed to same, August 26, 1915, AGC.
97. Trollinger to Lon A. Brooks, August 13, 1915; Assistant Attorney General to Billy Smith, August 18, 1915, AGC.
98. (2 tels) Colonel J. T. Stockton to J. A. McCalmont, August 12, 1915; Hutchings to Assistant AG, August 14, 1915; McCalmont to Stockton, August 13, 1915; Fox to same, August 11, 1915, AGC.
99. Funston telegram to AG, August 10, 1915, AGO.
100. Ibid.
101. For Rincones's statement, see *IMA*, 1284–1285; Captain A. V. P. Anderson to Major E. Anderson, August 11, 1915, AGO.
102. Funston telegram to AG, August 13, 1915, 590, AGO.
103. Barnes to Bielaski, August 12, 1915, reel 8, BI. The telegram is mistakenly dated August 12, 1914.
104. See, for example, Adjutant General H. P. McCain to Senator James A. Reed, September 14, 1915, 2322734, AGO; "Memorandum" by Brigadier General James Parker, September, 1915, FC.
105. AG to Reed, October 15, 1915, 2322724-A, AGO.
106. Funston to AG, August 8, 9, 11, 1915, AGO. See also Charles Cumberland's groundbreaking article, "Border Raids in the Lower Rio Grande Valley–1915," *Southwestern Historical Quarterly* 57 (January 1954): 285–311.
107. Funston to AG, August 14, 1915, no. 591, AGO.
108. Ibid.; Mann to same, August 14, 1915; Field Return, Battery E and Headquarters, 2nd Battalion, 5th Field Artillery, August 18, 22, 1915, Part 1, entry 4552, AGO; *BDH*, August 18, 1915.
109. Breckenridge to Commanding General, Second Division, August 14, 1915, no. 252; Field Return, 26th Infantry, Part 1, entry 4552, AGO; *BDH*, August 16, 1915.
110. Garrison to Funston, August 12, 1915, no. 525, AGO.
111. Funston to War Department, August 13, 1915, no. 590, AGO.
112. Funston to AG, August 13, 1915, no. 589, and Adjutant General McCain to Commandant, Service Schools, Fort Leavenworth, Kansas, August 14, 1915, AGO.
113. A. J. Bacevich, *Diplomat in Khaki: Major General Frank Ross McCoy and American Foreign Policy, 1898–1949* (Lawrence: University Press of Kansas, 1989), 61–64; Sterling, *Trails and Trials*, 44; "Proceedings," 1411–1412.
114. Sterling, *Trails and Trials*, 146, 177.
115. Ibid., 88.
116. Ibid., 260.
117. Ibid., 177.
118. Kirby F. Warnock, *Texas Cowboy* (Dallas: Trans Pecos Productions, 1992), 60–61.
    The Hidalgo County Historical Museum removed the book from its shelves because, according to the director, "Some passages in Mr. Warnock's book were in dispute." *Austin American-Statesman*, February 13, 1993.
119. "Scout Report, Co. D, Ranger Force for Oct, 1915," RRM.
120. Warnock, *Texas Cowboy*, 56–59, 125–126; *BDH*, October 2, 1915; State of Texas vs. W. W. Sterling and E. A. Sterling, Jr., *ex parte*, Habeas Corpus, No. 1003, 79th Judicial District, March 4, 1916; Ed Sterling to Wells, March 9, 1916; both in the James B. Wells Papers, CAH.

121. AG to Ransom, October 11, 1915, AGC.
122. Ransom to Hutchings, October 14, 1915, AGC.
123. Sterling, *Trails and Trials*, 419.
124. *BDH*, August 16, 1915.
125. See, for example, Scout Report for Captain Ransom's Company D, August, 1915, RRM; MR, Company D, August 31, 1915; MR, Company A, August 31, 1915; MR, Company B, August 31, 1915, AGC.
126. The *Herald* was consistently excellent in its coverage of the Bandit War. Under deadline pressure, it occasionally published stories that later turned out to be either erroneous or incomplete, but in these instances the newspaper would correct its account in later editions. Advertisers and the economic elites in the Brownsville area undoubtedly requested that the *Herald* downplay coverage of the raids, but it published accounts that were page one, top of the fold, and were generally accurate.
127. *BDH*, August 12, 1915.
128. Ibid., August 16, 1915.
129. *SAE*, June 18, 1916; *BDH*, August 5, 1915.
130. *BDH*, August 14, 25, 1915; "Weekly reports," September 16, 1915, 812.00/16256, September 22, 1915, 812.00/16319, and October 7, 1915, 812.00/16457, RDS.
131. *BDH*, August 16, 1915.
132. Scout Report of Ranger J. L. Anders, August, 1915, RRM.
133. "Proceedings," 1329. See also *BDH*, August 18, 1915.
134. *BDH*, August 19, 1915.
135. Fox to Hutchings, August 24, 1915, AGC.
136. Fox to Hutchings, August 20, 1915, AGC.
137. AG to Fox, August 23, 1915, AGC.
138. Kleberg to Hutchings, August 25, 1915, AGC.
139. Hutchings to Kleberg, same to Fox, Fox to Hutchings; all three dated August 23, 1915, AGC.
140. Fox to Hutchings, August 25, 1915, AGC.
141. Hutchings to Fox, August 28, 1915.
142. Ibid., August 18, 1915.
143. Ferguson to Wilson, August 16, 1915, FP.
144. Ferguson to Garner, August 17, 1915, FP.
145. Sanders was at Norias with Sergeant Grimes and Privates Brooks, Aldrich, Price, Cole, Blackwell, Hurst, Heinrich, Frances, Faubion, Dillard, and Webb, while Willis was at Del Rio and Cardwell at San Angelo. Sanders to Hutchings, August 22, 1915, AGC.
146. *BDH*, August 21, 1915.
147. Ibid., August 19, 1915.
148. Ibid., August 12, 21, 1915.
149. L. W. Edwards, Paul More West, Frank P. Baker, and Joe Davenport.
150. Scout Report of L. W. Edwards, Company D, August, 1915, RRM; Sanders to Hutchings, August 25, 1915, AGC; "Weekly report," August 28, 1915, no. 128, 545-B-7, AGO.
151. "Weekly report," no. 127, 545-A-7; Funston to AG, August 17, 1915, AGO.
152. J. H. Rogers report, November 16, 1915, reel 6, BI.
153. Ibid.; *BDH*, August 27, 1915.
154. J. H. Rogers report, November 16, 1915, reel 6, BI; *BDH*, August 27, 1915.
155. J. H.Rogers report, November 16, 1915, reel 6, BI; *BDH*, August 30, 31, 1915.
156. *BDH*, August 27, 1915.
157. Sanders to Hutchings, August 29, 1915, AGC.
158. Sanders to Hutchings, August 25, 1915, AGC.
159. *BDH*, August 26, 1915.
160. See A. J. Peters to William Phillips, September 9, 1915, 812.00/16194, RDS. There is a photograph of de la Rosa in the Huntington Library in Pasadena, California, dated 1914 and

referring to him as "captain." We have included this photograph.

161. Garrett to Lansing,, August 27, 1915 (812.00/15946), RDS; Canada to same, September 6, 1915 (812.00/16275), RDS.

162. Charles H. Harris III and Louis R. Sadler, "The Plan of San Diego and the Mexican-United States War Crisis of 1916: A Reexamination," *Hispanic American Historical Review* 58, no. 3 (August 1978), 387–388.

163. Ransom to Hutchings, August 30, 1915, AGC.

164. Sanders to Hutchings, August 22, 1915, AGC.

165. Hutchings to Sanders, August 31, 1915, AGC.

Chapter 10

1. *BDH*, September 2, 1915.
2. J. H. Rogers report, November 16, 1915, reel 6, BI.
3. Funston to AG, September 5, 1915, 650, AGO.
4. Cumberland, "Border Raids," 299.
5. Funston to AG, September 4, 1915, 649, AGO.
6. Baker to Hutchings, September 4, 1915; Hill to same, September 4, 1915, AGC.
7. *BDH*, September 1, 1915.
8. McCoy to AG, September 21, 1915, 11838-A52, AGO; *BDH*, September 4, 5, 1915.
9. Funston to AG, September 4, 1915, AGO; MR, Company D, September 30, RRM; J. L. Anders to Hutchings, September 4, 1915, AGC. Private Anders's telegram was, in the tradition of the Rangers, laconic: "While patrolling river with Sheriff Baker and deputies we were fired on from the Mexican side. We returned the fire. Soldiers have gone to the place where the battle occurred." *BDH*, September 4, 1915.
10. Sterling, *Trails and Trials*, 139–140; *BDH*, September 7, 1915.
11. Johnson, *Revolution in Texas*, 111.
12. *BDH*, September 8, 1915.
13. Funston to AG, August 27, 1915, 261, AGO.
14. *BDH*, August 31, 1915; U.S. vs. Miguel Saiz, no. 268, U.S. Commissioner, Brownsville, and no. 2178, U.S. District Court, Brownsville, FRC-FW.
15. *BDH*, August 31, 1915. Bureau of Investigation Special Agent in Charge Robert Barnes investigated the incident prior to filing federal charges.
16. Puig to Secretary of State, August 29, 1915, Southern Department, United States Army, 1913–1920, Correspondence Relating to the Mexican Revolution, 1913–16, Record Group 393, National Archives and Records Service, Washington, D.C.
17. Funston to AG, August 30, 1915, 629, AGO.
18. Funston to AG, August 30, 1915, 628, AGO.
19. *BDH*, September 7, 1915.
20. Aldrich to Hutchings, September 4, 1915, AGC.
21. *BDH*, September 10, 1915; Rogers report, November 16, 1915, reel 6, BI. Rogers noted in his report that the Guerra killing was the first of a series of revenge killings targeted against the Deyos.
22. *BDH*, September 10, 1915.
23. Funston to AG, telegram 670 [September 11?, 1915], AGO.
24. Rogers report, November 16, 1915, reel 6, BI; *BDH*, September 15, 1915.
25. *BDH*, September 21, 1915.
26. Funston to AG, September 10, 1915, 664, AGO.
27. Scott to AG, September 11, 1915, AGO.
28. Funston to AG, September 10, 1915, 664, AGO.
29. (tel) Ferguson to Funston, September 12, 1915, AGO.

30. Ferguson to Hutchings, September 13, 1915, FP.

31. Funston to Robertson, September 13, 1915, FP.

32. Ferguson to Funston, September 13, 1915, FP.

33. Hay to Commanding Officer, September 15, 1915, 14318, Southern Department, AGO.

34. Rogers report, November 16, 1915, reel 6, BI.

35. Funston to Ferguson, quoted in telegram 676, Funston to AG, September 16, 1915, AGO.

36. Ibid.

37. Ferguson to Vann, September 20, 1915, FP.

38. Ferguson to H. L. Yates and to Lawrence Bates, September 10, 1915, FP.

39. Ferguson to Vann, October 1, 1915, FP.

40. Carranza to Arredondo, September 20, 1915, in 23286552, box 7645, October 1, 1915, AGO.

41. *BDH*, September 15, 1915.

42. Ibid., September 14, 22, 1915.

43. Ibid., September 14, 1915; *LWT*, September 19, 1915.

44. *BDH*, September 11, 15, 1915.

45. Funston to AG, September 17, 1915, 679, AGO; "Weekly report," no. 131, 545-E-7, AGO; *BDH*, September 17, 1915.

46. "Weekly report," no. 31, 545-E-7, AGO.

47. Gregory to Garrison, September 20, 1915, 90755–24501/2, RDJ.

48. *BDH*, September 23, 1915.

49. Captain A. V. P. Anderson to Commanding Officer, September 24, 1915, AGO.

50. Funston to AG, September 24, 1915, telegram 698, AGO.

51. *BDH*, September 24, 1915.

52. Funston to AG, September 27, 1915, telegram 711, AGO. These were lightweight guns that could be broken down and carried by mules or horses over difficult terrain. See Field Return, Battery D, 4th Field Artillery, October, 1915, Part I, Entry 4552, Southern Department, United States Army, 1913–1920, Correspondence Relating to the Mexican Revolution, 1913–16, NA.

53. *BDH*, September 27, 1915.

54. Funston to AG, September 29, 1915, telegram 716, 2328806, October 2, 1915 (filed with 221235), AGO. A copy of Cuéllar's sworn statement, which Captain McCoy secured, can be found in *IMA*, 1289–1290, and Mayfield's testimony before the Fall Committee is on pages 1287–1296.

55. Sterling, *Trails and Trials*, 38–42; *BDH*, September 25, 27, 1915. See also Warnock, *Texas Cowboy*, 46–48, who gives a somewhat different account of the raid.

56. Warnock, *Texas Cowboy*, 49–50, 125, 127.

57. Rogers to Gregory, September 30, 1915, in AGO 2329053, October 2, 1915, and Southern Department no. 15062, October 13, 1915.

58. Ransom to Hutchings, September 22, 24, 1915, AGC.

59. Ransom to Hutchings, September 3, 1915; Hutchings to Ransom, September 4, 1915; same to Baker, September 4, 1915, AGC.

60. L. W. Edwards, Cole K. Brunner, Bert C. Veale, George A. Glick, Joseph E. Baker.

61. F. P. Baker, I. S. Chadick, Ben B. Dubose, J. L. Anders.

62. Sanders to Hutchings, September 4, 17, 1915; AG to Sanders, September 20, 1915.

63. Kleberg to Hutchings, September 25 [?], 1915, AGC.

64. Ibid.

65. Hutchings to Kleberg, October 2, 1915, AGC.

66. J. H. Johnson to Secretary of State, January 25, 1916, 812.00/17186, RDS.

67. *BDH*, October 2, 1915.

68. See, for example, Paul J. Vanderwood and Frank N. Samponaro, *Border Fury: A Picture Postcard Record of Mexico's Revolution and U.S. War Preparedness, 1910–1917* (Albuquerque: University of New Mexico Press, 1988), 121–122.

69. *BDH*, September 27, October 1, 1915.

70. Sanders to Hutchings, October 9, 1915, AGC.

71. Funston to AG, Second Indorsement, October 13, 1915, in 2329053, AGO, October 4, 1915.

72. Robert Lansing to Charles Parker, October 19, 1915, 812.00/16518a, RDS.

73. *BDH*, October 19, 1915; the testimony of District Attorney Kleiber that Luis de la Rosa actually participated in the attack is quite persuasive. See *IMA*, 1269–1277.

74. *BDH*, October 20, 1915; *IMA*, 1269–1277.

75. *BDH*, October 19, 20, 1915.

76. *IMA*, 1276–1277.

77. Ibid., 1272; *BDH*, October 19, 1915.

78. "Weekly report," October 23, 1915, no. 136, 545-J-7, AGO; Scout Report, Company D, October 31, 1915, RRM.

79. *BDH*, October 20, 1915.

80. "Weekly report," October 23, 1915, no. 136, 545-J-7, AGO.

81. Ferguson to Lansing, October 25, 1915, FP.

82. "Proceedings," 562; *BDH*, October 21, 1915.

83. Sterling, *Trails and Trials*, 42–43.

84. "Proceedings," 573–575.

85. *BDH*, October 21, 1915.

86. Funston to AG, October 22, 1915, no. 754, AGO.; *IMA*, 1303–1307.

87. Hidalgo County Deputy Sheriff Tom Mayfield had several informants whom he would send across the Rio Grande to report on the activities at de la Rosa's camp. Mayfield testified that de la Rosa had four Japanese who fashioned crude hand grenades by pouring black powder and pieces of metal on green cowhides, tying the cowhides into a bundle, and inserting a fuse. See *IMA*, 1290, 1293. Japanese involvement in the Mexican Revolution is a topic that bears investigation.

88. Funston to AG, October 22, 1915, no. 756, AGO. Funston's request was first cited by Charles Cumberland in his seminal article "Border Raids," 285–311, an article that has not received the scholarly recognition it deserves.

89. Funston to General Hugh Scott, October 22, 1915, no. 757, box 7645, 2311838, A59, AGO.

90. Garrison to Funston, October 23, 1915, no. 674, box 7645, AGO. The Southern Department commander was not the only one concerned by events. The commanding officer of the 26th Infantry, which covered an area from Kingsville to Olmitos to Mercedes to the Gulf of Mexico, in a report dated October 30, 1915, warned that "The wide use of arms by white citizens and the extreme difficulty of the civil authorities supervising their use, leading to personal aggression, revenge and terrorism by white upon Mexican citizens, are . . . complicating the situation. . . . There is unquestionably a growing separation and distrust between white and Mexican races. Some intelligent citizens of Mexican blood are beginning to realize that existing conditions in this district cannot . . . last a great deal longer without resulting in a race war." "Weekly Report" no. 137, 545-K7, AGO.

91. Funston to AG, October 24, 1915, no. 761, box 7645, AGO.

92. Field Returns, 28th Infantry, October 25, 1915, Part 1, Entry 4552, Southern Department, Correspondence Relating to the Mexican Revolution, 1913–16, NA.

93. Funston to AG, October 20, 1915, no. 746, AGO.

94. Gregory to Secretary of War, October 23, 1915, AGO.

95. For a full discussion of the assassination plot see Charles H. Harris III and Louis R. Sadler, *The Archaeologist Was a Spy: Sylvanus G. Morley and the Office of Naval Intelligence* (Albuquerque: University of New Mexico Press, 2003), 8–9, 387–388.

96. Scout reports, Companies A and D, October, 1915, RRM.

97. Spears to Hutchings, October 20, 1915, AGC.

98. See D. W. Glasscock, Caesar Kleberg, Sam Spears, Lon Hill et al. to Culberson, October 29, 1915. A copy was forwarded by Culberson's office to Secretary Garrison, 2338926, AGO.

99. See 1st and 2nd endorsements to AGO 2338926, dated November 5 and 16, 1915, respectively.

100. Secretary to the Governor to Fred Henry, FP; Funston to the AG, November 16, 1915, 2nd endorsement to AGO 2338926.

101. *BDH*, October 28, 1915.

102. Harris and Sadler, "Plan of San Diego," 391.

103. Ribb, "José Tomás Canales," 80, 8.

104. "Proceedings," 866–868.

105. Johnson, *Revolution in Texas*, 106.

106. Ibid., 2.

107. Harris and Sadler, "Plan of San Diego," 390.

108. Don Carroll, of the Bureau of Vital Statistics, Texas Department of Health Resources, graciously tabulated for the present authors the violent deaths for the period of the Bandit War in Cameron, Hidalgo, Jim Hogg, Kennedy, Starr, Webb, and Willacy Counties. Almost all of the reported deaths concerned soldiers killed fighting the raiders. Hidalgo County, where most of the fighting occurred, did not report a single violent death of a "WSS (white Spanish surname)." These deaths were simply not reported, although required by Texas law.

109. Pierce's list is in 812.00/17186, RDS. See also the "Memoirs of Jesse Perez," pp. 57–58, Center for American History, University of Texas at Austin. Pérez names sixty-two of the men who were killed.

110. Webb, *Texas Rangers*, 478.

111. Tyrrell to Chief, U.S. Secret Service, November 25, 1915, Records of the U.S. Secret Service, Daily Reports of Agents, 1875 through 1936, Microcopy no. 3.158, Record Group 87, National Archives and Records Service, Washington, D.C.

112. Harris and Sadler, "Plan of San Diego," 391–392.

113. Ibid., 392.

114. Ibid., 405–406.

Chapter 11

1. Clifford G. Beckham report, September 4, 1915, reel 8, BI; U.S. vs. Victoriano Huerta et al., no. 2185, U.S. District Court, San Antonio, and U.S. vs. Aristarco Carrascosa et al., no. 1536, U.S. Commissioner, El Paso, FRC-FW.

2. Meyer, *Mexican Rebel*, 124–130, and *Huerta*, 214–224.

3. *EPMT*, August 31, September 1–5, 1915. The best account of Orozco's death is the series of reports by Customs officials, especially that by mounted Customs Inspector Herff A. Carnes, a member of the posse. See Zack Cobb to Secretary of State, August 30, 1915, 812.00/15971; same to same, August 31, 1915, 812.00/15982; same to same, September 2, 1915, 812.00/16008 and /16046, all in RDS.

4. Meyer, *Mexican Rebel*, 131. See also Kenneth J. Grieb, *The United States and Huerta* (Lincoln: University of Nebraska Press, 1969), 191.

5. Alberto Calzadíaz Barrera, *Hechos reales de la Revolución*. III, 2nd ed. (México: Editorial Patria, 1972), 67–68.

6. *EPMT*, August 27, 1915.

7. "Weekly report," September 4, 1915, no. 129, 545-C-7, AGO. The possemen were: Sheriff John A. Morine, Jack Finlay, A. B. Medley, Dave Allison, George Love, H. A. Carnes, Robert C. Love, B. N. Love, Price Love, J. W. Millard, Will Shrock, and Pete Wetzel.

8. Carlo D'Este, *Patton: A Genius for War* (New York; HarperCollins, 1995), 158.

9. According to one account, it was Dave Allison who killed most, if not all, of the Orozco party. See "The Last Days of Pascual Orozco," E. A. "Dogie" Wright Papers, CAH.

10. *EPMT*, October 8,9, 1915.

11. [Hutchings] to Senator John H. Bailey, October 27, 1915; same to Ransom, December 17, 1915; same to Fox, December 18, 1915; Sanders to Hutchings, December 19, 1915; Smith to same, December 23, 1915, AGC.

12. [Hutchings] to N. P. Houx, November 20, 1915, AGC.

13. [Hutchings] to Ferguson, February 10, 1916; Ferguson to Hutchings, February 26, 1916, AGC.

14. [Hutchings] to Carlos Bee, March 22, 1916, AGC.

15. (tel) [Hutchings] to Captain Fox, March 13, 1916, RRM.

16. Fox to Hutchings, March 14, 16, 1916; Hutchings to Postmaster General A. S. Burleson, March 21, 1916, AGC.

17. *EPMT*, March 11, 12, 15, 1916.

18. Ibid., March 22, 23, 1916.

19. Ibid., March 28, 1916.

20. Walter Rushin to Hutchings, March 10, 1916, AGC.

21. Harris and Sadler, "The Plan of San Diego," 392–393.

22. Corpus Christi *Caller and Daily Herald*, May 9, 1916.

23. Memorandum, June 8, 1916, Expediente Brigada Fierros; General Esteban Fierros to General Pablo González, June 9, 1916, Expediente Esteban Fierros, PGA.

24. General Pablo González to A. Valdés, December 30, 1915; General Esteban Fierros to González, November 23, 1916; Expediente Esteban Fierros; J. N. Galbraith to Fierros, August 30, 1915; Expediente Brigada Fierros, PGA.

25. U.S. vs. Abel Sandoval et al., U.S. Commissioner, no. 309, Brownsville; U.S. vs. Felipe Sandoval et al., no. 2208, U.S. District Court, Brownsville, FRC-FW.

26. General Pablo González to Carranza, June 17, 22, 24, 1916, Telegrams, State of Morelos, 1916, VCA.

27. González to Carranza, June 24, 1916, Telegrams, State of Morelos, 1916, VCA.

28. Receipts in Expediente Brigada Fierrros, PGA. For a more detailed account of the 1916 crisis see Harris and Sadler, "The Plan of San Diego."

29. State of Texas vs. Norberto Pezzar [sic] et al., no. 5204, District Court, Laredo; *LWT*, July 15, 1916.

30. Jose Antonio Arce et al. vs. State of Texas, no 4314, Texas Court of Criminal Appeals, Austin; *LWT*, May 24, 1918.

31. Johnson, *Revolution in Texas*, 142.

32. Howard P. Wright reports, May 2, 4, 5, 1916; "Statement of Jose Morin," May 12, 1916, reel 12, BI. In 1912, José Morín and his brother Alcidio reportedly enlisted in Kenedy, Texas, for service with Pascual Orozco's revolutionary forces and recruited men in San Antonio for that movement. H. A. Thompson report, March 30, 1912, reel 1; Robert L. Barnes reports, May 17, 18, 1912, reel 2, BI.

33. R. L. Barnes report, May 11, 1916; J. B. Rogers report, May 25, 1916, reel 12, BI.

34. See, for example, Howard P. Wright report, May 30, 1916, and R. L. Barnes report, June 2, 1916, reel 12, BI.

35. Howard P. Wright report, May 6, 1916, reel 12, BI. See also Harry Berliner report, May 9, 1916, reel 12, BI.

36. Howard P. Wright report, May 11, 1916, reel 12, BI; *La Prensa*, May 12, 13, 16, 1916; Corpus Christi *Caller and Daily Herald*, May 12, 13, 1916.

37. "Statement of Jose Morin," May 12, 1916, and "Statement of Victorino Ponce," May 12, 13, 1916; Robert L. Barnes to Howard P. Wright, May 11, 1916; Howard P. Wright report, May 13, 1916; Wright to Barnes (two letters), May 14, 1916, reel 12, BI; *SAE*, May 16, 1916.

38. Corpus Christi *Caller and Daily Herald*, May 13, 1916.

39. Howard P. Wright reports, May 30, June 5, 1916, reel 12, BI; see also Sheriff Scarborough's testimony in "Proceedings," 253–267.

40. J. B. Rogers report, May 25, 1916, reel 12, BI.

41. Ibid.; *SAE*, May 27, 30, 1916.
42. R. L. Barnes report, May 29, 1916, reel 12, BI.
43. Howard P. Wright report, June 5, 1916, reel 12, BI.
44. Ibid.
45. Ibid.
46. Ibid. See also *La Prensa*, May 29, June 1, 1916.
47. Howard P. Wright report, June 5, 1916, reel 12, BI; *AA*, June 5, 1916; *La Prensa*, June 8, 1916.
48. Testimony of Hook, "Proceedings," 335–336, and of Sanders, "Proceedings," 1396–1398.
49. Garrison to Gregory, June 19, 1916, reel 12, BI.
50. Captain Fox to Hutchings, May 16, 1916; AG to Fox, May 19, WC; *EPMT*, May 15, 16, 20, 1916; AG to Hotel Dieu, June 12, 1916, AGC.
51. Almond to Hutchings, May 21, 1916, AGC.
52. AG to Almond, May 27, 1916, AGC.
53. Almond to Hutchings, May 31, 1916, AGC.
54. AG to Almond, June 2, 1916, AGC.
55. *EPMT*, July 4, 1916.
56. Ibid., August 16, September 28, 1916.
57. Ibid., September 9, 1916.
58. [Hutchings] to Ferguson, July 7, 8, September 7, 1916, AGC.
59. AG to J. L. Lubbock, September 30, 1916; Same to Sheriff John W. Almond, October 10, 1916, AGC.
60. Edwin R. Huck to Hutchings, September 7, 1915, AGC; [Hutchings] to Ferguson, September 8, 1915; "Additional Testimony in Charges Against Captain E. H. Smith," September 8, 9, 1915, WC.
61. Wells to Hutchings, June 9, 1916, AGC.
62. Kleberg to Hutchings, September 25, 1915; [Hutchings] to Ferguson, September 30, 1915; Ferguson to Hutchings, October 1, 1915; AG to McAlister, October 2, 1915, AGC.
63. Hutchings to Kleberg, October 2, 1915, AGC.
64. Kleberg to Hutchings, November 30, 1915; Hutchings to Kleberg, November 22, December 4, 1915, AGC.
65. Parr to Hutchings, January 12, 1916, AGC.
66. Hutchings to Ferguson, January 14, 1916; (tel) Same to Paul McAlister, January 14, 1916, AGC.
67. Sanders to Hutchings, December 11, 12, 1915; (tel) Judge V. W. Taylor to same, December 13, 1915; Hutchings to Taylor, December 13, 1915; Same to Sanders, December 13, 1915, AGC; "Scout Report of Company A, Ranger Force for December, 1915," December 31, 1915, RRM; *LWT*, December 19, 1915.
68. White to Hutchings, April 28, 1916, AGC.
69. Frederick Guy reports, December 13, 15, 1915, reel 6; John Wren report, June 10, 1916, reel 12, BI.
70. Mrs. A. Alderete to Ferguson, August 28, 1916, AGC.
71. (tel) Hutchings to Fox, September 7, 1916, AGC; Fox moved the Ysleta camp to Eagle Springs, between Hot Wells and the Rio Grande. (tel) Fox to Hutchings, September 7, 1916, AGC.
72. AG to Fox, September 7, 1916, AGC.
73. (tel) Edwards to Hutchings, September 8, 1916, AGC.
74. (tel) Hutchings to Edwards, September 8, 1916, AGC.
75. Hutchings to Commanding General, Massachusetts Militia, September 9, 1916, AGC.
76. Fox to Hutchings, September 10, 1916, AGC.
77. Hutchings to Ferguson, September 14, 1916, AGC.
78. Steve L. Pinckney reports, May 5, 6, 1916, reel 12, BI.
79. U.S. vs. George Holmes et al, nos. 1979 and 2053, U.S. District Court, El Paso. See also no.

121, U.S. Commissioner, El Paso, all in FRC-FW; *EPMT*, October 9, 14, 1916. George Holmes was sentenced in 1919 to three years in Leavenworth for perjury and five years for conspiring to export munitions to Mexico. On March 16, 1927, he was killed in the mountains of Chihuahua. *EPMT*, December 21, 1919, and March 19, 1927; *LWT*, October 24, 1920.

80. Captain R. E. Grinstead to District Commander, October 27, 1916, 8532-49, MID.
81. Ibid. See also E. B. Stone report, June 12, 1916, reel 12, BI.
82. *EPMT*, August 29–31, October 18, November 2, December 1, 4, 1916.
83. W. L. Barler to Hutchings, April 9, 1916, WC; *EPMT*, April 10, 11, 1916.
84. There is a photograph of the Coney Island Saloon in Sonnichsen, *Pass of the North*, between 370 and 371.
85. *EPMT*, September 22–27, 29, 30, 1916; "Proceedings," 987–988.
86. *EPMT*, October 19, 20, November 21, December 5, 14, 19, 1916, January 17, 1917.
87. *BDH*, May 30, 1917; Sands's service record does not specify the date of his discharge.
88. McGregor to Ferguson, September 23, 1916; Hutchings to same, September 28, 1916, AGC.
89. *EPMT*, December 17, 19, 1916.
90. (tel) W. A. Merrell to Ferguson, December 20, 1916; John L. Wroe to AG, December 21, 1916, AGC.
91. E. B. Spiller to Hutchings, November 1, 4, 1915; AG to Spiller, November 2, 1915; Hamer to AG, November 7, 19, 1915; AG to Hamer, November 7, 22, 1915, AGC.
92. W. W. Weems to Ferguson, December 21, 1916, WC; see also [Hutchings] to Ferguson, December 21, 1916, AGC.
93. Ibid.
94. John L. Wroe to AG, December 21, 28, 1916, AGC.
95. J. D. White to Hutchings, December 27, 1916; AG to J. D. White, December 28, 1916, AGC.
96. W. A. Merrell to Ferguson, January 1, 1917; AG to W. W. Weems, January 3, 1917; same to W. A. Merrell, January 5, 1917, AGC.
97. AG to E. B. Spiller, November 2, 1915, AGC.
98. Frank A. Hamer to Hutchings, January 10, 1917; AG to Sam H. Hill, January 10, 1917; same to Hamer, January 11, 1917, AGC.

Chapter 12

1. Katz, *Secret War*, 350–378. See also Barbara Tuchman, *The Zimmermann Telegram*. New York: Viking Press, 1958.
2. See, for example, Charles H. Harris III and Louis R. Sadler, "The Witzke Affair: German Intrigue on the Mexican Border, 1917–18," *Military Review*, LIX, no. 2 (February 1979): 36–50.
3. Harley to Senator Morris Sheppard, January 30, 1918, AGC.
4. Chief of Staff, Southern Department to Adjutant General of the Army, January 10, 1917, copy in 812.00/20395, RDS.
5. J. García report, January 2, 1916 [sic—1917], reel 11; J. P. S. Mennet report, April 30, 1917, reel 6, BI; Weekly Intelligence Report, Southern Department, January 20, 1917, copy in 812.00/20454, RDS; Philip Hanna to Secretary of State, January 16, 1917, 812.00/20405, RDS; "Weekly reports," July 28, 1917, 10014-5; September 1, 1917, 10014-6; September 8, 1917, 10014-7; December 8, 1917, 10014-20; December 29, 1917, 10014-26; January 12, 1918, 10014-30; January 18, 1918, 10014-32; February 2, 1918, 10014-39; February 16, 1918, 10014-46, MID; *BDH*, January 18, December 6, 1917.
6. J. H. Lege report, October 16, 1917, reel 12 BI; Agent #40 [J. P. S. Mennet] report, December 6, 1917, reel 18, BI.
7. G. N. Lynch to Ferguson, April 11, 1917, AGC.

8. T. Vard Woodruff to Ferguson, July 10, 1917, AGC.

9. Ed P. Eason to Hobby, January 28, 1918, AGC.

10. Fox to Hutchings, January 11, 1917; Hutchings to Daugherty, January 12, 1917; J. D. McGregor to Hutchings, January 18, 1917; Daugherty to Fox, undated [January, 1917], AGC.

11. W. L. Amonett to Ferguson, May 5, 1917, AGC.

12. See, for example, AG to Hudspeth, May 31, 1917; same to C. E. Miller, May 31, 1917; same to Charles K. Smith, May 31, 1917; Hudspeth to AG, June 13, 14, 16, 1917; AG to Hudspeth, June 13, 19, 1917, AGC; "Proceedings," 964, 982, 985.

13. Caesar Kleberg to Hutchings, May 10, 1917; same to Governor, May 17, 1917, AGC.

14. "Stations of National Guard Organizations in the Southern Department Including changes since memorandum no. 15, June 30, 1917," RRM.

15. Bill Connally to Hutchings, June 23, 1917, AGC.

16. James H. Taylor to Ferguson, August 13, 1917, AGC.

17. On the subject of draft dodging see: Oscar Roberts to Ferguson, May 1, 1917; W. R. Burnett to AG, May 1, 1917; same to Ferguson, May 1, 1917; W. T. Jones to Hutchings, May 3, 1917; Guy L. Edison to Ferguson, May 4, 1917; J. H. Tallichet to Hutchings, May 4, 1917; Hutchings to Tallichet, May 5, 1917; Ferguson to Hutchings, undated [April 1917]; J. T. Runyon to Hutchings, May 22, 1917; A. B. Wilson to same, May 24, 1917; same to Ferguson, May 24, 1917; J. Frank Wallace to same, May 28, 1917; P. G. Dabney to same, May 28, 1917; Byron Jarrell to Hutchings, May 31, 1917; L. S. Schluter to same, June 15, 1917; W. T. Armistead to Ferguson, June 27, 1917; Charles Clements to same, August 6, 1917; Scott Eubanks to same, August 6, 1917; John L. Culp to AG, August 10, 1917, AGC; *AA*, June 14, 1917.

18. James O. Winborn to J. C. Jones, August 4, 1917, AGC.

19. Dick Hatcher to AG Department, December 3, 1917, AGC.

20. John R. Banister to AG, August 8, 1917, AGC.

21. J. C. White to Hutchings, January 18, 1917; [Hutchings] to J. C. White, January 19, 1917; same to L. D. Boynton, February 2, 1917; E. B. Hendricks to Ferguson, January 19, 1917, AGC. Captain E. H. Smith was commissioned in 1915 in Company C and transferred in 1916 to Company D. On December 20, 1917, he was reinstated as a Regular Ranger without pay. His Ranger connection ended on January 15, 1919, after which he became a special officer for the Katy Railroad in Waco.

22. Hutchings to Pat Craighead, February 2, 1917; Craighead to Hutchings, January 31, 1917, AGC.

23. Hutchings to J. D. Jackson, March 29, 1917, AGC.

24. AG to Chairman, Finance Committee, April 12, 1917; see also same to Tom R. Hickman, April 14, 1917, AGC.

25. *BDH*, April 9, 17, 24, 25, 1917; W. W. Turney to Ferguson, May 2, 1917; R. B. Slight to same, May 3, 1917, AGC.

26. *BDH*, May 9, 1917.

27. *AA*, May 10 and 17, 1917.

28. *General and Special Laws of the State of Texas Passed at the First Called Session of the Thirty-fifth Legislature Convened at the City of Austin, April 18, 1917 and Adjourned May 17, 1917* (Austin: A. C. Baldwin & Sons, 1917), 57–59; *Biennial Report of the Adjutant General of Texas From January 1, 1917, to December 31, 1918* (Austin: Von Boeckmann-Jones Co., 1919), 56.

29. *Biennial Report*, 58–59.

30. E. H. Parker report, April 24, 1917, reel 17, BI.

31. *BDH*, May 9–11, 16–19, 21, 24, 29, 30, June 2, 4, 7, 1917; *LWT*, May 27, 1917.

32. J. T. Dodson to Ferguson, May 18, 1917; E. K. Register to same, May 18, 1917; Harley to Dodson, May 28, 1917; same to Register, May 28, 1917, AGC.

33. *Handbook*, II, 956; S. Adamson and W. A. Merrell to Hutchings, August 2, 1917; B. L. Russell to James A. Harley, December 3, 1917; J. R. Hollis to same, December 27, 1917, AGC.

34. S. Adamson and W. A. Merrell to Hutchings, August 2, 1917; W. W. Beall to Hobby, November 22, 1917; Harley to Ransom, December 14, 1917, AGC.

35. Hugh Smith to Ferguson, April 19, 1917; Jerry Gray to same, May 11, 1917, AGC.

36. Carroll Bates to Ferguson, April 20, 1917, AGC.

37. W. P. McLean, Jr., to Ferguson, May 19, 1917; C. B. Hudspeth to same, May 26, 1917; James Cornell to same, May 20, 1917; W. D. Davis to Whom It May Concern, May 21, 1917; J. N. Latham to Ferguson, May 22, 1917; Brown Harwood to same, May 22, 1917; William A. Hanger to same, May 23, 1917; C. E. Dubois to same, May 24, 1917; J. W. Johnson to same, May 24, 1917; Carroll Bates to same, May 24, 1917, AGC.

38. C. B. Hudspeth to Ferguson, April 30, 1917; John F. Robinson to same, May 22, 1917, AGC.

39. *EPMT*, August 16, 1917; *BDH*, August 13, 15, 20, 1917.

40. Clark, *Tactful Texan*, 67–74; *BDH*, September 22, 25, 1917.

41. *BDH*, September 26, 1917.

42. Ibid., September 24, 1917.

43. Hobby to Oscar Calloway, September 3, 1917; same to P. F. Dunn, September 14, 1917, HP.

44. Brigadier Gen. Henry Hutchings to General Manager, I&GN Railway, October 6, 1917, AGC.

45. John D. McCall to C. J. Bartlett, October 2 and 15, 1917, HP.

46. *Biennial Report*, 59.

47. Hobby to F. A. Chapa, January 5, 1918, HP.

48. *A Twentieth Century History*, II, 479–480; Stevens to Hutchings, June 30, 1917; Hutchings to Chapa, July 3, 1917; J. H. Rogers to Hutchings, July 14, 1917; D. H. Hart to same, July 14, 1917; J. F. Carl to Ferguson, July 24, 1917, AGC.

49. W. M. Hanson to Harley, February 26, 1918, AGC; C. F. Stevens reports, September 5, 11, 16, 1913, reel 4; R. L. Barnes reports, September 7, 1914, reel 6, November 21, 1914, reel 5, January 17, 1916, reel 8; E. M. Blanford reports, October 7, 1914, reel 6, and December 3, 1914, reel 5; Charles Breniman report, November 3, 1915, reel 8; Clifford S. Beckham report, February 16, 1916, reel 8, BI.

50. *BDH*, December 18, 1917; *LWT*, December 9, 1917.

51. Barker to Harley, December 3, 1917, AGC.

52. Harley to Clifford Belcher, October 4, 1917; same to W. P. Fennell, October 4, 1917; Belcher to Harley, October 11, 1917, AGC.

53. Harley to Captains W. L. Barler, J. J. Sanders, and J. M. Fox, October 8, 1917, AGC.

54. Sanders to Harley, October 10 and 19, 1917; Harley to Sanders, October 12, 1917, AGC.

55. Barler to Harley, October 12, 1917, AGC.

56. Harley to Captains W. L. Barler, J. J. Sanders, and J. M. Fox, October 9, 1917, AGC.

57. Woodul to James Callan, December 21, 1917; Harley to J. H. Bailey, December 22, 1917, AGC.

58. Moses and Rowe to Harley, October 9, November 13, 1917; Harley to N. H. Lassiter, October 12, 1917; same to General Manager, Rock Island Lines, October 12, 1917; same to Moses and Rowe, October 20, 1917, AGC. Moses and Rowe, the attorneys for the Cattle Raisers Association of Texas, was a Fort Worth law firm.

59. Harley to Captains Barler, Sanders, Fox, and Ransom, October 11, 1917; see also Sanders to Harley, November 11, 1917; Barler to same, October 12, 1917; Harley to Sanders, October 15, 1917, AGC.

60. Harley to Fox, November 24, 1917, AGC.

61. Woodul to Mayor [George J. Bird], November 27, 1917, AGC; see also Hobby to Jack Stephens, September 1, 1917, HP.

62. Bates to Woodul, November 27, 1917, AGC.

63. [Harley] to W. H. Fryer, December 3, 1917; see also same to H. J. Ellis, December 6, 1917, AGC; Hobby to Robert M. Insall, November 15, 1917, HP.

64. Fred Pearce to Harley, October 18, 1917, AGC.

65. Rawlings to Hobby, December 6, 7, 8, 11, 15, 1917, AGC. Rawlings's company was disbanded in February, 1918.

66. *EPMT*, October 16, 1917; *BDH*, October 27, 1917.
67. Sheriff, Mason County to Harley, December 3, 1917, AGC.
68. D. S. Barker to Harley, December 3, 1917, AGC.
69. J. S. Scarborough to Harley, November 30, 1917; see also same to Ferguson, June 4, 1917, AGC.
70. Edgar T. Neal to Harley, December 18, 1917; Hugh Smith to same, December 18, 1917; J. L. Sheppard to same, December 18, 1917; J. S. Scarborough to same, December 19, 1917; J. F. Ray to same, December 19, 1917; Harley to W. W. McCutcheon, December 18, 1917, AGC.
71. See Harley to Chief Special Agents, December 18, 1917, AGC.
72. Woodul to R. J. Noonan, December 20, 1917, AGC.
73. See, for example, Captain Fox to Woodul, December 31, 1917, AGC.
74. Woodul to Captain W. L. Barler, December 18, 1917; same to T. G. Barnett, December 18, 1917, AGC.
75. See, for example, Woodul to Captain Fox, December 18, 1917, AGC.
76. Harley to Sheriff, Mason County, December 5, 1917, AGC.
77. *EPMT*, January 1, 1917.
78. Ibid., May 20, 25, 31, 1917.
79. Ibid., August 18, 1917.
80. Fox to Hutchings, May 19, 1917, RRM.
81. Hutchings to Fox, May 22, 1917, RRM.
82. Woodul to John A. Hulen, December 15, 1917, AGC.
83. Cano and Sochat, *Bandido*, 18, 116, 117, 231.
84. *EPMT*, May 20, September 28, 1917; *AA*, May 24, 1917.
85. *IMA*, 1538–1540, 1648–1650; *AA*, December 13, 1917.
86. *IMA*, 1543.
87. Ibid., 1540–1547.
88. Ibid., 1526–1531; *BDH*, December 26–28, 1917.
89. Statement of Raymond Fitzgerald, undated [March, 1918], WC.
90. See, for example, A. H. Allen to Vice Consul Newman P. Blocker, September 3, 1917, AGC.
91. Vice Consul Newman P. Blocker to Secretary of State, August 27, 1917, copy in WC; A. H. Allen to Blocker, September 3, 1917, AGC; "Weekly report," September 8, 1917, 10014-7, MID.
92. "Weekly report," December 15, 1917, 10014-25, MID.
93. Harley to Barler, December 1, 1917, AGC.
94. Cunningham to Harley, December 28, 1917, AGC.
95. Woodul to Cunningham, December 29, 1917, AGC.
96. Cunningham to Harley, December 31, 1917, WC; same to same, January 5, 1918, AGC; see also R. G. Barnes to same, January 7, 1918, WC, and J. M. Lege report, December 30, 1917, reel 17, BI. For the army's report on the incursion see Assistant Secretary of State to Secretary of War, December 30, 1918, Records of the Adjutant General's Office, 1917–, Central Decimal Files Project Files, 1917–1925, Countries–Mexican Border, 000.51, RG 407, NA.
97. Newman P. Blocker to Secretary of State, December 31, 1917, and to Brig. Gen. Fernando Peraldi, December 31, 1917, copies in AGC.
98. Cunningham to Harley, January 30, 1918, WC.

Chapter 13

1. *AA*, January 3, 1918; Harley to Davis, December 31, 1917; Davis to Harley, December 31, 1917, January 1, 1918; Gray to same, January 1, 1918, AGC.
2. Davis to Harley, January 2, 1918, AGC.

3. Woodul to J. W. Favela, January 3, 1918, AGC; "Proceedings," 1509–1510.

4. Woodul to T. P. Hull, January 8, 1918, AGC; see also Harley's comments on the Rangers in reply to an inquiry by the Governor General of Australia, in Hobby to Secretary of State, January 16, 1918, HP.

5. Dr. I. E. Clark to Harley, June 21, 1918, AGC.

6. Harley to J. F. Carl, February 13, 1918, AGC.

7. Woodul to Captain W. W. Davis, January 31, 1918, AGC.

8. Hobby to M. B. Smith, September 13, 1917; same to Secretary of War, December 8, 1917; same to General W. C. Gorgas, December 7, 1917; same to John N. Garner, December 26, 1917 and January 5, 1918; same to H. E. Porter, January 7, 1918; same to C. McWhirter, January 8, 1918; same to J. R. Mills, January 11, 1918; For Hobby's comments on how the press had distorted Harley's mission see Hobby to John H. Kirby, January 21, 1918, HP.

9. W. A. Webb to Dear Sir, February 7, 1918, AGC.

10. Sheppard to Harley, January 29, 1918; Garner to same, January 29, 1918; same to Hobby, February 11, 1918; Hobby to Interstate Commerce Commission, February 12, 1918; same to Garner, February 12, 1918; J. F. Carl to Hobby, February 5, 1918; Harley to Carl, February 13, 1918; Marshall Hicks to Gregory, February 15, 1918; Gregory to Hicks, February 21, 1918; Harley to Joseph Mansfield, February 22, 1918; Garner to Harley, February 23, 1918, AGC; Hobby to W. G. McAdoo, January 31, 1918; same to Interstate Commerce Commission, February 12, 1918, HP.

11. Brite to Sheppard, February 7, 1918; Kleberg to Garner, February 9, 1918, AGC.

12. Harley to Sheppard, January 30, 1918, AGC.

13. (tel) Hobby to Interstate Commerce Commission, February 19, 1918; (tel) same to W. G. McAdoo, undated [February 1918]; (tel) same to John N. Garner, February 12, 1918, HP.

14. Woodul to J. C. Rawlings, January 31, 1918, AGC.

15. Harley to Fox, February 23, 1918; same to Manager, Gulf Coast Lines, March 20, 1918; A. G. Whittington to Woodul, March 21, 1918, AGC.

16. Woodul to Garrett, February 5, 1918; Harley to same, March 5, 1918, AGC.

17. Harley to C. P. Engelking, March 5, 1918, AGC.

18. Hobby to J. M. Woolridge, January 11, 1918, AGC.

19. Woodul to Davis, December 26, 1917, AGC.

20. Woodul to Davis, January 4, 1918, AGC.

21. Davis to Harley, January 2, 1918, AGC.

22. Ibid.; same to same, January 4, 1918; Woodul to Davis, January 4, 1918, AGC.

23. Davis to Woodul, January 10, 1918; Woodul to Davis, January 14, 1918, AGC; Hobby to Davis, January 23, 1918, HP.

24. P. A. Cardwell to Davis, January 17, 31, 1918; Davis to Cardwell, January 28, February 3, 6, 8, March 1, 1918, AGC.

25. Davis to Harley, January 26, 29, February 4, 1918; Harley to Davis, January; 29, 1918; Fox to Woodul, January 22, 1918; Woodul to Fox, January 28, 1918; same to Davis, January 31, February 11, 14, 1918; Davis to Woodul, February 8,9, 1918; Same to Cardwell, February 8, 21, 1918, AGC.

26. Davis to Harley, March 18, 1918, AGC.

27. Davis to Woodul, February 25, 1918, AGC.

28. Eickenroht's tenure proved all too brief. On April 9, Harley ordered him back to Austin. Harley to Davis, April 9, 1918, AGC.

29. Davis to Harley, March 7, 1918; Harley to Davis, March 7, 1918, AGC.

30. Davis to Harley, March 14, 1918, AGC.

31. Harley to Davis, March 16, 1918; Davis to Harley, March 17, 1918, AGC.

32. Harley to Davis, March 21, 1918, AGC.

33. Harley to Davis, April 1, 1918; Davis to Harley, April 4, 1918; see also same to same, March 23, 27, 31, 1918, AGC.

34. Davis to Harley, March 23, 1918, AGC. Pennington's service record states that he died of Spanish influenza on October 12, 1918.
35. Woodul to Davis, March 26, 1918, AGC.
36. Davis to Cardwell, March 27, 1918; [Cardwell] to Davis, April 2, 1918, AGC.
37. Davis to Harley, April 4, 1918; see also same to Cardwell, April 1, 1918, AGC.
38. Davis to Harley, March 18, April 27, 1918, AGC.
39. Davis to Harley, April 27, 1918; same to Woodul, April 30, 1918; Woodul to Davis, April 30, May 8, 1918; Harley to same, May 10, 1918, AGC.
40. R. E. Thomason and R. M. Dudley to Harley, May 31, 1918, AGC.
41. Davis to Cardwell, May 9, 1918, AGC. Private Robert E. Hunt of Company L died of Spanish influenza on October 15, 1918.
42. Davis to Cardwell, May 13, 1918, AGC.
43. Holbrook to Hanson, May 29, 1918, AGC.
44. Harley to Knight, August 26, 1918; Special Orders No. 33, August 26, 1918; Knight to Harley, Hanson to Harley, May 29, 1918; Woodul to Davis, June 5, 1918, AGC.
45. Woodul to Holbrook, June 5, 1918, AGC.
46. Davis to Woodul, June 10, 1918; Woodul to Davis, June 14, 1918, AGC.
47. Woodul to McGregor, May 10, 1918, AGC; "Proceedings," 968, 975, 982, 989–990.
48. McGregor to Woodul, May 13, 1918, AGC.
49. Gray to Harley, June 23, 1918, AGC.
50. Dudley to Harley, July 17, 1918, AGC.
51. Knight to Harley, August 14, 1918, AGC.
52. Harley to Knight, August 26, 1918; Special Orders No. 33, August 26, 1918; Knight to Harley, August 12, 30, 31, 1918, AGC.
53. Captain Jerry Gray to Woodul, June 9, 1918, AGC.
54. Fox to Johnston, January 31, 1918, AGC.
55. MR, Co. B, January 31 and February 28, 1918, AGC.
56. Harley to Fox, January 2, February 21, 1918; Woodul to R. F. Stevenson, Jr., January 3, 1918; Fox to Captain Johnston, January 22, 1918, AGC.
57. Woodul to Fox, February 16, 1918, AGC.
58. Harley to Fox, November 10, 1917, RRM.
59. Fox to Harley, February 22, 1918; same to Woodul, March 2, 1918, AGC. Senator Hudspeth on May 31 had wired Governor Hobby urgently demanding that Trollinger be kept on. Hobby's notation on the telegram was: "Jim [Harley], This must be important, so will do it. W.P.H." Yet Harley stood up to Hobby. Trollinger was fired, and Harley wired Hudspeth: "If you can determine some good way to make party keep his promise to remain sober, I will put him on." Harley to Hudspeth, June 2, 1918 AGC.
60. Fox to Harley, February 22, 1918; C. O. Finley et al. to same, February 22, 1918, AGC.
61. Fox to Harley, February 10, 1918, AGC. Scullin held the Special Ranger commission from February 10, 1918, to January 15, 1919.
62. This account of the Porvenir raid is based on the sworn statements of Bud Weaver, Raymond Fitzgerald, and John Pool, undated but March, 1918, and John Pool's statement dated March 11, 1918, WC. See also Cano and Sochat, *Bandido*, 161–182.
63. (tel) Hobby to Robert Lansing, February 27, 1918, HP; see also Colonel George Langhorne to Commanding General, Southern Department, January 31, 1918, 8531-41-1, MID. Fox's account of the Porvenir affair is in his report to Harley, February 18, 1918, in "Proceedings," 834–835; Robert Keil, ed. Elizabeth McBride, *Bosque Bonito: Violent Times along the Borderland during the Mexican Revolution* (Alpine, Texas: Sul Ross State University, 2002), 27–34; A good account of the Porvenir affair is in Justice, *Revolution*, 35–47.
64. Kenneth C. Miller to Harley, March 18, 1918, AGC.
65. Colonel G. T. Langhorne, Memorandum for Captain W. M. Hanson, State Ranger, March 12, 1918, WC.

66. Biographical sketch, in "Guide to Manuscript Collections, Archives of the Big Bend, Sul Ross State University—Alpine, Texas," 16–17.

67. *IMA*, 1510–1515, 1650.

68. Fox to Woodul, March 29, 1918, AGC.

69. Fox to P. A. Cardwell, March 30, 1918, AGC.

70. Fox to Woodul, March 30, 1918, AGC.

71. Fox to Woodul, April 9, AGC.

72. Benjamin F. Berkeley to Hobby, May 10, 1918, AGC; Harley to Berkeley, May 23, 1918, WC.

73. Affidavits regarding Porvenir are in "Proceedings," 841–849.

74. "Proceedings," 849–852.

75. Colonel G. Langhorne to Hanson, May 22, 1918, WC; see also Hanson to Woodul, April 22, 1918, AGC, and the open letter from Harley to Fox, *EPMT*, July 11, 1918.

76. Fox to Harley, May 31, 1918; MR, Co. B, May 31, 1918; Woodul to Fox, May 27, 1918; Fox to Woodul, May 27, 1918, AGC; Hobby wired Woodul: "Accept resignation of Ranger Fox." (tel) Hobby to Woodul, undated [May 1918], HP.

77. "Proceedings," 836.

78. Ibid., 838–839.

79. Ibid., 837.

80. Ibid., 837–838.

81. Ibid.

82. Barker to Hobby, June 17, 1918, AGC.

83. Harley to Barker, June 29, 1918; [John D. McCall] to same, June 26, 1918; C. E. Mead to W. J. Crawford, June 15, 1918, AGC.

84. Gray to Harley, April 2, 1918; same to Woodul, May 17, 1918, AGC.

85. Gray to Woodul, June 9, 1918, AGC.

86. Gray to Woodul, June 18, 1918; Woodul to Gray, June 20, 1918, AGC. Trimble became controversial in 1921 for allegedly abusing a Mexican. See Trimble Vertical File in TRH. For a feature story on Trimble's law enforcement career see the *San Antonio Express-News*, August 29, 1981.

87. W. D. Smithers, *Chronicles of the Big Bend: A Photographic Memoir of Life on the Border* (Austin: Madrona Press, 1976), 59.

88. MR, Co. F, February 28, 1918, AGC.

89. Hunnicutt to Johnston, February 27, 1918, AGC.

90. William P. Stillwell was born in March, 1870, in Live Oak County. He was a stockman in Alpine when he enlisted in Company F on February 15, 1918.

91. Bates to Harley, April 6, 1918; same to same, April 3, 4, 1918; Harley to Bates, April 3, 1918, AGC.

92. John C. Palmer was born in Dewey County, Oklahoma, in 1873. A moulder by occupation, he enlisted in Austin on January 3, 1918.

93. Bates to Harley, April 6, 1918, AGC.

94. Bates to Harley, April 7, 1918, AGC.

95. Bates to Harley, April 14, 1918, AGC.

96. Harley to Bates, April 15, 1918, AGC.

97. District Intelligence Office, El Paso, to Department Intelligence Office, Southern Department, May 16, 1918, 532-891-1, MID.

98. Woodul to All Ranger Captains, May 17, 1918, AGC.

99. Woodul to Hanson, June 18, 1918, AGC.

100. Hunnicutt to Woodul, July 5, 1918; see also Frank Oltorf to Harley, July 12, 1918, AGC.

101. Jerry D. Hall had been a deputy U.S. marshal for eleven years, a Brewster County deputy sheriff for two years, a soldier in the Spanish-American War, and a cowboy. He had enlisted in Company F on April 12, 1918.

102. Harley to I. L. Martin, Jr., August 23, 1918; same to J. A. Walton, August 15, 1918, AGC.

103. Charles E. Breniman to Hanson, October 16, 1918, Gus T. Jones reports, October 21, 31, 1918, reel 17; D. L. Tinklepaugh reports, September 2, 30, 1918, reel 17, and September 3, 1918, reel 20, BI; Colonel G. T. Langhorne to Department Intelligence Officer, June 4, 1919, 5384-234-6, MID.

Chapter 14

1. Barler to Woodul, January 7, 1918, WC.
2. Woodul to Captain James B. Murrah, February 4, 1918, AGC.
3. Barler to Woodul, January 9, 1918, AGC.
4. Barler to Woodul, February 15, 1918; Woodul to Hanson, February 18, 1918, AGC.
5. Harley to Cunningham, January 3, 31, 1918, AGC
6. Cunningham to Harley, February 13, 1918, AGC.
7. Subsistence and Forage Return, Company M, January 1–February 4, 1918; C. P. Engelking to Captain Harry Johnston, January 31, 1918; Harley to Cunningham, February 5, April 3, 25, 1918; Woodul to same, February 5, April 8, 25, 1918; Cunningham to Harley, February 14, April 24, 1918; [P. A. Cardwell] to Cunningham, April 18, 1918, AGC.
8. Cunningham to Harley, February 12, 13, 15, 19, March 5, April 24, 1918; Woodul to Cunningham, February 27, 1918; Harley to same, February 9, 21, 1918; Cunningham to H. M. Johnston, January 16, April 25, 1918, AGC.
9. Cunningham to Harley, January 31, February 28, 1918, AGC.
10. C. G. Hunter to Harley, February 26, 1918, AGC.
11. Eugene Buck, ex-Dimmit County sheriff and deputy sheriff and captain of the Company C Volunteers, was stationed at the Indio Ranch.
12. Cunningham to Harley, January 31, 1918, AGC; R. G. Barnes to same, January 7, 1918, WC.
13. T. A. Coleman to Hobby, February 6, 1918, AGC.
14. Burwell, who had become a Ranger on September 1, 1917, had strong Ranger connections. Captain John H. Rogers was his uncle by marriage; his uncle, William M. Burwell, had been a Ranger sergeant, was Captain Rogers's brother-in-law, and was sheriff of Potter County; Burwell's father, Charles B. Burwell, was sheriff of La Salle County.
15. Strong Memorandum Report, February 16, 1918, AGC.
16. Cunningham to Harley, March 4, 1918, AGC.
17. *BDH*, July 1, 1915.
18. Harley to Cunningham, April 20, 1918, AGC.
19. Cunningham to Harley, March 5, 1918, AGC.
20. Ibid.
21. Ibid.
22. Cunningham to Harley, March 16, 1918, AGC.
23. Ibid.
24. "Cresse" [Charles E. Jones] report. May 16, 1918, reel 20, BI.
25. Cunningham to Harley, March 17, 1918, AGC.
26. D. W. Cox to Harley, March 26, 1918; Woodul to Cox, April 1, 1918; C. P. Engelking to Cunningham, March 16, 1918; W. D. Hale to Harley, March 31, 1918; Harley to Hale, April 1, 1918, AGC.
27. Cunningham to Harley, March 16, 1918, AGC.
28. Claude Darlington to Cunningham, April 1, 1918; R. M. Miller to same, March 19, 1918; Cunningham to Harley, March 30, April 1, 1918; C. P. Engelking to same, February 28, 1918; Harley to Engelking, March 5, 1918, AGC.
29. Harley to Cunningham, March 25, 1918; Cunningham to Harley, March 25, 1918, AGC.
30. Cunningham to Harley, April 2, 1918, AGC.
31. "Cresse" [Charles E. Jones] report, May 13, 1918, reel 20, BI.

32. *LWT*, June 16, 1918; T. A. Coleman to Hobby, March 25, 1918, AGC.

33. *LWT*, September 29, 1918.

34. Ryan to Harley, January 3, 1917 [sic—1918], AGC. Besides Willis there were only two other members of the company with Ranger experience: Richard L. Morris, who'd served from 10/05/11–06/30/12 and who'd reenlisted on 12/14/17, and Otho Vivion, 06/20/16. The rest were recruits: Charles B. Burwell, 09/01/17; Clyde Jennings, 12/14/17; J. E. Faubion, 01/26/18; James P. Chessher, 12/10/17; R. H. Johnson, 12/15/17; Irwin C. Harris, 12/14/17.

35. Hanson to Harley, March 22, 1918, AGC.

36. John A. Valls to Woodul, July 19, 1918, AGC.

37. W. M. Hanson to Harley, February 15, 1918, AGC.

38. Hanson to Harley, February 16, 1918, AGC.

39. *LWT*, January 27, February 10, 1918.

40. Sterling, *Trails and Trials*, 411–412.

41. Wright to Woodul, February 10, 1918, AGC.

42. Hanson to Harley, February 20, 1918, AGC.

43. Harley to Edds, February 14, 1918, AGC.

44. "Report on the bandit raid on the East Ranch, March 7, 1918," AGC; for sensational accounts of the raid see *LWT*, March 10,17, 1918.

45. Harley to Wright, March 23, 1918, AGC.

46. East to Woodul, March 11, 1918, AGC.

47. Woodul to East, March 15, 1918, AGC.

48. East to Woodul, April 18, 25, 1918, AGC.

49. East to Woodul, undated [April, 1918]; Woodul to Thompson, April 25, 1918, AGC.

50. W. A. Dannelley to Woodul, March 16, 1918, AGC.

51. Wright to Harley, May 12, 1918, AGC.

52. Woodul to East, June 3, 1918, AGC.

53. East to Woodul, June 14, 1918, AGC.

54. Woodul to East, June 18, 1918, AGC.

55. East to Woodul, undated [June, 1918], AGC.

56. Hanson to Harley, March 28, 1918, AGC; Charles E. Breniman to Hanson, March 28, 1918, reel 20, BI.

57. Stevens to Woodul, January 13, 1918, WC; MR, Company G, December 31, 1917, AGC.

58. Stevens to Harley, December 12, 1917, AGC.

59. Stevens to Harley, January 4, 1918, WC.

60. Stevens to Johnston, December 27, 1917, AGC.

61. Johnston to Stevens, January 3, 1918, AGC.

62. Stevens to Harley, December 27, 1917, AGC.

63. J. F. Garza to Stevens, January 4, 1918, WC.

64. Stevens to Harley, January 5, 1918, WC.

65. Ibid.; Woodul to Stevens, January 9, 1918, WC.

66. Stevens to Harley, January 5, 1918, WC; see also same to Woodul, January 23, 1918, AGC.

67. Stevens to Harley, March 19, 1918, WC.

68. See, for example, Stevens to Woodul, March 27, 1918, WC.

69. Stevens to Harley, January 4, 1918, AGC; Scott then became a lieutenant in the 10th Cavalry.

70. Stevens to Harley, February 19, 27, 1918; same to Woodul, May 3, 1918, AGC.

71. Stevens to Woodul, May 3, 1918, AGC.

72. Captain Daniel J. Keane to Stevens, April 8, 1918, WC; Unfortunately, Stevens had to fire Gentry on August 30, 1918, "for the good of the service."

73. Hanson to Harley, March 5, 1918, AGC.

74. Ibid.; On December 21, 1918, Slocum wrote Harley a letter commending the Rangers. Harley was so pleased that he included it in his *Biennial Report* (January 1, 1917–December 31, 1918), 63–65.

75. Stevens to Woodul, March 27, 1918; W. T. Vann to Harry Wallis, April 23, 1918, WC.
76. Stevens to Woodul, March 23, 1918, AGC.
77. Stevens to Woodul, March 31, 1918, AGC.
78. Stevens to Woodul, April 6, 1918, AGC.
79. Stevens to Woodul, April 23, 1918, WC; same to same, May 6, 1918, AGC.
80. Stevens to Woodul, April 25, 1918, AGC.
81. Ibid.
82. Stevens to Harley, April 26, 1918, WC.
83. Stevens to Woodul, May 14, 1918; see also John P. Gause to Hanson, May 16, 1918; Hanson to Gause, May 20, 1918, AGC.
84. J. Z. Garza to Captain W. M. Hanson, May 2, 1918, AGC.
85. Stevens to Woodul, May 23, 1918, AGC.
86. Stevens to Woodul, May 25, 1918, AGC.
87. J. Z. Garza To Whom It May Concern, May 31, 1918, WC.
88. Stevens to Woodul, June 2, 1918, AGC.
89. Stevens to Woodul, June 4, 1918, WC.
90. Woodul to Stevens, June 5, 1918; Stevens to Woodul, June 7, 1918, WC.
91. Baker was the brother of (ex-Ranger) Sheriff A. Y. Baker of Hidalgo County. He had served in Company D in 1915 but was fired for drunkenness and conduct unbecoming. He presumably reformed, for he reenlisted in 1916, being discharged the next year because of a reduction in force. He was working as a jailer for his brother in Edinburg when Stevens enlisted him on December 31, 1917. On May 1, 1918, Baker was promoted to sergeant. Joseph E. Baker came from a law enforcement clan. Besides his brother A. Y., his brothers Frank P. and Alfred R. served in the Rangers, as did his cousins Lawrence H. Bates and Winfred F. Bates. Another cousin, Arthur S. Bates, was a Texas quarantine guard.
92. Stevens to Woodul, June 10, 1918, WC.
93. Stevens to Woodul, June 12, 1918, WC.
94. Stevens to Woodul, June 18, 1918, WC.
95. Hanson to Harley, March 28, 1918, RRM.
96. Grimes to W. D. Cope, January 12, 1918, AGC.
97. Grimes to Sanders, May 13, 1918; same to P. A. Cardwell, May 19, 1918, AGC.
98. "Personnel Record Members of Company 'A' Ranger Force," undated [September 1917?]; Sanders to Harley, March 10, 1918, AGC.
99. Harley to Sanders, April 27, 1918; Sanders to Harley. December 13, 1918; Captain Harry Johnston to Katie Moran, December 13, 1918; Ben Tumlinson, Jr., to Captain Johnston, December 23, 1918, AGC.
100. See, for example, Woodul to Hanson, June 10, 1918; same to Sanders, June 10, 1918; Stevens to Woodul, July 17, 1918; Harley to Sanders, July 12, 1918, AGC.
101. Sanders to Woodul, June 13, 24, 1918, AGC.
102. Woodul to Ransom, February 13, 1918; Ransom to Woodul, February 16, 1918; W. E. Hodge to Harley, February 17, 1918, AGC.
103. Ransom to Harley, March 26, 1918, AGC.
104. Koon to Harley, April 1, 1918, WC; Harley to Koon, April 2, 1918; McKenzie to Harley, April 2, 1918, WC; Harley to McKenzie, [April 2, 1918], AGC; "Record of Inquest," Ransom Vertical File, TRH. The *Houston Chronicle*, one of whose reporters Ransom had assaulted several years earlier, gave him a rather chilly obituary headlined "Henry Ransom Long Known As a Gunfighter" and dwelling on his violent past. *HC*, April 2, 1918.
105. Petition to Hobby, April 3, 1918; Hickman to Harley, April 2, 1918; Woodul to Hickman, April 3, 1918, AGC.
106. McKenzie to Woodul, May 3, 1918, AGC.

Chapter 15

1. *IMA*, 3223–3230.
2. Luther Ellsworth to Secretary of State, March 3, 1911, 812.00/884, May 6, 1911, 812.00/1717, and May 11, 1911, 812.00/1779, RDS; J. T. Canales to Hobby, December 12, 1918, 10487-1311-1, MID; "Proceedings," 888–893; Ribb, "José Tomás Canales," 142–143. One of Hanson's operatives was Roy N. Adams, a future Ranger. Adams to Harley, August 23, 1919, AGC.
3. Hanson to Harley, February 1, 1918, AGC.
4. Joe H. Grimes to War Department, June 15, 1915, Box 2, entry 4439, SD.
5. Hanson to Harley, December 20, 1917, AGC.
6. J. F. Carl to Harley, December 9, 1917, AGC.
7. Woodul to Hanson, December 21, 26, 1917; Hanson to Woodul, December 23, 24, 1917, AGC.
8. Willard Utley report, April 30, 1917, reel 7; R. L. Barnes report, May 5, 1917, reel 11; Manuel Sorola report, December 1, 1917, reel 17; Louis De Nette reports, April 18, 27, 1918, reel 20, BI.
9. See, for example, Martín de León to Hanson, January 6, 1918; Hanson to Woodul, December 23, 24, 26, 1917, January 19, 1918, AGC.
10. Woodul to Hanson, January 7, 1917 [sic–1918], AGC.
11. Woodul to Hanson, January 26, 1918; Hanson's oath of office, January 31, 1918, AGC.
12. Harley to Lansing, January 31, 1918, AGC.
13. Roswell Gillett to Hanson, January 30, 1918; Hanson to Harley, February 2, 4, 1918; Engelking to same, February 2, 1918, AGC.
14. Hanson to Harley, February 2, 1918, AGC.
15. Hanson to Harley, February 8, 1918, AGC.
16. Ibid.
17. Hanson to Harley, February 11, AGC.
18. Hanson to Harley, February 13, 1918, AGC. This letter, with Hanson's name deleted, is in reel 19, BI.
19. Spellacy to Hanson, February 14, 1918; Hanson to Harley, February 17, 1918, AGC.
20. Hanson to Harley, February 20, 1918, enclosing a letter from "A Friend" to Hanson, February 16, 1918, AGC.
21. Hicks to Gregory, February 21, 1918, AGC.
22. Hanson to Harley, February 22, 1918, AGC.
23. Hanson to Harley, February 26, 1918, AGC.
24. Ibid. See also "Cresse" [Charles E. Jones] report, November 30, 1918, reel 20, BI.
25. Hanson to Harley, February 28, 1918, AGC; Charles E. Breniman report, May 13, 1918, reel 18, BI.
26. Engelking to Hanson, February 10, 1918; same to Harley, February 9, 10, 1918; Hanson to Harley, February 10, 1918; [same] to Engelking, February 11, 1918, AGC.
27. Hanson to Harley, February 28, 1918, AGC.
28. Ibid.
29. Ibid.
30. Hanson to Harley, March 4, 1918, AGC.
31. Hanson to Harley, March 4, 1918, AGC—a separate letter from the one cited in note 30.
32. Ibid.
33. Ibid.
34. García to Hanson, March 4, 1918, AGC.
35. Hanson to Harley, March 5, 1918, AGC.
36. Hanson to Harley, March 7, 1918, AGC.
37. Hanson to Harley, March 10, 13, 16, 1918; Woodul to Hanson, March 15, 1918, AGC.

38. "Memorandum for Captain W. M. Hanson, State Ranger," March 12, 1918, WC.
39. Hanson to Harley, March 22, 1918, AGC.
40. Ibid.; Woodul to Hamby, March 26, 1918, AGC.
41. Woodul to Hanson, March 26, 1918, AGC. For further details about the East Ranch raid, see "Proceedings," 1167–1187, 1191–1192.
42. (tel.) Hobby to Major General Ruckman, March 26, 1918, HP.
43. Hanson to Woodul, March 26, 1918, AGC.
44. Hanson to Harley, March 27, 1918, AGC.
45. Hanson to Harley, March 28, 1918 (two reports); Woodul to Hanson, March 28, 1918, AGC.
46. Hanson to Harley, undated [March, 1918], AGC.
47. General Luis Caballero, one of the two candidates for the governorship, both claiming to have been elected.
48. Hanson to Harley, April 20, 1918, AGC.
49. Manuel Sorola report, April 25, 1918; Fred Marks report, April 17, 1918; Van Curtis report, April 13, 1918; J. P. S. Mennet report, April 12, 1918, reel 20, BI.
50. Hanson to Harley, April 1, 1918, AGC.
51. Hanson to Woodul, April 1, 1918, AGC.
52. Vann to Hanson, April 3, 1918, AGC; Hobby to Vann, December 10, 1917, HP. Archie Parr also endorsed Anglin for Ranger captain. Hobby to Parr, January 2, 1918, HP.
53. Vann to Hanson, April 19, 1918, AGC.
54. Stevens to Woodul, July 15, 1918, AGC.
55. Hanson to Harley, April 11, 19, 20, 22, 1918, AGC.
56. *General and Special Laws of the State of Texas Passed by the Fourth Called Session of the Thirty-Fifth Legislature Convened at the City of Austin, February 26, 1918, and Adjourned March 27, 1918* (Austin: A. C. Baldwin and Sons, 1918), 12–15. Disloyal statements could get one into a lot of trouble. A corporal in El Paso who expressed the hope that Germany would win was court-martialed and sentenced to ninety-nine years at hard labor at Leavenworth. *BDH*, August 3, 1918. The Texas Court of Criminal Appeals ruled the Hobby Loyalty Act unconstitutional in 1920, *LWT*, March 21, 1920.
57. *Biennial Report of the Adjutant General of Texas From January 1, 1917, to December 31, 1918* (Austin: Von Boeckmann-Jones Co., 1919), 63; Captain H. M. Johnston to G. C. Wood, October 17, 1918, AGC.
58. Hanson to A. Bruce Bielaski, September 27, 1918, reel 21, BI.
59. "Duties of Special Rangers," undated but filed with December, 1918, AGC.
60. Hanson to Woodul, June 12, 1918, AGC.
61. See, for example, Hanson to Woodul, June 4, 1918; [P. A. Cardwell] to Hanson, June 4, 1918; John R. Hill to Harley, July 17, 1918, AGC.
62. See, for example, James E. Booth to Harley, June 5, 1918, AGC.
63. Hanson to W. T. Duncan, May 25, 1918; same to Harley, May 9, 19, 1918; same to Woodul, May 13, 1918 (two letters); Woodul to Hanson, May 23, June 5, 1918, AGC.
64. Stevens to Woodul, May 6, 18, June 4, 1918, AGC.
65. [Hanson] to John P. Gause, May 20, 1918, AGC.
66. [Walter J. Crawford?] to Hanson, June 5, 1918, AGC.
67. Hanson to Davis, June___, 1918, AGC.
68. A. J. Robertson to General W. D. Cope, April 6, 1920, AGC.
69. Hanson to Harley, June 27, 1918, AGC.
70. "Proceedings," 838–839.
71. C. E. Mead to W. J. Crawford, June 15, 1918, RRM. See also (tel) Hobby to W. Threadgill, May 9, 1918, HP.
72. Mrs. Hal W. Green to W. J. Crawford, June 25, 1918, AGC.
73. *EPMT*, July 11, 1918.
74. Sol Rubenstein to Harley, July 17, 1918; Harley to Colonel H. J. Slocum, July 30, 1918, AGC.

75. Hutchings died in Austin on July 27, 1939, being executive officer in charge of the Narcotics Division of the Texas Department of Public Safety. *Handbook*, III, 803.

76. Walter J. Crawford to Harley, June 20, 1918, AGC

77. Woodul to Hanson, June 10, 1918; G. Huston to Harley, June 10, 1918; Hanson to Woodul, June 11 (two letters), 18, July 2, 1918; same to Harley, June 29, 1918; same to Martin Arnold and F. A. Chapa, July 8, 1918; J. Arnold to Harley, July 10, 1918, AGC.

78. Walter J. Crawford to Harley, July 12, 1918, AGC.

79. Stevens to Woodul, July 17, 1918; George B. Hurst to Harley, July 29, 1918, AGC.

80. Harley to J. Fennell Dibrell et al., July 25, 1918, AGC.

81. Hanson to Judge Advocate, Camp Travis, October 3, 1918, WC.

82. Captain R. E. White had been sheriff of Travis County for many years, later was county judge and mayor of Austin, and currently was a county commissioner. *EPMT*, July 13, 1918; (tel) Hobby to R. E. White, July 13, 1918, HP.

83. Anders to Harley, July 12, 1918; Harley to Anders, July 12, 1918; same to Sanders, July 12, 1918, AGC.

84. Hanson to Harley, July 14, 1918, AGC.

85. Erby E. Swift report, July 25, 1918, copy in AGC; Chester B. Collins to Harley, July 20, 1918. See also statements by L. B. Harvey, July 13, 17, 1918, WC; *EPMT*, July 17, 1918; W. A. Harvey and E. G. Hart to Harley, July 16, 1918, WC.

86. Canales to Woodul, July 22, 1918, AGC.

87. *Brownwood News*, July 26, 1918, clipping in AGC.

88. Stevens to Woodul, July 27, 1918, AGC.

89. Clark, *Tactful Texan*, 95.

Chapter 16

1. James H. Beall report, July 11, 1918, 10080-1543-38, MID; Walter Acher, Jr., report, April 17, 1918, 10080-1543-9, MID.

2. Woodul to Caldwell County Exemption Board, January 22, 1918, AGC.

3. Harley to Davis, March 7, 13, 1918, AGC.

4. Harley to Davis, March 16, 1918; Davis to Harley, March 18, 1918, AGC.

5. Davis to P. A. Cardwell, April 1, 1918, AGC.

6. Harley to Davis, April 9, 1918, AGC.

7. L. E. Bates report, April 16, 1918, 10080-1543-3, MID.

8. L. E. Bates report, April 18, 1918, 10080-1543-6, MID.

9. Department Intelligence Officer to Chief, Military Intelligence Branch, April 24, 1918, 10080-1543-11, MID; Memorandum, District Intelligence Office, El Paso, April 25, 1918, 10080-1543-12, and May 16, 1918, 10080-1543-20, MID.

10. Chief, Military Intelligence Branch to Intelligence Officer, Southern Department, June 3, 1918, 10080-1543-26, MID.

11. Department Intelligence Officer to Chief, Military Intelligence Branch, July 29, 1918, 10080-1543-40, MID; R. L. Barnes to J. F. Walters [sic], July 31, 1918, 10080-1543-45, MID; E. V. Spence to Department Intelligence Officer, 10080-1543-43, MID; Department Intelligence Officer to Director, MID, September 28, 1918, 10080-1543-46, MID; Intelligence Officer, Camp Mabry to Acting Director of Military Intelligence, 10080-1543-50, MID.

12. Department Intelligence Officer to Chief, Military Intelligence Branch, June 11, 1918, 10080-1543-32, MID.

13. Harley to Moses and Rowe, September 10, 1918, AGC.

14. Moses and Rowe to Harley, September 13, October 8, 1918, AGC.

15. *Biennial Report of the Adjutant General . . .* (January 1, 1917–December 31, 1918), 63.

16. "Memorandum for Captain Keppel," August 23, 26, 27, 1918, 8532-1155-6, 7, 8, MID.

17. ". . . favor informar al Sr. Presidente que entre Laredo y Matamoros se están organizando diariamente partidas de cinquenta y sesenta hombres montados y armados siendo ayudados para esta organización plenamente comprobado por W. M. Hanson, Jefe de Rangers. Este individuo es el que más ayuda a los rebeldes del otro lado, habiendo sido expulsado por el Gral. González en el tiempo que estuvo en Matamoros por ser este de los más enemigos de nuestra causa y ahora del Gobierno. Espero la contestación." Ricaut at Monterrey to General Juan Barragán, August 13, 1918, Telegrams, State of Nuevo León, 1916 [sic—the telegram is misfiled], VCA. See also Lieutenant Colonel R. M. Campbell to Director of Military Intelligence, January 15, 1919, reel 21, BI.

18. "Cresse" [Charles E. Jones] report, May 13, 1918, reel 19, BI.

19. See, for example, W. M. Burnett to Hobby, August 2, 1918; Mack Kercheville to same, July 30, 1918; Hobby to Kercheville, August 3, 1918; Woodul to same, August 5, 1918; Walter J. Crawford to Harley, August 6, 1918; I. A. Patten to Woodul, August 7, 1918; Woodul to Walter J. Crawford, August 9, 1918; Ira P. Hildebrand to Harley, August 10, 1918, AGC.

20. *BDH*, August 22, 24, 28, 1918. Shaw was born in 1890 in Yoakum, Lavaca County, and was a rancher when he enlisted in Company G on July 5, 1918.

21. Captain H. M. Harrison to Stevens, August 24, 1918, AGC.

22. Hanson to Harley, August 1, 1918, WC; *BDH*, September 2, 6, 1918. Fred Tate had been a Special Ranger from April 26, 1917, to December, 1917. His son, Tom Tate, was a Regular Ranger 11/25/10–9/15/11 and 1/8/26–2/1/27, and a Special Ranger 8/25/15–2/6/19.

23. Stevens to Woodul, August 22, 1918 (telegram and letter), AGC.

24. Stevens to Woodul, August 26, 1918, WC; E. H. Parker reports, August 26, 29, 1918, reel 21, BI.

25. Anders, *Boss Rule*, 255.

26. Alba Heywood to Hobby, August 28, 1918, WC.

27. Canales to Harley, August 31, 1918, AGC.

28. (tel) Hanson to Harley, August 31, 1918, AGC.

29. (tel) Chapa to Hobby, September 2, 1918, AGC; (tel) Hobby to Chapa, September 4, 1918, HP. For Harley's concern over the Mexican labor situation see Harley to O. E. Dunlap, September 14, 1918; same to J. F. Carl, September 14, 1918; Carl to Harley, September 19, 1918, AGC. For praise of Chapa see A. A. Browne to Harley, September 16, 1918, AGC.

30. *BDH*, August 29, 1918.

31. (tel) Hobby to Chambers of Commerce, Rio Grande City and McAllen, September 5, 1918, HP.

32. Hanson to AG, January 29, 1919, WC.

33. "Proceedings," 1071–1073.

34. Ibid., 1531–1556.

35. Pedro Támez affidavit, August 14, 1918, Ibid., 824–826.

36. Ibid., 1056–1068; see also Robert Lansing to Hobby, September 11, 1918, Ibid., 820–821, and Hobby to Lansing, September 18, 1918, Ibid., 826.

37. Report to the Consul of Mexico, August 15, 1918; Ygnacio Bonillas to Robert Lansing, August 31, 1918, Ibid., 821–824.

38. Statement of Thomas Hester, October 13, 1918, Ibid., 829–831; see also Statements of Sam Bernard and G. M. Abney, October 13, 1918, Ibid., 826–829.

39. For Captain Stevens's testimony see Ibid., 1428–1429, 1433–1434.

40. Hanson to Harley, October 24, 1918, Ibid., 816.

41. Hanson to Harley, November 8, 1918; Special Rangers G. M. Abney and Thomas Hester to Hanson, November 7, 1918, WC.

42. Deposition of María González, September 25, 1918; Robert Lansing to Governor, November 27, 1918, WC; Hobby to Robert Lansing, December 5, 1918, HP.

43. Hanson to Harley, November 15, 1918, WC; see also I. Bonillas to Robert Lansing, November 15, 1918, WC; Hobby to same, March 20, 1919, HP. W. Stillwell took the oath

of service on February 15, 1918, "Index to Service Records, Ranger Headquarters, Dept. of Public Safety, 1900———," Ranger Archive, Texas Department of Public Safety, Austin, Texas, copy in Texas State Library.

44. Hanson to Harley, December 10, 1918; same to Tom East, December 10, 1918, WC.

45. *Revolutions in Mexico*, 588.

46. Hispanics in the Big Bend were also disarmed. See, for example, Love and Patterson to Hobby, August 30, 1918; Chisos Mining Co. to AG, September 3, 1918, AGC.

47. Stevens to Harley, September 14, 1918, AGC; *BDH*, August 31, 1918.

48. Cardwell to Johnston, September 27, 1918, AGC.

49. George W. Saddler [sic] to Harley, September 15, 1918, AGC; "Memoirs of Jesse Pérez," 61–62.

50. (tel) Captain W. W. Davis to Harley, November 8, 1918, AGC.

51. Major Sam D. W. Low to Davis, November 8, 1918, AGC; Davis to Low, November 12, 1918, WC; *EPMT*, November 8, 10, 1918.

52. "Weekly report," October 20, 1916, 812.00/19654, RDS.

53. Hanson to Harley, October 15, 1918, WC; "Proceedings," 565; E. H. Parker report, October 11, 1918, reel 21, BI; Sterling, *Trails and Trials*, 423–425.

54. Hanson to Harley, October 15, 1918, WC.

55. Ibid.

56. "Proceedings," 481.

57. Edds to Paul Perkins or Oscar Thompson, September 3, 1918 and "To Whom It May Concern," September 3, 1918, Ibid., 770–771.

58. Captain W. L. Wright to Harley, September 7, 1918; statements of Captain W. L. Wright, J. J. Edds, Ed Yzaguirre, and Sabás Osuna, all undated, Ibid., 771, 763–769; for Hanson's report on the affair see Hanson to Harley, September 16, 1918, Ibid., 761–762.

59. Statements of J. J. Edds, Monroe Wells, Jesús Sánchez, and Zaragoza Sánchez, October 18, 1918, Ibid., 782–787.

60. Hanson to Harley, October 10, 1918, WC; see also (tel) Fred E. Marks to Hanson, October 7, 1918, AGC.

61. Wright to Major Sam D. W. Low, October 9, 1918, WC.

62. Captain H. H. Dunn to Hanson, October 21, 1918, AGC.

63. R. Osterveen to Hobby, October 18, 1918, AGC.

64. Hanson to Harley, October 15, 1918; Wright to Major Sam D. W. Low, October 9, 1918, WC.

65. Hanson to AG, October 9, 1918, AGC; "Proceedings," 216, 220–221, 751–757.

66. Secretary [Ralph Soape] to Hanson, December 21, 1918, HP.

67. Anders, *Boss Rule*, 255–265, 283; Captain W. M. Ryan to Hobby, November ___, 1918; "Report of Special Ranger Redway," November 5, 6, 1918; Fred Marks to Hanson, November 7, 1918; Hanson to Harley, November 8, 1918; same to Captains Sanders, Wright, and Taylor, November 19, 1918, WC. For a detailed account of this affair see *In the Senate of Texas. D. W. Glasscock, Contestant vs A. Parr Contestee. Supplement to the Senate Journal; Regular Session of the 36th Legislature 1919. Published by Authority of the Senate.* Austin: A. C. Baldwin & Sons [1919].

68. Anders, *Boss Rule*, 265. See Stevens to Harley, September 14, 1918, AGC.

69. Robert A. Caro, *The Years of Lyndon Johnson: Means of Ascent* (New York: Alfred A. Knopf, 1990), xxxii.

70. Ibid., xxxi.

71. Ibid., 303–384. Some historians of Texas politics consider Caro to be biased against Johnson. See, for example, Evan Anders, "Robert Caro's Lyndon Johnson and the Pitfalls of Political Biography: A Critical Evaluation of *The Years of Lyndon Johnson: The Path to Power* and *Means of Ascent*," *Southwestern Historical Quarterly* 94 (1991): 581–598. Yet the fact remains that Johnson stole the 1948 election.

72. McKenzie to Captain J. L. Anders, December 20, 22, 1918, WC.

73. W. D. Suiter et al. to Hobby, December 22, 1918, WC; Hobby to J. H. Beavers, December 27, 1918, HP.

74. Statements of C. T. Christopher, Mrs. Viola Christopher, W. H. Bowers, S. J. Yearly, Frank Douglas, and C. E. Boothe, December 29, 30, 1918, "Proceedings," 773–779, 137.

75. Special Orders No. 1, January 9, 1919, "Proceedings," 773.

76. Walter R. Allen to Adjutant General Cope, January 23, 1920, AGC.

Chapter 17

1. Hanson to A. Bruce Bielaski, September 27, 1918, reel 21, BI.

2. Ralph Soape to M. V. Bentley, December 6, 1918, HP; "Comptroller's Department, Appropriation Numbers for fiscal year 1918–1919," September 1, 1918, AGC.

3. Hanson to AG W. K. Weaver, October 10, 1918, WC; J. M. Dunn to Harley, December 30, 1918; Robert R. Mullen, Jr., to same, December 31, 1918, AGC; "Proceedings," 1460–1476. According to the service records there were 458 Special Rangers, from a very wide variety of occupations. Still, the number is approximate because in a few cases the service records are incomplete or unclear.

4. Hobby to Oscar Dancy, January 10, 1919; same to Sheriff W. T. Vann, January 10, 1919, HP. Captain William W. Taylor again served in the Rangers as sergeant of Companies B, C, and A from 1925 until he resigned in 1928. In 1932, he served as an unassigned captain. In 1918, 1931–1932, 1933–1935 he held a Special Ranger commission.

5. Hanson to Harley, September 1, 1918; Harley to Taylor, December 27, 1918, WC.

6. Hanson to Captain H. M. Johnston, November 19, 1918; see also Johnston to Hamer, November 22, 1918, AGC.

7. Ribb, "José Tomás Canales," 56. See also Richard Ribb, "Patrician as Reedemer: José Tomás Canales and the Salvation of South Texas, 1910–1919," *The Journal of South Texas*, 14, no. 2 (Fall 2001): 189–203. For another treatment of Canales bordering on hagiography see Carlos Larralde, "J. T. Canales and the Texas Rangers," *The Journal of South Texas*, 10, no. 1 (1997): 38–68.

8. Anders, *Boss Rule*, 246–247; "Proceedings," 855.

9. Anders, *Boss Rule*, 266.

10. "Proceedings," 1416–1419. See also Ibid., 925–927.

11. Ibid., 885–886.

12. Ibid., 887.

13. Ibid.

14. Ibid., 888.

15. Ibid., 888–890.

16. Ibid., 891.

17. Ibid., 892–894.

18. Ibid., 894–895.

19. Canales to Garner, December 12, 1918, 10487-1311-2; Garner to Joseph P. Tumulty, December 16, 1918, 10487-1311-3, MID.

20. Colonel John M. Dunn to Intelligence Officer, Southern Department, January 16, 1919, 10487-1311-4, MID.

21. Captain E. V. Spence to Department Intelligence Officer, February 10, 1919, 10487-1311-3, MID.

22. Colonel John M. Dunn to Adjutant General of the Army, February 19, 1919, 10487-1311-4, MID.

23. "Proceedings," 392.

24. Ibid., 898.

25. Ibid., 1568.

26. Ibid., 1560–1561.
27. Anders, *Boss Rule*, 267–268.
28. Quoted in Ibid., 268.
29. *LWT*, February 2, 1919.
30. Canales to Woodul, July 22, 1918, AGC; see also "Proceedings," 857.
31. Woodul to Canales, July 26, 1918, AGC; see also Hanson to same, July 31, 1918, "Proceedings," 1016.
32. "Proceedings," 676–721, 713.
33. Anders, *Boss Rule*, 268; William T. Burnett to Harley, January 31, 1919; John C. Ray to same, February 24, 1919; Tom M. Ross to same, February 9, 1919, AGC. Ex-Ranger Captain Tom Ross held a Special Ranger commission from May 8, 1929 to May 8, 1930. He served as interpreter for the U.S. District Court in San Antonio from 1925 through 1945. Ross died at the age of 74 on January 1, 1946, at his home in Rossville, Atascosa County. It is claimed that Canales supported Parr out of loyalty because he was a longtime family friend and neighbor. Ribb, "José Tomás Canales," 52–53.
34. "Proceedings," 869.
35. Quoted in Virginia Duncan, "The Life of Captain Roy W. Aldrich, " (M.A. thesis, Sul Ross State Teachers College, 1942), 53.
36. Anders, *Boss Rule*, 268–269.
37. "Proceedings," 135, 1085–1088.
38. Ibid., 167–189, 195–206.
39. For example, he tried to lead a witness to say that the killer of Ranger Joe Shaw was just acting in self-defense. Ibid., 387.
40. Ibid., 3, 156, 1557–1558.
41. Benjamin Johnson, who bashes the Rangers at every opportunity, uses Virginia Yeager's letter accusing the Rangers in the affair regarding water rights, (*Revolution in Texas*, 109) but not her letter admitting that she had misinterpreted the whole thing (attached to Fox to AG, August 27, 1914, CP), as discussed in Chapter 6 of this book.
42. "Proceedings," 301–352, 1390.
43. Ibid., 13–14, 34, 87.
44. Ibid., 135, 156, 467–478, 493, 496, 503, 508, 910–911, 1341–1363.
45. Ibid., 136, 479–507, 911, Statements of John Edds, Zaragoza Sánchez, Jesús Sánchez, Federico Saldaña, Monroe Wells, October 18, 1918, 782–787; Hanson to Harley, October 23, 1918, 780–781.
46. Ibid., 136, 738–745, 1298–1319, Statements of J. J. Edds, Sabás Osuna, Eduardo Yzaguirre, Captain Will Wright, 763–769; Edds's letter to Ranger Paul Perkins and his "To Whom It May Concern" note, 770–771; Wright to Harley, September 7, 1918; Harley to Wright, September 12, 1918, 771–772.
47. Ibid., 912–914.
48. Ibid., 136–137, 157, 541–547, 553–558, 596–597, 1056–1079, 1118–1119, 1364–1379, 1431–1433, 1531–1538, 1541–1556.
49. Ibid., 481.
50. Ibid., 1044–1053, 1026–1028, 1034.
51. Ibid., 137, 157, 221–237, 288–296, 394–458, 511–525.
52. Ibid., 123–124, 137, 158.
53. As previously noted, the Rangers weren't big on record keeping, and some of the adjutant general's files were in disarray. Ranger P. A. Cardwell, who had been the assistant quartermaster for years, telegraphed Captain H. M. Johnston, the quartermaster, that he "Took all letters and put in big box and put them in basement in little room but when Selective [Service] people moved down they tore up everything so badly is doubtful whether you can find them." (tel) Cardwell to Johnston, February 6, 1919, AGC.
54. "Proceedings," 788–793.

55. Ibid., 754–757.
56. Hanson to AG, October 9, 1918, AGC.
57. "Proceedings," 220–221, 751–757, 916, 1453–1458.
58. Ibid., 928–929.
59. Ibid., 140–141, 159, 208–220, 759–762, 773, 780, 794–798, 804–806, 917–930, 942, 1017.
60. Ibid.,141.
61. Ibid., 142, 985.
62. Ibid., 985.
63. Hudspeth to Harley, April 21, 1918, AGC.
64. (tel) Hudspeth to Harley, February 1, 4, 1919; (tel) Harley to Hudspeth, February 4, 5, 1919, AGC.
65. "Proceedings," 160.
66. Ibid., 189, 192, 934.
67. Ibid., 856–857.
68. Ibid., 997, and see also 932–934, 1581–1582.
69. Captain Aldrich to Ben Tumlinson, Jr., April 8, 1919, AGC. Captain Sanders took the two .30-30s home with him to Lockhart, and only after repeated inquiries by the owners did he finally pay $40 for them, in 1920. That same year the shotgun was returned to its owner. Aldrich to Ben Tumlinson, Jr., March 15, 1920, AGC.
70. Lea, *King Ranch*, 639.
71. "Proceedings," 145–146.
72. Ibid., 832–852.
73. Ibid., 146.
74. Ibid., 820–831, 940, 1056.
75. Ibid., 816.
76. Ibid., 1428–1429, 1434.
77. Ibid., 962–963.
78. Ibid., 819.
79. Ibid., 366.
80. Ibid., 944.
81. Ibid., 1561–1562.
82. Mayberry was the sergeant of Headquarters Company, assigned to the Superintendent of Public Buildings and Grounds as custodian of the Ranger facility at Camp Mabry.
83. *Austin American*, February 8, 1919; *SAE*, February 8, 9, 1919; *Dallas Morning News*, February 9, 1919.
84. Ibid., 1562–1563.
85. Captain R. W. Aldrich to S. E. Rosengren, February 28, 1919, AGC.
86. Special Orders No. 13, February 13, 1919, AGC.
87. Cardwell to Harley, March 24, 1919; The Petmecky Company to same, February 10, 1919; Harley to Petmecky, February 21, 1919; Aldrich to W. R. Caldwell and Co., January 29, 1920, AGC.
88. "Proceedings," 1564–1566.
89. Ibid., 946.
90. Ibid., 1477–1478.
91. Ibid., 132.
92. Ibid., 885–886.
93. Ibid., 900–901.
94. Ibid., 150–154.
95. Ribb, "José Tomás Canales," 353.
96. Hughes to AG, December 4, 1911, WC.
97. See, for example, A. M. McFaddin to Hughes, March 5, 1913; Hughes to AG, March 6, 1913, AGC.

98. *AA*, July 2, 1914; MR, Company A, June 30, 1914, AGC; "Proceedings," 164.

99. *EPMT*, January 27, 1914, January 17, 19, 20, 22, 1915.

100. "Proceedings," 979–980, 989; *EPMT*, November 30, December 1–5, 7, 14, 19, 1915, April 23, June 17, 1916.

101. Sterling, *Trails and Trials*, 379–380; Weston A. Pettey, "The Seminole Incident and Tom Ross," *West Texas Historical Association Year Book*, LVI, (1980), 133–140. The Tom Ross referred to in this article is not Tom M. Ross, the sometime Ranger captain.

102. "Proceedings," 980–983, 987–988.

103. Ibid., 372.

104. Quoted in L. H. Flewellen report, February 17, 1919, reel 21, BI.

105. Bielaski to Breniman, February 12, 1919, reel 21, BI.

106. L. H. Flewellen report, February 17, 1919; C. E. Breniman to W. E. Allen, March 4, 1919, reel 21, BI.

107. Anders, *Boss Rule*, 270.

108. Ibid.

109. (tel) Hanson to Everett Anglin, February 19, 1919; Harley to Frank Robb, February 19, 1919, AGC.

110. Anders, *Boss Rule*, 270–271; Dayton Moses to A. B. Robertson, February 20, 1919; Harley to Senator Paul Page, March 13, 1919, AGC.

111. Anders, *Boss Rule*, 272–273.

112. Ibid., 273; Handbook, I, 953.

113. Ribb, "José Tomás Canales," 191, 429.

114. Justice, *Revolution*, 46.

115. James W. Robinson, *The DPS Story: History of the Development of the Department of Public Safety in Texas* (Austin: Texas Department of Public Safety, 1974), 6.

116. Montejano, *Anglos and Mexicans*, 127.

117. Harry Krenek, *The Power Vested: The Use of Martial Law and the National Guard in Texas Domestic Crisis . . . 1919–1932* (Austin: Presidial Press, 1980), Preface, n.p.

118. Ben Proctor, *Just One Riot: Episodes of Texas Rangers in the 20th Century* (Austin: Eakin Press, 1991), 7.

119. Ribb, "José Tomás Canales," 366.

120. Anders, *Boss Rule*, 273.

Chapter 18

1. Ribb, "José Tomás Canales," 369.

2. *Supplement to Vernon's Texas Civil and Criminal Statutes . . .* 3 vols. (Kansas City, Mo.: Vernon Law Book Company, 1922), II, 1906–1909.

3. Captain R. W. Aldrich to J. B. Chambers, April 17, 1919; same to J. A. Richter, July 24, 1920; same to John J. Dowling, December 8, 1919; same to V. A. De Vaughan, February 26, 1920, AGC; Hobby to C. M. Cureton, May 28, 1919, HP.

4. "Proceedings," 243–245, 1396–1398, 1403–1406.

5. Harley to Harbert Davenport, March 15, 1919, AGC. See also "Proceedings," 1382, 238–252; John W. McClintock to Harley, February 4, 1919, [Harbert Davenport] to same, March 7, 1919, AGC.

6. Harley to Barler, March 24, 1919, AGC.

7. Harley to Frank Hamer, March 26, 1919, AGC.

8. Special Orders No. 21, March 10, 1919, WC.

9. Duncan, "The Life of Captain Roy W. Aldrich," passim.

10. Aldrich to S. S. Hutchison, April 26, 1920, AGC.

11. Aldrich to Frank Hamer, February 28, 1919; same to A. T. Hamilton, June 5, 1919; A. T.

Hamilton to Aldrich, June 11, 1919, AGC; "Proceedings," 1584. Apparently none of these daily reports has survived, or if they have they are not among the Adjutant General's Correspondence.

12. Hays M. Wallis to Captain H. M. Johnston, October 19, 1918; Johnston to Wallis, October 22, 1918, AGC.

13. Aldrich to C. J. Hanson, June 10, 1919; same to Byron B. Parrish, January 24, 1920; Captain H. M. Johnston to J. M. Arrington, October 22, 1918, AGC. For a sketch of a privately designed badge see R. A. Scheultz to Harley, September 18, 1918, AGC; Gilliland, *Wilson County*, 46, has a photo of a badge made in 1909 from a Mexican silver peso. See also George E. Virgines, "Heraldry of the Texas Rangers," *Password*, XXXVII, no. 2 (Summer 1992), 83–88.

14. Cardwell to Harley, March 24, 1919; Harley to Cardwell, March 27, 1919, AGC.

15. Aldrich to Captain W. M. Ryan, July 19, 1919; same to John J. Edds, February 27, 1920, AGC.

16. Aldrich to Otho D. Vivian, April 18, 1919; same to Ben Tumlinson, April 18, 1919, AGC.

17. Dr. H. B. Ross to Aldrich, April 2, 7, 1919; Aldrich to Ross, April 4, 1919, AGC.

18. Aldrich to S. E. Rosengren, February 28, 1919; same to George W. Sadler, February 28, 1919; same to Forrest Campbell, April 4, 1919; Forrest Campbell to Aldrich, April 1, 1919, AGC.

19. Special Orders No. 36, September 24, 1918, AP.

20. Harley to Judge E. T. Branch, April 16, 1919, AGC; "Proceedings," 1583–1586.

21. Aldrich to J. R. McMillan, March 27, 1919; J. R. Hunnicutt to Aldrich, March 29, 1919, AGC.

22. Sergeant B. L. Schramm to Officer in Charge of State Rangers, March 27, 1919, AGC.

23. Aldrich to J. R. Hunnicutt, April 4, 1919, AGC.

24. Edds to Harley, May 3, 1919; Harley to Edds, May 15, 1919; Aldrich to Edds, September 10, 1919; Edds to Aldrich, September 15, 1919, AGC; Hanson to Hobby, August 2, 1919, WC; Edds to Aldrich, August 17, 1919, AP.

25. Harley to M. London, May 17, 1919, AGC.

26. Horton B. Porter and Earl Carter to Hobby, January 13, 1919, AGC.

27. J. Y. McDaniel to Horton B. Porter and Earl Carter, January 13, 1919, AGC.

28. Special Orders No. 2, January 14, 1919, AGC.

29. Hobby to Horton B. Porter, January 22, 1919; same to E. A. Berry, January 23, 1919; same to C. M. Cureton, January 23, 1919, HP.

30. (tel) Harley to County Attorney, April 3, 1919; (tel) Tom C. Hicks, D. M. Maynor, Webster Jarvis to Harley, April 3, 1919; Special Orders No. 29, April 4, 1919, AGC.

31. Special Orders No. 43, July 19, 1919, Hanson vertical file, TRH.

32. *Biennial Report of the Adjutant General of Texas, From January 1, 1919 to December 31, 1920* (Austin: Knape Printing Co., n.d.), 27–28.

33. Hanson to AG, July 17, 1919, WC; J. R. McMillan to Colonel W. D. Cope, July 29, 1919; Judge E. M. Bramlette to Hanson, August 14, 20, 1919; Hanson to Bramlette, August 18, 27, 1919; same to Sheriff Meredith, August 25, 1919, AGC; William Tuttle, "Violence in a 'Heathen' Land: The Longview Race Riot of 1919," *Phylon*, 33 (1972): 324–333; Krenek, *Power Vested*, 105–113.

34. Judge J. R. Warren to Hobby, August 2, 1918; (tel) Harley to Judge Felix McCord, August 1, 1919; (tel) same to J. R. McMillan, August 1, 1919, AGC.

35. Hanson to W. E. Powers, August 8, 1919; same to J. T. Martin, August 8, 1919, AGC.

36. "Minutes of meeting of Sheriff [sic] of Houston District with Captain Hanson, representing the Adjutant General's Department of Texas, held August 23rd, 1919 at 10 a.m.," AP; Frank W. Matthews to Hanson, August 12, 15, 19, 1919, WC; same to same, August 16, 18, 1919; (tel) Hanson to C. E. Breniman, August 22, 1919; R. P. Littlejohn to Harley, August 24, 1919; Harley to Littlejohn, August 26, 1919, AGC; Gould, *Progressives*, 253; Special Orders No. 53, August 21, 1919, Hanson vertical file, TRH.

37. See, for instance, Aldrich to Sheriff E. P. Bemer, August 6, 1919, AGC.

38. Hobby to Harley, May 19, 1919, AGC.

39. Lackey to Hobby, May 2, 1919; see also same to Harley, May 2, 1919, AGC; Hobby to W. H. Bledsoe, May 1, 1919, HP.

40. Harley to Stevens, March 27, 1919; Stevens to Harley, March 29, 1919, AGC; Hobby to same, April 3, 1919; same to Stevens, April 9, May 1, 1919, HP.

41. Hudspeth to Harley, May 20, 1919, AGC.

42. Harley to Hudspeth, May 25, 1919, AGC.

43. Hudspeth to Harley, May 26, 1919, AGC.

44. Hudspeth to Harley, May 31, 1919; Richard F. Burges to same, May 3, 1919; T. J. Jackman to same, May 25, 1919; Harley to Hudspeth, May 30 and June 5, 1919, AGC.

45. Aldrich to Charles H. Wright, May 16, 1919, AGC.

46. Aldrich to Walter I. Rowe, June [illegible but after the 18th], 1919, AGC.

47. Aldrich to A. T. Hamilton, June 24, 1919, AGC.

48. Douglas W. Richmond, *Venustiano Carranza's Nationalist Struggle, 1893–1920* (Lincoln and London: University of Nebraska Press, 1983), 220–228.

49. Harley to Albert Browne, Robert McComb, C. O. Fokes, R. F. Vaughan, Charles Davis, R. M. Dudley, R. E. Thomason, June 5, 1919, AGC.

50. Marks to Harley, May 6, 1919, AGC.

51. Hobby to Major General DeRosey C. Cabell, May 28, 1919, AGC; William P. Blocker to Secretary of State, May 26, 1919, no. 1727, copy in 5384-234-8, MID; Hobby to General Cabell, May 29, 1919, HP.

52. C. E. Breniman to Harley, June 12, 1919, AGC.

53. Harley to C. E. Breniman, June 19, 1919, AGC.

54. *Report of the Adjutant General* (January 1, 1919—December 31, 1920), 44. There was also Ranger R. D. Shumate, who was based in Brownwood and worked directly under the adjutant general as a troubleshooter, mainly in the oilfields.

55. Hobby to Dr. M. P. Cullinan, June 5, 1919; same to S. V. Edwards, June 6, 1919; same to Charles Davis, June 5, 1919, HP.

56. Rowe to Harley, June 6, 1919, AGC.

57. Rowe to Harley, (two letters), undated [June, 1919]; Aldrich to Rowe, July 2, 1919, AGC. Osterveen was the son of Adolph Osterveen, who was the assessor in Starr County. See Osterveen to Aldrich, July 28, 1919, AGC.

58. Rowe to Harley, undated [June, 1919], AGC. See also same to same, June 24 and 28, 1919, AGC.

59. June 5, 1919, AGC. Rowe's brother, S. C. Rowe, was a partner in the Fort Worth law firm of Moses and Rowe, attorneys for the Cattle Raisers Association of Texas. Rowe was subsequently assigned to light duty, guarding the governor's mansion. He then carried out investigative assignments, and on February 7, 1921, he resigned for a better-paying job as a Special Agent for the Saint Louis and Southwestern Railway in Fort Worth. D. E. Singleton to Aldrich, October 13, 1919; W. I. Rowe to AG, February 3, 1921, AGC.

60. Stevens to Hanson, June 11, 1919, AGC.

61. Stevens to Hanson, June 14, 1919, AGC. This was also the opinion of attorney R. E. Thomason, one of Harley's El Paso informants. Thomason to Harley, June 13, 1919, AGC.

62. Katz, *Pancho Villa*, 706–709. For a detailed account of the battle see Donna Lynn Durham, "Francisco Villa's Attack on Juarez, June 15–16, 1919," M.A. thesis, New Mexico State University, 1994.

63. Charles H. Harris III and Louis R. Sadler, *Bastion on the Border: Fort Bliss, 1854–1943* (Historic and Natural Resources Report No. 6, Cultural Resources Management Program, Directorate of Environment, United States Army Air Defense Artillery Center, Fort Bliss, Texas, 1993), 99.

64. Stevens to Harley, July 19, 1919, AGC.

65. Stevens to Harley, August 24, 1919, AGC.

66. Aldrich to Captain W. M. Ryan, July 19, 1919, AGC.

67. Aldrich to Will Alsobrook, August 16, 1919. See also Hanson to C. E. Breniman, August 22, 1919, AGC.
68. Ben Tumlinson, Jr. to Aldrich, August 21, 1919, AGC.
69. Aldrich to D. E. Singleton, October 15, 1919, AGC.
70. August 31, 1920, AGC.
71. Aldrich to D. P. Scarborough, September 10, 1919, AGC.
72. Colonel G. T. Langhorne to Department Intelligence Officer, June 4, 1919, 5384-234-6, MID.
73. W. D. Cope to Langhorne, August 20, 1919, AGC.
74. W. D. Cope to Langhorne, August 19, 1919; Harley to General DeRosey Cabell, August 13, 1919; same to Langhorne, August 13, 1919; Langhorne to AG, September 10, 1919, AGC.
75. Complaint filed by Sergeant H. A. King, Company A, at Marfa before U.S. Commissioner H. O. Metcalfe, October 27, 1919, FRC-FW.
76. Ronnie C. Tyler, *The Big Bend: A History of the Last Texas Frontier* (Washington, D.C.: National Park Service, U.S. Department of the Interior, 1975), 183–184.
77. Ibid., 184–185.
78. For a detailed account of these events see Cano and Sochat, *Bandido*, 198–210, and Smithers, *Chronicles*, 34–55.
79. Aldrich to Ben Tumlinson, Jr., September 2, 1919; same to J. C. Perkins, September 3, 1919; same to J. R. McMillan, September 8, 1919, AGC.
80. V. L. Snyder report, August 16, 1919, reel 23, BI.
81. Gus T. Jones to Charles E. Breniman, September 22, 1919, reel 23, BI.
82. B. C. Baldwin report, August 27, 1919, reel 23, BI.
83. C. E. Breniman to Frank Burke, August 21, 1919; same to B. C. Baldwin, January 20, 1920, reel 23, BI.
84. Gus T. Jones reports, August 12, 1919, reel 18, and August 21, 1919, reel 23, BI.
85. Cano and Sochat, *Bandido*, 206.
86. V. L. Snyder report, August 18, 1919, reel 23, BI.
87. Gus T. Jones report, August 21, 1919, reel 23, BI.
88. B. C. Baldwin report, August 21, 1919, reel 23, BI.
89. L. Lanier Winslow to Frank Burke, September 10, 1919, reel 23, BI.
90. V. L. Snyder report, August 14, 1919, reel 23, BI.
91. C. E. Breniman to B. C. Baldwin, October 4, 1919, reel 23, BI.
92. Gus T. Jones report, October 4, 1919, reel 23, BI.
93. Hanson to Breniman, August 18, 1919, AGC.
94. J. E. Vaughan to AG W. D. Cope, February 17, 1920, AGC.
95. Aldrich to Alsobrook, September 8, 1919, AGC.
96. Alsobrook to Aldrich, September 13, 1919, AGC.
97. Aldrich to J. L. Anders, December 9, 1919, AP.
98. J. R. McMillan to Aldrich, September 4, 1919, AGC.
99. G. M. Millard to Captain Hanson, August 25, 1919; Hanson to Millard, August 19, 1919, AGC.
100. (tel) E. A. Hill to Hobby, December 19, 1919; (tel) Sam McKenzie to W. D. Cope, December 22, 1919; (tel) Cope to Hill, December 23, 1919; Hill to Cope, December 24, 1919; Captain J. B. Brooks to Sam McKenzie, December 24, 1919, AGC.
101. Special Orders No. 59, September 4, 1919, Hanson Vertical File, TRH.
102. Charles H. Boynton to Charles A. Safford, December 3, 1919, ABF, enclosing Hanson's correspondence with Thomson. Also see W. M. Hanson to W. F. Buckley, November 24, 1919, William F. Buckley Papers, Benson Latin American Collection, University of Texas at Austin.
103. Luis de la Rosa offered his and his men's services. Ribb, "José Tomás Canales," 117.
104. Hanson to Charles A. Safford, December 4, 1919, ABF.
105. Hanson to Senator Albert B. Fall, December 22, 1919, ABF. See also same to Charles A. Safford, December 2, 1919, reel 24, BI.
106. Ibid.

107. Director of Military Intelligence to Department Intelligence Officer, Southern Department, December 5, 1919, 257-5-1, MID.
108. Copy made for file 257-5, MID.
109. District Intelligence Officer, Laredo, to Department Intelligence Officer, December 19, 1919, 257-5-2, MID. The Bureau of Investigation was also interested in Lino Caballo and Agustín Garza. See J. J. Lawrence report, December 20, 1919, reel 24, BI.
110. "Report by Captain Hyde, Rec'd 12/24/19" 257-5-4, MID.

Chapter 19

1. Aniceto Pizaña was living quietly in Matamoros as of 1955. Carlos Larralde, *Mexican-American: Movements and Leaders* (Los Alamitos, Calif.: Hwong Publishing Co., 1976), 145, note 3.
2. (tel) Chapa to Cope, December 8, 1919, AGC.
3. Marks to General W. D. Cope, January 5, 1920, AGC.
4. Marks to Cope, January 7, 1920, AGC.
5. Ibid.
6. Cope to Marks, January 10, 1920, AGC.
7. Cope to Marks, January 13, 1920, AGC.
8. Marks to Cope, January 15, 1920, AGC.
9. (tel) Colonel H. C. Smith to Marks, January 19, 1920, AGC.
10. Marks to Cope, January 19, 1920, AGC.
11. Chapa to Colonel H. C. Smith, January 23, 1920, AGC.
12. (tel) F. A. Chapa to Hobby, April 1, 1920, AGC.
13. Edds to Captain R. W. Aldrich, February 5, 1920, AGC.
14. Marks to Cope, February 12, 1920, AGC.
15. Edds to Aldrich, March 3, 1920, AGC.
16. Aldrich to Edds, March 10, 1920, AGC.
17. Cope to Marks, March 13, 1920, AGC.
18. Cope to Chapa, March 13, 1920, AGC.
19. (tel) Chapa to Hobby, April 1, 1920, AGC. Marks's name, incidentally, was misspelled in the telegram as "Morris."
20. Cope to Chapa, April 13, 1920, AGC.
21. (tel) F. A. Chapa to Cope, October 12, 1920, AGC.
22. Marks to Cope, January 5, 1920, AGC.
23. Gray to Cope, January 13, 1920, AGC.
24. Hanson to Colonel H. C. Smith, February 9, 1920, WC; Colonel H. C. Smith to Hanson, February 7, 1920, AGC. See also *IMA*, 1558–1560.
25. Fuller to Aldrich, February 11, 1920, AGC.
26. Fuller to Cope, February 20, 1920, AGC.
27. Cope to Neill, April 29, 1920. See also Neill to Aldrich, April 21, 1920, AGC.
28. Memorial by the Mexican agent to the General and Special Claims Commission, included in Charles Kerr to Commander of the Texas Rangers, November 14, 1925 (filed with April, 1920); Sergeant H. A. King to Cope, April 3, 1920; S. Diego Fernández to Bainbridge Colby, April 26, 1920; Hobby to same, May 20, 1920, AGC.
29. King to Cope, April 3, 1920.
30. Edds to Aldrich, February 15, 1920, AGC.
31. S. S. Hutchison to Aldrich, April 24, May 30, 1920; Stanley Morton to same, March 10, 11, 1920, AGC. See also Ben Tumlinson, Jr., to same, May 20, 1920, AGC.
32. Oscar Thompson to Cope (April, 1920), AGC.
33. (tel) Ralph Soape to Hobby, April 20, 1920, HP.

34. (tel) Hobby to Bainbridge Colby, April 19, 1920, HP.

35. (tel) Hobby to Colby, April 24, 1920, HP.

36. See, for example, R. M. Dudley to Cope, April 18, 26, 1920; Cope to Dudley, April 29, 1920; same to Captain W. W. Davis, April 16, 1920; Davis to Cope, April 17, 1920, AGC; Raymond Brooks to Ralph Soape, April 17, 1920; Hobby to Elbert C. White, May 4, 1920, HP.

37. (tel) Hobby to Mayor Charles Davis, February 2, 1918; (tel) same to Secretary of State, February 2, 1919, HP.

38. Davis to Cope, April 10, May 22, 1920; Cope to Davis, April 16, 1920, AGC.

39. Claude Franklin to Aldrich, March 30, 1920, AGC.

40. Aldrich to Claude Franklin, May 4, 1920, AGC.

41. Stanley Morton to Aldrich, June 11, 1920, AGC.

42. (tel) Ryan to Cope, May 10, 1920; Cope to Ryan, May 12, 1920, AGC.

43. Cope to H. P. Taylor, May 16, 1920, AGC.

44. Ribb, "José Tomás Canales," 385–386.

45. *NYT*, March 16, 1924.

46. Ibid., February 5, 1926.

47. *Congressional Record*, 69th Congress, 1st sess., Senate, April 30, 1926 (Washington, D.C.: Government Printing Office, 1926), 8500–8502.

48. *SAE*, February 20, 1931.

49. Captain R. W. Aldrich to J. Matthews, October 28, 1920, AGC.

50. (tel) Cope to Stevens, December 29, 30, 1919, WC; (tel) Hobby to R. M. Dudley, R. E. Thomason et al., January 3, 1920; (tel) same to E. C. Davis, January 3, 1920, HP.

51. Stevens to Hobby, February 3, 1920; (tel) Same to Cope, February 3, 1920, AGC.

52. Stafford E. Beckett to Cope, February 3, 1920; Van D. Hargus to same, February 3, 1920; J. A. Miller to same, February 17, 1920, AGC.

53. Aldrich to John T. Moore, August 8, 1920, AGC.

54. Chris Strachwitz, *Corridos y Tragedias De La Frontera* (El Cerrito, California: Arhoolie Productions, Inc., 1994), 115–121. The corrido is found in the accompanying compact disc, 7020.

55. Hobby to Cope, January 19, 1920, AP.

56. (tel) Colonel H. S. Smith to Cope, January 23, 1920; (tels) Cope to Lone Star Oil, March 23, 24, 1920; (tels) same to Ticket Agent, March 23–25, 1920; J. Shuler to Cope, March 18, 1920, AGC.

57. Special Orders No. 6, March 16, 1920, AP.

58. Aldrich to T. J. Jackman, February 15, 1920, AGC.

59. G. M. Millard to Aldrich, February 12, 1920, AGC.

60. Frank Matthews to Aldrich, March 31, 1920; Aldrich to George M. Millard, March 10, 1920, AGC.

61. Aldrich to Ben T. Tumlinson, Jr., April 30, 1920, AGC.

62. (tels) Aldrich to Cope, April 12, 14, 1920, AP.

63. E. A. Hill to Hobby, May 18, 1920, AGC.

64. Shumate to Aldrich, May 19, June 10, 22, July 7, 1920; Perry E. Taylor to Adjutant General, June 10, 1920; Horace Soule to Hobby, June 14, 1920; Shumate to Cope, June 17, 1920; (tel) Colonel H. C. Smith to Shumate, June 19, 1920; Aldrich to Shumate, June 30, 1920; (tel) Cope to same, July 14, 1920; AGC.

65. W. M. Molesworth to Cope, July 13, 14, 1920; Aldrich to Shumate, September 16, 1920, AGC.

66. Shumate to Cope, August 24, 1920; Cope to H. A. Turner, August 27, 1920; Cope to Shumate, August 27, 1920, AGC.

67. *Biennial Report* (January 1, 1919–December 31, 1920), 67. See William D. Angel, Jr., "Controlling the Workers: The Galveston Dock Workers' Strike of 1920 and Its Impact on Labor Relations in Texas," *East Texas Historical Journal*, 23, no. 2 (1985): 14–27.

68. *Biennial Report*, 68; Aldrich to R. D. Shumate, May 29, 1920, AGC.
69. Hobby to Cope, September 21, 1920 and attachment, AGC.
70. *Biennial Report* (January 1, 1919–December 31, 1920), 69–80; Krenek, *Power Vested*, 5–29.
71. Colonel John W. Heavey to General J. F. Wolters, October 5, 1920, AGC.
72. Aldrich to Colonel J. T. Stockton, October 1, 1920; Southern Pacific Lines invoice, October 5, 1920, AGC.
73. Aldrich to Captain A. M. Hendricks, October 28, 1920, AGC.
74. Governor to Jacob Singer et al., January 4, 1921, WC; Cope to Captain Joe B. Brooks, January 15, 19, 1921, AGC.
75. (tel) T. A. Coleman to Hobby, September 23, 1920; (tel) Pat Craighead et al. to Cope, September 23, 1920; (tel) Robert J. Kleberg to same, September 23, 1920; (tel) Cope to T. A. Coleman, September 23, 1920, AGC.
76. Fletcher S. Jones to Hobby, August 27, 1920, AGC. See also J. A. Russ to same, September 19, 1920, AGC.
77. Aldrich to Stanley Morton, October 25, 1920, AGC.
78. Cope to J. A. Russ, October 7, 1920; (tel) same to Charles T. Williams, October 15, 1920; Aldrich to Major C. M. Crawford, October 20, 1920; same to M. L. Langford, October 25, 1920; Hubert P. Brady to Aldrich, October 25, 1920; Aldrich to Brady, November 18, 1920, AGC.
79. Aldrich to Harold J. Matthews, October 28, 1920, AGC.
80. Aldrich to James A. Bracewell, November 16, 1920; same to J. J. Edds, November 18, 1920; same to H. P. Brady, November 26, 1920; Major T. J. Powers to E. A. Carroll, Jr., November 18, 1920; T. J. Powers to Jim P. Morrow, November 18, 1920; H. P. Brady to Aldrich, undated [November, 1920], AGC.
81. Aldrich to H. P. Brady, November 26, 1920, AGC.
82. Sterling, *Trails and Trials*, 194–202.
83. Ibid., 209.
84. Ibid., 189, 190, 425.
85. Ibid., 517.
86. Duncan, "The Life of Captain Roy W. Aldrich," 66–69; *Handbook*, I, 98.
87. Aldrich to M. F. C. Damaske, November 20, 1920, AGC.
88. Aldrich to H. P. Brady, December 23, 1920, AGC.

Epilogue

1. *HC*, January 8, 1922.
2. Hobby to Cope, January 11, 1921, WC; Aldrich to J. J. Edds, January 14, 1921, AGC.
3. Wright to Barton, September 13, 1921, WC.
4. Wright to Barton, November 24, 1921, WC. For photos of Wright's Rangers and the captured pack train see *HC*, January 8, 1922.
5. Webb, *Texas Rangers*, 554–557.
6. Gilliland, *Horsebackers*, 15–68 gives a good account of the Rangers' clashes with tequileros throughout the 1920's. See also Peavey, *Echoes*, 206-passim.
7. Sterling, *Trails and Trials*, 416.
8. Gilliland, *Horsebackers*, 111–112.
9. Sterling, *Trails and Trials*, 183.
10. *LWT*, July 10, 1921.
11. Brigadier General Thomas D. Barton officially became adjutant general on January 20, 1921. *Annual Reports of the Adjutant General of Texas for the Periods from January 1, 1921 to December 31, 1921 and January 1, 1922 to August 31, 1922* (Austin: Von Boeckmann-Jones Co., n.d.), 28.

12. *Annual Report of the Adjutant General of Texas for the Period from January 1, 1922, to August 31, 1922* (Austin: Von Boeckman-Jones Co., n.d.), 38–39; Krenek, *Power Vested*, 59–81.

13. Krenek, *Power Vested*, 33–56.

14. *Annual Report . . . January 1–August 31, 1922*, 53–58.

15. Draper, "Twilight of the Texas Rangers," 76–82, 107–113, 118; Art Chapman and Peyton D. Woodson, "A Breed Apart," Fort Worth *Star-Telegram*, October 27, 2002; Harold J. Weiss, Jr., "The Texas Rangers Revisisted: Old Themes and New Viewpoints," *Southwestern Historical Quarterly*, 97, no. 4 (April, 1994): 620–640.

Conclusion

1. For example, Frank Hamer and three other Rangers couldn't control a lynch mob in Sherman in May, 1930. Krenek, *Power Vested*, 114–127.

2. They also committed an atrocity unrelated to the Bandit War, the Porvenir massacre.

3. Interpretations vary considerably on this point. Douglas Richmond states that "Undoubtedly the major reason for the defeat of the Plan de San Diego movement was the ruthless response of local authorities" but then declares that "Having achieved his diplomatic objective, Carranza temporarily halted the fighting." ("La Guerra de Texas," 19, 20). Rodolfo Rocha takes a somewhat different approach, writing that "Carranza may have allowed the raids to continue in his attempt to obtain U.S. recognition for his government," but never "officially" [sic] endorsed the raids. ("The Tejano Revolt of 1915," 103–119, in Emilio Zamora, Cynthia Orozco, and Rodolfo Rocha, eds. *Mexican Americans in Texas History: Selected Essays* (Austin: Texas State Historical Association, 2000). Of course the reason Carranza did not "officially" endorse the raids was because he was not a fool. Regarding Carranza and the Plan, James Sandos is all over the landscape. He first declared that the Plan de San Diego "began with followers of Huerta, then was taken over by the Germans, who later shared their control with Carranza ("Plan de San Diego," 10). Then Sandos dropped the Germans, retained the Huerta connection, but absolved Carranza of any involvement ("The Mexican Revolution and the United States, 1915–1917: The Impact of Conflict in the Tamaulipas-Texas Frontier upon the Emergence of Revolutionary Government in Mexico," Ph.D. dissertation, University of California at Berkeley, 1978, 179, 211–215, 223). Sandos's next interpretation was that Carranza's favorite and most loyal general, Pablo González, was running some kind of rogue operation by sponsoring the raids, much against Carranza's wishes. ("Pancho Villa and American Security: Woodrow Wilson's Mexican Diplomacy Reconsidered," *Journal of Latin American Studies*, 13, no. 2 (November 1981): 304–311). Lastly, Sandos asserts that the Plan de San Diego was an attempt to implement the anarchist principles of Ricardo Flores Magón, who "did not comprehend the situation" and "failed to recognize his intellectual progeny" (*Rebellion*, 100). He concludes that the Plan did not succeed because it was "strangled by the military and political authorities of the U.S. and Mexican governments." (Ibid., 172).

4. Paredes, *With His Pistol*, 24.

5. See the interesting discussion of Hispanic-black relations in James N. Leiker, *Racial Borders: Black Soldiers along the Rio Grande*. College Station: Texas A&M University Press, 2002.

6. Barbara Tuchman, *Practicing History: Selected Essays* (New York: Knopf, 1981), 34.

BIBLIOGRAPHY

Archives and Manuscript Collections

National Archives and Records Service, Washington, D.C. and College Park, Maryland

 Record Group 60: Records of the Department of Justice

 Record Group 65: Records of the Federal Bureau of Investigation—Old Mex 232, Microcopy, no number

 Record Group 94: Records of the Adjutant General's Office, 1780's–1917

 Record Group 165: Records of the War Department General and Special Staffs, Military Intelligence Division

 Record Group 204: General Records of the Pardon Attorney's Office

 Record Group 393: Records of the United States Army Continental Commands, 1821–1920

  Adjutant General's Office, Department of Texas, Record Cards, 1909–12

  Southern Department, United States Army, 1913–1920, Correspondence Relating to the Mexican Revolution, 1913–16

  General Correspondence, Department of Texas, 1870–1913

 Record Group 407: Records of the Adjutant General's Office, 1917—Central Decimal Files Project Files, 1917–1925, Countries—Mexican Border

 Record Group 59: Records of the Department of State, Decimal Files, Internal Affairs of Mexico, 1910–1929. National Archives Microfilm Publication, Microcopy no. 274.

Centro de Estudios de Historia de México, Departamento Cultural de Condumex, Mexico City
 President Venustiano Carranza Archive

Kansas State Historical Society, Topeka, Kansas
 General Frederick Funston Collection (microfilm)

Archive of the Big Bend, Sul Ross State University, Alpine, Texas
 Roy Aldrich Papers

Center for Southwest Research, General Library, University of New Mexico, Albuquerque, New Mexico
    A. B. Fall Papers (microfilm)

Benson Latin American Library, University of Texas at Austin
    General Pablo González Archive (microfilm)
    William F. Buckley Papers

Center for American History, University of Texas at Austin
    Lon Hill Papers
    Walter Prescott Webb Collection
    "Memoirs of Jesse Perez"
    Governor Oscar B. Colquitt Papers
    James B. Wells Papers
    E. A. "Dogie" Wright Papers

Archives Division, Texas State Library, Austin, Texas
    Adjutant General's Correspondence
    Governor Thomas M. Campbell Papers
    Governor Oscar B. Colquitt Papers
    Governor James E. Ferguson Papers
    Governor William P. Hobby Papers
    "Proceedings of the Joint Committee of the Senate and the House in the Investigation of the Texas State Ranger Force," 3 vols., 1919
    Texas Rangers, Service Records (microfilm)

Texas Court of Criminal Appeals, Austin, Texas
    Jose Antonio Arce et al. vs. State of Texas, no. 4314

Texas Department of Public Safety, Austin, Texas
    Ranger Archive

Texas National Guard Archives, Camp Mabry, Austin, Texas
    Ranger Records

Texas Ranger Hall of Fame and Museum, Waco, Texas
    Vertical Files:
        Francis Noel "Frank" Johnson
        Henry Lee Ransom
        Lafetra "Lee" Trimble
        William M. Hanson

Texas State District Courts

    Brownsville (Cameron County)
        State of Texas, *ex rel* Louis Cobolini vs. A. B. Cole, no. 2353, District Court, Cameron County.
        State of Texas vs. Ramón Pizaña et al., no. 3657, District Court, Cameron County.

    McAllen (Hidalgo County)
        State of Texas vs. W. W. Sterling and E. A. Sterling, Jr., no. 1003, District Court, Hidalgo County.

Cotulla (LaSalle County)
   State of Texas vs. J. M. Rangel, et al., no. 1032, District Court, LaSalle County.

Laredo (Webb County)
   State of Texas vs. Norberto Pezzar [sic] et al., no. 5204, District Court, Webb County.

Federal Records Center, Fort Worth, Texas

   U.S. District Court Files
      Western District of Texas
         El Paso

            U.S. Commissioner
               El Paso
               Marfa

         Southern District of Texas
            Brownsville
            Laredo
            San Antonio

            Judge's Bench Dockets: Criminal Cases. vols. 6 and 7, U.S. District Court, Brownsville

            U.S. Commissioner
               Brownsville
               Laredo
               San Antonio

   U.S. Customs Letter Press Book, Saluria District, 1913

Government Documents

Texas

Biennial Report of the Adjutant General of Texas for the Period Ending December 15, 1910. Austin: Austin Printing Co., 1911.

Biennial Report of the Adjutant General of Texas, from January 23, 1911, to December 31, 1912. Austin: Von Boeckmann-Jones Co., 1913.

Biennial Report of the Adjutant General of Texas, from January 1, 1913, to December 31, 1914. Austin: Von Boeckmann-Jones Co., 1915.

Biennial Report of the Adjutant General of Texas, from January 1, 1915, to December 31, 1916. Austin: Von Boeckmann-Jones Co., 1917.

Biennial Report of the Adjutant General of Texas, from January 1, 1917, to December 31, 1918. Austin: Von Boeckmann-Jones Co., 1919.

Biennial Report of the Adjutant General of Texas, from January 1, 1919, to December 31, 1920. Austin: Knape Printing Co., n.d.

Annual Reports of the Adjutant General of Texas for the Periods from January 1, 1921, to December 31, 1921 and January 1, 1922, to August 31, 1922. Austin: Von Boeckmann-Jones Co., n.d.

General Laws of the State of Texas Passed at the Regular Session of the Twenty-Seventh Legislature Convened at the City of Austin, January 8, 1901, and Adjourned April 9, 1901. Austin: Von Boeckmann, Schutz & Co., 1901.

General Laws of the State of Texas Passed by the Thirty-fourth Legislature at its Regular Session Convened January 12, 1915, and Adjourned April 20, 1915. Austin: A. C. Baldwin & Sons, 1915.

General and Special Laws of the State of Texas Passed at the First Called Session of the Thirty-fifth Legislature Convened at the City of Austin, April 18, 1917, and Adjourned May 17, 1917. Austin: A. C. Baldwin & Sons, 1917.

General and Special Laws of the State of Texas Passed by the Fourth Called Session of the Thirty-Fifth Legislature Convened at the City of Austin, February 26, 1918, and Adjourned March 27, 1918. Austin: A. C. Baldwin and Sons, 1918.

General and Special Laws of the State of Texas Passed by the Forty-fourth Legislature at the Regular Session Convened at the City of Austin, January 8, 1935, and Adjourned May 11, 1935. Vol.1. Austin: The State of Texas, 1935.

Annual Report of the Adjutant General of Texas for the Period from January 1, 1922, to August 31, 1922. Austin: Von Boeckmann-Jones Co., n.d.

In the Senate of Texas. D. W. Glasscock, Contestant vs. A. Parr, Contestee. Supplement to the Senate Journal; Regular Session of the 36th Legislature 1919. Published by Authority of the Senate. Austin: A. C. Baldwin & Sons [1919].

Robinson, James W. *The DPS Story: History of the Development of the Department of Public Safety in Texas.* Austin: Texas Department of Public Safety, 1974.

United States

Expense of Patrolling the Boundary in Texas. Senate Documents no. 404, 62nd Cong., 2nd sess. Washington, D.C.: Government Printing Office, 1912.

Investigation of Mexican Affairs. Senate Documents no. 285; 2 vols, 66th Cong., 2nd sess. Washington, D.C.: Government Printing Office, 1920.

Revolutions in Mexico. 62nd Cong., 2nd sess. Washington, D.C.: Government Printing Office, 1913.

Congressional Record, 69th Congress, 1st sess., Senate, April 30, 1926. Washington, D.C.: Government Printing Office, 1926.

Harris, Charles H., III, and Louis R. Sadler. *Bastion on the Border: Fort Bliss, 1854–1943.* Historic and Natural Resources Report No. 6, Cultural Resources Management Program, Directorate of Environment, United States Army Air Defense Artillery Center, Fort Bliss, Texas, 1993.

New Mexico

Laws of the State of New Mexico Passed at the First Regular Session . . . 1912. Albuquerque: Albright and Anderson, Printers, 1912.

Books

Acuña, Rodolfo. *Occupied America: The Chicano's Struggle Toward Liberation*. San Francisco: Canfield Press, 1972. A later edition is entitled *Occupied America: A History of Chicanos*. New York: Longman, 2000.

Anders, Evan. *Boss Rule in South Texas: The Progressive Era*. Austin: University of Texas Press, 1982.

Bartra, Armando, ed. *Regeneración, 1900–1918: La corriente más radical de la Revolución de 1910 a través de su periódico de combate*. México: Hadise, S. A., 1972.

Beezley, William H. *Insurgent Governor: Abraham González and the Mexican Revolution in Chihuahua*. Lincoln: University of Nebraska Press, 1973.

The Blue Book for Visitors, Tourists and Those Seeking a Good Time While in San Antonio, Texas. San Antonio, n.p., 1911–1912.

Brown, Norman D. *Hood, Bonnet, and Little Brown Jug: Texas Politics, 1921–1928*. College Station: Texas A&M University Press, 1984.

Bruce, Leona. *Bannister Was There*. Fort Worth: Branch-Smith, Inc., 1968.

Calzadíaz Barrera, Alberto. *Hechos reales de la Revolución*. III, 2nd ed. México: Editorial Patria, 1972.

Cano, Tony, and Ann Sochat. *Bandido: The True Story of Chico Cano, the Last Western Bandit*. Canutillo, Tex.: Reata Publishing, 1997.

Caro, Robert A. *The Years of Lyndon Johnson: Means of Ascent*. New York: Alfred A. Knopf, 1990.

Chamberlain, Samuel E. *My Confession*. New York: Harper, 1956.

Clark, James A., with Weldon Hart. *The Tactful Texan: A Biography of Governor Will Hobby*. New York: Random House, 1958.

Coerver, Don M. and Linda B. Hall. *Texas and the Mexican Revolution: A Study in State and National Border Policy 1910–1920*. San Antonio: Trinity University Press, 1984.

De la Garza Treviño, Ciro. *El Plan de San Diego*. Ciudad Victoria, Tamaulipas: Universidad Autónoma de Tamaulipas, 1970.

———. *La Revolución Mexicana en el Estado de Tamaulipas*. México: Editorial Porrúa, 1973.

D'Este, Carlo. *Patton: A Genius for War*. New York: HarperCollins, 1995.

Durham, George. *Taming the Nueces Strip: The Story of McNelly's Rangers*. Austin: University of Texas Press, 1962.

Fehrenbach, T. R. *Lone Star: A History of Texas and the Texans*. New York: Macmillan, 1968.

Frazer, Robert W. *Forts of the West: Military Forts and Presidios and Posts Commonly Called Forts West of the Mississippi River to 1898*. Norman: University of Oklahoma Press, 1965.

Frost, H. Gordon, and John H. Jenkins. *I'm Frank Hamer: The Life of a Texas Peace Officer*. Austin: Pemberton Press, 1968.

Gilliland, Maude T. *Horsebackers of the Brush Country: A Story of the Texas Rangers and Mexican Liquor Smugglers*. [Brownsville: Springman-King Co.], 1968.

_____. *Rincon (Remote Dwelling Place): A Story of Life on a South Texas Ranch at the Turn of the Century*. Brownsville: Springman-King Co., 1964.

_____, comp. *Wilson County Texas Rangers 1837–1977*. Brownsville: Springman-King Co., 1977.

Gonzales, Manuel G. *Mexicanos: A History of Mexicans in the United States*. Bloomington: Indiana University Press, 2000.

Gould, Lewis L. *Progressives and Prohibitionists: Texas Democrats in the Wilson Era*. Austin: Texas State Historical Association, 1992. Originally published by the University of Texas Press, 1973.

Grieb, Kenneth J. *The United States and Huerta*. Lincoln: University of Nebraska Press, 1969.

Harris, Charles H., III, and Louis R. Sadler. *The Archaeologist Was a Spy: Sylvanus G. Morley and the Office of Naval Intelligence*. Albuquerque: University of New Mexico Press, 2003.

Jennings, N. A. *A Texas Ranger*. Norman: University of Oklahoma Press, 1997.

Justice, Glenn. *Revolution on the Rio Grande: Mexican Raids and Army Pursuits 1916–1919*. El Paso: Texas Western Press, 1992.

Katz, Friedrich. *The Life and Times of Pancho Villa*. Stanford: Stanford University Press, 1998.

_____. *The Secret War in Mexico: Europe, the United States and the Mexican Revolution*. Chicago and London: University of Chicago Press, 1981.

Kearney, Milo, and Anthony Knopp. *Boom and Bust: The Historical Cycles of Matamoros and Brownsville*. Austin: Eakin Press, 1991.

Keil, Robert, ed. Elizabeth McBride. *Bosque Bonito: Violent Times along the Borderland during the Mexican Revolution*. Alpine, Texas: Sul Ross State University, 2002.

Krenek, Harry. *The Power Vested: The Use of Martial Law and the National Guard in Texas Domestic Crisis . . . 1919–1932*. Austin: Presidial Press, 1980.

Larralde, Carlos. *Mexican-American: Movements and Leaders*. Los Alamitos, Calif.: Hwong Publishing Co., 1976.

Lea, Tom. *The King Ranch*. 2 vols. Boston: Little, Brown and Company, 1957.

Leiker, James N. *Racial Borders: Black Soldiers along the Rio Grande*. College Station: Texas A&M University Press, 2002.

Martin, Jack. *Border Boss: Captain John R. Hughes, Texas Ranger*. Austin: State House Press, 1942.

Means, Joyce E. *Pancho Villa Days at Pilares*. El Paso: Guynes Printing Co., 1976.

Meyer, Michael C. *Huerta: A Political Portrait*. Lincoln: University of Nebraska Press, 1972.

_____. *Mexican Rebel: Pascual Orozco and the Mexican Revolution 1910–1915*. Lincoln: University of Nebraska Press, 1967.

Montejano, David. *Anglos and Mexicans in the Making of Texas, 1836–1986*. Austin: University of Texas Press, 1987.

Paine, Albert Bigelow. *Captain Bill McDonald, Texas Ranger*. New York: Little and Ives, 1909.

Paredes, Americo. *"With His Pistol in His Hand:" A Border Ballad and Its Hero*. Austin: University of Texas Press, 1958.

Proctor, Ben. *Just One Riot: Episodes of Texas Rangers in the 20th Century*. Austin: Eakin Press, 1991.

Quirk, Robert E. *An Affair of Honor: Woodrow Wilson and the Occupation of Veracruz*. New York: W. W. Norton & Co., 1967.

Raat, W. Dirk. *Revoltosos: Mexico's Rebels in the United States, 1903–1923*. College Station: Texas A&M University Press, 1981.

Reid, Samuel C., Jr. *Scouting Expeditions of McCullough's Texas Rangers. . . .* Philadelphia: G. B. Zieber, 1847.

Reyes, Rodolfo. *De mi vida: memorias políticas*. Vol. 1 (1899–1913). Madrid: Biblioteca Nueva, 1929.

Richmond, Douglas W. *Venustiano Carranza's Nationalist Struggle, 1893–1920*. Lincoln and London: University of Nebraska Press, 1983.

Robinson, Charles H., III. *The Men Who Wear the Star: The Story of the Texas Rangers*. New York: Random House, 2000.

Rosenbaum, Robert J. *Mexicano Resistance in the Southwest: "The Sacred Right of Self-Preservation."* Austin: University of Texas Press, 1981.

Samora, Julian, Joe Bernal, and Albert Peña. *Gunpowder Justice: A Reassessment of the Texas Rangers*. Notre Dame: University of Notre Dame Press, 1979.

Sandos, James A. *Rebellion in the Borderlands: Anarchism and the Plan of San Diego, 1904–1923*. Norman: University of Oklahoma Press, 1992.

Smithers, W. D. *Chronicles of the Big Bend: A Photographic Memoir of Life on the Border*. Austin: Madrona Press, 1976.

———. *Early Trail Drives in the Big Bend*. El Paso: Texas Western Press, 1979.

Sonnichsen, C. L. *Pass of the North: Four Centuries on the Rio Grande*. El Paso: Texas Western Press, 1968.

Spellman, Paul N. *Captain John H. Rogers, Texas Ranger*. Denton: University of North Texas Press, 2003.

Sterling, William Warren. *Trails and Trials of a Texas Ranger*. Norman: University of Oklahoma Press, 1959.

Strachwitz, Chris. *Corridos y Tragedias De La Frontera*. El Cerrito, Calif.: Arhoolie Productions, Inc., 1994.

Supplement to Vernon's Texas Civil and Criminal Statutes. . . . 3 vols. Kansas City, Mo.: Vernon Law Book Company, 1922.

Timmons, W. H. *El Paso: A Borderlands History*. El Paso: Texas Western Press, 1990.

A Twentieth Century History of Southwest Texas. 2 vols. Chicago: Lewis Publishing Co., 1907.

Tuchman, Barbara. *Practicing History: Selected Essays*. New York: Knopf, 1981.

———. *The Zimmermann Telegram*. New York: Viking Press, 1958.

Tyler, Ronnie C. *The Big Bend: A History of the Last Texas Frontier*. Washington, D.C.: National Park Service, U.S. Department of the Interior, 1975.

Utley, Robert M. *Lone Star Justice: The First Century of the Texas Rangers*. Oxford: Oxford University Press, 2002.

Vanderwood, Paul J. *Disorder and Progress: Bandits, Police, and Mexican Development*. Lincoln: University of Nebraska Press, 1981.

Vanderwood, Paul J., and Frank N. Samponaro. *Border Fury: A Picture Postcard Record of Mexico's Revolution and U.S. War Preparedness, 1910–1917*. Albuquerque: University of New Mexico Press, 1988.

Weaver, John D. *The Brownsville Raid*. Rev. ed. College Station: Texas A&M University Press, 1992.

Webb, Walter Prescott. *An Honest Preface and Other Essays*. Cambridge: The Riverside Press, 1959.

_____. *The Texas Rangers: A Century of Frontier Defense*. 2nd ed. Austin: University of Texas Press, 1965.

Wilson, Neill C., and Frank J. Taylor. *Southern Pacific: The Roaring Story of a Fighting Railroad*. New York: McGraw Hill, 1952.

Articles

Anders, Evan. "Robert Caro's Lyndon Johnson and the Pitfalls of Political Biography: A Critical Evaluation of *The Years of Lyndon Johnson: The Path to Power* and *Means of Ascent*." *Southwestern Historical Quarterly* 94 (1991): 581–598.

Angel, William D., Jr. "Controlling the Workers: The Galveston Dock Workers' Strike of 1920 and Its Impact on Labor Relations in Texas." *East Texas Historical Journal*, 23, no. 2 (1985): 14–27.

Chapman, Art, and Peyton D. Woodson. "A Breed Apart." Fort Worth *Star-Telegram*, October 27, 2002.

Collier, Walter, as told to Bill Leftwich. "Germans' 'Plan of San Diego' Worked Good—On End of a Rope." *The Southwesterner* (May 1963): 6–7.

Colquitt, O. B. "The Texas Ranger As He Is." *Leslie's Illustrated Weekly Newspaper*, April 16, 1914: 367.

Crawford, Charlotte. "The Border Meeting of Presidents Taft and Diaz." *Password* 3, no. 3 (July 1958): 86–96.

Cumberland, Charles. "Border Raids in the Lower Rio Grande Valley—1915." *Southwestern Historical Quarterly* 57, no. 3 (January 1954): 285–311.

Day, James M. "El Paso's Texas Rangers." *Password* 24, no. 4 (Winter 1979): 153–172.

Draper, Robert. "The Twilight of the Texas Rangers." *Texas Monthly* (February 1994): 76–83, 107–108, 110, 112–113, 118.

Friend, Llerena B. "W. P. Webb's Texas Rangers." *Southwestern Historical Quarterly* 74 (January 1971): 293–323.

"The Future is Texas." *The Economist* (December 21, 2002): 29–31.

Gerlach, Alan. "Conditions Along the Border—1915: The Plan de San Diego." *New Mexico Historical Review* 43 (July 1968): 195–212.

Gómez-Quiñones, Juan. "Plan de San Diego Reviewed." *Aztlán: Chicano Journal of the Social Sciences and the Arts* 1 (Spring 1970): 124–132.

Hager, William M. "The Plan of San Diego: Unrest on the Texas Border in 1915." *Arizona and the West* 5 (Winter 1963): 327–336.

Hammond, Matthew Carlton. "The Posse Comitatus Act: A Principle in Need of Renewal." *Washington University Law Quarterly* 75, no. 2 (Summer 1997): 1–32.

Harris, Charles H., III, and Louis R. Sadler. "The 1911 Reyes Conspiracy: The Texas Side." *Southwestern Historical Quarterly* 83, no. 4 (April 1980): 325–348.

_____. "The Plan of San Diego and the Mexican-United States War Crisis of 1916: A Reexamination." *Hispanic American Historical Review* 58, no. 3 (August 1978): 381–408.

_____. "The 'Underside' of the Mexican Revolution: El Paso, 1912." *The Americas: A Quarterly Review of Inter-American Cultural History* 39 (July 1982): 69–83.

_____. "The Witzke Affair: German Intrigue on the Mexican Border, 1917–18." *Military Review* 59, no. 2 (February 1979): 36–50.

Larralde, Carlos. "J. T. Canales and the Texas Rangers." *The Journal of South Texas* 10, no. 1 (1977): 38–68.

Meyer, Michael C. "The Mexican-German Conspiracy of 1915." *The Americas: A Quarterly Review of Inter-American Cultural History* 23 (July 1966): 76–89.

Pettey, Weston A. "The Seminole Incident and Tom Ross." *West Texas Historical Association Year Book* 56 (1980): 133–142.

Ribb, Richard. "Patrician as Reedemer: José Tomás Canales and the Salvation of South Texas, 1910–1919." *The Journal of South Texas* 14, no. 2 (Fall 2001): 189–203.

Richmond, Douglas W. "La Guerra de Texas se renova: Mexican Insurrection and Carrancista Ambitions, 1900–1920." *Aztlán: Chicano Journal of the Social Sciences and the Arts* 2, no. 1 (Spring 1980): 1–32.

Rocha, Rodolfo. "The Tejano Revolt of 1915," in Emilio Zamora, Cynthia Orozco, and Rodolfo Rocha, eds. *Mexican Americans in Texas History: Selected Essays.* Austin: Texas State Historical Association, 2000: 103–119.

Sandos, James A. "Pancho Villa and American Security: Woodrow Wilson's Mexican Diplomacy Reconsidered," *Journal of Latin American Studies* 13, no. 2 (November 1981): 304–311.

_____. "The Plan of San Diego: War and Diplomacy on the Texas Border, 1915–1916." *Arizona and the West* 14 (Spring 1972): 5–24.

Tuttle, William. "Violence in a 'Heathen' Land: The Longview Race Riot of 1919." *Phylon* 33 (1972): 324–333.

Valadés, José C., ed. "Los secretos del reyismo: diez años de intensa lucha." *La Prensa* (San Antonio), October 23–December 11, 1932.

Virgines, George E. "Heraldry of the Texas Rangers." *Password* 37, no. 2 (Summer 1992): 83–88.

Warburton, L. H. "The Plan de San Diego: Background and Selected Documents." *The Journal of South Texas* 12, no. 1 (1999): 125–155.

Weiss, Harold J., Jr. "The Texas Rangers Revisited: Old Themes and New Viewpoints." *Southwestern Historical Quarterly* 97, no. 4 (April 1994): 620–640.

BIBLIOGRAPHY

Reference Works

"Guide to Manuscript Collections, Archive of the Big Bend, Sul Ross State University, Alpine, Texas."

The New Handbook of Texas. 6 vols. Austin: The Texas State Historical Association, 1996.

Theses and Dissertations

Duncan, Virginia. "The Life of Captain Roy W. Aldrich." M. A. thesis, Sul Ross State Teachers College, 1942.

Durham, Donna Lynn. "Francisco Villa's Attack on Juarez, June 15–16, 1919." M.A. thesis, New Mexico State University, 1994.

Huckaby, George Portal. "Oscar Branch Colquitt: A Political Biography." Ph.D. dissertation, University of Texas, 1946.

Johnson, David H. "Exiles and Intrigue: Francisco I. Madero and the Mexican Revolutionary Junta in San Antonio, 1910–1911." M.A. thesis, Trinity University, 1975.

Ribb, Richard Henry. "José Tomás Canales and the Texas Rangers: Myth, Identity and Power in South Texas, 1900–1920." Ph.D. dissertation, University of Texas at Austin, 2001.

Rocha, Rodolfo. "The Influence of the Mexican Revolution on the Mexico-Texas Border, 1910–1916." Ph.D. dissertation, Texas Tech University, 1981.

Sandos, James A. "The Mexican Revolution and the United States, 1915–1917: The Impact of Conflict in the Tamaulipas-Texas Frontier upon the Emergence of Revolutionary Government in Mexico." Ph.D. dissertation, University of California at Berkeley, 1978.

Newspapers

Alpine Avalanche

Austin American

Austin Statesman

Brownsville *Daily Herald*

Corpus Christi *Caller and Daily Herald*

Corpus Christi *Democrat*

Dallas Morning News

El Paso *Herald*

El Paso Morning Times

Houston Chronicle

Laredo *Weekly Times*

New York Times

San Antonio *Express*

San Antonio *Light*

San Antonio *News*

La Prensa (San Antonio)

INDEX

Rangers photographs are identified with bold page numbers. Please note that only Rangers mentioned in the text are found in the index. For other Rangers, see the Appendix which lists alphabetically the Texas Rangers that served during this period.

A

B

D

E

ABOUT THE AUTHORS

Charles H. Harris III and **Louis R. Sadler** are emeritus history professors at New Mexico State University, Las Cruces. Harris (pictured right) and Sadler (left) have coauthored several books including *The Archaeologist Was a Spy: Sylvanus G. Morley and the Office of Naval Intelligence*.

Photograph by Darren Phillips.

ALSO AVAILABLE FROM UNM PRESS

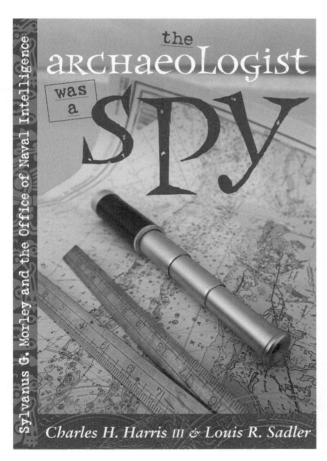

Praise for the book:

"In this remarkable story of a remarkable man and his colorful associates, Harris and Sadler bring to vivid life an unknown story of early American intelligence. They illuminate the start of today's vast spy apparatus. A lively, scholarly, and useful job."—*David Kahn, author of* The Codebreakers *and* Hitler's Spies.

"This is superior scholarship. Harris and Sadler have written the most significant book available on U.S. intelligence during World War I in Latin America."—*William H. Beezley, University of Arizona*

University of New Mexico Press

www.unmpress.com   1-800-249-7737

673